Armoured Trains

Armoured Trains

An Illustrated Encyclopedia 1825–2016

Paul Malmassari

Translated and Edited by Roger Branfill-Cook

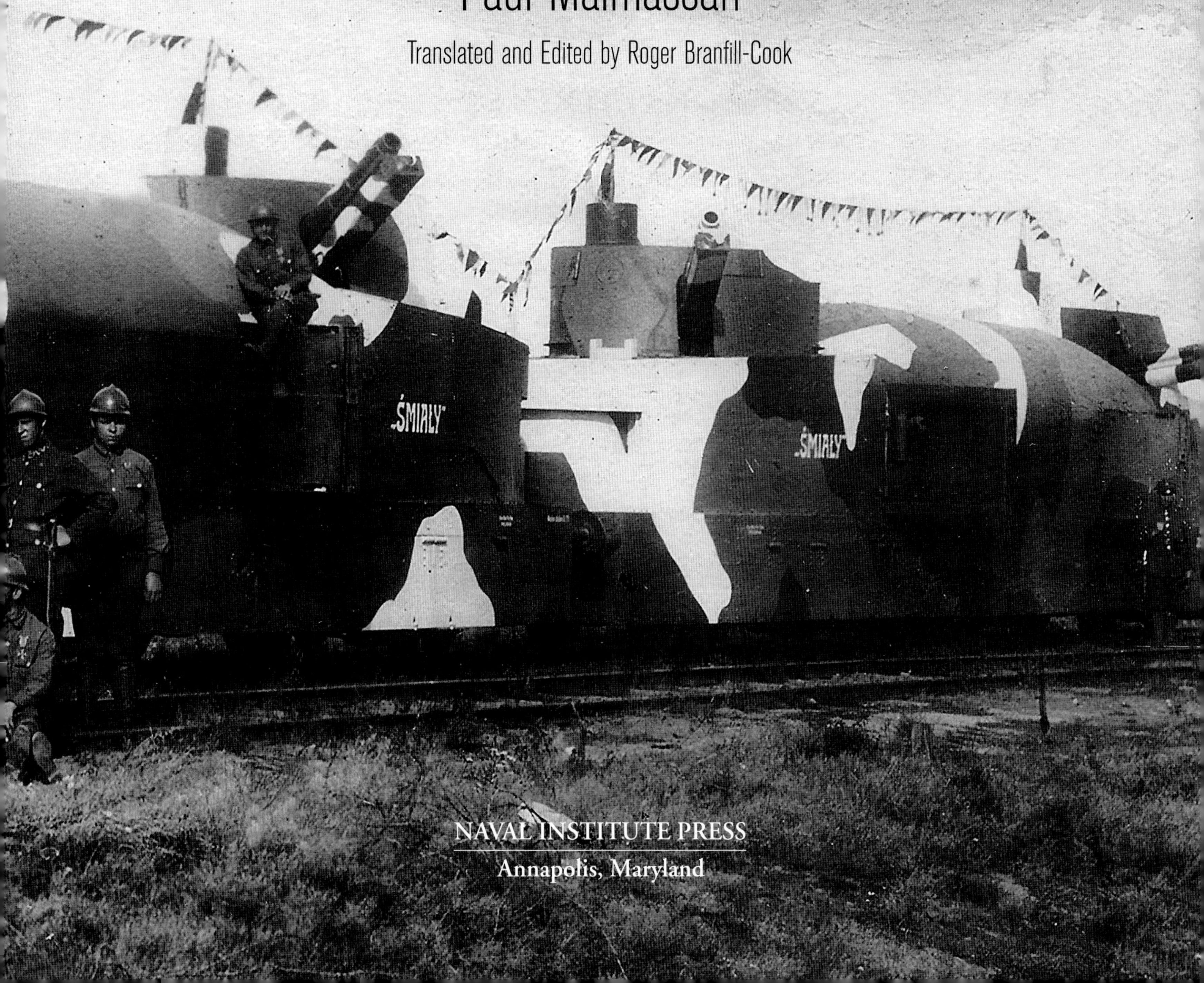

NAVAL INSTITUTE PRESS

Annapolis, Maryland

Half-title page: Close-up of the embrasure for the 57mm chase gun in the Swedish armoured train *Boden*, which gives an idea of the thickness of the armour. *(Photo: Sveriges Järnvägs Museum)*

Title page: Armoured Train PP 53 *Śmiały* dressed overall for Polish Army Day, on 15 August 1921. *(Photo: Adam Jońca Collection)*

Copyright © Paul Malmassari 1989 & 2016

First published in French as *Les Trains Blindés 1826–1989* in 1989
by Editions Heimdall

This revised and expanded edition first published
in Great Britain in 2016 by
Seaforth Publishing,
An imprint of Pen & Sword Books Ltd,
47 Church Street,
Barnsley
South Yorkshire S70 2AS

www.seaforthpublishing.com
Email: info@seaforthpublishing.com

Published and distributed in the United States of America and Canada
by the Naval Institute Press, 291 Wood Road, Annapolis, Maryland
21402-5043
www.nip.org

Library of Congress Cataloging Number: 2016945670

ISBN 978 1 59114 607 0

Designed by typeset by Mousemat Design Ltd

Printed and bound in China by Imago

CONTENTS

INTRODUCTION

In my native France, for many of us of the generation born before the Internet and the fall of the Berlin Wall, our first meeting with armoured trains was the screening of René Clement's classic film *La Bataille du Rail* (1946).[1] The famous German armoured train depicted in the film, which has come down to us through the magic of the cinema, would have become the icon of the armoured train, had it not been cut up by the breakers' torches.

Two decades later, we witnessed the destruction of another German armoured train, in the Burt Lancaster film *The Train* (1964), but it was the dramatic arrival of Strelnikov's armoured train in *Dr Zhivago* (1965) which imprinted itself on countless imaginations as it punched across our screens, with the scream of its whistle in a forest of red flags, much more than a military machine, in fact a projection of pure power.[2]

The armoured train – which we will use here in the general sense, only referring to 'rail trolleys', 'railcars' and so on in specific cases – is neither an armoured vehicle like the others, nor a train like the others. Neither fish nor fowl, and difficult to classify in the range of military technology, the fall from favour of this weapon probably results from this paradox. The armoured train has usually been denigrated by railway enthusiasts, who have been more inclined (in a Saint-Simonian fashion) to emphasise the social advantages of the railways. Even the famous French author Stendhal expressed the pious hope that 'The railway will render war impossible'.[3] For their part military historians have paid the armoured train scant attention up until recent times: traditionally they dismissed it as the poor relation of the tank, unable to manoeuvre freely, unsuited to offensive missions, and only suitable for policing duties. In sum, in Western culture the armoured train seems to be unworthy of inclusion in any line-up of major weapon systems.

However, even a brief review of the regions, the different historical periods and the conflicts in which armoured trains served will show that they were present almost everywhere, from a single, unique light armoured rail trolley, to heavy trains operating in groups, and even in 'fleets'. Obviously, the approach to their use differs according to the nations involved and the chronological period under consideration. Despite their widespread use, especially since the end of the nineteenth century, the first concise work, written by an Italian, dates only from 1974,[4] followed by an English publication in 1981.[5] In 1989, we in our turn published a detailed study of the subject, opening it up to all countries on all continents.[6] Since then, having taken the measure of the scope of the subject – from a geographical as well as a chronological standpoint – we decided to undertake this new study of the employment of armoured trains across the whole world, from the birth of the railways up until the most recent conflicts, and in as much detail as the existing sources permit.

The bibliographical references, which we have quoted in the Sources for each country's chapter, show that many studies of the armoured trains of individual countries have been published in recent years. However, few of their authors have attempted to set them in the overall context of armoured trains or to make comparisons with other units and their employment. There are many omissions in the links between different chronological periods on the one hand, and on the other, the different means of employment according to geographical area. Historical technical material in museums and archives is widely dispersed, is not referenced on a standard basis, or is often extremely rare. In this encyclopaedia we have therefore decided to follow a logical progression for each separate country, rather than attempt to write exhaustive national histories, which only a historian fluent in the language of the country concerned will be qualified to undertake. Again, where a national work exists, we will not attempt to duplicate the text, but will restrict ourselves to the pictorial aspects.

Why Study the History of Armoured Trains?

There are three principal reasons.

Firstly, the contemporary use of these units (as in recent years in the former Yugoslavia, in Colombia, in the Caucasus and in Chechnya . . .) awakens our curiosity and leads us to want to link these events with historical precedents.

[1.] '*The Battle of the Railways*'.

[2.] The idiom continues in the modern Russian film *The Last Armoured Train*, where the true hero is the armoured train itself, which comes through to win at the very end.

[3.] In *Mémoires d'un touriste*, published in 1837. It would be several decades before the ability of the rail network to facilitate rapid mobilisation and the concentration of forces would dash his hopes.

[4.] Pierangelo Caiti, *Atlante mondiale delle artiglierie: artiglierie ferroviairie e treni blindati* (Parma: Ermanno Albertelli Editore, 1974). Two previous volumes by D Bishop and K Davis, *Railways and War* (London: Blandford Press Ltd, 1972 and 1974) had included some armoured trains.

[5.] George Balfour, *The Armoured Train, its development and usage* (London: B T Batsford Ltd, 1981).

[6.] Paul Malmassari, *Les Trains Blindés 1826–1989* (Bayeux: Editions Heimdal, 1989).

Secondly, armoured trains are the victims of a paradox which can be summed up as follows: in light of the common perception that, in order to defeat an armoured train, it simply suffices to cut the tracks, why is it that the armoured train has continued to be widely employed without interruption, and with varying degrees of success, ever since railways were invented? There is obviously a multitude of answers, depending on the mentality and the geography of each user nation, and on their perception of each of the threats the armoured train was intended to counter.

Thirdly, the armoured train is an inseparable part of the railway and military heritage of the nation concerned. Again, a train can be armoured for other than specific military uses, for example as official transport or for transfer of cash and specie. Various numbers of units were built, differing in quality according to the period and the armament mounted. On the other hand, the very design of the units was a reflection of the industrial capacity of the nation concerned and the doctrine for their use: the latter varied depending on the geographical area of influence, later the colonial experience, the various alliances entered into, and an evaluation of the capacities of likely opponents.

An Overview of the Use of Armoured Trains

Before examining armoured trains on a country-by-country basis, it is sensible to present a general panorama of how armoured trains evolved. Obviously, this panorama will allow us to link technical advancement to the innovations applied to armoured trains, and in particular to attempt to identify trends caused by the observation of equivalent enemy units, their battlefield recovery and repair, and finally by an analysis of the enemy's capabilities. Three major periods can be discerned, each one subject to varying availability of source material:

1825–1917: APPEARANCE OF THE RAILWAY AND ITS ADAPTATION TO MILITARY REQUIREMENTS

The appearance of the railway is a Western and European phenomenon. The introduction of the steam engine and its use in industry had already generated many projects (that of Cugnot among others), but the perfection of the iron rail allowed the creation of a homogenous artificial roadway, finally guaranteeing easy transportation. A brief study of the pre-1825 period is thus justified.

1765–1825: Pre-history of the motorised vehicle: steam creates the automobile era

The steam engine was invented by James Watt in 1765, then in 1769 Cugnot built and tested the first steam-powered automobile. Apart from his artillery tractor, this period was hardly propitious to military automobile applications. Nonetheless, surviving sources indicate a growing intellectual interest in the notion of a 'tank' or 'armoured vehicle' in the true sense of these terms.

1825–1871: First adaptations of the railway to military use, appearance of the armoured train

Many projects conceived during this period show the influence of the American Civil War, as much by the proposed methods of employment as in the actual construction details. The first appearance of armoured trains in Europe dates from the Franco-Prussian War, and their perceived effectiveness depends on which side prepared the evaluation. Several contemporary projects proposed in France and Great Britain were intended for coastal defence.

1871–1917: Colonial use and methodical studies for future armoured trains

An analysis of the Franco-Prussian War led to the creation of armoured trains or wagons around the turn of the century by the major Powers. This period also saw the expansion of colonial empires, and armoured trains would be employed in the colonies to maintain internal security, then ultimately to conquer the German colonies in southern Africa in 1914. Great Britain was in the lead, experimenting with and using armoured trains on a large scale, notably during the Second Boer War. On the other hand, it is difficult today to evaluate the significant thought given to developments in Germany.[7] 1917 seems to be a propitious date to end the first period of the history of armoured trains, as the Russian Civil War was about to break out, and 1917 was also the year when the first tanks entered service.

1917–1945: THE 'GOLDEN AGE', WITH ARMOURED TRAINS IN ACTION ON MULTIPLE FRONTS

The Russian Civil War would be the first time that relatively modern armies would confront each other on such vast continuous open spaces (from Germany and Poland to the ends of Siberia), which were beyond the capabilities of contemporary armoured vehicles, mainly designed for use on roads. In addition, the Bolshevik Revolution, and the Chinese Revolution which followed, both created a new need for mobile artillery.

During this period, new nations were born from the dismemberment of the Austro-Hungarian Empire on the one hand, and on the other the independence of provinces which had previously been part of Russia. The centre of gravity of the users of armoured trains moved to the East. Thus the Baltic States and Poland based their artillery firepower principally around armoured trains, while Czechoslovakia, Austria, Hungary and Yugoslavia shared the former Austro-Hungarian units. And finally the Revolutionaries inspired by the October Revolution all began to build new armoured trains.

[7.] The majority of the German archives were destroyed during the bombing of Potsdam in 1945, along with the destruction of Breslau where PZ BP42 and BP44 had been built.

1917–1922: Standardisation of the role of armoured trains in combat
The young states continued to develop their trains, with national characteristics which became more and more marked, notably in the Baltic States. The employment of the armoured train as the principal weapon system became the norm in the battles which followed the victory of the Entente Powers in 1918, from all the operations in the Russian Civil War, to the Russo-Polish War, the German Revolution and the Baltic Freikorps, the uprisings in Silesia, Hungary, and the Ukraine, and the Civil War in China.

1922–1941: Equipping the armies and modernising the armoured trains
These efforts begun in the early 1920s were put into effect in the countries of central and eastern Europe. In Germany, after the destruction of the armoured trains ordered by the Inter-Allied Armistice Commission, a new generation was created with the object of maintaining internal security. In Asia, the Sino-Japanese incidents all took place around strategic rail lines, requiring the use of armoured trains by the opposing sides. The Spanish Civil War saw their use by the Republicans, and the Second World War in Europe began at 02.00 in the morning of 1 September 1939 with co-ordinated attacks by armoured trains and trolleys on either side of the Danzig Corridor.

1941–1945: The peak of technical and doctrinal development facing widespread partisan warfare
With the Wehrmacht's attack on the USSR, for the next four years armoured trains took on an importance which has never been equalled. On the one hand Soviet technical know-how influenced German designs, and on the other, the widespread partisan warfare which broke out behind Axis lines in Russia, the Balkans, France and Poland led to a sense of insecurity which only armoured trains could alleviate. For one side the armoured train had become a 'progressive' political weapon and for the other a symbol of fascist oppression.

1945–2016: DECLINE AND REGULAR REAPPEARANCES
1945 marked the end of the fundamental importance of the railway networks. The ALVF[8] disappeared from the military inventory to be replaced by missiles, and while armoured trains lived on as major weapons in certain Communist countries, they mainly continued in an anti-guerrilla role, this time in the overseas possessions of the Western countries. They came to the fore in certain conflicts, but never regained their former primary role despite excellent propaganda successes.

1945–1962: Armoured trains during revolutionary struggles
Despite the arrival of air superiority and missiles partly replacing conventional artillery, armoured trains did not disappear completely. They remained in use in Russia up until the 1970s and probably also in China. But it was in the front line of the endless crises, conflicts and civil and decolonisation wars that they would play their last and most brilliant card: in the Korean War, the Malaysian Emergency, Cuba, Indochina, Algeria, Netherlands East Indies and the Vietnam War, all of the railway networks virtually without exception made use of them. In the case of France, which had never truly believed in their effectiveness, the armoured trains of Indochina (all erroneously called 'Rafales') would become legendary, while those in Algeria ensured the security of the rail network up to the very end.

1962–2016: Railway networks proof against nuclear warfare and frequent reappearances for political ends
The immediate effects of nuclear warfare are impressive. On the other hand, the harmful effect of the radiation is the very real enemy of the troops who have to exploit the breakthrough facilitated by the initial strike. To counter the physical effects, attempts to adapt armoured vehicles were undertaken but without any real success.[9] The crossing of contaminated zones by vehicles remained virtually impossible, so in about 1970 in the USSR, special armoured trains were developed, three of which later saw service in the Caucasus. A journey of the North Korean leader to Russia, and the conveyance of Euro banknotes have been the subject of intense media coverage and have helped to keep the armoured train in public awareness, to say nothing of the intense speculations about the supposed discovery of a Nazi armoured train loaded with gold hidden 'somewhere in Poland', and which remains to be proved.

Finally, complete coverage of our subject requires that we consider the perception of the armoured train in the minds of the public, and that we show several examples of their impact on popular culture by way of novels, poems, comic books, films and song.

Armoured Train Design and Construction Techniques
All the functions united in the crewing of an armoured train give it an all-arms character, bringing together all the various armed services of the nation concerned. And this feature was present from its very beginnings: the ability to manufacture and assemble large armour plates, the use of turrets, and finally the selection of crewmen trained in the use of heavy artillery, pointed to the use of sailors to serve in these land battleships.[10] So it was during the Siege of Paris in 1871, during the British intervention in Egypt in 1882, in the Cameroons and before Antwerp in 1914, in the Russian arsenals . . . Coast-defence armoured trains, which were the subject of several proposals,

---

[8.] ALVF: *Artillerie Lourde sur Voie Ferrée* = Heavy Railway Guns.
[9.] Such as the Russian 'Object 279' prototype tank, with its quadruple track system and armoured hull specially contoured to resist being overturned by a nuclear shockwave.
[10.] The same reasons led the British to ascribe a 'naval' connotation to the first tank developments: the project was the responsibility of the Admiralty, the first tanks were described as 'land battleships', their tactical employment was initially copied from naval rules of engagement, etc

would have been the responsibility of the Navy. However, the significant use of armoured trains in operations on the battlefield turned them into an essential arm of land warfare, since in many conflicts they supplanted tanks and other armoured vehicles.

From the moment that aircraft were employed for military purposes, an 'air' component became essential, either in the form of specialised armoured or unarmoured anti-aircraft trains, or by permanently mounting anti-aircraft guns in existing armoured trains. Just as in the case of anti-aircraft ground artillery units, on the trains these pieces were manned in most cases by air force personnel (for example in German armoured trains up until 1942, and British armoured trains from 1940 to 1944). There was also the special case of an improvised armoured train built and manned by the Royal Air Force during the Mau Mau Uprising in Kenya.[11]

The varied appearance of armoured trains remains one of their main characteristics, even if several countries attempted to rationalise the overall design features of these units, which were often assembled in a haphazard manner. The variations could be found at two levels: that of the whole train and that of individual wagons. In the first case, the original configuration would vary following the destruction of wagons on the one hand, and their replacement – or not – by repaired or improved wagons, or by wagons originating in other trains, enemy or friendly, on the other. As for the individual wagons, the availability of the weaponry was more important than the availability of a particular platform to be armoured. The case of Soviet armoured trains (as much for those of the Civil War as for the Second World War) shows that the design of the wagons, despite constants which were obviously imposed under official programmes, varied from one workshop to another, and it is often impossible to ascribe them to any standard regulation type of train. In a similar way, the design features of 'BP 42' and 'BP 44' German armoured trains were applied in the same manner to the trains produced by LHW as to those built in workshops close to the front lines, their silhouettes differing even if the armament was standardised.

The Role, Missions and Classification of Armoured Trains

Orinally, the mounting of armament on railway wagons arose from the basic need to provide this armament with mobility, which would otherwise be impossible to achieve on the ground due to lack of adequate motive power. As it was necessary to protect the gun crews, the units were armoured. The first armoured trains can therefore be classed in the same category as railway guns.

When each side began to damage railway lines to prevent their use by the opposition, the primary role of the trains became that of protecting the network. This defence was assured by providing a random presence at any point on the line, as well as by bringing down heavy and light firepower while allowing troops and vehicles

[11.] George Balfour, *The Armoured Train, its Development and Usage*, (London: B T Batsford Ltd, 1981).

carried on board to disembark and extend the combat capabilities of the trains. With the increasing intensity of ground firefights, especially towards the end of the Second World War, the armoured and anti-aircraft trains saw their armour protection augmented to the point where they were able to take part in close-range combat, similar to tanks. To this end, their tactics evolved continually since the American Civil War, and specialist units were conceived, tested and developed by all the countries concerned.

Globally, and depending on the specific period, the following missions can be defined, which are not mutually exclusive, as each armoured train was required to be autonomous:

– breakout train (especially in the case of towns or fortresses).
– reconnaissance train.
– artillery train (field and anti-aircraft artillery, light or heavy).
– internal security train/riot control train.
– command train.
– supply train (living quarters, logistics)
– train/railcar for carrying out repairs
– troop training duties.

In order to carry out these missions, each train should be autonomous and thus carry on board, or in close proximity, specialised equipment and crews:

– command element.
– driving element.
– communications element.
– field artillery/mortars (indirect fire).
– anti-tank guns (direct fire).
– anti-aircraft armament.
– flamethrowers.
– assault group (infantry), also for close-in defence.
– possibility of a mobile armoured unit (tank or armoured vehicle carried onboard).
– technical repair unit (engineers).
– scouting element (rail trolley or troops on foot).
– reconnaissance unit (trolley).
- support element (accommodation, galley, medical etc).

CLASSIFICATION OF ARMOURED TRAINS

In the absence of an international standard we need to propose a method of classifying armoured rail units to be able to use a common base to describe them. An armoured train is a combination comprising:

– the intended use.
– the offensive and defensive armament carried.
– the makeup of the train (the order of each successive wagon and motor unit).

– the characteristics of the wagons (specialised type, level of protection etc).

– the means of propulsion (steam, diesel-electric, electric, exceptionally, animal power).

According to their intended missions, their zone of deployment and the tactics of each country, the trains can be classed as light, medium, heavy and special. In general, trains carrying a heavy armament, intended for long-range fire are less-heavily protected than trains armed with field guns or anti-tank guns, which bring their armament to bear at close range, which are therefore more exposed, and thus carry thicker armour. The weight, and the power, of the guns to be carried will often decide the choice of the rolling stock to be used as the base for armoured wagons:

– flat wagons, bogie platform wagons = safety wagon, command wagon, anti-aircraft platforms.
– high-sided bogie wagons = wagons armed with tank turrets.
– covered bogie vans = idem, plus machine-gun wagons, assault group transports, galley, infirmary, command . . .
– four-wheel vans, brake vans = used for their short length, often to separate two major units, or to carry light armament.
– coach = for transporting officers or officials, or when a long armoured unit is required.

This non-exhaustive and particularly unsystematic division of types does not apply to those units built in factories or in well-equipped workshops. On the other hand, for its newer trains (BP 42 and BP 44) the Wehrmacht decided to only use four- or six-wheel rolling stock, wartime experience having revealed that the bogie types were too difficult to lift and put back on the tracks once derailed.

The Rail War

Before describing the armoured trains and trolleys of each individual country, we will review certain general aspects common to rail warfare, beginning with the raison d'être of armoured trains, namely sabotage on the line.

Mines could be detonated by simple pressure, or by a rack and pinion delay device, which would be set to operate after the pressure of the passage of a certain number of axles, for example to let a safety wagon pass over them but then explode under the engine.

The actual physical destruction of the tracks is not desirable when one intends to use them for one's own trains, notably during the phase of an advance into enemy territory, which of course is not the case for guerrilla forces who do not operate trains. In the 1930s the Russian Army perfected a type of rail torpedo capable of destroying, or at least derailing, an enemy train. Hence the value of safety wagons at the front of trains.

An example in Russia of rails unbolted and left in place, which can appear safe from a distance, but which will twist under the weight of a passing train, or even rails refastened with a slight offset, undetectable by the naked eye but sufficient to drop the wheels of the train onto the sleepers.
(Photo: Paul Malmassari Collection)

Removing a mine placed under a length of track, seen here in Russia. The unhappy sapper appears to be a Russian PoW.
(Photo: Paul Malmassari Collection)

Sabotage of a set of points, much more difficult to replace than a simple length of rail, again in Russia.

(Photo: Paul Malmassari Collection)

Placing of an obstacle (here a wheel rim) after unbolting and refastening the fishplate, in Russia.

(Photo: Paul Malmassari Collection)

Use of small explosive charges in the centre of a length of rail, sufficient to cut it, but easy to repair, in Russia.

(Photo: Paul Malmassari Collection)

A similar type of sabotage, this time in Algeria in 1957, which targeted the armoured train commanded by Sub-Lieutenant Loiseau.

(Photo: Dominique Loiseau)

Sabotage carried out by the guerrillas under Lawrence of Arabia on the Hejaz Railway: the characteristic 'tulip' shape of the rail bent under the force of a very small explosive charge.

(Photo: N V Salt)

In Indochina, the Viet Minh used the cattle from nearby villages to pull a section of rail to one side, the inertia effect of which would cause hundreds of metres of track to overturn, or else to drag entire sections off to disappear in the jungle. Here in the distance is the train which has reversed and is ready to use its firepower to protect the repair gang.

(Photo: BORDAS)

Reversing the process reset the sections of rail, but it was the troops and often the passengers who had to do the hard work.
(Photo: BORDAS)

A Soviet ZhDT-3 rail torpedo, designed in the Podolsk factory in 1938. This simple, cheap 'fire and forget' device could cause considerable damage with its 100kg (220lb) explosive charge, launched at 50km/h (30mph) with a range of some 10km (6 miles). Although five examples of this device were issued to each armoured train in 1941, it is not known whether any were actually used in action. Its principal tactical drawback would have been that in 'Barbarossa', the Germans attacked using tanks, whereas the rail torpedo was most useful against enemy railway traffic, armoured or not, using the Russian broad gauge.
(Photo: Maxim Kolomiets Collection)

The primary means of detecting, or better still preventing, a sabotage attempt, is to patrol the line in a random manner. Since the armoured trains were too heavy, only the rail trolleys could carry out this work of scouting and reconnaissance. The panoply of these machines included a myriad of different types, from original railway inspection trolleys to road vehicles converted for rail use. A noteworthy development dating from the First World War period was the specific pairing of a reconnaissance railcar with an armoured train: the armoured train of Captain Schober in Austria and Armoured Train *Orlik* of the Czech Legion in Siberia, would lead to the NKVD trains coupled to railcars in 1941.

The following list of this type of rolling stock covers the main classifications. The difference between the various types, as well as between heavy, medium and light vehicles, depends on the dimensions of the machines and national predilections, and finally the civil designation of the machine from which the military version is derived.

– reconnaissance trolley (unarmoured, ultimately armed).
– light armoured trolley (with or without turret).
– heavy armoured trolley (with or without turret).
– armoured railcar (without turret).
– multi-turreted railcar (one, two or three turrets, or even four in a Soviet project).
– chase railcar (anti-tank turrets).
– motorised wagon or van.
– armoured car on rails (combined road/rail machines, with integral rail conversion system or with a wheel change, with or without provision for carrying troops for ground combat).
– rail tank.
– design for amphibious road/rail machine.
– expendable remote-controlled vehicle.

The complete Czech armoured train *Orlik*, with two artillery wagons behind the engine, and the railcar (ex-Russian *Zaamurietz*) at the front, capable of patrolling on its own, and itself preceded by a safety flat wagon.
(Photo: Paul Malmassari Collection)

Unarmoured reconnaissance trolleys in Finland during the First World War, adequate for use in low-intensity combat zones.

(Photo: Paul Malmassari Collection)

A good example of an integral rail conversion system for a road/rail vehicle, on condition that the vehicle's track on the road was the same as the rail gauge. This was the case with this unique SdKfz 231 (6-rad) attached to PZ 3.

(Photo: Paul Malmassari Collection)

A completely different approach, these Ford motorcars of the King's Own Royal Regiment converted by the British in Palestine in 1938, were intended only for rail use. This scene also illustrates the fate of numerous trolley crews, sacrificed in order to ensure the safe passage of the trains.

(Photo: Paul Malmassari Collection)

Posed propaganda shot, but useful in showing the use envisaged for these trolleys, more to cover working parties than for offensive reconnaissance.

(Photo: Paul Malmassari Collection)

Diesel-electric locomotive 060 DY of the *Chemins de fer d'Algérie* (CFA) which cab has been fitted with armoured shields. Note the vertical sliding door fitted to the side windows.

(Photo: Paul Malmassari Collection)

Here in Krapina (25 miles north of Zagreb), the Panzerzug (s.Sp.) 202 is an illustration of the tactical trend which countries confronted with railway warfare were gradually developing, namely self-propelled units capable of employment either in full armoured trains or detached as individual combat units.
(Photo: Paul Malmassari Collection)

First introduced by the Soviets with their NKVD railcars, then more widely by the Wehrmacht from 1944 with the PZ le.Sp and PZ s.Sp, reconnaissance units composed of trolleys capable of independent action, coupled together in a small group or in a complete train, seem to have become the norm at the end of the Second World War.

SECURITY: ANTICIPATION, DISCRETION, ARMOUR, ADAPTABILITY

Armour, as with all armoured fighting vehicles, is not the sole guarantee of survivability. It is always combined with other functions and capabilities. For the sake of simplicity, we can consider that the rolling stock is either protected, or armoured, or armoured and also armed. The following examples will illustrate several solutions adopted.

Coupled in a German train in Russia, two high-sided wagons have been crudely armoured by fastening steel plates on the inside, rising 50cm above the planking and pierced with loopholes.
(Photo: Paul Malmassari Collection)

The use of wooden sleepers to protect the crew of this 2cm FlaK 38 AA gun at the head of a convoy, covered by a PzKpfw III tank. The protection has been left deliberately low to permit fire against ground targets.
(Photo: Paul Malmassari Collection)

Based on their previous combat experience, the Poles crewing British armoured trains in 1940 insisted on having a means of entry/egress through the floors of the wagons.
(Photo: IWM)

An example of simple necessity: the armouring of only the driving cab of 4-6-2 engine No 231 501, seen at Phnom Pen on 1 December 2001. The track in Vietnam and Cambodia has never been sufficiently robust to allow the complete armouring of engines and locomotives.
(Photo: Gérard Pouille)

Armoured driving cab on this diesel locomotive No BB 1005 in a depot in Cambodia. Note the space left between the armour plate and the cab, which increases the protection through causing the projectile to fragment.
(Photo: Florian Grupp)

The importance of camouflage

Camouflage is intended to deceive the eye of the enemy observer, either by disrupting the shape or by making the object disappear. It should be noted that maximum efficiency requires static non-moving machines, emitting neither smoke nor light. The moment a tank or a train begins to move, no camouflage can hide it, and all that can be hoped for is that land-based observers have difficulty in determining its precise position and its nationality. On the other hand, one must consider the psychological aspects: one cannot leave a military train unpainted (metal will rust, wood will rot), and since it is essential to paint it, one can profit from the use of paint intended for other military vehicles. And its crew will always feel less visible in camouflage paint than without it.

In a Russian forest, two lines cross at right angles: a railway line, on which a train is burning, and a forest track. It is useless to try to hide an armoured train. But at least one can delay the moment when it will be clearly identifiable.
(Photo: Paul Malmassari Collection)

The plume of black smoke from the steam engine will give away the exact position of this armoured train (PZ 26 to 31) running on the Russian gauge during Operation 'Barbarossa'. Note the armour protection formed from rail lengths fitted to the front of the safety wagon, transforming it into an observation platform.
(Photo: Paul Malmassari Collection)

Smoke deflector apparatus on the ex-Austro-Hungarian steam engine of the Polish PP *Smialy*. This unarmoured fitting has suffered from shell or bomb fragments or machine-gun rounds.
(Photo: Wawrzyniec Markowski Collection)

An impression of rails and sleepers painted on the roofs of these Finnish armoured wagons, apparently in two different colours.
(Photo: SA-Kuva)

Thousands of miles away, but the same principle: this smoke deflector equips a Chinese armoured train of the Fengtian Army in the 1930s. The smoke could be diverted under the engine or along the side of the train.
(Photo: All Rights Reserved)

An interesting camouflage scheme on Soviet Armoured Train No 47 of the 12th Armoured Train Battalion.
(Photo: Paul Malmassari Collection)

First used in Spain, and lastly up until the end of the war in Indochina, the painting of false rails and sleepers on the vehicles seems to us to be a way of boosting the morale of the crews, rather than an effective camouflage technique.
(Photo: Paul Malmassari Collection)

Towards the end of the Second World War, Allied air superiority obliged the Germans to heavily camouflage their trains. Here it is difficult to make out a train composed of s.Sp heavy trolleys at the moment of its surrender to the Americans in 1945.

(Photo: Paul Malmassari Collection)

Perfect camouflage for an armoured train in a static position. Seen here in 1914, one can just make out to the left of the gunner one of the wheels of this French train armed with a 95mm gun.

(Photo: Paul Malmassari Collection)

Above: The front section of SSZ *Blücher* in June 1943 reutilising a static PzKpfw I (armed with two 7.92mm MG 13s, in the more distant wagon) and a PzKpfw II (armed with a 2cm KwK 30 or 38) encased in outer armour protection, for anti-partisan duties.

(Photo: Paul Malmassari Collection)

Left: Partial camouflage on a Russian armoured train captured near Kiev in 1941. Camouflage based on foliage is difficult to keep attached to moving vehicles, and moreover deteriorates badly, dying leaves being easily spotted in the middle of nearby growing vegetation.

(Photo: Paul Malmassari Collection)

Offensive capability

Ever since the birth of armament carried on the railways, the object was to be able to transport artillery pieces. The evolution of the armoured train having given it an offensive role, it combined all or parts of the three following types of artillery: anti-aircraft, indirect fire (light guns, heavy guns, howitzers, mortars, rockets) and direct fire (notably anti-tank guns). These combinations are found on wagons dedicated to a single type, or on specialised wagons, with in every case close-in defensive armament, distributed along the whole length of the train. The armament is carried either in a casemate firing ahead or to the rear of the train, or in a turret. In the latter case, either the turret alone is mounted, or the turret is mounted on the complete hull of a tank. The type with the complete tank can be in a static version, with only the turret remaining operational, or in a mobile version, in which the tank can fight on board or disembarked, greatly extending the combat radius of the train. Here are several examples, again only a small part of the multiple variations.

PZ BP 42 and 44 were equipped with two PzKpfw 38(t) tanks. Here we see one mounting aboard the Panzerträgerwagen facing forwards, whereas normally they are seen facing the ramp, ready for rapid deployment. In addition to supplying firepower, the tank served as a command post and forward look-out post. Note the Soviet PPSh sub-machine gun carried by the pipe-smoking crewman.
(Photo: Paul Malmassari Collection)

Here a BT-7 tank with its engine removed adds to the protection of the wagon and provides the firepower of its 45mm M32 gun and its 7.62mm anti-aircraft machine gun.
(Photo: Paul Malmassari Collection)

Obsolete tanks were also used by the French Army in Algeria. Here, following an FLN ambush, the tank wagon has remained upright by some miracle, while the rest of the train has been overturned.
(Photo: Guy Chabot)

One of the first stages in introducing anti-tank armament: a 7.5cm L/41 gun replacing the limited traverse casemate on PZ 3.
(Photo: Paul Malmassari Collection)

One of the more advanced design concepts: the Polish Trolley R (for Renault) which fulfilled the dual mission of rail reconnaissance while preserving its ability to disembark without docking facilities in the open countryside to fight at some distance from a train. Following their capture, it appears that these machines influenced the tank transporter wagons of PZ BP 42/44.
(Photo: Jońca Collection)

The ultimate stage in anti-tank armament on armoured trains: a PzKpfw IV turret armed with the 7.5cm KwK40 L/43 or L/45 (here seen attached to PZ 3 between July and October 1944). A previous stage involved using turrets from T-34s in a similar fashion, by both the Germans and the Soviets.
(Photo: Paul Malmassari Collection)

Anti-aircraft defence

The ability of an armoured train (and in general of all military trains) to survive in modern warfare relies also on the manner in which its anti-aircraft defence is organised. In many armoured trains (Polish, Baltic States, Spanish) the defence of the train itself was provided by machine guns installed either on wagons or on the engine tenders. On several Soviet armoured trains, specialised anti-aircraft wagons were added to the rake. On the other hand, the Wehrmacht, the Soviets from 1943 onward then later in the 1970s, and the Canadians with their Armoured Train No 1, armed certain wagons with anti-aircraft guns, capable also of firing against ground targets.

The anti-aircraft position of PZ 32 (the German armoured train used in the 1946 film *La Bataille du Rail*) with a 3.7cm FlaK 36. A quad 2cm Flakvierling 38 was standard equipment on PZ BP 42 and BP 44.
(Photo: Paul Malmassari Collection)

Twin Maxim SPM 7.62mm machine guns, or in rarer cases a quadruple set, were carried on turrets mounted on the tenders of Soviet steam engines and on railcars. Here is a captured train made up of NKVD D-2 railcars. Note the complete lack of protection for the AA machine gunners, who even lack any form of safety rail to prevent them from firing on each other or into their own train.
(Photo: Paul Malmassari Collection)

A twin mounting with 7.62mm ItKk 31 VKT[11] MGs on a Finnish anti-aircraft wagon which allows freedom of movement for the gunners.
(Photo: Paul Malmassari Collection)

11. ItKk, or *Kaksoisilmatorjuntakonekivääri* = Twin anti-aircraft machine gun.
KKT or *Valtion Kivääritehdas* = State rifle manufacturing factory.

At the southern edge of Europe, during the Spanish Civil War, the installation of this anti-aircraft machine gun mounting on either diesel armoured train No 7 or No 8 is very different, favouring the protection of the gunners more than their ability to spot and follow a target. The militiaman is fixing a protective cover over the muzzle of the 70mm Schneider Model 1908 gun.
(Photo: BN from Rojo y Azul, via Jacinto M. Arévalo Molina)

The original anti-aircraft trains had been designed to provide strong defences around strategic points such as towns, railway centres, refineries, industrial complexes etc, with no or light armour protection. Over time, they had evolved as the anti-aircraft units drew closer to the front lines, or as the partisans had become bolder and had begun to sabotage the lines used by these trains. Further research is required into whether these developments resulted from specific programmes on the part of the Russians and the Germans.

This captured Soviet train was armed with 85mm ZP obr.1939g guns, one of the most efficient Russian anti-aircraft guns.

(Photo: Paul Malmassari Collection)

Russian anti-aircraft train, with only the sides protected against bomb and shell fragments. These captured wagons have been rearmed with 88mm guns.

(Photo: Paul Malmassari Collection)

An integral feature of the artillery wagons was the rangefinder in the foreground. Note the rustic nature of the wagon interior.

(Photo: Paul Malmassari Collection)

The barrel stuck in the recoil position would indicate that the crew had rendered the gun inoperable prior to abandoning the train.

(Photo: Paul Malmassari Collection)

One can make out the origins of this German anti-aircraft wagon: the folding sides of the Russian bogie wagon used as the base have been increased in height by a double skin of planks. The gun is a 7.62cm FlaK M31 or a 7.62/8.8cm FlaK M31(r).

(Photo: DGEG-Malmassari Collection)

Seen here in firing position, at the base of the mounting the wagon is now twice the width.

(Photo: DGEG-Malmassari Collection)

One of the more developed versions is this wagon with an 8.8cm FlaK 36. In travelling mode, the side nacelles have been lifted and the wagon will now conform to the loading gauge.

(Photo: DGEG-Malmassari Collection)

The wagon seen in the previous shot, here in the final stages of construction. The 50-tonne capacity bogie flat wagon used as the basis of this unit is of Russian origin, as per the following drawing.

(Photo: DGEG-Malmassari Collection)

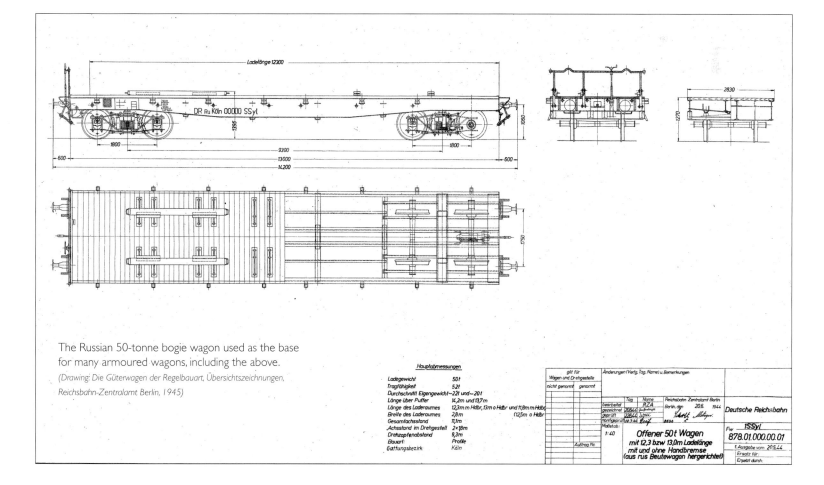

The Russian 50-tonne bogie wagon used as the base for many armoured wagons, including the above.

(Drawing: Die Güterwagen der Regelbauart, Übersichtszeichnungen, Reichsbahn-Zentralamt Berlin, 1945)

Close-up of one end of the wagon under construction, showing its similarity with the wagons of PZ BP 42 and BP 44.
(Photo: DGEG-Malmassari Collection)

A common feature which runs through all the pages of this encyclopaedia is the durability and the capacity of railway rolling stock – and in particular the armoured trains – to be re-used. Observing and following certain wagons and railcars through the various conflicts adds a new dimension compared to that of other armoured vehicles. Thus we can follow the itinerary of many armoured wagons, Austro-Hungarian from 1914 to 1945, Polish and Czech from 1938 to 1945, Russian from 1916 to the Chinese Civil War and then from the 1970s to the present day, French from 1950 to 1975 in Indochina.

This continual regeneration owes much to the solidity of the base platforms, but also to the relative lack of hits on the vital parts of the trains, and finally to the inventiveness of the front-line workshops. The psychological dimension, and by extension the political dimension, form part of the attractiveness of the armoured train.

As a combat platform, the armoured wagon has carried, and still carries, practically all types of existing armament. One can therefore refer to general works for details of the specific armament of a particular period. Again, few wagons or railcars were built for the purpose of being armoured, the vast majority of armoured units being created by fastening a framework covered with armour plates to a standard item of rolling stock. Further details can be sought by reference to the motive power units and the rolling stock of the different countries involved.

Conclusion

It is not our intention in compiling this encyclopaedia to trace a linear history of the evolution of the armoured train. Nor is it our intention to describe each and every engagement involving armoured trains or the specific confrontations which gave rise to their invention. Our aim is to examine how each individual country invented, experimented with, utilised and, in some cases, abandoned this military weapon system, while not ignoring the effects on states outside the countries of origin. If, as we believe, military progress consists of destroying the adversary by engaging him at longer and longer ranges while remaining better and better protected, then the armoured train has a significant place in the history of military technology and in the genesis of the tank in particular.

Armoured trains (and the armoured railcars and trolleys derived from them) are at the same time a common arm and an atypical arm. The longevity of their success was first and foremost due to their ability to supplant the tanks and armoured vehicles that many nations lacked the means to design or acquire; then to their ability to neutralise or at least minimise the threats to the railway networks on which the logistics of the armies of the Second World War and the wars of decolonisation relied; finally to their capacity for regeneration through repairs, innovation and re-use of captured units. To demonstrate and study armoured trains, over the swathe of the battlefields on which they participated, illustrates the industrial history and the economic, social, cultural and political makeup of a nation.

To conclude, we feel that interest in armoured trains remains strong, whether in order to lift the veil on fascinating and still mysterious military machines, or to encourage the continued design and construction of armoured units, the use of which has never ceased – and will never cease while railway networks continue to be an efficient modern means of transport, and therefore a tempting target of attempts at destruction and obstruction. If as Plato said, necessity is the mother of invention, the story of the armoured train is one of the best proofs that he was right.

An extremely rare shot of an armoured Flak wagon, with a profile which appears to allow the gun to fire at low elevation to either side of the cabin.
(Photo: DGEG-Malmassari Collection)

Despite continuing research and analysis, the subject of armoured trains still has many mysteries to be solved: many machines are still unexamined, either because their existence is documented but no photos or drawings have come to light, or the converse such as this photo of an unidentified trolley, which is almost certainly Russian.
(Photo: Paul Malmassari Collection)

SOURCES:
Books
Caiti, Pierangelo, *Atlante mondiale delle artiglierie: artiglierie ferroviarie e treni blindati* (Parma: Ermanno Albertelli Editore, 1974).

Dupuy, R Ernest, and Dupuy, N Trevor, *The Harper Encyclopaedia of Military History* (New York: HarperCollins Publishers, 1993).

Heigl, Fritz, *Taschenbuch der Tanks*, 4 vols (Munich: J F Lehmanns Verlag, 1935 [re-edited in 1970]).

Malmassari, Paul, *Les Trains blindés 1826-1989* (Bayeux: Editions Heimdal, 1989).

Westwood, John, *Railways at War* (San Diego: Howell-North Books, 1980).

Zaloga, Steven J, *Armored Trains* (Oxford, Osprey Publishing Ltd, 2008).

Journal articles
Aiby, Lieutenant André, 'L'emploi des trains blindés', *La Revue d'Infanterie* Vol 83 (November 1933).

'Du XIXᵉ au XXᵉ siècle l'histoire des trains blindés', *Champs de Bataille thématique* No 43 (November 2015).

Ferrenz, Tirell J, 'Armored Trains and Their Field of Use', *The Military Engineer* Vol XXIV, No 137 (Sept–Oct 1932).

Gallacher, Ian, 'Armoured Trains', *Military Illustrated* No 191 (July 2004).

'Les Trains blindés', *La Nature* No 2150 (12th December 1914).

M., Capitaine, 'Les Trains blindés', *La France militaire* No 11795 (23 May 1924).

Malmassari, Lieutenant-Colonel Paul, '1914: Quand la voie ferrée annonce le char', *14-18, le magazine de la Grande Guerre* No 20 (2004), pp 22–7.

Mayer, Major Franz, 'Introduction à l'histoire des trains blindés', *Militär-Wissenschaft und technische Mitteilungen* (Nov–Dec 1929).

Purdon, Charles J, 'Fortress on steel wheels', *Trains* Vol 41, No 11 (September 1988), pp 30–1.

Urbański, Hauptmann August, 'Über die Verwendung von Panzerzügen im Feldkriege', *Mitteilungen über Gegenstände des Artillerie- und Genie-Wesens* (1900), pp 402–12.

Van Volxum, Major, 'Le rôle des trains blindés dans les opérations de guerre', *La Science et la Vie* No 25, (March 1916), pp 305–12.

University Studies
Malmassari, Paul, *Etude comparée des trains blindés européens (1826-2000)*, DEA en Histoire militaire, défense et sécurité, Université Paul Valéry, Montpellier III, under the guidance of Professor Jean-Charles Jauffret, 2004.

Conferences
Malmassari, Lieutenant-Colonel Paul, *Les Trains blindés et la fortification au XIX° siècle,* communication au colloque de l'artillerie, Draguignan, 9 April 2005.

NOTES ON THE SOURCES AND REFERENCES
No author can hope to master all the publications in a multitude of foreign languages. Therefore many of the quoted sources are French, but we have listed at the end of each country's chapter all the pertinent references we know of, a certain number of which have been made accessible through translations often supplied by our correspondents. Here we warmly thank them for their efforts. We have made a particular effort to include the maximum number of previously unpublished photographs or those from private collections. Even when making use of archival documents or those kept by museums we have given priority to less-well-known photographs. We must emphasise the aid provided by the Internet, on a worldwide basis, through the ease of correspondence, and the use of online auction sites to acquire items, or the use of search engines to identify documents.

The level of support we have received for this project has been extremely widespread: we have been able to study the majority of the countries thanks to the documents supplied by the archival centres (and which the author has patiently collected over more than thirty years), or by enthusiastic correspondents, historians, eyewitnesses and enlightened amateurs. Sometimes, lacking original documentation on certain units, we have resorted to using unedited photographic evidence furnished by their military opponents of the period, which has left us with serious historical lacuna due to the lack of reliable references.

Again, the level of detail which we can provide varies according to the country under review. For example it is not possible in one volume to name all the commanding officers of the various trains, except for a very few, nor to list each and every single armoured train, railcar and trolley for the major user countries we have covered. We therefore assume full responsibility for the selections we have made, just as we accept any errors that readers may find in this study. They are the responsibility of the Author and not of those who have helped him.

We would therefore like to seize this opportunity to welcome any positive criticism which will allow us to make further progress in our research.

NOTES ON THE PLANS
Except where indicated to the contrary, the plans are here reproduced to 1/87th (HO) scale, which is the most popular scale in worldwide railway modelling. Certain plans were previously published in 1989 in our encyclopaedia of *Les Trains Blindés 1826-1989*. We have decided to not reproduce those which suffer from too many inaccuracies, which we discovered as the result of research in the interim, but we have added new plans drawn since then. M. Frédéric Carbon kindly agreed to prepare several plans of vehicles from newly discovered documents. M. Francisco Cruzado Albert kindly authorised us to publish several plans of Spanish armoured trains. Finally, wherever possible we have preferred to reproduce original technical drawings, accepting some minor loss of definition.

ANGOLA

ARMOURED TROLLEYS

The end of the war of independence[1] saw the beginning of the civil war which lasted up until 1991. Several ex-Portuguese Wickham Type 42 armoured trolleys (see the chapter on Portugal) continued in service, notably on the southern rail network, the C.F.B. (*Caminho de Ferro de Benguela*). Here their role was to counter possible incursions by the South African armed forces supporting UNITA.[2]

A Wickham Type 42 armoured trolley photographed outside the Huambo railway workshop in January 1987.
(Photo: DuSewrer)

[1.] Independence from Portugal was declared on 11 November 1975.
[2.] *União Nacional para a Independência Total de Angola.*

SOURCES:
Defensa No 33.

ARGENTINA

AUTOVIA PAGADOR PE-1 ARMOURED RAILCAR

In 1941 the *Ferrocarril del Sud* put an armoured railcar into service. Built by Buxton Ltd in Buenos Aires on the chassis of an Austin truck, it was designed to transport cash on the railway network at a maximum speed of 50km/h (30mph), and weighed 7.52 tonnes. Light weapons could be fired through slits, and security was enhanced by automatic doors, which were quite rare at the time. It was used to convey cash collected at the railway stations. This vehicle was restored by the Ferroclub Argentino between September 2001 and September 2007.

Left: Front view of the PE-1 Railcar. It has a wheelbase of 4m (13ft 1½in), was 6.78m (22ft 3in) long overall, and 1.88m (6ft 2in) wide.

Right: Despite appearing almost symmetrical, the PE-1 has only one driving position (here on the left), and has to be turned by means of a turntable seen here resting on top of a wooden block.

(Photos: Ferroclub Argentino)

ARMENIA

First Democratic Republic of Armenia – Armoured Trains (1918–1920)

Towards the end of the First World War, the collapse of the Russian Empire and its forces in the Caucasus left the Armenians exposed to Ottoman attack. Following the break-up of the short-lived Transcaucasian Federation, the First Democratic Republic of Armenia was proclaimed on 28 May 1918. The Treaty of Versailles did not resolve the question of the frontiers of the new Armenian state, which was in conflict with its neighbours in a tangle of ethnic and religious issues.

In the course of these conflicts, during the Turkish-Armenian War of September to November 1920 and the subsequent invasion and takeover of Armenia by Bolshevik forces, several armoured trains – no doubt having their origins in the Russian Civil War – were employed. The lack of reliable independent sources does not allow us to construct an accurate historical record of these trains and the actions in which they were engaged.

Soviet Armenia

During the Second World War, an armoured train bearing the name *Soviet Armenia* recalled the status of this nominally autonomous Republic (1936–91).

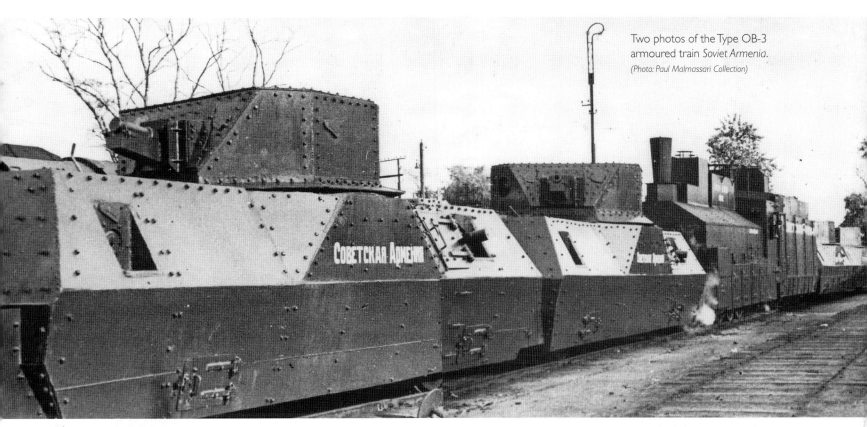

Two photos of the Type OB-3
armoured train *Soviet Armenia*.
(Photo: Paul Malmassari Collection)

The turrets are armed with 76.2mm
Model 27/32 guns, identical to those
mounted in T-35 tanks, plus a
quadruple 7.62mm machine-gun
mounting.

(Photo: Paul Malmassari Collection)

AUSTRIA

Before considering the history of Austrian armoured trains, it is first necessary to detail the successive states that succeeded the Empire, then the separate countries which arose from it. The armoured trains of the latter will be found in the corresponding country's chapter.

The Austrian Empire lasted up until 1867. In that year Emperor Franz Josef I was crowned King of Hungary, and the new Empire (the Dual Monarchy) thus created lasted until 1918. It united the Imperial Crown of Austria (Austria, Bohemia and Galicia) with the Royal Crown of Hungary (Hungary and Croatia-Slavonia), and in 1908 Bosnia-Herzegovina officially joined the Dual Monarchy. After 1918 the Austro-Hungarian Empire, dismantled by the Treaty of St Germain, fractured into five separate nation-states: Austria, Hungary, Czechoslovakia, Poland and the Kingdom of Serbia (which included the territories of the Croats and the Slovenes). Parts of former Imperial territory were also annexed by Romania and Italy. The Treaties of St Germain (10 September 1919) and Trianon (4 June 1920) established the new frontiers of Austria and Hungary. The First Austrian Republic existed until 12 March 1938 when it was absorbed into the German Reich.

Concerning the first armoured trains of the Austrian Empire, an article in a French military journal published in 1851 stated that in Austria 'for several years now wagons [have been built] so arranged as to allow infantry platoons to bring into play their weapons as necessary'. This probably refers to trains built to counter the revolution of 1848.

After November 1918, the First Austrian Republic was affected by problems caused in large part by the Empire's defeat, and then by the Wall Street Crash of 1929. Demonstrations in 1918–19 led to the construction of an armoured train in January 1919 in the state railway workshops in Villach. The train, designated PZ XIII (following on from the numerical series of the Austro-Hungarian armoured trains), went into action in Carinthia and lost its locomotive (one of the Class 29 C-n2 series). Wagons Nos 1 and 2 were converted from Types G and O respectively, with improvised ballast protection and armed with heavy machine guns. After derailing on 31 May 1919, Wagon No 2 was rebuilt, this time with improved armour protection and an observation cupola. In addition, it could now deploy a 37mm Italian M 15 gun. The train was disarmed following the cessation of hostilities between Austria and Yugoslavia on 6 June 1919.

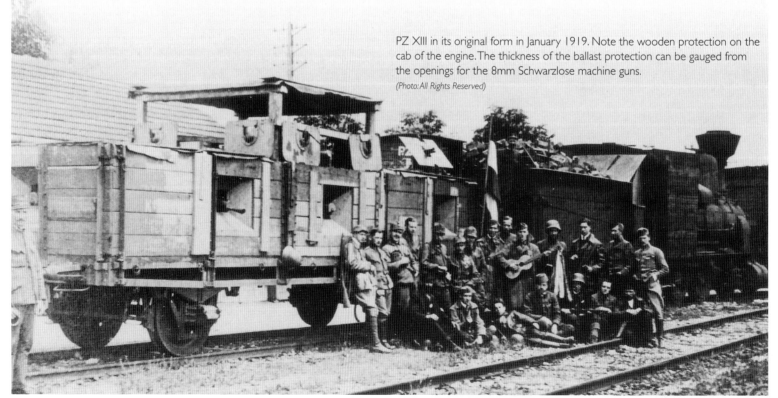

PZ XIII in its original form in January 1919. Note the wooden protection on the cab of the engine. The thickness of the ballast protection can be gauged from the openings for the 8mm Schwarzlose machine guns.
(Photo: All Rights Reserved)

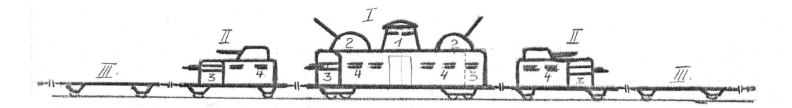

I Triebwagen,

1 Beobachtungsturm,

2 Geschütze,(Flamkn)

3 MG Erker,

4 Lucken,für Wirkungsmäßigkeit von MG und Gewehr,

II Artilleriewagen,

III Plattformwagen, zur Zugsicherung und Beförderung von Strecken-material.

Civil war broke out in February 1934, setting government supporters against the socialists and revolutionaries. At that time trains were armoured to ensure the security of the lines of communication.

On 27 January 1938 Panzerzüg M 39, a modern armoured train with electric propulsion, was designed by *Abteilung PV*[1] which produced the sketch above. At that stage the armour protection had not been finalised, in contrast to the optical equipment and the armament.

The 1938 sketch shows the overall layout of the projected train. The central railcar would have mounted 40mm M 36 anti-aircraft guns (licence-built Bofors) and four M7/12 heavy machine guns. Each artillery wagon was to have been armed with a turret-mounted 100mm M 14 or M 38 howitzer and two heavy machine guns. Finally, thirteen men were to form the crew of the railcar and an assault group would be divided between the two wagons. Work on the project was brought to a halt by the *Anschluss*.

SOURCES:

'Des Chemins de Fer considérés au point de vue militaire', *Le Spectateur Militaire* Vol 50 (June 1851), p 306.

[1]. *Pionier und Verkehrstechnik*, Engineers and Transport Technical Section.

One of the six Panzerzüg Types M 33 ordered by the Bundesheer, photographed on 13 February 1934 in Vienna-East Station. In front and rear of the 2-6-2 Class 73 kkStB engine (with armour protecting the upper part of the cab door) are two Type O wagons, with internal armour protection. Trench shields protect the riflemen, while in the centre of the wagon is a Schwarzlose M1907/12 machine gun behind its characteristic shield.

(Photo: Paul Malmassari Collection)

AUSTRIA-HUNGARY

ARMOURED TRAINS AND RAILCARS

Austria-Hungary formally came into existence on 29 May 1867 and was dissolved on 31 October 1918.[1] When the Empire went to war on two fronts in 1914, the Army possessed no armoured trains. During the first months of the war, the Austro-Hungarian Army was forced to pull back in the face of Russian forces which outnumbered them three-to-one, and they were unable to transfer sufficient men from their second front due to initial Serbian Army successes. In view of the serious situation, local commanders organised improvised armoured trains, such as the one formed by Captain Schober, commander of the 15th Railway Company. These improvised trains served as the basis of experiments leading to the production series which was built during the Winter of 1914–15.

These eight standardised armoured trains were built by MÁV in the Budapest-North workshops. In his study published in 1992,[2] Professor Dr Wolfgang Sadowny showed that no official classification had in fact existed. The author had previously accepted an incorrect classification commonly used in the 1980s. To rectify the situation, we can now use Dr Sadowny's classification system, as follows, to describe the makeup of the three types of armoured train (from front to rear):

– Infantry wagon/engine/infantry wagon = Type A, of which the prototype was PZ II.
– Wagon with turret-mounted gun/engine/infantry wagon/second engine/wagon with turret-mounted gun = Type B.
– Artillery wagon/infantry wagon/engine/infantry wagon = Type Ae or Ae* according to the type of artillery wagon.

The ten standard armoured engines were all of the MÁV Class 377 (overall length of 8.105m [26ft 7in]), while Dr Sadowny classifies the infantry wagons into three types:

– Type 1: using Type 140 wagons, with handbrakes, lockers for equipment mounted beneath the body, and an observation cupola (six examples built).

– Type 2: using wagons Types 148 to 150, without handbrakes, water tank carried centrally, locker for additional coal supply (seven examples built).
– Type 3: using Type 150 wagons, with a water tank at the end nearest the leading engine, and machine-gun positions at the ends (two examples were built, and were used only with PZ VII and VIII).

The first five armoured trains (Type A) were divided between the *Eisenbahn-Linienkommando Debreczen* (three units) and the *Feldtransportleitung*[3] at Miskolcz (the remaining two units), to carry out reconnaissance missions and cover troop withdrawals. The first two trains reached the Front on 10 November 1914, and the three others, apparently with a sixth train added, followed at intervals up until 20 November. The Type B trains, PZ VII and VIII, entered service in March 1915. These two armoured trains included armoured wagons with a turret (approx 270 degrees horizontal field of fire) mounting a 7cm L/30 gun (the actual calibre of these guns, designed for use on torpedo boats, was 66mm). Five such wagons were built, one going to reinforce PZ V, while PZ I and II each received an artillery wagon built in 1915 on tender chassis.

Following Italy's entry into the war on 23 May 1915, two armoured trains were built in the workshops at Villach, in Carinthia.

The first armoured train designed by Captain Schober, commander of the 15th Railway Company, seen here in Galicia in 1914. The intention is obviously to provide the train commander in the armoured engine with an elevated position compared to the low profile of the infantry wagons (with their less comfortable firing positions), for him to be able to see over both ends of the train.
(Photo: Paul Malmassari Collection)

[1.] The Austrian and Hungarian armoured trains after this date are covered in their individual chapters.
[2.] Sawodny, 'Die Panzerzüge Österreich-Ungarn und ihre Verblieb', p 26.
[3.] Debreczen Line Railway Command and Campaign Transport Directorate.

Initially numbered I and II, to avoid confusion they were subsequently renumbered as PZ IX and X in late October 1915.

In the Spring of 1915, the workshops at Neu-Sandec began construction of the second armoured train designed by Captain Schober. Initially it was composed of a Class 59 engine and two six-wheel wagons. On 1 May 1915 the train was ready, and after several tests, the Class 59 engine was replaced by fully-armoured engine No 97.247 coupled to tender No 76.177. A new motorised six-wheel wagon was also included, armed with a turret mounting a 7cm L/30 QF gun. This wagon was powered by a petrol-electric engine driving the central axle, and when detached on reconnaissance it could run at up to 40km/h (25mph). The complete train was crewed by sixty-five officers and men, and in addition to the main gun it was armed with eight machine guns. After modifications, it returned to service in July 1915, initially under the name of its designer, as *Panzerzüg Schober*, then in the Spring of 1916 it was redesignated PZ XI.

The numerical series contained another train, PZ XII, of which no trace remains in the official archives. Powered by a Class 229 engine, it appears to have comprised two armoured wagons built on Series O originals, to a design closely resembling that of Captain Schober's first armoured train.

Aside from the standard armoured train designs, several experiments were carried out, such as adding a high-sided bogie wagon protected with lengths of rail and armed with an 8cm gun to PZ VII; or again mounting a 10cm naval gun on a wagon attached to PZ V. In addition, improvised armoured trains were also built to meet local needs: in the Spring of 1915, an armoured train was built at Cracow using armoured engine No 229.85 and two wagons armed with machine guns. When Romania entered the war on 28 August 1916, the Railway Command at Bucovina ordered the construction of a train to protect the Jakobeny-Dorna Völgy line.

This photo shows the prototype train PZ II just out of the shop, without its artillery wagon which would not be built until 1915, and also lacking its observation cupola. Note that the machine-gun embrasures in leading wagon No 140.914 are inset at the top at an angle, whereas later photos of PZ II show that they were modified to sit flush with the armoured sides.
(Photo: Paul Malmassari Collection)

Lastly, at least one narrow-gauge armoured train was put into service on the metre-gauge network in Bosnia.

Tactically, the armoured trains were operated in pairs for mutual support, as proposed by Captain Kossowicz, commander of the 5th Railway Company. The same deployment would be adopted by the Red Army.

Following the relative stabilisation of the various fronts, the need for armoured trains lessened, and in September 1917 it was decided to demobilise six trains: thus PZ I, III, VI, X, XI and XII were laid up, and only PZ II, IV, V, VII and VIII remained in service (PZ IX having been destroyed during the previous month). The remaining trains were organised in a new manner, with the artillery wagon leading, then the engine, followed by an infantry wagon. A second infantry wagon would be held in reserve in the support train. The existing rolling stock was redistributed, making the later trains difficult to identify in photographs. In the Spring of 1918, a number of armoured trains were built to the Russian broad gauge for operations in Russia, but at the time of writing no trace of their deployment and fate has come to light.

At the end of the war, the surviving trains (PZ I to VII and PZ XI) were shared out between the following countries (refer to the corresponding country chapters for their subsequent use):

– PZ IV, VII (1917 numbering), XI (less its engine) and parts of PZ I, VI and VIII to Hungary.
– PZ III and part of PZ VIII to Poland.
– PZ II and parts of PZ VI and VII to Czechoslovakia.
– PZ V and part of PZ I to Yugoslavia.

The Class 59 engine of Captain Schober's first armoured train, with hastily-added armour which covers only the most vital parts.
(Photo: Paul Malmassari Collection)

The excellence of their basic design, their capacity for further development and their underlying durability are proved by their continual employment up until 1945, often in adverse conditions.

Drawing of MÁV Class 377 engine.

(Paul Malmassari)

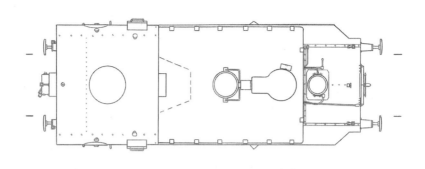
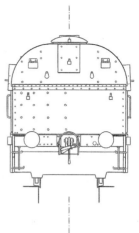

© Paul MALMASSARI 1986 1/87 (HO)

The rear wagon (No S 150.003) of PZ II before modification of the machine-gun embrasures. Note the arrangement for the machine-gun fitting in the door facing away from the engine, and also the coupling rail, doubtless attached to a safety wagon. There were no cowcatchers/stone guards fitted to the infantry wagons of PZ I, II and III.

(Photo: Paul Malmassari Collection)

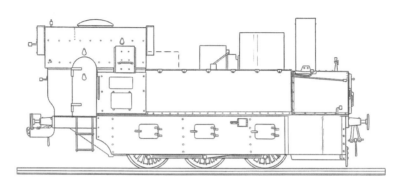
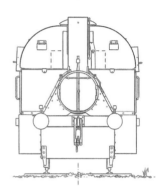

PZ I entered service with only two wagons and the engine, but in 1915 this artillery wagon was added. Note the safety flat wagons in front.

(Photo: Paul Malmassari Collection)

A rare interior view of an infantry wagon, with the shield for the lateral machine gun. The external armour was 12mm thick, fitted over a 40mm layer of wood, plus an internal layer of armour.

(Photo: Paul Malmassari Collection)

Here is PZ I apparently leading a part of a different armoured train.

(Photo: Paul Malmassari Collection)

PZ II has here received its header wagon built on a tender chassis and armed with a 7cm L/30 chase gun.
(Photo: Paul Malmassari Collection)

Here the side machine-gun positions of the infantry wagons are clearly vertical and flush with the armour sides. The header wagon is armed with a 4.7cm gun on each side, and these, plus the 7cm chase gun, gave it formidable firepower.
(Photo: Paul Malmassari Collection)

Two views of PZ II (with the number painted on the engine) being inspected by Archduke Karl, who would become Emperor on 21 November 1916 as Karl I. Note that the cab window is not yet protected by armour.
(Photos: Paul Malmassari Collection)

Above: At the rear of PZ II can be seen a high-sided bogie wagon which appears to be carrying a field gun. Behind engine MÁV 377.116 is wagon No S 150.003 and in front, No 140.914.
(Photo: Paul Malmassari Collection)

Left: A superb photo of one of the side-mounted 4.7cm I.F.K. guns in the header wagon of PZ II.
(Photo: Paul Malmassari Collection)

Below: PZ II photographed on 5 August 1915, festooned with tra-ditional decorations for a public celebration.[4] The Austrian flag flies proudly in front of the left-hand wagon, on which the column on the rear facing the engine denotes the handbrake. Note also the rectangular armour plate covering the engine cab.
(Photo: Paul Malmassari Collection)

4. Probably in commemoration of the battle of Petrovaradin in 1716, a victory over the Ottoman Empire.

Probably a view of wagon No S 148.105 of PZ V in camouflage, fitted with the cowcatchers used on PZ IV, V and VI.
(Photo: Paul Malmassari Collection)

An overall view of a Type B PZ. Four hooks seen on the armour skirt around the turret were used to clamp the turret in place when travelling.
(Photo: Paul Malmassari Collection)

Left: A fine attempt at camouflage on PZ VII, easily recognisable by the circular ventilator cowls on the turret.
(Photo: Paul Malmassari Collection)

Below: The artillery wagon with its 70mm turret was characteristic of Type B armoured trains. On this wagon, which is carrying sleepers and lengths of rail, is painted the name 'Oberleutnant Becker', perhaps the commander of the train.
(Photo: Paul Malmassari Collection)

Top: This overhead view is interesting because it allows us to see the horizontal armour on the top of the engine. Detailed differences sometimes allow us to tell one MÁV Class 377 engine from the others. The lighter tone of certain armour plates tell of more recent additions. This is PZ VII, and the artillery wagon in the foreground is No 141.172, fitted with angular ventilator cowls on its turret.

(Photo: Paul Malmassari Collection)

Above: This armoured wagon mounting a 10cm L/50 naval gun, seen here at the exit from the Montfalcone tunnel in the Summer of 1916, was temporarily attached to PZ V.

(Photo: Paul Malmassari Collection)

This view of PZ VII allows us to see the shape of the rear face of the artillery turret of wagon No 141.963 which precedes one of the engines, either MÁV 377.455 or 377.118. Between the two engines is wagon No S 150.271.
(Photo: Paul Malmassari Collection)

PZ VII was immediately recognisable by the round shape of the armoured ventilator cowls on wagon No. 140.963, while the wagon at the other end of the train had angular ones.
(Photo: Paul Malmassari Collection)

Above: Some time in 1915 this high-sided bogie wagon MÁV No Ikn 169.011 armoured with a double row of rails was coupled to PZ VII. The chase gun was an 8cm[5] Feldkanone M 05. The wagon was dismantled in December 1915 as it blocked the field of fire of the wagon behind it.

(Photo: Paul Malmassari Collection)

Right: A fine photo of life on the Italian or Russian Front, with a Škoda 30.5cm Model 1911 howitzer and the pensive crew of a Type B armoured train observing the piece. No doubt some are wondering how they could carry off the howitzer for some additional firepower.

(Photo: Paul Malmassari Collection)

Below: Red Cross postcard representing an attack on the Russians, specifically the Cossacks, with a certain amount of artistic licence.

(Postcard: Paul Malmassari Collection)

5. The actual calibre was 76.5mm.

Above: The Carinthian PZ I which would become PZ IX, seen here on 1 October 1915, with its original number 'I' painted on its sides. The embrasures allowed the crew to bring to bear two Russian machine guns and thirty personal weapons. The engine is probably a Class 97.

(Photo: Paul Malmassari Collection)

Below: Several months later, an 'X' has been added beside the 'I' to form the number 9 in Roman numerals. The crew complement of each of these Carinthian PZ was two officers and thirty-three men. PZ IX would be destroyed by Romanian artillery fire on 29 August 1916.

(Photo: Paul Malmassari Collection)

Above: The second of the Carinthian armoured trains, with its engine No 63.07, was given the designation PZ X in the revised numbering system. The armoured wagons are Ke 65.370 (on the right) and K 802.163 (on the left). Here it is seen at Tarvis.

(Photo: HGM)

Below: The engine of the improvised armoured train built by the 19th Railway Company in the Summer of 1916, probably a Class 94 of the Bucovina Railway.

(Photo: Paul Malmassari Collection)

This improvised armoured train was employed in 1916–17 in the Jacobeny region of Bucovina, before being destroyed in May 1917.

(Photo: Paul Malmassari Collection)

The header wagon bearing the inscription '19 E.K.' after the 19th Railway Company which built it.

(Photo: Paul Malmassari Collection)

An overall view of the train.

(Photo: Paul Malmassari Collection)

Right: The initial configuration of PZ *Schober*, with a Class 59 armoured engine, identical to the one which powered the original armoured train designed by Captain Schober. The two wagons are numbered 314.706 and 334.457.

(Photo: Paul Malmassari Collection)

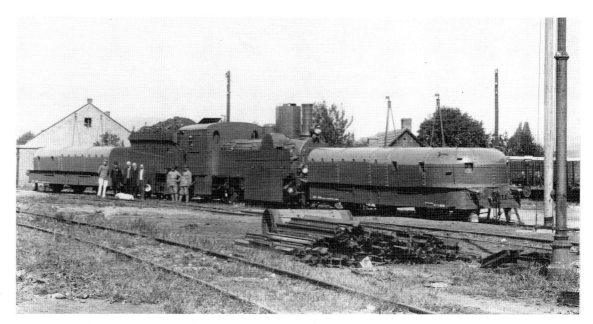

Below: The improved version of PZ *Schober* was built in the Spring of 1915 and was renumbered PZ XI in 1916. The new engine (its lower armour protection not yet in place) was No 97.247 coupled to tender No 76.177. Here the train has not yet been fitted with the antennae on the wagon roofs.

(Photo: Paul Malmassari Collection)

This view of the entire train allows us to compare the two sides of the motorised armoured wagon, and to note the presence of the radio masts, as shown in the drawings below, and which would ultimately be removed. Also, in this configuration the motorised wagon is coupled to the rear of the train.

(Photo: Paul Malmassari Collection)

The front end of the wagon is differentiated by having only three firing embrasures, compared to five at the rear end, plus the radiator grill. Here the searchlight can be clearly seen, together with its power cable which feeds it at all angles of training of either its housing or the turret.
(Photo: Paul Malmassari Collection)

Rear view of motorised wagon No 303.343 (in German a *Motorkanonenwagen*). It weighed 45 tonnes and was 9.86m (32ft 4in) long overall. The cylinder on top of the turret contains a trainable searchlight.
(Photo: Fortepan)

Left: An inspection by Archduke Friedrich, Duke of Teschen, on the Carpathian Front in February 1917. Commander-in-Chief of the Austro-Hungarian Army, he would be dismissed from his post by the Emperor just a few days later.
(Photo: Paul Malmassari Collection)

Above: In this photo dated March 1916 note the machine guns mounted in the firing embrasures, the stone guard fitted in front of each end wheel, and the Austro-Hungarian flag proudly flown. On each of the three wagons in the train, access was by hatches in the roof, reached by means of the handrails and steps at each corner.
(Photo: Paul Malmassari Collection)

In this previously unpublished photo, from a glass-plate negative, note the flat face of the low-profile infantry wagon facing the tender. On each of the two infantry wagons, this end had a machine-gun port in the centre. In the diagram reproduced below the lead wagon is shown running with this flat face forward, so this position would then become the chase gun.

(Photo: Paul Malmassari Collection)

Probably the only photo showing the wreck of PZ XI, perhaps as the result of an artillery bombardment to judge by the churned-up earth. PZ XI was withdrawn from service in September 1917.

(Glass-plate negative, date and place unknown: Paul Malmassari Collection)

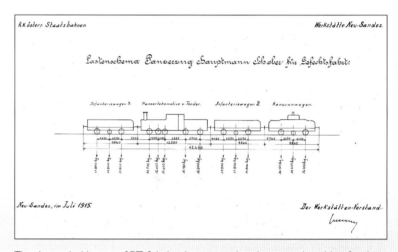

Engine No 97.247 of PZ XI with its fully-armoured tender seen at Roveretto. Under the canvas sheeting is railcar No 303.343.

(Photo: HGM)

The theoretical layout of PZ *Schober*. It appears that the normal position for the motorised wagon was at the rear of the train, perhaps to enable it to manoeuvre independently in case the train was immobilised.

(Plan: Private Collection)

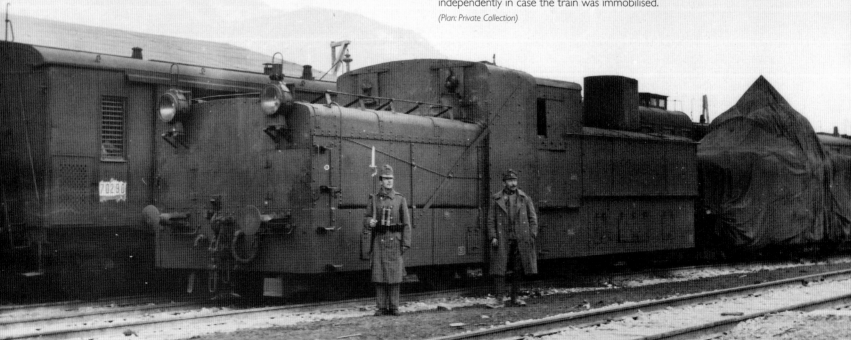

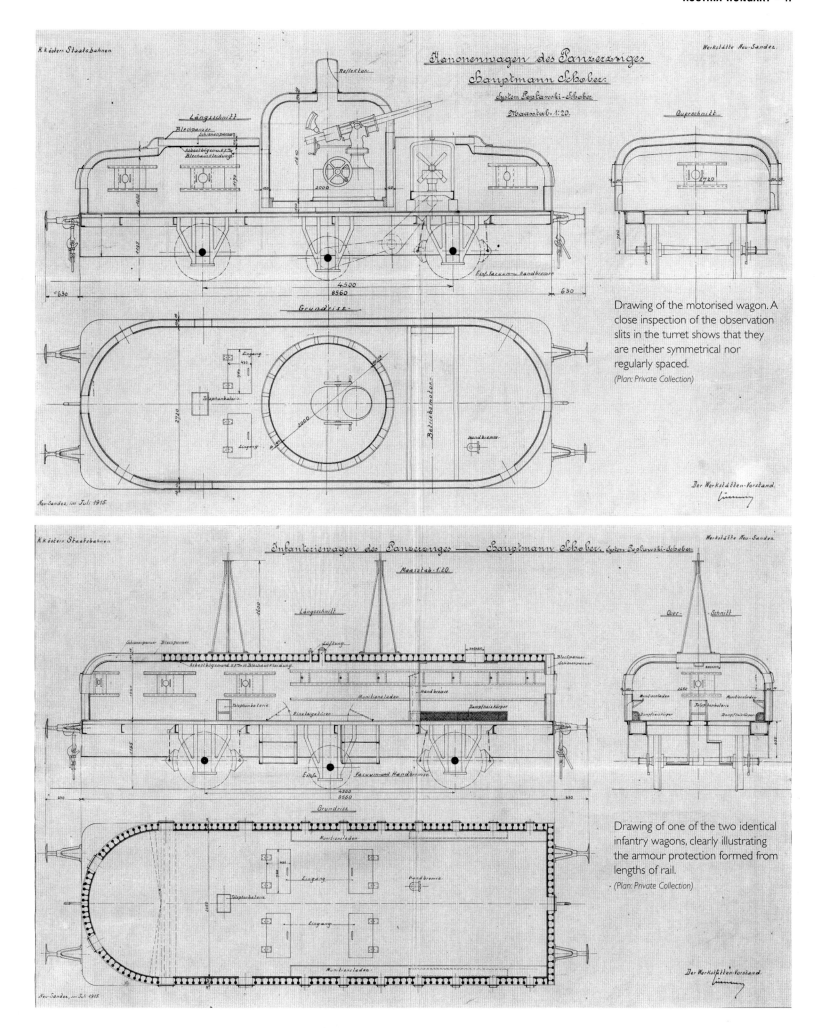

Drawing of the motorised wagon. A close inspection of the observation slits in the turret shows that they are neither symmetrical nor regularly spaced.

(Plan: Private Collection)

Drawing of one of the two identical infantry wagons, clearly illustrating the armour protection formed from lengths of rail.

(Plan: Private Collection)

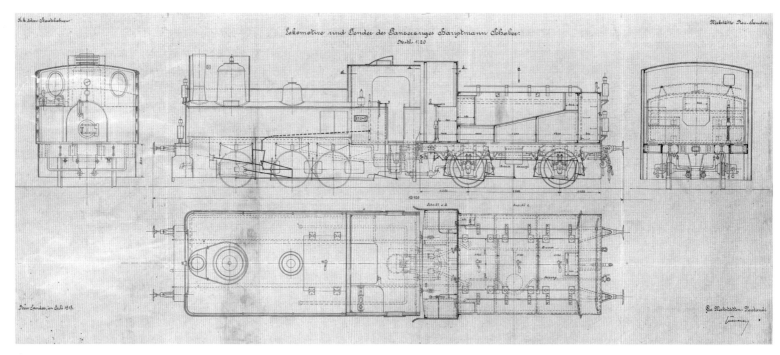

Above: Drawing of engine No 97.247 with its tender No 76.177.
(Plan: Private Collection)

Left: In 1916 the train which would later be numbered PZ XII was attached to XXV Army Corps, powered by a Class 229 2-6-2 tank engine, coupled to an auxiliary armoured tender. The appearance of the armoured wagons is very similar to those of Captain Schober's first train, illustrated at the beginning of the chapter.
(Photo: Hungarian Historical Service)

Below: PZ IV (new numbers in 1917) was put together with units from PZ VII. Here we can clearly see one of the hooks which held the turret in the travelling position.
(Photo: Paul Malmassari Collection)

Above: An unidentified armoured train, which we believe to be an Austro-Hungarian unit in Galicia, perhaps dating from after the Russian retreat in May 1915. Close inspection of the original photo reveals an inscription in Cyrillic letters on the door of the building visible between the chimney and steam dome of the engine.

(Photo: Paul Malmassari Collection)

Right: An unofficial badge produced for the Hungarian crews of armoured trains in 1914–16.

(Badge: Paul Malmassari Collection)

Below: An unofficial badge issued to commemorate 'Christmas at the Front' in 1916.

(Badge: Paul Malmassari Collection)

Above: Two Type B armoured trains were built. But in this photo we are looking at either a reorganisation, or rolling stock brought together at the end of the war. Note the smoke deflector on the left-hand engine.
(Photo: Paul Malmassari Collection)

Left: In 2003 the Austrians commemorated their armoured trains by issuing this postage stamp, showing the artillery wagon which was perhaps the most iconic image of these trains.
(Photo: Paul Malmassari Collection)

ÖSTERREICH 65

SOURCES:

Books:

Hauptner, R, and Jung, P, *Stahl und Eisen im Feuer* (Vienna: Verlagsbuchshandlung Stöhr, 2003).

Scopani, Paolo, *L'Ultima guerra dell'impero austro-ungarico, Storia fotografica delle operazioni militari sul fronte russo, serbo-albanese ed italiano 1914-1918* (Novale-Valdagno: Gino Rossato Editore, 2002).

Journal articles:

Lankovits, J., 'Panzerzüge in Österreich und Ungarn', *Eisenbahn* (Austria) (1986), No 8, pp 142–6; No 9, pp 164–7; No 10 pp. 184–6.

Sawodny, Wolfgang, 'Die Panzerzüge Österreich-Ungarn und ihre Verbleib', *Eisenbahn* (Austria) (1992), No 2, pp 26–8; No 3, pp 44–6; No 4, pp 64–6; No 6, pp 105–8.

Website:

http://www.heeresgeschichten.at/

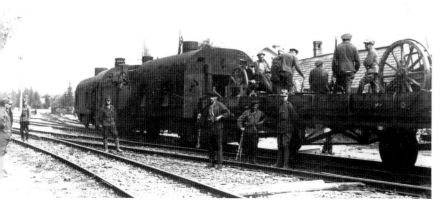

An armoured train assembled by the Czechs: the engine is probably No 377.362 from PZ VI (recognisable by the cupola on the cab roof), coupled between the wagons of PZ II which was captured in Prague. The nearest wagon is No 140.914, and the one behind the engine is No 150.003. The Czech soldiers are wearing Italian uniforms.
(Photo: Paul Malmassari Collection)

BELGIUM

ARMOURED TRAINS 1914–1915

A small country sandwiched between the two main belligerent powers of the First World War, in 1835 Belgium had embarked on the construction of an extensive railway network, just five years after the country had won its independence. By 1914 the network included some 4400km (2700 miles) of main line, backed up by around 4000km (2500 miles) of branch lines. Its sovereign territory was invaded on 4 August 1914, and the armoured trains (constructed primarily for the defence of Antwerp) would play a significant role in the conflict, as much from a psychological viewpoint as from their military impact. And this especially when one compares their numbers and their actions with the size of Belgium. The railway troops were formed in 1913, as an integral part of the Corps of Army Engineers, but the notion of 'armed trains' had been considered as far back as 1871, and the concept had been the subject of courses at the Belgian War College.[1]

The railway war was considered to be first and foremost defensive in nature, involving the destruction or blocking of numerous tunnels, and the cutting of bridges in the provinces directly menaced by an enemy attack, while at the same time seeking to avoid obstructing the movement of one's own troops. 'Phantom' (or 'ram') trains would be sent to crash into enemy trains or crucial elements of infrastructure such as turntables, in order to block the free circulation of enemy traffic.

The Siege of Antwerp

In September 1914, the decision was taken to link together the different forts around Antwerp by a single track circular rail line. The construction of the line took from 7 September to 1 October. In particular it would allow the movement of armoured trains during the final days of the siege.

Four Light Armoured Trains, for patrol and protection duties, were ordered by the Army High Command, and were constructed out of metal sheets meant for ship construction in the Antwerp

North workshops with the aid of the Engineers' Railway Company (CFG[2]). They were to be followed by three Heavy Armoured Trains, to be armed with naval guns provided by the British, to act as mobile artillery in advance of the line of forts.

The first Light Armoured Train was completed in ten days, the second in eight days and the third in just six days. The fourth train, however, was captured incomplete when Antwerp fell to the German Army.

The first train (No 1, Light, commanded by Lieutenant Michel then, when he was wounded, by Sub-Lieutenant Goutière) became operational on 5 September and was in action[3] continuously right up to 8 October, in particular on 25 and 26 September 1914 when it supported the operation to block the Brussels-Tournoi line, by means of 'phantom trains' launched in the direction of Enghien and Hal. This operation was repeated on 7 and 8 October, when the target was Duffel. In addition to their

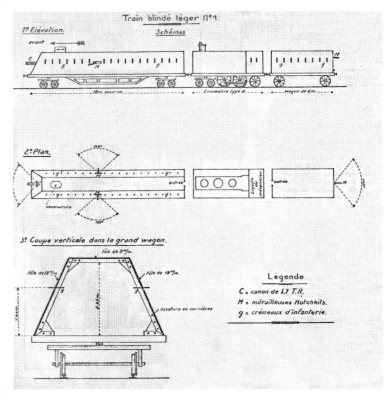

The only known plan of the Light Armoured Trains. Although schematic, it gives a good idea of the overall dimensions on the one hand, and of the layout of the armament (a 57mm chase gun firing straight ahead and three machine guns, including one firing to the rear). We have never seen a photo of the four-wheel van.

(Drawing: Bulletin belge des sciences militaires, July 1932)

[1.] Wauermans, Major H, *Fortification et travaux du Génie aux armées* (Brussels: Merzbach & Falk, 1875).

[2.] CFG = Compagnie de Chemins de Fer du Génie.

[3.] On 5 September 1914, the region of Boom and Tisselt; on the 7th, the region of Puurs; the 8th, at Beveren-Waes and Lockeren; the 9th, at Zele and Termonde; from the 11th to the 14th (with Armoured Train No 2), destruction of the bridges at Denderleeuw and Alost on the River Dendre; from the 25th to the 26th, the region of Gand, Grammont, Lessines; the 27th, launching of phantom trains from Muizen towards Louvain; 2 and 3 October, protection of the engineers demolishing the Duffel railway bridge.

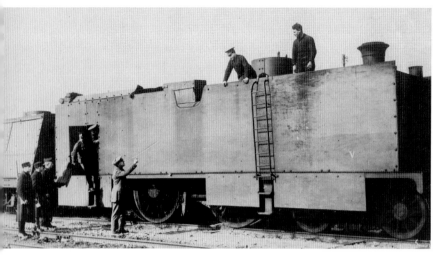

Class 16 armoured engine. These 4-4-2 tank engines were among the most modern of their day.
(Photo: Paul Malmassari Collection)

The other type of engine used with the Belgian armoured trains, the Class 32 Etat, an 0-6-0 tender engine also used on French railways.
(Photo: Paul Malmassari Collection)

Armoured wagon of a Belgian Light Armoured Train. The chase gun is a 57mm QF model on a casemate mounting with a severely restricted field of fire, its embrasure closed by sliding shutters. Of the three machine guns on the train, one fired to the rear from the van at the tail of the train. Each wagon carried six rails 6m (19ft 8in) long, ten pairs of fishplates and repair gear.
(Photo: Paul Malmassari Collection)

normal ammunition load of 12,000 rifle cartridges, 240 shrapnel shells and 120 57mm HE rounds, the armoured trains also carried 25kg (55lbs) of explosives for blowing up key installations.

Armoured Train No 2 (commanded by Lieutenant Deleval) went into action for the first time between 11 and 14 September, along with Armoured Train No 1. It participated in the destruction of the bridges at Denderleeuw and Alost on the River Dendre. It then operated on several occasions at Alost, Renaix and Audenaerde, at Eine and Zingem, at Tielt, and at Deurle. On 8 October, the crew launched phantom trains from Mortsel in the direction of Lierre.

Despite these actions, the German advance forced the Belgian Army to retreat. It entrenched itself in the fortified stronghold of Antwerp, from which the armoured trains also stationed there took part in sorties, in particular that of 9 to 13 September towards

One of the results of a 'phantom train' launched against German rail transport. The CFG driver and fireman of the ram engine jumped to safety before the collision and were only slightly injured. They were both later decorated by King Albert.
(Photo: All Rights Reserved)

Close-up of the armoured bogie wagon of Armoured Train No 1 after its capture by the Germans. Note the armour protection for the bogies and the buffer beam, which now has no buffers. It is uncertain whether this modification was carried out by the Belgians or the Germans. In addition, although the armament is not in evidence, the horizontal sliding armoured shutters have been removed, giving way to a much larger embrasure opening.
(Photo: Paul Malmassari Collection)

Above: A Belgian Light Armoured Train following its capture by the Germans near Boom. It was subsequently used by them for some time, as shown by the postcard below.
(Photo: Paul Malmassari Collection)

Right: This postcard is in fact German, showing PZ No 1. The armoured van on the left is the one seen in the background in the two photos above, indicating that the Germans rearranged the order of the train units, as the engine now brings up the rear.
(Postcard: Paul Malmassari Collection)

Below right: Here on the left one can just make out the rear of the artillery wagon with its larger embrasure.
(Photo: Paul Malmassari Collection)

Vilvorde, Louvain and Aarschot. On 7 and 8 October, a violent bombardment struck the fortress, but it held firm, allowing the evacuation of an enormous quantity of stores and virtually all the troops. On 9 October, the last Belgian and British troops pulled out, heading west. On that date, the unfinished Armoured Train No 4 was abandoned in Antwerp and captured. The demolition of the railway bridge at Boom cut off the retreat of Light Armoured Train No 1, which was sabotaged by its crew who were evacuated on Armoured Train No 2. They reached Ostend on the evening of the 9th, and formed the crew of Armoured Train No 3 which had been evacuated to Ostend the day before. The two surviving armoured trains were sent to Dunkirk on 13 October 1914. Then on the 19th, Armoured Train No 2 returned to Dixmude. Its crew were then employed in repairing the lines, notably on 21 and 22 October, in order to re-establish the rail link on the Caeskerke-Nieuport line.

Above: Class 32 engine captured at Antwerp.
(Photo: Paul Malmassari Collection)

Below: Another captured Class 32 engine. Note the armour plating which extends much lower than is seen on other engines in service, together with the inspection hatches.
(Photo: Paul Malmassari Collection)

The role of the Belgian Light Armoured Trains came to an end in late October 1914. The two trains were sent back to Calais where their armour protection was removed, apart from the armour on one Class 32 engine used to haul a British heavy railway gun, and on two armoured engines allocated to the French 200mm artillery battery 'Pérou'.[4] There was also a special train armed with a 21cm mortar originally mounted in the Blauwgaren Redoubt, double-headed by two armoured engines, which was in action during the battle of the Yser.

The Heavy Armoured Trains

From 8 September 1914 the construction of these three trains in Antwerp was entrusted to Lieutenant-Commander[5] A. Scott Littlejohns, who was acting as attaché to General Deguise, the Military Governor of Antwerp. This co-operation resulted in the trains often being referred to as 'Anglo-Belgian Armoured Trains', notably in the newspapers of the day. Some days earlier, it had been agreed to cede to the Belgian Army several British naval guns, which were the only ones capable of counter-battery fire against the German artillery.

Of the three trains planned,[6] two were constructed in the Hoboken workshops (by the British Engineering Company) and the third in the North Antwerp workshop. The first two were armed with three 4.7in (120mm) naval guns and armoured from the outset. Each train was composed of three Class 32 or 32S Etat Belgian engines (of which one could be detached for track reconnaissance), three 40-tonne artillery platform wagons 18m (59ft) long, and three Bika Type vans. The mixed nationality crews comprised one Royal Navy officer and six senior gunnery ratings, seventy NCOs and gunners from the Belgian fortresses, and finally railway personnel of the CFG. The armament of the third train was to comprise two heavier 6in (152mm) naval guns without shields, which at first were simply bolted onto unarmoured platform wagons (one with girder chassis underpinnings and the other with bar-type chassis underpinnings).

The first armoured wagon was completed on 15 September[7] and its firing trials were successfully carried out the same day. The next ten days were spent fixing the armour protection in place, training the crews and reconnoitring the railway lines and the Belgian positions. On the 23rd, the first train with one armoured wagon left Antwerp at 11.00, carrying Lieutenant-Commander Littlejohns who was the overall commander of the Heavy Armoured Trains, Captain Servais, French and Belgian officers, and the British Military Attaché. An observation aircraft was to correct the fall of shot on the German batteries which were thought to be in Epperghem. In spite of the mist which interfered with observation, based on the interrogation of prisoners and refugees the shoot actually took place.

From their base in Antwerp, the first two trains went into action at Malines between 24 and 27 September, co-operating with

spotting aircraft and balloons. One of the trains was even able to approach within 1800m of the German lines. On the 28th and 29th, they were in action in front of Forts Waelhem and Wavre-Sainte-Catherine (Sint-Katelijne-Waver), as the guns of the forts were unable to reach the German batteries. At one point, a German 42cm[8] shell only just missed one of the trains, whose movements were followed by German Drachen balloons. In spite of the trains taking shrapnel fire which fortunately burst too high, the Allied fire was effective, and forced the Germans to pull back.

On 4 October, the trains were fired on by German artillery, and one balloon was shot down by a 4.7in gun, served by Gunner's Mate T. Potter. On their withdrawal, still under fire, the trains were visited by Winston Churchill, then First Lord of the Admiralty,[9] accompanied by Admirals Horace Hood and H F Oliver. On 5 and 6 October, they went into action around Kleine-Miel, supported by two French armoured trains. But on the evening of the 6th, near Buchout, the artillery wagon at the head of one of the trains derailed on a section of line which had been cut by artillery fire. The derailed wagon was detached from the train and left there until the rails could be repaired, which took several hours. In the meantime the remaining five guns of the two trains engaged the

A direct hit on the shield of a 4.7in gun of a Heavy Armoured Train, possibly that on 21 October when Lt Robinson's train was hit.
(Photo: Le Miroir, 1 November 1914)

[4.] No 17 MT (0-6-0) of the Compagnie Malines-Terneuzen, and No 3479, a Belgian Class 32 Etat.

[5.] The equivalent of a Major in the Army (*Commandant* in French).

[6.] From 9 November they were allocated the following names: HMAT (His Majesty's Armoured Train) *Deguise* (after the Lieutenant-General who was the Military Governor of the Fortress of Antwerp, commanded by the Belgian Captain Servais; HMAT *Jellicoe* commanded by Lieutenant Lionel Robinson RN, and finally HMAT *Churchill*, commanded by Lieutenant Ridler RN. The train names were also painted on the wagons. Note that the Belgians serving on these trains wore British uniforms.

[7.] The first two armoured trains were completed by 25 September.

[8.] Evidently fired from an M-Gerät 'Big Bertha'.

[9.] Churchill was in Antwerp from the afternoon of 3 October to the evening of the 6th.

One of the 6in guns mounted on a Belgian platform wagon, seen here in Ostend on 9 October 1914.

(Photo: IWM)

A rare postcard, showing the armouring of a wagon of a Heavy Armoured Train. The vertical armour was 15mm thick compared to 10mm for the horizontal plates. Note however the chassis reinforcement system, which is different from that on the other Heavy and Light wagons. This is one of the two British 6in guns.

(Photo: Paul Malmassari Collection)

A photo dated with certainty to 13 November 1914, the square bearing the number '23' is not painted on the train but is a kilometre marker.

(Photo: From J'ai Vu, 13 December 1914)

German positions and silenced three batteries. On the 7th, the trains were successfully evacuated with reduced crews towards Saint Nicolas, before the lines were cut.

At Ostend from 12 October the armoured trains covered the withdrawal of troops from Gand. Then on the 15th, one leading and the other as rearguard, they protected the British troops marching on either side of the tracks between Roulers and Ypres. On entering the latter town, the lookouts posted on the engine fired on a scouting party of six German cavalrymen, killing an officer and a trooper. From 19 and 31 October, the trains were made available to General Rawlinson. Armoured Train No 3 (Lieutenant Robinson) went into action in the attack on Menin on the 19th and in the direction of Passchendale on the 20th. On the 21st, the train went into action on the Ypres-Roulers line, where it was fired on by German artillery, which failed to pierce its armour, but which prevented it from advancing further. From the 26th to the 31st, the trains were in action at various locations in support of the Belgian 3rd and 4th Divisions, fighting to the east of Dixmude and to the west of the bend of the Yser.

The 6in guns which had been mounted on bogie platform wagons in Antwerp, were evacuated to Ostende on 7 October, and received their full armour protection in late October. They were formed into a new train which, under the command of Lieutenant-Commander Ridler RN, rejoined the two other trains in the Ypres sector. From 1 to 7 November, the trains went into action against the German lines, and notably against an observation balloon on the 3rd. German prisoners even indicated that the 6in shells from the trains had killed eighty-seven soldiers in a trench on the 6th. Then HMAT *Deguise* left for Boulogne to be repaired. When it reached Oostkerke on the 11th, it was targeted by two salvoes which fell just 15m short of the train, forcing it to retreat 500m behind the station. But on the 13th, while the train was stationed at Km 23 on the Caeskerke line, a shell hit the second engine, killing the driver. From the 15th, HMAT *Jellicoe* came under the orders of I Corps, and went into action each day to the east of Ypres. It was also the target of German artillery on the 17th, and one man was wounded. The heavy rail traffic evacuating casualties had prevented the train from quickly manoeuvring out of range. On the 18th, a German shell damaged an engine and one of the 6in guns. The train pulled back towards Ypres Station but the German artillery succeeded in following it and ended up also firing on the station itself. The German bombardment was renewed on the 19th, but the tracks were undamaged.

For its part, HMAT *Churchill* went into action in December in the area around Oostkerke against German batteries to the south of

Dixmude. On 18 December, a shell wounded Commander Littlejohn's second-in-command. Between the end of December and March 1915, the three armoured trains were continuously in action, sometimes in support of an assault (*Jellicoe* at la Bassée on 10 January), but in particular in counter-battery or bombardment missions and in actions to neutralise trench lines (*Jellicoe* at Beuvry between 20 and 24 January, *Churchill* at Oosterkerke on 28 and 29 January, and against an observation post at Ennetières on 11 February, *Déguise* at Beuvry firing on a rail junction on the 15th, among other targets, *Churchill* against a battery at Fleur d'Ecosse on 3rd March). The guns of the trains were extremely effective, notably against troop concentrations: on 18 February, HMAT *Deguise* fired seven shells at German troops to the South-West of la Bassée. These actions brought the trains within range of the German artillery. The Germans scored hits, but the armour protection and swift manoeuvring of the trains normally protected the crews, except on 25 January when *Jellicoe* was hit, with two men wounded and the Belgian engine driver killed. Between 10 and 13 March the three trains supported the action at Neuve Chapelle. On that occasion, Field Marshal Sir John French paid a surprise visit to HMAT *Churchill*, which was the command train for Commander Littlejohns.

Above: The extreme length (18m/59ft) of the bogie platform wagons used in the trains is evident in this side view of a 6in gun wagon. Note the name 'Leman' painted on the side armour.
(Photo: Paul Malmassari Collection)

Left: A well-known shot of a Heavy Armoured Train. The length of the protruding rifle barrels adds to the offensive look of the train, even against troops on the ground.
(Photo: Paul Malmassari Collection)

A popular postcard, showing the 6in gun wagon with girder underpinning, where it appears that one of the side doors is missing.
(Postcard: Paul Malmassari Collection)

Another postcard which shows the armoured van between the engine and the gun wagon, beyond which is the second train engine.
(Postcard: Paul Malmassari Collection)

A fine view of the open breech of the 4.7in gun on one of the Heavy Armoured Trains.
(Photo: La Guerre de 1914–1918)

Above: This view, again from *La Guerre de 1914-1918*, is interesting as it shows the relative lack of comfort for the crews of the gun wagons, even if they are glad of the protection given by the armour!

Left: Here we can see the girders joined in an 'X' which support the gun mounting.
(Photo: La Guerre de 1914-1918)

We lack information on the armoured trains after March 1915. Nevertheless, a well-illustrated article was published by the magazine *Sur le Front* No 18 on 8 May 1915. The photos used in the article show the Light Armoured Trains, which leads us to think that the Heavy Armoured Trains were no longer in use at that time (otherwise they would have been shown), and this was probably because the front lines had become fixed. Finally, the armoured trains were formally taken out of service in September 1915.

In the section of Commander Littlejohns' report dealing with the radio sets installed in the trains, he mentions the names of three armoured trains: H.M.A.T. *Sinclair*, which entered service at Boulogne on 26 December 1914, and which, after the succesful trials conducted up to 7 January 1915, led Commander Littlejohns to introduce H.M.A.T. *Singer* on 15 January, followed by H.M.A.T. *Sueter* on 23 January. In addition to their radio sets, they were equipped with a radio mast 8m (26ft 3in) high which could be erected in three minutes, plus 15m (49ft) of aerial cable. This installation gave radio reception over a range of 50km (30 miles) by day and 70km (40 miles) by night. The defence of these trains was provided by a machine gun installed on the roof. We must conclude that the designation 'HMAT' was used for convenience in the report but did not correspond with actual armoured trains.

Above: An anti-aircraft gun obviously mounted in the position formerly occupied by a shielded 4.7in gun. There is no documentary evidence to show when this conversion was carried out.
(Photo: All Rights Reserved)

Above left: The observation ladder used by the armoured trains in conjunction with observation from balloons and vantage points such as factory chimneys and belfries, which had become priority targets for the gunners of both sides.
(Photo: All Rights Reserved)

Left: An illustration from a German publication, based on the principle known since the times of Julius Caesar, namely to emphasise the courage of one's own side by demonstrating the threat or the power of the enemy.
(Illustration: Paul Malmassari Collection)

Top: This postcard seems to have inspired many variations and derivatives, as much by the Belgians and the other Allies as by their enemies.
(Postcard: Paul Malmassari Collection)

Above: Virtually the same view, in an American postcard which places the action at Antwerp.
(Postcard: Paul Malmassari Collection)

Above right: This German postcard correctly attributes the train as belonging to the Belgian Army, but sites the scene as being in front of Dixmude; another, this time attributing the train to the German Army, can be seen in the colour section, page 499.
(Postcard: Paul Malmassari Collection)

Below: The engine at the head of a Belgian Armoured Train was not usual. However, certain sources do indicate that each armoured train had one engine which could be used for reconnaissance.
(Postcard: Paul Malmassari Collection)

SOURCES:
Archives:
SHD, carton 9 N 464 SUP

Books:
Littlejohns, Commander A Scott, RN, *Royal Naval Air Service: Armoured Trains, Report on Operations Sept. 1914 to March 1915*, Air Department, June 1915 (MRA B.1.178.4).
Ministère des Chemins de Fer, Marine, Postes et Télégraphes: *Compte-rendu des opérations 04/08/1914 - 04/08/1917*.
Scarniet, Vincent, *D'Anvers à l'Yser. La Compagnie de Chemin de fer du génie et les trains blindés* (Jambes: ASBL Musée du Génie, 2014).
Wauwermans Major H., *Fortification et travaux du Génie aux armées* (Brussels : Merzbach & Falk, 1875).

Journal articles:
Harlepin, J., 'Les Trains Blindés', *Newsletter of the Centre liégeois d'histoire et d'archéologie militaires* Volume IV, No 7 (July–September 1990), pp 45–66.
_____, 'Les Trains Blindés', *Militaria Belgica* (1998), pp 69–88.
'Trains blindés et "trains fantômes" pendant l'investissement d'Anvers', *Belgian Bulletin of Military Sciences* Volume II, No 1 (July 1932), pp 1–14.

Website:
http://pages14-18.mesdiscussions.net/pages1418/forum-pages-histoire/autre/trains-blindes-sujet_12036_1.htm

BOSNIA AND HERZEGOVINA

When civil war broke out in Yugoslavia in 1991, the tensions which had been building up over a long period caused the breakup of the country. On the territory of the new Bosnia and Herzegovina (Herzeg-Bosnia), each of the three ethnic groups – Serbs, Bosnians and Croats – attempted to create their own zone of influence with the ultimate aim of becoming autonomous. Along with other improvised armoured vehicles, armoured trains played an important role.

Republica Srpska[1]

At Gradačac, an important railway junction 45km (28 miles) to the south-east of Slavonski-Brod and the River Sava (which serves as the frontier), and 30km (18.6 miles) to the west of Brčko, one can see the Bosno-Serbian armoured train which was used as a 'Trojan Horse' in an attempt to capture the town in October 1992. The attack failed when the train was stopped by the Muslim defenders, who have since preserved it as a monument to the fighting.

Note in the third photo the camouflage pattern on the left which positively identifies the wagon as the same in the two previous photos. Here the side armour protection is intact, which would suggest that the explosion of the charges which caused the impressive damage visible on the museum train occurred at a later date – either to prevent the risk of the train being put back into service by its previous owners, or for propaganda purposes.

Our research has unearthed another armoured train, probably Serb, at Brčko in 1995.

[1.] A self-proclaimed enclave, covering half of Bosnia and Herzegovina, and whose autonomy within the Republic was recognised by the Dayton Accords in 1995

The camouflage scheme is irregular patches of red-brown and dark grey on pale-green.
(Photo: Michael Hansson)

Brčko lay between the two Serb regions of Bosnia during the civil war, and was an entry point from Croatia via the Republic of Krajina. The Serbs therefore seized the town in May 1992 after six days of fighting, and it is likely the armoured train photographed there had been used to protect supply lines between the various Serb enclaves.

The train at Gradcačac on the day it was captured.

(Photo: All Rights Reserved, via Yves Debay)

The train at Brčko. The camouflage pattern of sky blue on a mid-blue background was apparently created by rolls pasted on like wallpaper, continually repeating the motifs.

(Photo: All Rights Reserved)

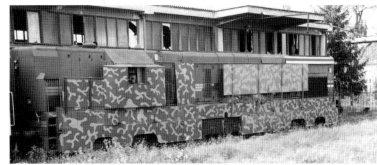

The train at Brčko 1995. A view of the armoured diesel locomotive with the Serbian flag visible at the front end.

(Photo: All Rights Reserved)

A view of one of the armoured wagons at Gradcačac, showing the armour plating deformed by explosions.

(Photo: Michael Hansson)

A view of the front and right-hand side of the Muslim-Croat Federation trolley, which well illustrates the asymmetrical protection, when one considers that the coupling is fitted on the centre line. The initials HVO stand for 'Hrvatsko Vijeće Obrane' or Croat Defence Council, formally dissolved in November 1995.
(Photo: ECPA–D)

The left-hand side of the trolley, with the added protection of sheets of rubber and tyres, fitted on the side facing the enemy, who here would be Muslims.
(Photo: ECPA–D)

French and Croatian soldiers inside the trolley. The internal lining of sheets of plywood can be seen, and at the far end, one of the driver's cabs which is identical to that of the Končar trolley described elsewhere. To the right, there appears to be a hatch in the roof, maybe for observation?
(Photo: ECPA–D)

Moslem-Croat Federation

We have discovered no details of this armoured trolley, apart from the fact that it was used during 1996 in Mostar, on the Bosnian-Croat side of the lines. At that time, French troops of the 3rd Engineer Regiment (Charleville-Mézières) used it for movements in high-risk zones.

SOURCE:

https://www.youtube.com/watch?v=TY3ODhgFtMc

BRAZIL

Armoured trains of the Constitutionalist Revolution,[1] 1932

In the fallout from the financial crash of 1929 which triggered an economic recession in Brazil, in October 1930 President Vargas deposed his discredited predecessor and established a provisional government. But his increasingly dictatorial style alienated him from the people, and in particular the inhabitants of the State of São Paulo, who called for autonomy from the federal government. The 'Unique Front' (*Frente Única*) which contained several senior army officers began an armed revolt against the federal forces. Alongside the Air Force and the Navy, improvised armoured vehicles and armoured trains were built, principally for the 'Paulist' forces, by both the railway workshops and the Technical College.

The latter institution supervised the construction of six armoured trains. In principle, each train would comprise an armoured wagon in front of and behind the locomotive, plus a safety pilot truck at the head of the unit, the crew of which would include fifteen men in each of the two wagons. There is no information on where trains Nos 1 and 6 were first employed; Nos 2 and 3 served in the Sorocaba region to the west of São Paulo, and Nos 4 and 5 served around Mogiana in the north of the state.

[1.] Also known as the Autonomist Revolution or the Paulist Revolution (from the name of the State involved).

Armoured Train No 1 of the Sorocabana sector, which became Armoured Train No 3 after modifications, and was christened *Phantom of the South*. The engine is a 2-8-2 Mikado, No 216.
(Photo: Periodical Section of UFDF/Defesa)

Armoured Train No 3 wagon with its 7mm machine gun in a square turret. The camouflage was inspired by contemporary French schemes using olive green/dark green/grey/chestnut brown.
(Photo: Periodical Section of UFDF/Defesa)

Armoured Train No 3, showing the cowcatcher on the leading safety wagon.
(Photo: Reginaldo Bacchi)

Another view of a wagon from Armoured Train No 3.
(Photo: Periodical Section of UFDF/Defesa)

Baldwin 2-8-0 No 730 armoured locomotive of Armoured Train No 4, built
in the workshops of the Companhia
Paulista de Estradas de Ferro in
Campinas, São Paulo State. It was
operated by the Mogiana railway
company, and was considered to be
the best of the armoured train designs.
(Photo: Periodical Section of UFDF/Defesa)

Armoured Train No 4 showing the
symmetrical layout typical of these
armoured trains, with an armoured
machine-gun wagon in front and
behind the locomotive, and a pilot
wagon at the head of the unit. The
turret at the rear of the left-hand
wagon is square.
(Photos: Reginaldo Bacchi)

Baldwin 2-8-0 locomotive from one of
Armoured Trains Nos 3 to 5, seen
from the left-hand side.
(Photo: Reginaldo Bacchi)

A photo which despite its below-average quality is still a fine shot of a machine-gun wagon from one of Armoured Trains Nos 3 to 5, armed with two 7mm Hotchkiss in square turrets.

(Photo: Reginaldo Bacchi)

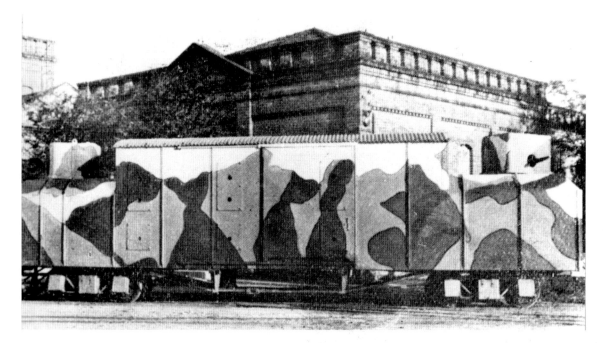

Armoured Train No 5 of the Companhia Mogyana, with Baldwin 2-8-0 No 732.

(Photo: Periodical Section of UFDF/Defesa)

Armoured Train No 6 *Phantom of Death*, built in the Central do Brasil Company's workshops in Pindamonhagaba. Two notable features are the roof sloping down towards each end of the armoured wagons, and the leading wagon armed with an unidentified gun firing forward.

(Photo: Police Military Museum of São Paulo via UFJF/Defesa)

Armoured locomotive of Armoured Train No 6, showing the overall armour protection on the tender, leaving a firing loophole in the side. This type of train was designed by Clément de Baujaneau, a French engineer living in Brazil.
(Photo: Reginaldo Bacchi)

The same train seen from the opposite side, revealing that the design was symmetrical. The sloping roof armoured wagon is based on a bogie wagon. In the following photo, the forward 75mm Krupp gun is clearly visible.
(Photo: Reginaldo Bacchi)

Close-up of the 75mm Krupp gun of Armoured Train No 6. The cowcatcher carries its lamp in an unusually low position, indicating that the two-plank safety wagon seen in the previous photo was not always attached – unless this view shows the rear of the train.
(Photo: Periodical Section of UFDF/Defesa)

SOURCES:

Bastos, Expedito Carlos Stephani, *Blindados no Brasil – Um Longo e Árduo Aprendizado, 1921/2011*, Vol I (Bauru e Juiz de For a: Taller Editoria e UFJF/Defesa, 2011).

Duarte, Paulo, *Palmares pelo avêsso* (Sao Paulo: Instituto Progresso Editorial, S.A., 1947).

Walsh, Paul V, *The 1932 Paulista War : An Example of Conventional Warfare in Latin America during the Inter-War Period*, lecture presented in 2001 at the annual conference of the Society for Military History of the University of Calgary.

Website:

http://netleland.net/hsampa/epopeia1932/blindados1932.html

BULGARIA

ARMOURED TRAIN PROJECT

It would appear that Bulgaria began a project for at least one armoured train. In 1936 the General Staff ordered a train from the Varna workshops, to comprise six wagons, armed with a total of four 75mm guns and eight anti-aircraft machine guns. Interestingly, the armour protection was to be reinforced concrete.

Delivery was planned for 1937, but no information has come to light as to whether it was actually built.

SOURCES:
SHD, 7 N 2751.

BURMA-MYANMAR

Annexed by the British Empire after three wars between 1824 and 1886, Burma became a Crown Colony in 1937. Five years later, Burma was invaded by the Japanese, who were driven out in July 1945. On 4 January 1948 Burma regained its independence, but the security situation remained highly unstable due to continuing ethnic and religious conflicts. In 1962, a *coup d'état* brought General Ne Win to power.

[1.] The name Myanmar was adopted in 1989 by the Burmese government and recognised by the UN, with the exception of the United States and the United Kingdom. Myanmar is a local variant of the ancient name Burmah.

Two of the Wickham armoured trolleys probably supplied by Malaysia, photographed here in February 1995.
(Photos: Olaf Güttler and Florian Grupp)

As late as 1994, the security situation on the railway network required that trains be preceded by a safety wagon, here seen with a cowcatcher. The locomotives are Alsthom DF[2] diesels.

(Photos: Olaf Güttler)

[2.] D = Diesel, F = six axles, delivered in 1987.

CAMBODIA

ARMOURED TRAINS

Under the French protectorate, the railway network was defended by armoured trains and trolleys (see the chapter on France). It is likely that similar measures were used during the Khmer Rouge uprising btween 1967 at 1975. Following the intervention of Vietnamese forces and the overthrow of the Pol Pot regime, in 1979 the Khmer Rouge carried out a systematic destruction of the country's infrastructure, including harassing attacks on the rail network. Armoured wagons were hastily built and added to each civilian train.

The Paris Peace Accord signed on 23 October 1991 allowed for the despatch of a UN contingent (MIPRENUC then UNAMIC), which promised a return to normality despite the millions of mines which had been laid and the continuing presence of pockets of resistance. Nevertheless, trains continued to be the target of attacks, and improvised armour was added to the locomotives, including the veteran Pacifics[1] left over from the French period.

<hr />

[1.] Built in Mulhouse by SACM and in Haine-Saint-Pierre in Belgium.

A scene from everyday life on the railway, with passengers piled onto the leading flat wagon, intended as a safety wagon to detonate explosive devices. Rather than indicating a return to more peaceful times, the passengers seemed to be motivated by the fact that travel on these wagons was free of charge, despite the continuing danger.
(Photo: Olaf Güttler)

Pacific No 231-501 with its armoured cab, practically identical to the types used during the war in Indochina.
(Photo: Olaf Güttler)

In 1966, the railway received thirteen BB diesel-electric mainline locomotives and eight shunting/branch-line locomotives from Alsthom. On the mainline locos only the front and side faces of the cabs at each end were armoured, and the observation slits show several variations.
(Photo: Olaf Güttler)

Above: In 2013 BB No 1055, photographed here in 1991, was being rebuilt in the Phnom Penh workshops.
(Photo: Olaf Güttler)

Close-up of an armoured wagon taken in July 1991 near Phnom Penh, showing the internal armour plating clearly.
(Photo: Olaf Güttler)

Left: On the right is armoured BB No 1055 seen at a junction north of Phnom Penh. The BB shunter No 1005 on the left has only an armoured cab.
(Photo: Olaf Güttler)

SOURCES:

Chlastacz, Michel, 'Les 50 ans de malheur du rail cambodgien' ('50 troubled years of the Cambodian railways'), *La vie du rail* No 2237 (22–28 March 1990), pp 16–17.

Roussel, Daniel, 'Cambodge, les trains de la guerre' ('Cambodia, the trains at war'), *La vie du rail* No 2237 (22–28 March 1990), pp 11–15.

CANADA

The first project for a Canadian armoured train dates back to 18 April 1867,[1] when the Great Western Railroad Company proposed the construction of an armoured wagon, equipped with a turret 2.5m (8ft 4in) high at the front end, and at the rear an armoured casemate with firing loopholes for the crew. The project was intended to counter the incursions of the Fenians, an Irish republican organisation based in the United States, which had carried out several raids on Canadian territory, which at the time consisted of a collection of colonies before amalgamation into a British Dominion on 1 July 1867. However, this armoured wagon never got beyond the planning stage.

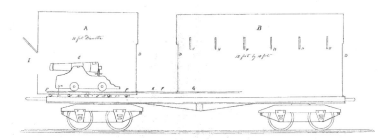

Canadian troops were among the crews of British armoured trains during the Second Boer War, but their participation was purely incidental. Less than twenty years later, Canadian units were sent to Russia[2] to fight the Bolsheviks, in the north near Murmansk and Arkhangelsk[3] and in the east in Siberia.[4] In the north, the Canadians manned an armoured train armed with an 18pdr field

The crew of this armoured train (three officers and twenty-six men) were from the 68th Field Battery of the 16th Artillery Brigade, and formed the railway detachment in the region of Vologda (170km [107 miles] to the south of Archangelsk). What at first sight appears to be a machine gun on a tripod just placed on the roof next to the armoured cupola is more likely a portable rangefinder.

(Photo: Paul Malmassari Collection)

gun and two naval guns in the region of the important rail junction of Vologda.

Canadian Armoured Train No 1

The impetus for construction of the first Canadian armoured train during the Second World War was the fear of a Japanese landing on the Pacific Coast (guided or aided by the Japanese fishermen who had traditionally trawled as far as the Skeena Estuary). The initial project was for two infantry companies patrolling in light trolleys, but in late March 1942 it was agreed to construct an armoured train, and the Canadian National Railway was charged with its design and construction. The work was carried out by the Transcona workshops near Winnipeg.

The train was designed symmetrically around the central locomotive unit, and consisted of four bogie artillery wagons (two with field guns, two with anti-aircraft guns) and two carriages for infantry, with the addition of a mess carriage. After numerous delays due to the difficulty of supplying armour plating, the availability of guns and their mountings, the locomotive to be used, etc., the train conducted its first patrol[5] on 29 July 1942, some four months after it had been ordered, but the service carriage with its radio installation did not join until 7 August. On 31 July 1944, the train was withdrawn from service and its individual components were returned to the CNR.

The cowcatcher wagon which was mirrored at the other end of the train. Note the total absence of armour protection (apart from the minimal gunshield) around the mount. The weapon is the American 75mm Model 17 (derived from the British 18pdr field gun, rechambered for the French 75mm round) on Mounting Mk I.
(Photo: Public Archives of Canada – PAC)

[1] Public Archives of Canada, Public Archives Canada (Ottawa), RG9, IC8, Vol 18.
[2] The first Canadian contingent left Victoria on 11 October 1918, and arrived at Vladivostok on the 26th. The last Canadian soldier left Russia on 5 June 1919.
[3] CNREF = Canadian North Russian Expeditionary Force.
[4] CSEF = Canadian Siberian Expeditionary Force.
[5] With 4-6-0 steam engine CN 1426.

Above: The four 40mm Bofors were of Canadian manufacture.[6] In this photo of the brand-new train, they are seen mounted directly onto the planking of the wagons, but between September and November 1942 their mountings were fixed higher up, allowing them to engage ground targets.
(Photo: PAC)

Below: Bogie wagon, 15m (49ft 2½in) long by 2.85m (9ft 4¼in) wide, with sides 1.05m (3ft 5¼in) high. The armour protection for the bogies on all the wagons was 8mm thick.
(Photo: PAC)

6. Built by Otis-Fensom in Hamilton from 1942 onwards.

Above: The kitchen/mess section of the service carriage. At the other end was the radio compartment, the train commander's office and a first-aid post.
(Photo: PAC)

Right: Stripped of their civilian fittings, the carriages were armoured on the inside faces up to a height of 0.95m (3ft 1½in) under the window openings and 2m (6ft 6¾in) between them. The bench seats would be reinstalled prior to November 1942.
(Photo: PAC)

Below: Two general views, showing both ends, but without either the locomotive or the service carriage. The whole train (inside and out) was painted matt khaki-green overall.
(Photos: PAC)

Left: On the end wagon, the second in this shot, is one of the train's two 90cm (3ft) Mk III searchlights, powered by a Leyland Westinghouse petrol generator, which in November 1942 would be replaced by 1.20m (4ft) diameter searchlights.
(Photo: PAC)

Right: The anti-aircraft wagon at the other end of the train. No higher armour protection was planned, and the tubes are safety rails limiting the firing angles of the Bofors.
(Photo: PAC)

The anti-aircraft positions on the roofs of the infantry carriages (Mounting Seat AA .303 MG Mk II), intended for a Bren Gun with a 100-round drum magazine.
(Photo: PAC)

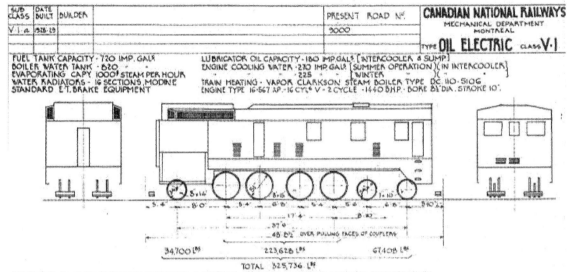

The typical central automatic coupling found on trains in North America, protected by articulated armour plates.
(Photo: PAC)

Above and below: Armoured diesel-electric loco CN-9000,[7] initially intended for the Santa Fe Railroad, which was not completed until August 1943 and never saw service with the train. In April 1943, it was fitted with a new motor as well as the armour protection, and pending discussions re the future of the train, it was stored at the Transcona workshops.
(Photos: PAC)

SOURCES:
Books:
Lucy, Roger V, *The Armoured Train in Canadian Service* (Ottawa: Service Publications, 2005).

Stevens, G R, *History of the Canadian National Railways* (New York: The Macmillan Company, and London: Collier-Macmillan Co.,1973).

Journal articles:
Anonymous note (untitled), *Canadian Rail* No 291 (April 1976), pp 126–7.

Anonymous, 'Canada's Armoured Train', *Canadian Rail* No 297 (October 1976), pp 300–4.

Grimshaw, Major Louis E, 'No.1 Armoured Train', *Canadian Defence Quarterly* Vol 21, No 2 (October 1991), pp 40–4.

Purdon, Charles J, 'Fortress on steel wheels', *Trains* Vol 48, No 11 (September 1988), pp 30–1.

_____, 'Canada's Armoured Train No.1', *Canadian Journal of Arms Collecting* Vol XVII, No 1 (1979), pp 14–18.

Website:
http://laughton.ca/documents/ww1/pub7.pdf

[7.] The first diesel-electric locomotive built in Canada along with No 9001 in 1928, by the Canadian Locomotive Company of Kingston, it had been laid up since October 1939.

CHILE

1891 ARMOURED TRAINS

In January 1891 a revolutionary struggle broke out between the 'Constitutionalists' or 'Congressists' (the revolutionaries, who were in fact the supporters of the Parliament) and the 'Balmaceditas' (the loyalists, named for President Manuel Balmaceda, who favoured a strong executive). The principal Congressist combatants were naval units, but on the presidential side the railway network was widely used in the movements of troops on land. On 15 February, locomotives sent to break through Congressist lines were used by presidential troops to concentrate at Huara, where Colonel Robles was victorious.

In the struggle for the northern ports, the Congressists used an armed locomotive and an armoured train with two machine guns. It carried out reconnaissance missions leading up to the battle of Pozo Almonte on 7 March, then took part in the battle itself, which saw the rout of the Presidential troops under Colonel Robles and the death of the latter. The civil war ended on 28 August 1891 with the victory of the insurgents.

It should be noted that an armoured wagon for the transport of explosives is currently kept at Copiapó Museum in Atacama Province, but there is no indication that this wagon was involved in the civil war.

CHINA

ARMOURED TRAINS 1920–1951

The very first Chinese armoured trains had appeared at the start of the 1920s during the Zhili-Anhui War.[1] Writing in March 1930 an American military attaché described an armoured train he had seen at that time on the Beijing-Hankow line: ordinary flat wagons protected by two thicknesses of mild steel plates. The rapid development of Chinese armoured trains would have to await the arrival of the White Russian mercenaries, notably on the side of the warlord Zhang Zongchang.

White Russian Armoured Trains

In October 1922, the Red Army laid waste to Vladivostok and a large number of White Russian soldiers fled to China with their weapons (it is thought that the famous *Zaamurietz/Orlik* crossed into China during this period), and took up service as mercenaries in the army of Marshal Zhang Zuolin (Chang Tso-Lin) and one of his subordinates Zhang Zongchang. On 15 September 1922 the latter had been sent to Vladivostok to buy arms. One of his contacts was a certain Nikolai Merkulov,[2] who moved to China and became the first commander of the White Russian armoured trains.

The very early White Russian armoured trains were improvised for the most part from bogie wagons reinforced with sandbags. Near the end of the Second Zhili-Fengtian War,[3] in October 1924, the forces of Zhang Zongchang (which were part of the Fengtian Army) carried out a surprise attack on the part of the Zhili forces commanded by Dong Zhengguo, and seized the important railway junction of Luangzhou. By blocking the bridge over the Luan River, they surrounded a huge number of men and large amounts equipment. The absorption of these troops increased the size of

[1.] This war which lasted one week in July 1920, between the two rival factions named for the respective provinces of their leaders (today in the region of Hebei), was fought to control the Chinese government in Beijing: the Zhili faction came out the winner.
[2.] Nicolai Merkulov was a merchant who, along with his brother Spiridon Dionisovich, headed the short-lived Government of Pryamure (from May 1921 to October 1922), the last White enclave in Siberia.
[3.] A conflict which was started by the *coup d'etat* of General Feng Yuxiang in Beijing.

Zhang Zongchang's army to 60,000 men in only a few days. The captured railway rolling stock was immediately recovered by Russian engineers, who improvised their first armoured trains (which would be immortalised on film by White Russian cameramen[4]).

A *coup d'état* in Beijing had temporarily put Duan Qirui in power. The latter, in order to strengthen the position of his ally Lu Yongxiang in south-east China, and at the same time to crush Qi Xieyuan (the warlord of the Zhili clique), sent Zhang Zongchang to attack towards the south. On 14 November 1924, his troops arrived at Pukou. In the absence of any ferryboat link on the Yangtze between Pukou and Nanjing,[5] his soldiers fitted railway tracks aboard barges, and thus ferried their armoured train across the river at night. The resistance they encountered at Jiangsu was weak, and with the armoured train in support the troops of Zhang Zongchang arrived in Shanghai on 28 January 1925. As there were many White Russian émigrés in the town, the Russian soldiers on the train were the subject of a great deal of attention, and it was then that the famous Russian artist Sapajou sketched the armoured train for the North China Daily News.

Note the rustic nature of this armoured wagon, obviously reinforced by armour plates and sandbags, and armed with a French 75mm APX field gun.
(Sketch by Sapajou, in North China Daily News, *30 January 1925)*

One example of the rolling stock transferred to China at the end of the Russian Civil War: this machine-gun wagon is of White Russian origin. Note the sliding armoured door which was less common than the hinged type.
(Photo: Paul Malmassari Collection)

The Battle of Guzhen (in the North-West of the Province of Anhui)

After Zhang Zongchang had become Tuchun[6] of Shandong in early 1925, he discussed with Merkulov the possibility of building classic armoured trains in the Tianjin-Pukou Railway workshops at Jinan, the capital of the Province of Shandong.

One of the most notable actions in which the White Russian armoured trains took part, and in which they suffered badly, occurred during this period. In September 1925 the provisional head of state Duan Qirui decided that two officers of the Fengtian clique, named Yang Yuting and Jiang Dengxuan, should take over as heads of the Provinces of Jiangsu and Anhui. Their appointments infuriated the warlord Sun Chuanfang who was in *de facto* control of these two provinces, and he immediately sent them away. Zhang Zongchang sent Shi, his highest-ranking officer, to launch a counter-offensive using his White Russian mercenaries, but they were defeated at Bengbu. Shi did not accept this defeat, and with his general staff boarded Armoured Train *Chang Jiang* (the Yangtse river), and headed for Guzhen to the north of Bengbu to continue the fight. The bloody battle fought there was described as follows by a former regimental commander in the forces of Sun Chuanfang:

After Shi retreated North from Bengbu, he did not admit defeat but continued to command from his armoured train. He was unaware that a regiment of Sun's forces had marched to the North of the Guzhen railway bridge, thus cutting off his intended escape route, while a second regiment launched a major attack from the South. When he became aware of the southern force, Shi ordered his armoured train to attempt to cut a way through to the North. When he approached the bridge, he saw it was completely blocked by his own troops who were desperately trying to escape to the North. Not wishing to run them down, he decided to change direction and ordered the train to return to the South. He quickly came into contact with the forces of the army of Sun, in overwhelming numbers, and he had to once more reverse course towards the North. Although the railway bridge was still blocked by the throng of his escaping troops, the powerful attacks of his opponents finally convinced Shi that he should ignore the fate of his men and force the crossing of the bridge to save his own skin. Over a thousand men trying to cross were either crushed by the train or thrown into the river. The terrible scene beggared description . . .

Shell damage to a White Russian armoured train of the army of Zhang Zongchang during the fighting in 1926 between the latter and Feng Yuxiang.
(Photo: Yichuan Chen Collection)

7.7cm FK 96 (German) or 75mm Type 38 (its Japanese version), crewed by White Russians.
(Photo: Philip Jowett Collection)

Despite this ruthless action, the armoured train carrying Shi did not escape its fate. Sources differ as to the manner in which the forces of Sun managed to destroy the train, but one suggests that Sun Chuanfang's artillery played a major role: the White Russian armoured train was hit by shells which caused its ammunition to explode. Most of the White Russians fought to the death, but others chose to surrender along with Shi himself. Very few of the mercenaries escaped. To show his fury at the way the fighting had developed, Sun Chuanfang immediately ordered that Shi be beheaded, and all the prisoners executed. One officer of his army who inspected the battlefield wrote that: 'The wreck of the armoured train of Zhang Zongchang was lying on its side, blocking the track. The White Russian soldiers, apart from a few who had escaped, had been burnt alive inside the armoured train. Their remains resembled piles of coal, and they were completely unrecognisable.'

Note the mixed Russian and Chinese crew of this armoured train.
(Photo: Paul Malmassari Collection)

The Composition of the White Russian Armoured Trains

In early 1926, a number of completely redesigned armoured trains were built at Jinan. According to a Chinese source these trains (the *Tai Shan*, the *Shan Dong*, the *Yun Gui* and the *He Nan*[7]) were converted from 40-tonne bogie flat wagons, passenger coaches and steam engines, armoured with steel plates 20mm thick. Following the lesson of the Battle of Guzhen, all these trains included flat wagons carrying searchlights and materials for track repairs.

The armoured trains[8] were composed of eight wagons:

1. Safety flat wagon carrying rails and sleepers.
2. Artillery wagon converted from a 40-tonne flat wagon.
3. Machine-gun wagon.
4. Armoured engine.
5. Mess and living quarters wagon for the officers, converted from a First Class coach.
6. Machine-gun wagon.
7. Artillery wagon converted from a 40-tonne flat wagon.
8. Safety flat wagon carrying rails and sleepers.

It was possible to pass between wagons (2) to (7) via armoured gangways. Finally, a wagon carrying two sections of Chinese infantry for close-in protection brought up the rear of the train.

In theory, their armament was to consist of seven 75mm Japanese Type 38 field guns and twenty-four Maxim heavy machine guns, but evidence from photographs shows that in fact there were major divergences from this. The floors of the artillery wagons of *Tai Shan* were protected by a layer of reinforced concrete poured

---

[7.] Respectively: Mount Tai, Shantung, the regions of the Provinces Yunnan and Guizhou, Ho Nan. It is difficult to know whether the armoured trains of the same name photographed several years later were the same ones, modernised, or completely different trains.

[8.] The White Russian armoured trains were commanded by a certain Tchekov.

The safety wagon carrying a hand trolley, at the head of a White Russian armoured train, captured at Chin Wang Tao, seen here in 1928.
(Photo: Paul Malmassari Collection)

The train's engine, on which the simple form of the armour is intended to enable it to blend in with the wagons.
(Photo: Philip Jowett Collection)

One of the artillery wagons from the same train. The turrets here are both armed with Russian 76.2mm Putilov guns. On the original photo it is just possible to make out the former Russian roundel in the centre of the side armour, under the new coat of camouflage paint.
(Photo: Paul Malmassari Collection)

This artillery wagon has two different turrets, both apparently armed with 75mm Type 38s.
(Photo: Paul Malmassari Collection)

The next wagon in line is perhaps the command wagon, coupled directly in front of the engine.
(Photo: Paul Malmassari Collection)

onto a steel plate fastened to the metal floor of the wagon. Also the vertical side walls were formed from two metal plates with the intervening space filled with concrete. To carry the increased weight, additional springs had to be fitted to the bogies. These trains were finished in a three-colour camouflage scheme. Two other armoured trains were also built in the workshops of the Beijing-Hankow Railway at Chang Xin Dian, to an identical design to the trains of the Province of Shandong, by order of Chu Yupu, the main ally of Zhang Zongchang and Governor of the Province of Chili during this period.

In early 1927, a White Russian armoured train, the *Chihli*, was placed in service at Tienstin by the forces of the Fengtian.[9] Composed of six wagons arranged symmetrically on either side of the engine, it was armed with 75mm guns (in the lower turrets of

9. Described in 'Manchurian Armored Train', *Coast Artillery Journal* (USA), Vol 66, No 5 (May 1927).

artillery wagons Nos 2 and 6, with a horizontal field of fire of 270 degrees) and 47mm guns (in the upper turrets, with a 360-degree field of fire). Wagon No 3 carried a Stokes mortar in a circular tub mounted centrally on the wagon. According to certain other contemporary sources, it carried a different armament: as with other White Russian trains it carried eight to twelve heavy machine guns, and the artillery was 76.2mm Putilov models with between 200 and 300 shells per gun. As for the engine, its armour was designed to give it a similar outline to the machine-gun wagons.

The Armoured Trains of Wu Peifu

Wu Peifu and Zhang Zuolin were the two most important warlords who used armoured trains other than those of the White Russians. Their crews were primarily Chinese. Wu Peifu began to use armoured trains in the mid-1920s, after he had rebuilt his forces following the defeat he had suffered during the Second Zhili-Fengtian War in 1924. They were probably inspired by the White trains of Zhang Zonchang and of Chu Yupu, but it appears, however, that their technical characteristics and operational doctrines were inferior to those of the Whites. The only information we have is that they were built at Hankow by the Mechanical Workshops of the Yang Tze, specialists in ship construction, including the gunboats of the Chinese Navy. The financial investment in the trains was so heavy that it brought about the bankruptcy of the Workshops in 1926.

In 1925, the principal adversary of Wu Peifu was the Kuominchun,[10] whose Second Army commanded by Yue Weijun occupied Xinyang in the Province of Henan. Kou Yingjie, one of Wu Peifu's commanders, had used armoured trains during the siege of that town in the Winter of 1925. According to the memoirs of an officer, Kou had planned to embark a large number of shock troops in an armoured train. The train was to have been used as a battering ram, supporting the main assault on the city by disembarking its troops to overwhelm the defences constructed along the line of the railway. Despite the advice of one of his subordinates that the enemy's dispositions could be intended as a trap for any such action, the order was given to attack. Barely had it begun to penetrate the enemy lines, when the train plunged into a large ditch prepared by the defenders. Although the sides of the train were armoured with iron plates, the wooden roof offered scant protection, and the troops inside were wiped out by the enemy firing from the high ground on either side of the ditch.

[10] A Nationalist Army created in 1924 and commanded by Feng Yuxiang.
[11] This campaign carried out between 1926 and 1928 by the Kuomintang, commanded by Generalissimo Chiang Kai-shek, had as its objective the reunification of China, which was completed by October 1928, with Nanking as capital.
[12] Certain sources believe that Jin Yun-é was secretly preparing to negotiate with the Nationalists.

The Armoured Trains of Zhang Zuolin and the First Battle between Armoured Trains

Paradoxically, the first battle between armoured trains did not involve the modern trains such as those of the White Russians, but rather the trains of Wu Peifu and Zhang Zuolin. Very little information survives on the trains of the latter. According to the memoirs of Marshall Zhang Xueliang, these improvised trains were built on the Central East Railway by the troops of Zhang Zongchang, when his army was in Manchuria in the early 1920s. Sleepers and lengths of rail had been used as armour by pouring cement between them, and their armament consisted of artillery and machine guns. The crews were Chinese.

Although Wu Peifu allied himself with Zhang Zuolin and the letter's subordinates Zhang Zongchang and Chu Yupu in their common struggle against the forces of the Kuominchun, the year 1926 had seen the rout of Wu Peifu's main forces faced with the rapid advance of the Nationalist 'Expedition of the North'.[11]

It was now, with Wu at a disadvantage, that once again Zhang Zuolin looked on the troops of Wu as standing in the way of his ambitious plan to conquer the whole of China. He therefore declared war in February 1927, sending his elite troops into Henan Province to attack those of Jin Yun-é who was loyal to Wu.[12] This would be the last great battle between the 'historic' Warlords of the North. For his part, Jin Yun-é launched his own counter-offensive against the city of Zhengzhou, led by his most loyal commander, Gao Rutong. At least one armoured train was used by his main force along the Beijing-Hankow railway line, guarded on each flank by the infantry. The official report of the Fengtian Army, preserved in the archives, describes the battle as follows:

On the morning of 24th March, the enemy commander Gao Rutong, accompanied by his bodyguard and his shock troops, took personal control of an armoured train, and led a major attack. After advancing towards Wu-shi-li Pu along the

A fascinating view of an armoured train built of cardboard on 1 September 1926, in honour of the dead of the Fengtian and Chili-Shantung Armies during the war against the Kuominchun. Interestingly, modern-day Chinese still leave presents such as televisions and microwaves made of card and paper as symbolic offerings on the graves of their ancestors.
(Photo: Yichuan Chen Collection)

Beijing-Hankow railway, the enemy was surrounded and their armoured train destroyed by our artillery. Gao and his head of staff Shen Qichang, his brigade commander Song Jiaxian and 40 other officers were killed inside the armoured train. The enemy forces thereafter retreated towards Xinzheng. After the battle, over 1,000 men were taken prisoner, and their armament, including one armoured train, eight artillery pieces and a large quantity of small arms, were captured. The bodies of General Gao and the other officers were sent to Zhengzhou and buried with all due honours.

The above official report does not mention the role played by the Fengtian armoured train. But several descriptions prove that it was involved in a rather curious train-versus-train combat. In the 1960s, Xu Xiangchen, a close subordinate of Jin, wrote on the subject of this battle:

A major obstacle to the advance of the troops of Jin was a Fengtian armoured train positioned to the South of Zhengzhou. Goa had planned to use the coupling hook of his own armoured train to harpoon that of the Fengtian Army's train in order to capture it. Gao's train was able to make its approach to the Fengtian train and managed to couple to it. However, he possessed only one engine as against the enemy's two (although individually of less power). After stalling for a moment, the coupling on the engine of Gao's armoured train let go, and the whole of his train was pulled towards the Fengtian lines, with Gao still on board. The latter ordered his on-board artillery to fire on the enemy train. The gunners on the Fengtian train replied, and the whole of Gao's train was destroyed, Gao being killed during the fight.

Marshal Zhang Xueliang, fighting on the other side, recounted this episode in his memoirs:

Cao Yaozhang, commander of the squadron of armoured trains, gave me the following report of the fighting. When in action our armoured train was always accompanied by the infantry, and in fact two companies of infantry had supported the train on the previous day. Following hard fighting, the infantry retreated, abandoning the train which had no engine attached. The troops on the train reported this to their commanding officer, who told them not to panic as he believed the engine would return to find them the next morning. In the morning, the train in fact began to roll, but the crew quickly noticed that they were going in the wrong direction. After checking on the situation, they concluded they were being towed by an enemy train – the mobile command post of Gao Rutong. At one end of our train was a Russian cannon, originally installed by the men under Zhang

This remarkable photo of Gao Rutong's armoured train allows us a view of the cement backing to the vertical steel armour plating. One or more shells have evidently penetrated and exploded inside, with devastating effect.
(Photo: History Illustrated, [June 1927], Yichuan Chen Collection)

Zongchang. A section head in charge of the cannon fired desperately on the enemy train. The shock effect on the closed-up wagons killed many of the soldiers in the enemy train.

Although the reports differ in the details, the accounts from both sides agree on the main features of the incident. A photo of Gao Rutong's wagon damaged by artillery fire appeared in various Chinese and Japanese publications.

The Birth of the Nationalist[13] Armoured Trains

The first armoured trains of the Nationalist Government in Canton, including the famous 'armoured train squadron of the Grand Marshal' (in other words, Sun Yat-sen, who was proclaimed

[13]. Depending on which historical period is under consideration, the term 'Nationalist' could also be applied to the Communist forces, since their objectives and those of the Kuomintang included opposition to the Warlords. Chiang's rupture with the Communists and his war against them began in April 1927.

An armoured train photographed between 20 and 27 February 1927 in Beijing by a British married couple. Note the artillery wagons inserted between the armoured machine-gun wagons.

(Photo: Paul Malmassari Collection)

Grand Marshal of the Army and the Navy by the government run by the Communists), were all of improvised construction. A Soviet adviser[14] described one of the trains on which he had travelled in 1925: 'The equipment of these trains was very rudimentary, consisting of goods wagons armoured with iron plates, and they even lack flat wagons.' Perhaps these were trains put in service to counter the bandits who had roamed around Canton since the beginning of the twentieth century. They remained extremely active, and the railway was their target of choice. In 1925 the managers of the Canton Railway had sent four recommendations to the Nationalist Government for the protection of the railway, and the first one concerned the establishment of armoured trains to protect the passenger trains.

The commanders of the National Revolutionary Army responded rapidly, and by 1926 the protection of all the commercial trains on the main lines around Canton was assured by armoured wagons. According to the newspapers of the period, these 'armoured trains' comprised a single armoured wagon, manned by soldiers, and hauled by a small steam engine.

One armoured train, probably of the same improvised type (with protection consisting of sleepers and sandbags) was put into service by the volunteer workers of the Canton-Hankow Railway during the difficult siege of the town of Wuchang, controlled by the forces of Wu Peifu, by the Fourth Army of the National Revolutionary Army (ANR). In order to defeat the ramparts, the sappers carried out a mining operation under the protection of the

14. Soviet advisers had been sent by the Comintern as early as 1923.
15. Recorded in the archives preserved in Taiwan.
16. The central element of André Malraux's novel *La Condition Humaine*.
17. 'Zhong Shan' was the most famous surname of Sun Yat-sen, given to him by the Japanese philosopher Töten Miyazaki, one of Sun's supporters during the Revolution.

armoured train. But during an enemy sortie, the forces of Wu Peifu surrounded and temporarily captured the armoured train. After the town fell, General Chiang Kai-shek ordered the Hanyang Arsenal to build armoured trains after consulting with Soviet advisers.[15]

The Battle of Shanghai (March 1927)[16]

The armoured trains of the ANC employed during the attack on Shanghai were still of the improvised type. In his memoires, General Bai-Chongxi tells that an armoured train armed with Russian 76.2mm guns had been used at Songjiang near Shanghai, to cover the assault sappers tasked with clearing the barbed wire entanglements which were blocking a railway bridge, and at the same time to destroy enemy machine-gun nests.

According to the photographic record, the improvised trains of the ANR were simply reinforced vans, with loopholes for firing rifles and machine guns cut in the side walls. 82mm trench mortars were mounted on revolving platforms protected by iron plates, probably inspired by the heavy 150mm mortars on the White Russian armoured trains.

After the fall of Shanghai, several White Russian armoured trains were captured by the ANR. According to the memoires of Zhang Pei, a staff officer of the ANR, hundreds of White Russian soldiers were captured at Songjiang along with their armoured trains, on which 'the wagons used by the officers were richly decorated, and contained expensive cigarettes and perfumes'. A Soviet adviser demanded that all the White Russians be decapitated, which was then carried out.

The captured White Russian armoured trains were all reused by the ANR against their former owners and were often renamed *Zhong Shan* in honour of Sun Yat-sen,[17] differing only by a following number. One source indicates that during the Expedition of the North, twenty armoured trains bearing this name were created from captured wagons.

One of the very early improvised Nationalist armoured trains, photographed at Canton.

(Photo: Yichuan Chen Collection)

Seen near Shanghai in 1927, this tub shelters a 150mm mortar served by the White Russian crew of the *Chang Chen* ('Great Wall').

(Photo: Paul Malmassari Collection)

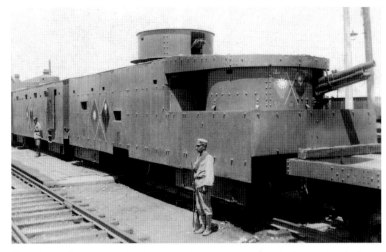

The Nationalist armoured train *Zhong Shan*, photographed in August 1927 after being captured from the Northern forces.

(Photo: Paul Malmassari Collection)

Chang Chen seen at Shanghai in April 1927, preparing to repulse the attack by Communist troops. The gun is a 7.5cm/L14G 'Shanghai-Krupp' mountain gun.

(Photo: Yichuan Chen Collection)

One of the 82mm mortars on the *Zhong Shan* No 1 photographed in July 1927.

(Photo: Yichuan Chen Collection)

The Golden Age of the Chinese Armoured Trains (Part I): Hand-to-hand Fighting against Armoured Trains in 1927

After having captured the cities of Shanghai and Nanking in April 1927, the Nationalist Government of Chiang Kai-shek broke with the rival Government of Wuhan and began eliminating the Communists. At the same time the Nationalist forces continued their progression against the forces of Zhang Zongchan and the other Warlords, in what was known as the 'Continuation of the Expedition of the North'.

Their primary objectives were the minor towns around Nanking to the north of the Yangtze. The Northern forces had placed their best units, including the 65th Division consisting of White Russian soldiers and armoured trains, near the railway junctions of Hua Qi Ying and Dong Ge.[18] Despite their dispositions, they found themselves unable to check the advance of the numerically superior Nationalist forces, who continued to advance northwards. The two sides clashed again in the town of Linhuai,[19] where according to reports, an armoured train named *Hubei* was captured.

These actions formed only a minor part of the great advance across the northern province of Jiangsu and the Province of Anhui to the north-east. Although the Northern forces were superior technically, employing armoured trains, White Russian cavalry units and aircraft in their defensive actions, the town of Xuzhou finally fell on 2 July 1927. According to the report by General Bai Chongxi, three Northern armoured trains were destroyed in the course of the fighting. The Nationalists were finally stopped when they entered Shandong, when the troops of General Wang Tianpei found themselves held up to the south of the Grand Canal.[20] The

18. Today in the District of Pukou, Nanking.
19. Today in the County of Fengyang, in the town of Chuzhou.
20. Which linked Beijing to Hangzhou, built between AD 605 and 609.

An overall view of *Hubei* (from the name of the Province, Hopei) captured by the Southern Army, seen here at Tientsin in 1927.
(Photo: Paul Malmassari Collection)

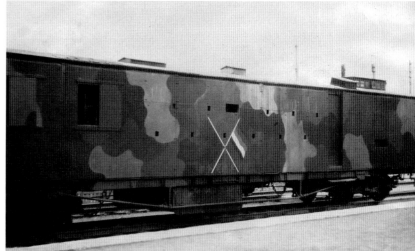

The command wagon of *Hubei* bearing the inscription 'Armoured Trains General Staff' on its side.
(Photo: Paul Malmassari Collection)

latter wrote in his memoirs that 'the enemy was bolstered by his barbaric armoured trains and bombarded us night and day, our efforts to cross the Canal being countered at every turn by overwhelming firepower'.

Chiang Kai-shek and Feng Yuxiang (known as 'the Christian General') concluded an alliance at Xuzhou. However, the rear of the forces of the Nanking Government were threatened by their opponents in the Government of Wuhan, which also possessed powerful armies. Accordingly, Xuzhou was abandoned on 7 August and the Nationalist troops rapidly withdrew to Nanking. Seizing their opportunity, the Northern troops returned from Jinan, supported by armoured trains, and very soon after reached Pukou, leaving the Yangtze River as the only obstacle before the capital of the Nanking Government. It appeared that at this moment the course of history was about to change.

According to contemporary reports, the armoured trains in

Pukou Station were used by the joint forces of Sun Chuanfang and Zhang Zongchang as mobile artillery batteries, supporting the amphibious attack attempted against Nanking. But the guns of the trains could not neutralise the heavy naval guns positioned along the bank of the Yangtze to the north of the city. The coastal batteries repulsed not only the armoured trains, destroying one of their steam engines, but also the infantry attempting a landing. Finally the forces of Sun Chuanfang crossed the river and landed beside the town Longtan, out of range of the coastal defence batteries. But just as Nanking seemed on the point of falling, the Nationalist forces launched a desperate counter-attack, encircling the forces of Sun Chuanfang. Nanking had been saved.

Needless to say, the fighting continued, bloodier than ever. The most serious combat involving the White Russian armoured trains took place in Linhuai and Fengyang. These two towns fell to the Nationalists on 11 and 12 November 1927 respectively, but the

An anti-aircraft gun on the forward flat wagon of *Hubei*, devoid of armour protection apart from the low side plates here seen in the raised position.
(Photo: Paul Malmassari Collection)

Close-up of one of the artillery wagons of *Hubei*, armed with a 75mm Model 38.
(Photo: Paul Malmassari Collection)

A Nationalist trolley converted locally from a Japanese road-rail truck, captured in Jinan Station in August 1927. Note the road wheels on the hull and the searchlight on top of the dome-shaped turret.
(Photo: Yichuan Chen Collection)

The Golden Age of the Chinese armoured trains (Part II): Train versus Train Combat and the End of the White Russian Armoured Trains

The war rapidly spread in the south of the Province of Shandong and as usual, the Northerners made effective use of their armoured trains. According to Nationalist documents, two tanks and four armoured trains were used by the forces of Zhang Zongchang. However, at this point we should pause to consider the use of artillery and armoured trains by the Nationalists. On the night of 17/18 April 1928, the Nationalist armoured train *Shandong* (perhaps an ex-White Russian armoured train, from its name) and artillerymen with six Krupp guns (also captured from the Northerners) were ordered to advance to protect the line near Tengxian (today a city in south Shandong), and to destroy enemy armoured trains. However, they arrived too late to engage the latter, as the following report describes:

> During the attack on Tengxian on 17th April, the Engineer Corps of the 9th Army had destroyed a length of track to the south of Tengxian, and had succeeded in surrounding an enemy armoured train. At this juncture, our artillery had not arrived, and our armoured train could not advance due to the damaged track. If our artillery had arrived in time, or if the track had been repaired more quickly, we would certainly have captured the enemy armoured train.

In the days which followed, the Nationalist armoured trains were primarily used for counter-battery fire, particularly against the enemy armoured trains. In the battle around Tai'an, two Nationalist armoured trains, *Zhong Shan No 4* and *Ping Deng* ('Equality'), engaged three White Russian armoured trains. At the same time, armoured trains were employed by the Kuominchun

crucial strategic site of Ma An Shan[21] changed hands several times. It was finally held by the Northern forces, and blocked the Nationalists' advance towards Bengbu. Four troop trains protected by two armoured trains had been sent to reinforce the Northern forces.

The armoured trains terrified the Nationalist soldiers: Nationalist General Xu Tingyao even declared that the White Russian crews were cannibals who killed captured soldiers in order to eat them. On their own side, the Nationalists had no artillery capable of inflicting any serious damage to the armoured trains. The General wrote:

> On the third day we were at Linhuai, the number of enemy armoured trains increased to four. The White Russian crews, after having drunk wine,[22] fired on us furiously and when our offensive had been stopped, they arrived to repair the tracks and advanced. Two of the armoured trains advanced up to 4 km behind our lines and fired on us from behind. On the fourth day, seven enemy divisions completely surrounded us, and the situation was only improved on the fifth day thanks to the arrival of nine of our divisions.

On 16 November 1927, the Nationalists broke through into Bengbu, while the White Russian armoured trains continued to support the Northern troops during the street fighting. All combat finally ended at 16.00 on the same day.

The Nationalists' next objective was Xuzhou. Although no descriptions of the actions involving the White Russian armoured trains have come to light, several Nationalist reports, and various publications, referred to the power of the enemy trains in their accounts of the fighting during the second battle for Xuzhou. The armoured trains, together with the air element and the trench mortars, were the three most formidable arms deployed by the Northern troops. But this time, the battle lasted only four days and ended with the Nationalists seizing Xuzhou, in the process capturing at least one armoured train.

---

21. To the south-west of Nanking. The name literally means 'horse saddle mountain'.
22. More likely vodka.

Armoured Train *Beijing*.
(Photo: Philip Jowett Collection)

An artillery wagon of Armoured Train *Chang Jiang* ('Yangtse River') at Tianjin (Tientsin) in around 1928. Note the two French soldiers, probably from the *Corps d'occupation de Chine* (COC = China Occupation Force) which in 1929 became the *Troupes françaises en Chine* (French Troops in China).
(Photo: Paul Malmassari Collection)

Armoured train at Mukden (the modern Shenyang) in 1928. The second wagon in line has an armoured tub on the roof, perhaps for a mortar. The flat wagon in the foreground is loaded with sleepers.
(Photo: Paul Malmassari Collection)

Another artillery wagon of the *Chang Jiang*, with the hull armour extended upwards probably to offer increased protection to the gunners serving the gun in its open-backed shield.
(Photo: Paul Malmassari Collection)

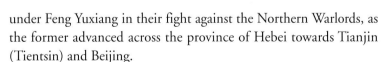

Nationalist armoured trolley employed in September 1928 at Tang Shang. Standing front left is General Bai, whose son wrote a book containing his father's memoirs.
(Photo: All Rights Reserved)

under Feng Yuxiang in their fight against the Northern Warlords, as the former advanced across the province of Hebei towards Tianjin (Tientsin) and Beijing.

Tientsin and Beijing fell to the Nationalist forces in June. On 4 July 1928, Marshal Zhang Zuolin who was the major supporter of the Northern forces (by this time consisting principally of the troops of Zhang Zongchang and Chu Yupu) was assassinated by the Japanese. Almost immediately, Zhang Zongchang and Chu Yupu fell out with the 'Young Marshal' Zhang Xueliang, who allied himself with the Nationalists and ordered the Northern warlords to

cross the River Luan to reorganise their forces as part of the Fengtian Army. Zhang Zongchang made his last address to his troops, who still numbered some 70,000 men, in his brutal bandit chief style, asking them to attack their former allies, the Fengtian Army. The attack by Nationalist forces supported by the armoured trains *Honan* and *Min Sheng* put a stop to his plans.

According to a Nationalist report, the Northern forces still possessed at least three armoured trains. Heavy fighting took place between Nationalist and Northern armoured trains. On 12 August 1928, the remaining Northern forces crossed the River Luan, only to be defeated by a combination of the Northern Warlords and the Fengtian Armies. Surviving documents of the latter indicate that the three remaining armoured trains of the Northern troops, with their White Russian crews, changed sides and joined the Fengtian Army, in passing wiping out the last Northern troops who had not surrendered. Thus a page of history was closed, the adventure of the armoured trains of Zhang Zongchang coming to an end there where it had begun four years earlier.

The Last War between the Dragons: the 1930 War of the Central Plains

An obscure chapter in the history of the Chinese armoured trains was written in Northern China between 1925 and 1928. It involved the struggle between the White Russian armoured trains of Zhang Zongchang and their lesser-known adversaries, the Soviet-designed armoured trains of the Kuominchun under General Feng Yuxiang. According to Russian sources, five armoured trains designed by Soviet advisers working with the Kuominchun were built in the Kalgan workshops (the modern Chang-chia-k'ou) in May 1925. The existence of the trains and the advisers is confirmed in the journal of General Feng Yuxiang, but information on and photos of these trains and their operations are extremely rare.

Like the Nationalists in the south, in 1927 and 1928 the forces of the Kuominchun made rapid advances against the Northern warlords, and several White Russian armoured trains were captured. With these trains and others built locally, the Kuominchun rapidly consolidated an armoured train force which equalled the Nationalist trains of Chiang Kai-shek. In May 1929, Fen Yuxiang formally declared war on Chiang, and in March 1930 Yan Xishan from Shanxi allied himself with Feng. China was once more plunged into civil war.

Chinese crew members of the *Ho Nan*, of the army of General Feng Yuxiang.
(Photo: Philip Jowett Collection)

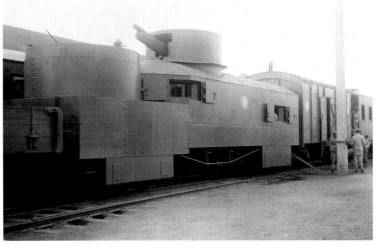

This armoured train was the escort for the special train which transferred the remains of Sun Yat-sen[23] when his ashes were repatriated from Beijing to Nanking in June 1929.
(Photo: Paul Malmassari Collection)

A rear wagon of the *Ho Nan*, with the now classic layout of two artillery turrets.
(Photo: Philip Jowett Collection)

During the war between Chiang Kai-shek, Feng Yuxiang and Yan Xishan, known as the 'War of the Central Plains', many battles between armoured trains took place. According to contemporary documents, the two principal objectives of the armoured trains were to silence or destroy enemy trains and to act in support of the infantry, missions which closely followed the classic role of the armoured train. On 24 May 1930 a typical battle took place, as described by General Xu Tingyao of Chiang Kai-shek's forces:

[23.] 12 November 1866 – 12 March 1925, he was one of the founders of the Kuomintang, and in 1912 had become the first President of the Republic of China. In June 1929 his ashes were buried in the mausoleum specially built to receive them.

During the fighting on the Longhai railway line, I was second-in-command of the 1st Division, and I was responsible for the leading echelon of the attack. An enemy armoured train, the *Zhongshan*, was positioned on the line and completely blocked our advance, which caused me a great deal of anxiety. Later I recovered two trains, the *Yun Gui* [the Provinces of Yunnan and Guizou] and the *Chan Cheng* [Great Wall]. These armoured trains could not match the enemy train in terms of firepower, but had more powerful engines. Thus I conceived the plan to combine our two trains – making a total of four engines – then to ram the enemy train with two engines, to couple it up and drag it back to our lines. I climbed aboard the leading train and personally supervised the operation. The enemy crew spotted our trains and fired on us without hitting us. Our own fire was also unsuccessful. However, when our trains came within 400m [almost 400 yards] of the enemy train, two shells struck our leading train, causing many casualties and appearing to knock it out of the fight. I therefore disembarked to lead the troops on the ground. The enemy train continued to fire and I was severely wounded by the explosion of a shell beside me.

Epilogue: the Chinese armoured trains 1931 to 1951

While the different factions were fighting each other in Central China, the Fengtian forces (the future Army of the North-East) had put together a formidable force of armoured trains in north-east China. As with the trains of the Kuominchun, details are hard to come by. Nevertheless, by the beginning of the 1930s, the Fengtian trains demonstrated remarkable features. Their main characteristic was the semi-cylindrical form of the artillery and infantry wagons, which provided superior protection compared with previous Chinese armoured trains. In addition, the ex-White Russian armoured trains were also used by the Army of the North-East. The armoured trains were in the vanguard when the Army of the North-East conquered Peiping and Tientsin under the command of Marshal Zhang Xueliang, thus putting an end to the war of the Central Plains.

They also fought the Japanese during the Manchurian incident in 1931, and showed themselves to be as effective as contemporary Japanese trains. Later, several were obliged to withdraw to the south to the areas still held by Chinese troops, such as Peiping and Tientsin.
(Photo: All Rights Reserved)

An armoured train photographed near Shanghai in 1932. Note the unusual profile of the artillery wagon, which allows a wide field of vision for the armoured observation cupola on the following wagon.
(Photo: Paul Malmassari Collection)

Above: Armoured Train *Chang Jiang*, with a wagon the hull of which is identical to that in the previous photo, but with a single gun protected by a shield which appears to be open at the rear. Note the hand trolley carried on the flat wagon.
(Photo: Paul Malmassari Collection)

The characteristic form of the Fengtian trains is well in evidence here, with their semi-cylindrical shape topped by turrets or an observation tower.
(Photo: Paul Malmassari Collection)

Right: 37mm Type 94 gun mounted aboard a Chinese armoured train captured by the Japanese.
(Photo: Paul Malmassari Collection)

Communist armoured train on the Hunan-Guangxi line in 1949. The Japanese wagons have been modified to carry turrets from Type 97 Chi Ha tanks,[24] but armed with 57mm Type 97s in place of the 47mm gun normally mounted. It appears that a cylindrical nacelle has been fitted to the left-hand wagon.
(Photo: Yichuan Chen Collection)

On the Nationalist side, from 1930 onwards there was virtually no renovation of the fleet of armoured trains, and their importance declined. The Chinese armoured trains, once a formidable force, had ceased to be the principal arbiter of the battlefield. They played a minor role during the war against the Japanese between 1937 and 1945. From the photographic record, the Chinese trains of that period were either the former trains of the Army of the North-East or ex-White Russian trains.

When the civil war between Nationalists and Communists began in 1946, Chinese armoured trains seem to have undergone a renaissance. As the Communists' principal tactic against the Japanese had been the destruction of the railway lines, they continued this against their new adversary, while the Nationalists inherited the tactics and the techniques of defence of the railway network from the Japanese, and even several Japanese armoured trains. From late 1947, the Communists began their counter-offensive with attacks against the cities held by the Nationalists. At that time the Nationalist armoured trains, rather than patrolling the railway network, were frequently used as a mobile force within the defensive systems of the cities. One of the first confrontations between the Communist besiegers and an armoured train took place in November 1947 during the battle for Shijiazhuang. The Nationalist force was composed of between four and six trains, including one of Japanese origin. The remainder were improvised from goods wagons and flat wagons reinforced with concrete and steel plates, often considered as being better protected than the Japanese trains, and carrying tanks. To fight them, the Communists employed captured weapons which were new to them, such as bazookas and anti-tank guns. Similar fighting occurred during the sieges of Jinan, Tianjin (Tientsin) and Taiyuan.

24. Known as Gongchen in China.

The last chapter in the history of armoured trains in China was written by the Chinese Communists. In the late 1940s and early 1950s, a few armoured trains were retained in service to guarantee the security of the rail network against bandits. In July 1951 all the armoured trains from the different regions of China were recalled and stocked at Shenyang. Their crews were distributed among infantry units and sent to Korea. Thus ended the thirty-year history of armoured trains in China.

Communist armoured train in north-east China, also converted from former Japanese wagons, on which armoured cupolas have been installed. These hemispherical cupolas were originally from bunkers, some of which are today on public display in the Museum of the Battery of the West at Yingkou (Liaoning Province).
(Photo: Yichuan Chen Collection)

Nationalist armoured train derailed during the battle for Taiyuan in 1949. The turret is armed with a 75mm mountain gun.
(Photo: Yichuan Chen Collection)

This scene purporting to show an armoured train captured by the Communists in the Shanxi has perhaps been posed for propaganda purposes, but it illustrates the method of attack in those zones where it was possible to dominate the trains from high ground.

(Photo: Yichuan Chen Collection)

A Nationalist armoured train captured during the battle for Taiyuan. Originally a Japanese safety flat wagon, the wagon shown in the centre has been converted by adding wooden walls pierced by loopholes.

(Photo: Yichuan Chen Collection)

This Nationalist armoured train was captured during the Zheng-Tai campaign in 1949 on the Zhengding-Taiyuan line. Note the familiar form of the ex-Japanese safety wagon with its armoured lookout cabin.

(Photo: Yichuan Chen Collection)

SOURCES

Books:

Jowett, Philip, *The Armies of Warlord China 1911-1928* (Altglen, PA: Schiffer Publishing, 2014).

_____, *China's Wars: Rousing the Dragon 1894-1949* (Oxford: Osprey Publishing, 2013).

Krarup-Nielsen, Aage, *The Dragon Awakes* (London: J. Lane, 1928).

Malraux, André, *La Condition humaine* (Paris: Gallimard, 1933).

Journal Articles:

'Chine: Trains blindés', *Revue d'Artillerie* Vol 99 (January–June 1927), pp 694–5.

Girves, Captain, 'La Guerre civile en Chine', *Revue militaire française* Vol 1 (1927), p 190.

'Manchurian Armored Train', *Coast Artillery Journal* (USA) Vol 66, No 5 (May 1927), pp 481–2.

Rouquerol, General J, 'Chine: Les trains blindés en Asie Orientale', *Revue d'Artillerie* (July–December 1927), pp 605–9.

Zaloga, Steven, 'Armour in China', *Military Modelling Manual* (1983), pp 4–9.

Website :

http://www.chinaheritagequarterly.org/features.php?searchterm=sapajou_page12.inc&issue=022

Film:

Russian-made film of the advance of the forces of Marshal Chang Tso-Lin, Warlord of Mukden, South towards Nanking, 1924-1925. (1925), IWM 172.

An interesting view of a Communist armoured train used for track repairs, with the red star surrounded by the slogan 'Our work takes us where the frontiers lie'.
(Photo: Yichuan Chen Collection)

This photo is not what it seems. Here is film star George Sanders with a 'Chinese armoured train' from the 1938 Hollywood film *International Settlement*, set in Shanghai. The ideograms on the side of the wagon read 'Government Property Do Not Touch'. Sadly, the scene with the armoured train seems to have ended on the cutting-room floor, so this is the only surviving record.
(Photo: Paul Malmassari Collection)

COLOMBIA

It appears that the only use of armoured locomotives in Colombia is the recent protection of coal trains in the region of the El Cerrejón opencast mine in the north of the country. The company of the same name was created in the 1970s and a railway line was built to transport the coal 150km (93 miles) to Puerto Bolivar. The original eight locomotives were General Electric type GE B36-7. Additionally five Type AC4400CW locomotives have been employed to work alongside the original units. In 2009 the guerrillas of the FARC[1] and also certain elements of the Wayuu Tribe began to attack the trains, causing several derailments. The fitting of armour to the locomotives, which is still in place at the time of writing, was carried out by two Bogotá-based companies, ISBI Armoring and Armor International.

A superb frontal view of a GE AC4400CW, showing how the armour protection blends in well with the overall silhouette of the loco.
(Photo: Armor International)

Two diesel locos of the Cerrejón Company with armoured cabs, on the left a GE B36-7, and on the right a GE AC4400CW.
(Photo: Armor International)

The team of fitters in front of a GE AC4400CW in the process of being armoured.
(Photo: Armor International)

Fitting the armoured windscreen on a GE AC4400CW by the company ISBI. The original glass has been replaced by 50mm-thick armoured glass panes.
(Photo: ISBI Armoring)

One of the 50mm-thick windscreens ready for fitting.
(Photo: ISBI Armoring)

[1]. *Fuerzas armadas revolucionarias de Colombia – Ejército del Pueblo*, A communist guerrilla movement.

CONFEDERATE STATES OF AMERICA

ARMOURED RAILWAY GUN AND COTTONCLAD SHARPSHOOTER CARS (1862)

The Dry Land *Merrimac*

In June 1862 the Union Army of the Potomac advanced on the Confederate capital of Richmond. General Robert E Lee looked for a means of countering the enemy's preponderance in heavy siege artillery, which they would be transporting into position by rail. On 5 June he asked Colonel Josiah Gorgas, the Chief of Ordnance, if it would be possible to mount a heavy gun on a railway car.[1] The challenge was taken up by the Navy, who already had experience of armouring the famous *Virginia* (ex-*Merrimac*), which had taken on the Union blockaders and fought the first ironclad battle with USS *Monitor*.

On 26 June, Captain M Minor reported to Lee: 'The railroad-iron plated battery designed by Lieutenant John M. Brooke, C.S. Navy, has been completed. The gun, a rifled and banded 32-pounder of 57 cwt,[2] has been mounted and equipped by Lieutenant R.D. Minor, C.S. Navy, and with 200 rounds of ammunition, including 15-inch solid bolt shot,[3] is now ready to be transferred to the Army.'[4] The railway gun was manned by Lt James Barry CSN, Sergeant Daniel Knowles and thirteen gunners of the Norfolk United Artillery Battery, many of whom had previously served on the *Virginia*.

The Battle of Savage's Station, fought on 29 June 1862, was a Union defeat, watched by Confederate Major General Magruder from the rail overbridge. The railway gun was propelled towards the Union lines along the track of the Richmond & York Railroad by an unarmoured steam engine, with obstacles being removed or pushed aside by the gun itself. Firing explosive shells as it advanced, it forced the Union troops to abandon their lines across the track and take up flanking positions beside it, which the gunners could not counter as they had no means of training the gun to one side.

Note that no means of propelling the railway gun, other than manpower, has been depicted in this illustration. The design is based on the memories of Charles S. Gates.

Eventually, the gun had progressed so far in front of the Confederate lines that it risked being lost due to the Union flanking fire, and Lieutenant Barry ordered it to pull back.

Fifty-nine years after the event, the Confederate veteran Charles S. Gates described from memory the famous 'Dry Land *Merrimac*', as the railway gun was called by Richmond newspapers in 1862. Later descriptions, and reconstructions in model form, have been based on his recollections,[5] including the painting above.

Fortunately we also have an eyewitness to the action, who fixed the scene in a watercolour. Private Robert Knox Sneden of the Union Army was a topographical engineer, who produced maps for the Army of the Potomac. Among his almost 1000 watercolours, sketches and maps was a painting of the Battle of Savage's Station, with the railgun as the centrepiece. While answering many questions, his depiction poses others.

Private Sneden may have painted this scene from memory afterwards, as the Army of the Potomac was forced to withdraw from in front of Richmond in some disorder. He certainly stretches the platform wagon to a unbelievable length, which would be too weak to support the weight of the gun, never mind withstand the recoil. As he obviously observed the event from a considerable distance away, his rendering of the moving flatcar may not be all that accurate. Nevertheless, what his illustration does reveal is the '*Virginia*-like' armoured casemate surrounding the cannon and its gunners, with armour on the sides as well as the front. He has

[1.] Official Records, Series I, Volume 11, Part III, Serial 14, p 574.

[2.] The US Navy had standardised all its guns as '32-pounders', being the weight of solid shot each one fired. Small, medium and large guns all of the same calibre (6.4in /16.256cm) were built, and only the powder charge and therefore the propulsive force varied between models. Each size was described by the weight of the gun barrel, expressed in cwt (hundredweight, or 112lbs/50.8 kg, of which twenty made up one Imperial ton). 57cwt = 2896kg.

[3.] A curious choice of ammunition, only useful against armoured ships, the projectile being a cylinder rather than a ball. Against infantry the gun would fire an explosive shell weighing 26lbs (11.8kg).

[4.] Official Records, Series I, Volume 11, Part III, Serial 14, p 615.

[5.] Lt Col H W Miller, *Railway Artillery, A Report on the Characteristics, Scope of Utility, Etc., of Railway Artillery*, Volume I (Washington DC: Government Print Office, 1921), p 8.

correctly depicted the Union force being obliged to take up position flanking the railway track, which would ultimately oblige Lieutenant Minor and his men to pull back, for fear of being fired upon from the rear.

There has been some confusion in the minds of railway enthusiasts between this gun and the Union railway gun used at the siege of Petersburg, mounted on a fourteen-wheel wagon (see the United States of America chapter). The latter gun, however, is clearly protected by timber baulks alone, even if they do cover the sides as well as the front, and there is no covering of iron as mentioned in all the accounts of the Confederate piece.

Accounts differed as to its effects in action, and certainly the Union commanders did not make much of it in their reports. But then, mentioning the attack of an unstoppable railway weapon adding to the debacle of the battle would be like rubbing salt in one's own wounds. After the battle, presumably recognising its tactical drawbacks, the Confederate Navy retrieved their valuable gun and the platform would be returned to freight work.

Cottonclad Sharpshooters[6] Cars

Whatever its value or otherwise, the railway gun has completely over-shadowed another Confederate innovation, the cottonclad armoured Sharpshooters Car, two of which can clearly be seen in Sneden's watercolour, coupled between the railway gun and the engine

Protection of these cars with cotton bales at first sight seems a strange choice.[7] Certainly raw cotton was far more readily available to the Confederacy than iron.[8] But how effective would it be against rifle fire? The British Army certainly recognised that bales of cotton waste could absorb the impact of .303 projectiles which would not penetrate a certain thickness.[9] That would leave the risk of the bales being set on fire by exploding shells. Apart from the fact that tightly-packed cotton, like stacked paper, is extremely difficult to set on fire, if a Sharpshooters Car were to be struck by a shell, the risk of subsequent fire would be a minor consideration. These early experiments in using cotton as protection would continue in the form of bulletproof vests, resulting in modern textile body armour.

The height of the Battle of Savage's Station, painted by Private Robert Knox Sneden.
(Painting: Diaries, Volume 3, 29 June –25 October 1862, Virginia Historical Society, Richmond, Va.)

A representation of a Sharpshooters Car in HO scale in the livery of the Richmond & York River Railroad.
(Model & Photo: Scott Cameron)

SOURCES

Archives:
Private Robert Knox Sneden Diaries, Volume 3, 1862 June 29–October 25, Virginia Historical Society, Richmond, Va.
The War of the Rebellion: a Compilation of the Official Records of the Union and Confederate Armies (Official Records), Series I – Military Operations, Volume 11, Part III, Serial 14, Cornell University.

Books:
Alexander, Edwin P, *Civil War Railroads & Models* (New York: Clarkson N Potter Inc., 1977).
Miller, Lt Col H W, *Railway Artillery, A Report on the Characteristics, Scope of Utility, Etc., of Railway Artillery*, Volume I (Washington DC: Government Print Office, 1921), p 8.

Websites:
http://scooters-stuff.blogspot.fr/p/a-sketch-of-csa-gun-car-followed-by.html
https://markerhunter.wordpress.com/2012/06/29/railway-arty-savage-station/
http://ebooks.library.cornell.edu/m/moawar/waro.html
http://www.civilwar-online.com/2011/06/civil-war-naval-artillery-part-one.html

[6.] Named after Union marksmen using Sharps breech-loading rifles, the original term was 'Sharps-shooters'.
[7.] This type of protection was also used on Confederate river gunboats, the famous Cottonclads, to protect the boiler, engine, ammunition and other vulnerable areas.
[8.] Towards the end of the Civil War the South was even forced to salvage and re-use obsolete inverted-U section rails.
[9.] Described to the Translator by Major George Geear, Royal Artillery (retired), Chapel Bay Fort, Pembrokeshire, UK.

CONGO-LEOPOLDVILLE

ARMOURED TRAINS AND TROLLEYS (1960–1965)

On 30 June 1960 Congo-Léopoldville was declared independent. On 5 July the Force Publique, the former colonial gendarmerie, mutinied and civil unrest broke out, with white civilians coming under attack and many being forced to flee to neighbouring countries. There began a period of instability characterised by murder and rape,[1] fuelled by anti-colonialist resentment and tribal rivalries. At the same time the integrity of the country was threatened by the breakaway of Katanga (11 July 1960 to January 1963), with the aid of mercenaries, and of South-Kasaï (20 August 1960 to 30 December 1961), and finally UN Forces intervened to aid Congolese forces in resisting the breakaway of these two provinces.

Maintaining freedom of traffic was vital for the provisional Katangese government, to be able to maintain the flow of copper exports, and for the supply needs of the UN contingents. The rail network (originally built to the metre gauge, but converted in 1955 to 1067mm [3ft 6in] gauge) came under attack, leading to the introduction of armour protection for rolling stock, at first by the railway staff and the remaining Belgian troops, then finally by all the belligerent parties. A Wickham armoured trolley (No 8453 built 1960) had also been acquired prior to independence.

In the centre, a trolley armoured by the workshops of the BCK,[4] on the line between Lubudi and Kamina in February 1961. A close examination of the photo suggests that the Wickham on the left is the same as the one in the previous photo.
(Photo: CEDOMI)

In the station at Kongolo, two trolleys fitted locally with armour protection, using as a base Wickham Type 18 inspection trolleys, six of which had been delivered between 1956 and 1959. Under the shed roof is diesel locomotive Class 200 1-D DH[2] with an armoured cab, leaving two observation slits. The gauge on the CFL[3] network was 1.067m (3ft 6in).
(Photo: Cegesoma-Bruxelles Collection Ref 280703)

An armoured train used by the Katangan forces, employing an American M8 Greyhound armoured car.
(Photo: Ltc Young, via Denis McCarthy)

Unidentified armoured trolley, supporting Katangan or Belgian troops ensuring the BCK line is clear.
(Photo: CEDOMI)

1. For descriptions of these dramatic events, see the 1965 novel *The Dark of the Sun* by Wilbur A. Smith, the 1968 film *The Mercenaries*, and *Chimères noires* by Jean Lartéguy, published in 1963 by Presses de la Cité.
2. DH = Diesel-Hydraulic. A locomotive built in Haine-St-Pierre in 1955.
3. CFL = Chemin de Fer des grands Lacs (Great Lakes Railway).
4. BCK = Companie du Bas Congo au Katanga.

Inspection trolley which formed the basis of the armoured versions, seen here in 1959 between Elisabethville and Kamina.

(Photo: Paul Malmassari Collection)

The same units seen from the locomotive end, with No 2305 of the KDL here operating on the BCK lines.

(Photo: CEDOMI)

A photo taken some time in March or April 1961, showing an armoured train during Operation 'Conga' on the Kongolo-Kabalo axis.

(Photos: CEDOMI)

Armoured wagon bringing up the rear of the train on the Benke to Kamina line (Operation 'Banquise').

(Photo: CEDOMI)

In February 1961, during Operation 'Banquise', the railway networks provided rapid deployment and needed protecting: here an armoured wagon is propelled by locomotive 2305 of the KDL,[5] seen here in Luena Station. Following this operation, the BCK network which had profited from the heightened security, could henceforth operate without an escort.

(Photo: CEDOMI)

The United Nations intervened[6] with contingents of troops from thirty-two nations. Here men of the Swedish contingent are fitting protection to open bogie wagons of the KDL. They were tasked with train protection in August 1960.

(Photo: CEDOMI)

(Photo: CEDOMI)

Three photos of the armoured train carrying the 1st Shock Unit (6th Foreign Commando Battalion), bearing the insignia of the 'Affreux' (a red devil's head on a white triangle), which supported Operation 'Ommegang'[7] in November 1964.
(Photo: CEDOMI)

The makeshift protection of the locomotive can clearly be seen in this shot, which is reminiscent of the film *The Mercenaries*.
(Photo: CEDOMI)

The 6th Battalion was formed of mercenaries commanded by the famous Bob Denard. The 0.615m (2ft) gauge line of the CVC[8] appears hardly suitable to carry combat units. The operation was in support of a Belgian battalion, and a parallel movement by a motorised column opening up the road leading to Buta-Aketi, to clear the Simba rebels out of the Upper Congo.
(Photo: CEDOMI)

SOURCES:

Blanchart, Charles, *Le rail du Congo belge 1945-1960, Volume III* (Brussels: Editions Blanchart & Co, 2008).
Malmassari, Paul, *Les Blindés de l'ONU* (Guilherand Granges: La plume du temps, 2000).
Film *The Mercenaries*, Director Jack Cardiff, 1968, running time 100 minutes.

[5.] KDL = Compagnie du Katanga-Dilolo-Léopoldville.
[6.] ONUC, the United Nations Operation in the Congo, deployed troops to support the Congolese Government from 14 July 1960 to 30 June 1964.
[7.] In January 1964 the Simba ('Lion' in Swahili), rose in revolt, and carried out indescribable atrocities in all the territory they overran. The revolt was crushed in November by Operation 'Ommegang' conducted by the Belgian Para-Commando Regiment supported by two columns of mercenaries.
[8.] CVC = Chemins de fer Vicinaux du Congo.

INDEPENDENT STATE OF CROATIA

ARMOURED TRAINS AND TROLLEYS 1941–1945

The Independent State of Croatia,[1] initially a monarchy, later a republic, was created following the break-up of Yugoslavia in 1941.

Armoured trains (*oklopni vlak*) were envisaged for anti-partisan operations from the very start. In September 1941 an improvised armoured train operated on the stretch of line between Maglaj and Doboj, and it remained in service up until December in the Tuzla region, assisting with the encirclement of the partisans in the Orzen Mountains.

The Slavonski Brod railway centre specialised in the repair and construction of armoured trains and trolleys, of which twenty were ordered in April 1942. At the same time, an 800-man Railway Battalion was formed. The armoured trains would not become an independent arm of service but were attached to and formed part of infantry regiments, each being designated a half-company to undertake this specialist role.

In November 1942 the Croatian trains came under the tactical control of the Wehrmacht, and records for 1943 indicate the existence of seven or eight armoured trains, grouped into five Armoured Train Companies (*Satnija Oklopljenih Vlakova Nos 1-5*). Each train was composed of several armoured wagons and of one or two static Renault FT tanks (armed with a 37mm gun), carried on three-plank wagons. A mortar, two heavy and four light machine guns made up the rest of the armament. In all, 364 officers and men, a mixture of Croats and Germans, commanded and crewed the trains.

At the time of writing details of the exact makeup of each train, specifying the type of wagon, are not available. Equally it has not been possible to correlate the known numbering and naming of individual trains.[2] Although we know that armoured trains were built for both standard gauge and narrow gauge, it is sometimes difficult to differentiate between them in photos. The sole indicator is that narrow-gauge armoured trains used central automatic couplings, whereas the standard-gauge units were fitted with buffers and screw link couplings.

A rough indication of the trains' geographical distribution is as follows:

– 1st Company: HQ at Doboj at the time it was formed in 1942; by September 1944 it was based at Slavonski Brod.
– 2nd Company: Created in 1942, by 1943 it operated to the north and east of Zagreb with Armoured Trains Nos 1 and 2.
– 3rd Company: Created in 1942, operating in the III Corps zone in Bosnia-Herzegovina with Armoured Trains *Ris*, *Vuk* and *Lisac*.

– 4th Company: No details at the time of writing.
– 5th Company: Formed in late 1943, operating in the Karlovac region with two armoured trains, then in 1944 on the Karlovac-Zagreb-Ozalj-Recica line.

Finally, two improvised armoured trains bearing the numbers 412 and 432 operated during 1941 in Bosnia-Herzogevina.[3] Because of the through connections of the different railway networks, several of these trains also operated in Greece, and perhaps as far away as Italy, where Croatian-type armoured wagons were photographed.

Armoured trolleys built at Slavonski Brod on the chassis of Steyr 1500 trucks.
(Photo: Wolfgang Sawodny)

Narrow-gauge armoured train with a mixed German-Croat crew. The initials HDŽ stand for *Hrvatske Državne Želejnice* or Croatian State Railways.
(Photo: Paul Malmassari Collection)

[1.] *Nezavisna Država Hrvatska* or NDH (August 1941–May 1945).
[2.] Thus we find several trains bearing the same number but serving under different commands, and the following designations, which are either the name of the station where the train was based, or the name of an animal: *Lisac* (No 3), *Ris*, *Gabela*, *Lašva*, *Neretva*, *Travnik*, *Vareš*, *Vuk* (No 2) and *Zenica*.
[3.] It is possible that an attack on one of these trains is commemorated by the plaque beside the Sarajevo-Vareš road, since no report mentions the presence of a German armoured train during the period mentioned on the plaque.

Above left: Protection improvised from sleepers on a pilot truck armed with an Italian 20mm Breda Model 35 cannon, seen in Katerini Station in Greece.
(Photo: Paul Malmassari Collection)

Above: The same train on patrol in Greece, seen here in Tembi in 1943. The turret is an APX from a French tank, in original condition without the opening top hatches usually fitted by the Germans.
(Photo: Paul Malmassari Collection)

Left: On the left, a standard-gauge armoured train, and on the right, a narrow-gauge track.
(Photo: Paul Malmassari Collection)

Below: Running along the coast at Palatamon in Greece.
(Photo: Paul Malmassari Collection)

A fine view of a standard-gauge wagon, with an APX turret.
(Photo: Paul Malmassari Collection)

Major-General Johann Fortner (1884–1947), commander of the 718th Infantry Division from May 1941 to March 1943, seen in front of an armoured wagon.
(Photo: Paul Malmassari Collection)

The same wagon photographed from the opposite side, showing the offset position of the lookout. The inscription 'O.V.T.102' may be the wagon's number.
(Photo: Paul Malmassari Collection)

A more distant view of the same wagon, showing the arrangement of firing loopholes. In the centre of the train is the armoured engine.
(Photo: Paul Malmassari Collection)

German and Croatian soldiers pose for the camera in front of an armoured train.
(Photo: Paul Malmassari Collection)

An armoured wagon of an unidentified armoured train. The wagon's origins are obscure; is it an old Austro-Hungarian armoured wagon modified in the inter-war period, or a more recent model? The Croatian coat of arms can be seen on the right. The inscription 'O.V.A.12' may be its serial number.
(Photo: Paul Malmassari Collection)

Above left: The artillery element of the trains in the Balkans and in Italy was usually furnished by the 37mm guns of Renault FT tanks on three-plank wagons.
(Photo: Paul Malmassari Collection)

Above: A different type of armoured wagon attached behind an FT Tank three-plank wagon, clearly showing the Croatian coat of arms.
(Photo: Paul Malmassari Collection)

Left: Another view of the same train.
(Photo: Bojan Dimitrijevic)

Below: Beside the road from Sarajevo to Vareš is a plaque commemorating the heroism of the partisans who appear to have attacked an armoured train in 1941.
(Photo: Paul Malmassari Collection)

Above and below: Two interesting views of typical Croatian armoured trains, with their different types of wagon and the engine with only the driving cab being armoured.

(Photos: Bundesarchiv – BA)

Above: Armoured train derailed by partisans on 4 August 1943.
(Photo: Yugoslav Railway Museum)

Right: A narrow-gauge armoured engine as captured at the end of the war. Note the second engine which is only partially armoured.
(Photo: Bojan Dimitrijevic)

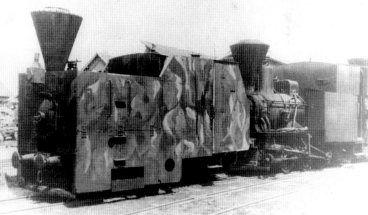

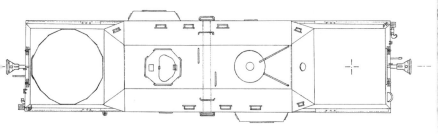

SOURCES:
Dimitrijevic, Bojan and Savic, Dragan, *German Panzers and Allied Armour in Yugoslavia in World War Two* (Erlangen: Verlag Jochen Vollert – Tankograd Publishing, 2013).
Article by H.L. deZeng IV, on the website http://www.axishistory.com.
DGEG Archives/ W. Sawodny Collection.
Author's archive.

Three photos of the narrow-gauge Croatian armoured wagon preserved in the Museum of the Revolution in Sarajevo, as seen in 2006.

(Photos: Paul Malmassari Collection)

CROATIA

CROATIAN WAR OF INDEPENDENCE[1] (1991–1995)

On 25 June 1991, following several years of rising tensions between the constituent republics of Yugoslavia, Croatia declared its independence.[2] In July, the Yugoslav Army, which by then was composed mainly of Serbs following desertions by the other nationalities, went into action to try to keep the country together. The civil war which broke out lasted until 12 November 1995.

Croatian Armoured Trains[3]

The young Croatian Republic put into service the following armoured trains, in chronological order: OV No 1 *Šišmiš* ('Bat'); OV No 2 in Osijek; OV *Split I* and an armoured trolley.

The first armoured train, *Šišmiš*, was completed on 17 August 1991 and went into action in the Novska region, then in the Sisak-Sunja sector. To date no photos of it have come to light.

The second armoured train went into service on 30 September 1990 in the Osijek-Vrpolje zone. It was organised in four sections, two combat and two anti-aircraft, carrying a crew of some forty men. The anti-aircraft wagons were armed with triple 20mm PA 20/3 M55 mountings. The train was demobilised on 10 July 1992.

The third, *Split I*, was built by the naval shipyard in Brodosplit and was shown to the authorities on 31 January 1992, but it was never called upon to go into action. It is now part of the collection of the Zagreb Railway Museum.

A view of the diesel locomotive of the Osijek armoured train, in a siding in 2013. The brick-red livery was the scheme carried during the war and not a subsequent repainting. Of note is the lower armoured skirt consisting of reinforced rubber sheets.

(Photo: All Rights Reserved)

[1.] Official Croatian name: *Domovinski rat*, the Homeland War.
[2.] Slovenia declared itself independent on the same day but the fighting on its territory lasted only two months.
[3.] In Croat: *oklopni vlak*, or OV.
[4.] HŽ = *Hrvatske Zeleznice*, Croatian Railways created in 1991 from parts of the ex-JŽ (*Jugoslovenske Zeleznice*) network.

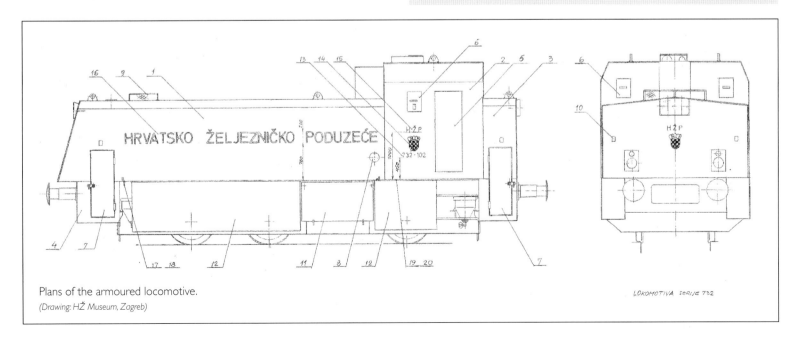

Plans of the armoured locomotive.

(Drawing: HŽ Museum, Zagreb)

End view of 0ne of the armoured wagons of *Split 1*, which is reminiscent of the wagons of the German BP 42 and 44. One must suppose that additional wagons were planned, since the train as it stands has no specific units to protect the ends.
(Photo: All Rights Reserved)

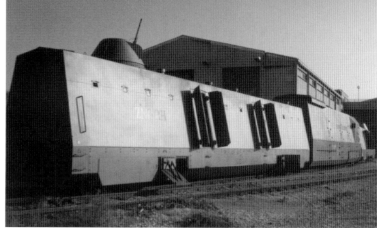

The second armoured wagon of *Split 1*, armed with a 12.7mm machine gun. The armour protection is formed of two layers of armour plates, one of 6mm and the other of 8mm, with gravel ballast sandwiched between the two plates. The bogies are protected by 10mm plates. The wagons used as the base were 22.5-tonne Series G, one being 16.52m (54ft 0½in) long and the other 16.79m (55ft 1in).
(Photo: HŽ Museum, Zagreb)

The leading wagon of the *Krajina Express*, with the Hellcat carried on the front platform.
(Photo: Wide World Photos)

Left-hand side of diesel-electric locomotive HŽ 2062-045 seen from the rear.
(Photo: HŽ Museum, Zagreb)

The armoured locomotive viewed from the front right-hand side, showing the cab.
(Photo: HŽ Museum, Zagreb)

Close-up of the cab of the armoured locomotive.
(Photo: HŽ Museum, Zagreb)

A detailed close up showing the insignia of the *Krajina Ekspres*: the four Cyrillic letters 'C' in the coat of arms of the Nemanjić dynasty stand for *'Samo Sloga Srbina Spasava'* or 'Only Union Will Save the Serbs'.
(Photo: Paul Malmassari Collection)

Armoured Train *Krajina Ekspres* of the Serb Republic of Krajina[5] (1 April 1991–August 1995)

The railway line linking Zagreb with the Dalmatian Coastline by way of Knin crossed Bosnian territory, passing through Bihać. The line's strategic importance led to the construction of an armoured train known as the *Krajina Ekspres* ('Krajina Express'). Its name gave rise to a popular song, and even in late 1994, to widespread press coverage, somewhat surprising for a train which long ago dropped out of sight of the popular media![6]

The train was built in Knin during the Summer of 1991 and was brought into service by the twenty men of the Railway Company of the 7th Motorised Brigade. From 27 November 1992, it was operated by the Railway Company of the 75th Motorised Brigade of the VII Corps (Dalmatia) of the SVK.[7] In late 1994, it became Armoured Train No 7, reporting directly to VII Corps.

Initially it was made up of two wagons protected by sandbags, with 25mm armour plate added, propelled by diesel locomotive JZ 664-013. The first wagon carried a 20mm M38 cannon (ex-FlaK 38) and a 40mm Bofors M12. The second wagon carried two AT-3 rocket launchers and a second 40mm Bofors M12. In the Autumn of 1991 a third wagon was added, armed with a 20mm M55A4B1 triple mounting and a single 20mm M75 mounting. A 7.62mm Zastava M84 MG was mounted on each side. In early 1992 the 20mm cannon on the rear wagon was replaced by a 76.2mm ZiS-3 field gun, and two L-57-12 rocket launchers replaced the 40mm Bofors on the front wagon. In 1993 an American M-18 Hellcat Tank Destroyer from the stocks held by the JNA (*Jugoslovenska Narodna Armija* – the Yugoslav People's Army) replaced the 76.2mm ZiS-3, its turret-mounted 76mm having a much greater traverse. At the same time the original 25mm armour protection was reinforced with rubber sheets fixed at approximately 10mm from the plates, the space between being filled with ballast. Finally, a fourth wagon carrying two 120mm mortars was attached to the train. On the other hand, a project to build a wagon armed with an 88mm gun did not see the light of day. During the operations around Bihać, three safety pilot wagons were pushed ahead of the train.

In 1991 the train was employed near Gradačac, on the Knin-Drnis line, then at Lika. In 1992 it was in action near to Zemunik Airport at Zadar, at Maslenica and at Ravni Kotari where two crew members were killed. In early 1993, it operated notably at Škabrnja, where it was to be the delivery system for a wagon loaded with 3.5 tonnes of explosives and 5 tonnes of shrapnel, with the aim of blowing up an ammunition dump at Zadar: a landmine

5. *Republika Srpska Krajina*.

6. Examples of press coverage are *Ouest-France* edition of 19–20 November 1994, the *Washington Post* of 26 November 1994, the *VSD* of 3 August 1995 etc.

7. *Српска Бojcka Краjине / Srpska Vojska Krajine (CBK/SVK)* = Serbian Army of Krajina, formed on 19 March 1992.

attached to one of the wagon buffers was meant to initiate the explosion of the load when the wagon was released to roll downhill from the village of Nadin towards its target.[8] The train was in action near Bihać where it was hit by an anti-tank missile, and it was deployed on numerous occasions during the siege of the town up until December 1993.

Finally in 1995, the train was sent in the direction of Lika, but during Operation 'Oluja' (Tempest) which took place from 4 to 7 August,[9] to avoid its being captured by the Croatian Army the crew sabotaged the train by running it off the rails into a ravine alongside the track, before they sought refuge in the *Republika Srpska*.

Two photos of below-average quality but nevertheless unique: this train was secretly photographed in 1992 near Benkovac. At the time not yet camouflaged, this is almost certainly the wagon armed with a 76.2mm field gun, added to the *Krajina Ekspres* in early 1992.
(Photos: Paul Malmassari Collection)

The accommodation coach of the armoured train, with its name on it in Cyrillic letters, with the flag of the Serb Republic of Krajina in the centre (from top to bottom the colours are: red-blue-white).
(Photo: Medija centar Odbrana)

Note the efficient construction of the train, which consisted of mounting precisely-measured armoured superstructures on standard bogie wagons.
(Photo: Medija centar Odbrana)

In this view looking back along the length of the train, the armoured wagons have not yet been fitted with the rubber panels which were to break up their silhouettes. Note the armour plates which protect all the lower parts of the locomotive apart from the bogies.
(Photo: Medija centar Odbrana)

8. The author does not know the outcome of this operation.
9. August 5th, the anniversary of the recapture of Knin, is now a national holiday in Croatia.

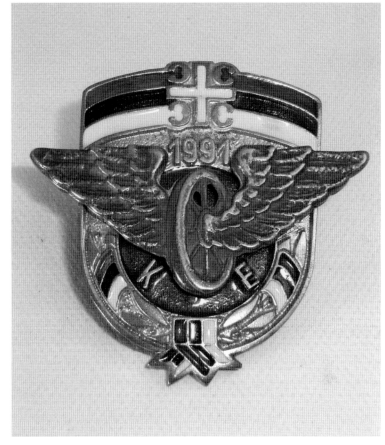

Above: The badge of the *Krajina Ekspres*, featuring, as would be expected, the arms of Serbia, the initials of the train, and the winged wheel, typical of the symbol used to represent armoured trains in many Eastern European countries.
(Photo: Paul Malmassari Collection)

Below: The crew of the train celebrating Mass on 11 March 1994.
(Photo: Paul Malmassari Collection)

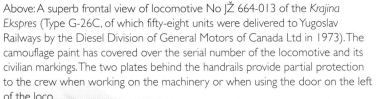

Above: A superb frontal view of locomotive No JŽ 664-013 of the *Krajina Ekspres* (Type G-26C, of which fifty-eight units were delivered to Yugoslav Railways by the Diesel Division of General Motors of Canada Ltd in 1973). The camouflage paint has covered over the serial number of the locomotive and its civilian markings. The two plates behind the handrails provide partial protection to the crew when working on the machinery or when using the door on the left of the loco.
(Photo: Medija centar Odbrana)

One of the train's 57mm rocket launcher pods photographed beneath its overturned wagon.

(Photo: Paul Malmassari)

One of the wrecked wagons in the ravine. Some of the armour plates carry NVA (*National Volksarmee* = former East German Army) markings. The black shape on the left is one of the reinforced rubber sheets which covered the sides of the train, giving it a rounded profile.

(Photo: Paul Malmassari)

The author standing inside one of the wagons of the *Krajina Ekspres*. The wagon platform was 2.51m (8ft 2¾in) wide.

(Photo: Paul Malmassari)

The curve where the crew of the *Krajina Ekspres* derailed it into the ravine to avoid its being captured by the Croatian Army. The wreckage can be seen on the left-hand side of the embankment.

(Photo: Paul Malmassari)

SOURCES:

Radic, Alexandre, 'Historia – *Krajina Ekspres*', *Arsenal* (Defence Ministry) No 14 (15 February 2008), pp 51–4 (in Serbian).
National Railway Bulletin, Vol 60–1 (National Railway Historical Society, 1995).
Medija Centar Odbrana via Bojan Dimitrijevic.
Notes and photos by the author (March 1998)
Video: https://youtu.be/qj6OSOAmYyM

'Domoljub 101' Armoured Rail Trolley

Designed in a few hours by Mr Ivica Zigolić, one of the Directors of Rade Končar in Zagreb, and built in seven days, this armoured unit was based on a TMD 22-119 locotractor, normally used on private branch lines. The initial plan was to provide an armoured railcar capable of defending the factory grounds against snipers posted on the roofs of surrounding buildings during the opening weeks of the war. This plunging fire led to the adoption of armour protection which was inclined inwards at the base, compared to the classic layout where the armour is inclined inwards at the top.

'Domoljub 101' had a large armoured compartment capable of carrying fifteen men. It was driven from the original cab, reached by a door on the right-hand side, and has no provision for a rear-facing driving position. The locotractor, immediately requisitioned by the Defence Ministry, went to the front and was employed as far as Nova Gradiska, where the railway network had been seriously damaged. It was the very first armoured rail vehicle of the Homeland War.

Technical Details:
Length (over buffers): 8.1m (26ft 7in)
Armour: 10mm
Motor: Diesel TDM 22-119
Power: 148hp
Weight: 11 tonnes
Load capacity: 6 tonnes
Maximum speed: 60km/h (37mph)

Above: A TMD 22-119 identical to the one used as the base for *Domoljub 101*.
(Photo: Paul Malmassari)

Above right: Three-quarters front view of *Domoljub 101*. The attached emblem was not used during its combat deployment, but a national flag was carried on a pole in the socket seen to the left of centre.
(Photo: Paul Malmassari)

Right: Sketch plans drawn by the author from actual measurements taken by him.
(Drawing: Paul Malmassari)

Close-up of the buffers, almost completely covered by the armour. Also note the two stone catchers to clear the rails of minor obstacles, and the feed pipes of the sanding gear.
(Photo: Paul Malmassari)

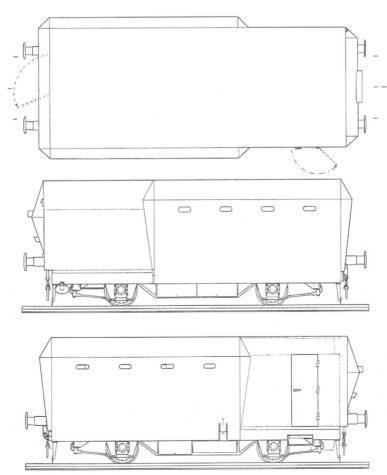

© Paul MALMASSARI 1999 1/87 (HO)

Two views of the rear of the unit, with the personnel access door. The unusual disposition of the inclined armour can clearly be seen in these shots.
(Photos: Paul Malmassari)

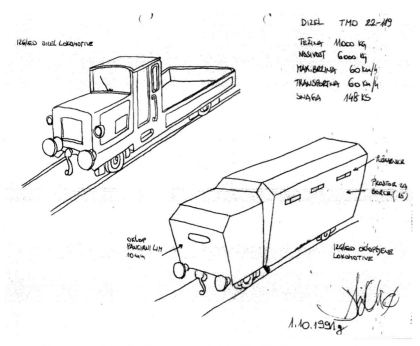

The access door to the driving position. The central slot clearly has only a limited field of vision. This vehicle is preserved in the museum devoted to improvised armoured units of the Homeland War.
(Photo: Paul Malmassari)

The stark interior of the locotractor, showing the structure, the rudimentary benches and the firing loopholes closed by sliding shutters.
(Photo: Paul Malmassari)

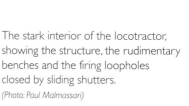
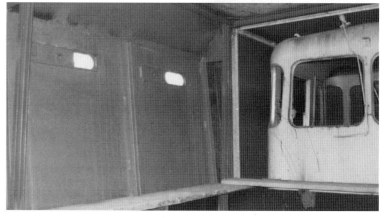

Photocopy of the sketch drawn by Mr Ivica Zigolić which served as the basis for the construction by Končar. Note that his original plan showed a locotractor with driving cab in the middle.
(Document: Končar)

SOURCES
Lajnert, Siniša, *Hrvatske Željeznice u Domovinskom Ratu* (Zagreb: 2010).
The author's visit and discussion with Mr Ivica Zigolić, Director of the Končar factory, 1998.

CUBA

SANTA CLARA 1958

During the Cuban Revolution (1956–9), the railways came under attack by the Castro revolutionaries, who aimed to cut the supply lines of the government troops. Accordingly, in 1958 the Ferrocarriles Occidentales Company built an armoured train. The attack on Santa Clara, defended by the 6th Regiment 'Leoncio Vidal', began on 20 December 1958, and on the 29th the armoured train, commanded by Colonel Florentino Rosell y Leyva was tasked with defending the north-eastern part of the town. Withdrawing in the face of an attack by Castro's forces, the train was derailed on a stretch where some 20m (65ft) of the rails had been torn up, and its crew were captured. Several armoured wagons from the train are among the main attractions in the Museum of the Revolution in Santa Clara.

The rear and underside of the armoured loco in the centre of the scene of devastation.
(Photo: Paul Malmassari Collection)

The site of the derailment, at the level crossing on the Camajuani road. Centre left, behind the armoured wagon, is the rear end of the locomotive which is lying on its side.
(Photo: Paul Malmassari Collection)

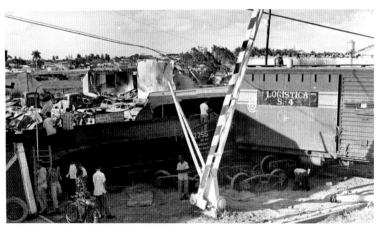

The nose of the overturned armoured loco seen behind the crossing barrier.
(Photo: Paul Malmassari Collection)

The armoured driving cab of the locomotive, a 1350hp GMC diesel.
(Photo: Paul Malmassari Collection)

SOURCES:
Book:

Batista y Zaldivar, Fulgencio, *Cuba Betrayed* (New York: Vantage Press, 1962).

Above, one of the armoured wagons from the train and below, the bulldozer said to be the one used to rip up the tracks and derail the train, on display at the 'Monumento a la Toma del Tren Blindado' at Santa Clara.
(Photos: Cairns, 1997)

Websites:

Discussion of the armoured train battle, at: http://trenblindado.com/Story.html

Visit the Museum, at: http://www.tripadvisor.fr/LocationPhotos-g671534-d2718318-w2-Monumento_a_la_Toma_del_Tren_Blindado_Santa_Clara_Villa_Clara_Province_Cuba.html#63606290

EL PUEBLO VILLACLAREÑO ERIGE
STE MONUMENTO A LOS COMBATIENTES
E LA BATALLA DE SANTA CLARA.

Julio de 1986

CZECHOSLOVAKIA

ARMOURED TRAINS[1] 1918–1950

Born from the geographical reordering of Europe at the end of the First World War, Czechoslovakia was formerly a part of the Austro-Hungarian Empire. The efforts to meet the national aspirations of the Czechs and Slovaks and to integrate them into the Allied camp had begun in 1916.

The Birth of an Army and a Nation in Russia and France

The key to understanding how this army came into being, before the birth of its nation state, is the fact that the Czechs and the Slovaks had long been submerged in a multi-national empire, which paid scant attention to their individual aspirations, power being vested in the more populous constituent nations. Two famous individuals laboured to promote the interests of these two peoples: Thomàs G Masaryk, a philosophy professor, and Edouard Beneš, one of his pupils who himself became a philosophy professor. In the course of numerous negotiations, the Allies, who at that point included the Russian Empire, began to consider that the enmity the Czechs and Slovaks bore towards the Austrians could be turned to their advantage. As early as 18 October 1914, the Czechs and Slovaks in Russian prisoner-of-war camps began to be separated from other Austro-Hungarian prisoners. Then in February 1915, the 11th Austrian Regiment, composed of a majority of Slavs, refused to fight the Serbs, and the 36th Regiment mutinied against its officers.

The National Council of the Czech Peoples was created in Paris with the support of Aristide Briand. Also in Paris, the popular artist and illustrator Alphonse Mucha also laboured tirelessly to promote Czech nationhood. At the Front, the embryonic Czech Army, the *Ceska Družina* scored its first victories and took its first prisoners. In 1915, there were 4000 Czech prisoners of war in France, 50,000 in Russia and 10,000 in Italy. Their potential employment against the Austro-Hungarians would weigh heavily against the Central Powers. By 1916, there were 300,000 in Russia, and the decree recognising the existence of the Czech Army was signed. The Russian Revolution upset the existing situation, however, and an agreement between the Bolsheviks and the Czechs allowed for the latter to move to the Western Front. The Germans, however, stood in the way of this redeployment, and the Czechs began their long withdrawal to the East over the Trans-Siberian Railway, with the 1st Regiment acting as rearguard throughout.

[1] In Czech: *Pancéřový vlak*, or PV. Alternatively in Slovak; *Obrněný vlak*.

Czech Armoured Trains, 1918 to August 1920

Their route followed the railway, and their primary concern was the security of the rearguard, especially when the Reds began attacking them. To hold the critical junction at Bakhmach, Captain Cervinks, commanding the 6th Regiment, set in hand the construction of an armoured train in March 1918, comprising a steam engine, a van and three mineral wagons. Protection was provided by sandbags, and it was armed with machine guns and the crews' rifles. On 1 June the train gained a field gun in the chase position, greatly improving its firepower, and its patrol missions ensured the safe passage of the Czech troops. Thus the armoured trains were born out of the mission assigned to the Czechoslovaks by General Janin, head of the French Military Mission, which was to guard the railway lines. The territory they controlled extended for 10km (6¼ miles) on either side of the tracks, and by 1919 this so-called neutral band was the only territory not in the hands of the Reds. The protection of certain parts of the line was assured by the Polish Legion, which deployed three armoured trains.

Of the twelve regiments taking part in the withdrawal, it appears that only two, the 5th and 11th, did not possess armoured trains. Construction and entry into service of the armoured trains took place principally from May to September 1918, even though certain trains did not see the light of day until 1919, such as those of the 8th and 9th Regiments. Other trains were not incorporated into regiments, such as the anti-aircraft train built by Captain Kulikovski in late September 1918 at Chaytanka. The armoured train of the Attack Battalion was built between the 16 and 20 June 1918 at Kansk, and took part in the battles covering the retreat as far as Lake Baikal in July–August 1918.

The 1st Regiment possessed one train, built near Kinel in June 1918, armed with a 76.2mm Putilov gun in the leading wagon. Designated No 3, it was destroyed during the battle of Bouzoulouk on the 25th of the same month.

Of the four armoured trains of the 2nd Regiment, the two equipped and manned by the First Platoon were destroyed, one on the Volga on 23 October 1918, and the other on the River Ik. The train commanded by Lieutenant Netik had to its credit a Red armoured train knocked out on 26 June 1918.

The 3rd Regiment was the most prolific user of armoured trains, but the size and armament of each of its trains was relatively modest: in general one single wagon with a chase gun, and several bogie wagons protected by sleepers and sandbags. These trains were all built in June 1918, and instead of individual train names they were known by the name of their commander: Malek, Lt. Iijnsky, Lt. Sembatovic, Captain Nemcinov, Captain Urbanek (of which the command passed to Captain Troka on 6 July) and Nepras.

The 4th Regiment possessed the most famous armoured train of the Civil War period, *Orlik*[2] (see also the chapters on Russia and China). Bearing the name *Lenin*, it was captured intact from the Reds at Simbirsk on 22 July 1918 and was renamed *Orlik* two days later. It immediately went into action on the Simbirsk-Tchita line. In October 1918 it was split into *Orlik I* and *Orlik II*, which operated from Priytovo and Abdulino respectively. Once more combined into one train, it assured the security of the Trans-Siberian during the Summer of 1919, at a time when the line was suffering continual sabotage. When the train was based at Irkoutsk Station, General Janin noted that the area was calm and that 'Armoured Train *Orlik* . . . guaranteed order'. At Tchita on 8 April 1920, it was involved in an incident when the Japanese forced the crew of four officers and 100 men to hand over the train to them. Following diplomatic exchanges, the train was handed back to its crew on the 13th. After the last Czech troops departed on 20 May 1920, the train once more came into the possession of the Japanese, who were occupying the region, but the Americans insisted it be handed to the White Russians. The latter used it up until Autumn 1922, but when Vladivostok fell to the Reds, *Orlik* joined the army of Zhang Zongchang in China.

The name of this train was popular with the Czechs, as the 4th Regiment possessed another *Orlik*, built at Penza in May 1918. Commanded by Captain Sramek, it had a crew of sixty men, and carried an armament of nine machine guns and two armoured cars. In late May a flat wagon carrying an artillery piece was added, but the train was seriously damaged the very same day. In a single night, it was rebuilt using new wagons. Its crew was reinforced, to a total of six officers and 200 men. It took part in the battles of Abdulino and Tchichma on 3 July. On that date it assumed the name of *Orlik I* to avoid confusion with the ex-*Lenin* of the same name, and was in action continuously up until the battle of Simbirsk on 8th and 9th September, where its leading wagon was destroyed and its gunners killed or wounded, along with the train commander. Shortly after withdrawing to Kindiakovka it was taken out of service.

The 4th Regiment built an *Orlik II* which was in action from July to November 1918. After the fighting before Bougoulma in early August, it was hit by fire from a Red train and was forced to retreat. It then covered the retreat from Bougoulma to Zlatoust, where its combat damage was repaired, then on 20 November it was decommissioned.

Armoured Train *Grozny*, built at Penza in May 1918 and armed with an artillery piece and three machine guns, had a crew of 107 men. It was given the unenviable role of covering the rearguard

of the 4th Regiment during the retreat, this regiment being now the rearguard of the entire Czech Legion. The most powerful part of its armament was the rear flat wagon, on which was mounted a Putilov-Garford armoured truck. It was reorganised twice: on the first occasion its crew was increased to 160 men and its armament to two guns and ten machine guns. Two armoured bogie wagons were added on 24 June. In August 1918 it was again transformed, being split into two: the part retaining the name *Grozny* kept the armoured truck. Its crew were forced to sabotage it on 23 October 1918. The other part kept the second gun and the ten machine guns, under the designation 'Armoured Train No 29'. It too had to be sabotaged in September.

Little is known about Armoured Train *Sirotek*, but a last train operated by the 4th Regiment was improvised by Captain Snajor to replace *Grozny* and continue its mission of supporting the rearguard.

The 6th Regiment, in addition to its first train built in March 1918, equipped three armoured trains (two in early June and the third in August). One 'Train of the 6th Regiment' counted among its battle honours the destruction of a Red armoured train on 27 June.

The sole train operated by the 7th Regiment was built on 25 May at Mariinsk. During its first action it comprised just one bogie wagon armed with two machine guns. Its armament was then increased by the addition of an artillery piece. On 26 June, it was hit by fire from a Red train but was able to retreat to Lake Baikal, where it took part in the fighting at Koultouk on 18 July, before continuing to cover the withdrawal.

The 8th Regiment operated Armoured Trains *Mariinsk* and *Těšín*, and also a train formed on 1 July 1918 at Ougolnaya in Manchuria, at first armed just with machine guns, but later naval guns were added. Towards the end of the fighting, it operated in the Oussouri sector between Vladivostok and Khabarovsk.

Armoured Train *Údernik* of the 9th Regiment saw service in May–June 1919.

The 10th Regiment lost its only armoured train, built at Nijne-Oudinsk in June 1918, when it was captured by the Reds on the 22nd of that month.

The 12th Regiment employed an armoured train about which little is known, apart from it taking part in the battle of the Ekaterinenbourg junction in October 1918.

Six trains were deployed in May–June 1919 to secure the central line of the Trans-Siberian to the west of Ienissei and assure the freedom of movement so vital to the Czechs. They were: the train of the Light Battery (not attached to a regiment), Armoured Train *Údernik* of the 9th Regiment, and Armoured Trains *Těšín* and *Mariinski* of the 8th Regiment; the zone to be patrolled extended from Taiga/Tomsk to Atchinsk, a distance of some 300km (190 miles), and in the Summer of 1919 this became the responsibility of Armoured Trains *Tajšet* and *Spasitel* of the 1st Regiment.

In conclusion, during their withdrawal to Vladivostok via the Trans-Siberian Railway, which was their only chance of returning to

2. '*Little Eagle*' in Czech, and also the name of a castle.

Western Europe, the Czech Legion used thirty-two armoured trains, three of which were captured from the Reds. In all, in the course of the campaign, they captured twenty-five Bolshevik armoured trains, and destroyed two more.

OTSTRAŇOVANÍ NEPŘÁTELSKÉHO BRONEV.
STRATI

One of the first improvised armoured trains, probably No 6, seen here at Tcheliabinsk in 1918. Note the limited protection, even on the engine which has only the cab protected, but sufficient at the start of the conflict to cut a path through the bands of marauding Bolsheviks.
(Photo: Paul Malmassari Collection)

Seen from this angle, the train appears unarmoured, but over and above those trains formally designated as 'armoured', all the Czech trains were fitted with a certain minimum level of protection.
(Photo: Paul Malmassari Collection)

Despite the apparent sense of security in the open countryside, the trains, armoured or otherwise, used by the Czech Legion in its long journey towards Vladivostok suffered continual attacks.
(Photo: Paul Malmassari Collection)

A well-known photograph taken at Oufa. It is interesting as it shows the considerable firepower provided by at least six machine guns mounted on each side of the wagon. On the left are 7.62mm Maxim Model 1905/1910s, and on the right the first machine gun is a Colt-Browning M1895 'Potato Digger', of which several thousand were ordered by Russia in 1914 in 7.62mm calibre.
(Photo: Vojenský Ústřední Archív, Vojenský historický archiv – VÚA-VHA)

A typical shot of one end of an armoured bogie wagon armed with a Russian 76.2mm gun. Note that only a small amount of training is possible. Obviously, the work to fit the internal armour has not yet been completed.
(Photo: VÚA-VHA)

Perhaps another shot of the same wagon. The 76.2mm Putilov Model 1902 gun, with a range of more than 8000m (5 miles), was the standard armament of the Czech trains.

(Photo: VÚA-VHA)

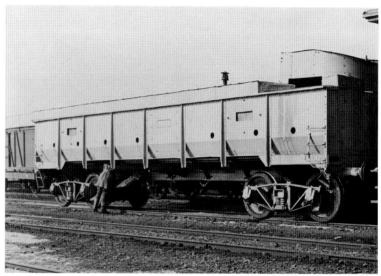

This wagon coupled behind the engine shows the typical features of the first armoured trains: increasing the height and roofing over of the sides, particularly to protect the crewmen against the extreme cold (note the stove chimney). Clearly visible are the diamond bogies which were particularly adapted to the often-irregular track found on the Trans-Siberian.

(Photo: ECPA-D)

One of the various types of armour protection on the bogie wagons used by the Czech Legion. The sides have been raised, and the V-shaped armour prevents projectiles from remaining on the roof before exploding. In addition, loopholes have been pierced in the wagon sides. Unusually, the armament appears to be a German 7.58cm Minenwerfer (trench mortar) neuer Art.

(Photo: VÚA-VHA)

A wagon from Armoured Train *Praha*, proudly displaying the national flag. The armour is well-designed, again fitted on a standard Russian Railways wagon.

(Photo: ECPA-D)

A well-known postcard of the period showing a Czech armoured train assembled from Russian rolling stock. The protection on the engine, seen here from the front right, is relatively simple, and the armoured wagons have all been built on the base of standard high-sided bogie wagons. As time passed, the design of the armour protection would evolve significantly.

(Photo: Paul Malmassari Collection)

Another example of an armoured bogie wagon on the Trans-Siberian. This one is perhaps a captured Bolshevik wagon, with its 76.2mm gun in the chase position.
(Photo: Paul Malmassari Collection)

On the other hand, this wagon is instead devoted to close-in protection of the train, with loopholes for small arms, and perhaps also a machine gun, as suggested by the larger central embrasure.
(Photo: Paul Malmassari Collection)

Seen in 1918, one of the revolving casemates of the armoured train of the Second Battery of the 1st Artillery Regiment. The van to the right bears the usual 'X' marking denoting explosives.
(Photo: VÚA-VHA)

This interesting view allows us to clearly see the roof protection provided by lengths of rail, and through the rear opening more rails arranged to form an internal partition, separated from the sides of the wagon by a layer of wood.
(Photo: Paul Malmassari Collection)

It is difficult to tell whether this train is Czech or White Russian. Nonetheless, the revolving casemate is rudimentary but interesting. Note the the cowcatcher, and also that the van next in line has an upper firing position and an observation cupola.
(Photo: Paul Malmassari Collection)

An interesting shot showing the final version of *Orlik*, on 2 June 1918. The Austin armoured car was used as a machine-gun wagon. Note the open door of the van in which a field gun is installed.
(Photo: VÚA-VHA)

The other casemate of this battery shows the construction technique used, with plates fastened over an internal framework.
(Photo: Paul Malmassari Collection)

Orlik as a complete train, with the railcar *Zaamurietz* coupled immediately behind the engine. Note the Czech flag.
(Photo: VÚA-VHA)

This photo of the leading wagon of the same train, probably taken later in the campaign, show how it has evolved, notably in the profile of the casemate. Cowcatchers have by now become standard, and also double as snowploughs.
(Photo: Paul Malmassari Collection)

One of several views of the self-propelled element which made up *Orlik I* when operating independently of the rest of the train.
(Photo: VÚA-VHA)

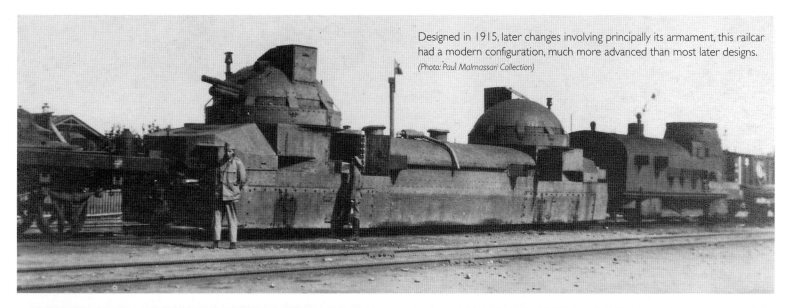

Designed in 1915, later changes involving principally its armament, this railcar had a modern configuration, much more advanced than most later designs. *(Photo: Paul Malmassari Collection)*

A shot showing the interior of an end compartment on *Orlik*, with the two corner machine guns and the access hatch open.
(Photo: VÚA-VHA)

The machine-gun positions in the central section of the railcar. Note the essential element present in all the armoured trains and even the wagons on the Trans-Siberian, the stove.
(Photo: VÚA-VHA)

As the inscription in Czech confirms, this wagon belongs to the part of the train made up of the wagons and the engine (Vuz cis. 2 = Part No 2, Part No 1 comprising the railcar operating independently). The turret is armed with a Russian 76.2mm Model 02, which can train through approximately 270 degrees.
(Photo: Paul Malmassari Collection)

A view of the other end of the artillery wagon, here coupled to the railcar.
(Photo: Paul Malmassari Collection)

The other artillery wagon of *Orlik*. Despite the fact that the two wagons were built on the same base vehicle, the turret with all-round traverse installed in place of the original chase gun has a different armament, a 76.2mm Model 1904 mountain gun.

(Photo: Paul Malmassari Collection)

A fact never previously published: Armoured Train *Orlik* received the French Croix de Guerre (top left of the pennant) from General Janin on 24th March 1920, for its service during the entire Trans-Siberian conflict. This pennant bearing *Orlik*'s insignia no longer exists.

(Photo: VÚA-VHA)

Interestingly, a postal service was set up to convey the correspondence of the Czech Legion, but also that of the local Russians, whose postal service had collapsed because of the Revolution. It began to operate on 18 September 1918, over an initial distance of 4000km (2500 miles), and was then extended to 7000km (4375 miles), taking two weeks to travel the length of the line to Vladivostok. Among several different images used on the stamps was one featuring Armoured Train *Orlik*, on a stamp of the second issue which appeared in 1919.[3]

A series of three stamps, printed in red, bistre and green, was also issued to commemorate the Czech soldiers who made the epic crossing of Siberia to build their nation, here featuring the bi-colour flag of the period flying from the armoured wagon at the head of the troop train.

(Stamp: Paul Malmassari Collection)

The yellow-gren 50-kopeck issue.

(Stamp: Paul Malmassari Collection)

[3.] The stamp issue, known as 'silhouettes', was printed at Irkoutsk by printers Makusin and Posochin: 35,520 examples of the 50-kopeck yellow-green stamp were printed. The third issue (for the Yugoslavs) and the fourth series (commemorative, which appeared between October 1920 and March 1921) show slight variations in the design.

The Czechoslovak Army during the Inter-War Period

While the *Družina* was forging the national spirit of Czechoslovakia by fighting its way across Siberia, the new army was also being created in the homeland. Called to fight on the new national borders, it used armoured trains firstly of foreign origin then those produced at home. The Czech Army subsequently maintained a force of six standardised armoured trains up until 1938.

With the defeat of the Central Powers in 1918, PZ II (MÁV engine 377.116, wagons Nos 140.914 and S150.003) and several wagons and a steam engine from Austro-Hungarian PZ I and IV were captured in Prague. On 18 November 1918 the first Czech armoured train, numbered II, left for the Slovak Front and added a new infantry wagon (S150.271) from the ex-Austro-Hungarian PZ VII. It was then divided into two, one part forming the principal armoured train proper (PV II-a) and the other the support train (PV II-b). The first part remained in Slovakia from December 1917 to the following Spring, to secure the new borders. It next fought

the Hungarians, and on 12 June in particular, it employed a technique unique to armoured trains, sending a safety wagon loaded with ballast to crash into a Hungarian armoured train parked in Hronská Breznice Station. The Hungarian train was certainly damaged, but having expended its safety wagon, the Czech train set off a mine the following day. Renumbered as No 1 on 21 July, it defended the border between Lučenec and Filakovo up until March 1920.

PV II-b went into service on 15 December 1918 and left Prague for the Sudetenland border. In the region of Kosice, it was integrated into the 6th Division of the Italian Legion until May 1919. On 1 May it attacked the Hungarian station of Miœkolec and enabled the Czechs to recover engines and wagons captured by the Hungarians in the Slovak zone. It was renumbered as No 2 on 21 June 1919.

A composite of two ex-Austro-Hungarian armoured trains, as confirmed by the presence of a wagon on the left from a Type B (see the chapter on Austria-Hungary) and from a Type A on the right.
(Photo: Paul Malmassari Collection)

Engine 179.01 of Armoured Train *General Štefányk* seen here in 1919.
(Photo: All Rights Reserved)

Armoured engine 310.440 (ex-MÁV 377.362). The name 'Libuše' refers to a legendary prophetess, granddaughter of Cech, the mythical founder of the Czech people, who chose a husband to favour the national interest over her personal feelings. Note the observation cupola above the cab, as well as the pipe enabling the transfer of water between the engine and the wagons.
(Photo: VÚA-VHA)

Armoured Train *Bratislava* at Slovensky Meder Station.
(Photo: VÚA-VHA)

An unidentified armoured train, dating from the period when the Czechs were forced to intervene militarily against their new neighbours. Its construction is interesting: the body has symmetrical openings at both ends, probably mounting two 76.2mm Putilov guns, and two-thickness wooden protection visible. Either the van at the rear is badly overloaded at one end, or the springs at that end have seen better days.

(Photo: All Rights Reserved)

On the left, wagon Kn 141.172, on the right wagon 149.902, and in between engine 377.455 of PV No 3. Note that this postcard features the tricolour Czechoslovak flag and not the bicoloured (red and white) original version, which dates this photo to later than 30 March 1920.

(Postcard: Paul Malmassari Collection)

In late 1918 Armoured Train *Brno* was built in three weeks in the state armament factory in the Moravian capital. It comprised an armoured engine and two wagons. The leading wagon was armed with two Maxim machine guns in the chase position, and a 75mm M15 Škoda mountain gun in a turret; the other wagon was armed with two Schwarzlose machine guns. After having seen action against the Poles, it remained in service up until December 1920 when it was demobilised and put in reserve. Profiting from the experience gained, it was decided to build two similar trains, No 3 *Bratislava* and No 4 *General Štefányk*. Each train included a safety wagon, an artillery wagon and two infantry wagons.

Bratislava went into action in Slovakia in July 1919 against the Hungarians. Seriously damaged at Nové Zámky, it was dismantled at the Škoda factory in August and its number transferred to the Hungarian train being repaired in the same workshops. *General Štefányk* was completed too late to take part in the fighting against the Hungarians, but remained in service until 1925, with PV 1 first at Lučenec then at Milovicer.

In 1919, the railway workshops at Vrútky built a fourth armoured train following the pattern of the Austro-Hungarian trains (engine No 377.83, but flat wagons protected with concrete slabs), carrying the No 7. Then in January 1920 PV 3 went into service, being the units of the Hungarian train captured at Sečovce which had been repaired by Škoda.

Škoda built two complete armoured trains in 1919, *Pilzen* (No 5) and *Praha* (No 6), each one having two Class 99 armoured engines with protection 6mm thick, two safety wagons, two artillery wagons, two infantry wagons and an ammunition wagon, all the wagons being protected by 8mm of armour. Each train could also be divided up into two smaller units. Their crews numbered three officers and eighty-eight men.

The period 1919 to 1938 also saw the introduction of the Tatra-Škoda armoured trolley. During the 1920s the firm of Koprivnice built a reconnaissance trolley, which also interested the Poles, who purchased some twenty examples in 1926. It could be used coupled to a train (with the driving axle disconnected) or as an independent vehicle. The Armoured Trains Company received the only example purchased by the Czechoslovak Army in 1927.

Tatra-Škoda Czech Armoured Trolley	
Technical specifications:	
Overall length:	3.68m (12ft 0¾in)
Width:	1.75m (5ft 9in)
Overall height:	2.14m (7ft 0¼in)
Ground clearance:	0.14m (5½in)
Armour thickness:	6mm to 10mm
Weight empty:	2.5 tonnes
Crew:	3 to 5 men
Armament:	2 x 7.92mm Hotchkiss machine guns
Motor:	2-cylinder 4-stroke water cooled
Cylinder capacity:	1.1 litre
Fuel capacity:	80 litres (21 Imperial gallons)
Maximum speed:	45km/h (28mph)
Range:	700km (435 miles)

Opinions differ as to the existence of a reconnaissance road-rail vehicle. According to Major Heigl,[4] Tatra was to have designed a 6x6 armoured vehicle of this type, with the following specifications, armament: two machine guns in diagonally-offset turrets; length: 7.6m (24ft 9¼in); width: 1.86m (6ft 1¼in); height: 3.1m (10ft 2in); speed: 60km/h (37mph) on roads, 80km/h (50mph) on rails.

The Czech model
Tatra, here armed with
two Schwarzlose
vz.7/24 machine guns.
(Photo: VÚA-VHA)

A rare photo showing the Czech Tatra armoured trolley with a modified turret,
mounted on a special flat wagon which perhaps could allow it to dismount
without external support. Note that when it is so mounted, its armour descends
to the level of the flat car (it is also possible that the hull has been mounted
without its wheels). Of interest is the complex camouflage scheme carried by
Czechoslovak armoured trains, which remained unchanged when they were
taken over and reused by the Wehrmacht.
(Photo: Paul Malmassari Collection)

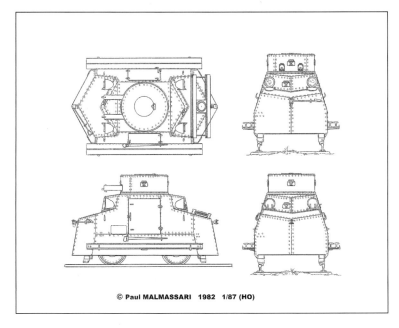

© Paul MALMASSARI 1982 1/87 (HO)

The artillery wagon of Armoured
Train No 4, seen from the safety
flat wagon. It possessed a powerful
armament capable of end-on fire,
comprising a 75mm gun and two
machine guns.
(Photo: Paul Malmassari Collection)

Armoured Train No 3 in Slovakia.
(Photo: All Rights Reserved)

According to M. Caiti,[5] this vehicle could have been created from
the conversion of all the PA 1 and PA 5 armoured cars. To date we
have found no evidence as to the existence of such a road/rail
vehicle.

[4.] Heigl, Fritz, *Taschenbuch des Tanks*, Vol II p 577.
[5.] Caiti, Pierangelo, *Atlante mondiale delle artiglierie: artiglierie ferroviarie e treni
blindati* (Parma: Ermanno Albertelli Editore 1974), p 25.

The six armoured trains remained in southern Slovakia
between 1919 and 1923. On 7 July 1922 they were formed into an
armoured battallion based at Milovice. In order to reduce the cost
of hiring rolling stock, the railway company reclaimed the unarmoured wagons in 1925, leaving just the armoured engines and
wagons. Then the armour plating was dismounted from the Class
99 engines and put into store, on condition that it would be
refitted on the engines after giving two days' notice to the railway
authorities. Finally, in 1933 the unit became a regiment.

By 1934, the existing armoured trains were wearing out, and
plans were made to build new units. The first option was the construction of armoured railcars weighing between 54 and 70 tonnes,
with 32mm of armour and armed with 66mm and 80mm guns in
turrets. ČKD and Škoda proposed designs, that of the latter firm
was chosen, and and a model was built. The German occupation
put a stop to these plans. The second option considered was to put
improvised armoured trains into service to defend the frontiers, with
rapidly-added protection, to be manned by reservists. Their
armament was to be the classic 8cm vz.5/8 in the chase position plus
several machine guns. A total of twelve such trains was envisaged.

This type of wagon was designed and built by Škoda. Here is PV No 4. The machine-gun armament initially came from four different countries, standardised on 7.92mm German Maxim Model 08s, replaced in 1925 by 8mm Hotchkiss, and ending in 1929 with Schwarzlose vz.7/24 models.
(Photo: Paul Malmassari Collection)

Overall view of a train with the second infantry wagon (also designated a machine-gun wagon) coupled at the rear , followed by a Class 377 engine, then the first infantry wagon and finally the artillery wagon. A safety wagon is only coupled at the front end of the train.
(Photo: Paul Malmassari Collection)

The Munich Crisis of 1938

Long before the negotiations leading up to the Munich agreement, separatist agitation broke out in Slovakia and Ruthenia. But on 30 September, the day before the agreement was signed, Czechoslovakia mobilised and put on alert the twelve improvised armoured trains to contain the *Freikorps* insurgents in the Sudetenland.

In this rare photo of an improvised armoured train at the time of mobilisation in 1938, note the hastily-applied camouflage on the wagon, and the ill-fitted armour plates on the engine. The gun is an 8cm Feldkanone M.5. The large number of crew members probably comprise the personnel of both the armoured train and the (unarmoured) support train. On the right in the front row is a railway employee of the CSD. In the centre of the front row is the train commander with the rank of captain (five-pointed star) and his sub-lieutenant assistant (three-pointed star). Finally, it appears that these reservists, assembled for the occasion, are wearing new uniforms.
(Photo: Paul Malmassari Collection)

Order of Battle of the Czechoslovak Armoured Trains in March 1939

Train No	Safety Wagon	Artillery Wagon	Infantry/MG Wagon	Engine	Infantry/MG Wagon	Armament
1	In 707.016	7-89499	Kn 140.914	310.412 Ex-377.116	Kn 150.003	1 x 7.5cm 1 x 4.7cm (removed in 1929) 9 then 11 x HMGs 2 x LMGs
2	In 700.820	Ik 315.784 Škoda	Ke 140.872 Ex-A-H	310.440 Ex-377.362	Ke 150.271 Ex-Hungarian	2 x 7.5cm 11 x HMGs 2 x LMGs
3	In 707.126 Ex-Hungarian			310.450 Ex-377.455	Kn 149.902 Ex-Hungarian	1 x 7.5cm 8 x HMGs 2 x LMGs
4	In 707.691 Škoda	Ke 306.809 Škoda	Ke 302.591 Škoda	To rejoin on mobilisation	Ke 62.339 Škoda	2 x 7.5cm 20 then 12 x HMGs 2 x LMGs
5	In 707.626 Škoda	Ik 307.901 Škoda	Ik 334.623 Škoda	To rejoin on mobilisation	Ik 309.364 Škoda	2 x 7.5cm 20 then 12 x HMGs 2 x LMGs
6 Training	Ik 622.616 Škoda	Ke 355.267 Škoda	Ke 309.218 Škoda	310.453 Ex-377.483 Škoda	Ik 314.850 Škoda	1 x 7.5cm 20 then 12 x HMGs 2 x LMGs
Company Level	2 armoured ammunition wagons (Škoda) Gg 28.922 and Gg 143.314 (from Armoured Trains No 5 *Pilzeň* and No 6 *Praha*)					

Each train had a crew of two officers, one NCO and between eighty and ninety-one men (apart from Train No 3 which had only seventy-four men).

The Munich agreement did not put a stop to Hitler's ambitions, and his annexation of Bohemia and Moravia led to the collapse of Czechoslovakia on 15 March 1939. This led to the incorporation of the Czechoslovak trains in the list of German armoured trains, and at that period these units comprised the most modern elements of it. Their component wagons would continue to be divided up and regrouped until the end of the Second World War.

In March 1939, German soldiers photographed the depot at Milovice where all the armoured trains were gathered together (on the right, an artillery wagon of Train No 4, and on the left, the sole Tatra trolley mounted on its flat wagon).

(Photo: Paul Malmassari Collection)

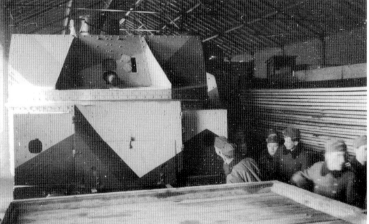

Inside the depot, the artillery wagon (photo above) and the trolley (next photo) have aroused a great deal of interest. Several months later these units, still wearing their distinctive camouflage, would form new German armoured trains.

(Photo: Paul Malmassari Collection)

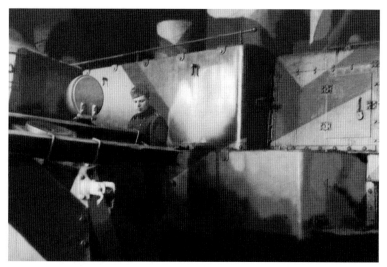

Note the device for moving from one track to the other, mounted on the bonnet of the trolley.

(Photo: Paul Malmassari Collection)

PZ 23 formed from ex-Czechoslovak units. The flat wagon which carried the Tatra trolley seen earlier is on the right of the photo, now used as the safety wagon.

(Photo: Paul Malmassari Collection)

The German trains composed of Czechoslovak elements would be PZ 23, PZ 24 and PZ 25. On the other hand, one of the improvised armoured trains of 1938, No 40, stationed at Zvolen, would join the newly-formed Slovak Army on 14 March 1939.

The Slovak National Uprising, 29 August – 28 October 1944

This uprising which started in Slovakia had as its aim the restoration of the former Czechoslovakia created in 1918, as proved by the names given to the three armoured trains taking part.

In Slovakia, resistance to the pro-German puppet government had begun during the invasion of the Soviet Union, when Slovak tank commanders and maintenance units deliberately returned broken-down tanks to Slovakia for possible future use against the regime. The initial 'anti-fascist' units were formed in late 1943, in the mountain regions. Their development was accelerated under the impetus given by the approach of the Red Army, by way of Poland towards north-east Slovakia. Two divisions of the Slovak Army officially tasked with supporting the Wehrmacht in reality were part of the plans for the Uprising, and were to make contact with the advancing Russians. The centre of gravity of the whole operation was the Banská Bystricka–Brezno–Zvolen triangle. The uprising began on 27 August, the towns were seized, and railway traffic was halted. In addition to equipment recovered from the Slovak Army, three armoured trains were built to compensate for the lack of armoured vehicles, since the majority of the Slovak tanks belonged to the two divisions in the East, which were immediately disarmed by the Germans. On 1 October, the insurgents deemed themselves to be the First Czechoslovak Army in Slovakia, in order to mark their return to their former country. On 18 October, the Germans counter-attacked from Hungary, and Banská Bystricka, the epicentre of the uprising, had to be evacuated on the 27th. The end of the uprising was notified to the government-in-exile in London the following day. The conflict

then devolved into a guerrilla campaign which ended on 3 November.

The three improvised armoured trains (IPV = *Improvizovaný pancierový vlak*) bearing the names of famous national personalities, *Štefánik*,[6] *Hurban*[7] and *Mazaryk*,[8] were built in that order, in record time (five weeks in total) in the Zvolen workshops, under the direction of Colonel Štefan Čáni, with the technical assistance of Engineer Lieutenant Hugo Weinberger. Lacking recent experience, the technicians and workers turned to an old regulation laying down rules for the construction of improvised armoured trains. The faults shown up in the first train, in particular the insufficient armour protection, were corrected in *Hurban* and *Masaryk*, which were of superior construction. It is our opinion that the description of these trains as 'improvised' should by no means be considered pejorative, as they demonstrated practices found on contemporary production armoured trains.

Each armoured train was accompanied by a support train, with sleeping accommodation, sickbay, kitchen etc. The makeup of each train differed, but all were powered by a Class 320.2 steam engine, and included a leading gun wagon plus several artillery wagons mounting turrets from Czech LT-35 tanks.[9]

Armoured Train *Štefánik*[10] was built between 4 and 18

6. Milan Ratislav Štefánik (1880–1919), airman, Vice-President of the Czechoslovak National Council then War Minister, Slovak General.
7. Jozef Miloslav Hurban (1817–86), one of the leaders of the Slovak Uprising of 1848, Member of the Slovak National Council.
8. Tomáš Garrigue Mazaryk (1850–1937), President of the Czechoslovak National Council in Paris, then President of Czechoslovakia from 1920 to 1935.
9. Several LT-35 tanks were stationed in the Slovak zone on the partition of Czechoslovakia.
10. *Štefánik* and *Hurban* were popular subjects for photographers, and a comparison of the resulting images shows that often the captions were attributed in error, which means that it is not possible today to be absolutely certain of positively identifying either train.

September. Commanded first by Lieutenant Anton Tököly then Captain František Adam, its crew numbered seventy men. On 27 September it went into action on the line from Hronskà to Kremina, and on 4 October supported a counter-attack from Stará Kremnička. Its engine was hit, but following repairs it operated on the line from Zvolen to Kriváň up until the end of October. On the 25th, it left Zvolen in order to reach Ulmanka, where it found itself trapped. The crew destroyed the train's armament and joined the partisans.

Armoured Train *Hurban* was begun on 25 September and completed in just eleven days. Under the command of Captain Martin Ďuriš Rubansky, it went into action on line from Hronská Dúbrava to Žiar nad Hronom up until 4 October, when it moved to the line from Banska Bystricá to Diviaky. On the same day, it fought German forces near Čremošné, where it suffered several casualties. At the end of October it had to be abandoned in Horný Harmanec Station.

Armoured Train *Masaryk* was completed on 14 October. It was the most sophisticated of the three units, and its engine had complete armour protection. The high-quality armour plates came from the Podbrezová steelworks. Under its commander Captain Jan Kukliš it operated on the line from Brezna to Červená Skala where it was damaged on 21 October. On the 24th, the engine was destroyed by a direct hit, and the commander, driver and fireman were killed. Beyond repair, it was towed to the tunnel at Horný Harmanec Station, where its crew destroyed its armament and joined the crew of *Hurban*. Captured when that town fell, both trains were sent to Milowitz for repairs before being shared out between SSZ *Max* and *Moritz*.

To celebrate the 300th anniversary of the Treaty of Utrecht (1713), Utrecht Museum organised an exhibition on trains in warfare. For the occasion, *Štefánik* was restored and partly reconstructed. After having been one of the major attractions at the exhibition, it returned to Zvolen in September 2013.

The handing-over ceremony of *Štefánik* at the Zvolen workshops on 18 September 1944. Engineer Lieutenant Hugo Weinberger (codename 'Velan') is second from the right. The civilian in the centre is Engineer Ivan Víest, Director of the Railways of Slovakia, with Colonel Štefan Čáni immediately to his left. *(Photo: Múzeum SNP)*

At the head of IPV I *Štefánik* is the 80mm vz 5/8 gun, seen during a halt at Viglas. The safety platform wagon is not coupled directly to the train, but is propelled by a timber beam. *(Photo: Múzeum SNP)*

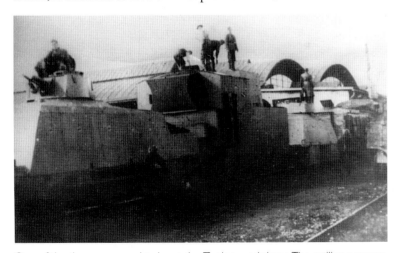
One of the three armoured trains at the Zvolen workshops. The artillery wagons were built using as a base Type U coal wagons. The protection was formed from two sheets of wood each 5cm thick separated by 15cm of gravel ballast. *(Múzeum Slovenského nároného povstania, SNP)*

An overall view of IPV I *Štefánik* seen from in front, with its safety platform wagon, the leading cannon wagon, the two turret wagons armed with 37mm guns and the tail wagon. *(Photo: Múzeum SNP)*

Štefánik seen from the rear.

(Photo: Múzeum SNP)

This shot of *Štefánik* and the photo on the right clearly show the difference between the tail wagon (with an embrasure for a 37mm gun) and the leading wagon with its large opening for the 8cm FK.

(Photo: Múzeum SNP)

Above: The Class 320.2 steam engine of *Štefánik*. The initial camouflage tones were white, green and red-brown. Subsequently, all the trains would be repainted an overall green shade.

(Photo: Múzeum SNP)

Left: Interior view of the infantry wagon of IPV I *Štefánik*, with one of the lateral 7/24 Schwarzlose machine guns.

(Photo: Múzeum SNP)

Štefánik in its overall green paint scheme under foliage camouflage, far more discrete than the original three-colour scheme.
(Photo: Múzeum SNP)

The chase gun mounted on all three trains (here we see IPV II *Hurban*) was an ex-Austro-Hungarian 8cm FK M 05 or 05/08, also used by the Wehrmacht during the Second World War. Thanks probably to the successive improvements included in each of the trains, the embrasure of *Hurban* is virtually closed by an armour plate which was not present on *Štefánik*.
(Photo: Múzeum SNP)

A fine view of the tail wagon of *Hurban*. The cupola does not appear to have observation slits, but it has a frame to mount a machine gun for close-in or anti-aircraft protection.
(Photo: Múzeum SNP)

An impressive view of *Hurban* wearing camouflage, with its crew disembarked. After the uprising was crushed, they would be forced to join the partisans in the mountains.
(Photo: Múzeum SNP)

Above: Leading safety wagon of IPV III *Masaryk* in camouflage, which however fails to disguise the fact that the wagon sides are vertical.
(Photo: Múzeum SNP)

Left: The main armament of the trains – seen here on *Hurban* – was an LT-35 tank turret armed with a 37mm gun and a co-axial 7.92mm machine gun. In Wehrmacht service, this tank was designated the PzKpfw 35 (t). Note in this photo the roof of the hull of the tank, enveloped in the armour protection which leaves only the hatches visible.
(Photo: Múzeum SNP)

The armoured steam engine of *Masaryk* seen in 1946, in one of the depots where all the equipment retrieved from the various wartime fronts was collected.
(Photo: All Rights Reserved)

Hurban restored during the post-war period. Note the cupola of the infantry wagon to the right.
(Photo: Múzeum SNP)

A monument to the Slovak National Uprising, in the form of a reconstruction of IPV I *Štefánik* at Zvolen with T-34/85 turrets altered to resemble those of PzKpfw 35(t)s.
(Photo: Fréderic Guelton)

In 1974 this medal was struck to commemorate the thirtieth anniversary of the uprising.
(Private Collection)

The Czech Uprising (1945)

On 6 April 1945, the day after the liberation of Bratislava in Slovakia, a coalition government was established in Košice, and on 5 May Prague rose up and the Wehrmacht was driven out in the course of fighting which lasted until 11 May. A large quantity of German rolling stock was captured, including PZ 27, PZ 80 and PZ 81, the PZ (s.Sp trolleys) 205 and 206, including several heavy railcars, security train *Moritz*, PT 36 (*Littorina*) and several anti-aircraft trains. The latter units were put back into service and formed twelve improvised armoured trains. Two other armoured trains (ex-German vehicles) were activated in Prague and Milovice (Milowitz, the former Czechoslovak armoured train base). Lastly, Type BP 44 wagons were discovered at Česká Lipa during the reconquest of the Sudetenland at the end of the month. One complete ex-German armoured train, less certain elements, was put back into service and used up until 1948.

Armoured Train *Praha* ('Prague') made up from assorted wagons, including this hull of a Panzerjäger IV placed on a four-wheel mineral wagon.
(Photo: Tomáš Jakl Collection)

A fine view of the 20mm Flugabwehr-MG 151/20 (Drilling) mounted on the anti-aircraft trains in concrete tubs.

(Photo: Tomáš Jakl Collection)

A completely improvised low-sided wagon, with earth piled up between a central compartment and the side planking. Notwithstanding, earth would be quite effective in stopping small-arms projectiles. Note the German helmets worn by the crew.

(Photo: Tomáš Jakl Collection)

Complete view of an anti-aircraft wagon.

(Photo: Tomáš Jakl Collection)

Armoured Train *Uhřiněves* composed of various flak wagons grouped together in 1945. The engine is unarmoured.

(Photo: VÚA-VHA)

Type 1 FlaK wagon, with the armour strengthened by the addition of a layer of wood.

(Photo: Tomáš Jakl Collection)

The Armoured Trains of the Second Czechoslovak Republic

The new Czechoslovak Army included an Armoured Train Company in its establishment, created on 1 October 1945, based at Nymburg (modern Nymburk), and placed under the command of the 11th Tank Brigade. This company had two platoons. One platoon was comprised of armoured trains, with each unit organised as follows: one artillery wagon, two infantry wagons, two tank transporter wagons, command wagon, engine and a trolley. The other platoon was composed of reconnaissance trolleys, made up into rakes comprising a command wagon, PT 36, two artillery wagons, and three infantry wagons. In addition, an armoured train and a trolley intended for training were activated. With the addition of new armoured rolling stock, the Company became a Battalion in September 1946, with a separate command structure, support units and three companies:

- 1st Company (steam engines): Armoured Trains *Benes*, *Masaryk*, *Štefánik* and *Svoboda*.
- 2nd Company (petrol locotractors): Armoured Trains *Pavlik*, *Stalin*, *Hurban* and one armoured trolley.
- Reserve and Training Company: Armoured Train *Orlik*.

These trains included five artillery wagons with a 2cm Flakvierling but with different main turrets: one with a 10.5cm le.Fh 18, two PzKpfw IIs and two PzKpfw IVs. The tank transporter wagons carried LT vz.38 tanks (ex-PzKpfw 38 (t)). The remaining units were infantry, mortar and command wagons.

The Battalion was reorganised in Autumn 1949: the 2nd Company was based at Sopot (100km/ 63 miles to the south-east of Prague) while the 1st remained in Nymburg, these two centres bringing together all the armoured trains, which on this occasion lost their names and were thereafter referred to by numbers. However, the armoured train units were dissolved in 1954–5 and the rolling stock was scrapped, except for several infantry wagons used in a stationary role, notably by the Air Force.

Reduced to a propaganda weapon, these trains had not been able to play a decisive role in the battles of liberation which stressed the actions of the partisans and paratroops.

This view shows the tool set of an infantry trolley, with the jack which is identical to that carried by tanks.
(Photo: VÚA-VHA)

The elements of two Panzerzüg (s.Sp) formed a train which comprised three turret-equipped trolleys, a command trolley (with frame aerial) and an infantry trolley. Note the Czechoslovak flag on the side of the leading unit.
(Photo: VÚA-VHA)

The opposite view of a turreted trolley, to be able to compare the two ends. Here is the motor end, identifiable by the semi-spherical armoured domes.
(Photo: VÚA-VHA)

The command trolley, with its frame aerial.

(Photo: VÚA-VHA)

Note the lack of a coupling hook on this unit. Regretably, none of these vehicles have been preserved in a museum.

(Photo: VÚA-VHA)

SOURCES:

Archives:

SHD, boxes 17 N 629.

Múzeum Slovenského nároného povstania, Banská Bystrica.

Vojenský Ústřední Archív, Prague.

Vojenský historický ústav, Bratislava.

Books:

Catchpole, Paul, *Steam and Rail in Slovakia* (Chippenham: Locomotives International, 1998).

Hyot, Edwin P., *The Army without a Country* (New York: MacMillan Company, 1967).

Jakl, Tomáš, Panuš, Bernard, and Tintěra, Jiří, *Czechoslovak Armored Cars in the First World War and Russian Civil War* (Atglen, PA: Schiffer Publishing, 2015).

Janin, General, *Ma Mission en Sibérie 1918-1920* (Paris : Payot, 1933).

Kliment, Charles K, and Francev, Vladimir, *Czechoslovak Armoured Fighting Vehicles 1918-1948* (Atglen (PA): Schiffer Publishing, 1997).

Kmet, Ladislav, *Povstalecké Pancierové Vlaky* (Zvolen, Slovakia: self-published, 1999).

Lášek, Pavel, and Vaněk, Jan, *Obrn ná drezína TATRA T 18* (Prague: Corona, 2002).

Richet, Roger, *Les émissions de la Légion Tchécoslovaque en Sibérie (1918-1920)* (Bischwiller: L'échangiste universel, nd).

Rouquerol, Général J., *L'Aventure de l'amiral Koltchak* (Paris: Payot, 1929).

Uhrin, Marian, *Pluk utocnej vozby v roke 1944* (Zvolen, Slovakia: Múzeum Slovenského Národného Povstania, 2013).

Journal articles:

'Československé obrněné vlaky 1818 až 1939', *Železnice* No 3/94 (1994), pp 23–6.

Chen, Edgar & Van Burskirk, Emily, 'The Czech Legion's Long Journey Home', *MHQ: The Quarterly Journal of Military History* Vol 13, No 2 (Winter 2001), pp 42–53.

Kudlicka, Bohumir, '*Orlik* Armoured Train of the Czechoslovak Legion in Russia', *The Tankograd Gazette* No 15 (2002), pp 27–30.

Militär-Wochenblatt, No 44 (1937), pp 2744–5.

'Povstalecky improvizovany pancierovy vlak *Stefanik*', *Modelar Extra* No 20 (June 2013), pp 37–49.

In 1948, the Czechoslovak authorities published this postcard, which tended to overlook the exploits of the Czech Legion in favour of the Reds, using a fictional portrayal of an armoured train.

(Postcard: Paul Malmassari Collection)

EGYPT

AHMED ARABI'S ARMOURED TRAIN 1882

British troops began landing in Alexandria on 17 July 1882, and on 5 August they made a probing attack on the main Egyptian lines at Kafr-el-Dawwar[1] which blocked the route to Cairo. Perhaps inspired by the British use of an armoured train, on 25 August the Egyptian forces of Colonel Ahmed Arabi assembled an armoured train of their own to support their position. Once the British under Sir Garnet Wolseley had moved the main thrust of their attack to Ismailia on the Suez Canal, the Kafr-el-Dawwar front became a

side-show, and there is no mention of the Egyptian armoured train after 29 August.

SOURCES:
Hawera & Normanby Star (NZ), Volume III, No 294 (30 August 1882), p 2.

[1] One also finds the name written as 'Kafradowar'.

ESTONIA

ARMOURED TRAINS[1] 1918–1940

The War of Independence (28 November 1918 – 2 February 1920)
Estonia declared its independence from Russia on 24 February 1918, but the capital Tallinn was occupied by German troops the following day. The Estonians had to wait for the Armistice of 11 November to gain their autonomy, and began to build up their own armed forces five days later. Profiting from the chaotic situation at the end of the Great War, on 28 November the Red Army attacked a German unit and troops of the Estonian National Guard, and the War of Independence began. In some areas the armoured trains were the most powerful armament available to the Estonians. The standard gauge was widespread apart from the narrow-gauge network which connected the southern part of Estonia with the northern part of Latvia.

The very first Estonian armoured train was in fact German, found abandoned at Tallinn in November 1918. It was made up of two artillery wagons (76mm guns) and two infantry wagons, with improvised protection which the Estonians upgraded. This train, allocated the number 1, arrived at the front on 30 November. It was made up of the following units: artillery wagon + two infantry wagons (one protected by sandbags, the other with iron plates) + unarmoured engine[2] + the same units in reverse order. The crew

was composed of 120 troops, made up of artillerymen, machine-gunners, and a strong infantry assault contingent.

The next five trains (on the standard gauge) went into action in the following order: on 15 and 23 December 1918, and then 21 January, 19 March and 12 August 1919. Armoured Trains Nos 5 and 6 included modern wagons (one artillery wagon + three machine-gun wagons + five infantry wagons). In August 1919, an Armoured Trains Division was created, which formed the strategic reserve of the Commander-in-Chief. By the end of 1919, the Armoured Trains force had fifty-five standard gauge wagons, and each of the artillery wagons was individually named.

Five armoured trains were built to operate on the narrow-gauge network. These were delivered on 1 January (SR No 1), 18 to 26 January, 21 February, 1 May (replacement SR No 4[3]), and 2 July 1919 respectively. Several narrow-gauge trains were protected by trench shields, which gave them a distinctive appearance. In general these trains were made up of two artillery wagons, one or

[1] In Estonian: *Soomusrong*, abbreviated to SR.
[2] Used with the tender leading.
[3] The original narrow-gauge SR No 4 was destroyed in action on 7 April 1919.

two machine-gun wagons and three or four infantry wagons. They carried a lighter armament than the standard-gauge units, with 47mm and 57mm guns, but included several 76.2mm Russian field guns.

After the Russian forces had been repulsed, the Estonians concentrated their military efforts against the *Landeswehr* who were attempting to maintain German influence throughout the Baltic States. Peace with Russia was signed on 31 December 1919. By the ceasefire date, the Estonian armoured trains numbered eleven: six armoured trains on the standard gauge (numbered from 1 to 6, the first bearing the name *Kapten Irv*[4]), and five trains for the narrow gauge (numbered 1 to 5). Between them these eleven trains carried twenty-seven artillery pieces and 118 heavy machine guns.

The Peacetime Army (1920 – June 1940)

On 1 February 1921, several trains were demobilised and the Division was reformed as a Brigade, with the following units: (standard gauge) SR *Kapten Irv*, SR No 2 and SR No 3, (narrow gauge) SR No 1 and SR No 2. In total the Brigade had three armoured engines, twelve artillery wagons, sixteen machine-gun wagons and twelve infantry wagons. In 1922, the narrow gauge SRs were demobilised and stored in depots, and then finally disbanded during the 1930s (certain units would resurface in modernised form in 1941 to face the Wehrmacht).

In addition to the formed armoured trains, there were certain individual wagons which could be attached to or detached from any existing train as need be. As these wagons each carried their own name, it is often difficult to identify a specific train solely from the name of the wagon seen in a photo.

On 1 February 1923, the Brigade was reorganised into two Regiments each comprised of two trains, then in December 1934 these two Regiments were merged into the Armoured Trains Regiment, comprising trains *Kapten Irv*, SR No 2 and SR No 3, the long-range railway gun battery, two engineer companies and two machine-gun companies. In 1936 the railway gun battery comprised one gun truck ('Suur Tõll') armed with a 152mm Canet gun, and two ('Müristaja' and 'Tapper') each armed with a 4in (102mm) gun. The plan was to combine the armoured trains with the railway gun but the financial situation of the country slowed down progress, to the point where, when the Soviets invaded Estonia on 17 June 1940, three gun trucks were still under construction, a part of the armament of the trains had been dismounted, and the acquisition of certain wagons had been put on hold.

---

4. Captain Irv, the first armoured train commander, in charge of SR No 1, was killed in action on 27 April 1919.
5. Made up of an engine + two combat wagons with a 76.2mm field gun, a 45mm anti-tank gun and nine machine guns + munitions wagon. The railway gun battery had three 130mm coast-defence guns on unarmoured 50-tonne platform wagons.

Armoured Trains incorporated into the Red Army (September 1940 – August 1941)

The former Estonian Army became a corps of the Red Army and on 12 February 1941, the armoured trains were attached to the Baltic Sea Military District. Although their ultimate fate is unknown, it appears that several wagons were sent to the front around Leningrad. At the start of Operation 'Barbarossa', the Russian High Command ordered the construction of new armoured trains at Tallinn where the rail workshops had the necessary experience. Two narrow-gauge trains[5] and a standard-gauge railway gun battery were built, and these units took part in the defence of Tallinn up until it fell on 28 August 1941.

Despite details given in the following sources, it is extremely difficult to identify a particular train from the names painted on the wagons, given the transfers between trains and successive modernisation schemes. The photo captions which follow are therefore indicative only.

SR No 1

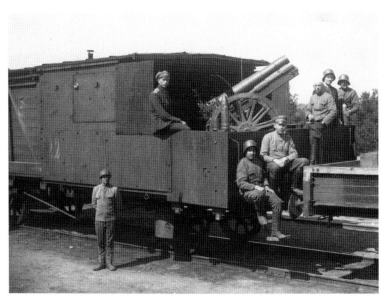

One of the wagons of the train captured from the *Landeswehr*. Note the assorted headgear: Russian caps, German Stalhelm and French Adrian helmets.
(Photo: Paul Malmassari Collection)

A telescopic observation platform extending up to 25m (82ft) high could be attached to an armoured train. Here the unit is shown lowered in the travelling position. The elements of the trains are heavily camouflaged with branches.
(Photo: Paul Malmassari Collection)

'Tommi', the leading wagon of *Kapten Irv*, showing its 6pdr (57mm) gun.
(Photo: Paul Malmassari Collection)

The pennant of SR *Kapten Irv* on an unidentified wagon, probably part of SR No 5. In the left background is the telescopic observation tower in the raised position.
(Photo: Paul Malmassari Collection)

The wagon 'Pisuhänd' of SR No 1 *Kapten Irv*. This photo shows the later configuration of the wagon fitted with a gun cupola.
(Photo: Paul Malmassari Collection)

Captain Irv, who gave his name to the armoured train he commanded.
(Photo: Paul Malmassari Collection)

An artillery wagon forming part of SR No 1. An armoured box encloses one end of a long-wheelbase outside-framed wooden wagon. The vulnerable axle boxes are protected by simple rectangular plates.
(Photo: Paul Malmassari Collection)

This view of 'Pisuhänd' appears to show its final configuration circa 1939.
(Photo: Paul Malmassari Collection)

Kapten Irv in original condition.
(Photo: Paul Malmassari Collection)

SR No 2

SR No 2 in 1919. Note the assorted collection of machine guns: From left to right, a Lewis, a Madsen (Russian calibre), a Russian Maxim on a wheeled carriage, and a Colt Browning 'Potato Digger'. A second Maxim is mounted inside the wagon. Note also the accordion held by the crewman on the right.

(Photo: Paul Malmassari Collection)

The crew of SR No 2 in front of artillery wagon 'Uku', built on the chassis of a Russian wagon, probably in 1919. Their armband bearing the number of the train is a feature which appears in many photos. In addition to the fir trees attached as camouflage, 'Uku' carries a wreath for an official ceremony attended by August Rei (the civilian in the centre), Chairman of the Constituent Assembly 1919–20, and his wife. Note the letters 'Uku' painted in shadow to give the impression of relief.

(Photo: Paul Malmassari Collection)

SR No 2 in winter camouflage. Note the smoke from the heating stove in the second wagon.

(Photo: Paul Malmassari Collection)

Vickers 130mm railway gun 'Kalewipoeg' attached to SR No 2.

(Photo: Paul Malmassari Collection)

One of several postcards dedicated to SR No 2, this one bearing the armoured train's pennant.

(Postcard: Paul Malmassari Collection)

SR No 3

75mm gun on wagon 'Onu Tom' of SR No 3. The gun appears to be a British naval 3in HA, for anti-aircraft use. Later, this wagon would be rearmed with Vickers 152mm howitzers.

(Photo: Paul Malmassari Collection)

A view of 'Onu Tom' of SR No 3, on 15 April 1919, showing the naval 3-inch HA gun. It was also armed with a 76.2mm Russian field gun at the opposite end.

(Photo: Paul Malmassari Collection)

SR No 5

Left: Wagon 'Tasuja' of SR No 5, armed with British 18pdr (84mm) and 13pdr (76mm) field guns.

(Photo: Paul Malmassari Collection)

Below left: A view of the end of 'Tasuja' carrying the 18pdr in the lower position. Note that the wheels of the field gun are bolted to a plate on which it revolves.

(Photo: Paul Malmassari Collection)

Below: A view of 'Tasuja' rearmed with a Russian 76.2mm field gun.

(Photo: Paul Malmassari Collection)

An interesting photo of SR No 5, showing a Russian bogie wagon with the armour increased in height and pierced for four firing positions for machine guns and lookout hatches. This type of wagon would not be kept in service once the fighting had ended.
(Photo: Tiit Noormets Collection)

Close-in anti-aircraft defence of the armoured trains was provided by Russian Maxim heavy machine guns, here seen on SR No 5 with a five-man crew. The mount has been given the necessary elevation by the simple expedient of propping the front legs of the tripod on a pile of empty cartridge boxes, stacked on a two-plank wagon. This improvised solution would give only limited traverse to avoid the mount toppling over on its side. The planking and roof in the background belong to a goods wagon on the neighbouring track.
(Photo: Paul Malmassari Collection)

6in (152mm) railway gun 'Lembit', attached to SR No 5.
(Photo: Paul Malmassari Collection)

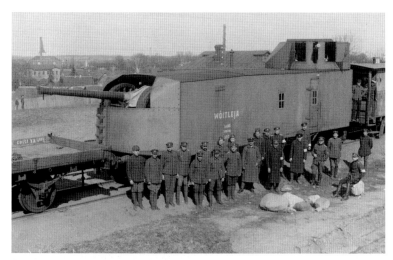

'Woitleja' in October 1919, equipped with what may be a Canet 120mm Pattern 1892 gun in its end casemate. Note that the field piece has retained its wheeled mounting, which severely limited its horizontal field of fire.
(Photo: Tiit Noormets Collection)

Closeup of the 'Lembit' gun. The combination of fixed round and screw breech indicate this is a Russian Canet 6in/45 built to a French design. Similar guns can still be seen on board the museum ship *Aurora*.
(Photo: Paul Malmassari Collection)

SR No 6

SR No 6 in action in 1919. The artillery wagon in the foreground is 'Rummu Jüri', armed with a Russian 76.2mm field gun. The artillery wagon with the long gun is 'Leitnant Sabolotnõi'.

(Photo: Paul Malmassari Collection)

Inset: An overall view of the latter artillery wagon with its long-barrelled 4.7in (120mm) British gun. Several crew members wear armbands specific to the train. The wagon carries camouflage paint panels in addition to the standard pine tree.

(Photo: Paul Malmassari Collection)

Narrow Gauge Armoured Trains
SR (narrow gauge) No 1

SR No 1 (narrow gauge) in January 1919. Each infantry wagon appears to be equipped with one Lewis Gun. Note the medical orderly, and the wounded crew member in the centre of the group.

(Photo: Paul Malmassari Collection)

SR (narrow gauge) No 2

Artillery wagon 'Suur Tõll' armed with a Russian 76.2mm field gun, part of SR No 2.

(Photo: Paul Malmassari Collection)

A closeup of the type of armour protection used on some narrow-gauge infantry wagons, comprising Russian trench shields. This type of wagon formed part of Armoured Trains Nos 2, 4 and 5. Note the riflemen have fixed bayonets. At first sight this seems incongruous, as they are fighting from behind armour and would not expect to use bayonets in close combat. But the Mosin-Nagant was never issued with a bayonet scabbard, so the bayonet is usually seen fixed.

(Photo: Paul Malmassari Collection)

SR (narrow gauge) No 4

The crew of SR (narrow gauge) No 4 in front of the artillery wagon armed with a 76.2mm Russian field gun.

(Photo: Paul Malmassari Collection)

SR (narrow gauge) No 5

An overall view of SR (narrow gauge) No 5.

(Photo: Paul Malmassari Collection)

SR (narrow gauge) No 5 wearing camouflage.

(Photo: Paul Malmassari Collection)

SR (narrow gauge) No 5 showing one
of its 76.2mm Russian field guns.

(Photo: Paul Malmassari Collection)

Modernised Armoured Trains of the 1930s

A bronze plaque on the wall of the station at Tapa, mounted on 9 June 1934 (restored to its position on 20 February 1993), bearing the insignia of the Armoured Trains Regiment.

(Photo: Paul Malmassari Collection)

Trolley No 145 of the 2nd Armoured Trains Regiment, used for the high-speed liaison role away from combat zones. The crew are lightly armed, with one rifle and pistols, probably Brownings. One occupant in the rear seat is talking on a field telephone, the cable reel for which is on the ground beside the track.

(Photo: Paul Malmassari Collection)

Armoured wagon No 212 in 1930. The two ends are symmetrical, with the machinegun embrasures diagonally opposed.

(Photo: Paul Malmassari Collection)

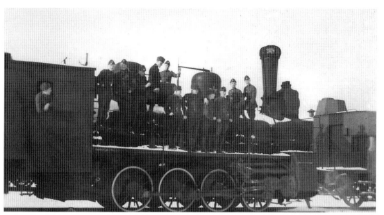

Steam engine Od-130, with only the driving cab armoured, used in armoured trains in the 1930s. Here it is propelling wagon No 212.

(Photo: Paul Malmassari Collection)

Gunners on artillery wagon 'Vanapagan' around their 76.2mm Russian field gun.

(Photos: Paul Malmassari Collection)

The leading wagon on this train photographed in 1925 is No 302 'Maru', here armed with a 76.2mm Russian field gun on the right, and a 3in(75mm) HA gun on the left. Note the Estonian flag.

(Photo: Paul Malmassari Collection)

Wagon 'Tommi' as modernised in 1929, with two 152mm M1910 Schneider howitzers.

(Photo: Paul Malmassari Collection)

Armoured wagon No 303 'Võitleja' armed with two 76.2mm field guns.

(Photo: Paul Malmassari Collection)

During the modernisation of the armoured wagons in the 1930s, 'Onu Tom' and 'Lembit' were rearmed with two Vickers 6in (152mm) 26 cwt BL howitzers. Serving these pieces required that the extending side armour walls be jointed to provide continuous protection. Note the presence of a Latvian officer with his Estonian colleagues.

(Photo: Tiit Noormets Collection)

Armoured wagon No 102 'Wapper', built to the same design.

(Photo: Paul Malmassari Collection)

In this photo of the same wagon, note the observation cupola with its four semi-conical sections which hinge open at the top to expose the lookout slots, a design which it seems was unique to Estonia.

(Photo: Tiit Noormets Collection)

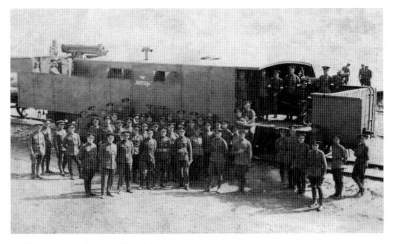

Artillery wagon No 2 'Hävitaja'.

(Photo: Paul Malmassari Collection)

SOURCES:

Helme, Mehis, *Eesti Kitsarööpmelised Raudteed 1896-1996* (Tallinn: self-published, 1996).

Õun, Matti, Noormets, Tiit, and Pihlak, Jaak, *Eesti Soomusrongrid ja Soomusronglased 1918-1941* (Tallinn: Sentinel, 2003).

An experimental armoured shield for a 76.2mm gun, using Russian trench shields bolted together. These trench shields were also used to protect several narrow-gauge armoured trains.

(Photo: Tiit Noormets Collection)

FINLAND

ARMOURED TRAINS[1] 1918–1945

The story of the Finnish armoured trains began with the War of Independence of 1918, which saw the birth of the state freed from its bonds with Russia. The Finnish railway network had not seen major growth, but at least it linked the different regions reasonably well, and had a good connection with Russia via the Viipuri-Petrograd line. The Finnish railway workers were easy prey for Communist ideology, and the Finnish High Command paid special attention to the security of the network from the very beginning. Armoured trains would thus come to play a major role in the three wars fought against Soviet Russia.

The War of Independence of 1918

Finnish independence was initially viewed by the Bolshevik leaders as a good thing, in the name of the 'right of the people to self-determination'. Almost immediately, however, the evidence that the country was determined to reject Communism led the Bolsheviks to change their minds and to try to reassert their domination by means of a 'Fifth Column'.

Under the overall command of Kullerco Manner, the President of the People's Commissariat, the Red forces were composed of Red Finns, bolstered by Russian troops commanded by Colonel Svetchnikov. At the outset armoured trains were almost exclusively used by the Reds, apparently up to ten in number. It is thought that four of these were of Russian origin, well-designed and solidly built, and that the remainder were constructed locally. It seems the first trains entered Finland only after the start of hostilities manned by Russian crews, which were not replaced by Finns until later. Nevertheless, on all the trains the Russian volunteers continued to serve as gunners and machine gunners. The crews were all part of the elite of the Red Guards, which helped to boost their morale, and the support of armoured trains helped to win many a battle.

The Red trains of Finnish origin were improvisations converted from bogie wagons in the workshops at Pasila, Viipuri and Fredericksberg (Helsinki). The steel plates used in their construction, although reasonably thick, had not been intended to be used as armour, and their lack of resistance could have been a serious weakness. Apart from small arms, their armament comprised naval guns of 37mm, 47mm, 57mm and 76mm calibre, with the mounting bolted directly to the floor of the bogie or flat wagon. On some trains, the guns were fitted with shields, as in the photo centre right, but on several others they were not. Tactically, the armoured trains formed a sub-division in the Red Guards and were used exclusively for artillery fire support. Their ultimate commander-in-chief would be G Tamlander who was previously the commander of Armoured Train No 1. Certain trains were designated by number (for Nos 1 to 4), and two others by a typical revolutionary name, which indicates that the last two were of Russian origin. They were PSJ *Kerenski* and *Partissani*. If the first four numbered trains had a name, these have not been passed down in the historical records. On the White side, apart from trains they captured, there was a train improvised to meet the Red offensive of 11 February 1918, named *Karjalan Pelastaja* ('Saviour of Karelia').

Red armoured train, built in the Fredericksberg workshops in Helsinki, armed with 75mm Canet guns originally intended for warships or coastal defence.
(Photo: Jean-Gabriel Jeudy Collection)

Fitted with rudimentary armour, the Class G1 engine of *Karjalan Pelastaja* is nevertheless equipped with a smoke deflector.
(Photo: All Rights Reserved)

[1.] In Finnish: *Panssarijuna* (PSJ).

A wagon from *Karjalan Pelastaja*, its armour protection comprising two layers of planks with the interval between filled with bricks. Its armament is a 76.2mm Model 76 VK/04 mountain gun with a shield.

Three Red attacks on Viipula led by Russian Colonel Svetchnikov were repulsed. On 7 February 1918 an armoured train was engaged in support of 1300 men with seven artillery pieces, but again the attack failed. During their renewed attempts on the 21st and 22nd, Armoured Train No 1 bombarded the White lines, but without visible results. On 13 March the Reds tried again to break through, with a train loaded with explosives in the forefront of the attack. After these repeated failures, the Reds planned to bring up a second armoured train, but the Whites had blown a railway bridge, preventing the capture of the town. In the Savo sector, the White-occupied station at Mäntyharju fell to a Red attack supported by a Latvian infantry company and an armoured train from the south. But the town was recaptured by the Whites on 14 February and remained in their hands thereafter.

In the Karelian Isthmus, *Karjalan Pelastaja* successfully went into action between 2 and 12 February, while in the south the Red Guards from Helsinki used a train in support of an infantry attack aimed at eliminating the Whites stationed on the Helsinki-Karjaa line at the strategic junction of the lines to Turku, Tampere and Lahti.

On 15 March the Whites launched their counter-offensive to block the Reds from reaching northern Häme. The fighting took place around the railway lines, and on the 15th the Whites blew up the track at Orivesi, preventing the Red trains from coming up from the south. On the 18th, the Whites were on the point of capturing Orivesi Station, but the intervention of a Red train coming from Lyly forced them out. This train, soon supported by a second, held back the Whites' attempts to recapture the station for two days before it finally fell. On the 21st, Armoured Train No 1 and a company of infantry defended Siitama on the line to the east of Tampere, and were soon joined by Armoured Train No 3. Damaged by White artillery, the trains withdrew into Tampere where they would later be captured. On the 24th, the Whites advancing from Orivesi reached Lempäälä and circled round to the east of Tampere. With the line to Helsinki thus cut, the Reds

attempted to re-establish the link by sending an armoured train, but in vain. The White encirclement continued by their capture of Ylöjärvi and Sivro Station, which blocked the arrival of Red reinforcements from the west. Several Red armoured trains were sent to break through, one of them coming directly from Helsinki and going into action between that city and Tampere. At the same time, it was decided to complete the trains being built in Helsinki which still lacked their armament.

During the final fighting, the Red train guarding the Tampere-Lampäälä line was engaged by White artillery on the 25th and destroyed, and two days later Armoured Train No 3 suffered several direct hits, its commander being killed. The line to the south having been cut on the 24th, two Red trains sent from Lampäälä went into action, without being able to reach Tampere. From that moment on, the encirclement was complete, and among the trains cut off, the one defending Näsinlinna was seriously damaged on 4 April then destroyed by a direct hit to its engine. On 5 April Armoured Train No 3 was sabotaged by its crew to avoid it falling intact into the hands of the Whites. On the fall of Tampere on the 6th, the Whites captured thirty artillery pieces and two armoured trains.

German intervention in the fighting began with a landing at Loviisa, 60km (38 miles) to the east of Helsinki. On 11 April the von Brandenstein Brigade advanced towards the Lahti-Kouvola railway line in order to cut it, with the help of 400 Civil Guards. The fate of Lahti was decided only on the 17th. The Reds fled to the west, guarding their rear with a train on the Lahti-Helsinki line. On 20 and 21 April, Armoured Trains *Kerenski* and *Partissani*, supported by infantry, tried to cut a way through to Helsinki by attacking from the east. They failed, and tried again on the following day, without succeeding in breaking through. One of the trains had to withdraw to Viipuri for repairs. On 2 May Lahti finally fell, and the two abandoned armoured trains were recovered intact by the Whites in Herrala Station.

The typical outline of the engine of a Red armoured train, with armour plates fitted directly to the running board. Note the lifting ring beside the cab.

The general aim of the Whites in their offensive in the east of the country was the definitive elimination of the Reds by cutting their lines of communication with Petrograd, as the Viipuri-Petrograd line was the Reds' umbilical cord. Their advance to the south, which began on 19 April 1918, led to the capture of the stations of Raivola, Kellomäki and Kuokkala. The latter station was defended by an armoured train which was forced to withdraw after suffering hits, while the Red resistance crumbled. At Raivola, the withdrawal of another armoured train led to the infantry retreating, and by the 24th, 40km (25 miiles) of track were in White hands, thus cutting off the Communists from Russia.

At the same time, another White force advanced on Viipuri itself from the north and the east. At dawn on the 24th, near Tali, a Red attack supported by two armoured trains failed. It seems that two armoured trains were involved in the defence of Viipuri, one crewed mostly by Russians escaping to the north, and the second withdrawing into the town.

To the south an armoured train was sent to try to break through to Petrograd. After Säiniö a broken rail forced it to halt, then as a temporary repair did not hold, to retreat. In withdrawing, it derailed, and its crew abandoned it. Re-railed by the Whites, it was taken away by them but does not seem to have seen service in their ranks. On the 27th, the Reds made another attempt to break through, but a destroyed bridge at Tienhaara forced their armoured train to retreat. A last train continued to defend Viipuri to the west of the town, patrolling as far as Simpla. Viipuri finally fell on the morning of the 29th, leaving three armoured trains in the hands of the Whites, and ending all hope of aid coming from Russia.

Three more armoured trains were included in the spoils recovered by the Whites at the end of the Civil War: two were captured intact at Kotka on 5 May and one when Helsinki capitulated on 14 April. The latter train was used on 19 April by the Germans on the Helsinki-Riihimäki-Lahti line.

One of the long artillery wagons probably built by the Reds during the Civil War, seen here with a flat roof, and a front turret armed with a 37mm Maxim pom-pom. These wagons would undergo continual modifications, reaching their definitive form in 1944.
(Photo: Kari Kuusela)

An interesting shot of one of the two mountain-gun wagons built in 1919, originally armed with a German 75mm VK/L14 mountain gun and two machine guns, and intended as the chase wagons for each of the armoured trains. The German mountain gun has been removed, and the wagon is now obviously used for training. It is coupled at the tail end of PSJ 1, and the observers appear to be controlling the fire of the gun turret of the short artillery wagon, now rearmed with a 76.2mm VK/04 mountain gun. This would date the photo to between 1932 and 1939. Interestingly, these wagons would continue in use for some years, included with the service trains accompanying the armoured trains. Note the Adrian helmet worn by one of the soldiers. The national insignia (the 'Cross of Liberty', a yellow short-armed swastika over a blue Maltese Cross, designed by Askeli Gallen-Kallela in 1918) is painted on each of the wagons.
(Photo: Paul Malmassari Collection)

One of the two wagons of the Russian armoured train, either *Voloi Kapitalism* ('Down with Capitalism') or *Partisaani*, which was captured at Säiniö on 24 April 1918. The wagons were initially used by German troops as in the photo. The wagon shown here had already been modified by the addition of a fixed observation cupola (see the chapter on Russia) but retained its 76.2mm K/02 gun up until the 1935–9 period. Each of these wagons would be attached to a Finnish armoured train when the Germans left Finland in late 1918, and this one would join PSJ 2.
(Photo: Paul Malmassari Collection)

At some time between 1935 and 1939 the (short) artillery wagon of PSJ 2 (recognisable by its two-level observation cupola) was rearmed with a 76.2mm VK/04 mountain gun, while PSJ 1 had received this modification in 1932.
(Photo: Paul Malmassari Collection)

Class Sk3 steam engine of PSJ 2. Of these goods engines, only two remained armoured after the Civil War. Initially, the engine of PSJ 1 was not fitted with a smoke deflector, which allowed Soviet aircraft to easily find the train in its various hideouts during the Winter War. Their armour was 10mm thick.
(Photo: Paul Malmassari Collection)

Closeup of the front (long) artillery wagon of PSJ 2 seen on 1 January 1940. The 37mm pom-pom has been replaced by a 76.2mm VK/04 mountain gun. Note the upper part of the shield which elevates with the barrel. The armament of this wagon also included twenty 7.62mm machine guns, one of which is visible protruding from the observation cupola on the roof. Two more could be mounted alongside the 76.2mm mountain gun, firing through the oval ports.
(Photo: SA-Kuva)

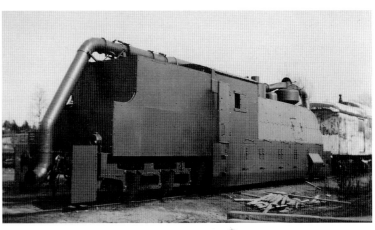

In 1940, K5 Class engine No 884 (redesignated as Class Tk3 in 1942) was armoured to reinforce the trains. The 77 plates which formed the armoured carapace were from 16mm to 22mm thick (16mm on the tender). This engine was allocated to PSJ 1, but also served with PSJ 2.
(Photo: Paul Malmassari Collection)

Armoured trains during the Russo-Finnish Winter War (1939–1940) and the Continuation War (1941–1944)

During this period, the two Finnish armoured trains were controlled by the High Command at Mikkeli, and were directly subordinate to the Army Corps Artillery Command. Used offensively during the Winter War, they were afterwards relegated to the role of mobile anti-aircraft batteries, and their armament was modified accordingly. Even then, the impression of power possessed by these units brought encouragement to the ground troops. The trains also aided the troops directly by transporting them in security, and by warding off traps and attacks by partisans. They were used against the Russians in the east of Finland, in the region of Lake Ladoga. During the Continuation War, PSJ 1 was transferred to Kollaa and PSJ 2 to the Isthmus of Karelia, then to the north of Lake Ladoga, which was armoured train country, where their fields of fire extended out to 6km (over 6500 yards).

Armoured Train No 1 (*Panssarijuna* 1)

Armoured Train No 1 consisted of two separate components, an armoured train armed with artillery and machine guns, plus an unarmoured support train.

In 1939 the armoured unit comprised:

1) safety wagon
2) safety wagon
3) long artillery wagon armed with a 76.2mm VK/04 mountain gun with a horizontal field of fire of some 270 degrees for firing against ground and aerial targets, plus two 7.62mm machine guns mounted at the sides of the turret and capable of forward fire, and six 7.62mm machine guns mounted three each side of the hull
4) machine-gun wagon armed with eight to ten 7.62mm machine guns mounted at the sides and two 7.62mm anti-aircraft machine guns mounted in tubs on the roof

5) unarmed armoured steam engine
6) armoured wagon (ammunition and various stores) serving also as a first-aid post
7) short artillery wagon armed with a 76.2mm VK/04 mountain gun and several 7.62mm machine guns
8) safety wagon
9) safety wagon

The unarmoured support unit comprised three or four Types Gb and T Third Class coaches, a kitchen wagon and various wagons containing a sauna, mess, radio compartments etc. The overall crew of the combined train was around ninety men, and the complement of the armoured unit alone was three officers, twenty-five NCOs and fifty men.

On 1 November 1939 the train made contact with the 34th Infantry Regiment of the 12th Division, in order to provide fire support during the delaying action against the Russians, and on 2 December, it covered the withdrawal of the 1st Battalion of the 36th Infantry Regiment to Suvilahti, the train forming the rearguard. On the 3rd, a counter-attack was launched with the train supporting the 3rd Battalion of the 36th Infantry Regiment, which withdrew at around 17.00 under the cover of its guns. On the 4th, Russian tanks attacked in the direction of the railway, but despite local penetrations, by the end of the day their attack had failed. Armoured Train No1 next participated in the destruction of the Russian forces attacking the front lines of the 34th Infantry Regiment between 8 and 16 December, and on the latter date the train received orders to restrict its patrols. Air attacks followed the ground attacks, and Russian artillery prevented the armoured train from reaching the front line. Between 17 December 1939 and 13 March 1940 the train was the target of twenty-five daytime and fifteen night artillery bombardments, and twenty-five air attacks, one of which caused it to derail, the track having been destroyed in a dozen places.

Between the two wars, PSJ 1 remained in reserve, until on 28 July 1941 it left for the Karelian Isthmus, then provided security on the Leningrad-Viipuri line. Before the outbreak of the Continuation War, it received several modifications: a new targeting system allowed indirect fire by the artillery, and an intercom system enabled communication between the wagons and the engine. In view of the main threat faced by the armoured trains during the Winter War the two 76.2mm mountain guns were replaced by two 40mm Bofors anti-aircraft guns. The armour protection remained between 15mm and 20mm depending on the different wagons. Finally, a deflector directing the engine's smoke towards the ballast as on PSJ 2 was installed.

On 28 November 1942, PSJ 1 and PSJ 2 were modified and transformed into two rail-mounted anti-aircraft batteries (*1. & 2. Rautatieilmatorjuntapattereri*). As the main threat posed by the Soviet air force came in the form of ground-attack aircraft, both

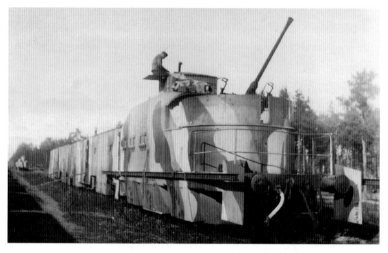
PSJ 1 seen after the Winter War. The short artillery wagon has been rearmed with a 40mm ItK/35-39 B Bofors, and an additional central axle has been added between the original two. Note the spare lengths of rail mounted on the sides of the wagon.
(Photo: Paul Malmassari Collection)

PSJ1 in July 1941. The roof of the long artillery wagon been modified by sloping the sides to increase the anti-aircraft firing angles of the Bofors. Note engine Tk3 at the tail end of the rake and the armoured axle boxes of the safety wagon.
(Photo: SA-Kuva)

The long artillery wagon of PSJ 1 seen from the front in 1942. The 76.2mm ItK/02/34 Obukhov anti-aircraft gun was installed in about September 1941, displacing the Bofors to the rear of the wagon where it was re-mounted directly on the wagon floor. The new larger gun tub for the Obukhov has opening panels allowing it to fire below the horizontal to each side of an elevated track.
(Photo: Paul Malmassari Collection)

The final version of the short artillery wagon (first two, then three axles) from PSJ 1 as exhibited at Parola. The set of wagons had been transferred to the Museum in 1984.

(Photo: Paul Malmassari Collection)

A fine view of the Class G 10 engine (the future Sk3) seen here with PSJ 2 during the Winter War. Note the armour extended to the rear of the machine-gun wagon on the left to protect the personnel entering or exiting by the rear door. These wagons were those originally built by the Reds in Helsinki and were subject to continual upgrading.

(Photo: SA-Kuva)

The final development of the long artillery wagon: In 1944, the wagon formerly from PSJ 1 was modified to optimise its anti-aircraft capabilities as part of Anti-aircraft Battery No 1. The rear part of the roof was sloped to increase the field of fire of the second 40mm Bofors. Seen here from the rear, as partially restored externally (the gun tub for the front Bofors is missing), and lacking armament, it is now on display at the Parola Armoured Museum. Note the revised national emblem, comprising a short-armed swastika painted black on white, as adopted by the armoured forces on 21 June 1941.

(Photo: Paul Malmassari Collection)

trains maximised their close-range automatic firepower by replacing the Obukhov guns with 40mm Bofors. By 30 August 1943, the armoured component of PSJ 1 carried the following armament:

– three 40mm ItK/39 Bofors, one on the short artillery wagon and two on the long wagon.
– two 20mm ItK/40 Madsens, mounted on two new unarmoured wagons (Type Git) modified in June 1943.

The Soviets attacked in force on 9 June 1943, and PSJ 1 was allocated first to the defence of the railway complex at Maaselkä, then that of Viipuri. For that specific mission, each wagon split from the others accompanied a goods train. An equivalent role was allocated to it between 28 March and 10 April 1944 when its individual wagons were used as stationary anti-aircraft artillery batteries, then from 28 May to 12 June in Lapland, where the units covered troop movements. The train next moved to Nurmi, then Simola, and finally Taavetti on 30 July, where its crew heard the news of the Armistice several days later. On 22 September, the train moved to Kouvola, and on 3 October a part of its crew was demobilised, the rest remaining with the train up until the following November. PSJ 1 was taken out of service on 17 November 1944.

Armoured Train No 2 (*Pansarijuna* 2)

Due to the loss of its war diary and its archive records during the retreat from Karelia in June-July 1944, it is difficult to retrace the operational history of this train.

In early April 1942, its armament consisted of:

– one 76.2mm ItK/02/34 Obukhov anti-aircraft gun (on the long artillery wagon)
– two 40mm ItK/38 Bofors (one on the long artillery wagon and one on the short wagon)
– seventeen 7.62mm kk 09 machine guns
– five 7.62mm kk 32 machine guns.

It was provided with a stereoscopic binocular rangefinder (as seen in the previous photo of the training wagon).

Transferred to Tohmajärvi from 1 July 1941 under the command of the VIIth Corps, it participated in the capture of Värtsilä in the company of the 2nd Heavy Railgun Battery. Then on the 28th, these two units joined the Army of Karelia where they came under the command of the 163rd Infantry Division of the Wehrmacht, to which they provided effective fire support. Ensuring the security of the logistical lines of the VIIth Corps, the train also provided the principal anti-aircraft defence of the towns of Vitska, Syväri and Karhumäki.

On 28 November 1942 the train was reformed as the 2nd Anti-Aircraft Battery. It then provided cover to the key points of the network, the bridge over the Uunista, the Station at Malu and the Mäki-Lisma branch line. Broken up into separate units, each element took on the designation of *1°, 2°, 3° etc Rautatiekone-kiväärikomppania* (abbreviated to *1°, 2°, 3° Raut. It. KKK.*) or Railway Anti-aircraft Machine-gun Company. As such it participated in the defence against the Soviet offensive in June directed against Karelia, and was then transferred to the Aunus Isthmus. It found itself trapped by the landing of the 70th Marine Brigade at Tuulos and the cutting of the rail line on 23rd June. To prevent it falling into enemy hands, the crew sabotaged the train on the same day near the station at Mäkriä.

Original drawing of an armoured SK3 locomotive.
(Private collection)

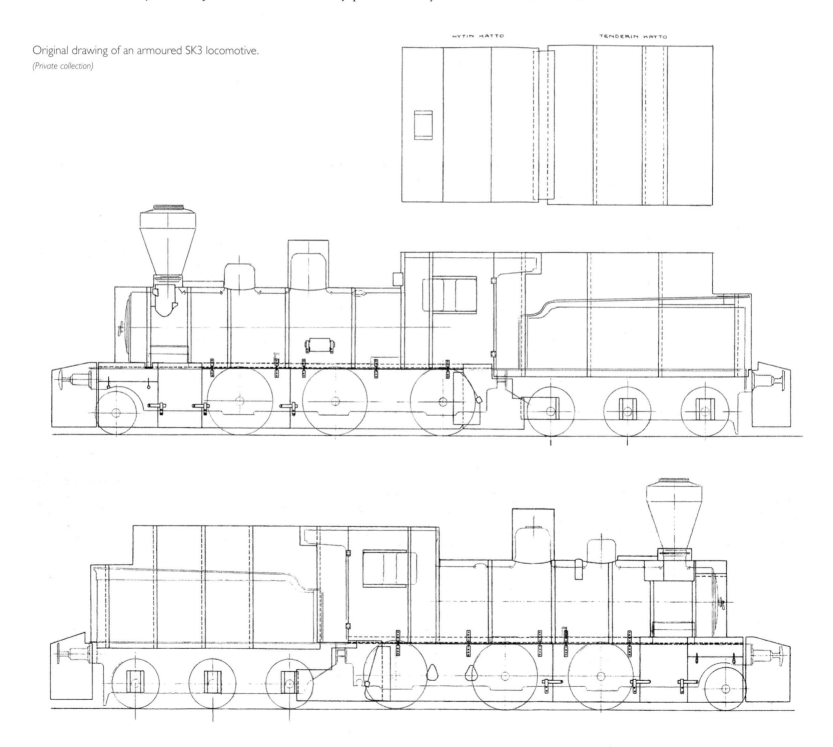

Right: The (short) anti-aircraft artillery wagon of PSJ 2, armed with a 40mm ItK/39B Bofors and seven machine guns. Note the searchlight on the stepped observation cupola. The following wagon is a machine-gun/kitchen wagon, with its machine-gun tub covered by a tarpaulin.
(Photo: Paul Malmassari Collection)

Above: On display at Parola is this example of a machine-gun wagon, which was common to both armoured trains, with minor differences over the life of the units. It is here preserved in its 1942 state, the final version of the wagons originally built for the Reds in Fredericksberg.
(Photo: Paul Malmassari Collection)

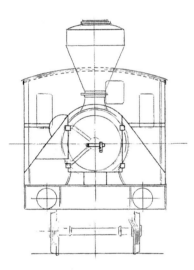

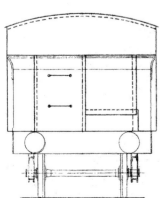
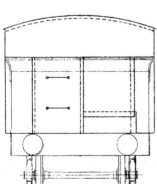

PSJ2 seen in March 1942 without its armoured engine. The second wagon from the right is the machine gun/kitchen wagon with two anti-aircraft machine gun tubs on its roof. The ex-Soviet PL-37 wagon has its turrets aligned fore and aft, but the anti-aircraft Obukhov and Bofors are elevated ready for action. The coach on the left is probably intended as a rest and recreation vehicle for the train crew.
(Photo: Paul Malmassari Collection)

The long artillery wagon of PSJ 2 photographed in October 1941 at Jessoila. The 76.2mm ItK/02/34 Obukhov anti-aircraft gun was installed on 23 September 1941, replacing the Bofors which has been re-positioned on the roof, in the tub which formerly held a 7.62mm anti-aircraft Maxim. The new gun tub for the Obukhov has opening panels allowing it to fire below the horizontal to each side of an elevated track. The next wagon in line is a machine-gun/kitchen wagon with two AA machine gun tubs on the roof.
(Photo: Paul Malmassari Collection)

The long artillery wagon of PSJ 2 photographed on 7 August 1941. It is heavily armed, with a 40mm Bofors, the barrel of which can be seen in the background, the three 7.62mm Maxim machine guns shown here, a fourth 7.62mm Maxim on an anti-aircraft mount in a tub at the rear of the roof, and several more firing from the wagon sides.
(Photo: SA-Kuva)

In September 1941, the Finns captured a Soviet armoured train at Äänislinna, and reused its PL-37 artillery wagon as part of PSJ 2. However, since its Russian armament did not possess sufficient elevation for anti-aircraft fire, it saw little action in Finnish hands. Note the barrel of the Obukhov AA gun at the far left.
(Photo: Paul Malmassari Collection)

The installation of an anti-aircraft 7.62mm Maxim M/32-33 inside one of the machine-gun/kitchen wagons. A twin 7.62mm ItKk/31 VKT mount was also used. It is possible this is a posed propaganda shot, as normally the AA machine gun would be mounted much higher, in the circular tub.
(Photo: SA-Kuva)

SOURCES:
Archives:
Finnish Photographic Archives (www.sa-kuva.fi).
Sotamuseo, Helsinki.
Rauttatiemuseo.
SHD, cartons 7 N 2788.

Books:
Hannula, General Josse Olavi, and Perret, Jean-Louis, *La guerre d'indépendance de Finlande, 1918* (Paris: Payot, 1938).
Sillanmäki, Jouni, *Panssarijunia Suomessa – Suomalaisia Panssarijunissa* (Jyväskyla: Gummerus Kirjapaino Oy, 2009).

Journal Articles:
Talvio, Paavo, 'Panssarijunat Talvi- Ja Jatkosodan Taiteluissa', *Sotahistoriallinen Aikakauskirja* No 5/1986, pp 193–235.
'Panssarijuna 2 : N Tuominta ja tuho', *Veturimies Magazine* No 11–12/1986, pp 474–82.

Website:
http://www.jaegerplatoon.net/MAIN.html

FRANCE

Armoured Trains 1825–1870

The first armoured train project of 1825

Inspired by the British plans for a railway to run the 28 miles (45km) from Stockton to Darlington, in 1825 *Capitaine de Frégate* (Commander) Montgéry launched the idea of 'a type of steam-powered defensive war wagon, or mobile casemates, which if employed on a large scale would be formidable fortifications, and would be capable of manoeuvring on railway lines more rapidly than the finest cavalry units. This machine would comprise three vehicles proof against cannon shot. One of these vehicles, placed centrally, would be equipped with a steam engine. Each of the two others would carry three howitzers . . . The all-up weight of a casemate thus equipped, with its small garrison, and the appropriate munitions, would be approximately 85,000 kg [almost 94 tons]. . . .' The inventor envisaged their deployment 'especially for the defence of defiles, of highways, of main roads in non-fortified strategic towns, the approaches to certain fortresses, and chosen beaches . . . '. Unfortunately, it appears that no plan of this armoured train has survived.

The Mexican Campaign (1861–1867)

In November 1866 during the Mexican Campaign plans were drawn up for a defensive wagon to counter the attacks of irregulars, which caused severe problems right up until the evacuation of the French Expeditionary Corps. The bogie wagon, protected by wooden cladding 12cm thick, was to have had eleven firing embrasures per side and three at each end. From the support pillars shown in the drawings it is possible the armament would have included large-calibre rampart guns, as befitting a 'mobile fortress'.

Proposals for armoured trains prior to the Franco-Prussian War

In 1841, M. Schwickardi proposed a 'cannon-wagon', proposed for the defence of fortresses, and also for the defence of Paris. The mixed road-rail 'armoured machine' of Zéphyr Toffin dates from March 1858: 4m (13ft 1½in) long by 2m (6ft 6¾in) wide, armoured including cones protecting the wheels, and to be armed with three *Mitrailleuses*. The design was presented by the inventor again in December 1870. In 1862 Captain Veillet proposed armoured 'wagon-batteries' 3.1m (10ft 2in) long by 2.1m (6ft 10½in) wide by 1.9m (6ft 3in) high, to be formed into convoys.[1]

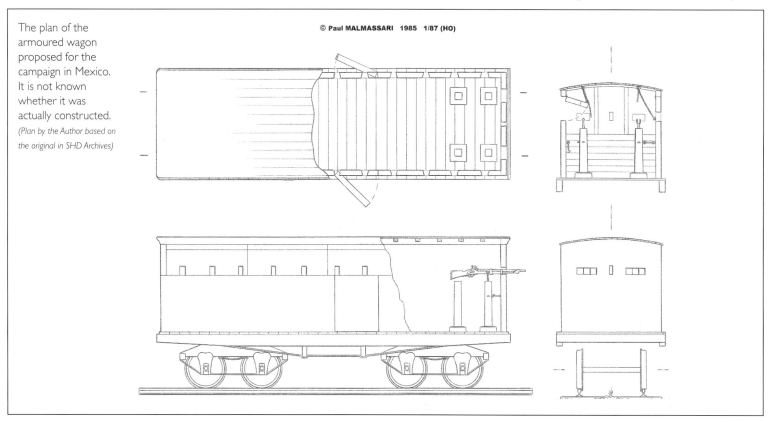

The plan of the armoured wagon proposed for the campaign in Mexico. It is not known whether it was actually constructed.
(Plan by the Author based on the original in SHD Archives)

© Paul MALMASSARI 1985 1/87 (HO)

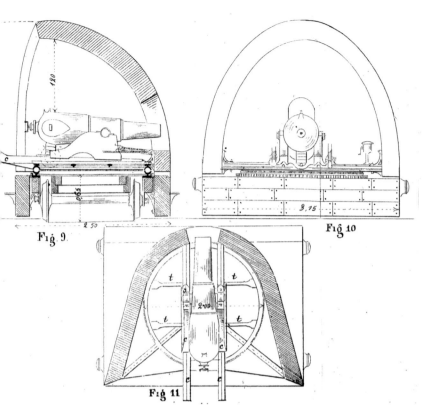

Layout of the armoured wagon (35cm of wood covered by 18cm of metal) proposed by Michel Body

(Plan: *Les Chemins de Fer dans leurs applications militaires*, Plate IV)

Two wagons of the Meudon Armoured Train. 13mm *Mitrailleuses* would have fired through the protected scuttles. The whole train weighed 85 tonnes.

(Photo: Musée Carnavalet)

On 10 November 1863, the Artillery Committee received from Thomas Wright, a British subject, his project for a battery on rails which 'apart from being suitable for the French coasts, is also proposed for Algeria, India and the French "colonies"'. These trains composed of three or four batteries, each armed with between ten and forty guns and mortars on pivoting mountings, would have formed a defensive barrier extending over a mile (1.5km).[2] Then in 1868, Michel Body presented his ideas of an integrated defensive system, encompassing railway systems, fortresses and armoured railway stations. He specified the construction of 'cannons mounted on trains and special motors proof against enemy fire [providing] this artillery with incomparable mobility',[3] as detailed in the plan above.

The Franco-Prussian War and the Siege of Paris (1870–1871)
The Meudon[4] Armoured Train

The origins of this train go back to 1867, when Colonel Brent, an American, had outlined to Napoleon III his ideas for railway war machines. Marshal Niel and General Leboeuf had considered the

---

[1.] In addition there were the projects of Baron Rystany (1864), M. Bukaly (1867), and M. Evrard (1868).

[2.] For further details of this project, see the chapter on Great Britain.

[3.] Michel Body, *Les Chemins de Fer dans leurs applications militaires* (Paris: Eugène Lacroix, 1868), pp 21–2.

[4.] Meudon was the workshop created by Napoleon III in 1860 to carry out secret research projects.

---

project, and had confided it to Captain de Reffye, Director of the Meudon Workshop, to be built in the utmost secrecy. The Armistice went into effect before the train could be used against the Germans. It was seized by the Paris Commune on 9 February 1871 and used on the *Chemin de Fer de Ceinture* (the peripheral railway line around the city centre). After the war, it was planned to keep the train for deployment at Douai, but weight and loading-gauge problems led to it being broken up by the *Chemin de fer du Nord* on 20 June 1872.

Armoured trains of the *Chemin de fer d'Orléans* (Dupuy de Lôme Batteries)

Out of all the numerous projects and inventions presented to the authorities, the one by Messrs Solacroup and Delannoy, two engineers of the *Chemin de fer d'Orléans*, caught the attention of the Paris Defence Committee. Their first design study consisted of one or two large-calibre guns mounted on a platform carried by two trucks placed side-by-side on the double track and pulled by horses. The second design study had a single platform carried on two parallel tracks, armoured on three sides with lengths of rail. Finally, their third design was a wagon fully armoured with rail lengths, roofed over by a curved plate. The front face was pierced by an embrasure allowing fire up to 30 degrees on either side of the central axis.

The Committee decided to build the fourth version proposed, being two four-axle wagons, armed with a 14cm gun firing *en barbette* over the top of the armour, 30 degrees to either side of the central axis, immediately followed by two other wagons, each armed with a 16cm gun mounted in a pivoting casemate. The firing embrasure in the 16cm battery had been much reduced in size compared with the previous proposals, and the roof was armoured.

In action two gun wagons were to be disposed side-by-side on parallel tracks. Behind the gun wagon on the track on the side facing the enemy was a second gun wagon. In place of the proposed armoured engines, two tank engines could be used to move the batteries. A tank engine would run on the track facing away from the enemy, propelling a leading gun wagon. On the side facing the enemy the engine would be protected by the second gun wagon in line, which was connected to the engine by a system of chains. After use for the defence of Paris, then by the Commune, these trains were broken up in 1871.

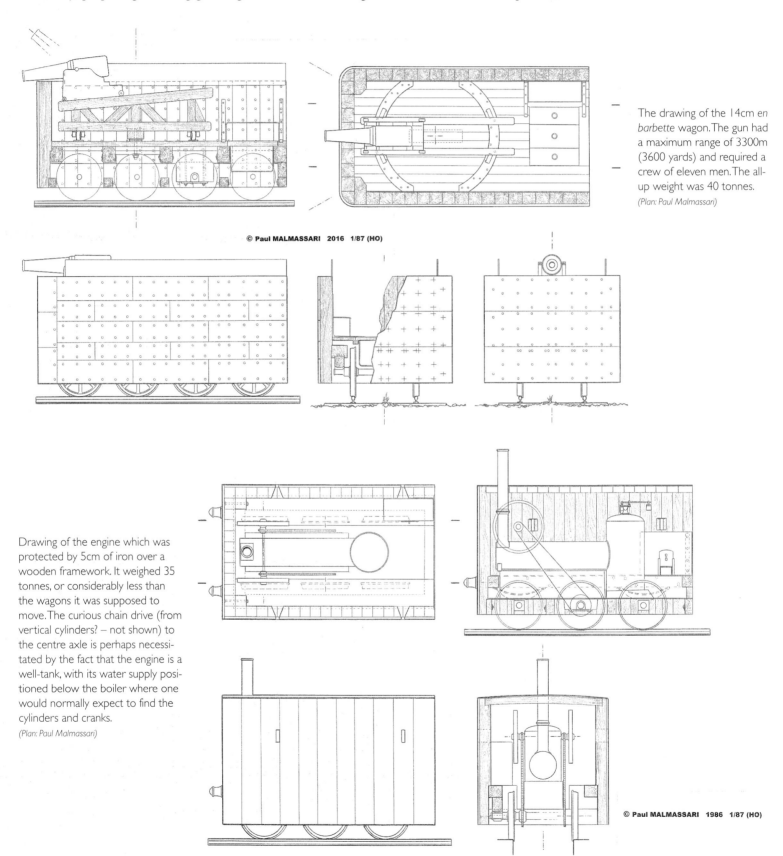

The drawing of the 14cm *en barbette* wagon. The gun had a maximum range of 3300m (3600 yards) and required a crew of eleven men. The all-up weight was 40 tonnes.
(Plan: Paul Malmassari)

© Paul MALMASSARI 2016 1/87 (HO)

Drawing of the engine which was protected by 5cm of iron over a wooden framework. It weighed 35 tonnes, or considerably less than the wagons it was supposed to move. The curious chain drive (from vertical cylinders? – not shown) to the centre axle is perhaps necessitated by the fact that the engine is a well-tank, with its water supply positioned below the boiler where one would normally expect to find the cylinders and cranks.
(Plan: Paul Malmassari)

© Paul MALMASSARI 1986 1/87 (HO)

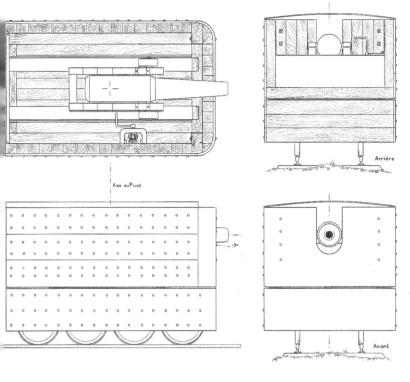

© Paul MALMASSARI 1982 1/87 (HO)

Axe du Pivot

Arrière

Avant

Drawing of the pivoting casemate battery armed with a 16cm gun, with a range of 3900m (4265 yards) served by a crew of 13 men. Total weight was 47 tonnes.
(Plan: Paul Malmassari)

Armoured trains in the French Provinces

An armoured train was ordered from the *Compagnie du Midi* at the end of 1870. At the time of writing, research had turned up no details of this train, which was constructed at Bordeaux. Again in 1870, the *Compagnie de l'Est* constructed armoured units. The main action undertaken by the *Est* armoured train was the capture of a goods train at Peltre, near Metz, on 27 September 1870. To the west, General Kératry, commanding the Army of Brittany, ordered the *Compagnie de l'Ouest* at Le Mans to construct three armoured trains, each comprising eight vehicles.

At Périgueux, beginning in early September 1870, the *Compagnie d'Orléans* had also built twenty-four wagons, identical to the Parisian models with pivoting casemates, which were intended to be used against the Prussians. But Paris capitulated before the train could intervene. Then on the morning of 11 April 1871, the Versailles Government ordered the train to make its way towards

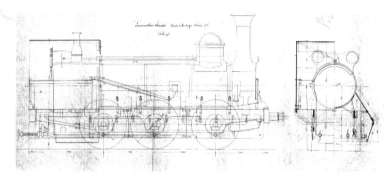

The original drawing for the engines of the Army of Brittany.
(Plan: SHD)

Canon Avant : champ de 50°.   Canons Latéraux : champ de 60°.

© Paul MALMASSARI 1985 1/87 (HO)

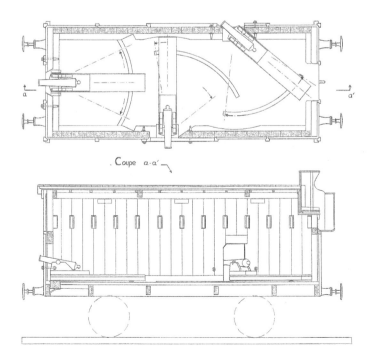

Coupe a-a'

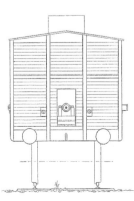

Drawing of the wagons of the armoured trains of the Army of Brittany.
(By the Author)

Paris to take part in the battle against the Commune. At the end of the morning, on hearing of this, the staff of the railway workshops deliberately overturned wagons on the tracks, delaying the departure of the train until 12 April, after which date it disappears from history.

The Period 1871–1914

Based on the lessons of the War of 1870–1, the future role of armoured trains would not be limited to defence alone, but would also encompass active employment designed to help push back the front lines. Numerous propositions dealing with this have come to light, like the project shown in the illustration below: the two rails of the central track are used by replenishment trains carrying munitions and coal. The gun battery and its engine run on the two outside rails. They make use of the firing embrasures let into the parapet at intervals, and the gun also uses a disappearing mounting. The artist appears to have imagined the small munitions locomotive – a Crampton – being fitted with a folding chimney, enabling it to take cover inside a tunnel in the body of the gun battery.

The armoured trains of the Armoured Wagons Commission

This Commission had been created on 11 June 1878, presided over by General Schnéegans. After having collated the existing documentation relating to the railway batteries during the Siege of Paris, the Committee decided to proceed with the construction of separate prototypes of wagon and engine, in order to evaluate the form and resistance of the armour protection, and the type of armament and the maximum traction effort to be adopted. Firing trials against the engine took place on 15 May 1879 in the sand quarry at Courbevoie, and led to armour protection designed by M. Mayer, Chief Engineer, Rolling Stock and Traction, of the *Compagnie de l'Ouest*. The wagons from the *Est* rail network were armoured with plates 10mm thick weighing a total of 4.5 tonnes. After three years of study, the decision was taken to create two types of train: reconnaissance trains (at first known as 'combat trains'), and trains intended for sorties from fortresses – but the latter type was quickly abandoned. The first train (which would remain the sole example), was assigned to Belfort in 1887.

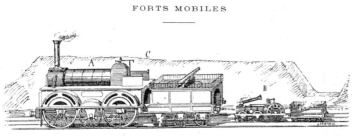

FORTS MOBILES

Wagons de guerre et de service sur un Chemin de fer à double voie.

A. Wagon de guerre sur roues de 4ᵐ de diamètre, occupant les rails extérieurs.
B. Wagon de service sur roues de 0ᵐ 50ᵉ de diamètre occupant l'entre-voie sur les rails du centre.
C. Terre-plein, banquette, crête, plongée et flanquements de peu de relief, de kilomètre en kilomètre.

An illustration from *Un bourgeois de Paris, Système de défense de Paris basé sur l'emploi des chemins de fer, des locomotives et des wagons blindés* (Saint-Nicolas-de-Port: E. Lacroix, 1871).

The experimental armoured train assigned to Belfort, seen here during manœuvres. The engine and flat cars were placed in the centre of four wagons to front and rear. The main defect was the deafening noise caused by the armour plates, which were hung on the wagon sides but not fixed firmly in place. *(Photo: La Vie du Rail)*

The armoured railway batteries of Commandant Mougin

At the request of General Brialmont, in 1885[6] Commandant Mougin had conceived an armoured battery on rails, an immense device weighing 330 tonnes! It was described as follows: 'this project may be considered as a hollow girder construction, armoured on four of its sides, and capable of resisting substantial external shocks without deforming. This girder structure is fixed to a strong platform carried on nine sprung axles, allowing the whole battery to change positions. Two end panels and two internal frames separate the battery into three compartments, each enclosing a cannon. The armour on the side facing the enemy consists of two thicknesses of 45mm laminated iron plates . . .'. It was intended to deploy these batteries principally on the parapet of a continuous defensive line, and between two neighbouring forts, to cover the intervals in the case of an attack on the forts.

The armament was to have comprised three 155mm guns, each able to traverse through an arc of 70 degrees, with elevation from –5 degrees to +20 degrees. The maximum range was 7000m (7655 yards). The track gauge was to have been 3.15m (10ft 4in) at a time when the standard rail gauge in France (prior to standardisa-

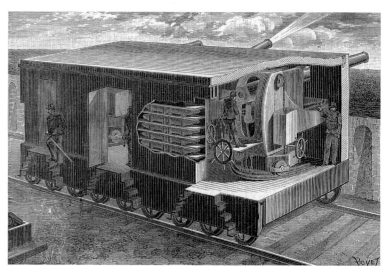

Armoured battery proposed by Commandant Mougin.
(Illustration: La Nature No 703 [20 November 1886], p 389)

tion) varied between 1.44m (4ft 8½in) and 1.5m (4ft 11in). Overall each battery would have measured 12.45m long x 3.5m wide (40ft 10in x 11ft 5¾in).

Armoured train and armoured rail torpedo projects by Louis Gregori[7] (1904)

Designed to run on rails and on roads, Gregori's 'armoured mobile battery' was intended to replace permanent and coastal fortifications, in Metropolitan France and also for defending the Colonies. The symmetrical layout was intended to protect the centrally-positioned engine, while the trucks at each end were used for observation and armament. In addition, the oval form of the vehicle's sides was supposed to offer superior protection compared with the usual vertical side walls. The secondary armament appears to be Hotchkiss revolver cannons, although Gatlings are also a possibility (they were being manufactured in France at that time for use in fortresses).

In the same year, this inventor proposed a 'land torpedo', inspired by naval torpedoes, propelled by a motor preferably powered by compressed air, and protected from rifle fire by a metal casing. The armament consisted of four 'warheads', which from the patent illustration appear to be large-calibre artillery shells with nose-mounted impact fuzes, covering four planes and intended to inflict all-round damage: to track, stations, platforms, enemy trains etc. The first shell exploding when its nose fuze struck a target – most likely the front one but one of the others could be activated if the enemy derailed the device – would then set off the remaining shells.

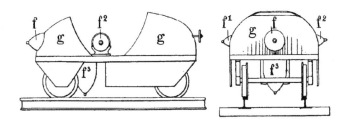

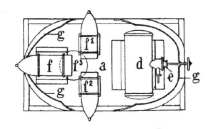

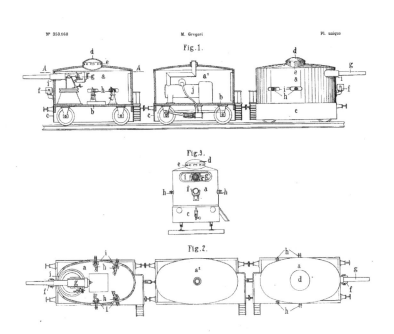

Detail from Patent No 350.168 submitted on 24 May 1904, granted on 13 September 1905.

Detail from Patent No 350.169, submitted on 28 May 1904, granted on 13 September 1904.

The rebellion in the Côte d'Ivoire (1906–1910)

The river system and the railway network were the two methods of transport in this colony. During the uprising, the rebels began attacks on the railway in January 1910. An armoured train service was put into service which helped suppress the revolt.

Basic protection but sufficient against the arms used by the tribes in the Côte d'Ivoire: note the timber cladding on the engine.

(Postcard: Paul Malmassari Collection)

---

6. Previously, in 1877 Mougin had proposed 155mm guns on disappearing mountings on rail platforms.
7. Also described in '*Panzerzug*', *Polytechnische Schau*, 1916, Band 331, Heft 19, p 299.

The First World War (1914–1918)
Armoured trains in the Colonies

The conquest of the German colonies in Africa involved the use of armoured trains of which no photos have so far come to light. While the Germans used armoured trains in Togo and Cameroon, the French deployed them only in Cameroon.

A naval gun was mounted on a wagon, probably armoured, for the advance on Medéa. Several wagons were fitted with armour protection for train escort duties and to fend off German harassing attacks, during which tracks and bridges were blown up. An armoured lorry was also built between 12 and 30 September 1915 and was used on the So-Dibanga–Eseka line.[8]

The armoured trains armed with 95mm guns (1914–1916)

Ordered on the declaration of war and designed very rapidly by Engineer General Gosselin in September 1914, with the initial aim of bolstering the ring of defences around Paris, three 95mm-armed armoured trains were built by the Batignolles Company using armour plates from the Commission in Gâvres. Each of the three trains comprised four wagons armed with a 95mm Model 1888 gun, plus corresponding ammunition wagons. A fourth train was assembled with two longer wagons each armed with two 95mm guns. They were delivered between the end of 1914 and the beginning of 1915, and remained in service until March 1916.

One of three armoured PLM Type B 111-400 4-4-0 engines requisitioned between 15 and 27 November 1914. The armour protection was designed by the Batignolles Company but installed by the PLM workshops. The front turret armed with a machine gun is a rare feature in the history of armoured trains, and must have made cleaning ash out of the smokebox a difficult task.
(Photo: Paul Malmassari Collection)

The following plans by the Batignolles Company show the 95mm armoured train. This is the first time these technical drawings, held by the SHD Archives, have been published.

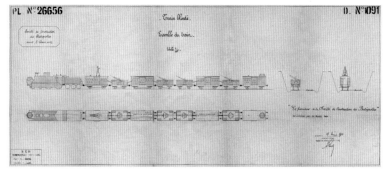

General arrangement drawing showing a complete 95mm armoured train. The leading van has an extending observation ladder, and the tail van is armed with a Hotchkiss machine gun in a turret.
(Plan: SHD Archives)

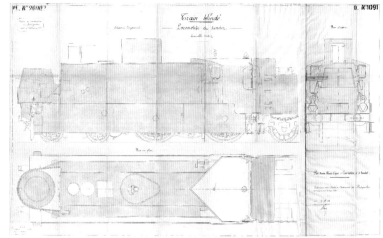

The PLM Type B 111 4-4-0 A engine.
(Plan: SHD Archives)

The lack of armour protection to the lower front end of this PLM engine shows that these trains were not intended for offensive operations. Of note is the miniature aircraft model mounted like a weather vane, but which we believe may be a visual indicator to the engine crew of the direction the turret is facing.
(Photo: Paul Malmassari Collection)

8. To complete the story of the overseas armoured trains, we must mention the armoured wagons built in Abyssinia in 1916, of which we have unfortunately found no photos.

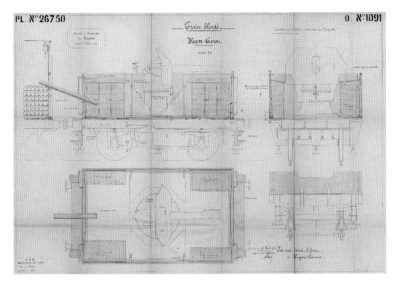

One of the 95mm gun wagons, with fixed side panels. Note the three jacks on each side for lifting the wagon wheels clear of the rails to relieve the stress on the springs when firing, and the clamps and spreader bars to fasten the wagon to the rails. Also the delivery chute from the ammunition van.

(Plan: SHD Archives)

It took only two minutes to prepare each wagon for firing, by jacking it up on sta-bilisers, and by clamping it securely to the rails. The 95mm cannon had a maximum rate of fire of eight rounds per minute. Each gun wagon carried 104 complete rounds. Note the number of the individual wagon painted above the builder's plate.

(Photo: SHD)

Batignolles built the armoured wagons in November 1914 on Nord 20-tonne flat wagon chassis.

(Photo: Guy François)

The armour protection of these wagons consisted of two 5mm steel plates spaced 5cm apart, with the gap filled with ballast gravel. Here the plates are partially dismantled, showing internal details.

(Photo: Guy François)

Wagons from a train with the Tenth Army in Artois. Each train had a crew of around forty men, including three officers. The armoured shields were fitted to the guns as early as 1893.

(Photo: Guy François)

An overall view of a train, compared with the plan. Note there are two tail vans with turrets, and in particular the exposed position of the artillery observers. Each ammunition van carried 1120 rounds.

(Photo: SHD)

On the right is a camouflaged gun wagon, and central a Bika van transferred from a Belgian armoured train. Next in line is a tail van followed by four ammunition vans specific to the 95mm armoured trains.

(Photo: Private Collection)

This view shows the 8mm Saint-Étienne Model 1907 machine gun in place. As on the Belgian trains, firing slots pierce the sides of the wagons, allowing us to see the thickness of the armour.

(Photo: Private collection)

Armoured Train No 4 was built in Dunkirk, and entered service in February 1915. It was composed of two bogie wagons each armed with a pair of 95mm guns.

(Photo: Private collection)

This photo shows the sliding armoured door giving access to the ammunition compartment. Armoured Train No 4 was decommissioned on 2 December 1918.

(Photo: Private collection)

The gun crew were from the 39th Battery of the 1er RAP (1st Fortress Artillery Regiment), and the engine crew were from the 5ème Génie (5th Engineering Regiment). Armoured Train No 4 was sent to the Third Army, where it carried out many fire missions, notably against a long-range 15cm K.i.S.L. gun, and was itself hit twice.

(Photo: Private collection)

A pair of 0-6-0 'Cuckoo' tank engines, identical to the ones which formed the motive power for Armoured Train No 4 from May 1915.

(Photo: Paul Malmassari Collection)

The 194mm TAZ[9] railway guns 1915–1940

Although related to the ALGP[10] and the ALVF,[11] this weapon, of which twenty-three examples were built, belongs in our study because it was completely armoured. The Schneider Works received four separate orders spread out between October 1914 and February 1915, aimed at an entry into service from April 1915 onwards. The gun was a 19cm Model 1870-93 coast-defence gun on coastal mounting Model 1886 PC, in a turret and placed on a 40-tonne chassis of the *Est* Railway Company. The wagon had an all-up weight of 65 tonnes and could be brought into action in 15 minutes, at any point on the tracks. Range varied from 11.8km out to 18.3km (12,900 to 20,000 yards) depending on the type of ammunition used.

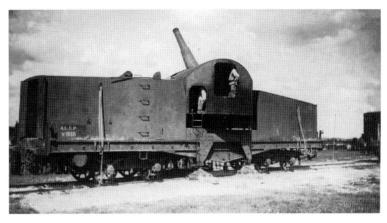

194mm TAZ Rail Gun No 1018 seen in the 1930s. These artillery pieces remained in service up until 1940, when certain units were captured and put back into use, notably twelve examples by the Italians. The openings in the revolving casemate are clearly seen here: on the left for the gun crew, in the centre for the ammunition.
(Photo: Paul Malmassari Collection)

Rail Gun No 1017 *La Revanche* ('Revenge') at Etrun (5km [3 miles] to the west of Arras) in October 1915. Overhead views are rare, and this one in particular shows the armoured shell replenishment corridor and the upper shutters on the revolving casemate. The firing stabilisers are in their lowered position.
(Photo: Paul Malmassari Collection)

1940: Rail Gun No 1003, one of the twenty-four put back into service, captured by the Wehrmacht and designated as '19.4cm Kanone (E) 486 (f)'. The outer stabiliser pads are here seen removed and stowed in the travelling position.
(Photo: Paul Malmassari Collection)

This view is interesting as it shows the configuration of a train with each individual gun battery and its ammunition van separated from the rest of the train for safety reasons. Photo taken at Somme-Suippes on 29 September 1915.
(Photo: Paul Malmassari Collection)

9. TAZ = *Tous AZimuts* (all-round fire).
10. ALGP = *Artillery Lourde à Grande Puissance* (High-Powered Heavy Artillery).
11. ALVF = *Artillerie Lourde sur Voie Ferrée* (Heavy Railway Artillery).

An unidentified armoured engine. The cutaway profile of the front armour is unusual, but the shape of the sliding shutter on the cab side suggests Belgian origins.
(Photo: Paul Malmassari Collection)

A mystery photo: The Renault FT light tank, on a flat wagon propelled by the Prussian G8 0-8-0, and which is clearly the centre of attention of the French soldiers, is not in transport configuration. On the back of the photo is written 'Kutina', which is in Croatia, at the time part of the new Yugoslavia. Perhaps this is a photo taken in the period 1919–20 when Communists, including mutinous regiments, rose up against the government. These revolts were suppressed by Serb troops supported by French units from Salonika.
(Photo: Paul Malmassari Collection)

French project to supply armoured trains to Latvia and Romania

See the relevant countries' chapters.

Armoured trains in the Levant (Syria – Cilicia)

At the end of October 1919, France took over Syria from Great Britain. The Hauran rose in revolt on 20 August 1920. French retaliation was supported by troops carried by trains protected by an armoured train. On 1 October 1920 there were three armoured trains: 'B', commanded by Captain Baumann (who was also in overall command of all the armoured trains), 'S' and 'D' (from the initials of their commanding officers?), which were joined by Train 'A' in December. After such a lapse of time it is difficult to identify them, therefore this list may be incomplete. On 13 March 1921, the London Accords put an end to the fighting, but the revolt of the Djebel Druze in 1925 required once more the presence of three armoured trains[12] on the lines leading to Damascus.

The artillery wagon (65mm mountain gun) of Armoured Train 'H'. *La Terreur des Druzes* ('The Terror of the Druzes') is perhaps the name of the train, while the turret is named *Chouquette* ('Cutie') a hangover from the 1914–18 War.
(Photo: Paul Malmassari Collection)

Damascus, 10 September 1926. A 65mm Schneider-Ducrest Model 1906 Mountain Gun, barrel in the rearward position ('*lancé*'), is in the turret. The two timber shelters also serve as accommodation. Note the shrapnel shell resting on its base, officially forbidden for obvious safety reasons!
(Photo: Paul Malmassari Collection)

12. Train 'F' at Damascus (Baranké Station), Train 'G' at Rayack, plus Train 'C'.

Armoured Train 'H' at Rayack, 17 May 1927. On the left is an unarmoured rail trolley. Note the makeshift nature of the protection on the wagons.
(Photo: Paul Malmassari Collection)

Laffly armoured cars converted into armoured trolleys.
(Photo: Pascal Danjou)

As part of this train photographed at Ezraa in September 1925 we see two armoured wagons assembled by mounting the hulls of captured Ottoman trolleys on bogie flat wagons (see the chapter on The Ottoman Empire).
(Photo: Paul Malmassari Collection)

An interesting shot taken in September 1925 which shows the smaller diameter of the rail wheels compared with the original road wheels, which often led to transmission and braking problems, and above all meant the speedometer reading was wrong.
(Photo: Delhalle)

Right: Finally, several traditional rail trolleys were constructed using the Laffly hull as a base, mounted on a flat wagon, complete with all-round armour plates.
(Photo: Paul Malmassari Collection)

For reconnaissance missions, several machine-gun armoured cars were converted into armoured trolleys, firstly by replacing their road wheels, then by surrounding them with armour plates.

After the end of the revolt, these trains were repaired, continually updated and kept in reserve. They would reappear in 1941 during the fratricidal fighting between troops loyal to Marshal Pétain and Gaullist troops.

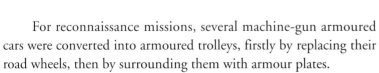

A view of the other side of Rail Motor No TF2 using a Laffly hull, on the Saïd Naïl-Yeferifa line on 22 March 1931.
(Photo: François Vauvillier Collection)

The Inter-War Period

This period is rich in armoured rail vehicles, but poor in surviving photographic evidence, particularly from 1924 to 1939.[13]

The armoured reconnaissance trolleys

In the early 1920s it was decided to employ reconnaissance trolleys. A light unarmoured type was ordered in 1924 and an armoured trolley for the standard gauge in 1927. Billard and Renault both proposed design studies for the latter unit, and the Billard proposal was accepted.

Technical specifications (Billard Archives)	
Height:	2.6m (8ft 6in)
Length:	4.25m (13ft 11in)
Width:	1.90m (6ft 2¾in)
Wheelbase:	2m (6ft 6¾in)
Wheel diameter:	0.6m (1ft 11½in)
All-up weight:	5 tonnes[14]
Motor:	Ballot 4-cylinder petrol; bore/stroke 75mm x 130mm; power 13hp at 1000rpm and 24hp at 2000rpm
Starting:	Crank handle or electric starter motor
Mobility:	The trolley could move equally in both directions, using three gear ratios giving 13, 26 and 40km/h (8, 16 and 25mph) respectively
Autonomy:	Sufficient petrol for a range of 200–300km (124–186 miles) depending on the gradients
Armour:	7mm
Turret:	Manual rotation
Armament:	Turret-mounted 8mm Hotchkiss machine gun, also adaptable on external pintle for anti-aircraft use

Trials were carried out with the prototype in late 1930, but it seems to have been abandoned in the third quarter of 1932, and disappeared without trace.

The prototype at the Billard Works in Toul, fitted with a dummy machine gun. Note the re-railing equipment carried on the lower hull.
(Photo: Paul Malmassari Collection)

One of the photos taken during anti-aircraft firing trials at Bourges, with an 8mm Hotchkiss machine gun installed.
(Photo: SHD)

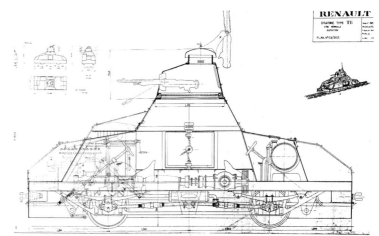

Cutaway profile of the rival Renault trolley proposed for the competitive trials of 1927 and not proceeded with. The weapon is an 8mm Hotchkiss machine gun. The presence of two steering wheels appears strange in a rail-only vehicle, but from the drawing they seem to be connected to the braking system.
(Document: Renault Foundation)

[13.] Concerning projects, in October 1924 a certain M. Mescherinoff proposed an armoured road-rail tractor unit. As it lacked workable technical details, the Army High Command did not follow up his proposal (SHD W 872).

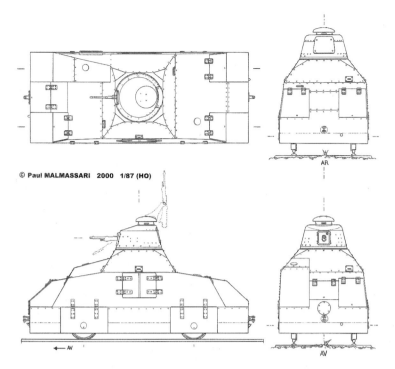

© Paul MALMASSARI 2000 1/87 (HO)

General arrangement drawing of the Renault design.
(Tracing: Paul Malmassari)

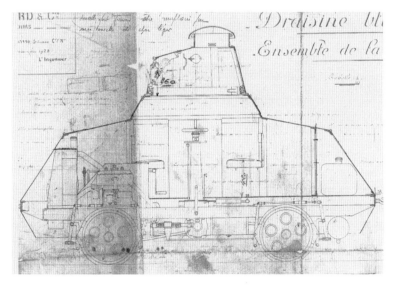

Cutaway profile of the Billard armoured trolley prototype proposed for the design competition in 1927. The handwritten notes suggest the turret was originally to be the type used on the Renault FT tank, whereas a new welded design, with a much lower ventilator cowl, was actually fitted. The machine gun is not shown, and a draughtsman has added a sketch of a possible 37mm TR Model 16 gun as fitted to many FT tanks.
(Drawing: Billard & Company calculations, undated Plan No 1751, Paul Malmassari archives)

Armoured train in China

An armoured wagon was put into service in 1929 in the Shanghai Concession, probably to act as escort for the International Train. Identification of this wagon is difficult (apart from a French source which indicates there were two wagons, but at Canton), and it is probable it was ultimately incorporated in one or other of the Chinese trains.

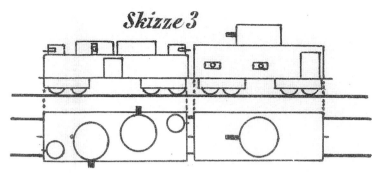

Sketch of the armoured wagons used in China by the French garrison, to a classic design typical of the period.
(Sketch: Militärische Wissenschaft und Technische Mitteilungen)

Armoured trains in Ethiopia and in the Côte Française des Somalis

During the period 1935 to 1937, the French had watched with concern the incidents involving Italians and Ethiopians which had begun in the Spring of 1935, followed by the Italian invasion of Ethiopia in April and May 1936, and the subsequent revolts and incidents of looting. They were obliged to plan for the protection of the railway by means of armoured trains and escorts, which was put into effect in 1938. With the addition of armoured trolleys the protection of the railway at Djibouti continued up until 1944. However, in the absence of surviving photos, we can only record these basic facts without being able to furnish specific details.

The Moroccan armoured train

During the Spanish Civil War, the French authorities feared incursions from Spanish Morocco. In August 1938 the project of an armoured train was mooted. General Charles Noguès[15] estimated 'that the creation of such an armoured train in times of peace would have a certain usefulness in the case of operations in Spanish Morocco', and on 23 September, a decision was taken to proceed. This train was to be made up of an armoured 0-6-0 engine (then

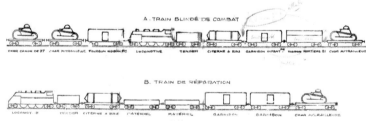

Two possible configurations of the armoured train, prepared by Lieutenant Mainguenaud, commanding officer of the *Formation spéciale de chemin de fer*, in June 1940. To the best of our knowledge this is the only surviving illustration of this train.
(Drawing: SHD)

14. Report No 6, meeting of 1 December 1931, dealing with firing trials with a machine gun on an armoured trolley (C.A.A. file not found).
15. Noguès commanded the XXIX Army Corps in Algeria in 1933 then from 1936 to 1940, he was resident general in Morocco.

later a 4-6-0), two Type NN bogie platform wagons, one armed with a 75mm gun (later a 37mm) and the other with a pair of 81mm mortars; two Type UU steel-sided bogie wagons for the engineer element and track repair equipment, plus the command post for the train. Reconnaissance in advance of the train would be carried out by a motorcycle on rails.

The train, built with the help of the Tangier-Fez Railway Company's workshops, was completed in March 1939, and given the designation *Formation spéciale de chemin de fer*. It was such a well-kept secret that apparently no photograph of the train was ever taken. Following the military collapse in Metropolitan France, the *Formation spéciale* was decommissioned on 3 July 1940.[16]

The Second World War (1939–1945)

Several armoured trains of various origins can be identified, in French overseas possessions[17] as well as in Metropolitan France[18] and during the fighting in Germany. They are listed here in chronological order.

Morocco

As part of the plan for the defence of Morocco, a train armed by the French Navy with two 75mm guns was stationed on the line to the north of Oued Sebou, and took part in the fighting on 8 November 1942 against the Allied landings, in the Green Beach[19] zone.

Indochina

In this colony 12,000km (7500 miles) from France, the use of 'armoured trucks' had already been envisaged back in 1905. Re the armoured trains used from 1940 to 1945, it is difficult to be specific as to their exact number. It appears that in total there were three armoured trains built: one in Tonkin, which took part in the fighting at Lang Son in September 1940 and was destroyed there during the Japanese *coup de force* in March 1945; a second train in Cochinchina; a third in Cambodia (Phnom Penh) which was deployed during the hostilities between France and Thailand in the period October 1940 and January 1941.

75mm gun wagon of the Tonkin Armoured Train in February 1942.
(Photo: Paul Malmassari Collection)

[16.] Service Note No 464/MC, of 3 July 1940, 3 H 1264/5 (SHD).
[17.] In October 1942 the British intelligence service at the post of Bathurst in the Gambia reported the presence of an armoured train, armed with twelve machine guns, on the Dakar-Thiès line.
[18.] During the Liberation fighting, in order to attack the German garrison at Ussel, plans were made to armour the 'Tacot' (the name for the Transcorrézian train), but this was never carried out.
[19.] Three landing beaches were designated by the colours Blue (South), Red (North) and Green (Centre).

Photographed by the Americans near Casbah Mehdia to the west of Port Lyautey on 17th May 1943, these two guns were the only ones mounted on railway wagons in Morocco.
(Photo: NARA)

In order to provide as wide a field of fire as possible for the 75mm gun seen in the background, a system of hinged platforms and vertical plates has been installed, forming a large firing platform for the gunners while retaining vertical armour protection.
(Photo: Paul Malmassari Collection)

The same train on gunnery exercises at P.K. 210 (Marker Km 210) on 28 March 1942. The railway line runs alongside the Red River. The hinged vertical plates for the sides of the firing platform can clearly be seen.
(Photo: Paul Malmassari Collection)

The armament of these three trains was identical: one 75mm gun, four heavy machine guns, five light machine guns and one 7-tonne tank, probably a Renault FT from the Tonkin Motorised Detachment and the 9th Colonial Infantry Regiment.[20]

Captured armoured train used by the 5th Armoured Division

During their entry into Austria in 1945, at Bludenz Station the 5th Armoured Division captured intact a German anti-aircraft train with concrete tubs. Reinforced by a Sherman tank on the leading flat wagon, it was used in reconnaissance sorties on 4, 5 and 6 May.[21]

The anti-aircraft wagons with a central concrete tub are instantly recognisable. Aside from the 75mm gun of the Sherman tank on the leading wagon, the armament consisted of 20mm Flak 38 and 20mm *Flakvierling* 38.
(Photo: Commandant Paqueteau)

The War in Indochina (1945–1954)

As concerned the railway network, the war in Indochina commenced in 1945/46 by reconnaissance runs to assess the tracks (badly worn), the infrastructure (destroyed by American bombing and sabotage by Vietnamese rebels), and the rolling stock (only 40 per cent of the engines remained in a usable state), following which railway traffic was gradually restarted. The Cambodian network was in the best condition. Essentially the railway network was the only viable means of transport in the colony, and its function was a gauge of economic recovery. To ensure success, the running of railway transport was delegated to the military, working in collaboration with tcivilian railway personnel.

Beginning in February 1946, armoured trolleys were sent out in front of the trains. For their part, the Viet-Minh set to work to destroy the network by laying mines, by tearing up the track, by demolishing the bridges and by simply removing the fishplates from sections of rails. To limit the damage, a system of static defence was established, with watchtowers, blockhouses and fortified stations in particular, to complement the active defences of the trains.

Track disrupted by overturning a complete section: to accomplish this it was necessary only to overturn a part of the track by pulling it with buffaloes or by requisitioning local villagers, and inertia would do the rest. Here the track has been tipped down a slope.
(Photo: Paul Malmassari Collection)

The result of a derailment. Clearly the rims of several driving wheels have been damaged, probably by the explosion of a mine.
(Photo: Michel Protat)

20. Order of battle of the French troops in Indochina, 23 November 1943; Order of battle of the troops of the Indochina Group, May 1944 (10 h 80/D1, SHD).
21. Paul Malmassari, *Les Trains Blindés 1826–1989* (Bayeux: Editions Heimdal, 1989), p 199.

Left: The Baika Viaduct (central Vietnam) was destroyed on 22 June 1953. At top right one can see an armoured wagon, and in the foreground the roof of the engine cab.

(Photo: Le Bris, Paul Malmassari Collection)

Right: This is definitely one of the four Belgian trolleys, seen here at Quang-Tri.

(Photo: Major Gricka)

The first step was to deploy armoured trolleys. Initially (February 1946), Japanese trucks (often armoured) and civilian trolleys were recovered. Then road-rail Jeeps (specially adapted to the metric gauge) were used despite their fragile construction and their light armament. The difference in diameter between their 50cm (1ft 7¾in) rail wheels and the 70cm (2ft 3½in) road wheels caused the motors to over-rev.

In view of the deficiencies evident in the existing vehicles, the

One of the rare surviving photos showing a trolley opening up a route in 1946 or 1947. It is not possible to identify its type.

(Photo: ECPA-D)

Jeep trolley in the region of the Col des Nuages, Lien-Chien Station in 1947. These machines remained in service up until late 1953. The 1990 book by Patrick Meney, *La Rafale*, includes a love scene which takes place in a Jeep running blind – a completely hair-brained notion which brings discredit to the book which is elsewhere quite vague.

(Photo: Jean-Gabriel Jeudy Collection[22])

French Army studied a project for an armoured trolley or rail tractor, with the following modern features: duo-directional, traction capability and turret-mounted guns, but this project would not be built. Equally a study of a Dodge 4x4 on rails was not followed up. In late 1949, four trolleys of Belgian manufacture were received by the CFL and entered service after they had been fitted with armour and armament.

Billard Trolleys

The Billard Works delivered at least three Type D 50 D 5 Trolleys for the metric gauge and six others designated D 50 D 5 V.[23] Compared with the standard production trolleys, they had a reinforced chassis, a petrol tank capacity increased to 100 litres (26.5 gallons), a floor armoured with 8mm plate, and a more powerful Panhard motor.

The introduction of the '*Rafale*' to ensure the safety of train journeys[24]

The '*Rafale*' was a traffic procedure involving the grouping together of two to five passenger and goods trains to run one after the other at 20km/h (12.5mph) or 25km/h (15mph) when preceded by an armoured trolley. A '*Rafale*' would be composed of a 'pilot' or

Type D 50 D 5 V trolley at Quang-Tri, fitted with anti-grenade wire mesh.

(Photo: Major Gricka)

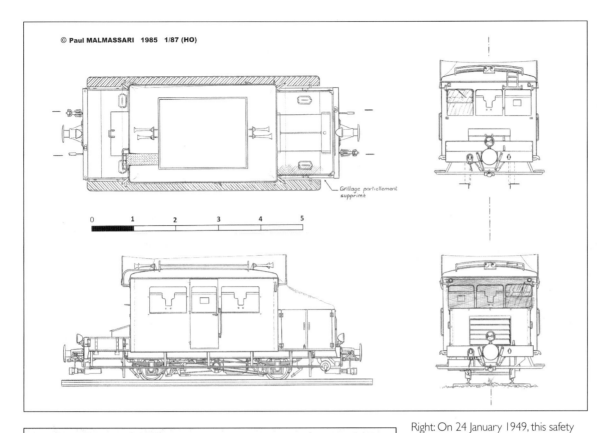

© Paul MALMASSARI 1985 1/87 (HO)

Grillage partiellement supprimé

The final version delivered to Indochina, which sports a camouflage scheme, an option rarely used in this theatre and all the more surprising because it features a representation of a railway track, as on certain Soviet or Spanish armoured trains.
(Photo: ECPA-D)

Right: On 24 January 1949, this safety flat wagon, fitted with a cabin armoured with steel rail sleepers, was derailed between Hué and Tourane. On the right is the front end of a Jeep trolley.
(Photo: Paul Malmassari Collection)

DRAISINE BILLARD BLINDEE
ECHELLE:1/20

An original drawing of the French Billard armoured trolley for Indochina.
(Builders' drawing: Paul Malmassari Collection)

'main' train, then trains '*bis*', '*ter*' and '*quater*', so named for the firing of successive rounds from an automatic weapon in a '*rafale*' (volley or burst of fire). The pilot train would be the most heavily armed (Bofors wagon, armoured car wagon etc).

But a '*Rafale*' was not capable of repulsing a major attack on its own, and it was therefore necessary to also deploy patrolling armoured trains. The first of these was built in Saigon and entered service on 16 December 1947. It had an engine and just two wagons. In 1948, the second armoured train was built with the help of the Foreign Legion, and the workshops of the C.F.I., under the command of Captain Raphanaud (who was not a member of the Legion).

The different armoured wagons: gun wagons, mortar wagons, command wagons etc.

The initial protection schemes added from mid-1947 were minimal (even using timber), but were followed by more solid and more efficient armouring. The safety wagon[25] at the head of the train and, if possible, at the rear, had an armoured shelter which allowed the detection of track damage and mines.

Heavy firepower was provided by the gun wagons, armed with tank turrets, Coventry armoured car turrets, mortars and AA guns,[26] and the following photos show several examples, demon-

[22.] From Jean-Gabriel Jeudy and Marc Tararine, *La Jeep, un défi au temps* (Paris: Editions Presse Audiovisuel (E.P.A.), 1981), p 182.

[23.] 'V' for 'Vietnam'. Three were delivered on 7 February 1953 (Nos 89, 90, 91), and the following three on 18 April 1953 (Nos 94, 95, 96). Notes taken by the Author at the SOCOFER Works in 1983.

[24.] A personal perspective has come down to us in the novel *La Vallée des Dieux* by Michel Tauriac. He travelled several times on '*Rafales*', and his eye-witness testimony worked into the narrative of his novel brings to life the dry facts reported in the Archives.

[25.] These Type MM or D bogie flat wagons were also called 'control platforms', 'shock wagons' or 'protection chassis'.

[26.] Range of the Bofors at high elevation was 9830m (10,750 yards) but British ammunition normally self-destructed at 3200m (3500 yards); max AP range of the Ordnance 2pdr (40mm) QF in the Coventry turret was 1370m (1500 yards) but no HE shell was ever mass produced, the turret relying on its co-axial 7.92mm Besa MG.

Type D wagon serving as control wagon for the pilot train of the *Rafale*. These platform wagons began to enter service in January 1947.
(Photo: Le Bris, Paul Malmassari Collection)

Type MM Wagon armed with a 40mm Bofors, put into service on 5 April 1947 on the line to Nha Trang. It was placed at the tail of the train and the flat wagon which followed normally ran unloaded.
(Photo: Le Bris, Paul Malmassari Collection)

Another version of the Bofors wagon which bears more than a passing resemblance to the Flak wagons with their central concrete tub.
(Photo: Michel Protat)

A third version of the Bofors wagon, here built up inside a high-sided Type HHff No 15415 bogie wagon.
(Photo: Yves Bernard)

Type HH[27] wagon with the turret of a Coventry armoured car, in the armoured train of the 4th Regiment, who had the habit of christening this 'rail tank' with the name of a memorable battle.
(Photo: Yves Bernard)

strating the inventiveness of troops confronted by two adversaries: the Vietnamese enemy and the scarce resources allocated by the home country in the process of reconstruction following the Second World War.

The use of turrets from tanks or armoured cars had two advantages: on the one hand they were protected by armour 14mm thick, superior to the available armour plates, and secondly they allowed all-round traverse of the arms carried. On the Cambodian rail network, ex-Japanese Type HA-GO tanks were also used (see the chapter on Japan). For indirect fire, 60mm then later 81mm mortars were used, which allowed the gunners to hit the enemy firing from trenches or behind cover. In the case of trains following one closely behind the other, in the '*Rafale*' configuration, they were also able to lob mortar rounds over the preceding train(s).

Type HHyf wagon built around a Coventry armoured car, with reinforced sides. The curved bands serve to deflect the cables stretched between trees to decapitate the unwary.
(Photo: Yves Bernard)

Recoving the wreckage of a Coventry wagon which has been blown up by a mine. Note that while the turret is standard (less its 2pdr gun), the armoured car hull has been lightened as much as possible.
(Photo: Yves Bernard)

One of the four Type H[28] wagons built in June–July 1949 with APX turrets from H 39 tanks (37mm Model SA38 gun), seen here on the Mandarin Road between the Col des Nuages and Tourane. The H 39 tanks had been captured in 1940 then re-used by the Germans who had modified the commander's cupola.
(Date unknown, photo: Paul Malmassari Collection)

Communications, whether to command posts, air support and stations or to other trains in the 'Rafale' and to the sections of the same train, were from the command wagons. In Indochina, several types of bogie wagon and van were used, all with a built-up casemate, and which from the outside were difficult to distinguish from the mortar wagons.

A fine shot of a mortar wagon (here a 60mm mortar, with a .303in Bren LMG), showing also the ammunition and equipment storage. As the mortars were mounted in elevated casemates, the remainder of the wagon could be put to other uses, and it is therefore difficult to distinguish between the different types of armoured wagons by appearance alone.
(Photo: Michel Protat)

In this view of an armoured train in central Annam, the intermediate flat wagon carries a shelter surrounded by aerials. To the right, a Type HH wagon is armed with a Coventry turret and on the left is perhaps a control van.
(Photo: Michel Protat)

GGc van of the first type to be built, in armoured train Sud of the 2nd REI (2nd Foreign Legion Infantry Regiment). The wooden exterior is doubled by an internal metal skin.
(Photo: Le Bris, Paul Malmassari Collection)

27. The Type HH wagons, wood or steel high-sided bogie wagons 10.1m (33ft 1½in) long, were principally used for wagons with a central armoured casemate such as for armoured cars, mortars or command posts.
28. The high-sided wagons Type H, 5.5m (18ft) long were specially used as gun wagons with turrets from armoured vehicles, and are not to be confused with the letter 'H' of the tank which corresponded to 'Hotchkiss'.

HH 15306 bogie wagon in Cochinchina with a central casemate for a mortar pierced by loopholes for firing fore and aft along the line. On the second wagon is a MAC 31 machine gun.

(Photo: Promotion Victoire via General Nicola-Vullierme)

An armoured van, well-supplied with firing loopholes which were always found at the corners, and which could be closed from the inside. On the casemate roof one can see opening vents, probably sheltering a mortar.

(Photo: Yves Bernard)

This shot gives a good idea of the dangers faced by the train crews, with dense vegetation which allowed the Viet-Minh to approach to within a few yards of the trains and then quickly vanish.

(Photo: Promotion Victoire via General Nicola-Vullierme)

Despite the increased difficulty of re-railing these bogie vans and wagons after a derailment, their much longer hull sides allowed for increased firepower.

(Photo: Yves Bernard)

Right: A typical view of a *Rafale*, with the armoured wagons inserted in a random manner in the middle of the train. The escort coach on the left is Type GGy No 12803.

(Photo: Institut du monde du travail)

Below: The armoured train of the 4th Dragoon Regiment in 1951–2, showing a classic wagon layout (which could be quickly varied). The engine is out of sight to the left, in front of the tank wagon, and from a distance the armoured train presents an appearance quite similar to that of a civilian rake.

(Photo: Yves Bernard)

The Madagascar Campaign

On 29 March 1947 an insurrection began, which included the railway network among its targets. The main railway stations were fortified and 'protected trains' carried out patrols on the TCE and the MLA.[29] Although lacking the firepower and protection of contemporary European armoured trains, they ensured the free circulation of traffic up until the end of the insurrection in 1948.

Quite adequate for fighting the Madagascan rebels, these patrol trains were far removed from the combat potential of the Russian and German types of the recent Second World War. The machine gun on the leading wagon is a Browning .50 Cal (12.7mm).

(Photo: Private collection)

The War in Algeria

The French railways in Algeria were permanently threatened by rebels, and the seriousness of such threats varied from year to year. The Press regularly alluded to the need for armoured trains, for example the edition of 5 July 1896 of *Le Monde du travail de l'Afrique Française*, in which a certain Francis Laure considered the use of armoured trains to be the only method of overcoming the Touaregs.

The war in Algeria began on 1 November 1954. At first the insurgents concentrated their attacks on individuals, and for the first year of conflict the communication infrastructure was left unaffected.[30] Then the attacks against the railways began in earnest, in the manner typical of pure terrorism. As Algeria was a French Department, the authorities could not let the insurgents gain the upper hand over the circulation of passenger and goods traffic. There were over 4500km (2800 miles) of track in use, with regular timetables and published operating procedures, which allowed the terrorists to plan their attacks, but at the same time the economic prosperity of Algeria depended on its railways.

[29] TCE = *Chemin de fer Tananarive-Côte Est*; MLA = *Chemin de fer Moramanga-Lac Alastre*.
[30] In December 1956 it was noted that '. . . the rebels are beginning to attack rail traffic' (Note from the military transport HQ in French North Africa to the Colonel who was Transport Director of the 10th Military Region, 1 H 2177/D1, SHD)

Derailment of a passenger train by a mine on 22 September 1957 at Km Post 135 + 200 on the Oran-Oujda line.

(Report of the Police Aux Frontières at Tlemcen)

An example of the armoured window openings applied to a derailed de Dietrich diesel-electric 060 YDA railcar of the S.N.C.F.A. (Algerian National Railway company).

(Photo: Nepveux)

Diesel locomotive 060DC-3 seen at Blida in September 1957, with all-round armour protection for the driving cabs.

(Photo: Gérard Pouillé)

Algerian Railways Alsthom diesel-electric locomotive BBB 060 YBD bearing the company's crest. The cab is armoured, and the holes in the buffer beam indicate that the locomotive was originally fitted with buffers for use on the main line, before being modified with central coupling knuckles.
(Photo: Private collection)

A rare shot of a steam engine on the metre gauge, a 2-8-2 named *MacArthur*.
(Photo: Paul Malmassari Collection)

An escort van partially-armoured with 7mm plates, lying beside a de Dietrich railcar after a successful ambush.
(Photo: ECPA-D)

The use of vehicles repatriated from Indochina was considered for the narrow-gauge lines.[31] Several narrow-gauge armoured trolleys had been recovered and in early 1956 they were undergoing overhaul. They would serve as sweepers preceding trains. The driving cabs of the locomotives and railcars were also fitted with armour protection, commencing with the region around Constantine. In addition, a certain number of wagons and vans included in the rakes of trains operating in danger zones, or attached at the tail end of mineral trains,[32] were also armoured.

In November 1955 the defence of the railway network was set in motion in earnest, with the creation of a battalion-sized specialist unit, supported by military specialists from the Algerian Railway Company. This move allowed the creation of an escort unit of Scout Cars (six pairs of coupled Scout Cars and six groups of trolleys of the C.F.A.), and three train escort units (or twelve sections, in specialised wagons of the C.F.A.). In summary, the fight against saboteurs was the role of the Army (surveillance and intervention by armoured train), and sweeping the track in advance of trains fell to the C.F.A. using the Billard Trolleys, the Dodge 4x4s on rails and the Scout Cars on rails.

By way of an example, the 587th Train Battalion was charged with three missions. The first was to ensure the regular running and the protection of the transport system. The second was to employ mobile means of sweeping, surveillance and intervention. The third and final mission consisted of supplying escort groups of up to a dozen men led by an NCO,[33] initially in wagons protected by sandbags or anti-mine carpets then, from February 1956, in armoured wagons.

What means were available to these units? In chronological order, the first seven Billard Trolleys were put into service at the end of 1955. The initial experience gained with these was used to improve subsequent vehicles.

Two views of the first Billard trolleys, with armour protection which followed the form of the basic vehicle. The armoured grille featured at the front end of all these trolleys. The opening to the upper left of the grille allowed a wider field of vision to the driver. Whether military or civilian, all these armoured trolleys carried a C.F.A. serial number.
(Photos: Paul Malmassari Collection)

31. 2227km (1384 miles) as against 2113km (1313 miles) of standard-gauge track.
32. Letter from the Director of the C.F.A. to the Governor General of Algeria, No IA8/67-15 dated 17 November 1955 (1 H 2177, sleeve 'Notes CGA 1955-1956', SHD).
33. Their armament consisted of a semi-automatic pistol, an LMG, five rifles and a rifle-grenade launcher.

Scout Car trolleys

Next, M3A1 Scout Car trolleys were introduced. They had been converted by the workshops of the C.F.A. to run on rails.[34] Well armed but slow and lightly armoured, their main drawback was that they had only one reverse gear. The solution was therefore to couple two Scout Cars back-to-back, or to pair one with a Billard Trolley.

The underditching rollers appear to have been removed during the final years of the war in Algeria. Note the .50 Cal (12.7mm) machine gun which is the main armament. The secondary armament of the Scout Car was either one or two .30 Cal (7.62mm) US machine guns.
(Photo: Paul Malmassari Collection)

To make up for the lack of a turntable, this coupled unit of Scout Car and Billard trolley nicknamed the '*Escargot*' or 'Snail' (by analogy with the train called '*Tortue*' or 'Tortoise') functioned with the Scout Car at the front driving forward, and with the gearbox in neutral when towed in reverse.
(Photo: Tallabardon)

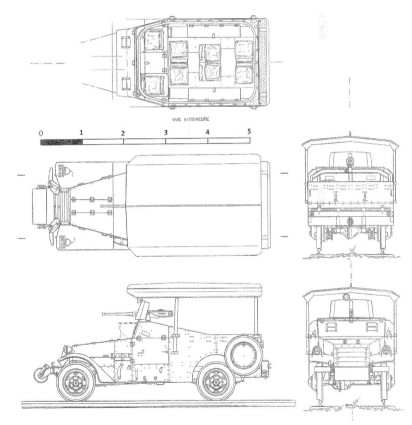

The front wheels of this Scout Car trolley have been fitted with additional armour. The shield is that of the 587th Transportation Battalion.
(Photo: Paul Malmassari Collection)

Right: The sad fate of a Scout Car, its wreckage recovered in a bogie wagon.
(Photo: Guy Chabot, 3rd Zouaves Association)

34. The special pneumatic tyres on flanged wheels were produced by Michelin (as used on their *Micheline* railcars).

Dodge trolleys

The Dodge Weapons Carrier WC51 converted to a railway trolley was used from February 1956 up until the end of the war. The rail conversion had been carried out for the C.F.A. and for the armed forces by two firms: VERARO[35] from 1951 and Desquesnes & Giral.

An early version of the Dodge Rail Trolley, with no side door.

(Photo: Paul Malmassari Collection)

Dodge trolleys of the Oran Army Corps, here seen coupled in pairs back-to-back to allow for travel in both directions without using a turntable, followed by a Scout Car.

(Photo: All Rights Reserved)

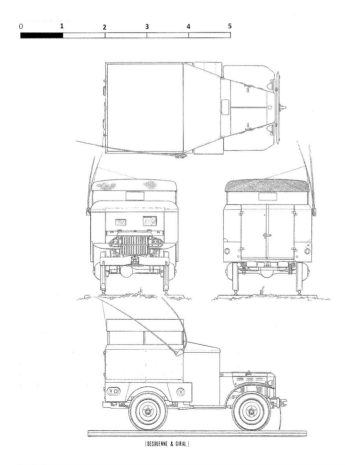

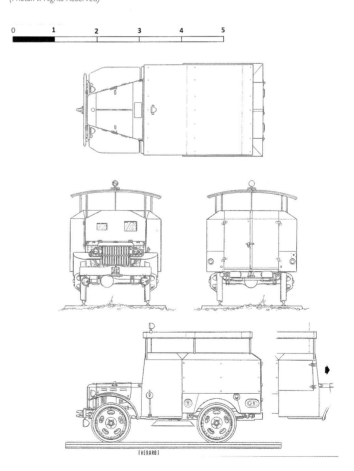

35. VEhicule RAil-ROute (Road-rail vehicles), the former Sibille company.

Jeep trolleys

Eleven Jeeps were converted for the metric gauge between May and November 1959, and they were sent to the zone to the south of Oran to form a surveillance screen against terrorist incursions. Although far from perfect, all the converted vehicles continued in service right up until the end, as there were never enough Billard trolleys to meet all operational requirements.

Later Billard trolleys

In addition to the machines of the C.F.A. mentioned earlier, the first additional trolleys were the metric gauge Type D 50 D 5 V[36] machines repatriated from Indochina, which were received in poor condition.

Six basic types of Billard Trolleys were used:

– D 50 D 5 V (initially for Indochina, then Algeria).
– D 50 D 5 (Algerian version).
– D 50 D 4 B (built as an armoured version only, for the standard and metric gauges).
– D 50 D 4 (armour protection added).
– D 50 D 6 B (armour protection added).

The complete vehicle park of twenty units was shared out between the C.F.A. and the Army.

Armoured Jeep trolley of the 2nd Company, 3rd Zouaves Regiment. Conversion for the standard gauge was not practicable, as it would have entailed fitting extensions to the brake drums which would have weakened the axles. Note the much larger diameter rail wheels compared with the Jeeps used in Indochina.
(Photo: ECPA)

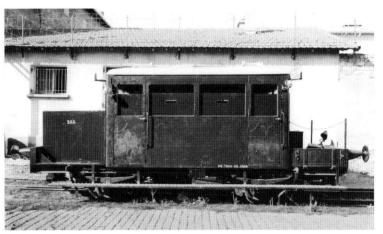

Armoured Billard Type D 50 D 5 trolley (standard gauge).
(Photo: Paul Malmassari Collection)

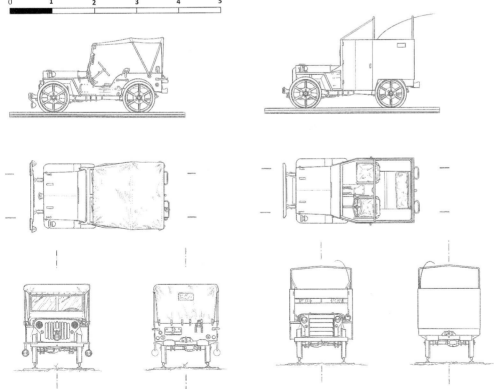

Front view, which shows that the armour protection was quite simple and followed the form of the original civilian bodywork. This is a Type D 50 D 5 trolley of the 587th Transportation Battalion.
(Photo: Paul Schneider)

The trolleys continued to evolve during the course of the conflict, but it is difficult to know whether this evolution resulted from the requirements of the Army High Command or from the availability of civilian chassis at the Billard factory. The final armoured versions were the Type D 50 D 6 B, built for both the standard and metric gauges, and which profited from the experience gained with the Type D 50 D 4. In the final models the 7mm armour plates were simply fastened to the body in such a way that the trolleys could easily be converted to civilian configuration.

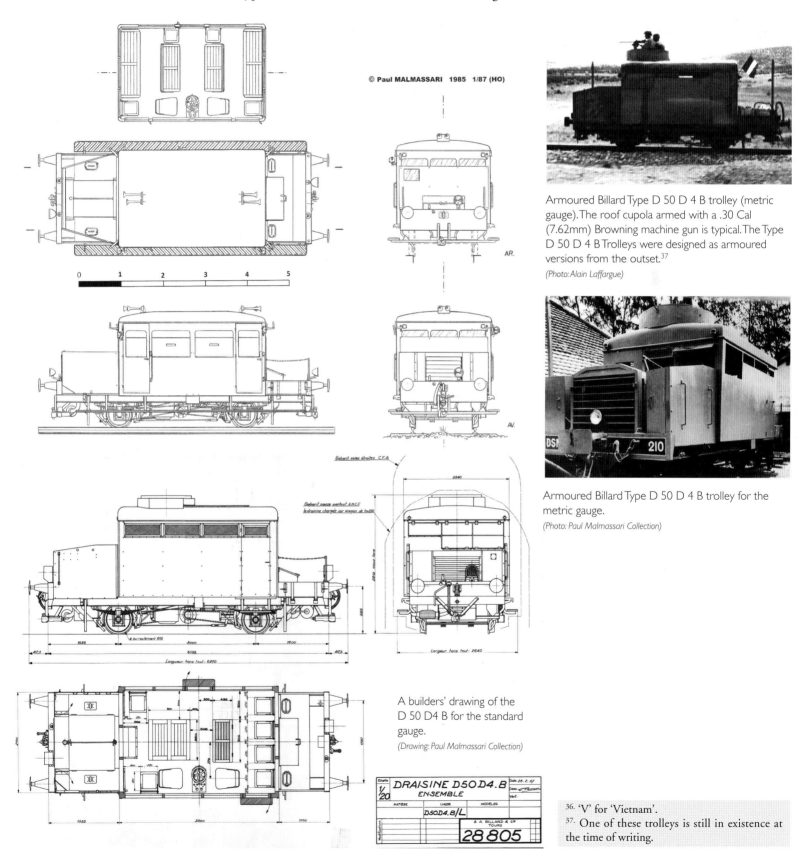

© Paul MALMASSARI 1985 1/87 (HO)

Armoured Billard Type D 50 D 4 B trolley (metric gauge). The roof cupola armed with a .30 Cal (7.62mm) Browning machine gun is typical. The Type D 50 D 4 B Trolleys were designed as armoured versions from the outset.[37]
(Photo: Alain Laffargue)

Armoured Billard Type D 50 D 4 B trolley for the metric gauge.
(Photo: Paul Malmassari Collection)

A builders' drawing of the D 50 D4 B for the standard gauge.
(Drawing: Paul Malmassari Collection)

36. 'V' for 'Vietnam'.
37. One of these trolleys is still in existence at the time of writing.

This Type D 50 D 6 B had a buffer beam which differed slightly from older models such as the trolley seen in the previous photo.
(Photos: Paul Malmassari Collection)

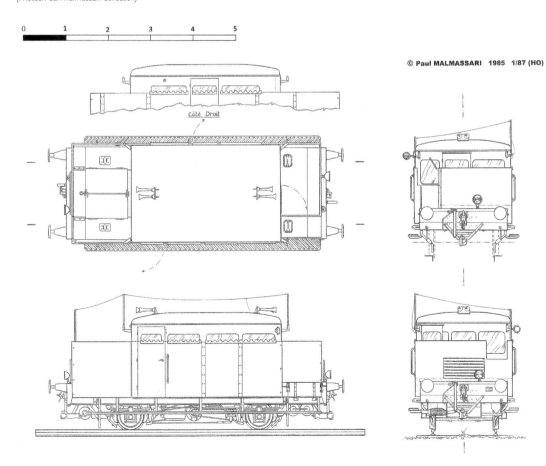

© Paul MALMASSARI 1985 1/87 (HO)

Armoured Billard Type D 50 D 6 B, seen from the rear. The windows are in 6mm plexiglass and the floor is formed from long bags filled with sand to provide a minimum of protection against mines. Note the searchlight attached to the machine gun.
(Photo: Paul Malmassari Collection)

This trolley was the victim of an attack on the Oued Tebarit bridge, and has fallen 20m (65ft).
(Photo: Tallabardon, 3rd Zouaves)

Radio-controlled trolleys

In a letter dated 12 April 1958, the Director General of the Algerian Railways admitted to being 'shocked by the degree of damage caused to the sweeper vehicles when they run over a live mine', and he expressed a wish that studies be undertaken into the production of a vehicle rolling with no-one on board, in other words a remote-controlled machine. In actual fact, the previous year the Billard Company had drawn up such a design to comply with an SNCF study of the use of shunters in marshalling yards. Two basic considerations for military use were, firstly to minimise the vehicle's profile so as to not overly obscure the view of the track when its controlling trolley followed close behind, and secondly to provide armour protection for all vulnerable parts so the controlling trolley could fire on the whole forward zone, which could involve rounds striking the radio-controlled trolley.[38] It was planned to

carry ten tonnes of ballast (worn-out rails) over each axle to ensure the detonation of mines. After several trials, ten trolleys were ordered, and the first was delivered on 10 April 1959. However, the results were far from satisfactory, and it appears that only two of these trolleys were used successfully.

In the course of the entire war in Algeria, between 190 and 201 armoured trolleys of various types had been employed, which was the greatest number of such vehicles of all the countries engaged in anti-guerrilla struggles.

[38] This scenario was far from uncommon in anti-guerrilla actions: in Indochina, tanks and even armoured railway wagons had been obliged to fire on their fellow units to sweep them clear of attackers who had scrambled on top of them.

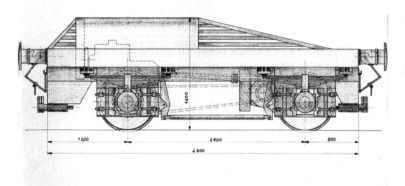

The initial design proposed by Billard. The superstructure would be modified, but the overall dimensions of the chassis would be retained in the production version.

(Builder's drawing: Paul Malmassari Collection)

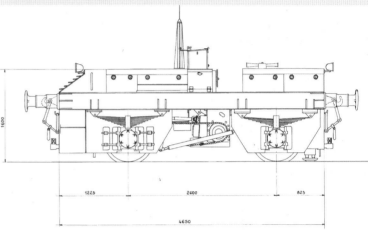

The production vehicle as delivered to the French army. The plan view is missing from the archives.

(Builder's drawing: Paul Malmassari Collection)

Billard Radio-controlled trolley (initial configuration). The armoured flap of the receiver unit has been left open.

(Photo: ECPA-D)

Billard Radio-controlled trolley equipped with an armoured cab. The obvious drawback of this configuration was that the cab obscured the view of the track from the following trolley or train.

(Photo: ECPA-D)

Armoured trains in Algeria

The first armoured train was built in Algeria in October 1956. Traction was provided by a 400hp shunter, enabling it to run at 35–40km/h (22–25mph). In 1957 the Army Engineers in Algeria began construction of an armoured train (ultimately nicknamed '*Tortue*' or 'Tortoise') for the 587th Transportation Battalion. The four drawings below by the author show elements of the 'Tortoise'. In total six or seven armoured trains would be built.

Algeria would be the last theatre of war in which France used armoured trains and trolleys of indigenous design. But other countries or regions in conflict have profited from the French experience: Mauritania, Portugal, the Bosno-Croat Federation etc, which we describe in the relevant chapters.

Two infantry firepower wagons of an armoured train of the 587th Transportation Battalion, in an atypical configuration.

(Photo: Dominique Loiseau)

Command van during a mission to escort a goods train (1st Company, 3rd Zouaves Regiment). The vehicle on the far right could be a Billard trolley, but the structure on its roof remains a mystery.

(Photo: Tallabardon)

Here the armoured train has been split up and wagon TTuw 25483 has been included as the escort of a goods train. Note that the cab of diesel electric locomotive 040-DC-13 has been armoured.

(Photo: Dominique Loiseau)

An escort van crushed between its train and the locomotive.

(Photo: Guy Chabot, 3rd Zouaves Association)

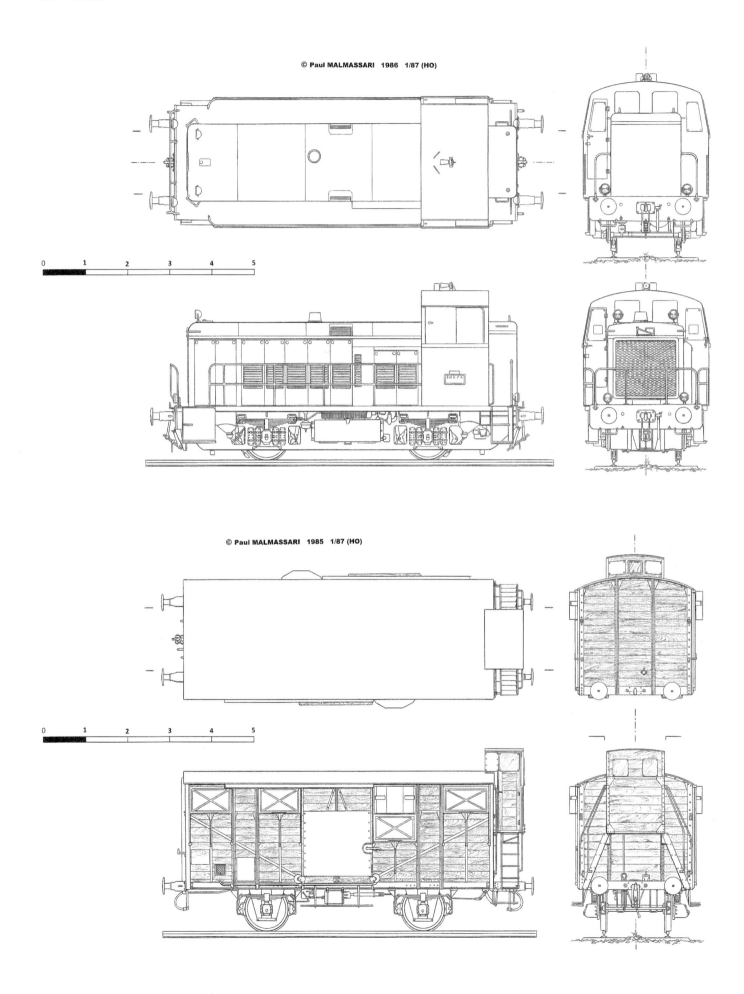

© Paul MALMASSARI   1986   1/87 (HO)

© Paul MALMASSARI   1985   1/87 (HO)

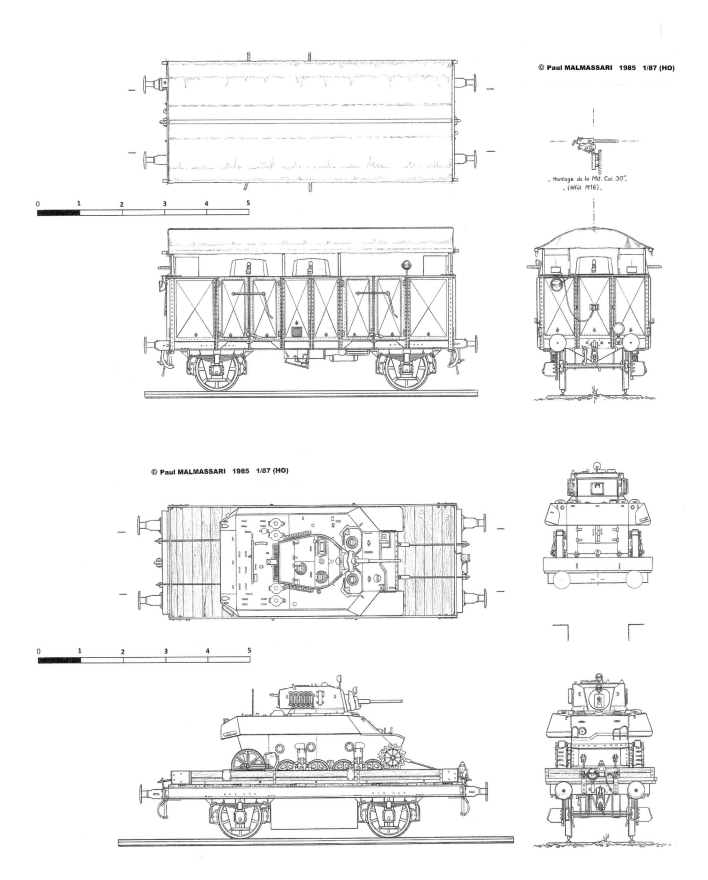

© Paul MALMASSARI 1985 1/87 (HO)

Montage de la Mit. Cal. 30"
(Affût M16)

© Paul MALMASSARI 1985 1/87 (HO)

M3A3 Stuart light tank mounted on a two-plank wagon. A photo of this combination in use in Algeria appears in the Introduction.
(Drawing: The Author)

SOURCES:

Archives:

Guy François.

Paul Malmassari.

Cercle généalogiste de la SNCF (album Emile Moret et Eugène Hallard)

Carton SHD 16 N 755.

Books:

Chabot, Guy, *Le Plus sale boulot – Guerre d'Algérie 1956-1962* (Coulommiers: Dualpha Editions, 2006).

François, Guy, *Les canons de la victoire, tome 2 : L'Artillerie lourde à grande puissance* (Paris: Histoire et collections, 2008).

Histoire militaire de l'Indochine française des débuts à nos jours (juillet 1930) (Hanoi-Haiphong, 1931), Vol 2, p 292.

Jeudy, Jean-Gabriel, and Tararine, Marc, *La Jeep, un défi au temps* (Paris: Editions Presse Audiovisuel (E.P.A.), 1981).

Malmassari, Paul, *Les Trains blindés français 1826-1962, étude technique et tactique compare* (Saint-Cloud: éditions SOTECA, 2010).

Conferences:

Malmassari, Lieutenant-Colonel Paul, '*La Défense dynamique des voies ferrées contre le terrorisme: l'exemple français*', actes du symposium Armée et technologie, Pully (Switzerland) 16 to 20 March 2004, pp 535–54.

Films:

http://www.britishpathe.com/video/french-gun-battery-on-railway/query/armoured+train

'*Les trains vus par le cinéma des armées*', ECPA-D, 2012, 61 min.

Kowal, Georges, '*Avec la Rafale*', 1952, ref. SCA No 0050.

Journal articles:

Aiby, Lieutenant André, 'L'emploi des trains blindés', *La Revue d'Infanterie* Vol 83 (November 1933), pp 775–95.

Dufour, Pierre, '1948 Rafale contre Viet-Minh', *Hommes de guerre* (January 1989), pp 27–32.

Dupont, Michel C, 'Trains blindés sur voie métrique en Indochine', *Le Rail* No 7/8 (December 1988), pp 72–5.

François, General Guy, 'Les Trains blindés français de 1914', *Ligne de Front* No 54 (March-April 2015), pp 20–9.

Le Bris, Pierre, 'Les Chemins de fer du Viet-Nam de 1945 à 1954', *VAUBAN, bulletin de liaison du genie* No 96 (3rd Quarter 1990), pp 6–11.

M., Captain, 'Les Trains blindés', *La France militaire* No 11795 (23rd May 1924), p 1.

Medard, Frédéric, 'Le soutien de l'armée française pendant la guerre d'Algérie', *Revue Historique des armées* No 4 (2002), pp 25–36.

Montgéry, M. de, 'Observations de M. Paixhans, avec les répliques de M. de Montgéry, au sujet de deux ouvrages intitulés: Nouvelle Force Maritime', *Bulletin des sciences militaires* Vol 3 (1826), pp 218—19.

Neviaski, Captain Alexis, 'L'audace du rail: les trains blindés du Sud-Annam', *Revue Historique des armées* No 234 (2004), pp 25–36.

Novels:

Meney, Patrick, *La Rafale* (Paris: Denoël, 1990).

Tauriac, Michel, *La Vallée des Dieux* (Paris: Flammarion, 1989).

Website:

http://www.forum-auto.com/automobiles-mythiques-exception/voitures-anciennes/sujet388213.htm

Two photos showing the opposite ends of armoured train *'Tortoise'* of the 587th Transportation Battalion. Although the wagons are of the same type, there are slight differences in the markings and also the position of the electric lamp sockets.

(Photos: Dominique Loiseau)

GEORGIA

THE FIRST REPUBLIC: ARMOURED TRAINS (1918–1921)

Created following the break-up of the Russian Empire, Georgia declared independence on 26 May 1918, supported by several countries which opened embassies and consulates. Already in January 1918, the nascent republic had put into service eight armoured trains under the command of a certain Valodia Goguadze, a Social Democratic Party activist. From January to March 1918 they intervened in support of the troops falling back before the Ottomans, then in March–April during the battles against the Turkish Army at Adjara, Guria and Borchalo Mazra.

Their final actions were against the Bolsheviks in 1920–1 when a total of some fifteen armoured trains were mobilised. The first Georgian Republic came to an end when, without having surrendered,[1] it was incorporated as an autonomous republic within the Soviet Union.

SOURCES:
https://icres.wordpress.com/2014/03/20/exhibition-soviet-occupation/

1. The government in exile was based in France up until 1934.

One of the Georgian armoured trains. An identical train, christened *Republican*, was commanded by Valodia Goguadze.
(Photo: Paul Malmassari Collection)

GERMANY

ARMOURED TRAINS, RAILCARS AND TROLLEYS[1] 1900–1945

At the beginning of the twentieth century, the German Army was no stranger to the armoured train, having had the chance to observe the French versions during the War of 1870–1, but despite the widespread reports of armoured trains during the Boer War, it took some time for the Germans to recognise the advantages this weapon could bring to them. Their country being sited at the heart of Europe, in time of war they would need to have the ability to rapidly move their forces between the various fronts. The only means of doing this was by the railway network, and therefore means had to be put in hand for its protection. A glance at a map showing the length of the front lines extending from the north to the south of Poland then on into the Ukraine, and the extent of the railway network inside Germany proper, would justify the deployment of armoured trains, the only force capable of intervening rapidly over the long distances involved, at a time when motor transport was neither fully developed nor highly regarded in military circles. Then during the Second World War, the armoured trains were the only effective means of countering the depredations of roaming bands of partisans. The German Army, with the bit between its teeth, wholeheartedly pursued the armoured train adventure, in the process continually perfecting or planning improvements up until the final defeat of the Third Reich.

The First German Armoured Trains

Following the Boxer Rebellion, the foreign Legations in China drew up a co-ordinated defence plan, and at Tsingtao the Germans commissioned a small artillery train with two wagons mounting naval guns.

Postcard showing the German armoured train in China in 1900, with its two 8.8cm F.K. guns.
(Postcard: Paul Malmassari Collection)

In 1904, the revolt of the Herero tribe in German South-West Africa led to the construction of a narrow-gauge armoured train. Under the command of a Lieutenant Bülow, the train was armoured at Waldau Station with corrugated iron sheets and sacks

PZ III, one of the 1910-Type armoured trains seen at Lille in December 1914. The armoured wagons were converted from 40-tonne Type Omk(u) mineral wagons. One wagon was always equipped with an armoured command and observation tower, for the train commander.
(Photo: Paul Malmassari Collection)

Armoured Class D XII engine built by Krauss at the turn of the century. It is not known whether this prototype was included in the 1910 Programme, but it had a relatively modern outline, even if the vertical arrangement of its armour plates betray its era.
(Photo: Krauss-Maffei)

[1.] In German: *Panzerzug and Panzerdraisine*. From 21 October 1944, the official designation changed from the original *Eisenbahnpanzerzug* to *Panzer Zug*, and for all the designations concerning armoured trains, the prefix 'Eisb.' disappeared. For the sake of simplicity, here we will use the generic term 'Panzerzug' or 'PZ'.

filled with earth; its armament comprised a 37mm revolver cannon from the landing detachment of the gunboat *Habicht*, plus the personal arms of the troops carried on board.

Apart from these local improvisations, in 1910 official German documents foresaw the necessity of building armoured trains in the case of hostilities. Based on the observations of Count von Schlieffen who had studied the Boer War, the Army High Command placed orders for thirty-two armoured trains. However, the financial situation that year obliged them to reduce the order to just fourteen. By the outbreak of war, manoeuvres carried out with the first trains had given some idea of their value. The standard composition of each train was:

– an armoured engine positioned centrally, in general a Class T 9.3 but also Prussian Class G 7.1, or a Class T.3 (as allocated to PZ IX), etc.
– twelve wagons protected against small-arms fire.
– an observation tower fitted on one of the wagons.

The trains required twenty-four hours' notice to prepare them for operations, crewed by railwaymen and soldiers from the regular army, up to a company in strength with four machine guns.

The First World War

In Belgium several improvised trains were built and used by the right wing of the invading armies. In September 1914 an 'intervention section' was created, its mission being to fight franc-tireurs, cyclist troops and Allied cavalry. One armoured train, built by the Engineers, participated in these actions, one of which involved foiling a Belgian 'phantom train'. If the employment of these armoured trains in Belgium could be qualified as satisfactory, on the other hand they were criticised for their thin armour and weak armament. The crews asked for internal telephones and searchlights. Beginning in November 1914 these defects were remedied, and in 1915 the number of trains reached the fourteen planned five years earlier. In that year, the front stabilised in the West, and the war of movement continued in the East. Out of the fourteen trains, seven were demobilised in 1916, and the seven others retained only their engineering crew members.

Between 1916 and 1918 a certain number of armoured trains were built to carry out different missions depending on the front where they were engaged. Some wagons now carried Gruson 53mm portable fortress turrets and others were roofed over.
(Photo: Paul Malmassari-DGEG Collection)

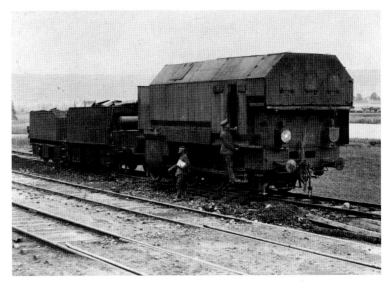

The Prussian Class T 9.3 was a tank engine, and the two additional unarmoured tenders were attached to increase its range. The practical speed of a Panzerzug in fighting configuration was in the range of 25–30km/h (15–18mph), whereas on the main lines, with the engine at the front, they could reach 60km/h (38mph).
(Photo: Paul Malmassari Collection)

In 1916, Panzerzug I and II, which had been sent to Romania, received a new wagon armed with a 76.2mm Putilov 02 in an armoured casemate pivoting on a set of rollers.
(Photo: Paul Malmassari-DGEG Collection)

Photographed in Hamburg in January 1918, this Class T 9.3 engine is armoured overall, which distinguished it from the other standard engines. It was attached to either PZ II, V or VII.
(Photo: Paul Malmassari Collection)

The leading wagon of PZ III ,converted from a 20-tonne mineral wagon. This train would be renumbered as PZ 54 in March 1919. Note the 37mm revolver cannon with a 180-degree field of fire. It is fitted with a front armour plate and muzzle cover with retaining chain, just as on the smaller Maxim 08. Also note the lateral machine gun in the upper casemate. The anti-aircraft machine gun is a 7.62mm Maxim which was not part of the original armament of this train.
(Photo: Paul Malmassari Collection)

Patrol train on which elements of armour can be seen, such as on the engine cab, and the wagon sides, photographed on 19 June 1918 at Potiflis.
(Photo: Paul Malmassari-DGEG Collection)

The German advance into the Ukraine involved building four trains for the Russian broad gauge, of differing design and with variable armour disposition, and also with the addition of captured wagons. Their armament was either German, using the 7.7cm field gun, or Russian with the 76.2mm.

On other fronts, armoured trains served in the German colonies: in the fighting in Cameroon against the French troops under General Dobell, a wagon was converted and used notably to defend the bridge over the Dibamda with its single machine gun. To the best of our knowledge, no photo of it was ever taken. In Palestine in 1918, German personnel of the *Asien-Korps* formed part of the crews of Turkish armoured trolleys (see the chapter on the Ottoman Empire). During the Finnish War of Independence, the Germans used only one train, captured from the Reds probably at Helsinki on or around 13 April 1918, armed with two Russian guns and four machine guns.

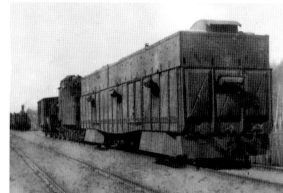

Armoured wagon captured during the advance into Russia and reused by German troops to the east of Gomel.
(Photo: Paul Malmassari-DGEG Collection)

A rare vehicle during the First World War, this armoured trolley captured by the Russians is an armoured Daimler lorry converted for use on rails. Note the firing ports in the rear side plating.
(Photo: Wolfgang Sawodny Collection)

Post-War Conflicts
The German Revolution and the Civil War

Humiliated by the terms of the Treaty of Versailles, undermined by their defeat and declining social conditions at home, Germany was easily destabilised by the export of the Bolshevik Revolution in Russia. Strikes, troubles and acts of sabotage multiplied, and led to the reactivation of the old armoured trains and the improvisation of many others. In late 1918, all the armoured trains, irrespective of the front where they were situated, were renumbered, beginning with 20 and ending in 55, plus several Roman numerals. The deployment of the trains became general in March 1919, when they operated principally in Halle, Magdeburg, Braunschweig, Leipzig and Munich. On the 'Red' side, in Leuna, where the factories were completely surrounded on 28 March 1919, a rudimentary armoured train was built by the revolutionaries, but it was captured intact.

The armoured train of the 'Leuna Arbeiter', converted from hopper wagons during the uprising inspired by Max Hoelz in Saxony between 23 and 29 March 1919. The industrial complex was recaptured by troops led by Colonel Bernhardt Graf von Paninski.
(Photo: Wolfgang Sawodny Collection)

The legend of Leuna was perpetuated by means of souvenirs such as a metal model train, and these plaques dated 1921, not 1919.
(Items: Paul Malmassari Collection)

In February 1919, PZ VII (the ex-PZ XII of 1914) added two wagons from PZ II and operated in Lithuania. When the German troops withdrew in November 1919, the Lithuanians took over the train and renamed it *Gediminas*. Note the searchlight in its armoured tower on the left.
(Photo: Paul Malmassari Collection)

The front part of PZ 45, seen in 1920. This train was built in March 1919 for the Lin. Kommando X (Stettin). From left to right: the machine-gun wagon (Type OmK) Breslau 55292; the artillery wagon (OmK) Essen 126 585, with its turret armed with a Krupp 8.8cm L/30 U-Boat gun on a C/16 mounting; a safety wagon; finally the machine-gun wagon (OmK) Cologne 62 455, with its armoured brakesman's cabin. The trooper sixth from the left in the front rank has an MP 18 sub-machine gun, and to his left is a soldier with a holstered Artillery Luger.
(Photo: Paul Malmassari Collection)

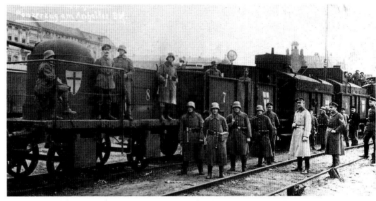

The Kapp Putsch in March 1920 involved six armoured trains in Berlin, numbered 30, 40, 46, 47, 55 and IV (seen here). The Gruson portable turrets were commonly used on armoured trains, but more usually inside a mineral wagon, and not mounted on a flat wagon as here.
(Photo: Paul Malmassari Collection)

PZ 48 (built in Dresden) was broken up at the end of 1920 after having intervened at Chemnitz among other places. Its 5.7cm Maxim-Nordenfelt L/36.3 gun seems to have been lifted complete from an A7V tank.
(Photo: Paul Malmassari Collection)

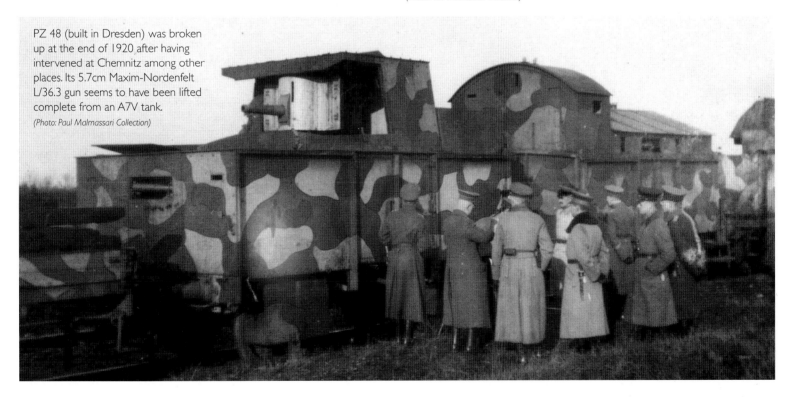

The rear half of PZ 45. On the right, armoured Class T.9.3, Stettin 7308; then the assault troop wagon, Cassel 14680; mortar wagon (OmK) Berlin 28630 with its characteristic inclined armour protection; finally machine-gun wagon (OmK) Cologne 64303. Note the two MP 18s, and the portable MG 08/15 beside the soldier sixth from the right.
(Photo: Paul Malmassari Collection)

An example of the armoured trains used during the Silesian uprising of 1921: this is the train of the Rossbach Free Korps. Behind the Type Om wagon is an armoured wagon fitted with an observation tower. Note the black-white-red flag of the German Empire, still used by the *Reichswehr* even when the black-red-gold flag was the official version.
(Photo: Paul Malmassari Collection)

The War of the Frontiers

These interventions were aimed at securing as much German territory as possible before the frontiers were definitively fixed. German troops were in action in the Baltic States, in Western Prussia and in Upper Silesia. Facing the three Polish uprisings, armoured trains were only deployed on the German side in the last two areas. In the Baltic States, a certain number of trains were also in action, including Panzerzug V in support of the Iron Division deployed in Riga in May 1919, and which was captured at Mittau.

For two years, Germany noted that armoured trains were not mentioned in the text of the Treaty of Versailles and demanded the right to keep some to maintain internal order and put down strikes. But on 5 May 1921, an ultimatum sent from London forced the German Government to accept 'without reservation' by letter of 20 May 1921 the handing over of all the trains. On 30 May 1925, the Inter-Allied Military Control Commission recorded having carried out the destruction of thirty-one armoured trains.

The Inter-War Period and the Rearmament Programme

The period 1921 to 1939 saw the renaissance of the German armoured trains. Even if the *Reichswehr* (which existed from March 1919 to March 1935) had no armoured trains, the *Reichsbahn* possessed twenty-two track security trains, which would form the backbone of the future Panzerzug. However, according to the Railway Department (Section 5) of the Army High Command, these trains were in poor shape, and only by amalgamating their individual rakes could they constitute 'two trains which could actually be used'. Hauled by unarmoured Class BR57 or BR93 engines, the wagons were simple units reinforced with sleepers, or with concrete poured between two layers of wood. The first military armoured trains (Panzerzug 1 to 4, 6 and 7) were created from these units, under the rearmament programmes launched in 1935, but Section 5 did not accord them a high priority. In fact,

the High Command thought these trains could be used to cover a withdrawal and that they would be expendable. For wartime operations they preferred armoured railcars armed with artillery and machine guns. Thus it was that during this intermediate period five Type VT railcars (Nos 807 to 811) were armoured, and at least one road-rail vehicle was the subject of a study based on the Schupo-Sonderwagen 21 from Daimler.

Wuppertal's armoured railcar No VT 809. The increase in weight required the installation of an extra central axle. Note the observation cupolas at each end of the roof and the wire of the radio antenna.
(Photo: BA)

Security train based in Munich, the future PZ 3, with its Type G vans armoured internally, and its radio masts deployed. Only the engine has overall armour. Note the observation cupola on the first van.
(Photo: Paul Malmassari Collection)

Armoured Trains of the Second World War, their Evolution and Construction Programmes

As military operations became imminent, on 23 July 1938 the seven *Bahnschtzzug*[2] (security trains) were reactivated. However, only four of them (Nos 3, 4, 6 and 7) were selected for combat operations on the basis of their offensive and defensive qualities and equipped accordingly, the others (Nos 1, 2 and 5) being reserved for railway security duties behind the front lines.

Panzerzug 41

This project begun on 13 December 1940 envisaged an armoured train comprising an armoured railcar capable of being used singly or coupled to other units, able to fight on road or rail, with the conversion even under fire taking only a few seconds. In addition, the armoured tank-transporter wagons would be self-propelled. In view of the complexity of the project, it was envisaged that production of the various units would extend over a period of time: as an urgent measure firstly the Type Omm flat wagons for carrying tanks, then the armouring of the locomotive, next the special wagons (auxiliary units, assault troop carrier, kitchen, infirmary), finally the conversion of all the wagons to self-propelled units. In actual fact only the Type Omm wagons would be built in 1941, and which were added to PZ 26-31.

Panzerzug SP 42

Also launched on 13 December 1940, this project included seven armoured wagons powered by a 1260hp diesel locomotive, which was capable of moving 600 tonnes at up to 50km/h (31mph) on the level. The train was to comprise: a command wagon, an assault section wagon, three tank-transporter wagons and two safety wagons, the whole being capable of running on standard and Russian broad gauge; the command wagon and/or any of the other armoured wagons was to be capable of independent operation. The tank-transporter wagons should be capable of unloading their tank in ten minutes and of re-embarking it in fifteen. The armament was to comprise 7.5cm guns in turrets, 2cm Flakvierling and machine guns. The diesel locomotive was to have been built by L-H-W and the rest by Berliner Maschinen Bau A.G. The design study was to have been finalised by September 1942 with the first train available by the Summer of 1943. The project was never started, and the designs were probably absorbed into those of Panzerzug BP 42/44 and PT 16.

Panzerzug BP 42 and BP 44

As the Panzerzug 1941 and SP 42 were not begun, in January 1942 the firm of Linke-Hofmann in Breslau was commissioned to build new armoured trains under the designation 'BP 42' (*Behelfmässiger Panzerzug* or 'makeshift armoured train', which suggests that this was to be a temporary solution), while Krupp was to fit the armour to the Class BR57 engines. The technical specifications were laid down in document K.St.N./K.A.N. 1169x[3] dated 17 August 1942. This document standardised the composition of the armoured trains along with their armament. Thus, in addition to those trains built in 1942, the previous trains would be brought up to the same standard at each major reconstruction.

The armament planned for these units was to be a 76.2mm F.K.-295/1(r) and a 2cm Flakvierling for the artillery wagons (A-Wagen), a 10.5cm le.F.H.14/19(p) for the gun wagon (G-Wagen), and machine guns. The PzKpfw 38(t) tanks to be carried should be capable of combat off the train. The armour protection was to be 30mm thick. Despite shortcomings in the armour thickness, for lack of suitable materials, the remainder of the armoured train corresponded to the standard laid down.

Combat experience quickly showed that the four 76.2mm or 10.5cm calibre guns were incapable of successfully engaging Russian tanks, and an expedient resorted to at the front was the mounting of the hull of a tank (PzKpfw IV or T-34) in order to use its turret armament. In parallel, a design study initiated by L-H-W resulted in the construction of a 'Panzerjägerwagen' (tank destroyer wagon) in 1944, equipped with the turret of a PzKpfw IV armed with a 7.5cm L/48 gun. On 6 September 1944 the Army High Command ordered the construction of 12 PZ of a new type to be designated BP 44, which complied with these latest standards. In parallel with the coupling of two Panzerjägerwagen at each end of the train, the 10.5cm guns were replaced with 15cm le FH 18 howitzers.

In use, the BP 42 and BP 44, which represented the high point of the art, proved themselves highly efficient at maintaining the morale of troops fighting bands of partisans, but suffered from the weaknesses due to their conservative design: steam power, their extreme length, lack of flexibility and limited armour protection. As a result, in August 1944 a front-line officer proposed an armoured train comprising a diesel locomotive coupled in the centre of two heavily-armoured wagons and six Panzerjägerwagen.

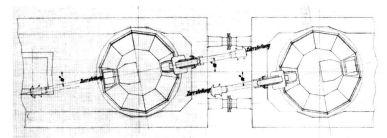

10.5cm guns on the G-Wagen (top) and the A-Wagen (bottom) of the BP 44-type trains.

(Drawings: Official German Military Archives)

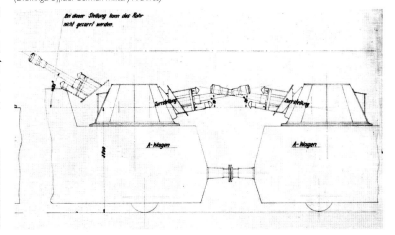

[2] For the record they were Frankfurt/Oder: PZ 1; Stettin: PZ 2; Munich: PZ 3; Breslau: PZ 4; Nuremburg: PZ 5; Königsberg: PZ 6 and 7 (the latter with railcar PT 15)

[3] K.st.n/K.A.N. = *Kriegs-Stärke-Nachweisung/Kriegs-Ausrüstung-Nachweisung*. These two documents listed the men and equipment allocated to a specific unit.

Track security trains

The trains in this category were not expected to comply with any existing standards apart from those required by combat in their particular locality. They were the improvised trains ('*Behelfmässiger Panzerzug*') which would be used particularly in Yugoslavia, in Italy and in Eastern Europe. Under the order dated 12 July 1943 they took on the designation of '*Streckenschützzug*' (SSZ or track protection train).

Railway reconnaissance units

The official German classification system laid down the following list:

– Gleiskraftträder = unarmoured self-propelled rail vehicle.
– Eisenbahnpanzerzug (leichter Spähwagen) = light reconnaissance vehicle.
– Eisenbahnpanzerzug (schwerer Spähwagen) = heavy reconnaissance vehicle.
– Eisenbahnpanzerzug-Triebwagen = armoured railcar.
– Panzerjäger-Triebwagen = tank destroyer railcar.

Trains comprising heavy and light self-propelled units

Trains were made up of a rake of these trolleys as follows: two sets of five trolleys (le.SP built by Steyr) or eleven trolleys (s.Sp also built by Steyr), alternating armed trolleys, command trolleys with radio antenna and trolleys with a tank turret. The train thus arranged was completed at each end by a Panzerjägerwagen slightly different to those used with the BP 42 and BP 44 type trains.

The organisation of the Eisb.Panz.Zg (le.Sp) was laid down in K.St.N. 1170P dated 1 October 1943, that of the Eisb.Panz.Zg (s.Sp) in K.St.N. 1170x dated 1 August 1944, that of the Pz. Triebwagen *Littorina* by K.St.N. 1170i dated 10 April 1944, and finally that for the Pz. Triebwagen 'a' and the Panzerjäger Triebwagen by K.St.N. 1170a dated 1 January 1945.

Road-rail armoured vehicles

Near the end of the war a road-rail vehicle project was studied, but the Nazi defeat put an end to it before any production vehicles resulted.

Organisation and command structure

Initially the armoured trains were under the control of the Railway Troops, up until 9 August 1941. On that date, with the attachment of Rapid Deployment Troops, it proved necessary to concentrate technical and tactical information in a single command centre, to permit their rapid deployment under a technician with intimate knowledge of armoured trains: the Armoured Trains Commanding Officer attached to the Army High Command, a function which remained in force up until March 1945. On 1 April 1942, the armoured train force, which by then counted some 2000 men drawn from different units, was grouped together administratively under the control of a new centre created at Warschau-Rembertow

(the Ersatz-Abteilung für Eisenbahn-Panzerzug-Warschau-Rembertow, or WK I). A further reorganisation came into effect on 1 April 1943, the armoured trains henceforth becoming an integral part of the 'Panzerwaffe'[4] instead of the Rapid Deployment Troops. In late 1944, the Armoured Trains Centre at Warsaw-Rembertow was transferred to Millowitz in the Protectorate of Bohemia.

Trains and railcars from 1938 to 1945

PZ 1 was created on 26 August 1939. It did not take part in the Polish Campaign and in 1940 was in the region of Düsseldorf on guard duty facing the West. It advanced into Holland on 10 May 1940 in the direction of Gennep, then Mill, where it was knocked out by a mine. It was repaired in Darmstadt, where it received wagons from the demobilised PZ 5. In 1941, it participated in the invasion of the Northern USSR, with the 4th Panzergruppe in the direction of Leningrad, then operated on the Central Front around Vitbesk and Smolensk. After suffering major damage on 28 November 1943, it was completely rebuilt in Königsberg to the new standards. Up until early 1944 it remained with Army Group Centre, notably carrying out security missions as part of the 221st Sicherung-Division based at Minsk. It was destroyed by its crew on 27 June 1944 during the Soviet summer offensive.

PZ 1 derailed at Mill on 10 May 1940. The armour on the engine has been deformed by the impact with the leading wagons. Note that all but one of the armoured wagons are converted from passenger coaches.
(Photo: Paul Malmassari Collection)

Even if the engine is still the same, most of the wagons have been replaced by captured Soviet wagons. By comparison with the BP 42 production versions, the number of field artillery and anti-aircraft pieces remains the same, but distributed differently. The command wagon with its armoured casemate is the original G-Wagen which has been modified.
(Photo: Paul Malmassari Collection)

[4]. The insignia colour therefore changed from black to pink and the 'E' for Eisenbahn was retained on the shoulder patch.

Close-up of the 2cm Flakvierling 38 mounting. All the trains brought up to the BP 42 standard had the same overall outline.

(Photo: Paul Malmassari Collection)

BR93 058 was the engine attached to PZ 2 ever since it was formed as the security train for Stettin. In 1945, the engine was the motive power for PZ 78.

(Photo: Paul Malmassari Collection)

PZ 1 (on the right) inherited a Polish Tatra T-18 trolley as proved by the camouflage scheme (see the chapters on Poland and Czechoslovakia).

(Photo: Paul Malmassari Collection)

PZ 2 seen from the rear. The original 75mm gun is still in place in the ex-Czech wagon but the turret behind it has been rearmed with a 2cm Flak.

(Photo: Paul Malmassari Collection)

The casemate destroyed at Könitz, with the 7.5cm F.K. M16 in the revolving turret.

(Photo: Paul Malmassari Collection)

Shortly after it was activated in July 1938 **PZ 2** participated in the occupation of the Sudetenland. It was next in action during the invasion of Russia. Between the Winter of 1941/42 and June 1944 it was under the orders of Army Group Centre in the region of Smolensk, then to the north-west of Kovel where it carried out anti-partisan security missions and troop transportation. It was updated to BP 42/44 standard, then was withdrawn from service in November 1944.

PZ 3 is one of the rare examples where it is possible to illustrate each phase of its career, which began prior to 1938 and ended in October 1944. PZ 2 (the former BSZ *München*) was reactivated on 23 July 1938 and placed under the orders of the General Kommando, VII.Armee-Korps in Munich. An SdKfz 231 railway reconnaissance vehicle was attached to it.[5] After 15 March 1939, when Germany invaded what was left of Czechoslovakia, PZ 3 returned to Brno passing through Austria. PZ 3 along with PZ 4 and 7 were in at the very start of the Second World War, going into action on 1 September 1939.[6] A direct hit from a Polish anti-tank gun destroyed the command turret, killing Lieutenant Euen, the train commander, and his second-in-command Lieutenant Zetter immediately took over. Withdrawing under fire, the train was stopped by a demolished bridge, whereupon Polish shells caused serious damage, destroying the leading wagon, setting fire to the wagons behind it, and knocking the train out of action. During subsequent repairs, the interior armour protection was enhanced and the destroyed turret replaced by a fixed casemate with an embrasure allowing a degree of training for the gun.

Following repairs, PZ 3 was sent to Lublin. On 10 May 1940 it crossed the Dutch frontier. But it could not fulfil its mission to seize the bridges over the Ijssel as the Dutch had sufficient time to blow them up. It then passed through the Halberstadt workshops where the wagons at each end were fitted with a turret from the abandoned BN10H programme for an anti-tank halftrack, mounting a 7.5cm L/40.8 gun, an elevated command/observation casemate and an anti-aircraft position (2cm Flak[7] in a tub, replaced in March 1941 by a 2cm Flakvierling[8]). To compensate for the subsequent increase in weight, a third axle was added centrally. PZ 3 thus became one of the better armed and protected of the first-generation trains.

SdKfz 231 armed with a 2cm cannon knocked out by anti-tank shells in front of the Ijssel bridges. This was the trolley attached to PZ 3, but the registration plate is a mystery, denoting a Bavarian Police unit.
(Photo: Paul Malmassari-Regenberg Collection)

PZ 3 at Veliki Luki in December 1942. The quadruple Flak mounting is clearly visible.
(Photo: Paul Malmassari Collection)

The leading artillery wagon of PZ 3 after leaving the repair shops in Danzig. Note the new command casemate and the replacement 7.7cm F.K. 96 gun in its fixed casemate. The painted death's-head is temporary.
(Photo: Paul Malmassari Collection)

For Operation 'Barbarossa', PZ 3 crossed the River Bug on the night of 22 June 1941 heading for Grajevo. In late October 1941, it returned to Königsberg for repairs. On 1 April 1942, it was blown up by a mine, and in the fighting which followed eight partisans were killed. On the 22nd, a remote-controlled mine destroyed an artillery wagon and derailed the two following wagons,[9] leaving seven dead and nine wounded among the crew.

Following serious battle damage in May, PZ 3 was sent for repair, then between 11 September 1943 and 12 July 1944 it was unavailable, being modernised to BP 42 standards in the Königshütte workshops in Upper Silesia (K.st.n./K.A.N. 1169x). The day after it left the workshops, the Russians launched an offensive towards the Baltic in the Dünaburg-Rositten zone, and on 24 July PZ 3 and PZ 21 counter-attacked at Kowno. On 1 August, a few kilometres after starting a mission, PZ 3 was derailed, and had to return for repairs.

[5.] This remained in use up until late 1940-early 1941.

[6.] This was the episode which inspired Pierre Thomas' comment 'The Second World War began in the middle of the railway lines' in Septembre 1939 mai 1940, des trains contre les Panzers, 1999, *La Voix du Nord* (1999), p 5. This may have been the first *combat* between the two opposing forces, but in fact the first shells of the Second World War were fired at 04.47 on 1 September 1939 by the battleship Schleswig Holstein against the Polish fortifications at Westerplatte.

[7.] Flak = *Flieger Abwehr Kanone* = anti-aircraft gun.

[8.] Flak Vierling = quadruple Flak cannon, also written as Flakvierling. This new mounting was fitted at the same time on PZ 1 to 4, 6, 7, 21 and 22.

[9.] The derailed wagons were not able to be recovered until a month later, when a crane was finally available.

A rare photo: the forward gun wagon was literally cut in two by a mine at Newel on 22 April 1942 and was recovered later, in this unusual configuration.
(Photo: Paul Malmassari Collection)

One of the few photos of PZ 3 in its final configuration, conforming to K.st.n./K.A.N. 1169x. From right to left, the G-Wagen armed with a 10cm le.F.H. 19(p), then the K-Wagen, and finally the A-Wagen with its 2cm Flakvierling 38.
(Photo: Paul Malmassari Collection)

One of the non-motorised Panzerjägerwagen of PZ 3. They were not equipped with *Schürzen* nor hull up-armouring. On the left is the tank-transporter wagon. This arrangement of these two wagons back-to-back is very unusual.
(Photo: Paul Malmassari Collection)

The ambush at Kowno in July 1944, where PZ 3 was derailed. Note the original form of the G-Wagen, and one can just make out the Flakvierling wagon in the background. It would seem that this view and the previous one are the last-known photos of PZ 3.
(Photo: Paul Malmassari Collection)

An impressive view of the engine from PZ 4, with its virtually integral armour, notably in the smokebox area which has streamlined armour protection.
(Photo: Paul Malmassari Collection)

This wagon, which is characteristic of PZ 4, is armed with a 3.7cm in the front turret (later replaced by a 4.7cm Pak) and a 7.5cm infantry gun in the rear turret, followed by an armoured rangefinder position. The semi-circular centre section is an ammunition shelter.
(Photo: Paul Malmassari Collection)

On 5 October 1944 the Russians attacked the front of the Third Panzer Army and cut the German forces in two when they reached the Baltic. On 10 October 1944, the train was cut off by Russian tanks and had to be sabotaged by its crew.

PZ 4 was put into service on 11 August 1939. During the Winter of 1941/42, PZ 4 was in the south of Russia in the region of Dniepropetrovsk. Between April and June 1944 it was under repair, then in December 1944 it no longer appeared in the active list, its units being broken up. Its number was passed to a new train.

Entering service at the same time as the other trains operated by the *Reichsbahn*, **PZ 5** crossed into Poland on 15 September 1939, then from the 20th carried out security patrols around Lvov during the discussions on the demarcation line between the Russians and the Germans. It was readied for the campaign against the Dutch in which it was to support commandos disguised as Dutch soldiers. On 10 May it was halted by the destruction of the bridge over the Ijssel and was severely damaged by Dutch anti-tank guns. It was broken up in June 1940 and its wagons were transferred to PZ 1.

PZ 6 was formed on 10 July 1939, and although incomplete, contributed to the capture of the town of Grajewo in Poland. Between 3 and 18 October 1939, it was in the Königsberg workshops being completed. It participated in the invasion of

An overall view of the complete train, which shows its rough-and-ready external appearance, even though the armour was effective against small-arms. But the absence of heavy guns and howitzers soon brought about improvised solutions by adding wagons. At the rear of the train is just visible one of the ex-Soviet MBV-2 railcars used as artillery wagons since the Autumn of 1942.
(Photo: Paul Malmassari Collection)

Holland but was blocked by a swing bridge being left open, and it then returned to Germany. During the Winter of 1941/42, it took part in 'Barbarossa' in Latvia then in Estonia, and finally in the region around Novgorod. Repaired after suffering serious damage, it was sent to Croatia. It was never brought up to BP 42 standards, and was destroyed in Serbia on 1 October 1944.

PZ 7 was created on 1 August 1939. It participated in the Polish campaign, then was used for security duties around Warsaw. On 8 March 1941 it was reinforced by 2cm Flak 38 mountings. In November, it participated in the invasion of the USSR (but on standard-gauge lines), then it returned to Germany for repairs. It returned to Russia and fought as part of Heeres-Gruppe Süd in the Kovel region. In June 1944, it was at the Warschau-Rembertow centre for modernisation, and was withdrawn from service in late 1944.

A rare view from above of the artillery position in the Type O wagon added after the Polish campaign, with the swastika added for aerial recognition. The gun appears to be a 7.5cm naval gun. Note the firing embrasures on the next wagon which seem to be useless in this configuration but which would have been used if the wagon was at the head or tail of the rake.
(Photo: Paul Malmassari Collection)

One half of PZ 7 probably being used as an artillery battery, profiting from the height of the line. The field gun is a 76.2mm F.K.295/1(r). One must suppose that the other half of the train is not far away.
(Photo: Paul Malmassari Collection)

Created on 26 November 1941, **PZ 10** was divided into two combat trains, Kampfzug I (one howitzer, two flak mountings, one anti-tank gun, two 10cm field guns and nineteen machine guns, from PP 53 *Śmiały*) and II (one flak mounting, one anti-tank gun, four 7.5cm and 10cm field guns and nineteen machine guns, from PP 51 *Marszalek*). The wagons were ex-Polish, adapted for the broad gauge. After entering the USSR, it moved to the Kiev region and became part of Army Group South up until early 1944. During this period it covered the retreat of the German forces after the defeat at Stalingrad. During operations near Sarny-Kovel, PZ 10a participated in the breakout from the Russian encirclement of that town, was heavily damaged but escaped. Intended to be repaired at Rembertow, it underwent an artillery bombardment in the second half of April. Its crew was therefore transferred to the ground troops and PZ 10 was abandoned.

When PZ 10 was separated into PZ 10a and PZ 10b on 1 April 1943, the latter was used on security operations on the Tarnapol (broad gauge) line, and received the number **PZ 11**. Between the middle of March and July 1944 it was taken out of service to be brought up to BP 42/44 standard. Railcars PT16 and PT18 were attached to it between the Summer of 1944 until January 1945. It was destroyed on 13 January 1945 near Chęciny to the south of Kielce, blocked along with PZ 25 by a destroyed bridge over the Nida.

Created on 10 June 1940 from ex-Polish rolling stock, **PZ 21** moved to the Eastern frontier where it was based in the 'Germano-Russian zone of interest' from 22 July 1940. It remained in Poland, under the orders of the 5th Panzer Division, up until April 1941 when it moved to France. There it came successively under the control of the 94th Infantry Division then the 337th Infantry

PZ 10 as it appeared between June 1942 and March 1944. The infantry wagon came from PZ 29. Between the ex-Polish wagon from *Śmiały* and the engine is an ex-Soviet wagon Type PL 35 or 37. On the far side of the engine is the infantry wagon from *Bartosz Głowacki*.

(Photo: Paul Malmassari Collection)

From June 1942, Class BR57 No 1064 from the series BR57$^{10\text{-}35}$ (armoured at Kharkov), was attached to PZ 11 as replacement for the ex-Polish Class Ti3 engine.

(Photo: Paul Malmassari Collection)

The ex-Soviet DTR trolley, used by PZ 10 as an armoured wagon. It had previously been used as a self-propelled reconnaissance vehicle.

(Photo: Paul Malmassari Collection)

An interesting view showing, in front of the artillery wagon, a Russian-type safety wagon, with armoured sides fitted with firing loopholes similar to those of the BP 44 trains.

(Photo: Paul Malmassari Collection)

Division up until July 1942. On 17 July it left for the Eastern Front and the Rshev sector, where it carried out anti-partisan missions for the 286th and 78th Security Regiments up until 6 February 1943. From 6 February 1943 up until the end, it remained in central Russia and in July, it went into action to the south of the Kursk Salient during that battle. In early 1944, it operated against partisans in the Pripet region to the east of Brest-Litovsk. PZ 21 was captured by the Russians on 30 October in Lithuania.

In its initial configuration, from front to rear PZ 21 was made up of: the artillery wagon from PP 54 *Groźny* (100mm howitzer and 75mm gun), then the assault group wagon from PP 11 *Danuta* (without its antenna frame), Class Ti3-13 engine No 54 654, the assault group wagon from PP 54 *Groźny* (with its antenna), and finally the artillery wagon from PP 52 *Piłsudczyk*.
(Photo: Paul Malmassari Collection)

The two Polish training wagons would join PZ 21. Here is the one without lower armour protection.
(Photo: Paul Malmassari Collection)

Two anti-aircraft flat wagons mounting 2cm Flakvierling were added in the Spring of 1941. The gun seen on the artillery wagon, on which the original armour has been reinforced by plates with loopholes, is a 100mm howitzer.
(Photo: Paul Malmassari Collection)

PZ 22 was created on 10 July 1940, using captured Polish rolling stock. It remained in Poland up until the end of March 1941, and on 10 April 1941 it arrived in France, where it was based at Tours. On 6 September, it was transferred to Niort, then moved to the Mediterranean coast. It remained there up until the middle of 1944 and only just escaped capture during the landings in Provence. It was then sent to Poland, where it was destroyed on 11 February near Sprottau.

Created on 1 March 1940 from captured Czechoslovak rolling stock, **PZ 23** took part in the invasion of Denmark then was stood down on 2 October 1940. Reactivated on 19 June 1941, on the 27th it officially received the number 23. It moved to the Balkans where it reinforced the three Croat armoured trains already there. It remained in Croatia up to the end of the war, notably operating in the Belgrade region.

PZ 22 at Lesparre (50km/30 miles north of Bordeaux) in 1942. Behind the safety wagons is the artillery wagon from PP 54 *Groźny* armed with two 75mm guns.
(Photo: Paul Malmassari Collection)

This 2-8-0 Class 140C armoured engine (from the Paris Depot, number unknown) powered PZ 22 from the Spring of 1944, replacing Polish Class Ti3-4 engine No 54651. The photo probably dates from June 1944, at Lons-le-Saunier.
(Photo: Paul Malmassari Collection)

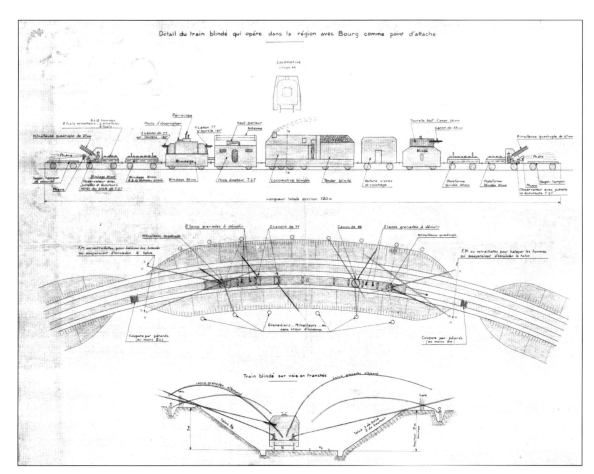

An exceptional document: a sketch made by the Resistance for the Allies, describing quite precisely the composition of the train, notably the Flak wagons and the ex-Polish training wagon.

(Drawing: Paul Malmassari Collection)

Below: A photo which illustrates the dramatic situation in Yugoslavia: the Royalist Chetniks finished up allied with the Germans in their common fight against the Communist partisans. By now PZ 23 had received Class BR93 engine No 220 which remained with the train up until late 1943.

(Photo: Paul Malmassari Collection)

The initial version of PZ 23, with only the death's-head insignia differentiating it from its Czechoslovak version. The leading flat wagon is the one which carried the Tatra T-18 trolley (see the chapter on Czechoslovakia).

(Photo: Paul Malmassari Collection)

Put into service on 1 March 1940, the early career of **PZ 24**, also composed of ex-Czechoslovak rolling stock, was identical to that of PZ 23. Reactivated on 19 June 1941, it took its number 24 on the 26th of that month. Up until 1943 it was in Serbia, then it moved to Italy. In early 1944 it was recalled to the rear for repairs. It moved to France where it was based from mid-1944 up until the landings in Provence on 15 August 1944. Recalled to the Eastern Front in the Winter of 1944/45, it was destroyed by its crew in Poland on 16 April 1945.

During the Winter of 1942/43, PZ 23 was rebuilt to BP 42 standards, including a Class BR57 engine. Here it is seen in Sisak (Croatia).

(Photo: Paul Malmassari Collection)

The rear of PZ 24. In front of the Czechoslovak artillery wagon is S Wagon 150.271 (ex-Austro-Hungarian PZ VII, afterwards Czechoslovak Armoured Train No 2), wagon 140.914 (PZ II, Czechoslovak Armoured Train No 1) and MÁV engine No 377.482.

(Photo: Paul Malmassari Collection)

Class BR57 engine No 2043 was attached to PZ 24 after December 1941. Note the Czechoslovak infantry wagon added in June, on which a 2cm anti-aircraft cannon position has been fitted.

(Photo: Paul Malmassari Collection)

A photo probably taken in August or September 1943, when PZ 25 had been transferred to Italy where it carried out coast-defence missions. The PzKpfw 38(t) tanks have replaced the Somuas.

(Photo: Paul Malmassari Collection)

Created on 1 March 1940 as No 9 from ex-Czechoslovak rolling stock, **PZ 25** was stood down, then reactivated on 10 December 1941 under the number 25. At that point, Eisb.-Panzer.-Triebwagen 15 was attached to it. The train was sent directly to France, at the moment when PZ 21 was sent from France to the Eastern Front. The main armament of PZ 25 consisted of two 7.5cm guns and two Somua S35 tanks, replaced later by PzKpfw 38(t) tanks. From late 1943 up until 1 March 1944, it patrolled

between Albenga and Nice, then from south-west of Nîmes to Montpellier. Following the landings in Provence, PZ 25 went to the Eastern Front where it was destroyed on 13 January 1945 in the region of Kielce.

Armoured trains for the broad gauge

As the start date for 'Barbarossa' approached, the Panzerzug 41 programme had not yet begun, and only the tank-transporter wagons had been designed. It was decided to use fifteen captured Somua tanks to create six armoured trains for the Russian broad gauge, to be numbered from 26 to 31. A lack of appreciation of the partisan menace (to say nothing of the weather, which was even more surprising) led the designers to provide open wagons, while only the cab of the Class BR57 engines was armoured.

PZ 26 was activated on 26 May 1941. It comprised a Class G 10 armoured engine, three Type Omm wagons (wheelbase 6m /19ft

The front of PZ 26, with two Somua tanks leading, a configuration used only on the first three trains. The tank was able to descend from the Type Omm wagon, but the procedure was not straightforward and hazardous when under fire: the safety wagon in front carried the ramp, and it was necessary to uncouple this wagon in order to lower the ramp for the tank.

(Photo: Paul Malmassari Collection)

In early 1942 a Soviet wagon of the 'Krasnoye Sormovo' type was added, and by modifying one of the two turrets it was possible to provide the train with an anti-aircraft defence position.

(Photo: Paul Malmassari Collection)

After the train was rebuilt in 1943, the 2cm Flakvierling was installed on a wagon converted from one of the old infantry wagons (with side armour protection extending below the level of the floor). The overall construction of the train was similar to that of PZ 1 and PZ 23.
(Photo: Paul Malmassari Collection)

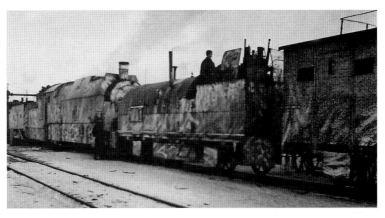

The assault group wagon from PP *Pierwszy Marszałek* has been converted to an anti-aircraft wagon in late 1942. The original Class BR57 engine No 2300 is now completely armoured.
(Photo: Paul Malmassari Collection)

8in; length over the buffers either 10.1m /33ft 1½in or 10.8m/ 5ft 5in) each carrying a Somua, and two safety wagons. In December 1941 it was in the Leningrad area. During the Summer of 1942, certain wagons and the engine were replaced by Soviet units. Shortly afterwards, it was modified to run on the standard-gauge lines that the German engineers were laying down as and when the front advanced, replacing the Russian tracks. Between March 1943 and April 1944 it was in Germany to be modified, then it returned to the Eastern Front where it was deployed in the region of Idritza and Polozk. During the Winter of 1944/45, it saw action in Courland as part of the H. Gr.-Nord. It was captured on 8 May 1945 at Libau in Latvia.

During the Winter of 1941/42, **PZ 27** operated in the region of Briansk and Kursk and was then reconverted to standard gauge.

PZ 27 at Roslavl, in its initial configuration. Here we see one of the reasons for the limited height of the vertical armour protection beside the Somua: while it protected the tracks it also needed to allow access via the side hatch. Note the rail which allowed alignment of the tank on its platform. Also, the Somua tank turret marked with the number of the train has not had its cupola replaced by a hatch.
(Photo: Paul Malmassari Collection)

On 30 May 1942 it was stood down and was not put back in service until 13 July using Soviet rolling stock, then in November 1942 it was converted to BP 42 standard. It was then engaged in the Pripet Marshes region and in March-April 1944 in the region of Brest-Litovsk to the north-west of Kovel. During the breakthrough at the 'Cauldron', it was immobilised by a direct hit to its engine, and several wagons were then destroyed. The remaining vehicles, together with those from PZ 66 took part in a counter-attack. Withdrawn to Warschau-Rembertow for repairs, it was abandoned there.

Commissioned on 1 June 1941 at the Police Barracks in Teschen-West, **PZ 28** entered Russia as part of Army Group Centre and operated with PZ 27 in the region of Terespol. During the Winter of 1941-42, it was in the zone Briansk-Orel-Kursk. In late March 1942, the Type Om infantry wagons were replaced with Soviet armoured wagons with 76.2mm guns. The engine was also ex-Soviet, an armoured Class O[b] or O[a]. Transferred to Army Group South in early 1944, it was at Nikolaiev for repairs then returned to the Warschau-Rembertow centre. It was destroyed in June 1944, during operations in the Carpathians.

Two captured Soviet wagons, the one on the right with the 2cm Flakvierling 38, and on the left, a 2cm Flak 36.
(Photo: Paul Malmassari Collection)

Faced with the threat of Russian tanks, before the anti-tank wagons were built, guns were placed on the leading flat cars: 7.5cm Pak, 3.7cm Pak etc. Here is a 76.2mm Soviet ZIS-3 installed in the Spring of 1944 at the head of PZ 28 in the place of a Somua tank.
(Photo: Paul Malmassari Collection)

PZ 29 was activated on 1 June 1941 and placed under the orders of Army Group Centre in the region of Platorow. It was partially destroyed on 21 December 1941 when it lost three wagons in a ditch dug by partisans. Various demolitions (track, bridges) prevented the recovery of the wagons, and finally the train was broken up, the engine returned to the depot and its remaining wagons were shared between PZ 27 and 28.

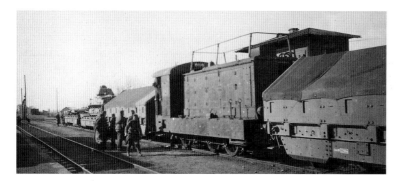

A rare view of the WR 360C diesel locomotive with its frame antenna.
(Photo: Paul Malmassari Collection)

PZ 30 entered Russia with Army Group North and operated in the Eydtkau region with Panzerzug 26. In December 1942, it left the front to be brought up to BP 42 standards, but using captured Soviet wagons. In early 1944 it was in southern Ukraine, then it was forced to retreat to the west of the Nicolaiev-Odessa line. Its engine was replaced by a Soviet Class S engine. In late April 1945, it returned to the Warschau-Rembertow centre for repairs, then participated in the defence of Danzig against the Russians. It was destroyed on 21 March 1945 near Gross-Katz.

Engine BR57 1504 on which the armoured cab is clearly visible.
(Photo: Paul Malmassari Collection)

PZ 30 in its final configuration. The Soviet wagon at the front has received an observation cab, and the Soviet origin of the infantry/command wagon, with its 2cm Flakvierling covered with a tarpaulin, is also evident. The armoured passages between wagons have been added at the same time as the protection for the couplings.
(Photo: Paul Malmassari Collection)

Very few photos of PZ 29 are known. Note that the flanks of the Somua lack protection, but that the infantry wagons have received protection from the weather. Note also the diesel locomotive fourth in line. In the background are a Soviet BP 35 wagon and engine.
(Photo: Paul Malmassari Collection)

PZ 31, the last of the trains specifically built for 'Barbarossa', was activated on 19 May 1941. Initially it was attached to the Sondertruppen, then as with the other trains, it came under the Heerestruppen. It entered Russia in 1941 in support of Army Group South and operated in the region of Zuravicav then Poltava. In early Summer 1942, it was equipped with Soviet vehicles, and soon afterwards was converted to run on the standard gauge. It was destroyed in December 1943 in Russia, but its crew escaped and were transferred to France, where they manned PZ 32.

Profile shot of PZ 31 with its BR57 engine between Soviet vehicles, in which the degree of comfort compared with the open Type Om wagons was certainly appreciated by the crew.

(Photo: Paul Malmassari Collection)

This photo is interesting as shows the conversion of one of the Soviet gun-armed turrets to an anti-aircraft position with a 2cm Flakvierling, the barrels of which have not yet been installed. From later photos it appears the 76.2mm gun was also retained on the mounting. Just visible on the left is one end of the (Russian) infantry wagon.

(Photo: Paul Malmassari Collection)

PZ 32 is probably the most famous of all the German armoured trains. It was immortalised by René Clément in his film *La Bataille du Rail* in which it – quite involuntarily – had the starring role. Its K-, G- and A-Wagen (the latter with 10cm 14/19 guns) were built in the Somua workshops at Lyon Vénissieux, the 0-10-0 engine (050A 33) was armoured in the Schneider workshops in Le Creusot, and the two tank-transporter wagons arrived complete from the Linke-Hofmann factory in Breslau. But as the Pz 38(t) tanks were delayed, they were replaced by two

122mm howitzers on GwLrs (Lorraine Schlepper). Its crew came from PZ 31. PZ 32 had an extremely short career in German hands: at 08.45 on 7 September 1944, as it entered Berain-sur-Dheune Station, the train came into contact with French tank destroyers from the 3rd Squadron of the 9th RCA. At around 11.00

0-10-0 engine 050A 33 of PZ 32 was armoured at Le Creusot. Its overall form followed the style of the engines of the BP 42/44 trains. Note that it was attached to the depot of Alès (Gard).

(Photo: Paul Malmassari Collection)

The A-Wagen of PZ 32 was in fact a Type BP42 G-Wagen, equipped with a 37mm Flak 36 anti-aircraft mounting. This modification reinforced the anti-aircraft defences of the train at a time when the Allies dominated the skies.

(Photo: Paul Malmassari Collection)

The K-Wagen. Note the shortened antenna, probably for the purpose of filming *La Bataille du Rail*.

(Photo: Paul Malmassari Collection)

a shell from a tank destroyer shattered one of the coupling rods of the engine, which was repairable, but at 13.50, a shell hit to the boiler finally immobilised the train. The crew escaped, but did not have time to destroy the train. With the end of the war, PZ 32 embarked on a cinema career which was mysteriously ended by the torches of the scrap merchants.

In January 1942, **PZ 51** was formed using Soviet rolling stock under the name of SSZ *Stettin*. It then became PZ 'A' on 10 May 1942, and finally PZ 51 on 16 June 1942. It operated within Army Group North, where it remained for the whole of the war. In early 1944 it was between Dno and Tchichatchevo, then in the region of Novgorod. In March it conducted operations against the partisans of the Idritza-Polozk region. It was destroyed in combat on 28 August 1944 in the region of Walk in Estonia.

PZ 60 (PZ R) was the training unit for the Rembertow Battalion. It was a Type BP 42 but does not appear in the official listing under that definition. In February 1944, it was in combat in the Lemburg region under the designation 'R'. Then it was engaged in security operations to the west of Tarnopol. Seriously damaged in March 1944 it returned to Warschau-Rembertow for repairs, which were never carried out.

These two views (above and below} show PZ 60, which had all the features of the new Type BP 42 trains. It served as the training unit and was then sent into combat.
(Photos: Paul Malmassari Collection)

PZ 52 was created in June 1944 by reinforcing the Streckenschützzug *Blücher* (seen here at Idriza). After fighting in Russia, it was destroyed near Danzig during the defence of that town in March-April 1945.
(Photo: Paul Malmassari Collection)

The armament of PZ 51 was made up of four 4.5cm KwK(r) guns in turrets from BT-7 tanks complete with coaxial machine guns, plus the turret guns of the PzKpfw 38(t) tanks carried on flat wagons after April 1944. In front of the engine is a Type OO wagon converted into a command wagon, and equipped with a Flak mounting.
(Photo: Paul Malmassari Collection)

The three specialised wagons (A-Wagen, K-Wagen and G-Wagen) were built on Type Omm wagons with 6m (19ft 8¼in) wheelbase, 10.1m (33ft 1½in) long overall, coupled symmetrically in rakes on the BP 42 trains and asymmetrically on the BP 44s.
(Photo: Paul Malmassari Collection)

Created on 1 September 1942, **PZ 61** was the first of the initial series (Nos 61 to 66) of the new Panzerzug BP 42-type trains. It joined its operational area during the counter-offensive towards Velikiye-Liki in late December 1942, and remained in the Velisch-Dorogobouch zone, then in that of Vitebsk, up until the end of 1943. On 22 February 1944 it had to undergo repair, then rejoined the fighting in the Polok-Molodetchno-Wilna zone. On 27 June 1944 it was destroyed in the region of Bobruisk during the Soviet summer offensive.

PZ 61 probably undergoing maintenance, with its tanks not present, the Flak mounting with its side armour panels folded down, and the muzzle-cover on the gun. Note the reinforcement under the sides of the tank-transporter wagon.
(Photo: Paul Malmassari Collection)

PZ 62 was created on 15 August 1942, and it received its official number on 1 September. Sent to the Eastern Front, it joined Army Group South, where it still was in 1944 on the Christinovka-Talnovie line. It next carried out security operations and joined in the counter-attacks launched to the South-East of Stanislav. During the Winter of 1944/45, it joined Army Group 'A' in Poland, where it was destroyed in January 1945.

This type of wagon was a modification of the Type R wagon, which allowed the tank to reverse into a protected well which sheltered its running gear. Extra protection was provided by four plates each side, folded outwards during the entry and exit of the tank. The permanently-fixed ramp required the adoption of mixed coupling types, a classic type at the rear and a Scharfenberg at the front. This arrangement allowed for a safety wagon to be coupled in front of the Panzerträgerwagen.
(Photo: Paul Malmassari Collection)

This photo of PZ 62 allows us to see a normally concealed feature, namely the raised central section of the floor which served to guide the tank into the well, and certainly increased the rigidity of the chassis.
(Photo: Paul Malmassari Collection)

As the tank itself was armoured, the armour of the tank-transporter wagon was very thin (only 10mm as against 30mm for the other wagons), as a crew member demonstrates here, following the impact of a Soviet anti-tank round.
(Photo: Paul Malmassari Collection)

A fine shot of one anti-tank wagon followed by a second, made up of the complete hull of a PzKpfw IV placed on the safety wagon, thus providing a second 7.5cm gun capable of firing over the top of the wagon in front. Note that the casemate of the anti-tank wagon is fitted with additional vertical armour.
(Photo: Paul Malmassari Collection)

PZ 63 was attached to Army Group North immediately on being commissioned, where it stayed until 1944, operating against the partisans on the Pleskau-Luga line. In early 1944 it transferred to the reserve of Army Group South and in April went into action around Lemberg. It was destroyed on 17 July 1944 to the East of Krasne. It was one of the trains most often photographed for propaganda reasons.

The A-Wagen of PZ 63, with its special camouflage scheme. The 2cm Flakvierling mounting is placed quite high, and by folding down the side armour it could engage ground targets.
(Photo: Paul Malmassari Collection)

The armoured tender was provided with hatches over the top of the coal supply. Nevertheless the demand was always greater than the standard quantity carried, as this extra pile of coal shows. On certain trains, the carrying capacity was increased with vertical planking. An identical tender was coupled to the front of the engine.
(Photo: Paul Malmassari Collection)

PZ 64 in Croatia in July 1943, probably at lunchtime judging by the crowd gathered next to the G-Wagen.
(Photo: Paul Malmassari Collection)

PZ 64 was created on 1 October 1942. It became operational on 18 June 1943 and was sent to the southern zone of the Eastern Front. In early 1944 it was required in the Balkans where it fought the partisans in Croatia, and in late 1944 it was sent to Hungary. During the Winter of 1944/45, it was reinforced by the attachment of Panzertriebwagen 19. During fighting in February 1945 one of its PzKpfw 38(t) tanks was destroyed. The train was captured 30km (18 miles) to the north of Graz on 9 May 1945.

Created on 1 November 1942, **PZ 65** immediately went to Croatia where it was placed under the orders of the Security Troops High Command. It ultimately withdrew into Germany where it was captured by the Americans at Hotlthusen.

PZ 66 was the last train of the first order for the Type 42. Sent to the East, it operated on the Minsk-Orscha line, then to the south of Mogilev. In April 1944 it participated in the counter-attack to the North of Kovel, and patrolled in the zone Brest-Barano-Vitchi. During the retreat in the Summer of 1944, it was destroyed near Warsaw on 30 July.

The first train of the second order for BP 42 types, **PZ 67** became operational on 15 March 1943 and was sent to the East. In early 1944 it was in the region of Polozk where it operated as part of the 281st Security Division. On 28 August 1944 it was damaged near Mitau in Courland and the crew sabotaged it. **PZ 68** was formed on 1 August 1943, and by early 1944 it was in the Pripet region where it operated against the partisans. It was destroyed in April 1945 during the battle for Danzig. On 22 March 1944, **PZ 69** was heavily damaged and was finally destroyed by its crew near Tarnopol. **PZ 70** operated from March 1944 in the region of Slobodka-Birsula (Army Group South). On 4 April 1944 its crew found themselves blocked by the destruction of the track in Radelsnaya Station, and they destroyed the train during the Soviet breakthrough. **PZ 71** was created on 16 September 1943 then operated in the region of Tarnopol in January-February 1944. In late April 1944 it was at Lublin for maintenance work, and it was sabotaged at Slanic (Romania) on 31 August 1944.

The case of **PZ 72** was different: created on 23 November 1943, in the Spring of 1944 it was converted into two armoured command trains, Befehls Panzerzug 72a and 72b. The former became part of Army Group Vistula from 2 February 1945 and participated in the defence of East Prussia. It was destroyed during the fighting for Kolberg on 16 March 1945. Befehls Panzerzug 72b was sent to the

This command train carried an unusual form of antenna on its K-Wagen.
(Photo: Frédéric Carbon Collection)

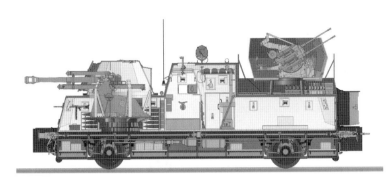

A sectional view (no scale) of an A-Wagen of a Type BP 44 PZ, in a special version where the quadruple Flak mounting was protected by a turret similar to that of the Wirbelwind (Whirlwind) anti-aircraft tank.

(Drawing: Marcel Verhaaf)

Here we see PZ 75 being emptied of its equipment and ammunition, which is being piled on the passage between wagons. The camouflage foliage appears reasonably fresh. One can only regret that practically no elements of any of these captured trains has survived, and that no technical reports – which must have been prepared at the time – have come to light.

(Photo: MHI)

The Panzerjägerwagen is the surest way to identify a Panzerzug BP 44 (and earlier trains brought up to that standard). Designed by the LHW Company, this wagon had a 5m (16ft 4¾in) wheelbase. Sloping armour protected the sides and the axle boxes, while a stoneguard in the shape of a snowplough was fixed to the front end. This wagon could propel itself independently at modest speed thanks to four rollers placed in front of the rail wheels. The coupling system was mixed: standard at the front and Scharfenberg at the rear.

(Photo: Frédéric Carbon Collection)

Warsaw region where it only just escaped being surrounded, only to be destroyed on 28 March 1945 near Danzig.

PZ 73 was created on 19 November 1943, then operated in Italy up until mid-1944, where it was captured intact at the end of the war. Powered by a Class BR93 engine with a different armour arrangement to the rest of the series, it had served as the prototype for the Panzerzug Type BP 44.

The first Type BP 44 train, **PZ 74** went into action on 25 July 1944 while it was still at Rembertow in an unfinished state, and on the 29th it was destroyed in an attack by T-34 tanks.

As with PZ 74, **PZ 75** went into action in an unfinished state, near Warsaw on 15 July 1944 then with Army Group Vistula, as Instructional Train No 5. In this capacity it transferred to the base at Millowitz in October 1944. It returned to operations on 31 December, and was captured intact by American troops at Hagenow.

PZ 76 was created in April 1944 and sent to Poland to join Army Group Centre, where it covered the retreat of the German

The turret from a PzKpfw IV AusF H, armed with a 7.5cm KwK40 L/48 was mounted on a well-shaped casemate, provided with firing and observation ports; in general the turret and casemate would have had additional external armour plates fitted.

(Photo: MHI)

Despite the camouflage, the shape of the 10.5cm turret is clearly visible. Note the two tubular structures which may be limiters to prevent the turret from firing into the tender. This photo seems to have been taken at Millowitz when PZ 76 was being demonstrated.

(Photo: Paul Malmassari Collection)

troops to the north of Warsaw. It was destroyed on 14 April 1945 near Königsberg in Sambie.

Created in May 1944, **PZ 77** was attached to Army Group Vistula and was at Millowitz from February 1945. It was destroyed on 26 February in Pomerania.

PZ 78 was created in late May 1944 and attached to Army Group South. In February 1945 it moved to Hungary where it remained for the most part. On 9 May, after the news of the German surrender, the train made its way to Thalheim where it was abandoned. Its crew succeeded in escaping to the American Zone.

Above: PZ 77 was destroyed in combat on 26 February 1945 at Bubitz. Note the creation of a storage space out of sleepers, on the rear of the anti-tank wagon in the foreground.
(Photo: Paul Malmassari Collection)

Below: PZ 78 captured intact at Thalheim on 9 May 1945. One special feature of this train was the A-Wagen with a turret similar to that on the Wirbelwind AA tanks.
(Photo: RAC-Tank Museum)

Armoured engine BR52 1965 K (Condenser) in Czechoslovakia post-1945. It is not known whether the armour was fitted by the Germans or the Czechoslovaks, and for which of three possible trains.

(Photo: Glöckner Collection)

BR52 K 2021 with partial armour protection. This engine was part of PZ 80. Here it is seen after the war, in the American Occupation Zone, in use by the 740th Railway Operating Battalion.

(Photo: Paul Malmassari Collection)

Railway modellers will know that the firm of Mikrometalkit used the same serial number for their BR52 K armoured engine.

(Photo: Paul Malmassari Collection)

PZ 81 seen after its surrender in Czechoslovakia, at Pisak in 1945. It was powered by BR52 7305. PZ 82 was completed just before the end of the war and included BR52 1965.

(Photo: Tomáš Jakl Collection)

Evidently taken in the Summer of 1945 (it is in the process of being dismantled: note the missing buffers) in this photo of a PzJgWn with an American soldier we see a forward observation position, which precludes the 7.5cm gun from depressing below the horizontal. This could be from PZ 73.
(Photo: Paul Malmassari Collection)

Here this PZ has shared the fate of so many armoured trains on the Eastern Front. Evidently several days have passed since it was destroyed, judging by the fact that the armament has been removed and there is a deal of rust on the overturned K-Wagen.
(Photo: Frédéric Carbon Collection)

Improvised armoured trains

Following the 1940 invasions, then the occupation, of various European countries, 'protected' trains were put into service as for example in Norway with trains *Norwegen*, *Bergen* etc . . .

The Russian Front saw the use of numerous makeshift armoured trains such as the security trains (Streckenschützzug) *Polko*, *Michael*, *Max* etc, and it is difficult to appreciate why they were not considered as 'regulation' armoured trains. Certain ones were later transformed into armoured trains and given a number, as with *Blücher* which became PZ 52, and others which were listed as Panzerzug.

In early 1945, security train '350' operated with Army Group Vistula and in February 1945 was in the Krupp-Drückenmüller workshops for upgrading.

In the final days of the war in Europe, armoured trains were being put together using a variety of materials, such as the trains under construction in the Linke-Hofmann factory in Breslau.

In Greece, security trains Nos 204 to 214 were put into service, but the actions they took part in are poorly documented.

One of the security trains in Norway, with an interesting method of mounting the gun, allowing it to fire at an angle forward, and small openings used as observation/firing slots, also on the following wagon.
(Photo: Paul Malmassari Collection)

A Norwegian 4-6-0 engine, probably a Class 18, hastily armoured. On later photos this engine was also named *Sandhase* ('Sand-hare', German slang for an infantryman).
(Photo: Paul Malmassari Collection)

Bergen, showing its unusually low silhouette compared with other contemporary armoured trains. Note that the two wagons in front of and behind the FlaK wagon are open-topped, despite the climate.
(Photo: Paul Malmassari Collection)

One of the wagons of *Blücher*, converted from a Russian bogie wagon on which a PzKpfw II was encased in wooden protection, no doubt doubled internally with steel plates.
(Photo: Paul Malmassari Collection)

SSZ *Polko*, formed out of captured Soviet rolling stock, including an artillery wagon from BP 1, the engine, a flat wagon equipped with an anti-aircraft mounting and safety wagons.
(Photo: Paul Malmassari Collection)

The front of S.S.Z.350, with its infantry wagon, a Flak wagon (in fact a wagon with sides protected by concrete, leaving firing slots, with a Flakvierling mounting), then a leading wagon carrying the hull of a PzKpfw IV.
(Photo: Wolfgang Sawodny Collection)

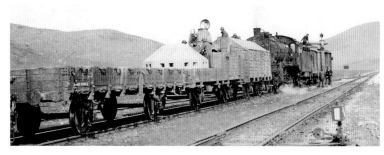

Security train in Greece, with its concrete blockhouse and a Renault FT tank, here armed with a 37mm gun. The engine is a Class Zd, obtained by Greece following the First World War.[10] Another such train was powered by a Class La engine.
(Photo: Paul Malmassari Collection)

On entering Germany, at Ohringen American troops found wagons probably intended for the anti-aircraft defence of train rakes, provided with a concrete tub protecting the gunners. Note the rungs to climb up into the fighting position.
(Photo: All Rights Reserved)

Security train *Leutnant Marx* made up by the 221st Sicherungs Division, which operated in the area of Orel and Livno. In 1942, this train was transferred to the 707th Infantry Division stationed at Rembertow.
(Photo: Paul Malmassari Collection)

10. The Class La and Zd were former Prussian P8 engines.

This wagon (ex-command wagon of PP *Pierwszy Marszałek*, No 3930.88) was the sole armoured element on this train.

(Photo: Paul Malmassari Collection)

Security train in Latvia, formed of several four-wheel wagons with the hulls of BT-5 tanks.

(Photo: Paul Malmassari Collection)

Steyr armoured trolleys

The light armoured reconnaissance trains Panzerzug (le.Sp) 301 to 304 created on 16 September 1943 were sent to the Balkans. No 301 operated in March and April in Serbia in the Ujse-Raska region and was destroyed at the end of the year. No 303 would be captured at the end of the war and No 304 was destroyed. To the best of our knowledge only one of these trolleys survives, in Trieste, being the one used by the British in their zone (see the chapter on Great Britain).

Steyr built the trolleys which would form the heavy reconnaissance armoured trains Eisenbahn-Panzerzug (s.Sp) Nos 201 to 210 on the mechanical base (chassis and motor) of the le.Sp. Train PZ (s.Sp) 201 was created on 5 January 1944 then was sent to the Balkans, where it would be captured at the end of the war. Nos

202, 203 and 204 became operational on 10 January 1944, 21 February 1944 and 23 March 1944 respectively, and were also sent to the Balkans. Nos 205 to 208 were built between April and June 1944. The last two in the series were not completed, at least one of them being captured at Millowitz in April 1945 (see the chapters on Czechoslovakia and Yugoslavia).

These machines are popular with enthusiasts who are passionate about armoured trains, probably because they resemble tanks on rails. In 2013 one was reconstructed by mounting a hull and turret built of plywood on a flat wagon. The turret revolved and could even fire blanks. It was planned to dismantle it in late 2015 to recover the original flat wagon for the railway preservation society collection.

PZ (le.Sp) 304 at Amorion in Greece on 30 August 1944, following its capture by partisans led by V Kassapis, seen here perched on the side of the vehicle.

(Photo: V Kassapis via Georges Handrinos)

A train formed of heavy trolleys being inspected by American soldiers at Dachau in 1945. Note that the coupling hooks have been removed. Although Steyr was responsible for building the hulls, the PzKpfw III turrets were fitted by Kraus Maffei in Munich.

(Photo: Paul Malmassari Collection)

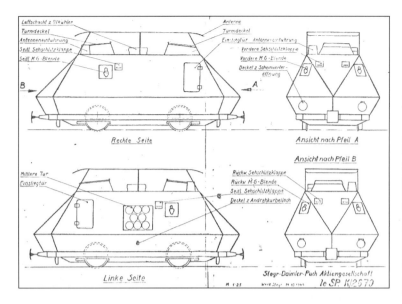

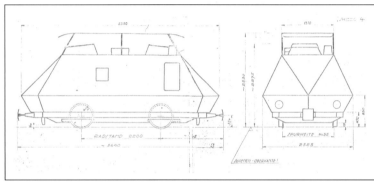

The reproduction s.Sp trolley named *Thor* built by the Levisham Historical Re-enactment Group (North Yorkshire) seen on 11 October 2013.
(Photo: Mark Sissons)

Two original drawings of the le.Sp Steyr trolley. The number 'K/2670' often found in literature is in fact the number of the plan drawing. Note that the form of the armoured air intakes corresponds to the final production model. The same chassis was used as the base for the heavy trolleys, and the difficulty of adapting it to carry the increased weight slightly delayed the production of the s.Sp.
(Drawings: Steyr-Daimler-Puch Archives)

'Eisenbahnpanzertriebwagen' armoured railcars

Eisb.-Pz.-Triebwagen 15, the only railcar put back into service after having been used by the *Reichsbahn*, was sent to France in 1942, then in 1944 to the Larissa region in Greece.

A rare shot from above showing a train of heavy trolleys captured by the Americans in South Germany. Why none of these units has been preserved and that no technical report has come to light (if one was established, which is unsure) remains a mystery.
(Photo: Stuart Jefferson Collection)

TR 15 seen in Greece.
(Photo: Wolfgang Sawodny Collection)

Eisb.-Pz.-Triebwagen 16, activated on 27 January 1944, was the most powerful railcar built for the Wehrmacht, by Schwarzkopf at Berlin-Wildau, on the base of diesel locomotive WR 550 D 14. The armour protection was fitted by Berliner Maschinenbau AG in Wildau. In the Summer of 1944, it was associated with PZ 11 (along with PT 18) and operated in the Ukraine. In July, the train and its two PTs broke out of a Soviet encirclement in the Rawa-Russka region then participated in the defence of Lublin. It retreated towards the River San on 27 and 28 July. On 12 January 1945, it was surrounded during the Soviet offensive, but succeeded in breaking out of the encirclement by a remarkable action on the part of its crew, who constructed a track on which to escape. Today PT 16 is preserved in the State Railway Museum in Warsaw (see the chapter on Poland).

Eisb.-Pz.-Triebwagen 17 to 20 were formed of ex-Soviet MBV D-2 railcars repaired, re-armed and re-engined. PT 17 was activated in April 1943. Remaining on the Eastern Front, it was destroyed in August 1944 near Warsaw. PT 18, 19 and 20 were activated on 20 November 1943 and were sent respectively to Poland, to Army Group Centre, and to the camp at Lissa on the Elbe. All were armed with 7.62cm F.K. 295/1(r) guns. PT 20 was attached to PZ 11 from the Summer of 1944, and was destroyed on 16 January 1945 at Kielce.

After PZ 29 was broken up, its diesel locomotive was used for other tasks, as here hauling ex-Soviet MBV D-2 railcars intended to be put back into service.
(Photo: Paul Malmassari Collection)

In its original form, PT 16 had no turrets, just two antiaircraft positions each with a 2cm Flakvierling mount but no shields. Hitler having found it to be under-armed for its size (200 tonnes, with two layers of side armour each 100mm thick!), the order was given to equip it with artillery turrets armed with 7.62cm F.K. 295/1(r) cannons.
(Photo: Paul Malmassari Collection)

Railcar from the PT 17 to 23 series. Note the frame antenna, the position of the exhaust silencers, and the additional armour added around the base of the turrets. The machine measured 10.30m (33ft 9½in) long on a wheelbase of only 3.90m (12ft 9½in).
(Photo: Paul Malmassari Collection)

An outstanding photograph taken in August 1944, showing probably for the first time PT 16 in its final form with one tank destroyer unit at each end, built around T-34 tank hulls secured on flat wagons. They are armed with one T-34/76 E Model 43 to the right, and T-34/76 Model 42 to the left. Note that the wagon side armour is low above the tracks, while the armour was only protecting the axles some months before. Here PT 16 is seen from the rear left, and the commander's cupola is open above the front compartment.
(Photo: Paul Malmassari collection)

In this photograph taken in August 1944, PT 18 is shown in its final version, namely with an additional armour covering the front half of each turret. Note the unusual camouflage scheme. PT 18 remained in service along with PT 16 until the 1945 fighting in Poland. It received several hits on 13 January 1945 and had to be abandoned in Kielce.
(Photo: Paul Malmassari collection)

Eisb.-Pz.-Triebwagen 30 to 38 were the Italian LiBli Type Aln-56 railcars, one of which had been seized at the Italian Armistice in 1943. Eight of the anti-aircraft version were ordered new from the Italian constructors, making a total of nine LiBli operated by the Wehrmacht. The first three units, TR 30 to 32, were activated on 12 May 1944.

Panzerjägertriebwagen 51, 52 and 53. Built in late 1944, but never put into service, these tank-destroyer railcars were armed with turrets from PzKpfw IV Ausf H or J. One of them was captured and put into storage in an American depot in Augsburg, and the other two were damaged by bombing in the Linke-Hofmann factory in Breslau.

One of the three railcars Nos 30 to 32, probably photographed at Millowitz.

(Photo: Paul Malmassari Collection)

Photographed in Augsburg at the end of the war in Europe were several rail vehicles, including the only complete example (in service?) of the tank destroyer railcar No 51. Note the unprotected buffers and couplings, perhaps intended to be armoured later, as well as the protected left headlight. As was done on all captured pieces of equipment, a white 'ALLIED FORCES' is painted on the side.

(Photo: Paul Malmassari Collection)

Either PT 30 or 31 in Serbia after extensive modification: apart from the installation of a 2cm Flakvierling in place of the roof armament of the Italian version, note the 2cm cannon in the turret and a new arrangement of the buffers.

(Photo: Aleksandar Smiljanic Collection)

This exceptional close-up allows us to note that the two sides were not the same, this side having only one door and the antenna base.

(Photo: Stuart Jefferson Collection)

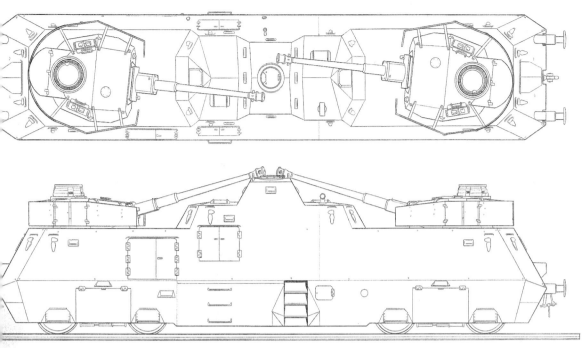
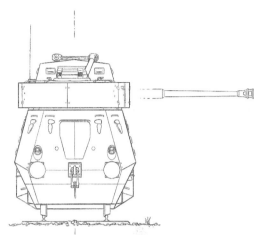

Panhard Panzerspähwagen
Trolley P204(f)

Forty of the 190 Panhard 178
armoured cars captured during the
Battle of France were converted to
trolleys and attached in pairs to
each Type BP armoured train. The
rail wheels were made by two
firms: Gothaer Waggonfabrik and
Bergische Stahlindustrie
(Remscheid). Certain examples
were fitted with buffers.
(Photo: Paul Malmassari Collection)

PzKpfw III SK 1 (1943)

Trials and demonstrations took place in the grounds at Arys[11] in October 1943, with two or three PzKpfw III Ausf L/N of the final series, armed with the 7.5cm KwK L/24. The machine was given the designation of 'SK 1' meaning *Schienenkampfwagen 1*' (Rail Tank No 1). The transmission, motor and cooling system were identical to those of the original tank, the last three torsion bars of the suspension needed modifying. With the added parts under the tank the ground clearance decreased from 48cm (1ft 7in) to 34.2cm (1ft 1½in). The drive on the rails was transmitted via the forward axle, the other being free-rotating. No matter how well the system performed, and the speed and haulage capacities were impressive, by 1943 the PzKpfw III was completely outclassed as a fighting vehicle.

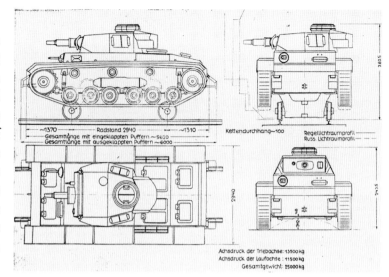

Drawing of the SK 1 tank.

(Saurer Archives)

SK 1 Technical specifications:	
Length (buffers folded):	5.62m (18ft 5⅛in)
Length (buffers extended):	6.00m (19ft 6¼in)
Width:	2.94m (9ft 7¾in)
Height (on road):	2.435m (8ft)
Height (on rails):	2.825m (9ft 3¼in)
Weight:	25 tonnes
Motor type:	12-cylinder Maybach HL 120 TRM
Horsepower:	320hp at 3000rpm
Transmission:	Fichtel & Sachs six-speed gearbox
Speed on rails (maximum):	100km/h (62mph)
Speed on rails (normal):	60km/h (37mph)
Wheelbase on rails:	2.94m (9ft 7¾in)
Gauge (European standard):	1435mm (4ft 8½in)
Gauge (Russian):	1524mm (5ft)
Fuel capacity:	350 litres (92½ Imperial gallons)

'Zepellin' trolley

This machine was built in Finland from Russian components: the doors came from Komsomoletz artillery tractors, the turret from a BA-10, and so on. It was used on the Kemijärvi-Salla-Alakurtti branch, which straddled the frontier with Russia.[12]

The trolley in Salla Station (Finland) which allows a good view of the camouflage scheme and allows an extrapolation onto the horizontal panels. The serial number marked on the hull side is 'WH-E.P. 1' which could indicate it was intended as the first of a series of such builds.

(Photo: Paul Malmassari Collection)

Left: The SK1 could act as a locomotive hauling four loaded wagons. Conceived as a 'rail security vehicle' ('Bahnsicherungsfahrzeug'), its rail power train pivoted on axles fixed in the interior face of the hull sides. Lowering and lifting were hydraulically operated, controlled from a lever beside the driver's seat, either operation taking only a few seconds.

(Photo: PKB)

11. Modern Orzysz in Poland.
12. To the east of this part of the frontier, the tracks torn up by the retreating Germans have never been replaced.

An interesting view showing the trolley being unloaded onto the track from an Sd. AH. 115 road trailer. Note the open access hatches for the crew.
(Photo: Paul Malmassari Collection)

A VT 137[13] railcar in Western Europe on an unknown date, with the glass panels of the cab replaced with armour plates. Note also the armoured window at the side rear. The fact that this particular train is composed of two railcars may indicate a railway gun battery.
(Photo: Paul Malmassari Collection)

The partisan threat: a German 'strike' trolley, unarmoured, captured by Resistance fighters, seen here at Bannalec Station, Brittany, on 7 August 1944.
(Photo: Bannalec City Hall Archives)

Probably a unique example, this SdKfz 223 reconnaissance armoured car has been converted for running on rails. We have no information concerning the date, place or usage. Note the serial number A-22225 (for Anhalt?) and the name *Bärbel*.
(Photo: Paul Malmassari Collection)

[13]. Construction of the 316 machines in the VT 137 series began in 1932 by several firms. On the outbreak of war, they were shared out between the different arms of service. In France, for example, fourteen VT 137 railcars were in use. After the war the surviving examples remained in service in many countries.

SOURCES:

Books:

Anonymous, *50ᵉ Anniversaire de la Libération*, 4 September 1994, brochure published by the town of Saint-Bérain sur Dheune (Panzerzug 32).

Dimitrijevic, Bojan, *German Panzers and Allied Armour in Yugoslavia in World War Two* (Erlangen: Verlag Jochen Vollert – Tankograd Publishing, 2013).

Gawrych, Wojciech J, *Panzertriebwagen Nr.16* (Warsaw: PROGRES Publishing House, 2003).

Gottwaldt, Alfred B, *Deutsche Kriegslokomotiven 1939-1945 (Die Eisenbahn im Zweiten Weltkrieg-2)* (Stuttgart: Franckh'sche Verlagshandlung, 1974).

Lauscher, Stefan, *Die Diesellokomotiven der Wehrmacht* (Freiburg: EK-Verlag GmbH, 1999).

Malmassari, Paul, *Les Trains blindés 1826-1989* (Bayeux: Editions Heimdal, 1989).

Porte, Lieutenant-Colonel Rémy, *La Conquête des colonies alleman-des* (Paris: 14-18 Editions, 2006).

Regenberg, Werner, *Panzerfahrzeuge und Panzereinheiten der Ordnungspolizei 1936-1945* (Wölfersheim-Berstadt: Podzun-Pallas-Verlag, 1999).

Roques, Paul, *Le Contrôle Interallié en Allemagne Septembre 1919 - Janvier 1927* (Paris: Berger-Levrault, 1927).

Sawodny, Wolfgang, *Deutsche Panzerzüge im Zweiten Weltkrieg* (Friedberg: Podzun-Pallas-Verlag GmbH, 1983).

_____, *Panzerzüge im Einsatz auf deutscher Seite 1939-1945* (Friedberg: Podzun-Pallas-Verlag GmbH, 1989).

_____, *Panzerzüge an der Ostfront 1941-1944* (Wölfersheim-Berstadt (RFA): Podzun-Pallas-Verlag, 2000).

_____, *German Armored trains on the Russian Front* (Atglen, PA: Schiffer Publishing Ltd, 2003).

_____, *Die Panzerzüge des Deutschen Reiches 1904-1945* (Freiburg: EK-Verlag GmbH, 2006).

_____, *German Armored Trains 1904-1945* (Atglen, PA: Schiffer Publishing Ltd, 2010).

_____, *Deutsche Panzerzüge* (Eggolsheim (RFA), s.d., Dörfler Zeitgeschichte, nd).

Trojca, Halina and Waldemar, *Panzerzüge Teil 1, (Pociagi pancerne cz.1)* (Warsaw: Militaria, 1995).

Trojca, Waldemar, *Panzerzüge Teil 2* (Zweibrücken: VDM, 2002).

Journal Articles:

Blümner, Oberst a. D., 'Panzerzüge', *Heerestechnik* 1st and 2nd Instalments (1916), pp 18–21.

_____, 'Panzerzüge in und nach dem Weltkriege', *Heerestechnik* (January & February 1925), pp 21–4 and 49–52.

Bolster, Hauptmann, 'Panzerzug und Panzerkraftwagen', *Militär-Wochenblatt* No 143 (1917), pp 3471–5.

'"Deutschland", Panzerzüge', *Schweizerische Zeitschrift für Artillerie und Genie* No 6 (1900), p 224.

'Eisenbahn in Krieg', *Bahn Extra* No2/2002, Special Number.

'Eisenbahnwaggons, gepanzerte', *Leipziger Illustrierte Zeitung* 154 Band (January-June 1920), p 296.

'German Armored Trains of WWII', *Ground Power* No 5 (1999), pp 102–47 (in Japanese).

Kopenhagen, Oberstleutnant Dipl. Journalist Wilfried, 'Panzerzüge-Schienen-Dinosaurien oder moderne Militärtechnik?', *Eisenbahn Jahrbuch* (1977), pp 155–65.

Malmassari, Paul, 'Panzerzug 3 1938-1944', *Batailles et blindés* No 48 (April-May 2012).

_____, 'Draisine SdKfz 231', *TnT* No 14 (July-August 2009).

_____, 'Panzer sur rails', *TnT* No 22 (November-December 2010).

_____, 'Panzerdraisine "Zeppelin"', *TnT* No 40 (November-December 2013).

_____, 'Panzerkampfwagen III SK 1', *World War Two Railway Study Group Bulletin* Vol 16 No 5 (2006), pp 16.131–16.133.

Pesendorfer, F, 'Im Panzerzug in die Sowjetunion', *Die Wehrmacht 5*, No 14 (1941).

Peters, Dr. Jan-Henrik, 'From Kassel via Schöneweide to the Eastern Front – The Class 52 Condensing Locos'(translated by Walter Rothschild), *World War Two Railway Study Group Bulletin* No 16/2 (March/April 2006), pp 16.48–16.58.

Sawodny, Wolfgang, 'Les Dinosaures de la guerre', *La Vie du rail* No 2314 (1991), pp 27–30.

Surlemont, Raymond, and Pied, Robert, 'Forteresses sur rails: les trains blindés allemands de la seconde guerre mondiale', *VMI* (Belgium) No 10 (1986), pp 36–9.

Wagner, Hauptmann a.D. Hans, 'Panzerzüge', *Militär-Wissenschaft und technische Mittellungen* (1929), pp 30–40.

_____, 'Gefechtwagen für neuzeitlische Panzerzüge', *Wehr und Waffen* (1933), pp 299–306, 349–51.

'Zukunftsentwicklung des Panzerzuges, *Militär-Wochenblatt* No 38 (1934), pp 1266–7.

Official Documents:

Dienstanweisung für Panzerzüge, 1910 (War Ministry).

Bulletin de Renseignements No 23, *Trains blindés allemands*, état-major de l'armée, 2ᵉ bureau, March 1945.

Note au sujet de l'emploi des trains blindés par l'Armée Allemande, s.d. (circa 1941, writer and addressees unknown).

University Studies:

Malmassari, Lieutenant-colonel Paul, *Etude comparée des trains blindés européens (1826-2000)*, DEA in Military History, Defence and Security, Université Paul Valéry, Montpellier III, under the academic guidance of Professor Jean-Charles Jauffret, 2004.

GREAT BRITAIN

ARMOURED TRAINS AND ARMOURED TROLLEYS 1859–1957

Britain has systematically deployed armoured trains in virtually all the regions where the interests of the country have been threatened, in the British Isles themselves and in its overseas possessions. Even if the British were not the pioneers of armoured trains, it is they who without doubt have made the most widespread use of them.

William Bridge Adams' Artillery Train

In August 1859 a certain William Bridge Adams, a civil engineer by profession, proposed the construction of a double ring of railway lines around London, 150 miles (240km) in circumference, on which heavy artillery pieces would circulate to defend the capital. To allow this circuit to be usable in times of peace, he planned for the rails to be let into the tarmac of a road surface, after the fashion of a tramway. The lower parts of the artillery wagons were to be protected, where practicable, by a parapet running around the outside of the lines. His plan was not taken up, but thirty years later a line of thirteen defensible positions was built along a stretch of the North Downs, the high ground to the south-east of London, to act as infantry concentration centres and as stores for mobile field guns.

Lieutenant Walker's Armoured Train

After introducing the subject in a letter to *The Times* on 16 July 1860, which he wrote under a pseudonym, in 1865 Lieutenant A Walker took up his idea once more in an article entitled 'Coast Railways and Railway Artillery'. He pointed out that, if an enemy landed on certain parts of the coast devoid of railway lines, they would meet no opposition for up to two days, the time it would take for British troops to march to the area. (He obviously thought little of the capabilities of the cavalry, although it was they who had thwarted the last invasion of the British Isles, in Pembrokeshire.) His proposal was to form a defensive train comprising armoured artillery turrets with two guns each, protected from enemy fire by thick armour on the upper parts and by an earth embankment shielding the lower parts. It seems the turrets were fixed, meaning that the guns would have very limited traverse. It also meant that they would always have to be positioned to fire seawards. Spades lowered on the landward side would absorb recoil. In summary, according to the writer, this type of rampart was advantageous since the trains 'would form a continuous fortress along the coast'.

Mr T Wright's Armoured Train

In August 1864, another civil engineer, Mr T Wright, proposed building trains with three or four artillery batteries, each containing between ten and forty guns and mortars, the whole forming a 'wall' of a large number of artillery pieces extending over a mile (1.5km). Each wagon would be built entirely of iron, containing one or more guns or mortars on a revolving base plate. The drawing clearly shows the method the inventor proposed to prevent the wagons from being overturned by the impact of enemy projectiles as well as to brake the recoil of firing, limiting the sideways displacement of the wagons with an inverted L-shaped guard rail running alongside the track on both sides. In addition, the mortar wagon in Fig. 2, subject to downward-acting forces from its armament, was to be supported by lowering wooden buffer plates onto the guard rail. The mortar would not be fired in the vertical position shown, and

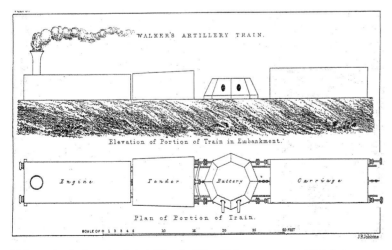

This moving fortress hauled at 30km/h (19mph) by an armoured 0-4-0 steam engine weighing 18 tons, carried on board ammunition for the guns and food for the crew.

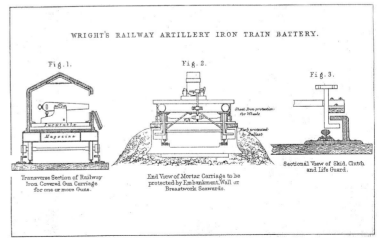

Thomas Wright's armoured train and railway battery (1864), showing a cross-section of the longitudinal guard rail.

it is probably depicted thus to emphasise the downward recoil to be buffered. The running gear was to be protected by vertical plates of sheet iron. From the proportions of the drawings, it is obvious the inventor was thinking of using broad gauge (7ft 0¼in) lines such as introduced by Brunel on the Great Western Railway rather than the much narrower standard gauge (4ft 8½in). Although having a greater load carrying capacity and being far more stable, the use of the broad gauge would have meant the trains would be unable to connect with the majority of the existing railway network.

John Smith's Armoured Battery

In 1871, a certain John Smith proposed and patented an armoured battery with the armour covering a wooden framework. The completely enclosed casemate pivoted on its axis by means of rollers running on a circular rail. The armament was to consist of either an artillery piece or a machine gun, or a mixture of both, and loopholes were to be arranged for rifle fire. As the casemate overhung the rear of its wagon, the design would be limited to a battery in front and possibly a second behind the engine. Mr Smith appears to have made no provision for handling the recoil when firing at 90 degrees to the track. The engine appears to be completely unarmoured. The revolving casemate could either be hauled by the engine, or be articulated to it by a common bogie – a curious arrangement, simple to draw but difficult to build, with perhaps the sole advantage of adding the weight of the front of the engine to stabilise the gun wagon when firing.

The basic problem with all these early coast-defence proposals, and presumably one reason why none were taken up, was the small calibre of gun which could be carried by the railways of the period, and the relatively light armour protection which could be fitted, compared with the increasingly heavy firepower of contemporary

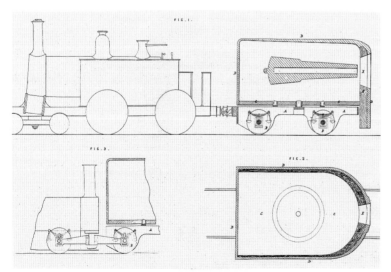

Note that no means of closing the gun embrasure is shown in the drawing, but a device would have had to be included to protect the crew when reloading. The engine depicted in the upper drawing is an early Adams 4-4-0, commonly known as the Metropolitan Tank.

(Plan attached to Patent No 1138)

warships. Despite building extensive fortifications around sensitive points, the British of course relied principally on their all-powerful fleet to deter a landing, or isolate a beachhead.

Armoured Trains in Egypt, 1882

In 1882 Egypt's failure to honour its international debt obligations led the British to intervene in the country, and gave rise to the use of two armoured trains, one at Alexandria and the other on the line from Ismailia to Tel-el-Kebir.

The train at Alexandria, crewed by men from the torpedo boat carrier HMS *Hecla*, in its usual form was made up of the following elements:

– Safety flat wagons.
– Six-wheel gun wagon *Hecla*, armed with a 5in 40pdr Armstrong breech-loader (the stern gun dismounted from HMS *Hecla*), fastened to a wooden platform 4in (10cm) thick. The wagon was protected at the front end only by metal plates 120mm thick, backed by 3ft (1m) of wood and sandbags. The sides and rear of the platform were left exposed.
– Steam engine protected by rails covering the boiler and by a rectangular plate 2ft x 4ft (60cm x 120cm) covering the steam cylinders and the reversing gear. The cab was also protected by armour plates.
– Infantry wagon, to carry fifty men. The protection was provided by removable wooden planks 2in (5cm) thick backed by ⅜in (1cm) of metal plus sandbags.
– Artillery wagon, protected as for the infantry wagon, armed with a Gatling gun at the front with 5000 rounds, and a Nordenfelt cannon at the rear, with 120 rounds.
– Transport wagon, protected as for the two previous wagons, carrying two 9pdr guns intended to be unloaded and used on the ground.

In addition, an observation platform could be raised on a system of ladders to a height of 18ft (6m) above ground level. A second unarmoured train followed a short distance behind in support of the first train.

In its first sortie on 27 July 1882, the train consisted of simply the gun wagon, the engine and the artillery wagon, but wagons continued to be added on each successive sortie, until finally by 5 August it totalled nine armoured wagons. At this point, it was divided into two parts, the armoured train proper retaining only two transport wagons in its rake, and the back-up train bringing along all the support wagons. On operations, the latter train was left behind at Gabarri.

Another armoured train was built by the crew of the armoured corvette HMS *Penelope*. It was first employed on 26 August, when sixteen horses towed it from Ismailia to Nefiche. After minor repairs, it was sent under power to Kassassine on 1 September, where it was unable to fire on the Egyptians for fear of

The engine which propelled *Hecla* was armoured with lengths of rail and iron plates, adequate in view of the limited capabilities of the enemy. The wagon name has been changed to 'HMS INVINCIBLE', apparently written on the photo when the crew was provided from this ship.
(Photo: Paul Malmassari Collection)

These trains made a big impression and the newspapers of many countries reproduced images of them, often with surprising accuracy. Here the artist has added 'HMS' to the name '*Hecla*'.
(Engraving: Paul Malmassari Collection)

hitting the British troops. It was itself hit several times, and its commander was killed, but after withdrawing a considerable distance the train was able to take part in repulsing the enemy. The train was manned by Royal Marines and comprised a flat wagon armoured along the sides with ½in (1.2cm) thick plates 3ft (90cm) high and 6ft (1.80m) long. The armament was a 5in 40pdr firing *en barbette* over the top of the armour. A second wagon, protected by sandbags packed tightly behind wooden sides, carried 230 rounds of ammunition. Its overhead protection consisted of ⅜in (1cm) plates covered by sandbags. When in action, this wagon stayed about 150ft (50m) behind the gun wagon, and its crew brought up the ammunition by hand.

Armoured Train on the Suakin-Berber Railway[1] (1885)

Planned in 1883 as part of the campaign against the Mahdi, in March 1885 the Suakin Berber Railway Corps, commanded by Captain Llewellyn Edge, was formed under the control of the 17th Squadron of the 22nd Engineer Regiment of the British Army, with the aim of building a railway from the Red Sea to Berber on the Nile, in anticipation of continuing efforts to avenge the death of General Charles Gordon, murdered two months earlier in Khartoum, and to reconquer the Sudan. The troops sent to save Gordon had been fatally delayed ascending the Nile Cataracts, and the railway appeared an attractive alternative way to penetrate deep into the Sudan. To defend the tracks against the marauding local tribesmen, an armoured train was formed, armed with a 3.75in 20pdr BL chase gun. During the short life of the railway, the train patrolled the track and guarded the construction and repair parties. Intended to run for 300 miles (480km), the tracks had only reached Otoa, just 15 miles (24km) from the port of Suakin, when the British Government decided to pull out of the Sudan, and the project was cancelled on 22 May 1885. After eleven months spent in Suakin, the final British troops of the garrison were withdrawn, but the railway was not forgotten: Rudyard Kipling mentioned the project in his novel *The Light That Failed*, written in 1890.

Early Armoured Trains in India

In 1885 and 1886 a prototype train with an armoured engine and nine wagons was the subject of experiments at the Exercise Camp, conducted by Captain W F G Moberley, on the metric gauge Rajputana-Malwa line. A 40pdr Armstrong gun weighing 1.7 tons, with a muzzle velocity of 1180ft/sec (360m/sec), was selected for trials, mounted on 13ft (4m) long four-wheel and 25ft (7.6m) long eight-wheel wagons. The results led to the conclusion that it was

The complete train with its artillery wagon in the foreground. Trials showed that it would even be possible to mount a 6in gun with a muzzle velocity of 1770ft/se (540m/sec) on an Indian wide gauge (5ft 6in /1676mm) wagon.

1. R Hill and R H Hill, '*The Suakin Berber Railway*'.

necessary to adapt a well-wagon to carry the gun, and to employ a system of stabilisers to absorb the recoil.

British and Anglo-Indian employees of the railways were required to join a militia force known as the 'Railway Volunteers', from which native Indians were deliberately excluded. The Volunteers attended annual camps where they were given basic military training to prepare them for security duties on the network. They were also called upon to crew the first armoured trains, which carried regular troops of the Indian Army.

Rudyard Kipling observed the firing trials of one of the first armoured trains built in the workshops in Lahore in December 1887. In 1890 he mentioned this train in his novel *The Courting of Dinah Shadd*, when during manoeuvres 'mounted infantry skirmished up to the wheels of an armoured train which carried nothing more deadly than a 25pdr Armstrong, two Nordenfelts, and a few score Volunteers, all cased in three-eighth inch boiler-plate'. By the end of the century the Armstrong guns would be replaced by 12pdr QF guns, the Nordenfelts by .455/.570 Martini-Henry calibre Gardiner machine guns, and finally by .303 Maxims. Some trains also included a second artillery wagon armed with a 6pdr QF gun.

Metre-gauge (3ft 3⅜in) armoured train preserved in the National Railway Museum in New Delhi. The initials 2ND BN. B. B. & C.I. RY. VOLS. along the side stand for the 2nd Battalion, Bombay & Baroda Central India Railway Volunteers.
(Photo: Prakash Tendulkar)

The preserved train, which is identical in layout to the standard type of train used on the Indian Broad Gauge, was built at Ajmer, in the workshops of the Bombay, Baroda and Central India Railway. No engine is coupled to it, but as displayed the train comprises:

- Low-sided bogie wagon (safety wagon) No 8952 of 1886, with cowcatcher, which would carry lengths of rail and tools.
- Bogie van No 9908 of 1890, armed with two Maxim machine guns, plus an armoured searchlight on the roof.
- Four-wheel van for the electricity generator set and its petrol tank.
- Bogie well-wagon for a 12pdr gun.
- Bogie van No 9919 of 1890, identical to No 9908, with two Maxims and a searchlight.
- Low-sided bogie wagon No 8956, identical to wagon No 8952.

The armour was formed of a 3in (76mm) layer of felt (for insulation) sandwiched between two steel plates ½in (12.7mm) and ¾in (20mm) thick.

In addition, the trains would also comprise an infantry wagon carrying ammunition, food and other supplies, with loopholes for rifles. Communication between the parts of the train was by telephone, and flags were used for co-ordinating movements with supporting infantry units. The train commander could remain in contact with the railway divisional headquarters, assuming the trackside telegraph wires had not been cut, by making a connection to the line with the aid of a long pole. The armoured trains were limited to a speed of 15mph (24km/h), the maximum allowed when an engine was propelling rolling stock.

The trains normally mustered one or two unarmoured civilian coaches to carry the troops, offering more comfort and especially a cooler environment than the confines of the armoured wagons. When action was imminent, these coaches would be parked in a siding at a nearby station. Mirroring the good practice introduced in other armies, which were beginning to operate armoured trains in pairs, when going into action the artillery wagon and wagons behind it could be detached and left some distance from the combat zone, with the engine propelling the machine-gun and infantry wagons forward, leaving the 12pdr gun to give fire support.

During annual exercises, and even when in action, the armoured trains provided an essential support function. They would include in the rake a dining car, specifically to provide tiffin to the officers. At lunchtime, having ensured that the troops were well-provided with sandwiches and curry puffs, the officers would converge on the dining car.

In British India armoured trains continued in widespread use, both for internal security and to guard the volatile North-West Frontier with Afghanistan, where the threat of Russian incursion occupied the Raj for many years. The North-Western Railway Volunteer Rifles, which later became the North-Western Railway Regiment, was responsible for protecting some 7000 miles (11,200km) of track. Its 1st Battalion kept an armoured train at Lahore, and the 2nd Battalion one at Karachi. An artillery practice range was built at Moghalpura for sub-calibre firing training, using .22 calibre rifles clamped to the 12pdr gun barrels on a 25-yard (23m) range.

William Smith's Armoured Battery (1887)

Having proposed a design of wagon chassis for the transport of heavy loads, including large artillery pieces, in 1887 William Smith proposed an imposing armoured wagon which was one and a half times wider than contemporary rolling stock. This huge wagon carried a naval gun in the centre and a fixed turret at each end armed with QF guns.

Jumping ahead several years to 1906 we once more find an armoured train used in exercises on Whale Island, the oldest coastal training ground for the Royal Navy.

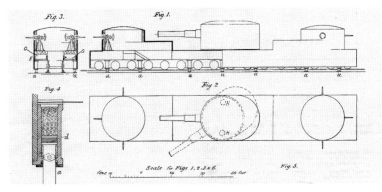

The plan attached to the patent shows the central turret supplied with ammunition on small wagons running inside the chassis. The presence of hydraulic jacks to stabilise the vehicle brings this design close to that of heavy railway guns.
(Drawing: Patent No 11,207)

Armoured trains became a standard part of the British military establishment. Here, the engraving shows a simulated attack by an armoured train during the Royal Tournament of 1887, a major military tattoo and pageant which had taken place each year since 1881 in the Royal Agricultural Hall in London. The Tournament was used to show off the military capabilities of the British Army to the general public.
(Engraving: Illustrated London News)

An exercise involving sailors dismounted from a (dummy) armoured train to repel an enemy landing party.
(Photo: Paul Malmassari Collection)

Richard Richardson Hutchinson's Armoured Train (1888)

This train was to have been formed of 'forts' with roofs shaped like the shell of a tortoise, armed with light guns and surmounted by observation turrets or revolving searchlights. Electricity for the latter was to be provided by dynamos, and a compressed-air system would provide ventilation. One major innovation introduced by this project was that the motive power would not come from coal, but by burning petroleum or 'hydro-carbon', with the fuel divided up between the various wagons and conveyed to the locomotive by means of armoured piping forming part of the coupling system.

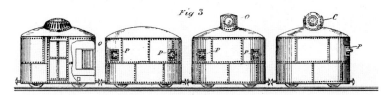

Plan attached to Patent No 6520.

The Brighton Casemate Wagon (1890–1900)

In 1891, at the instigation of Captain F G Stone of the 1st Sussex Artillery Volunteers, an armoured train was built for the defence of the Sussex coast, armed with a 40pdr Armstrong gun. The design of the cannon wagon, conceived by a Mr Billinton, closely resembled the 16cm cannon wagons of Dupuy de Lôme's armoured train, the gun being fixed to an armoured revolving platform (see the chapter on France). A pair of inclined chocks up which the wheels of the gun ran absorbed part of the recoil, the rest being damped by a centrally-mounted recoil cylinder as fitted on the fortress mountings used with this gun. A system of screw jacks stabilised the wagon during firing.

The gun crew travelled in one of the two armoured coaches, the other being reserved for the harness which would allow the gun to be moved when dismounted from the train. An armoured roof protected the troops, who were provided with low loopholes for

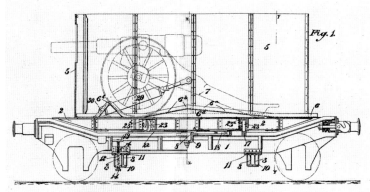

This plan attached to Patent No 2982 granted on 2 February 1895 differs only very slightly from the wagon as actually constructed, shown in the following photo.

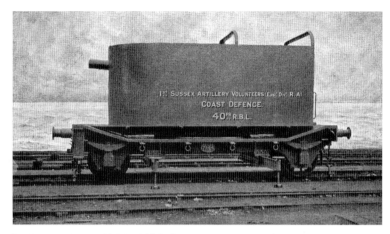

Put into service on 19 May 1894 after a short trial period, this train was normally made up of a 0-6-0 or 0-4-4 engine, followed by the artillery wagon and two armoured coaches. Note that no loopholes were installed in the armoured sides of the artillery wagon.

(Photo: Illustrated London News, No 2877, 9 June 1894, p 723)

The armoured train took part in many public demonstrations and accompanied the Volunteers on manœuvres. It was even mobilised for action in July 1898, during a French invasion scare at the time of the Fashoda Incident. It was dismantled in 1900, its armament being quite outmoded by that time. The good results obtained with the train would certainly have had an influence on subsequent developments of the same type.

(Photo: Illustrated London News, No 2877, 9 June 1894, p 723)

firing their artillery carbines from the prone position. The carriage walls were reinforced internally. The designer intended that a number of such mobile coast-defence batteries could continually be on the move to evade return fire.

Mr Billinton's Project (1894)

The designer of the successful Brighton prototype proposed two schemes for much heavier artillery vehicles, with two turrets mounted either on the same wagon, or on two wagons running on parallel tracks. Neither scheme progressed beyond the granting of the patent.

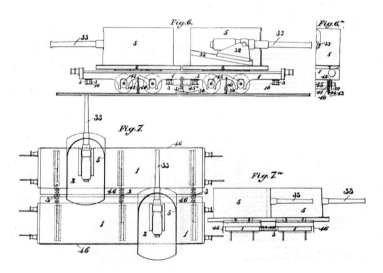

Plan attached to Patent No 2982. The inventor does not seem to have taken into account the destabilising effect of having the 6in guns recoil backwards and upwards on the Vavasseur mountings, when fired to one side. Compared with his earlier workable gun wagon, here the stabiliser pads rest on the rails, and the wagon is rigidly clamped to the same. The recoil from firing such large guns would have quickly destroyed the track. Again, presumably for added strength, the wagons are shown as rigid-wheelbase eight-wheelers, a definite anachronism by that time.

The Simms Armoured Trolley (1899)

This machine was designed by Mr F R Simms for Vickers and Sons and Maxim Ltd. in 1899. Intended for reconnaissance and as an auxiliary to armoured trains, the employment of twenty-five such trolleys on a stretch of track would cover a zone of action of some 20 miles (over 30km). The inventor considered that just 100 crewmen could do the work of the two or three regiments normally considered necessary to control 500 miles (800km) of track. This economy in trained manpower was also one of the sales ploys of Hiram Maxim when promoting his machine gun to colonial powers. The hull was made of laminated steel, mounted on spiral springs. The steel axles ran in ball bearings instead of the usual plain railway bearings. The 7hp Simms motor was water-cooled, and equipped with a Simms-Bosch magneto which was used to boost maximum speed in each gear. The Panhard gearbox had three speeds in forward and reverse, and final drive was by

The armament of the Simms Trolley was to consist of a .303 calibre Maxim machine gun, with 40,000 rounds. The weapon being demonstrated by Mr Simms is an air-cooled Light Maxim, and not the standard water-cooled version in contemporary use. A 1pdr Maxim pom-pom and a searchlight could also be mounted, although neither appears in any photo. The lower armour plates protecting the drive components were fixed by bolts passing through rubber blocks, to reduce vibration and noise levels. Weighing 1.422 tonnes, the trolley measured 6ft 8in (2.03m) long by 5ft 6in (1.68m) wide and 4ft (1.22m) high. The machinery was mounted at least 2ft (60cm) from ground level and was protected by a solid metal belt which greatly reduced the machine's vulnerability.
(Photo: The Autocar)

chain. One man alone was required to drive the machine, and a double system of foot and hand brakes could bring it to a halt in just 10ft (3m). In trails the maximum speed obtained in the gears at 1200 revolutions was 1st: 8mph (13km/h); 2nd: 15½mph (25km/h); 3rd: 23½mph (38km/h), with a short sprint up to 30mph (48km/h) in top gear using the magneto to boost the motor to 2000 revs. The trolley could normally carry sufficient fuel for 200 miles (320km). Three out of the crew of four men could find space to sleep in the vehicle, protected by a removable canvas roof. It seems that at least one trolley was sent to Nairobi in 1900 for operational employment.

The Boer War (1899–1902)

The incident when Winston Churchill, as a war correspondent, was involved in the ambush of an armoured train did a great disservice to the reputation of this weapon system in many countries. It was during the Boer War, however, that a formal doctrine for the use of armoured trains was first laid down, despite the fact that most military minds of the period remained wedded to the idea of the railway as a simple aid to mobility rather than as a weapon. South Africa was comparable to Russia in view of the great distances to be covered in a country lacking roads and tracks, and with a total dependence on rail transport. For his part the Boer was an intrepid horseman capable of long journeys, who in the darkest hours of

that war would sabotage the tracks and find refuge in the bush, or blow up the trains and pillage them for his essentials. Although built to a standard 3ft 6in (1067mm) gauge, the railway network in South Africa was far from continuous: a gap of some 500 miles (750km) existed between the Cape and Natal Province, blocking the movement of troops by rail, who had perforce to travel by road.

Thirteen armoured trains were in service before the war: five in Natal, five in Cape Province and three in Rhodesia. In Natal, the initial composition of each train was three armoured wagons with a steam engine (apart from one train which had only two wagons). The wagons were protected by plates 6ft (1.83m) high, giving a

An interesting view showing a detail often hidden by the camera angle: the communicating door at the end of the wagon. Note also the overhead protection from hastily-added roof plates held on with cables. These wagons were simple containers lacking any comfort, difficult of access and especially of egress.
(Photo: HGM)

The famous 'Hairy Mary' being fitted by sailors with her additional rope protection over the existing armour plates.
(Photo: The King, 17 February 1900)

total height above the rail level of 8ft 10¼in (2.7m), completely encasing a platform wagon 38ft 4½in (11.7m) long, and pierced by two rows of loopholes allowing for firing standing and kneeling. The wagons had inter-communicating doors. Each of the two trains in Durban were armed with a 3pdr QF gun, while for all the others, the armament consisted of the individual arms of the crew.

Haulage of the Natal armoured trains was provided by 4-8-2 engines with complete armour protection of 10mm thick plates, and they possessed an adequate reserve of power. One famous engine was No 48, christened 'Hairy Mary' which operated over the northern Natal railway network. Built in August 1888, 'she' was covered by a layer of ships' ropes providing a certain degree of resistance to Boer fire. Despite the ropes appearing flexible, this was deceptive, as on at least one occasion the excessive tension of the cables led to the tender derailing on a curve.

In Cape Province, four of the five trains dated from 1899. They were composed of an engine and two armoured wagons pierced by loopholes for individual arms, and each wagon carried three Maxim machine guns firing end-on and to the flanks. The poor disposition of the Maxims meant that unfortunately some 75 per cent of the ground surrounding the train was not covered.

Four trains were deployed as follows: two at Kimberley, one supporting the advance of Lieutenant-General Methuen towards that town, and one at Stromberg under the orders of Lieutenant-General Gatacre. One of the trains at Kimberley was destroyed by the Boers on the very first night of the war, and from the start the remaining trains were fully employed, within the limits of their inadequate capacity to engage the Boer artillery, as no artillery was mounted in the wagons. The trains were therefore reduced to the defensive role of mobile fortresses. The fifth train was put together at Mafeking to take part in the siege, and the gun it carried caused heavy Boer casualties.

One of the many armoured wagons built for inclusion in armoured trains, here with H. M. A. T. *Wasp.*

(Photo: Paul Malmassari Collection)

After the capture of a train between Vryburg and Mafeking, their employment was temporarily suspended. Their return to combat was due to Lord Methuen's requirement that they control the railway to the north of Kimberley while he carried out the conquest of the south bank of the Vaal at Fourteen Stream. The trains were then engaged once more to counter the tactics of the Boer General De Wet, who aimed at systematically destroying the tracks in the region of Kroonstadt followed by those of the whole network. The trains were given the secondary role of covering the construction trains despatched to repair sections of destroyed track. A construction train would be based at every one station in three. Armoured Train No 1 undertook over sixty missions of this nature.

The first attempts to arm the trains with effective artillery only began a year after the start of the war. In September 1900 the naval authorities of Simonstown mounted four 12pdr QF guns on two wagons. These were stationed at Pretoria, and then were attached to Armoured Train No 1. Just a few days later, the two hard-fought engagements against De Wet's troops on the Wolwehook-Heilbron line proved the worth of these artillery wagons. According to availability, the armoured trains then all received either a QF gun or a Maxim pom-pom.

Organisation of the armoured trains

In 1900, the number of trains reached their maximum of twenty, and Lord Kitchener, the new C-in-C, set in hand a reorganisation, leading to a more centralised command structure but with greater flexibility in the way they were employed. One of his staff officers was appointed to supervise the armament and equipment of the trains, and the recruitment of their crews. Through his rapid appreciation of reports from the field he could, on his own initiative, organise the despatch and movements of the trains. On the other hand, the sheer size of the Cape rail network required the appointment of two deputies, one for the southern part (Captain F G Fuller) and the other for the north (Lieutenant H O Mance), the Orange River forming the boundary between the two zones. Both came under the command of Captain H C Nanton, responsible for the armoured trains, and of Major Girouard, Railway Director. In addition, Captain R S Walker was responsible for the operation of the searchlight equipment. Three engine supervisors were also designated to supervise the maintenance and the general state of the locomotive stock.

The armoured trains were numbered from 1 to 20, and some bore names, although it is not always possible to correctly make the connection between a specific name and a train number. All carried the prefix 'H.M.A.T.' which derived from naval parlance, and signified 'Her Majesty's (and after the death of Queen Victoria in January 1901, 'His Majesty's') Armoured Train'.

The crews were made up of artillery detachments, engineers (one NCO, six railway sappers, three signallers, two firemen and two engine drivers), and infantry (each train always carried men drawn from one regiment). Each train was controlled by two officers: the train commander in the leading wagon and his deputy in the artillery wagon.

The rolling stock
ENGINES
Class 03 4-4-0 types at the beginning of the war, the Cape Railway engines were later replaced by Cape Government Railways 4-6-0 engines and Dutch Railways 0-6-4 engines, both types being much more powerful and capable of carrying and hauling additional armour protection. At first the armour only protected the cab, but as the war progressed and casualties mounted, the whole engine finished by being protected. On tender engines the gap between the cab and tender was protected by a curved overhead plate, and many engines on normal trains received armour protection which reached halfway up the cab sides and helped protect the crews. A code based on a series of whistle blasts signalled the need to brake in an emergency.

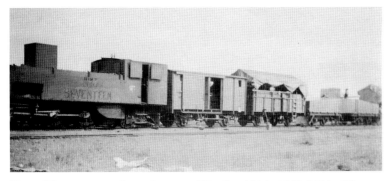

The well-known H.M.A.T. *Sweet Seventeen* ('Her Royal Majesty's Train' No 17), hauled by a Dutch South African Railways Class B 0-6-4 engine.
(Photo: Paul Malmassari Collection)

INFANTRY WAGONS
Often referred to as 'Maxim Wagons' because of their main armament, they were always positioned at the ends of the train, the leading vehicle being the command wagon. In general the space between the roof and the side armour was seldom used for firing, for fear of being hit by friendly fire from the unengaged side of the train. The preferred stance was firing from a kneeling position

Armoured Train No 13, with its 'Maxim Wagon' carrying two roof-mounted searchlights, followed by the artillery wagon.
(Photo: Paul Malmassari Collection)

through loopholes 3ft (1m) above floor level, spaced every 2ft (60cm) at the ends and every 5ft (1.5m) in the centre of the sides. Corner firing slits were provided for the Maxim machine guns, which were fitted with a shield. The machine gun compartment was separated from the infantry compartment by a wall pierced by a door 16in (40cm) wide.

Six special wagons were built under the direction of Captain Fuller. Their roof was formed of 10mm plates inclined at an angle. From his individual compartment, the train commander could operate the braking system without leaving the protection of his additional armour plating. Lastly, sliding doors were installed at each end, enabling easy circulation between wagons. For his part, Lieutenant Mance built wagons with armour protection using lengths of rail. These were placed one above the other on the wagon sides, reaching up 5ft (1.5m) above floor level and held in position by vertical strakes. At 4ft (1.2m) from the floor a rail was left out, to allow observation and firing. The wagon ends were built up with wooden sleepers on which rail lengths were fastened. These wagons were employed in the armoured trains and also as escort wagons in civilian rakes.

The header wagon of H.M.A.T No 18 *Coldstreamer*, with its upper armour protection formed of rails welded together.
(Photo: Army & Navy Illustrated, 6 September 1902)

ESCORT TRUCK

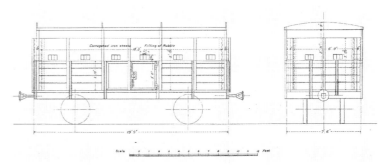

Drawing corresponding to the wagon in the previous photo.
(Drawing: Royal Engineers' Report)

The armour removed from the Fowler road trains is clearly visible on this wagon of H. M. A. T. No 2 *Disturber*.

(Photo: RAC Tank Museum)

The internal protection of these wagons was composed of a space filled with crushed stones. Note the armband worn on the left sleeve, signifying that the wearer is in mourning.

(Photo: Paul Malmassari Collection)

An overall view of an armoured train built at Kimberley. Note its symmetrical composition.

(Photo: Paul Malmassari Collection)

We must also mention the armour obtained by dismantling the Fowler road trains. These had been sent to South Africa following apparently satisfactory trials on the road between Leeds and Pontefract in England. Deemed too heavy for their intended role, their armour protection was removed and mounted on bogie wagons, finishing their armoured train career on rails, notably with Armoured Train No 2.

An examination of photos reveals a final form of armoured wagon, quite modern in appearance but dating from the early stages of the war, as the type was used at the siege of Kimberley. The overall armour protection covering the wagon is in fact pierced by loopholes closed by sliding shutters. A long gap just below roof level allows for firing and particularly all-round observation.

ARTILLERY WAGONS

12pdr, 6pdr and 3pdr QF guns were the armament used most often. In the course of the war 6in and 9.2in (152mm and 230mm) guns were added according to operational requirements. Although properly speaking not 'armoured wagons', these latter guns were attached to the armoured trains, mounted on lengthened tender chassis or on specially-designed platform wagons. Stability when firing was guaranteed by extending support arms fitted with screw jacks. One of the 6in guns was attached to Armoured Train No 2 and in action its experienced gunners vindicated the theories put forward by Captain Girouard.

Fifteen 12pdr guns were mounted on armoured wagons during the war. The first four were mounted diagonally on two bogie wagons, bolted down onto 6ft (1.8m) square steel plates to spread the shock of firing. Built at Simonstown, this type of wagon was certainly comfortable and was theoretically very efficient. However, the disposition of the armament did not allow both guns to be fired at the same time, as during an ambush the Boers logically took up position all on the same side of the track (so as not to fire into one

Artillery wagon named 'Bobs' (probably after Lord Roberts), armed with a 6in gun mounted on a lengthened tender chassis.

(Photo: Paul Malmassari Collection)

another). Thus this armament arrangement was abandoned in favour of a central mounting for the remaining eleven guns. The revised arrangement consisted of positioning the 12pdr on a naval or land Mark II mounting in the centre of a bogie platform wagon, surrounded by armour plates 3ft (90cm) high in the centre sloping down to 2ft (60cm) high at the wagon ends. The gun itself had a shield, the top of which was 9ft (2.75m) from the wagon floor. Each ammunition locker contained 100 rounds. In this revised version, the crew consisted of one officer and five gunners.

SPECIALISED ROLLING STOCK

A certain number of armoured escort wagons were also built to accompany civilian trains. The Pretoria workshops built one prototype which was followed by a series of eighty-four wagons, on which the armour protection consisted of two thicknesses of steel plate pierced by firing loopholes. This type of wagon was used in the Transvaal in particular. North of the Orange River, the wagons were instead armoured with lengths of rail. Lastly, the Imperial Railways workshops in Pretoria built passenger carriages on which the upper section of armour plating could be inclined at a 45-degree angle to protect against overhead fire (when, for example, passing through a ravine or a cutting), and they were pierced by loopholes allowing the crew to fire back at up to 45 degrees elevation. The brake vans were also armoured, in view of their essential security function.

The left-hand side of a 12pdr gun wagon, showing the four steel doors fitted only on this side, which give access to the ammunition lockers. The gunners are carrying out maintenance, and the lockers with wooden doors at each end of the wagon contain tools, oil and grease and cleaning materials.
(Photo: Paul Malmassari Collection)

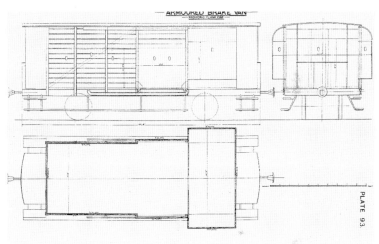

Drawing of a brake van included in the Royal Engineers' report on armoured trains in South Africa.

H. M. A. T. No 3 Cock O' The North shows another form of armoured gun wagon, with a pom-pom in the central position.
(Photo: IWM)

Right: A training ground was created on Fox Hills in Aldershot Camp in England specifically to prepare the troops for deployment to South Africa. One feature involved firing practice at moving targets fixed to an 'armoured train' running on a narrow-gauge track.
(Revue Universelle, No 66, 15 July 1902, in the Paul Malmassari Collection)

This huge 9.2in gun from the coast defences of the Cape was mounted on a railway truck in August 1900 in order to participate in the fighting at Belfast (to the north-east of Johannesburg). However, as the battle was over by 27 August, the gun never saw action.
(Photo: S.A.R.)

Representations and illustrations of armoured trains of the Boer War

The conflict aroused a wide range of international sympathy for the 'underdog' Boers: brand-new Krag rifles were smuggled to them from a consignment ordered by the Norwegian Army, and a host of international volunteers flocked to fight on the Boer side from many countries in Europe and the Americas. The armoured train in particular became an iconic symbol of this struggle.

The Boer War remains the first conflict in which armoured trains were systematically employed, despite early setbacks. British engineers and military men would draw inspiration from this war in order to conceive the First World War armoured trains *Norma* and *Alice*.

A typical scene favoured by the French press, showing the destruction of a British armoured train. Here the wagons are simplified – even the engine seems to be copied from a British tramway engine – and the armour protection has been emphasised to glorify the (very real) courage of the Boers.

(Illustration: Le Pélerin No 1289, 1901, in the Paul Malmassari Collection)

The characteristic shape of the 4-4-0 engines, and especially the curved armour over the top of the cab, used in the siege of Kimberley in 1899 made a lasting impression.

(Photo: Paul Malmassari Collection)

This engraving was made in a similar vein, and accentuates the sinister aspect of the wagons. Sadly, Boer women and children were the unintended victims of the first concentration camps, instituted by the British to starve the Boer commandos of their popular support in the countryside.

(Engraving: Paul Malmassari Collection)

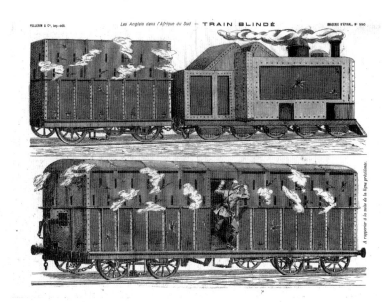

A magnificent Epinal image representing the first British armoured trains in South Africa. In the original colour print the officer wears the typical scarlet jacket, long since replaced by the more discreet khaki. The shape of the engine would inspire many later illustrations, even down to the post-Second World War period. On the other hand, the armoured roof and the chase gun were developments which would appear later in the Boer War. It has to be said that the engine bears more than a passing resemblance to the Märklin version shown opposite.

(Image: Pellerin & Co, in the Paul Malmassari Collection)

Caricature does not spare its own camp: a drawing by Harry Furniss evokes the difficult ordeal of Question Time in Parliament, where the Government passes through the House of Commons inside the wagons of an armoured train!

(Illustration: The King, 17 February 1900, in the Paul Malmassari Collection)

The toy industry often reflects the preoccupations or the key references of a particular epoch. Here is the engine of the famous O-Gauge armoured train produced by Märklin under reference No K 1020 in 1900.
(Model: Private Collection)

More basic but still immediately recognisable is the pull-along toy armoured train produced by Pinard in 1915, with its typical cab profile.
(Toy: Paul Malmassari Collection)

Armoured Trains in Uganda (1905)

In 1905, the decade-long resistance of the Nandi tribe in Kenya led to attacks on Europeans. At the same time they intensified their raids on the railway. The Ugandan Railways put in hand the construction of two armoured trains for internal security, and to protect their vital connection to the coast. However, before the trains could come into service, the death of the Nandi leader Arap Samoei at the hands of Colonel Richard Meinertzhagen on 19 October 1905 brought the revolt to an end.

The Armoured Garratt (1911)

In August 1911 the famous engineer Herbert William Garratt registered a patent for an armoured steam engine. Well-known for his articulated engines which operated throughout the world, he proposed a machine fully protected by armour, and carrying armament at both ends, where space was available thanks to the siting of the boiler in the centre. The inventor also suggested that additional armour could be fitted as and when required. The military version of his design did require certain modifications, such as the provision of a water tank under the central part of the engine, due to the armament taking up part of the space normally

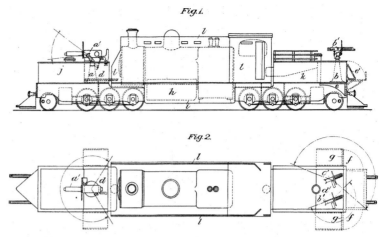

The diagram included in Patent No 19.338, showing the pom-pom at one end and two Vickers machine guns at the other. The firing platforms could be lowered to the horizontal to facilitate the gunners' training through wider angles of fire. If the armour plates were hinged downwards they could provide protection for the wheels, cylinders and motion gear.

used for feed water. Although his proposal would have resulted in an extremely powerful armoured railcar, it was an expensive solution and wasteful of the haulage potential of the engine. In any case, the engine of an armoured train was too valuable to risk at the head of a train.

The First World War in Europe, 1914–1918

The initial use of armoured trains by the British Army in the First World War was in Europe, and in fact the trains were Anglo-Belgian, as much from the composition of their crews as by the arrangement of their artillery wagons (see the chapter on Belgium). Their zone of operations, between Liège and Antwerp, was particularly vital for the Allies who relied on resupply by sea. The primary role of the Light and Heavy Armoured Trains was the protection of the railway network.

The name on this train leaves little doubt as to its nationality, even though one of the soldiers sitting on the gun barrel appears to be French or Belgian.
(Photo: Paul Malmassari Collection)

The British troops sent by Winston Churchill, then First Lord of the Admiralty, mounted available naval 4.7in and 6in guns on bogie wagons, protected by 3ft 3in (1m) high armour plates surrounding the centrally-mounted gun, although at least one gun was used initially without armour. Despite their designation as 'armoured trains', in actual fact the two trains in use prior to the evacuation of Antwerp were essentially used as mobile artillery.

Three armoured engines took part in the battle of Loos in 1916, as it was noticed that the glow from the firebox of unarmoured engines prevented any discreet approach near to the front lines. The armour plates around the cabs hid the glow from the firebox, even if the armoured cab was less comfortable for the crew. Immediately after the battle, the armour was removed and all three engines returned to normal use on the Hazebrook-Ypres line.

A Manning Wardle Armoured Petrol Mechanical Tractor in France. Some ten examples were built, initially to haul railguns into position.
(Photo: Paul Malmassari Collection)

More discreet than the steam engines, which allowed them to serve immediately behind the front line, the Simplex Tractors which the Motor Rail and Tram Company Ltd began to produce in 1916 were based on the original Simplex weighing 6 tons: a 'protected' version for the 60cm gauge tracks, an 'armoured' version and a 'protected' version for the Standard Gauge, weighing 8 tons. Several other makes of tractor were also used, in armoured or protected versions.

Armoured Trains *Norma* and *Alice*

Studies undertaken prior to the First World War, and based on experience in the Boer War, enabled the British Army and the railway companies to rapidly produce armoured trains for defending the British coastline. Their designs benefited from the fact that the British track gauge of 4ft 8½in permitted the carriage of a greater load than the South African 3ft 6in gauge.

Armoured Train No 1:
– artillery wagon.
– infantry wagon (No 53996).
– armoured engine (No 1587).
– infantry wagon (No 53986).
– artillery wagon.

Armoured Train No 2:
– artillery wagon.
– infantry wagon (No 53994).
– armoured engine (No 1590).
– auxiliary tender.
– infantry wagon (No 53981).
– artillery wagon.

The artillery wagons were 30-ton bogie wagons with a 12pdr gun mounted at one end immediately above the end bogie pivot. The gun shield, open at the rear, bore a striking resemblance to those used on the Belgian armoured trains. Armour protected the entire wagon, and there were four entrances, one behind the gun mounting, one on each side, and a fourth giving access to the infantry wagon. A number of loopholes placed at a height of 3ft 3in (1m) allowed for small-arms fire. Lastly, the ammunition compartment was placed in the centre of the wagon.

The two engines used were Class N1 0-6-2 tank engines, built in 1912 and therefore quite modern. Compared with their civilian configuration, their coal capacity was reduced to permit an increase in their water capacity to 1850 gallons ($7m^3$) compared to 3 tons of coal. In addition, a stock of one ton of coal was carried in one of the infantry wagons and four 200-gallon water tanks were slung beneath its frame. 15mm armour protected the whole engine including the moving parts.

On the train itself, the armour protection extended down to cover the wheels and chassis plus the couplings. The transmission of orders between the wagons was effected by speaking tubes as on board ship. One of their special features was the ability for the train to be driven from either end, for greater safety in traffic and when approaching signals. The driver at the front of the train could communicate with the fireman in the cab via a telephone link, and he could remotely control the engine via an intermediate regulator valve fixed on the smokebox, and operated through a link and lever.

The LNWR was given the task of assembling and armouring the trains at its Crewe workshops. They were not built at the same time: the first one (the future *Norma*) was completed in December 1914 and posted to North Walsham. The second train (*Alice*), completed in April 1915, was sent to Scotland, based in Edinburgh. Although they carried out many patrols, they obviously never engaged in combat, and both were dismantled in 1919. The armour was removed from the engines only in 1923, and both were retired from service in 1956.

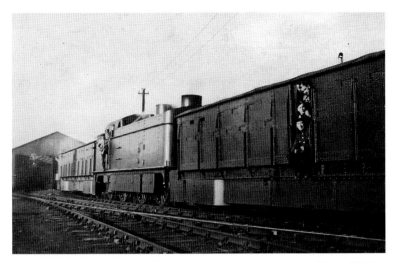

Armoured Train No 1 *Norma*. The infantry wagons were converted from GWR 40-ton coal wagons.
(Photo: Paul Malmassari Collection)

Armoured Train No 2 *Alice* sporting the characteristic cowcatchers fitted only to this train, in 1916. The artillery wagons were converted from 30-ton Caledonian Railway boiler trucks. The 12pdr QF guns of these trains were the same as those which armed the trains of the Boer War. Note the armour plates surrounding the gunshield, which could be folded down to allow the gun to train. They had firing loopholes for when they were secured in the upright position during reconnaissance missions.
(Photo: NRM)

Two views of one of the infantry wagons from *Alice*, showing (above) the firing loopholes open, and (top right), the loopholes closed. On the wagons of this train, No 2, the exterior reinforcing T-section strapping did not extend beyond mid-height on the wagon sides, while on *Norma* they continued to the roofline between the rows of loopholes.
(Photo: NRM)

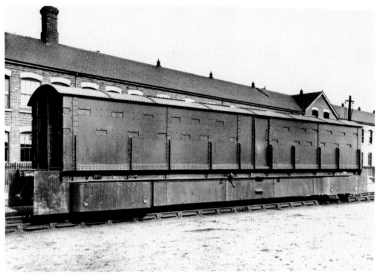

The two rows of loopholes were intended for simultaneous firing by troops in the standing and kneeling positions, which is why they are staggered horizontally. Note the modern appearance of the plates protecting the couplings. A horizontal plate allowed for communication between wagons. The interiors of both wagons were fitted out with folding tables, ammunition lockers, rifle racks, tanks for drinking water and a coal-fired stove for the troops.
(Photo: NRM)

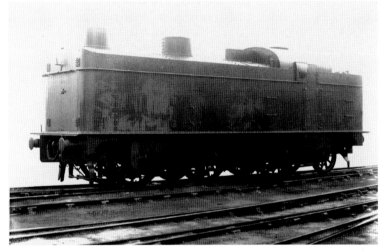

GNR Class N1 tank engine No 1587, seen here at Doncaster in December 1914. This 0-6-2 engine weighed 72 tons and was designed for hauling passenger trains.
(Photo: NRM)

Conquest and Occupation of the German Colonies (1914–1916)

Two improvised armoured trains were employed against the German colonies in Africa. One train was used by the British on the line heading west from Dar es Salaam[2] to Tabora and Oudjidji to take over German East Africa.[3]

On the other side of the African continent, when the British invaded German South-West Africa (the future Namibia) in April 1916, the Royal Navy supplied 4.7in (120mm) and 6in (152mm) guns mounted on wagons. The two sides competed with novel

[2] 'Place of Peace'.
[3] *Schutzgebiet Deutsch-Ostafrika*, subsequently divided between the British, the Belgians and the Portuguese.

Engraving from a contemporary German magazine at the time of the operations in German East Africa, showing the train built by Ugandan Railways operating out of Dar es Salaam.
(Illustration: Paul Malmassari Collection)

H. M. A. T. *Simba*, composed of an armoured engine, an armoured wagon at each end and a passenger coach which appears not to be armoured, was built in the Nairobi workshops in just ten days.
(Photo: The Sphere, 16 January 1915)

The rear wagon, showing the thickness of the armour protection.
(Photo: The Sphere, 16 January 1915)

ideas: when the British added a safety wagon, the Germans laid delayed-action mines; when the former sprayed whitewash on the ballast to spot areas where the track had been disturbed, the latter brought their own white paint with them. In the course of this guerrilla conflict there were more than fifty attacks which derailed trains or destroyed bridges. The armoured trains remained in use to the very end of the Great War.

The Sudan

After the defeat of the Khalifa at the battle of Omdurman,[4] the agreement of 19 January 1899 established shared sovereignty by Egypt and Great Britain over the Sudan. Order was restored but several expeditions were necessary to pacify the whole region. In 1914, Sultan Ali Dinar declared his allegiance to the Ottoman Empire and declared war on the British. A small force of 2000 men was despatched in 1915 and Ali Dinar met his death in March 1916 in the Darfour region. Armoured trains were utilised to defend the communication and resupply routes.[5]

British armoured train in the Sudan. Note the elaborate camouflage scheme on the engine which does not seem to extend to the armoured wagons, which are protected by lengths of rail, recalling their predecessors in the Boer War.
(Photo: IWM)

British Armoured Trains in Ireland (1916–1919)

Fearing uprisings and attacks, the British Government deployed a self-propelled armoured wagon in Haulbowline Docks, and ordered two armoured trains from the GNR(I). These trains comprised an engine and two wagons, with wooden sides doubled on the outside with steel plates. Two rows of loopholes were arranged for small-arms fire, and a safety platform was coupled at front and rear. Two additional armoured engines were built in 1918 by the GNR of Ireland, and they remained active until 1919.

Upper Silesia

In Upper Silesia, as part of the Allied forces supervising the Plebiscite, the British Army put together an armoured train in Oppeln Station in June 1921, to secure the railway network and support the British, French and Italian troops involved. Made up of an armoured engine and two armoured wagons, its armament comprised a Vickers HMG and two Lewis LMGs in each wagon, plus the personal arms of the crew of one officer and twenty men. This train, with sufficient supplies of food and water to undertake a mission lasting up to three days, was on two hour standby to intervene on the orders of the RTO (Railway Transport Officer).

---

[4] Fought on 2 September 1898.
[5] The rail gauge in the Sudan was 3ft 6in.

The engine was a Prussian Class T-14. The Type Om armoured wagons perhaps came from German trains.
(Photo: Krysztof Margarinski Collection)

The wagon preceding the one in the last photo, showing a well-executed piece of improvisation at the Front. The hull of an armoured Simplex Tractor, with an opening cut for a 75mm APX gun, has been converted into a revolving turret.
(Photo: IWM)

Another view of the BSF (British Silesia Force, also known as the Upper Silesia Force) train seen at Oppeln in 1919 following modifications. Note the wagon on the left on which the armoured side has been increased in height and the plates on the engine have been altered.
(Photo: Krysztof Margarinski Collection)

A 6pdr naval gun mounted as a chase piece.
(Photo: IWM)

Latvia (1918)

In November 1918, a British detachment helped crew a Latvian armoured train during the fighting against the Germans and the Reds (see the chapter on Latvia).

British Intervention in Russia

Following the Revolution, the British sent forces to North Russia to secure the two main ports of Archangelsk and Murmansk, the termini respectively of the narrow-gauge and broad-gauge

networks. In line with local tactics they improvised armoured trains which compared favourably with those of their Russian opponents: a 4.5in howitzer mounted on a circular platform, a Simplex Tractor cannibalised for use as a turret mounting a French 75, a casemate improvised out of steel plates and beams protecting a 6pdr naval gun, etc. The Allied intervention on behalf of the Whites ending in total defeat, their armoured trains ending up with the other Red war trophies.

Between August 1918 and April 1919, an independent force of 500 men under the command of General Wilfrid Malleson was sent from India to support the Transcaspian forces in what is modern day Turkmenistan. Two armoured trains were used by the Anglo-Transcaspians against three Bolshevik armoured trains.

Left: British 4.5in Howitzer Mk II installed on a cut-down bogie van. The side plates forming the armour protection could be lowered to the horizontal to form a platform for the gunners when firing to one side. This piece was extremely effective against opponents in trenches or bunkers.
(Photo: IWM)

The Middle East

When the First World War began, the Ottoman Empire extended from Turkey proper, to take in the Lebanon, Palestine, Syria, Mesopotamia (modern-day Iraq), as far as the Persian Gulf and down a coastal strip to the end of the Red Sea. Medina and Mecca were included. Turkey mobilised in the Levant on 15 August 1914, but entered the war on the side of Germany only on 29 October. The fighting took place in five zones: Palestine and Sinai, Mesopotamia, Persia, the Caucasus and Gallipoli. British armoured trains faced the Turks in the first three of these zones. For their part, the Turks defended the Hejaz Railway (see the chapter on the Ottoman Empire) and Palestine. In Egypt (to defend the Suez Canal), in Mesopotamia and then in Persia, it was the British who employed armoured trains. Following the end of the First World War, occupation forces and mandates were set up in the former provinces of the Ottoman Empire, which necessitated maintaining the security of the railway networks.

Mesopotamia (1918–1921)

The British Army entered Bagdad on 11 March 1917 but Mesopotamia was placed under British mandate only following the Armistice of 31 October 1918 and the surrender of the Turkish Sixth Army at Mosul. In this region dominated by tribal traditions, an undercurrent of continuous insurrection existed, with raids by armed bands, who were highly mobile and motivated by Turkish and Syrian agitators to fight for the establishment of an Arab government. The revolt grew in intensity, and the tribes had some successes in surrounding and even eliminating isolated British detachments. The railway network, vital for the movement of troops and their resupply, was constantly under attack, which led to the deployment of armoured trains and trolleys. Several armoured cars, notably Leylands and Austins, were converted for rail use by the simple expedient of changing their wheels. Often employed in pairs coupled back-to-back, they made up the 16th and 17th Railway Defence Batteries, which would come together to form the 1st Railway Armoured Motor Battery. The revolt was finally crushed in February 1921.

A patrol with two Leylands. Four machines were built in 1915 and were initially sent to East Africa, where it was found they were too heavy. They were therefore transferred to the Middle East and used to protect the rail network.
(Photo: RAC Tank Museum)

Two Austin trolleys coupled back-to-back. Note the protection for the couplings and the names of the machines: H. M. A. C. *Warspite* and *Valiant*, the initials standing for 'His Majesty's Armoured Car'.
(Photo: Sepia Images Collection)

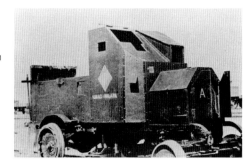

A FIAT armoured car converted to an armoured trolley. The name H. M. A. C. *Malaya* continued the tradition of naming armoured vehicles in the manner of warships: as with HM Ships *Warspite* and *Valiant*, *Malaya* was one of the *Queen Elizabeth* class super-dreadnoughts.
(Photo: RAC Tank Museum)

A fine view of one of the four Leylands converted for rail use. The device for turning the trolley can be seen beneath the chassis. Note the complete lack of the original vehicle fittings: mudguards, headlamps, trench-crossing rails etc. The vertical device made of sleepers seen behind the trolley does not appear to be part of it, except perhaps as a bulldozer blade to clear obstacles.
(Photo: All Rights Reserved)

Another view of a Fiat trolley, here seen manned by Australian troops.
(Photo: Australian War Museum)

Possibly one of the ugliest rail trolleys ever built! Six machines were ordered for use in Mesopotamia from the Drewry Car Company Ltd., with twin turrets each armed with a Lewis Gun plus a searchlight. The armour was 6mm thick. Note the armour panels protecting the running gear, seen raised in the photo. There is no information on their use in Mesopotamia.

(Photo: The Industrial Railway Society via Lichfield Record Office)

View of an armoured train on the Mesopotamia Railway (note the letters 'MR' on the leading wagon), armed with a 13pdr 6cwt anti-aircraft gun, of which four examples were recorded as being in Mesopotamia at the end of the First World War.

(Photo: Sepia Images)

The front of the machine, with the armoured hatch for the driver, the small aperture enabling him to see when driving closed down. At the bottom, the two radiator shutters are also openable, in order to increase the flow of air. The surface texture reveals a covering of asbestos, to help with heat insulation. The two photos were taken in January 1922 at the Baguley workshops in Shobnall Road, Burton upon Trent.

(Photo: The Industrial Railway Society via Lichfield Record Office)

A different armoured train with a 12pdr naval gun in a well wagon. The lack of tunnels and overbridges allowed the construction of unusually high observation towers.

(Photo: Private Collection)

Armoured wagon *Julius* of an armoured train on the Bagdad Railway, with a mixed crew of Scottish and English troops. It is armed with a 3in gun from HMS *Marlborough*, and a second similar wagon bore the name of the ship. *Julius* perhaps refers to the British naval base in Istanbul.

(Photo: Paul Malmassari Collection)

British armoured train derailed on 5 September 1920 at Samawah on the Bagdad line.

(Photo: Illustration No 46 in The Insurrection in Mesopotamia 1920, by Sir Aylmer L Haldane)

Egypt and Sinai

The British troops in Egypt were there to defend the Suez Canal, a vital supply artery for the forces of the Empire, against the Turks based in Palestine. In the Autumn of 1915 the first lines of a defensive network of 2ft (61cm) and 3ft (91cm) gauge track were laid in the Canal Zone between Port Said and Mohamedieh on the Egyptian bank of the Canal. After the Egyptian Expeditionary Force (EEF) won the battle of Romani on 4 and 5 August 1916, the network was extended as far as Rafah (reached in March 1917). But the Turkish withdrawal reduced the importance of the network, and its components were sent to Gallipoli. However, a 3ft-gauge line 15 miles (23km) long was built to support the advance into Palestine as an extension of the standard-gauge line which ended at Deir-El-Balah. In November 1917, Gaza was finally captured, Jerusalem fell to the British on 9 December and Jaffa on the 22nd. The Armistice put an end to the fighting on 31 October 1918.

Two armoured trains were built by the Royal Engineers. The design of those in Egypt was fairly basic. Here is No 2 at Zagazig with no engine attached. Note the uniforms drying on the armour plate!
(Photo: Paul Malmassari Collection)

The safety wagons were fitted with cowcatchers and protected by sandbags.
(Photo: Paul Malmassari Collection)

Below: A rare interior view of a chase artillery wagon. The small 2.95in QF Mountain Gun can train to fire through each of the three apertures. Note the telephone and notepad on the right.
(Photo: IWM)

Armoured Trains in British India (1919–1930)

In addition to the standardised purpose-built armoured trains, improvised armoured trains were also built during periods of crisis. Lacking overhead protection, they were much more vulnerable than the standard types, as shown during the Afghan War of 1920, when troops of a Sikh regiment were trapped in a cutting on the Peshawar to Jamrud line, and suffered heavy casualties.

After the First World War, the trains' armament was supplemented by the addition of 3in Stokes mortars carried in high-sided armoured wagons, such as the one in the photo below. They had a range of 800 yards (730m) and a rate of fire of up to thirty-two rounds a minute. The infantry were supplied with the .303 Lewis light machine gun which greatly augmented their firepower. The 12pdr guns remained in use up until 1939, when with the risk of invasion from Russia long since past, they were removed for mounting on merchant ships.

On 18 March 1919 the introduction of a new law, the Anarchical and Revolutionary Crimes Act, known also by the name of its author as the Rowlatt Act, caused revolts which although

A machine-gun 'barbette' wagon of the Punjab Rifles (IDF) Armoured Train Section, at Moghalpura in 1919. Note the basic similarities between the armoured wagon and those used during the Boer War. The rifles are .303 calibre P14s manufactured by Winchester and Remington during the First World War.
(Photo: Hal Walters Collection)

A pair of Commer trolleys seen in 1919. The broad-gauge examples above are mounted on four wheels, whereas on the narrow-gauge pair in the next photo the front axles have been replaced by a four-wheel bogie. This arrangement would reappear later, for example on Japanese SO-MO trolleys (see the chapter on Japan). Apart from the superior ride on uneven track, the bogies were easier to repair when damaged by mines.
(Photo: RAC Tank Museum)

Coupling these trolleys back-to-back was the classic arrangement in the absence of a rear driving position and suitable gearing, whereas to attempt to turn one vehicle under fire would be suicidal.
(Photo: RAC Tank Museum).

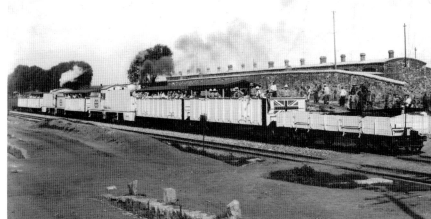

An overall view of the armoured train, with its two armoured engines back to back, separated by a central wagon. The security flat wagon was only coupled at one end.
(Photo: Paul Malmassari Collection)

localised, were sufficiently unsettling as to give rise to severe repression, culminating on 13 April 1919 in the incident which became known as the Amritsar Massacre. In the backlash after this tragic event, the troubles and countermeasures multiplied in Punjab Province. An armoured train based at Lahore had to intervene to ensure the repair of the line at Amritsar while other troops arrived from Jullundur. As always in such circumstances, the protection of the railway network had to be increased.

The UK General Strike of 1926

In 1926 in England, the derailment of a train in Northumberland led to the building of an armoured train, composed of a Type 4-4-4 engine and four wagons reinforced with steel plates. Intended to safeguard against possible sabotage, the two brake vans and two cattle wagons were provided with firing loopholes. The strike ended without the train having been used, and it was dismantled.

China

The British Army was charged with defending the possessions of Hong King and Kowloon (three battalions of which one was Indian), as well as the concessions at Shanghai (two battalions) and Tientsin (one battalion).[6] The permanent state of insecurity in China between the wars obliged the Great Powers to look to their own security and that of their supply routes, plus access to the sea. The British placed in service an armoured train. According to documents we have discovered, in 1928 this train was manned by the 1st Battalion the Bedfordshire & Hertfordshire Regiment. Part of the International Defence Force at Shanghai since February 1927, in May 1928 they moved to Kuyeh, where they were assigned to protect the mining facility there – where the following photos were taken. The unrest in the area had settled down by November, after which the battalion moved to Hong Kong.

Two views of one of the two Ordnance 3pdr QF Hotchkiss (47mm/L40) naval guns on the train, on a naval Model 1915 mounting. Note the Royal Navy gunners, and the internal armour in the wagon.
(Photos: Paul Malmassari Collection)

6. The British withdrew their troops from Tientsin in December 1939 then from Shanghai in August 1940.

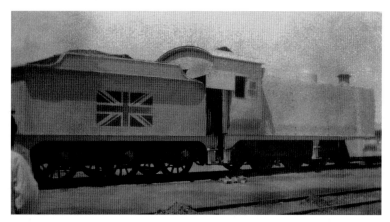

One of the two 4-6-0 engines.
(Photo: Paul Malmassari Collection)

Since the role of this train was as much political as military, the crew had not skimped on depictions of the flag.
(Photo: Paul Malmassari Collection)

One of the armoured trains in India during the 1930s, with its classic silhouette and notably a 12pdr naval gun on a bogie wagon. The rail gauge was the Indian broad gauge of 5ft 6in (1.676m).
(Photo: Military vehicles Museum)

Armoured Trains in India (1930s)

During the 1930s India was a hotbed of disaffection and revolt against the British, and the railway security units were always more numerous compared to the other regular regiments. Two armoured trains were permanently stationed in Lahore, up until 1939 when the Royal Navy reclaimed their guns for fitting to merchant ships. The troubles of 1930 on the North-West Frontier once more called for the presence of armoured trains. At least one of them was employed on the Peshawar line, crewed by the 4th Bengal Engineers Company.

A similar artillery wagon in 1930 at Peshawar, with a crew probably furnished by the North Western Railway Regiment, which was responsible for 1750 miles (2800km) of track. The 1st Battalion covered the North-West Frontier and the 2nd Battalion covered Baluchistan.
(Photo: Paul Malmassari Collection)

British Mandate in Palestine and Sinai (1923–1939)[7]

With the breakup of the Ottoman Empire, carved up between the victors under the Sykes-Picot Agreement, Palestine was to be ruled by the League of Nations under an International Mandate. However, secret discussions between Clemenceau and Lloyd George which had begun in 1918 led to Britain obtaining control of Mosul and Palestine.[8] The British Mandate over Palestine came into effect on 23 September 1923. Disturbances had already taken place in 1922, but it was during the Arab revolt of 1936–9 that the railway network was seriously threatened. On 26 September 1937 the British High Commissioner for Galilee was assassinated, and in 1938 alone, 340 attacks on the railway network were recorded, the aim of the Arabs being to cut communications between Egypt and Iraq. The British sent 20,000 men to maintain order, and in order to ensure the security of the railway network, they put armoured wagons and trolleys into service.

Model T Fords converted into rail trolleys, with minimum protection, to patrol the tracks. In September 1938 the 2nd Battalion the King's Own Royal Regiment was made responsible for protecting the Jerusalem-Jaffa line.
(Photo: Library of Congress)

[7.] The period from the Second World War to 1948 is covered later.
[8.] See the chapter on France for the French zone of responsibility.

Above: Before bomb attacks and gunfire targeting the crews became the norm, civilian vehicles were adapted for rail use, propelling a ballasted chariot, and with a machine gun on a pivot in the back of the pickup.

(Photo: Paul Malmassari Collection)

Below: One of the methods successfully used to put a stop to mines placed on the tracks was to sit local Arab leaders on the ballasted chariot. After the first two hostages were killed in October 1938, no more mines were laid.

(Photo: Paul Malmassari Collection)

Here the machine guns are Lewis Mk I in .303 (7.7mm) calibre, mounted in the back of Ford Model 1937 pickups.

(Photo: Library of Congress)

The fate of too many crews of reconnaissance machines was to be sacrificed to ensure that the trains, and especially those carrying civilians, would not be derailed.

(Photo: Paul Malmassari Collection)

Above: This train was used on the Samaria narrow-gauge line. Note the anti-grenade netting and the letters 'H.R.' standing for 'Hedjaz Railways'.

(Photo: Hans Kohit via Chen Melling)

Below: One of the great advantages of the train: the water tanks on the wagon which also served as the safety vehicle.

(Photo: Hans Kohit via Chen Melling)

Right: Three trolleys (official designation: Lightly Armoured Patrol Vehicle) for the metre gauge were ordered from the Drewry Car Co. Ltd. on 28 January 1938 and built by Baguley Cars Ltd. Note the wire netting protection, and the installation of a Lewis Gun.

(Photo: Lichfield Records Office)

Below: Two armoured escort wagons were built in Palestine. Here is the first one, *The Hillmen's Pride*, a concrete blockhouse mounted on 30-ton platform wagon No 3708, 24ft 3in (7.39m) long and 7ft 6½in (2.30m) wide.

(Photo: Library of Congress)

Above: A view of the other side of the flat wagon, showing the entry door. No glass or armour was provided for the openings. The concrete was 8¼in (21cm) thick.

(Photo: Uzi Raviv)

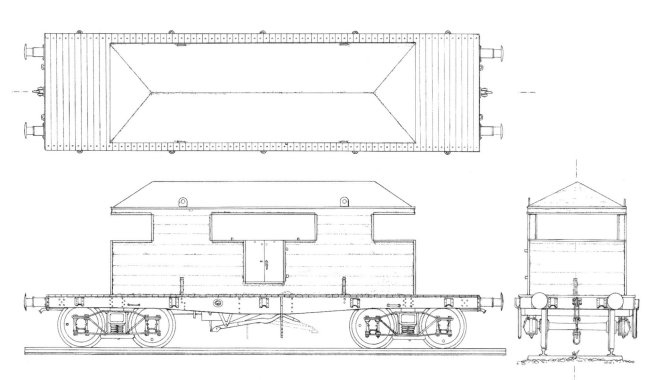

A second bogie flat wagon No 3702 was fitted with a steel bunker, and named *Noah's Ark*. Note the complete roof protection.
(Photo: Uzi Raviv)

Here the crew composed of men of the Black Watch have removed the metal roof, certainly due to the stifling heat in the interior.
(Photo: Library of Congress)

Armoured Trains in Great Britain during the Second World War

Reliving the old fear of a landing by enemy forces, the British decided in May 1940 to create a militia, which would become the Home Guard, and studied the possibility of building armoured trains to defend the coastline. A large number of proposals, proof of the British spirit of inventiveness, saw the light of day in the course of 1940, and on into 1941. Admiral Sir Frederic Dreyer wanted several trains to defend the north coast of Cornwall (which would in fact be defended by Trains A, D and F after July 1940) and the coastline of the Firth of Clyde south of Glasgow. In December 1940 Captain Kenneth Cantlie, of the Transport Bureau, proposed a train of modern construction, crystallising the various ideas on the subject discussed by the officers of the Armoured Train Groups

in Scotland on 24 August. The project was not proceeded with, and neither was the idea of armouring a certain number of railcars. On the south bank of the Humber, the docks of Grimsby and Immingham proceeded with the construction of an armoured train so heavy that it was barred from using the normal tracks. In February 1941 a project by the Home Guard in the Peterborough area for an armoured train comprising a shunting engine and an armoured wagon armed with Bren LMGs was turned down, as was the equally basic train proposed by the Home Guard in Essex. Finally, in June 1941 a super-heavy armoured train was proposed, with twin 4in (105mm) AA turrets and lighter anti-aircraft armament. Again, this project was not pursued.

In 1943 Austerity 2-8-0 engine No 7195 of the War Department[9] was fitted with experimental armour protection with a view to future employment on the Continent. Built by the North British Loco Co. in Glasgow, the engine was armoured in the same workshops. In the event, the aerial threat had decreased by the time the engine was sent to the Continent, and it was deployed without the armour.

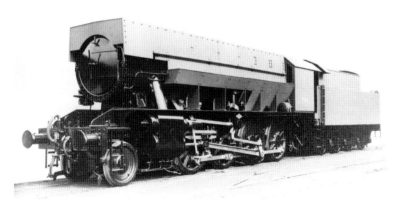

The armour covered only the upper parts of the engine and tender, an economical solution adapted with a view to protecting them from attacks by the Luftwaffe.
(Photo: University of Glasgow)

[9]. The Austerity was a wartime version of the Stanier 8F of the LMS (London Midland and Scottish Railway), designed by engineer Robert Arthur Riddles, but using non-strategic materials. In all, 935 Austerities were built for the MoS (Ministry of Supply).

The machine breathes an aura of raw power, and in addition allows the crew to carry out regular maintenance without having to hinge upwards or otherwise dismantle armour plates.
(Photo: University of Glasgow)

The standard armoured trains of the Second World War

The basic principle consisted of armouring a standard series of wagons by the addition of a layer of concrete in the interior. In fact, it was decided to pour the concrete inside a sandwich of two armour plates, to avoid the concrete spalling when the armour was struck. Depending on the planned use, the wagons would be cut away to allow the armament to be deployed.

The choice of base wagon fell on the 20-ton steel coal wagon of the LMS, which would have to be cut down at one end in order to allow the gun to train. The main armament was to be a 6pdr 6cwt Hotchkiss Mark II, as used in the side sponsons of the heavy tanks of the First World War. These had been in store ever since the tanks had been scrapped, and had the advantage that the original long barrel of the Hotchkiss naval gun used in the Mark I tanks, proving a distinct disadvantage in the confines of the trenches, had been reduced in length for the Mark IV and later tanks. In the armoured wagons, the guns could therefore be trained laterally without fouling the tight British loading gauge. At the suggestion of the Poles, the virtually cylindrical gun shields from the tank sponsons were cut down to a half-circle in section, and the two offcuts were welded back on, but reversed, thus extending the protection for the gunners.

At the rear of the gun compartment a door communicated with the infantry fighting compartment, which had sides extended upwards by armoured shields with sliding shutters. The rest of the train armament comprised three Bren LMGs and a Boys .55in (13.9mm) anti-tank rifle in each combat wagon, plus the personal arms of the crew. Later a Vickers machine gun would be added. No overhead protection was ever fitted throughout the life of the trains, as it was envisaged the machine guns would need to fulfil an anti-aircraft role. The later Vickers was admirably suitable for close-range AA actions, but trying to engage a fast-moving enemy aircraft with a Bren with a magazine containing only twenty-nine rounds was impractical.

In order to avoid encumbering the combat armoured wagons, lightweight intermediate wagons for ammunition, stores and the like were inserted between the armoured wagons and the engine, thus extending the length of each train and providing for virtual all-round observation from the combat units.

The engine was a 2-4-2 LNER tank engine, covered in armour except for the top of the boiler, the smokebox and the wheels. The crew was provided with vision ports closed by sliding shutters.

The normal composition of each train was as follows:

– gun wagon.
– lightweight wagon.
– armoured engine.
– lightweight wagon.
– gun wagon.

No safety wagon was included, as the threat of mines on the track was felt to be so slight as to not justify diverting goods rolling stock. One of the lightweight wagons, originally three-plank, was later replaced by a five-plank wagon, and there were minor differences in the armouring of the various engine whistles, pumps and valves.

It appears that construction of the trains was begun in May 1940 and proceeded at an extremely rapid pace, as the first seven engines were delivered from the Stratford workshops before the end of June, while the Derby workshops supplied the fourteen armoured combat wagons and an equal number of intermediate wagons before 27 June. The component units of the five other trains were delivered in July. During 1940, the protection was reinforced by adding wooden planking to the interior walls of the wagons, to avoid ricochets off the armour. At the same time, each train was fitted with fixed mountings for their Bren Guns, produced in local workshops, placed in the front part of the combat compartment.

In order to have spare engines to hand, apart from those which could be provided by local engine sheds in an emergency, an additional engine was attached to each Armoured Train Group between January and February 1941. In addition an armoured tender was added to each train in early 1941. Planned already in 1940, they provided an increase in water and coal capacity sufficient to increase the range of each train to over 106 miles (170km). The additional braking capacity of the tenders improved the overall stopping distances of the trains, with the aim of avoiding accidents such as the one involving Train F in September 1940, when the driver of a lorry was killed. In actual fact, only nine armoured tenders were delivered: five six-wheel tenders to Trains A, F, H, L and M, and four bogie tenders to Trains D, G and K.

As described in the relevant section of the chapter on Poland, when the trains were being operated by Polish crews, they began to receive armoured vehicles carried on flat cars, in order to train the Poles to operate armour.

ORGANISATION

Attached to the Royal Armoured Corps which supplied one officer, seven NCOs and twenty-nine men, each train also carried eight members of the Railway Engineers, responsible for the driving and other technical matters. Each crew was composed of active members and a reserve ready to take over as replacements as required. At least on paper, there was also supposed to be a flying reserve based at the command centre of each Group. A Group of armoured trains was composed of at least two trains which could each operate independently. The Group was commanded by a major of the Royal Armoured Corps assisted by an officer of the Transport Engineers.

Finally, on 21 September 1940, it was decided that all the crews would be Polish, a changeover which was completed in April 1941. When the Polish crews had accumulated sufficient experience with the armoured vehicles attached to their trains, the Poles were transferred to armoured units, and the trains were handed over to the Home Guard.

OPERATIONS

The trains were mobilised in two stages: the first batch of Trains A to G were mobilised on 30 June 1940, and the subsequent batch, Trains H to M, on 10 July.

According to operational requirements, and especially in view of the lack of defences in Scotland, the trains were divided between the following five regions: Scottish Command, Northern Command, Western Command, Eastern Command and Southern Command. It was even planned to build a further eight trains for the Scottish Command to protect the extremely long Scottish coastline, but the project was never begun.

Armoured Train A: Attached to Eastern Command on mobilisation, it joined Group No 1 (with Trains C, D and G) and carried out training missions in Norfolk in the vicinity of Norwich. It was then transferred to Southern Command on 25 July, where it joined the garrison at Newton Abbot, to the east of Plymouth. In July 1941 it moved to Cornwall to replace Train D which had been transferred to the east of England and took up garrison at Wadebridge. Its operational area took in practically the whole of Cornwall up until April 1943. On 20 April 1942 it moved to Hitchin, from where it patrolled on a 25-mile (40km) radius. It was dismantled in May 1943.

Armoured Train B: Designated as Armoured Train No 6, it was mobilised on 28 June 1940 and was part of Group 3 stationed in Scotland. It commenced patrols on 6 July on the north-east coast of Scotland, but on 28 July was transferred with Trains H and M to Northern Command. Its new area of operations extended from Newcastle to Berwick, with the various surrounding lines, where it remained for several months. In February-March 1941, the train was immobilised due to severe weather which was causing collisions and derailments in its area. It recommenced patrolling on 8 April, undertook a practice shoot on 23 August, and participated in a 'public relations exercise' on 1 February 1941. The remainder of the year passed without any particular incidents. On 8 November it suffered a bombing attack, which destroyed its base accommodation but only caused a few minor injuries among the crew. During the Winter of 1941/42, the armour on its engine was reinforced, but between 15 and 21 April 1942 it became the first of the armoured trains to be broken up, and its wagons were returned to civilian use.

Armoured Train C: Mobilised on 30 June 1940, it was part of Group 1 along with Trains A, D and G. On 3 July it began patrolling the east coast of Norfolk, and in late July 1940 it added to its area of operations that of Train D, which had been transferred to the west. In March 1941, it was transferred 19 miles (30km) further south to Westerfield, and shortly afterwards took on board its Polish crew. In August, its operational area was expanded further

east and in April 1942 it received three armoured Bedford trucks, followed by a fourth in June. It was broken up in June 1943.

Armoured Train D: Mobilised on 30 June 1940, it was part of Group 1 along with Trains A, C and G, and began patrolling on 3 July along the coasts of Essex and Suffolk. On 25 July it was transferred to Southern Command to operate in Cornwall out of Wadebridge in the north of the county. After a year of patrols, it was once more transferred to the east, to Essex, and received an operational area which reached within 12 miles (20km) of London. In April 1942 it also acquired armoured Bedfords, and was broken up in September 1943.

Armoured Train E: Mobilised on 30 June and attached to Group 2 with Train F, it began patrolling on 1 July in Kent, on the rail network south of the Thames Estuary. At the end of July, it was sent to Tonbridge and was given the dangerous mission of patrolling the whole of the south-east coast, in other words the region most menaced by the threat of invasion. In March 1941 it moved to Ashford and shortly afterwards received its Polish crew. It patrolled within a radius of 25 miles (40km). In addition, it was designated as the experimental unit used to test modifications to be applied to the armoured trains. During the Winter of 1941/42, the armour protection on the engine was reinforced at Ashford, and at the same time the train received its first armoured vehicles in the shape of Bren Carriers, followed in early 1943 by four Valentine tanks transferred from Train H. Train E was dismantled in July 1943.

Armoured Train F: Mobilised on 30 June and attached to Group No 2 with Train E, it patrolled in Kent along the axis Ashford-Dungeness-Appledore-Hastings-Lewes, operating to a fixed timetable, and thus covered the whole south coast of Kent. On 25 July it was transferred to Barnstaple in Devon, coming under the control of Southern Command, and patrolled there until early 1942. In February 1942 it received several Covenanter tanks and on 20 April it began patrols on the lines to the north of the Thames, without going as far as London. It was broken up in April 1943.

Armoured Train G: Mobilised on 30 June, it was part of Group 1 along with Trains A, C and D, and began patrolling the north coast of Norfolk on 3 July. It was based in this area until September 1941, when it moved further south to Cambridge. In April, it began to take delivery of three Bedford armoured vehicles, the last one arriving in June. It was dismantled in June 1943.

Armoured Train H: Attached to Scottish Command, Group 4, from 6 July 1940 it patrolled in the region of Aberdeen, but from the 28th of that month it was transferred to Northern Command with Armoured Train M. In April 1940 it was in position near the Humber estuary, one of the most vulnerable points in the event of a German invasion. But overall, Armoured Train H seems to have been relatively inactive. On 14 December 1940 it was transferred to Canterbury, to the south-east of London. Then when the Polish crews began to take over railway duties, Armoured Train H undertook its first mixed patrol on 5 April 1941 between Canterbury, Faversham and Minster then returned to Canterbury. In early 1943, Valentine tanks arrived to supplement the Covenanter tanks attached as patrol vehicles. One of the tanks was, however, destroyed by a direct bomb hit on the night of 31 May/1 June 1943. Armoured Trains D and H were the last to be broken up in September 1943.

Armoured Train J: Attached to Scottish Command on mobilisation, it was part of Group 4 and on 10 July it moved to the region around Stirling. Its area of operations extended from the Firth of Tay to the Firth of Forth. It remained there until late August. On 7 September, it was put on alert by mistake, which made the local population fear that German paratroops had landed in the area. It was one of the first three trains (with K and L) to receive Polish crews, following the decision of 21 September 1940. During 1941 it was the train which undertook the greatest number of operations. During the Winter of 1941/42, the armour protection of the engine was reinforced at Cowlairs, and in early 1942 the train was transferred to Thornton Junction. The order to dismantle it was issued on 5 November 1944.

Armoured Train K: Transferred to Scottish Command on mobilisation, it reached Edinburgh on 10 July with Group 4 and patrolled the south bank of the Firth of Forth. With Trains J and L, it was one of the first to receive its new Polish crew. Its operational area was extended in 1941 to take in stations 50 to 65 miles (80 to 90km) from its base. During the Winter of 1941/42, the armour protection of the engine was reinforced at Cowlairs. The train was then transferred to Saughton Junction in early 1942, where it was dismantled on 5 November 1944.

Armoured Train L: Attached to Scottish Command on mobilisation, it was part of Group 4, and on 10 July 1940 moved to the area around Glasgow. On the 18th, it moved to Dumbarton and carried out patrols in the direction of Stirling, then further north from the 21st. On 31 July it moved to Aberdeen to replace Train H which had been transferred further north, and it began patrolling from mid-August. Its operational area was the largest of any of the armoured trains. As with Trains J and K, it received its Polish crew and sent its engine to the Inverurie workshops, near Aberdeen, to have its armour protection enhanced. This would become its final base from 1942 until it was dismantled on 5 November 1944.

Armoured Train M: Attached to Scottish Command on mobilisation, it was initially designated Armoured Train 'I' before this was changed soon after to 'M'. On 12 July 1940 it moved to the town of Forfar to the north of Dundee, where it undertook patrols up until late July. On the 28th, it was transferred along with Trains B and H to Northern Command. On 30 July it reached Louth and began patrolling the east coast of Lincolnshire, undertaking various training activities such as firing its 6pdr guns on 27 October, and what we would today term 'public relations exercises'. In January 1941, the train was transferred further south, to Spalding, and

shortly after received its Polish crew. At the end of the year, its area of operations was increased to include the Humber. As a result, it was transferred 15 miles (25km) further north, to Boston, but its stay there was brief. During the Winter of 1941/42 the armour on the engine was reinforced at Stratford, and in mid-April the train was dismantled, the rolling stock being sent to Catterick to be returned to civilian use. The engine itself was for a time under repair in Kent, but its armour was removed by 5 November.

FINAL DISPOSITIONS

When the majority of the armoured trains were demobilised and dismantled (apart from the engines), Scottish Command wanted to retain its own trains after the Polish crews left, in view of the huge length of coast which needed watching. Approval was given in April 1942, railwaymen from the LNER taking over the running of the trains, while the Home Guard would take over the military side. But to ensure that sufficient personnel would be available, without overstretching the crews, the trains had to be relocated in more important Home Guard bases. Thus between June and July 1942, Armoured Train J left Stirling and moved to Thornton Junction (Fife Sub-Area), Armoured Train K moved to Saughton Junction to the west of Edinburgh (10th City of Edinburgh – 3rd LNER – Battalion) and Armoured Train L set up base at Inverurie (8th North & South Highlands Area Battalion). On 5 November 1944, with the Allies just six months away from completing the downfall of the Reich, the decision was taken to withdraw the last three trains from active service.

The Royal Navy armoured train project

This train was planned to act in support of the twelve armoured trains described above, especially in view of the meagre defences of the south coast of England, which was the area facing the greatest threat of German invasion. The Royal Navy Armoured Train, however, remained on the drawing board.

Armoured Train A, the first to come out of the workshops, seen here at Shoeburyness.
(Photo: IWM)

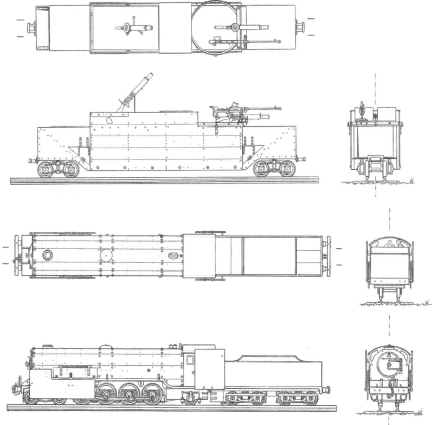

A fine view of a Vickers machine gun in a side mounting, manned by a sergeant of the Home Guard. The photo is obviously posed, as the ammunition belt contains no cartridges. The soldier behind him is armed with a P14 rifle. Note the internal wood cladding. The lack of overhead protection is glaringly obvious.
(Photo: IWM)

The miniature armoured train

This 'thirteenth' train was built for use on the 40cm gauge line of the Romney, Hythe and Dymchurch Railway (RH&DR), once this line had been requisitioned by the army on 26 July 1940. Work had already begun on 16 July on converting the locomotive originally chosen, a diesel shunter, but it became immediately obvious that the additional weight to be carried could not be supported by the bogie and the two driven axles. A steam engine was therefore selected for

conversion, the famous 4-8-2 *Hercules* of the RH&DR. The work of fitting the armour took one month, and protected the whole engine except for the driving cab, which was left open at the rear. The two armoured wagons, former mineral wagons, were coupled in front of and behind the engine. Each wagon was armed with a Boys anti-tank rifle and a coaxial Lewis LMG mounted behind a shield on a ring at one end, with a second Lewis on an anti-aircraft mounting in the central compartment, but without a shield.

For all its reduced dimensions, with its four Lewis Guns the Miniature Armoured Train was credited with one victory, a Heinkel III, and one probable, a Messerschmitt Bf 109 on 7 October 1940.
(Photo: IWM)

Between 30 April and 30 June 1943 the line and the rolling stock were progressively returned to their previous use, and the armour plating was removed. But this famous train has been recreated, with a steam engine and a single wagon, clad in wood to represent armour.
(Photo: RH&DR)

Armoured wagon 'HMS *Terror*', 1940–1944

During the Winter of 1940/41, the Home Guard unit at the Experimental Establishment[10] at Shoeburyness built an armoured wagon armed with a naval 12pdr QF gun in the central position and a 2pdr pom-pom at each end. Originally built in 1916, the bogie well wagon was intended to mount an anti-aircraft gun, and entered service during the First World War. Then in 1940 at Swindon, it had previously been used for the trial mounting of a 6in gun. As armed in 1940–1, it was intended to be used for the anti-aircraft defence of the Shoeburyness polygon, at the mouth of the Thames, and therefore on the route taken by German bombers, and was hauled by an unarmoured diesel shunter. Although of imposing appearance, its organisation left much to be desired: the large mast defiantly flying the Royal Navy ensign was doubtless good for morale, but seriously reduced the fields of fire of the three guns. To be even moderately effective against modern aircraft it would have required some form of fire-control system, and in the photos it appears to lack even a basic rangefinder. The pom-pom was recognised by some in the Navy as an ineffectual AA weapon from the early 1920s (due to its low muzzle velocity and short range) but it could put up a useful barrage to deter strafing and hit-and-run fighter-bombers. The well wagon survived the Second World War. It is now in the collection of the Railway Museum at Burnham-on-Crouch, but devoid of armament and armour.

Side views of the wagon taken in January 1941, the mast denoting an unequivocal naval origin. This gun battery falls halfway between an armoured train and an artillery battery.
(Photos: PE&E)

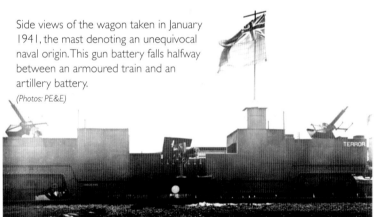

10. Also known as 'XP' for Experimental Establishment.

Armoured trolleys in Ulster (1940–1944)

In Northern Ireland, the British Army needed to protect troop movements against sabotage by enemy agents or IRA sympathisers. Trials of an armoured trolley built on a commercial chassis failed because of the excessive weight. The choice therefore fell on a freight flat wagon, motorised via a belt drive to one axle, on which was mounted an armoured box allowing the firing of light weapons plus Lewis light machine guns. These were also to be used in an anti-aircraft role firing through a part of the roof which slid open. Each Lewis Gun was to be provided with 1000 rounds of .303. Nine units were ordered, but only six were built in Northern Ireland workshops: three were sent to the north-east area of Ulster centred on Antrim, and the three others went to Portadown to patrol further to the south-west. In 1944 they were dismantled, and no trace of them survives.

Converted from GNR(I) wagons, these trolleys were disguised as cement wagons operating from Whitehead and later Magherafelt. Note the right-hand sliding portion of the roof armour, to allow anti-aircraft fire. The initials stand for the 'London Midland and Scottish Railway – Northern Counties Committee' following the union of the two companies in the Grouping of 1923.
(Photo: IWM)

Exercise disembarking to investigate a suspect location. The muzzles of the two Lewis Guns can be seen emerging from the front apertures. The soldier on the left has an SMLE, but the man on the right carries a P14.
(Photo: IWM)

'KROHCOL',[11] Malaya, 8–11 December 1941

During Operation 'KROHCOL', an armoured train from Padang Besar manned by thirty men of the 2/16th Punjab Regiment[12] entered Thailand[13] in an attempt to destroy a bridge near Khlong Ngae, in order to delay the Japanese advance. The train was part of the third British attack column.

East African Campaign, 1940–1941

Between June 1940 and November 1941, during the campaign conducted against the Italians (including a small German unit and colonial levies), launched from the neighbouring British colonies, an armoured train was used in the Sudan, about which no information has come to light.

British Occupation Forces in Italy, 1944–1945

In their occupation zone, the British used a Steyr le.Sp as transport, more out of availability than necessity, as the fighting in the area had ceased.
(Photo: Paul Malmassari Collection)

The same machine in June 1946 at Cormans, an early model recognisable by the rectangular shape of the protective covers over its ventilation intakes. It was named *Atom* by its users.
(Photo: from the Collection of the late Andrew Gillitt, seen here in the observation cupola)

Winston Churchill's Armoured Train,[14] 1944, and King George VI's Armoured Saloon

In the days leading up to the Normandy Landings, Churchill's special train (codename 'Rugged') was parked in the village of Droxford in Hants before returning to Waterloo Station. It was made up of eight coaches and was hauled by a 4-4-0 Drummond T9 engine. The LMS[15] coaches were armoured on the exterior.

In comparison, the Royal Saloon built for King George VI on the basis of an LMS dining car was armoured on the interior and had bullet-proof glass windows, looking for all the world like a standard coach. George VI's armoured coach still survives, in the collection of the Severn Railway Society.

General Eisenhower's Armoured Coach, 1945

In 1945 a special armoured coach was built in 1945 by the LNER[16] for General Eisenhower, Supreme Commander, Allied Forces Europe. Converted from a wagon-lits, out of the ten original sleeping compartments, six were transformed into a large conference room and an office, with radio communication facilities. Sides and windows were armoured, and the total weight after conversion was 51 tonnes, or 7.5 tons more than the coach in its original state.

Armoured Trolleys in Palestine up to the end of the British Mandate (1948)

After the end of the Second World War, during which the British Mandate in Palestine continued in force, the terrorist movement which was extremely active from 1945 to 1947 was Zionist. The Jewish revolt against British rule began in 1944 and continued through 1947, and was followed by the civil war in 1948.[17] The converted armoured cars used as rail escort vehicles were supplemented by trolleys built on commercial chassis, and armoured wagons were coupled in the trains. The most murderous terrorist attack on the railways took place on 22 February 1948, when a mine exploded on the Cairo to Haifa line, causing the deaths of twenty-eight British soldiers and wounding another thirty-five.

[11.] From Kroh, the starting point for the troops of the first, motorised, column (modern Pengkalan Huku) and 'Col' for Column. The second column was designated LAYCOL, Lay being the name of the commanding officer of the 6th Indian Infantry Brigade.

[12.] Led by Sergeant Eddie Augustin of the Railway Operating Maintenance Company (ROMC) of the Federated Malay States Volunteer Force (FMSVF).

[13.] A new name for the country decided upon in 1939 but not officially used before 1949, the former name Siam being used in parallel.

[14.] 'Winston Churchill's Train – Codename "Rugged"', *World War Two Railway Study Group Bulletin* Vol 24, No 3 (2014), pp 24.71–24.72.

[15.] London Midland & Scottish Railway.

[16.] London & North Eastern Railway.

[17.] The British Mandate ended when the State of Israel was proclaimed on 14 May 1948.

Humber LRC (Light Reconnaissance Vehicle) Mk III converted into a rail trolley. Production of this 3.7-ton machine began in 1941. The mudguards have been removed so the headlights have had to be mounted on the bonnet.
(Photo: RAC Tank Museum)

A pair of Marmon-Herrington Mk IV armoured cars on rails, mounted back-to-back in the classic configuration. In between the two there is a cab for carrying troops.
(Photo: All Rights Reserved)

Daimler Mk III serial number F351115, seen here in 1948. Certain reference sources state that a prototype trolley conversion had been tested but not adopted. In this photo there is a second machine probably attached back-to-back with No F351115. The men from the 21st Lancers are posing with a .30 cal (7.62mm) Browning machine gun and signal flags; almost certainly the lower one is green and the upper, red.
(Photo: Paul Malmassari Collection)

The blockhouse from *The Hillmen's Pride* seen dismounted and abandoned in the 1990s, on which the camouflage pattern can still be made out.
(Photo: Paul Cotterell)

The Hillmen's Pride restored and on show today, on a modern bogie flat wagon, in the Israeli Railway Museum in the former station in Haifa. Note the bars fastened over the window openings, which were never fitted in its original state.
(Photo: Israeli Railway Museum)

Land Rover Trolleys, Sudan (1952)

The Sudan became an Anglo-Egyptian condominium in 1899, after the country had been conquered by the British Expeditionary Force led by General Kitchener. Years of instability and revolt followed, until the accession of King Farouk who took the title of King of Egypt and the Sudan.[18] Finally, in 1953 a treaty was signed between Great Britain and Egypt, recognising the right of the Sudanese to self-determination.

The railway network was now more important to the Sudan than the road system.[19] It was therefore vital to ensure the security of the railway lines, and in about 1950 the British Army[20] converted Land Rover 80s into trolleys for the metric gauge.

[18.] British forces had remained in Egypt after the formal occupation of the country ended in 1936.
[19.] See H R J Davies, 'Les Chemins de fer et le développement de l'agriculture au Soudan', *Annales de géographie*, Vol 70, No 380 (1961), pp 422–7.
[20.] British units based in the Sudan in 1952 were: Sudan Signal Squadron; Eritrea Signal Squadron; 1st Btn South Wales Borderers; 1st Btn South Lancashire Regiment.

Two interesting views of the armoured Land Rovers converted for rail use. Note especially the folding side plates of the rear compartment and the doors, and the cage which was intended to offer protection against missiles thrown by a mob.
(Photos: REME Museum)

Armour plating added to the cab of the engine.
(Photo: Soldiers Magazine)

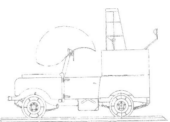

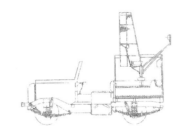

Drawing of the trolley prepared afterwards by the workshops of the East African EME at Nairobi.
(Plan: REME Museum)

Armoured Trains and Trolleys during the State of Emergency in Malaya (1948–1960)

The most widespread use of these units by the British Army was during the bloody conflict which began in Malaya in 1948 and which ended with the victory of the British over the Communist insurgents in 1960. Before standard production vehicles could be obtained, the urgency of the situation meant that many means were resorted to. Armoured Jeeps were used for the movement of individuals, armoured cars, driving along the ballast and skimming over the tracks (a procedure which required changing the tyres every evening after missions), were employed for track reconnaissance. As for the trains, apart from these same armoured cars carried on wagons at the head and tail of the rakes, the railway company mounted armoured cloches on flat wagons, permitting observation

A fine view of one of the cloches placed on a bogie flat wagon with the planking removed. The casting may have originated in heavy industry such as a foundry.
(Photo: Soldiers Magazine)

Humber Mk III armoured car photographed on 5 June 1950 in Kuala Lumpur Station. Note that the turret faces the rear.

(Photo: Paul Malmassari Collection)

Wickham armoured trolley (Armoured Wickham No 6) of the first series, designed by the Royal Engineers. A new turret would be fitted before the 1953 trolleys arrived in the country.

(Photo: Soldiers Magazine)

A remarkable transformation of a Jeep for the Telecommunications Department. Note the added stoneguards, and also what appears to be a re-railing device carried beneath the vehicle.

(Photo: Soldiers Magazine)

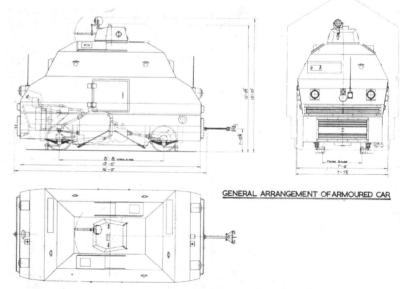

GENERAL ARRANGEMENT OF ARMOURED CAR

and the firing of individual firearms, and finally the engine driving cabs were armour-plated.

In 1950, the firm of Wickham supplied a dozen Type 40 Mk I chassis to the Malayan Railways. Once received, they were fitted with armoured hulls designed by the Royal Engineers. This was the first version of a much more sophisticated vehicle which would appear two years later. The design of this was begun after the receipt of an order on 29 July 1952, and was completed at the beginning of the following year. Between 2 March and 23 November 1953 the firm delivered forty-one units (Chassis Nos 6 538 to 6 679).

Technically, the vehicle was able to be re-railed with the aid of a second unit used as a tractor. In local use, the operators equipped

Drawing of the Wickham trolley, showing the coupling arrangement.
(Plan: Wickham)

it with a safety bogie, propelled in front to detonate mines. The motor was a Perkins P 6 diesel producing 60hp, which gave a maximum speed of 63mph (100km/h) in either direction. The crew comprised a commander, two drivers and one or two machine-gunners. The two drivers sat in tandem on the right-hand side, and each one was provided with a set of driving controls. The armour gave protection against small arms up to .30in (7.62mm) calibre. The main armament comprised a .30 cal (7.62mm) machine gun in the turret from a Ferret armoured car, mounted on the roof of the trolley. The searchlight was coupled to the machine gun by a mechanical linkage. On each side of the hull roof, sliding shutters allowed for ventilation and throwing grenades, while access was by two side hatches. Following independence, the trolleys were transferred to the Railway Police who used them for training. A certain number were also sold to South Vietnam and Thailand.

The Mau-Mau Revolt in Kenya

In 1953, the Royal Air Force was obliged to place in service two armoured mineral wagons protected by sandbags and armed with twin Browning machine guns on the line from Mombasa to Eldoret, an RAF base near to the frontier with Uganda.

The Royal Family's Armoured Train

In 1985, plans were drawn up for the building of an armoured train for the Royal Family, following on from the armoured Royal Saloon built in 1941 by the LMS. Essentially defensive, its role would be to counter attacks by IRA or other terrorist groups, employing Chobham-type armour as used on modern main battle tanks. It would also have been equipped with a sensitive radar capable of detecting irregularities in the track or obstacles placed on the line. The cost threatened to be prohibitive, and criticism from certain Members of Parliament, notably those with republican sentiments, caused the project to be abandoned.

Bullion Vans

In the days of the Gold Standard, bullion was physically transferred both ways across the Atlantic, and to and from Europe, so the UK railway companies owned specially reinforced Bullion Vans. For the USA traffic, the LNWR and successor company the LMS carried gold between London Euston and Liverpool; the LSWR and the GWR carried gold between London and Plymouth. The final special Bullion Vans were built in 1965, two years after the Great Train Robbery, when British Rail decided to convert five Mk I Brake Corridor Second Class coaches into Bullion Vans, installing internal protection, plating over most windows and fitting the remaining ones with armoured glass, and adding radio communications equipment. They were later painted Army Green and used for the high-security transfer of MoD ammunition.

Great Western Railway Bullion Van No 878 built in 1913 (in crimson lake livery) for the gold traffic between Britain and the USA, passing via Plymouth. These vans had doors only on one side for security reasons, and no other openings. A total of five GWR Bullion Vans were built between 1903 and 1913.
(Diagram M.17 and Official Photo: British Rail)

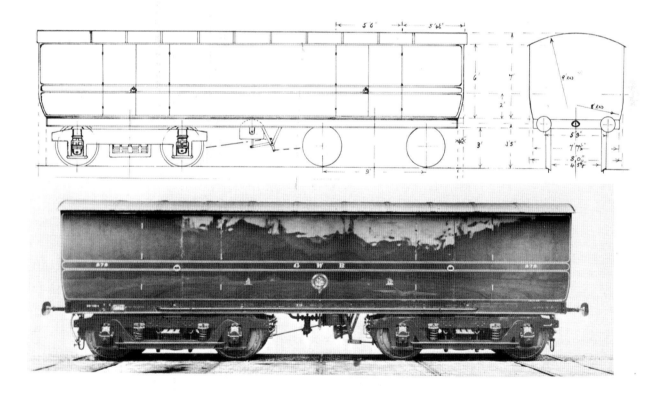

SOURCES:
Books:
Balfour, George, *The Armoured Train, its Development and Usage* (London: B T Batsford Ltd, 1981).
Danes, Richard, *Cassell's History of the Boer War 1899-1901* (London: Cassell and Company Ltd, 1903).
Fletcher, David, *War Cars: British Armoured Cars in the First World War* (London: HMSO, 1987).
Forty, George, *A Photo History of Armoured Cars in Two World Wars* (Poole: Blandford Press, 1984).

Girouard, Lieutenant-Colonel Sir E P C, *History of the Railways during the War in South Africa, 1899-1902* (London: Harrison and Sons, 1903).

Goodrich, Lieutenant-Commander Caspar F, *Report of the British Naval and Military Operations in Egypt, 1882* (Washington DC: Government Printing Office, 1883).

Hill, Tony, *Guns and Gunners at Shoeburyness* (Buckingham: Baron Books Ltd, 1999).

Jervois, Major-General Sir W F D, *Defences of Great Britain and her Dependencies* (Adelaide: E. Spiller, 1880).

Kearsey, A, *A Study of the Strategy and Tactics of the Mesopotamia Campaign 1914-1917* (Aldershot: Gale & Polden Ltd, nd).

Pakenham, Thomas, *The Boer War* (New York: Random House, 1979).

Pratt, Edwin A, *British Railways and the Great War, Vol 1* (London: Selwyn and Blunt, 1921).

RE Institute, *Detailed History of the Railways in the South African War, 1899-1902* (Chatham: 1904: new edition Arkose Press, 2015).

Sanders, Lt.-Col. E W C, *The Royal Engineers in Egypt and the Sudan* (Chatham: The Royal Engineers Institution, 1937).

Tourret, R, *Hedjaz Railway* (Abingdon: Tourret Publishing, 1989).

Townshend, Charles, *The British Campaign in Ireland 1919-1921* (Oxford: Oxford Historical Monographs, nd).

Journal Articles

'17th/21st Lancers Armoured Rail Detachment', *The White Lancer and the Vedette* (History of the 17th /21st Lancers) Vol XXIX, No 2 (November 1947), pp 51–3.

Aitken, D W, 'Guerrilla Warfare, October 1900-May 1902: Boer Attacks on the Pretoria-Belagoa Bay Railway Line', *Military History Journal* Vol 11 No 6 (December 2000), pp 226–35.

_____, 'The British Defence of the Pretoria-Delagoa Bay Railway', *Military History Journal* Vol 11 No 3/4 (October 1999), pp 80–6.

'Armoured Trains in South Africa', *The Navy and Army Illustrated* (6 September 1902), p 608.

'"B" Squadron letter', *The White Lancer and the Vedette* (History of the 17th /21st Lancers) Vol XXX, No 1 (May 1948), p 20.

'Blockhouses', *The Royal Engineers Journal* (2 November 1903), p 243.

Botha, Johannes, 'Armoured Trains of the Boer War', *Tank TV* (NZ) No 22 (December 1999), pp 11–13.

_____, 'The Fowler Roadtrain and Mobile Blockhouses', *Tank TV* (NZ) No 19 (June 1998), pp 10–11.

Conradie, Eric, 'The Firing of the First Shots in the Anglo-Boer War, 12 October 1899', *SA Rail* (March/April 1993), pp 58–9.

Cooke, Peter, 'Armour in the Boer War', *Tank TV (NZ)* No 2 (November 1992), pp 3–6.

Dillard, J B, 'Armoured Trains for Coast Defense', *The Engineer* (14 February 1919), pp 150–2.

Fletcher, David, 'Les Véhicules militaires de F. R. Simms', *Tank Museum News* (Belgium) No 13 (June 1986), pp 6–7.

Golyer, David G, 'The Miniature Armoured Train', *Bygone Kent* Vol 12, No 7 (1991), pp 378–88.

Hill, R, and Hill, R H, 'The Suakin-Berber Railway, 1885', *Sudan Notes and Records* Vol 20, No 1 (1937), pp 107–24.

Hussey, John, 'The Armoured Train Disaster, and Winston Churchill's Escape from Prison, South Africa, 1899', *British Army Review* No 123 (nd), pp 84–103.

'In Loyal Natal', *The Navy and Army Illustrated* (23 December 1899), p 369.

Lock, Ron, 'Churchill and the Armoured Train', *Military Illustrated* No 133 (1999), pp 52–8.

McLean, C H, 'Havelock-Hairy Mary', *S.A.R. & H. War Services Union Newsletter* (1975), pp 4–5.

Martin, Greg, 'LNER 2-4-2Ts on Armoured Trains', *World War Two Railway Study Group Bulletin* Vol 14, No 1 (2004), pp 14.13–14.17.

Napier, Paul, and Cooke, Peter, 'Armour in Emergency', *Tank TV* (NZ) No 4 (August 1993), pp 1–5.

Parsons, Major-General A E H, 'Railway Reconstruction by the Royal Engineers for the Military Railway Service, Allied Forces, Italy', *World War Two Railway Study Group Bulletin* Vol 9, No 4 (1999), pp 9.111–9.116.

Phillip, S M, 'The Use of our Railways in the Event of Invasion or a European War', *Railway Magazine* (May 1901).

Rue, John L, 'The Wickham Armoured Rail Car', *Army and Navy Modelworld* (July 1984), pp 103–6.

'Science at the Front', *The Navy and Army Illustrated* (15 December 1900), p 327.

'Tenders for Armoured Trains', *World War Two Railway Study Group Bulletin* Vol 11, No 3 (2001), p 11.57.

'The Outlook in South Africa', *The Navy and Army Illustrated* (7 December 1901), pp 273–4.

'The Siege of Ladysmith – Operations in Natal from 31st October to 19th November', *The Royal Engineers Journal* (1 February 1900), p 23.

'The War in South Africa – North to South', *The Navy and Army Illustrated* (20 October 1900), p 108.

'The Wide, Wide Veldt', *The Navy and Army Illustrated* (17 May 1902), p 213.

'War Trains', *The Navy and Army Illustrated* (9 December 1899), p 309.

Warner, Terry, 'Armoured Trains in Southern Africa', *Tank TV* (NZ) No 6 (June 1994), p 1.

Weaver, Rodney, 'The Petrol Locomotives of McEwan Pratt', *Model Engineer* (4 June 1971), pp 528–31, 554.

Zurnamer, Major B.A., 'The State of the Railways in South Africa during the Anglo-Boer War 1899-1902', *Militaria* No 16/4 (1986), pp 26–33.

GREECE

ARMOURED TRAINS[1]

After a long period of political instability, the Greek Civil War began in September 1946, sparked of by the refusal of the Communists[2] to accept the return of King George II to the throne. At first the Communist forces, supported by Yugoslavia and Bulgaria, overran almost all of Greece, while the Government forces were supported by the British and later the Americans. Tito, who had broken away from Stalin, withdrew his support, and following a series of defeats the Communists agreed to a ceasefire in October 1949.

Humber Mk IV armoured car mounted on a railway flat wagon during the Greek Civil War. Note the check rail preventing the turret guns from firing straight ahead and thus hitting the wagon in front.
(Photo: All Rights Reserved)

Two views showing the methods of protecting trains during the Greek Civil War. It appears that the photo above left shows the interior of the casemate partly visible behind the armoured car in the previous shot. The armour seems to be concrete.
(Both photos: L'Illustration)

SOURCES:
Metsovitis, Triantafyllos, '1945-1950', *NEA IMPS Hellas* No 2 (1999), pp 36–40.

[1.] In Greek: 'Τεθωρακισμένο Τραίνο', pronounced 'Tethorakismeno Treno'.
[2.] During the Second World War, EAM-ELAS, the armed wing of the Communist Party, had opposed EDES, the non-Communist resistance movement, and on the German withdrawal had risen in revolt, only to be crushed in February 1945 by an Allied force sent from the Italian Front.

GUATEMALA

ARMOURED WAGON

An attempted revolution against the rule of President Chacon broke out in January 1929 in western Guatemala. It failed, and the revolutionaries were dispersed, but they remained in control of certain towns. In February, in the course of their advance to regain control of the rebel towns, the government forces improvised an armoured wagon. It consisted of a field gun mounted on a platform wagon, protected by sleepers and sandbags.

SOURCES:

Ferrez, Major Turrel J, US Army, 'Armored Trains and Their Field of Use', *The Military Engineer* Vol XXIV No 137 (Sep–Oct 1932), p 472.

A view of the leading wagon, with its field gun behind a wall of sleepers.
(Photo: Philipp Jowett)

HONDURAS

IMPROVISED ARMOURED TRAIN USED IN THE 1897 UPRISING

In 1897 the Honduran government was taken by surprise by an uprising, during which the rebels seized Puerto Cortez on 13 April, and then advanced towards San Pedro Sula. Along the way, at the Laguna Trestle they captured a train along with its driver, an American by the name of Lee Christmas,[1] who was press-ganged into the service of the rebels, tasked with helping them enter the town. To that end, Christmas, turned mercenary somewhat against his will, organised the armouring of a flat wagon with walls of 20mm steel plates, reinforced by two layers of sandbags. A Hotchkiss gun was mounted at the front end.

The Federal army launched an attack on 14 April, but was driven off. The Federals were obliged to abandon San Pedro Sula and the train was able to enter the town. Lee Christmas was even promoted to the rank of Captain! His train was subsequently used to transport more rebel troops from Puerto Cortez, but the victory was short-lived: government troops, supported by Nicaragua,[2] retook the port and the rebels, threatened from two sides, were forced to retreat precipitately towards Guatemala. The revolt fizzled out in May.

SOURCES:

Deutsch, Hermann B, *The Incredible Yanqui* (London: Longmans Green & Co, 1931: reprinted by Pelican Publishing, 2012), pp 6–13.

[1.] Originally from Louisiana, Lee Christmas was the local representative in Honduras for United Fruit. Six years earlier, he had lost his job as a train driver following an accident on the Memphis-New Orleans railroad. In Honduras his narrow-gauge train was being used to transport blocks of ice to the coast and return to the provincial capital with loads of bananas. After his service with the rebels, Christmas pursued a career as a mercenary in Latin America for many years.
[2.] In 1895 Honduras, El Salvador and Nicaragua had agreed to form the Greater Republic of Central America.

HUNGARY

ARMOURED TRAINS 1918–1945

On 16 November 1918 the Kingdom of Hungary became the Democratic Republic of Hungary, and very quickly the new state lost border regions populated by non-Hungarian ethnic minorities. In April 1919 the government handed over power to Belá Kun who founded the short-lived Hungarian Soviet Republic, which was crushed on 3 August by the Czechs and Romanians. The country became a kingdom once more under the Regency of Admiral Horthy, who set about regaining the lost territories, a project which came to an end in 1945.

Austro-Hungarian armoured trains[1] IV, VI, VII and IX were stationed on Hungarian territory in 1918. They were renumbered I, II, III and IV respectively. Four new trains, numbered V to VIII, were built between December 1918 and January 1919. Due to the continuing fighting on the new frontiers of the country, six additional trains to be numbered IX to XIV were ordered from MÁVAG,[2] but the last two were never completed. The Communist regime intended to allocate these two trains, XIII and XIV, to the Red Railway Regiment, and a further five trains ordered in June 1919 were to be manned by the Hungarian Red Army. With the collapse of the regime, construction of these never even began.

On 12 June 1920 the new Hungarian Army reclassified the armoured trains as 'military surveillance trains',[3] and distributed them across the country.[4] In 1929, the four trains considered as worn out were broken up, and the four best trains, Nos I, II, III and V, were modernised. In 1938 smoke diverters were fitted on the engines, and turrets were mounted on the armoured wagons. Roman numbering was replaced by Arabic numerals. An armoured trolley, Type RÁBA Vp, was also put into service between 1932 and 1939. In the latter year, the trains were renumbered from 101 to 104, and came under the direct control of the Army High Command.

The four modernised trains went into action against Slovakia in March-April 1939, and took part in the reoccupation of Ruthenia[5] in March. In 1940 they were used in the invasion of Transylvania and then in 1941 against Yugoslavia. They then took part in the invasion of the USSR, and finished the war on Hungarian territory. On the Eastern Front, anti-aircraft wagons with minimal protection were added to the trains.

Above: Artillery wagon of the former Austro-Hungarian PZ IV or VI in use by the Hungarian Army in 1919.
(Photo: All Rights Reserved)

Above right: Armoured Train XII.
(Photo: Magyar Műszaki és Közlekedési Múzeum)

[1]. In Hungarian: '*Páncélvonat*', PV.
[2]. MÁVAG = *Magyar Királyi Államvasutak Gépgyára*, the Royal State Railway Manufacturers, Steelworks and Foundries.
[3]. *Katonai Őrvonot*.
[4]. On that date, the crews of the ten armoured trains totalled 41 officers and 662 men.
[5]. The eastern part of Czechoslovakia.

The engine of PV XII has only partial armour protection.

(Photo: Magyar Műszaki és Közlekedési Múzeum)

Austro-Hungarian PZ IX left in Hungary, seen in 1920 prior to being modernised. The two low-roof wagons would go to make up PV 102, and the powered railcar would go to PV 104.

(Photo: Paul Malmassari Collection)

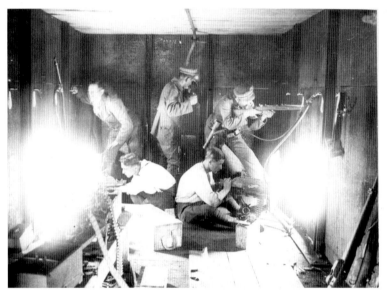

Interior shot of a Hungarian armoured wagon during the period of Communist rule. The armour protection extends down to the floor. Despite the spartan interior, note the communication system using voice tubes. The machine guns are Schwarzlose.

(Photo: Magyar Műszaki és Közlekedési Múzeum)

8cm forward turret of the type originally mounted on the river patrol boat *Győr*.

(Photo: http://militaryhistory.x10.mx)

Armoured Train IX of the Red (Hungarian) Army in 1919, with its anti-aircraft flat wagon sandwiched between two armoured wagons. On this train, the machine guns fired through gunports in the wagons in front of and behind the engine, but the crew of the end wagon were limited to using rifles and pistols.

(Photo: Magyar Műszaki és Közlekedési Múzeum)

PV 104 (ex-kkStB 303-343). In the 1930s, the turret was replaced by one taken from the Danube armoured river patrol boat *Győr*, when that vessel was rearmed with modern Bofors anti-aircraft weapons. Note the 'combat-type' coupling, which can be released from inside the hull.

(Photo: Paul Malmassari Collection)

Type RÁBA Vp armoured trolley , also designated a 'lightweight armoured train'. It does not appear to have been fitted with specific rail buffers or coupling gear.

(Photo: Barta Zoltan)

Engine MAV 377 of PV 101 seen at Roznyo in 1938.

(Photo: Magyar Mûszaki és Közlekedési Múzeum)

PV 102 seen in 1938, with engine MAV 377, and preceded by a lightweight trolley. Somewhat surprisingly, the national insignia is that used by the Hungarian Air Force between 1938 and 1941 (the colours being a green triangle then a white chevron and on the outside a red chevron), and in particular during the attack on Slovakia. Both 7cm guns taken from the *Gyór*[7] are now fitted to the reduced-height wagons of the former Austro-Hungarian PZ IX.

(Photo: Magyar Mûszaki és Közlekedési Múzeum)

In the Autumn of 1941, during the occupation of the Bačka region which Hungary had claimed since 1918, PV 101 or 103 was halted by the demolition of the Ba ko Gradište Bridge by the retreating Yugoslav Army.

(Photo: Muzej Vojvodine)

Closeup of the gun in the leading wagon of either PV 101 or 103. Note the cutout in the armour mantle which allows the gunsight to follow the movement of the 7.5cm F.K. Model 08.

(Photo: Muzej Vojvodine)

This photograph of either PV 101 or 103 shows the modifications to the shape of the roof on the artillery wagon. The lateral machine guns by this date would be the locally-manufactured 8mm Gebauer Type 34.AM.

(Photo: Magyar Mûszaki és Közlekedési Múzeum)

[7.] The armoured river patrol boat *Györ* was originally armed with two single turrets with 8cm guns (actual calibre 76.5mm).

The modernised wagons of PV 101 or PV 103. A turret armed with a 20mm Model 36 M has been installed on top of the roof, and a second 20mm Model 36 M is in a turret fitted at a lower level, the roof having been cut back. The smoke diverter was installed in 1938, and the Hungarian national insignia is now the white cross on a black square, which first appeared in late 1942.
(Photo: Paul Malmassari Collection)

A captured Soviet armoured wagon included in a Hungarian train.
(Photo: FORTEPAN)

Armoured train *Botund* with its mixture of different types of wagon.
(Photo: Hadtörténeti Intézey és Muzeum)

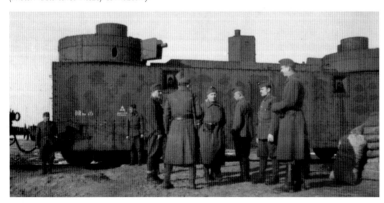

The artillery wagon of *Botund* on which is clearly visible the marking 'DR' denoting its previous inclusion in a Soviet armoured train, perhaps the *Leutnant Marx* of the 221st Security Division.
(Photo: Hadtörténeti Intézey és Muzeum)

Artillery wagon from PV 103 abandoned in Budapest (note the damaged observation cupola) in front of the arched entrance to the Eastern Railway Station. Note also the markings in Cyrillic letters added by the Soviets who had taken the city on 13 February 1945.
(Photo: All Rights Reserved)

Above: An anti-aircraft wagon seen in 1943, armed with a 40mm Bofors.
(Photo: Paul Malmassari Collection)

Right: The final illustration shows a 40-florin stamp commemorating the armoured trains of the Bolshevik Revolution, dated 7 November 1917 in the Julian Calendar (25 October for the countries using the Gregorian Calendar).
(Paul Malmassari Collection)

SOURCES:
Archive:
SHD: Box 7 N 2893.

Book:
Bonhardt, Attila, A *Magyar Királyi Honvédség fegyverzete 1919-1939* (Budapest: Zrínyi Katonai Könyvkiadó, 1992).

Journal article:
Villanyi, György, 'Magyar páncélvonatok', *Haditechnika* 1994/1, pp 69–71; 1994/ 2, pp 48–52.

INDIA

The Republic of India inherited several British armoured trains, one of which has been restored, and is today preserved at the National Railway Museum in New Delhi (see the chapter on Great Britain). On 15 August 1947, the very day of the declaration of independence which was to see the majority of the states of former British India merged into the new Indian Union, the State of Hyderabad declared its independence from the rest of India.[1] It was the largest of the princely states, situated in the very centre of the continent, and had a certain degree of administrative autonomy, having its own standing army and a militia, and running its own railway network. The new Indian Government refused to accept the situation, and after fruitless negotiations, on 13 September 1947 began Operation 'Polo' to annexe the state by force. Two main attacks were launched, from east and west, with a secondary attack from the south, the latter principally intended to secure the railway network, with three regiments of the Indian Army and two armoured trains. The whole operation benefitted from air cover, and Hyderabad was finally conquered on 17 September.

On 28 May 2010, the Jnaneswari Express derailed following sabotage of the track carried out by Maoist guerillas.[2] More than 170 passengers were killed. Initial responses included only running trains by day, which caused severe passenger disruption. Faced with the guerilla threat in the region of Jangalmahal, the state of West Bengal was obliged to introduce armoured locomotives, plus a widespread system of surveillance cameras along the most vulnerable stretches of track. Currently the railway network is guarded by the Railway Protection Force, an armed militia which is also a major employer.

SOURCES:

Sharma, Gautam, *Valour and Sacrifice: Famous Regiments of the Indian Army* (New Delhi: Allied Publishers, 1990).

[1.] For its part, the state of Kashmir refused to integrate into the new Pakistan, and requested Indian military assistance when the Pakistanis invaded.
[2.] No-one ever claimed responsibility for the attack, however. This guerilla movement which has affected virtually half of the states of the Indian Republic, began in 2005 after the formation of groups of Maoist insurgents, the 'Naxals', who preach revolt against the central government. Attacks against the trains began in 2006.

INDONESIA

Although the country unilaterally declared its independence from the Netherlands on 17 August 1945, formal recognition was not granted until 27 December 1949. The defence of the railway network during these four years is covered in the chapter on the Netherlands.

Newly-independent Indonesia suffered from several years of separatist agitation, notably in the south of Sumatra in the years 1951 to 1953. Armoured wagons accompanied the trains, and it appears that Dutch trolleys were put back into service, which would explain why several examples are displayed in Indonesian museums.

SOURCES:

http://www.overvalwagen.com
http://www.kaskus.co.id

A train double-headed by two 2-10-2 Type D52 engines, propelling two flat wagons carrying the hulls of BRAAT armoured trolleys, on a line in the south of Sumatra in the years 1951–3.
(Photo: All Rights Reserved)

This Panser Rel V16 armoured trolley has an aggressive and elegant appearance. It was constructed by joining two BRAAT (second version) vehicles together back-to-back. Traces of the original camouflage survive under the patches of rust on this vehicle parked out of service in a station. A restored example (perhaps the same vehicle) is now on display in the Bandoeng Museum.
(Photo: Tony Ford)

The Panser Rel V16 (perhaps from the designation of the motor) on display at Bandoeng in a new paint scheme. This vehicle measures 5.20m (17ft 0¾in) long and weighs 7 tonnes.
(Photo: http://www.kaskus.co.id)

IRAQ

Nominally an independent monarchy since 3 October 1932 but in practice under British control, the Kingdom of Iraq did not declare war on Germany in 1939 but did sever diplomatic relations. In 1941 British control of the Iraqi oilfields was threatened by proposed nationalisation and the formation of a national oil company run by representatives of the Axis powers. The British were determined to counter this threat to their vital oil supplies, and an infantry division was landed at Basra on 18 April 1941 to overthrow the Iraqi government. On 2 May 1941, an Iraqi armoured train, probably a veteran of the Mesopotamian uprising of 1920–2, was spotted on the metre-gauge line to the south of the town of Ur. Bombed by two Vickers Vincents. it was stopped outside Basra, and captured by the 3rd Sikhs. One report describes it as having been put back into service by the British.

SOURCES:

Northcote, H. Stafford, *Revolt in the Desert: Purnell's History of the Second World War*, Vol 2 No 4 (London: Purnell, 1967), pp 346–8.

IRISH FREE STATE

ARMOURED TRAINS AND TROLLEYS (1922–1941)

The Irish Free State was created by the Anglo-Irish Treaty signed in London on 6 December 1921, following the bloody Easter Rising of 24 April 1916 and the ensuing Irish War of Independence (21 January 1919 to 11 July 1921). The Treaty was intended to come into effect on 6 December 1922, but following its ratification by the Irish Parliament on 7 January 1922, opponents of the Treaty (the Republicans) rose in revolt, and were opposed by the Irish National Army (INA). The latter inherited armoured cars from the British (Rolls-Royces, Peerless and Lancias), and began constructing armoured trains and trolleys to counter Republican attacks on the railways. In addition, the Railway Protection, Repair and Maintenance Corps (RPR&MC) was created in October 1922.

The Irish Civil War

The first armoured train was based at Inchicore (Dublin) in July 1922, but it was destroyed by the Republicans. In August a second train was constructed in Limerick, using armour plates found in an abandoned British barracks, and other trains of variable effectiveness existed in Clonmel, Dundalk and Thurles. Following the creation of the RPR&MC, armoured trains were built in Cork and Dublin. The armoured train detachments organised by the RPR&MC and set up in Clonmel, Cork, Killarney, Limerick and Thurles had a total of nine trains, and in February 1923 they were stationed as follows: Clonmel: AT No 1; Thurles: AT No 2; Limerick: AT No 3; Cork: AT Nos 4, 5 and 6; Dublin: AT No 7; Dundalk: AT No 8; Mullingar: AT No 9.

The trains' main role was the protection of working parties repairing destroyed bridges and damaged track. In between the fixed bases, regular patrols were carried out by armoured trolleys. Of the various makes of Irish armoured cars, only the Lancia[1] armoured personnel carriers were converted for use on rails. Out of a dozen set aside for conversion, only seven (AL Nos 22, 23, 31, 32, 33, 47 and 51) were in fact fitted in September 1922 with flanged wheels. Their configurations varied between individual cars, and at least two of those converted at Inchicore were fitted with a turret armed with a machine gun.

The Republicans in general preferred to avoid combat with the trains and trolleys, leading to less attacks on the railway which nevertheless continued to suffer. The fighting which did take place was often hotly contested. For example, on 15 October 1922, it took the Republicans some four hours of fighting to force the surrender of the famous Lancia known as the *Grey Ghost* (from its

camouflage scheme and its near-silent approach). After being disarmed, the crew were set free, and the Lancia partly destroyed by fire. On 27 February 1923 the Lancia trolleys were based as follows: Cork: Lancias Nos 1, 2 and 3; Limerick: No 4; Dundalk: No 5; Dublin: Nos 6 and 7. In addition, a further five Lancias had been set aside for quick conversion to trolleys. At the end of the Civil War, the Lancia trolleys were restored to road use and passed to the Armoured Car Corps.[2]

Up to the Second World War

In 1931, the Irish Government expressed interest in the project by the Swedish firm of Landsverk, described in the chapter on Sweden, but no orders resulted.

The Army High Command envisaged the construction of an armoured train in 1941, to be built around a diesel locomotive. However, the GSR turned down the idea, because of the impossibility of obtaining armour plate, and the lack of a sufficiently powerful locomotive to carry armour in the first place.

Armoured train built by the Great Southern Railway, and crewed by its employees under military supervision.
(Photo: Irish Military Archives)

Armoured train photographed at Mallow in 1923. The engine is a 4-4-2 tank of the GSWR.[3]
(Photo: Walter McGrath Collection)

[1.] The Lancia armoured personnel carriers were originally British vehicles built on either Lancia 1 Z or Lancia Triota chassis, 100 examples of which were in service with the Irish National Army. Crew: eight or nine men; speed: 45mph (72km/h) forward, 20mph (32km/h) in reverse; armour: 6mm; armament: .303in Lewis LMG.

[2.] On the other hand, Peter Leslie states that several Lancia trolleys and an armoured train dating from the Civil War period were stored in a siding up until the 1950s.

[3.] GSWR = Great Southern & Western Railway.

Armoured train photographed on 14 February 1922. The internal wooden supports holding the armour plates are clearly visible at the front of the engine. With internal Stephenson valve gear, these tank engines carried no protection below the footplate.

(Photo: Paul Malmassari Collection)

Amusing play on words on 'the tank' engine of Armoured Train No 7. The discovery of the Pharaoh's tomb by Carter had taken place in 1923 and the news was all the rage at the time.

(Photo: Irish Railway Record Society)

A view of the armoured train of the DSER,[4] here in Grand Canal Street, Dublin in 1923. The engine is 2-4-2 No 64 *Earl of Bessborough*.

(Photo: All Rights Reserved)

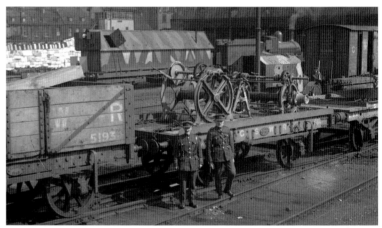

Behind the repair train we can make out the armoured train from Cork, and behind the horizontal capstan is the famous Lancia, the *Grey Ghost*.

(Photo: Irish Military Archives)

The complete armoured train from Cork, powered by a Class 101 GSWR 0-6-0 engine. The imposing armoured wagon at the rear had been built by the workshops of the CB&SC.[5] Note the carriage in front of the engine, armoured with plates over the windows, pierced by loopholes. On the other hand the engine crew are protected only by a simple plate at each side.

(Photo: Irish Military Archives)

Two Lancia armoured trolleys at Glanmire Road Station, Cork, in November 1922. The machine on the left is of the 'Hooded Terror' type, so-called from the nickname of the Lancia which had served as the prototype: the former open-topped crew compartment was now covered by an armoured roof. 'AL-23' on the rear of the body indicates 'Armoured Lancia' plus its original armoured car designation. It may in fact be Lancia Trolley No 1, and is ascribed to No 2 Company as marked on the left-hand cab door.
(Photo: Walter McGrath Collection)

The *Grey Ghost*, the famous Lancia which resisted a Republican attack for some four hours, before the crew surrendered, and the trolley was set on fire.
(Photo: Irish Military Archives)

SOURCES:

Archives:
Irish Army Ref 2/69329.

Books:
Share, Bernard, *In Time of Civil War, The Conflict on the Irish Railways 1922-23* (Cork: The Collins Press, 2006).

Conference Notes:
Walsh, Paul V, *The Role of Armoured Fighting Vehicles in the Irish Civil War, 1922-1923*. Lecture presented in September 1997 at the Cathal Brugha Barracks.

_____, *The Irish Civil War, 1922-1923: A Military Study of the Conventional Phase, 28th June-11th August 1922*. Lecture presented 10 February 2001 during the 6th Annual Conference of the Barnes Club of Temple University.

A variant of the Lancia armoured trolley, photographed at Inchicore, with armour similar to that of the *Grey Ghost*.
(Photo: Irish Military Archives)

The second Lancia trolley fitted with a turret, seen in the Inchicore workshops. The generous Irish track gauge of 5ft 3in (1600mm) is particularly noticeable here: the mudguards are no longer aligned with the road wheels. To fit the latter required an extension to each axle.
(Photo: All Rights Reserved)

Journal articles:
Bergin, Lieutenant-Colonel W J, 'Ambush on the *Grey Ghost*', *An Consantoir* (May 1978), pp 135–6.

Leslie, Peter, 'Armoured Rail Cars in Ireland', *Military Modelling Annual* (1974), pp 6–9.

McCarthy, Denis J, and Leslie, Peter, 'Armoured Fighting Vehicles of the Army No 3; The Lancia Armoured Personnel Carrier', *An Consantoir* (May 1976), pp 136–8.

Website:
http://railwayprotectionrepairandmainten.blogspot.fr/

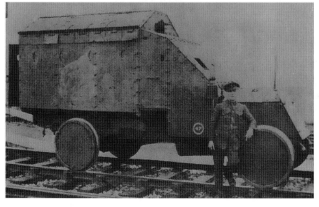

Yet another variant, with a different type of roof armour.
(Photo: All Rights Reserved)

[4.] DSER = Dublin & South Eastern Railway.
[5.] CB&SC = Cork, Bandon & South Coast Railway.

ITALY

ARMOURED TRAINS AND TROLLEYS 1891–1945

The first Italian foray into the realm of armoured trains occurred in 1891, when an Italian officer, conscious of the difficulty of defending the long coastlines of his country, laid before Parliament a proposal to defend Sicily with armoured trains. Although the idea was not taken up at the time, the Italians, like the British, were well aware of the possibilities offered by using armoured trains for coastal defence.

The Italians in Libya (1912[1])

The story of Italian armoured trains began after the Treaty of Lausanne was signed on 18 October 1912, recognising Italy's occupation of Libya. The conquest of Tripolitania and Cyrenaica had begun on 29 September 1911 with naval operations and landings. Benghazi was occupied on 20 October and Tripolitania was annexed on 5 November. There followed a year of fighting and an expansion of the revolt against the Ottoman Empire. The Treaty of Lausanne put an end to the war, but sporadic uprisings continued until 1931 when Sheikh Omar Al Mokhtar, the ally of the Senussi, was executed. Beginning in 1912, the Italians built a 95cm gauge network in Tripolitania and to guarantee security, put into service an armoured train comprising an engine and two armoured wagons based on a pair of flats used to transport long loads such as gun barrels.

The engine intended to haul the train, fitted with fairly comprehensive armour protection, including an armoured lookout on each side of the cab.
(This photo and the two following: Nicola Pignato and Filippo Cappellano, Gli Autveicoli da combattimento dell'Esercito Italiano (Volumes 1 and 2), by kind permission of the Ufficio Storico dello Stato Maggiore dell'Esercito – USSME)

---

[1]. The story of the Italian armoured trains in Libya ends in 1943, when Italy lost control of the country, renouncing all rights to Libya in 1947, the last Italian colonists being expelled in October 1970.

Two external views of one of the armoured wagons, with personal weapons (Carcano carbines) ready to fire from a standing position. This type of wagon would be effective against the types of light armament possessed by its opponents at the time it was introduced.

Note the access door at the engine end. The five Maxim machine guns could train over a wide arc. The central part of the roof was left open. Photographed in the workshop with the wagon on a short length of temporary track.

The Second World War

During the First and Second World Wars, the concern about coastal defence resulted in the '*Treni Armati*' ('Armed Trains') which were operated by the *Regia Marina* (Italian Navy). We will not study them in this work, as they are railway artillery rather than armoured trains in the true sense.

On the other hand, rail trolleys, not all armoured, were used in sensitive areas such as the Libyan-Egyptian frontier. In the

Armoured trolley used on the frontier between Libya and Egypt.
(Photo: Nicola Pignato & Filippo Cappellano, Gli Autveicoli da combattimento dell'Esercito Italiano, Volume 2)

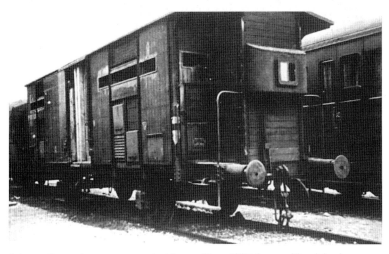

A type of escort wagon converted from a Type 1905 F van, with minimal armour protection and large loopholes.
(Photo: Nicola Pignato & Filippo Cappellano, Gli Autveicoli da combattimento dell'Esercito Italiano, Volume 2)

One of the first of the armoured trains, intended for coastal defence, with a Breda 20mm cannon and a 47mm Model 32 anti-tank gun.
(Photo: Nicola Pignato & Filippo Cappellano, Gli Autveicoli da combattimento dell'Esercito Italiano, Volume 2)

absence of other photographic records we have to return to the works of Nicola Pignato and Filippo Cappellano for a poor-quality but nevertheless unique image.

In the Balkans, the Italian zone of occupation included Slovenia, the Dalmatian coastline and the islands. Montenegro and Albania had already been included in the Italian Empire. At the time of the Italian invasion of Greece, Albanian resistance movements were disrupting communications routes, but when the Germans joined in the occupation of the Balkans, it was they who took over responsibility for the defence of the railway networks.

The *Compagnia Autonoma Autoblindo Ferroviairie* (Independent Railway Armoured Car Company) was created in Yugoslavia on 15 May 1942. In order for it to carry out its mission, which was to control the railway lines, several improvised armoured trains were converted from bogie wagons. The Littorina Blindate ('Libli') railcars, Model 42 trolley and the rail version of the AB 40 will be considered later.

The armoured trains

Separate from the escort wagons of the *Milizia Ferroviairia* (Railway Militia) which were included in goods trains, ten armoured trains were built, beginning in 1941, to assure the security of the lines in the Italian occupation zone in Yugoslavia. They were of simple design, converted from goods wagons, with armoured sides, and were initially armed with infantry weapons. In each train, two wagons were equipped with a 47mm 47/32 Model 35 anti-tank gun, able to fire at 90 degrees to the track by opening doors which gave a horizontal field of fire of around 120 degrees. Each gun covered one side of the track. Another wagon was armed with 20mm Breda Model 37 cannon. With the partisan threat increasing in intensity, the trains later incorporated wagons (up to six) with improved armour protection, having a central covered compartment (of wood or steel) with firing loopholes, and at either end an open-topped firing position for an 8mm Fiat/Revelli Model 14/35 machine gun. The armament was completed by a 45mm Brixia Model 35 mortar.

A goods wagon base armed with a 47mm Model 37 gun fitted with a small shield. The canvas covers add a degree of comfort in a region where the winters are particularly harsh.
(Photo: Nicola Pignato & Filippo Cappellano, Gli Autveicoli da combattimento dell'Esercito Italiano, Volume 2)

Above: A different form of protection on a Type L wagon, completely enclosed, the sides extended upwards and armoured, but once again armed with a 47mm gun with a very restricted field of fire.

(Photo: Nicola Pignato & Filippo Cappellano, Gli Autveicoli da combattimento dell'Esercito Italiano, *Volume 2)*

Below: Machine-gun wagon converted from a goods wagon. Note the camouflage scheme.

(Photo: Nicola Pignato & Filippo Cappellano, Gli Autveicoli da combattimento dell'Esercito Italiano, *Volume 2)*

This photo shows an interesting combination: the armoured body of a narrow-gauge wagon has been mounted on a standard-gauge wagon, leaving a slight gap between the two. The result is an armoured wagon which is perhaps more resistant to mines.

(Photo: Nicola Pignato & Filippo Cappellano, Gli Autveicoli da combattimento dell'Esercito Italiano, Volume 2)

An overall view of Armoured Train No 3 at Novo Mesto, where it was stationed from August 1943. The muzzle of a 47mm Model 32 can just be seen protruding from the side of the third wagon.

(Photo: Nicola Pignato & Filippo Cappellano, Gli Autveicoli da combattimento dell'Esercito Italiano, Volume 2)

Goods trains were hauled by modern Class 06 engines, with extensive armour protection on the cab, including the door for the crew. The armoured trains were powered by Class FS 910 tank engines.
(Photo: Nicola Pignato & Filippo Cappellano, Gli Autveicoli da combattimento dell'Esercito Italiano, Volume 2)

Saloon coach S 294 fitted with armour, seen here in July 1942.
(Photo: Archivo Ferrovie dello Stato Italiano)

In Slovenia and Dalmatia, the Second Army used several Series Dpz and DI coaches, armoured against small-arms fire, to form a command train with 'passive' protection, with no heavy armament and organised like a troop transport train, with sleeping accommodation, kitchen and so on. The windows were replaced by several armoured blinds.

A view of the end of the coach. The armour plates have been riveted to the original bodywork.

(Photo: Archivo Ferrovie dello Stato Italiano)

Although improvements to the protection and the armament of the wagons can be observed as the occupation continued, the Italian trains in the Balkans were not intended for an offensive role, which would be the province of the railcars and trolleys.

The 'Libli' railcars

In 1942 it was decided to armour the ALn-556 railcars of the Ansaldo firm, for service in Yugoslavia. The Railway Engineers chose models produced from 1936 to 1938. They had to be shortened by 5.60m (18ft 4½in). The prototype was tested in the Ansaldo-Fossati workshops in Genoa, and was adopted on 5 September 1942, with several recommended changes, with the designation '*Littorina blindata mod. 42 (Li.Bli 42)*'. The first production model was rolled out on 20 September and joined the *1º Compagnia Autonoma Littorine Blindate*. This company would receive eight railcars in total, and was made up of ten officers, twelve NCOs and 167 men. The 8.5mm armour protection was built in one piece, pierced only by access and maintenance hatches, and firing ports.

Armed with two tank turrets mounting 47mm guns, two versions were used at the same time. The first version had two openings in the roof to allow firing two 81mm Model 35 mortars, or flamethrowers through side apertures. The second had a circular tub with a pedestal-mounted 20mm Breda Model 35 cannon. The 8.5mm armour protection was built in one piece, pierced only by access and maintenance hatches, and firing ports.

When the Italian Armistice was signed, the 'Liblis' were based at Karlovac, Ogulin and Split (Croatia), Ljubljana and Novo Mesto (Slovenia) and Suse (in Italy, 30km/19 miles west of Turin). A series of machines was then ordered for the Wehrmacht in 1943 (see the chapter on Germany).

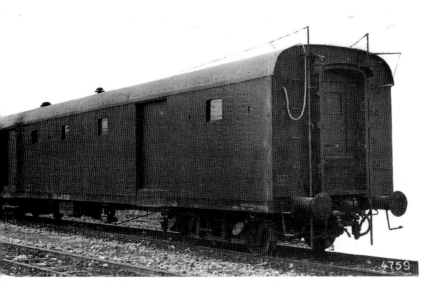

A view of the former baggage van Dpz 1913 converted into an armoured coach, intended for the command train *SLODA* (for SLOvenia-DAlmazia).

(Photo: Archivo Ferrovie dello Stato Italiano)

The Independent Railway Company saw hard service up until the Armistice of 1943, and suffered heavy losses. In particular two 'Libli' were destroyed, the first at Split in October 1942 and the second at Ogulin on 12 February 1943.

(Photo: Paul Malmassari Collection)

Technical specifications:

Length:	13.50m (44ft 7½in)
Width:	2.42m (7ft 11¼in)
Height:	3.57m (11ft 8½in)
Weight:	39.5 tonnes
Motor:	FIAT 355C, 80hp at 1700 rpm
Fuel:	Diesel
Maximum speed:	80km/h (50mph)
Range:	450km (280 miles)
Armour thickness:	8.5mm
Armament:	2 turrets similar to those fitted to the M13/40 tank, with 47mm/L32 gun with 195 rounds and 8mm Breda 38 machine gun
	Either 2 x 81mm Mod. 35 mortars with 576 bombs Or 1 x 20mm Breda Mod. 35 anti-aircraft cannon
	2 Mod. 40 flamethrowers
	4 x 8mm Breda 38 machine guns in side ball mountings with 8,040 rounds
	The personal arms of the crew and hand grenades
Crew:	1 officer, 2 drivers, 2 gunners, 2 loaders, 6 machine gunners, 2 mortar specialists, 2 flamethrower engineers, 1 radio operator
Radio equipment:	Marelli RF2CA or RF3M set
Various:	Turret searchlights, track repair equipment.

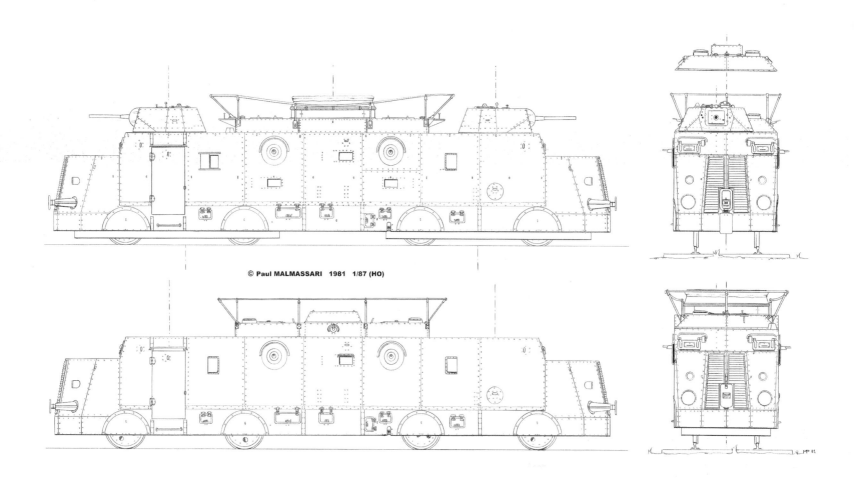

© Paul MALMASSARI 1981 1/87 (HO)

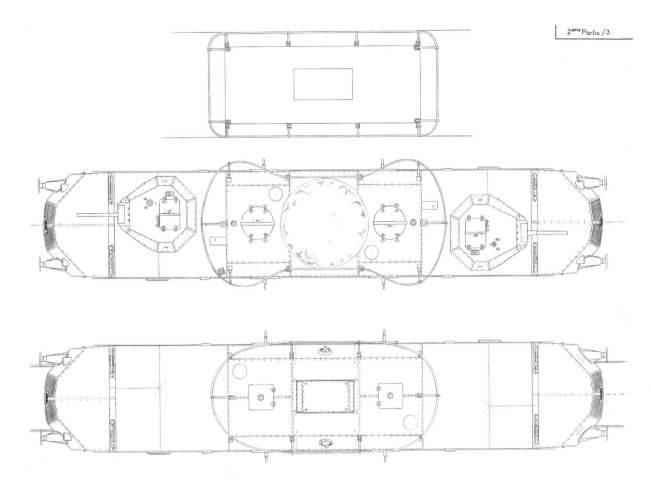

2ème Partie /3

The AB 40 and AB 41 trolleys

To supplement the 'Libli' railcars, a request was made on 24 July 1942 for the conversion of twenty AB 40 and AB 41 armoured cars into road/rail vehicles, to be used equally on the road or on rails simply by changing the wheelsets. The modifications also included adding sanding boxes to the front and rear wings, and one swivelling headlight. The first version could be recognised by its low turret armed with two 8mm Breda Model 38 machine guns. The AB 41 received a higher turret, an automatic 20mm 20/65 cannon and one Breda machine gun. Lastly, the AB 43, of which only an experimental model existed in road/rail form, mounted a 47mm gun.

Above: An AB 40 of the *2° Raggrupamento genio ferrovieri*. The sanding boxes and delivery pipes are clearly visible. The armament comprised three 8mm Breda 38 machine guns, two in the turret and one in the hull rear. Stoneguards were fitted in front of each rail wheel to aid in pushing aside small obstacles.
(Photo: Daniele Gugglielmi Collection)

Left: We are unable to say whether this camouflaged AB 41 is still in Italian hands or if it has been taken over by the Germans. The cannon is a 20mm Breda 35. This machine had a rear driving position, and therefore had no need for a turntable.
(Photo: Paul Malmassari Collection)

Technical specifications:

Length:	5.20m (17ft)
Width:	1.935m (6ft 4in)
Height:	2.44m (8ft)
Ground clearance:	35cm (13¾in)
Weight:	Between 6.9 tonnes and 7.7 tonnes
Motor:	FIAT-SPA ABM1, 6 cyl inline
Power:	AB 40: 88hp at 2700 rpm; AB 41: 108 hp at 2800 rpm
Fuel:	Petrol
Maximum speed (road):	78km/h (49mph) AB 40; 81km/h (51 mph) AB 41
Range (road):	400km (250 miles) AB 40: 350km (215 miles) AB 41
Armour thickness:	8mm
Armament:	3 x 8mm Breda 38 machine guns (AB 40); 1 x 20mm Breda 35 cannon and 2 machine guns (AB 41)
Crew:	4

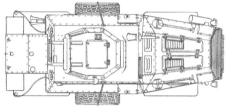

© Paul MALMASSARI 1982 1/87 (HO)

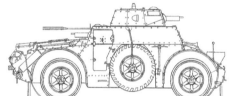
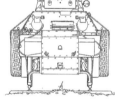
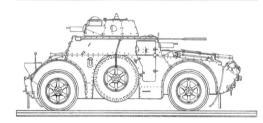
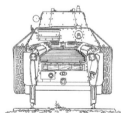

Autocarretta Ferroviaria Blindata Mod. 42 trolley

Derived from the Autocarretta OM36, twenty examples were built for the Railway Engineers. After prototype testing in late 1942, the machines were put into production in early 1943 and entered service in May 1943 on the narrow gauge (76cm/2ft 6in) lines in Dalmatia and Slovenia. After 8 September 1943, they continued in use with the Wehrmacht.

Technical specifications:

Length:	3.83m (12ft 6¾in)
Width:	1.535m (5ft 0½in)
Height:	2m (6ft 6¾in)
Ground clearance:	12.5cm (5in)
Weight:	3.2 tonnes
Motor:	FIAT-SPA AM, 4 cyl inline, 20hp at 2400 rpm
Fuel:	Petrol
Maximum speed:	15km/h (10mph)
Range:	350km (215 miles)
Armour thickness:	8mm
Armament:	1 x 8mm Breda 38 machine gun
Crew:	6

Above: This three-quarter front view shows clearly the turning mechanism of the type normally used on asymmetrical trolleys, but which was extremely dangerous to operate under combat conditions. Note also that the only means of access is via the roof, making a turning manoeuvre even more perilous.
(Three Photos: Daniele Guglielmi Collection)

Far left: The front view shows the modest dimensions of the machine, which would have been relatively uncomfortable for its crew. The front plate, pierced by the emergency starting-handle, protects the radiator air intake.

Left: In this rear view of the trolley, note the numerous firing and observation loopholes, plus the handrails which were the only means of climbing on the vehicle.

Two further projects were being studied in the Summer of 1943: the firm of Viberti had designed two trolleys (one for the narrow gauge and the other for the standard gauge) which did not go into production because of the Armistice. Extremely compact, they had probably benefitted from experience gained with the Autocarretta Mod. 42, despite the weakness of its armament and armour protection.

It would be simple to see in the defeat of the Axis Powers in the Balkans the failure of the means of defending the railway network. It is the case that the Italians were never able to prevent sabotage of the communications links, but the escort missions and the reconnaissance patrols carried out day after day by the Independent Company and the Railway Militia prevented the complete paralysis of the communications and supply lines in the Balkans. Lastly, the excellent qualities of the 'Liblis' are attested by the production orders and use by the Wehrmacht after 8 September 1943 in the zone which would now be known as the *OZAK* (*Operationszone Adriatisches Küstenland*, Adriatic Coast Operations Zone).

At some time, probably in the early 1920s, Anslado proposed an armoured engine, and also an armoured railcar. Although the drawing for the railcar is annotated in French, no record of a specific request for this project has come to light in the French archives. The inclusion of Saint Etienne Model 1907 machine guns in the plan suggest it was intended for use in French North Africa, probably Morocco. Interestingly, the plan also depicted the Ansaldo version of the stroboscopic observation device on the turret, similar in concept to that fitted to the French FCM Char 2C.

SOURCES:

Benussi, Giulio, *Treni armati treni ospedale 1915-1945* (Parma: Ermanno Albertelli Editore, 1983).

Guglielmi, Daniele, *Italian Armour in German Service 1943-1945* (Fidenza: Roadrunner, 2005).

Luparelli Albion, Filippo Ettore, *La Sicilia nella probabilità di una invasione francese* (Palermo: Michele Amenta, 1884).

Pignato, Nicola, *Atlante mondiale dei mezzi corazzati, i carri dell'Asse* (Bologna: Ermanno Albertelli Editore, 1971, 1983).

_____, *Un secolo di autoblindate in Italia* (Fidenza: Roadrunner, 2008).

_____, and Cappellano, Filippo, *Gli Autoveicoli da combattimento dell'Esercito Italiano (Volume 1)* (Rome: Uffico Storico SME, 2002).

_____, *Gli Autoveicoli da combattimento dell'Esercito Italiano (Volume 2)* (Rome: Uffico Storico SME, 2002).

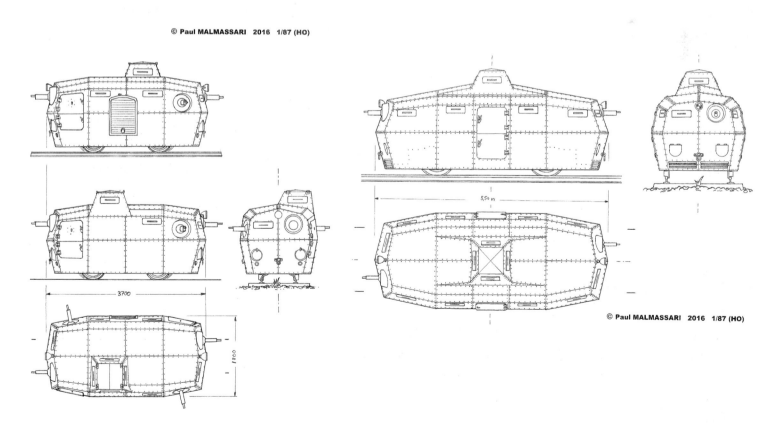

Plan of the Viberti trolley for the narrow gauge (76cm).

Plan of the Viberti trolley for the standard gauge.

JAPAN

ARMOURED TRAINS 1918–1945

Beginning in 1894, in moves to establish footholds and expand territorial gains on the continent of Asia, the Japanese Empire became embroiled in several conflicts, firstly with the Chinese Empire, and then with the Republic of China. Amongst other territorial gains, the Sino-Japanese War of 1894–5 gave Japan Formosa and Port Arthur in Manchuria. Korea became a Japanese colony. Then Japan participated in the Allied intervention in Siberia from August 1918 to October 1922. In 1931 Japan conquered Manchuria and renamed it Manchukuo. Finally, the Second Sino-Japanese War which broke out in 1937 became part of the wider Second World War.

As for Japanese armoured trains, from 1918 they intervened in Siberia, in 1931 in the invasion of Manchuria, then in 1932 in the move against Shanghai, and finally across the whole of occupied Chinese territory. After the Japanese defeat in 1945, Japanese armoured trains were used by Chinese forces during the Chinese Civil War, and perhaps even in Korea.

Intervention in Siberia (1918–1922)

Japan intervened in the Russian Civil War as part of an international force totalling 25,000 men. The Japanese first went into action in Siberia in July 1918 at the request of the American government, with the despatch of an initial contingent of 12,000 men under Japanese command.[1]

Once the troops were in place, the security of the railway network was assured by armoured trains, most of which had been brought to the region by the withdrawing Czech Legion. The Japanese, however, refused to become involved to the west of Lake Baikal, and their priority was basically to support the White Generals Ataman Semyonov and General Kalymkov, who themselves were well-equipped with armoured trains, and then later General Baron von Ungern-Sternberg.

On 5 April 1920 the Japanese contingent, the sole non-Russian force

remaining after the withdrawl of the American contingent,[2] launched an offensive to disarm the local revolutionary forces, with the ultimate aim of protecting the Japanese Home Islands, as well as its colonies in Korea and Manchuria, against the threat of the anti-monarchist Bolsheviks. The Japanese crossed the Transbaikal, withdrew their support from Semyonov, and finally in October 1922, giving in to international and domestic[3] pressure, withdrew their troops.

This gun crudely placed on an elevated platform, installed aboard a Russian bogie wagon and allowing for only head-on fire, appears primitive in comparison with other contemporary armoured trains with guns in turrets.
(Photo: Paul Malmassari Collection)

More in keeping with the standards of the day, this train which flies the Hinomaru, the Japanese flag,[4] is built on the base of a classic Russian railways' bogie wagon.
(Photo: Paul Malmassari Collection)

[1.] The 12th Division was the first to land on 3 August 1918 and went into action alongside the Czechs in the region of the Amur and the Ussuri Rivers. At their peak, the Japanese contingent numbered 72,000 men commanded by General Otani, who in theory was nominal head of all the Allied troops. In fact the Russo-Japanese War was still fresh in local memory, and the Russians mistrusted the growing power of Japan.
[2.] The AEFS, the American Expeditionary Force in Siberia, was withdrawn on 1 April 1920.
[3.] The Japanese intervention had cost their forces 5,000 dead from combat and disease.
[4.] Adopted in February 1870. The 'Hinomaru' differs from the better-known war ensign adopted in May 1870 which includes sixteen sun's rays.

This Japanese armoured wagon built on a Russian bogie wagon has rudimentary armour protection, but its armament is impressive.

(Photo: Paul Malmassari Collection)

A close-up of one end of the railcar of *Orlik*, which still bears its Czech name, with the inscription 'VUZ CIS.1' meaning 'Wagon No 1'.

(Photo: Paul Malmassari Collection)

A well-known photo of an interesting machine-gun wagon, with a mixed Czech and Japanese crew, typical of the forces defending certain sections of the Trans-Siberian Railway.

(Photo: All Rights Reserved)

The artillery wagon of *Orlik*, here in Japanese hands, as shown by the inscription painted on the sides. The gun is a 76.2mm Russian Model 1902 in a turret with a horizontal field of fire restricted to 270 degrees due to the armoured superstructure.

(Photo: Paul Malmassari Collection)

A fine view of the armoured railcar which operated with, or independently of, the armoured train *Orlik*. Note the Czech officer on the left, with a group of Japanese officers. Note also the latest modifications such as the searchlight mounted on the roof.

(Photo: Paul Malmassari Collection)

Above: This photo shows the ultimate appearance of a Russian armoured wagon, formerly part of Kalmykov's forces but now taken over by the Japanese. Note the 'Japanese touch' of the additional armour, and in the overall arrangement of the train, which appears less haphazard than in its original version.

(Photo: All Rights Reserved)

Right: A fine photo of a Japanese armoured trolley in service in Siberia. It is surrounded by Czech Legionnaires.

(Photo: Vojenský ústřední archive-Vojenský historický archive)

Japanese Armoured Trains in Manchuria, China and Korea (1931–1945)

The civil war which began in 1911[5] had left China fragmented. In Manchuria, where Japanese influence had replaced that of the Russians since the war of 1905, on 18 September 1931 minor damage caused to a railway line[6] passing close by a Chinese garrison, in what became known as the 'Mukden Incident',[7] gave Japan the excuse to strengthen its hold by launching an invasion.[8] By occupying Harbin on 5 February 1932, the Japanese completed their military conquest of Manchuria, one of the major Chinese provinces situated well to the north of the original Japanese zone of influence. Subsequently, on 18 February 1932 the Japanese created the puppet state of Manchukuo, ruled by Pu Yi, the last Emperor of China, which would never be recognised by the League of Nations.

In 1928, the Japanese had assembled six armoured trains in Manchuria, armed with 75mm Model 41 mountain guns. But following the Mukden Incident, the Railway Company of the Kwantung Army was created specifically to commission armoured trains and take over responsibility for their technical aspects. Alongside the growing number of armoured trains, 'guard trains' were brought into service, the latter composed of just one infantry wagon coupled to an artillery wagon. In addition, armoured wagons crewed by veterans of the Manchurian Railway Company were coupled in with scheduled trains. Thus by 1935, the Kwantung Army had a total of twenty-eight armoured trains and four guard trains.

A lack of detailed records prevents us describing all the actions in which armoured trains participated during the campaign, but several typical engagements were reported in the newspapers of the time. Although the Chinese Army in Manchuria had retreated in disorder, the railway lines were by no means secure. For example, on 15 November 1931, when the Japanese tried to outflank the Chinese lines near the bridge over the River Nonni, Chinese cavalry succeeded in cutting off the troop detachment which had disembarked from their armoured train, and only a few of the Japanese succeeded in rejoining the train, under the covering fire of its guns.

The whole of Manchuria was nominally occupied by the Japanese, but they in fact controlled only the towns and the railway lines, along with a large part of the Chinese Eastern Railway. The Japanese presence obliged the Russians to maintain 150,000 men along the length of the frontier between Vladivostok and Manchuli (the station closest to the Manchurian frontier). The Japanese garrison, in addition to tanks and artillery, maintained some thirty armoured wagons.

In reprisal for a boycott of Japanese goods by the Chinese authorities in response to the invasion of Manchuria in early February 1932, the Japanese decided to take military action in Shanghai. The Chinese resisted the Japanese aggression and among other means, brought an armoured train into use on the Shanghai-Nankin line, operating principally by night, and added armoured wagons to their troop trains. It appears that their use ceased once the Japanese landed heavy artillery.

On 7 July 1937 the Marco Polo Bridge Incident between Chinese and Japanese troops led to the outbreak of the Second Sino-Japanese War on the 28th of the same month, in which the Japanese captured several Chinese cities. In March 1940 a Central Chinese Government was installed by the Japanese, but the war gradually developed into a series of guerrilla and counter-guerrilla actions. This conflict ended on 8 August 1945 with the Japanese surrender,[9] the occupation of Korea by Soviet forces and the outbreak of a new civil war in China.

The lack of good roads in this immense territory meant that the railways were vitally important. The Japanese deployed large numbers of troops to protect the railways, and in turn these became a principal target for sabotage. The Imperial Army used several armoured trains[10] and armoured trolleys. These units were obliged to operate over two different rail gauges depending on the area:

1520mm (5ft nominal) Russian gauge in the northern zone of Manchuria, and 1435mm (4ft 8½in) European gauge in the rest of the territory.

The first Japanese armoured trains, which according to Antoine Baseilhac 'represented the only highly mobile powerful elements across the vast Manchurian plains', were improvised from existing Manchurian rolling stock. They also used elements of captured Chinese armoured trains, which were often better constructed, many being former White Russian armoured trains brought to China when the Whites had fled Russia at the end of the Civil War. But to meet the need for modern equipment, two unique designs of armoured train were built for use in Manchuria: the Temporary Armoured Train in 1932, and the following year the Type 94 Armoured Train. At the same time, a large number of self-propelled units were put into service for use by rail reconnaissance patrols.

This type of armoured wagon is typical of the Korean or Manchurian railway network. Its construction is straightforward, with an armoured body attached to a standard bogie flat wagon which is the same as in preceding photos.
(Photo: Konstantin Fedorov, Archivist, Collection)

Right: This photo should be compared to that shown in the chapter on South Korea (1950–3). The arrangement of the opening flaps on the firing nacelle is interesting, as is the tripod fixture for a searchlight on the roof. In fact, this photograph viewed in conjunction with the preceding two proves that the nacelles were diagonally offset.
(Photo: Paul Malmassari Collection)

A view of the other end of the wagon.
(Photo: Konstantin Fedorov, Archivist, Collection)

5. The Republic of China was created on 1 January 1912 by Sun Yat-sen.
6. The rail network in that region belonged to the Japanese Railway Company of Southern Manchuria.
7. The modern Shenyang.
8. See also 'Armoured Trains in Comic Books' in Appendix 1.
9. The island of Formosa had been Japanese since 1895, and only became Chinese again in 1945. We do not know if the defence of the island's railway network included armoured trains.
10. In Japanese: *Soko Ressha*.

Similar construction features are evident on other armoured trains, here lacking lateral MG nacelles. Note the front observation position separated from the main armoured hull.
(Photo: Paul Malmassari Collection)

Another similar view – perhaps the other end of the same train, showing the various different types of protection, riveted plates, welded plates, sandbags, etc.
(Photo: Paul Malmassari Collection)

In addition to armoured wagons intended to be included with normal trains, the Japanese put together armoured trains intended for offensive patrols. Here, the pilot/safety wagons have been uncoupled. The insignia on the side of the armoured wagon is that of the military railways.
(Photo: All Rights Reserved)

In these photos, we can see dark rectangles painted as a *'trompe-l'œil'* to represent false firing ports.
(Photo: Paul Malmassari Collection)

A different type of pilot/safety wagon, equipped with an armoured cabin for close observation of the track. The design of these cabins varied considerably, and there seems to be no standard pattern.
(Photo: Paul Malmassari Collection)

Two photographs of a typical armoured train on the Manchurian front. In this view, the train is lacking an artillery wagon which would normally be coupled to the wagon in the foreground.

(Photo: Paul Malmassari Collection)

Here is the front part of the same train showing the partial protection on the engine, but with a fully-armoured cab fitted with a sliding blind. The gun appears to be a 75mm Type 41 (1908).

(Photo: Paul Malmassari Collection)

Probably an earlier design of pilot/safety wagon, since the second wagon is a Russian high-sided bogie wagon of the type used during the Russian Civil War.

(Photo: Heiwa Kinen Tenji Shiryokan)

Another tactical feature of these trains is shown here: to provide sufficient water for the engine, a bogie tank wagon was inserted between the tender and the artillery wagon.

(Photo: Paul Malmassari Collection)

A view looking down on an artillery wagon, which would serve as the inspiration for a number of subsequent illustrations. For examples, see Appendix 1.

Here the horizontal board serves both as protection from the elements and as a recognition feature for Japanese aircraft. This photo was the inspiration for the postcard shown in Appendix 1.

(Photo: Paul Malmassari Collection)

The Japanese also put into service armoured trains on the narrow-gauge or metric lines within their occupied territory. These two views show two trains of this type, with a gun in a turret and with armour obviously tailored to the contours of the wagons. But it is just possible that these show a training unit (white armbands, irregular form of the armour etc)

(Two Photos: Wawrzyniec Markowski Collection)

Japanese protection wagon, converted from a van, seen as part of an unarmoured train photographed at Tientsin in August 1937. It is armed with a 6.5mm Type 11 light machine gun.

(Photo: Paul Malmassari Collection)

Above: Another van roof fitting seen in Manchuria, this time armed with a 6.5mm Type 3 heavy machine gun. The lack of the special ring sight would suggest this is not meant for anti-aircraft protection.

(Photo: All Rights Reserved)

Below: An imaginative postcard issued by an anti-aircraft unit, their stamp bearing two AA guns, a searchlight beam and sound locators. In fact the Chinese air force put up little real opposition.

(Postcard: Paul Malmassari Collection)

Right: In the course of their offensive, several Chinese armoured trains were captured by the Japanese and were immediately put back into service, as we can see in this photo, where the side of the wagon to the right bears Japanese markings. For other views of these units, refer to the chapter on China.

(Photo: Paul Malmassari Collection)

Temporary Armoured Trains (1933–1945)

'Temporary Armoured Train' was the official name given to this type of train, which was designed in 1932 as an experiment for service in Manchuria. In all, three of these trains were built, the first one being completed in July 1933. They were operated by the 3rd and 4th Railway Regiments. Each train was made up of the following elements:

– Pilot (track control) Wagon.
– Heavy Artillery Wagon.
– Light Artillery Wagon.
– Infantry Wagon.
– Command Wagon.
– Tender Engine.
– Auxiliary Tender.
– Technical Equipment Wagon.
– Infantry Wagon.
– Light Artillery Wagon.
– Howitzer Wagon.
– Pilot (track control) Wagon.

One of the Pilot (track control) Wagons, built on a 30-tonne bogie platform wagon, with its turret for close-in defence, armed with a 6.5mm Type 11 LMG. The two armoured doors protect a 60cm diameter searchlight.
(Photo: All Rights Reserved)

An overall view of the train, demonstrating the typical camouflage used on the Chinese front. Immediately obvious from this photo is the degree to which the plume of smoke from the engine, when it is not diverted to track level or otherwise dispersed, gives away the precise location of the train to enemy observers.
(Photo: All Rights Reserved)

The leading Artillery Wagon of the Heavy type, with its 100mm Type 14 anti-aircraft gun, in a turret with all-round traverse, and supplied with 500 shells. Its additional armament was composed of a heavy machine gun and ten rifles, served by a crew of one officer and fourteen men. Here the lower armour plates have been hinged upwards, allowing us a view of the means of stabilising the wagon when firing. Also visible are the seemingly excessive number of firing ports, closed by sliding shutters – although the total would allow for the full crew to bring their weapons to bear on one side.
(Photo: All Rights Reserved)

Of note are the rails and sleepers attached to the sides of the wagon, and the well-executed camouflage scheme.
(Photo: All Rights Reserved)

The same comments apply to the Light Artillery Wagon, whose crew of one officer and nineteen men served the two turrets, each mounting a 75mm Type 11 gun, supplied with a total of 500 rounds. The base for both units was the Type Ta-I 50-tonne coal wagon.

(Photo: All Rights Reserved)

A bogie platform wagon formed the base for the Infantry Wagon. Each turret was armed with a 13mm Type 92 HMG. The armament also included two 6.5mm Type 3 MGs (also known as the Taisho 14), two Type 38 rifles and a 30cm diameter searchlight. The crew consisted of one officer and eleven men.

(Photo: All Rights Reserved)

The Command Wagon had two levels, the lower for the radio compartment and the upper for the artillery command post – one can just see the binocular sight projecting from the roof. One of the observation nacelles is in the raised position, as is a radio aerial with its retractable mast passing through the roof. The light armament comprised two MGs and ten rifles.

(Photo: All Rights Reserved)

This view of the Command Wagon shows the two observation nacelles mounted on telescopic tubes. Note the plates protecting the sides of the open platform.

(Photo: All Rights Reserved)

There is no vertical armour over the boiler, but the steam dome is protected from horizontal fire.

(Photo: All Rights Reserved)

A passage ran behind the vertical armour plates on the Manchurian Railways 2-8-0 Type 'So-ri-i' tender engine, allowing crew members to pass from one end of the train to the other.

(Photo: All Rights Reserved)

The Technical Equipment Wagon converted from a Type Ha-2 coach. The generator-powered radio equipment required the fitting of frame aerials mounted on insulator blocks.
(Photo: All Rights Reserved)

The impressive Auxiliary Tender based on a 50-tonne coal wagon is fitted with two retracting turrets each armed with a 6.5mm Type 11 MG, which allowed observation and fire along the length of the train. Note the central access door.
(Photo: All Rights Reserved)

A fine view of the roof of the Technical Equipment Wagon.
(Photo: All Rights Reserved)

Above: The Auxiliary Tender carried enough coal for 600km (375 miles) and enough water for 300km (188 miles).
(Photo: All Rights Reserved)

At the rear end of the train was the Howitzer Wagon, based on the same commercial wagons as the other artillery wagons, but with a turret armed with a modified 150mm Type 4 howitzer. The armament also included four Type 3 MGs and ten rifles, for a crew of two officers and twenty men.
(Photo: All Rights Reserved)

Type 94 Armoured Train (1933–1945)

The Type 94 Armoured Train was conceived after feedback from operating the previous Temporary Armoured Train. Design began in October 1933 and in one year the train had been built. It would remain a unique example, as there was no follow-up. Although capable of running at up to 65km/h (40mph), it was essentially a coast defence/mobile artillery type of train rather than a track patrol unit. Compared to the other armoured trains used in China and Manchuria, its light armour protection of 6mm and 10mm plates shows that it was not designed for close-range combat.

Its eight elements were as follows, from head to tail:

– Pilot (track control) Wagon.
– Artillery Wagon No 1 (Kó).
– Artillery Wagon No 2 (Otsu).
– Artillery Wagon No 3 (Hei).
– Command Wagon.
– Engine.
– Tender.
– Electrical Generator Wagon.

The Pilot (track control) Wagon at the head of the train, equipped with a 30cm-diameter armoured searchlight. On can see the 7.7mm Type 92 MGs for close-in defence and the sliding shutters for the observation ports. The central coupling knuckle indicates that this wagon has been built on the base of a 30-tonne Type Ta-I mineral wagon.
(Photo: All Rights Reserved)

Turrets aligned fore and aft, here the train is photographed between Sakako and Furanten.
(Photo: All Rights Reserved)

A superb view of the complete train, which gives a feeling of invulnerability due to its homogenous design. It underwent running trials from 16 November to 16 December 1934, and in the interim its firing trials on 8 and 9 December.
(Photo: All Rights Reserved)

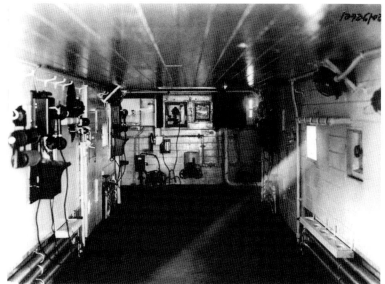

The interior of the Pilot Wagon, which appears to comprise a small command post. Its layout is similar to that of the Command Wagon of the Temporary Armoured Train, and it too carries rails and sleepers mounted on its sides.
(Photo: All Rights Reserved)

Interior view of the forward part of the Kó Wagon, with its armour plates backed with wood. In the background is the turret revolving basket, while on the left are some of the racks for the 200 shells the wagon carried.
(Photo: All Rights Reserved)

The Otsu Wagon was similar in design to the Kó Wagon, except that its superstructure was higher to enable it to fire over the latter. On this wagon all four MG turrets could be used against both ground and air targets. The same as used on board ship, the coincidence rangefinder and its crew are visible on the roof, with the binocular periscope to their left. In the camouflage pattern are yellow or ochre bands intended to break up the regular lines of the wagon.
(Photo: All Rights Reserved)

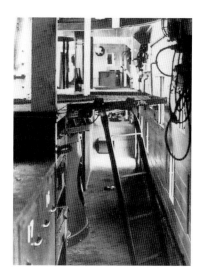

The interior of the Otsu Wagon. The ladder was needed for access to the rotating basket of the turret, set at a higher level than in the Kó version.
(Photo: All Rights Reserved)

The Kó Wagon is fitted with a single turret armed with a 100mm Type 14 anti-aircraft gun (here used solely against ground targets) with a 270-degree field of fire. Its maximum range was 15km (9.4 miles). The 7.7mm Type 92 MGs in the forward turrets are for use against ground targets, while those in the rear turrets are dual-purpose ground/AA.
(Photo: All Rights Reserved)

As with the other artillery wagons, the Hei Wagon was constructed on the base of a 60-tonne wagon Type Chi-i. The guns are 75mm Type 88 anti-aircraft guns, also capable of engaging ground targets, with a horizontal range of 14km (8.75 miles), provided with 300 rounds each.

(Photo: All Rights Reserved)

This interior view shows one of the turret baskets of Wagon Hei. At the very top of the photo the breech of the 75mm gun is just visible. Although it seems to be a relatively small weapon compared to the size of the wagon, each gun had a rate of fire of some twenty rounds per minute.

(Photo: All Rights Reserved)

Two views of the interior of the Command Wagon. Above, the upper level with the base of the periscope and various fittings. Below, the lower level, clearly the office for the train command staff.

(Photos: All Rights Reserved)

The Command Wagon, constructed on the base of a 60-tonne coal wagon Type Ta-sa. Each turret is armed with a 7.7mm Type 92 MG. On can just make out one of the lateral searchlights in its armoured enclosure, plus various optical instruments.

(Photo: All Rights Reserved)

The Mikado 2-8-2 tender engine has simple vertical armour protection, open at the top.

(Photo: All Rights Reserved)

The left-hand side of the tender showing the retractable nacelle in the outboard position, topped by a small rotating turret armed with a 7.7mm Type 92 MG. One can just make out the door at the right-hand end.

(Photo: All Rights Reserved)

The smokebox protection is completed by a plate fastened on the front. The cutout enables us to see the American-style smokebox door. The vertical cylinders are perhaps air pumps.

(Photo: All Rights Reserved)

A view seldom seen, of the front end of the tender facing the engine, to which it is normally attached by the drawbar clearly visible here. In this photo the MG nacelle is in the retracted, inboard position.

(Photo: All Rights Reserved)

Even the tender was armed: one can just make out the retracting turrets, centre-right and far-left. The water capacity (in the six tanks with circular hatches) and the coal carried sufficed for a range of only 150km (94 miles), showing that the train was never intended for long-distance patrols across the Manchurian plains.

(Photo: All Rights Reserved)

This side view of the Generator Wagon showing its roof-mounted aerial.

(Photo: All Rights Reserved)

End view of the Generator Wagon, bringing up the rear of the train, with its two 7.7mm Type 92 MGs for close-in defence and the armoured 30cm searchlight.
(Photo: All Rights Reserved)

The Kó Wagon having the wheelsets of its bogies changed.
(Photo: All Rights Reserved)

Two views of a Japanese armoured wagon captured at the end of the Second World War. It is not possible to determine the location, but the presence of a central knuckle coupling plus buffers is indicative of the Russian network.

The shoe used to accurately level the artillery wagons for firing.
(Photo: All Rights Reserved)

After the war, Japanese equipment was reused by the various combatants in China and in Korea. This is perhaps one of these armoured trains watched from afar by a group of children, while more adventurous adults scavenge in the wreckage of what appears to have been a head-on collision.
(3 Photos: Paul Malmassari Collection).

Japanese Armoured Trolleys

SUMIDA[11] RSW Armoured Trolley

It would appear that the Japanese Army authorised only the infantry and cavalry to use armoured vehicles armed with artillery, which would explain why armoured rail trolleys are only seen with machine guns in turrets.

The RSW trolley, based on an armoured truck, was designed in 1929 to carry out railway security missions in Manchuria. The armour was 6mm thick and covered the whole vehicle. Square ports were placed around the four sides of the hull for the personal arms of the crew. The armoured radiator slats could be fixed open to increase the flow of air. For it to run on rails, all that was needed was to remove the solid rubber tyres from the wheel rims. Three headlamps provided the lighting in front of the trolley.

Postcard showing an RSW trolley at the workshops in Paichengtzu in China.

(Postcard: Paul Malmassari Collection)

A view of an RSW Trolley with the crew disembarked. In this vehicle the driver sits on the right-hand side, which explains the larger hatch. The red sun (or 'Meatball' as the Americans called it) for air-recognition purposes is painted in the centre of the turret hatch.

(Photo: Paul Malmassari Collection)

Type 91[12] SO-MO armoured trolley

This heavy trolley,[13] with the official designation of '*91-Shiki Koki Kenisha*' or 'Tractor for Wide Gauge, Type 91', was identified by Allied wartime intelligence as the Type 93 'Sumida' Armoured Car, an incorrect designation used ever since (and which the author has himself used in previous works).

Built from 1930 onward, this 6x4 vehicle had plain wheels which could be fitted alternatively with solid rubber tyres for the road or with flanged rims for running on rails. Derived from the Naval Type 90 Armoured Car, it weighed 7 tonnes and carried 16mm of armour over its vitals.[14]

The road-rail conversion took around twenty minutes, and necessitated raising the vehicle by means of the four jacks fitted to the bumpers. In addition, the spacing of the wheels could be adjusted to suit the rail gauge. The trolley reached a maximum speed of 60km/h (38.5mph) on rails as against 40km/h (25mph) on roads. However, as the chassis was unidirectional and lacked a built-in turntable arrangement, it was necessary to couple two trolleys back-to-back to allow for rapid withdrawal under fire. It was armed with six 7.7mm Taisho Type 92 MGs, one of which was mounted in the turret.

Their principal zone of operations was the China and Manchurian theatres, but it seems that several examples were used in Indochina and Malaya. The stated production total of 100 examples could include the Naval Type 90 and the Army Type 91 versions.

The original Navy Type 90, which lacked the means of converting it for rail use. The inscriptions signify 'Vehicle No 1 offered by the town of Nagaoka'.[15]

(Photo: Matthew Ecker)

11. Named after the River Sumida which flows through Tokyo. Originally, the name Sumida was that of the first truck built in 1929 by the Tokyo Ishikawajima Shipbuilding & Engineering Co. Ltd. The name of the workshops is often confused with the name of the SO-MO trolley (see below).
12. The numbering system for Japanese armoured vehicles (and in fact, all weapons) related to the year the Empire was founded, i.e. 660 BC. The year 1931 therefore corresponded to the Japanese year 2591, of which the last two numbers were used, resulting in the designation '91'. For weapons introduced from 1941 onward, the 'zero' of '01' disappeared and the item became 'Type 1'.
13. The year designations of four vehicles were close together, as were their characteristics: Types 90 (naval version), 91 (SO-MO Trolley), 92 (Chiyoda Motor Car Factory of the Tokyo Gasu Genki K. K., but also a light tank), which added to the confusion on the Allied side.
14. 16mm on the turret sides and the front face of the hull; 11mm on the hull sides and rear; 6mm on the hull top and floor, and the turret roof.
15. 'Hokoku-Koto' was the name of the organisation which offered the vehicles to the Navy, while the corresponding organisation providing vehicles to the Army was the 'Aikoku-Koto'.

The Army Type 91 on solid rubber tyres for the road, with rail rims and re-railing ramps clamped to the hull sides.

(Photo: All Rights Reserved)

Close-up of the front end detail in the previous view.

(Photo: Heiwa Kinen Tenji Shiryokan)

A well-known view of the front of a SO-MO, showing the central knuckle coupling which was adjustable for height. The four lifting jacks for raising the vehicle above the rails are protected by sacking.

(Photo: Paul Malmassari Collection)

A Type 91 SO-MO of the Tsudanuma Railway Regiment seen in 1939, lacking the brackets for the re-railing ramps.

(Photo: Wawrzyniec Markowski Collection)

A later configuration, with the front axle replaced by a bogie, easier to repair after hitting a mine, and also providing a better-quality ride over uneven track. The original front wheels are carried on top of the bogie, for reconversion to road use.

(Photo: Wawrzyniec Markowski Collection)

A camouflaged version. The re-railing ramp is clearly seen, as is the built-in front railing jack.

(Photo: Heiwa Kinen Tenji Shiryokan)

The protection against the cold helps break up the lines of the vehicle and aids in camouflaging it. Note the two boxes (a field modification?) on the cab roof in front of the turret.

(Photo: Wawrzyniec Markowski Collection)

A group photo of SO-MO units with their proud crews, in a summer setting with the armoured flaps of the radiators open. A second photographer is at work capturing the line of four SO-MOs in the background, with one or more wagons coupled in the rake, and behind him is a convoy headed by a road-rail ISUZU truck. This scene demonstrates the wide use the Japanese made of the SO-MO for patrol work. Note the uneven track in the depot, devoid of ballast, laid on closely-spaced wooden sleepers.

(Photo: Heiwa Kinen Tenji Shiryokan)

A fine view of the rear of a trolley, from which one can see that the two rear doors were not symmetrical. The two units are connected in tandem, and this time the armament is in place.

(Photo: Paul Malmassari Collection)

A paperweight in cast iron or white metal, made for the Manchurian Railway Company.

(Private Collection)

Problems on the track near Jehol on 3 September 1933. Troops scan the countryside for any sign of the Chinese who have removed sections of rail.

(Photo: Paul Malmassari Collection)

A train crossing a box-girder bridge with no side railings in March 1941. It is possible this is a construction train.

(Photo: Heiwa Kinen Tenji Shiryokan)

The rail-convertible ISUZU truck gave rise to an armoured prototype which closely followed the form of the SO-MO. One difference is that the wheels shod with pneumatic tyres can be replaced by complete flanged rail wheels, and not simply the flanged rims as on the SO-MO.

(Photo: All Rights Reserved)

The kind of souvenir photo that every soldier in every army wants, standing with his comrades beside his combat vehicle!

(Photo: HeiwaKinenTenjiShiryokan)

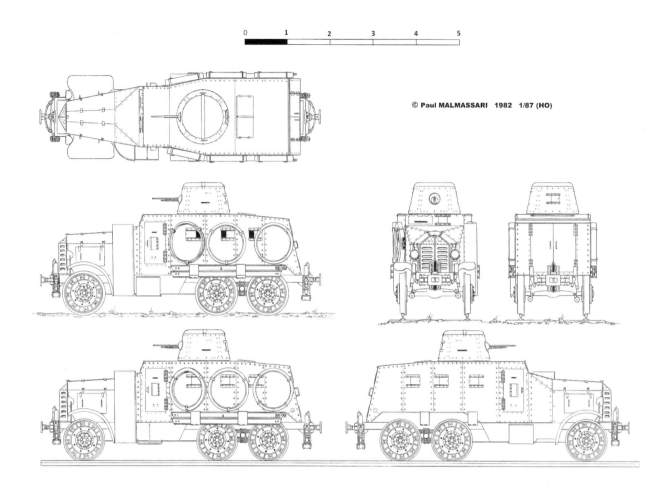

© Paul MALMASSARI 1982 1/87 (HO)

Length:	6.57m (21ft 7in)
Width:	1.9m (6ft 3in)
Height:	2.95m (9ft 8in)
Speed:	60km/h (37.5mph) on rails: 40km/h (25mph) on roads
Armour:	6mm min; 16mm max
Armament:	1 x 6.5mm Type 91 machine gun
Weight:	7.7 tonnes
Range:	240km (150 miles) on rails
Crew:	6

Japanese SO-KI Road-Rail Tank (1935)

In 1935 the Japanese designed the advanced SO-KI Type 95 Light Tank, of which sixty-five examples were built.[16] A number were captured by the Chinese Nationalists,[17] then taken over by the Communist forces, and one surviving example is now on display in the Beijing Military Museum. To the best of our knowledge this was the only tracked road-rail armoured vehicle to have seen operational use, in Manchuria and even perhaps in Burma.[18]

16. Some sources quote a total of 121.
17. A photo was published in the 1 January 1950 edition of *El Mundo*.
18. Paradoxically, the Japanese SO-KI Type 95 Light Tank ran slightly slower on rails than on roads, but on rails its range was much greater.

The SO-KI Tank in its 'rail' configuration. Its compact dimensions can be gauged by comparison with its crew members beside it.

(Photo: Wawrzyniec Markowski Collection)

Two photos of the SO-KI on display in the Beijing Military Museum.

(Photos: Yichuan Chen)

A fine interior shot of the SO-KI. In the centre is the vehicle commander's seat, directly beneath the turret.

(Photo: Wawrzyniec Markowski Collection)

The SO-KI could be employed as a rail tractor, as proved by its fittings: hook and tow chains etc.

(Photo: RAC Tank Museum)

When in rail configuration, it was necessary to secure the central part of the track to avoid it rubbing on the sleepers, and to immobilise the outer rollers. The SO-KI could be employed as a rail tractor, as proved by its fittings: hook and tow chains etc.

(Photo: All Rights Reserved)

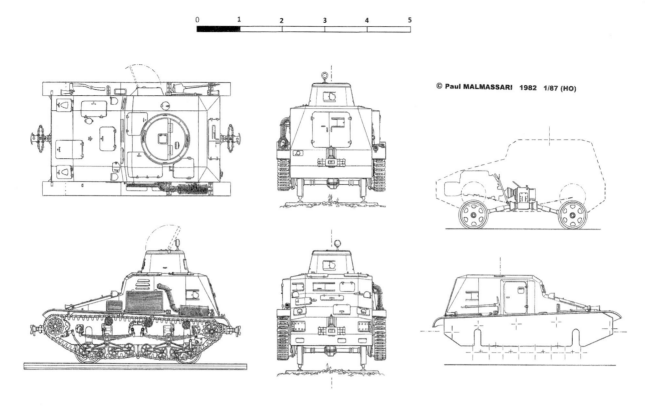

© Paul MALMASSARI 1982 1/87 (HO)

Length:	4.53m (14ft 10¼in)
Width:	2.50m (8ft 2½in)
Height:	2.45m (8ft 0½in)
Speed:	72km/h (45mph) on rails; 80km/h (50mph) on roads
Armour:	6mm min, 8mm max
Weight:	9 tonnes
Trench crossing:	1.50m (4ft 11in)
Range:	355km (222 miles) on rails; 123km (77 miles) on roads
Crew:	6

These unidentified armoured trolleys may be captured Chinese vehicles. The searchlight mounting is similar to the tripod seen in the previous photos of the armoured wagon in Manchuria.

(Photo: Paul Malmassari Collection)

Various Japanese armoured trolleys

Alongside the armoured trains, a certain number of armoured trolleys of different types were also constructed, some of which we are unable to formally identify. Nevertheless, their interesting designs merit inclusion here. In Manchuria, several radio-controlled trolleys were put into service to act as pilot/safety trolleys in front of the trains. No technical details have come to light.

Another unidentified armoured trolley, this time displaying more modern lines.

(Photo: Paul Malmassari Collection)

A well-known type of trolley, of which several examples were built by the Tokyo Gas and Electric Co., here in use as a scout vehicle for a train which is pushing a safety pilot wagon.

(Photo: Wawrzyniec Markowski Collection)

A pair of four-wheeled armoured trolleys, of which the design recalls aspects of the Temporary Armoured Train and the Type 94. The side extensions on the trolley do not have firing ports, only observation windows. The insignia on the officer's armband is that of the Combat Railways Command.

(Photo: Wawrzyniec Markowski Collection)

Above: The same type of armoured trolley in Chinese service after the war.
(Photo: Wawrzyniec Markowski Collection)

Right: The hull was constructed of plates 6mm and 8mm thick. Note the three headlights at each end to illuminate the track, and the masts holding the radio aerials to receive the control signals. The masts are remarkably similar to those used on the German radio-controlled Fernlenkboot (exploding motorboats) built by Siemens-Schuckert in 1917, perhaps indicating German technical help.
(Photo: Japanese Army Handbook) Above:

SOURCES:
Books:
Baseilhac, Antoine, *Recherches sur l'armée de terre japonaise 1921-1931*, Masters dissertation under the guidance of W Serman, Paris I Panthéon-Sorbonne, 1993–4.
Branfill-Cook, Roger, *Torpedo, The Complete History of the World's Most Revolutionary Naval Weapon* (Barnsley: Seaforth Publishing, 2014), pp 31–2.
Fujita, Masao, *Japanese Armoured Trains* (Kojinsha Co., 2013) (in Japanese).
Surlemont, Raymond, *Japanese Armour* (Brussels: A.S.B.L. Tank Museum V.Z.W., 2010).

Journals and Journal Articles:
Danjou, Pascal, 'L'automitrailleuse SUMIDA', *Minitracks* No 4 (4th Quarter 2002), pp 49–52.
Japanese Tanks up to 1945, Tank Magazine Special Issue (Tokyo: Delta Publishing Co. Ltd., April 1992) (in Japanese).
Lesser-Known Army Ordnance of the Rising Sun (Part 1), Ground Power Special 2005-01 (Cambridge: Galileo Publishing Co. Ltd., 2005) (in Japanese).
Malmassari, Paul, 'Le Char sur rails Type 95 SO-KI', *TnT* No 24 (March 2011), pp 54–5.
Merriam, Ray, and Roland, Paul, 'Japanese Rail-Riding Vehicles', *Military Journal* No 11, pp 12–13.

Panzer No 6 (1996).
Panzer No 9 (1996).
Panzer No 7 (1997).
Panzer Vol 13 No 9 (1990).

Tank Magazine No 2 (1987).
Tank Magazine No 4 (1987).
Tank Magazine No 7 (1987).

The Tank Magazine No 6 (1982).
The Tank Magazine No 7 (1982).
Panzer No 48 (June 1979).
Panzer No 49 (July 1979).

LATVIA

ARMOURED TRAINS[1]

The War of Independence (5 December 1919 – 11 August 1920)

The territory which would become the independent state of Latvia was occupied by German troops from March to November 1918. In the Russian Civil War, the majority of Latvian units fought on the Bolshevik side. In 1918,[2] two 'governments' claimed hegemony, one being a coalition of democratic parties and the other the Bolsheviks. Both sides armed their troops for the conflict. Alongside them the German troops stationed in Courland together with Germans who had settled in Latvia formed the *Landeswehr*[3] under the command of General Rüdiger von den Goltz. Their aim was to fight the Reds with the aid of the White Russian forces commanded by Colonel Pavel Bermondt-Avalow, and then to march on Moscow. In October 1919 they began their offensive, but the German troops were halted by the combined efforts of the Allied fleet and two Estonian armoured trains (the Estonians at that time occupying the northern part of Latvia). In November, the 'Bermondtists' were beaten, and retreated to Prussia. In January 1920, the Latvian forces went on the offensive against the Bolsheviks, and the subsequent Treaty of Riga signed on 11 August 1920 formally recognised the independence of Latvia, no longer part of Russia.

As the military and political situation evolved, German and Estonian armoured trains were engaged in combat either alongside or against the Latvian forces. On 22 May 1919, a Bolshevik armoured train was captured by the *Landeswehr* in Riga. It then fell into the hands of the Latvians at the battle of Cesis and was designated BV No 1. The future BV No 2 named *Komunistu iznicinātājs* ('Destroyer of Communists') went into action on 9 July 1919. These units, forming an Armoured Train Battery created on 21 July 1919, were joined by BV No 3 in September 1919 and by BV No 4 (captured from the Bermondtist forces) in November 1919.

The Inter-War Period

At the close of the War of Independence, Latvia possessed six trains,[4] but by 1921 only two remained in service, and these lacked anti-aircraft armament. In October 1923 the Latvian Government made overtures to France for the construction of six engines, four or six armoured wagons and twenty wagons mounting turrets. However, following a political crisis in Latvia the project was shelved in January 1924.

Between 1925 and 1930, as part of a major modernisation and rearmament programme, four new trains entered service and made up the Armoured Train Battery[5] based in Riga, which also included three 152mm Canet railway guns. The armoured trains were divided between the Russian gauge (1520mm/5ft nominal) and the standard gauge (1435mm/4ft 8½in) networks. The Latvian Guard (*Aizsargs*) which came under the authority of the Minister of the Interior, appears also to have used armoured trains as part of its railway regiment.

On 1 July 1926, the Battery was reorganised as an Armoured Train Regiment, and in 1939 it was planned to build two additional units. The Regiment was eventually dissolved on 3 February 1940, because of a lack of ammunition which up until then had been supplied by Czechoslovakia and Germany. The two trains still in service were allocated to the Coast Artillery Regiment.[6]

Occupation by Soviet then German Forces

On 17 June 1940, Soviet forces occupied Latvia, and the armoured trains were incorporated in the Red Army. The following year, the Soviet armoured trains of obvious Latvian conception were cut off and captured by the Wehrmacht, who set about converting the Latvian railway network from Russian gauge to standard gauge. This task was virtually complete by the end of 1941, and the majority of Latvian armoured train units were thereafter reused by the Wehrmacht.

The badge of the Latvian Armoured Trains Regiment.
(Photo: All Rights Reserved)

---

1. In Latvian: *Bruņoto'Vilcienu*, abbreviated as BV.
2. November 18th 1918 is recognised as Independence Day in Latvia.
3. Territorial Defence Force.
4. Included were two trains armed by the British who also provided training: *Kalpaks* (the future BV No 5) and *Pikols*. Both were discarded in December 1919.
5. BV No 3 was activated in 1928 and BV No 4 in 1930.
6. The static defences had been reinforced in the late 1930s by two railway guns.

PZ 5 of the *Landeswehr*.
(Photo: Paul Malmassari Collection)

Unidentified Latvian armoured train, probably photographed in the 1920s.
(Photo: Latvijas Kara Musejs)

In 1919, the Latvians captured a Bolshevik armoured train of the 'Krasnoye Sormovo' type, and put it into service with their own armed forces.
(Photo: Latvijas Kara Musejs)

A similar armoured loco, seen here at Daugavpils in 1923.
(Photo: Latvijas Kara Musejs)

Here is the same wagon, captured in turn by the Wehrmacht in 1941.
(Photo: Paul Malmassari Collection)

BV No 2 in 1919. Its armour protection consists of Russian trench shields, of which several thousand were available in the stores.
(Photo: Latvijas Kara Musejs)

Right: The armoured locomotive from BV No 2, demonstrating that it too was armoured using Russian trench shields.
(Photo: Latvijas Kara Musejs)

Left: The platform wagon *Kalpas* of BV No 5 in November 1919, with its crew of British sailors and Marines and their 3in HA gun.
(Photo: Latvijas Kara Musejs)

A classic shot of one of the later Latvian armoured trains.

(Photo: Paul Malmassari Collection)

Probably BV No 1 near the Viksna bridge in the Summer of 1924.

(Photo: Latvijas Kara Musejs)

Armoured train at gunnery practice in October 1931.

(Photo: Latvijas Kara Musejs)

One of the two armoured wagons designed by engineer Oskars Dzervitis in 1925. Interestingly, the turret gun (which is probably a German 7.7cm 16 field gun) still retains its wheels and gunner seats, possibly allowing for it to be dismounted for use off the train. In the same year, the older locomotives were replaced by new engines, fitted with arrangements to vent the steam and smoke at rail level.

(Photo: Latvijas Kara Musejs)

One of the 152mm Canet railway guns, photographed in 1937.

(Photo: Latvijas Kara Musejs)

Photographed in Cietoknis Station, a modern train evidently made up of elements of shorter trains, including the old platform wagons from PZ 5 still in use, but now armed with British guns.

(Photo: Latvijas Kara Musejs)

Above: One of the Canet guns seen here in travelling mode, attached in support of a complete armoured train.

(Photo: Paul Malmassari Collection)

Above right: An armoured train seen during the 1930s, armed with a 37mm Hotchkiss revolver cannon, a devastating close-range anti-personnel weapon despite its age.

(Photo: Paul Malmassari Collection)

SOURCES:

Book:

Lavenieks, J, *Bruņoto vilcienu pulks* (New York: Izd. Vera Laveniece, 1971).

Websites:

http://vesture.eu/index.php/Bru%C5%86oto_vilcienu_pulks

http://vesture.eu/index.php/Latvijas_armijas_Bru%C5%86oto_vilcienu_divizions

http://www.lacplesis.com/WWI_To_WWII/Pirmais_Pasaules_un_Brivibas_Kars/BRUNOTAIS_VILCIENS/index.htm

LITHUANIA

ARMOURED TRAINS

Lithuania waged three wars to gain its independence, beginning on 16 February 1918 and lasting for two years. The first was fought against the Bolsheviks, and ended in June 1919, the second against Russo-German forces invading Lithuania from neighbouring Latvia, and the third against the Polish Army which sought to seize Vilnius (Vilno) in defiance of the League of Nations' decision to cede that city to Lithuania. This third conflict ended in defeat for the Lithuanians. The latter used two armoured trains,[1] incorporating parts of captured Russian armoured trains.

The ST *Gediminas*[2] was built in January 1920 in Kuanas (Kovno) and was despatched to Varena to confront the Poles. On the 19th of that month it was on the front line at Suvalkai, but was forced to withdraw to Vilnius, where it was captured intact by the Poles. It saw further service as part of the Polish armoured train PP 1 *Marzalek*.

In October 1920 a replacement armoured train bearing the name *Gediminas* was built by the Lithuanians. On 21 November it was sent to Kedainai to confront the Polish forces, but the ceasefire took effect before it could go into action.

When the Lithunian army was formally established, it included a battalion with three armoured trains, all built at the Kaunas workshops: ST 1 *Gediminas*, ST 2 *Kęstutis*[3] and ST 3 *Algirdas*.[4] The layout of each train was standardised asd an engine, an artillery wagon with two guns, and two machine-gun wagons each armed with eight machine guns. In January 1924 the battalion became a regiment and was incorporated in the Armoured Group 'Sarvuociu Rinkine'. However, ST 3 *Algirdas* was broken up in early 1927. A directive dated 16 November 1927 fixed the establishment of the armoured trains as five officers, six NCOs and forty-one men. The armoured trains formation was finally dissolved on 14 August 1935. Certain sources give the name of the third armoured train as *Glezininku Vilkas*,[5] but at the date of writing we have been unable to confirm or refute this. Several wagons survived to be captured during the Soviet invasion, but they have not been identified as having been incorporated in later Russian armoured trains.

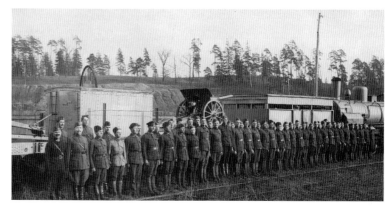

Artillery Wagon No 1 of ST *Gediminas*, armed with a pair of ex-German 7.7cm *Feldkanone* 16 field guns, retaining their original shields. The mixed armament reflects the tortuous frontier problems of this period of European upheaval. *(Photo: Paul Malmassari Collection)*

Artillery Wagon No 3 of ST *Gediminas*, armed with French 75mm Model 97 guns, again retaining their wheels but now fitted with large box gunshields. *(Photo: Paul Malmassari Collection)*

In the foreground is Artillery Wagon No 2 of the ST *Gediminas*, armed with ex-German Army 10.5cm *Leichte Feldhaubitze* 98/09. The light howitzers, retaining their wheels, appear to be mounted on turntables. Each gun has been retrofitted with a large box shield providing good protection for the gunners. Artillery Wagon No 3 in the centre is armed with a pair of French 75mm Model 97 field guns with their wheels and original small shields.

(Photo: Paul Malmassari Collection)

---

[1] In Lithuanian: 'sarvuotas traukinys', abbreviated to 'ST'.
[2] Gediminas (c. 1297–1341), Grand Duke of Lithuania in 1316.
[3] Kęstutis (1297–1382), son of Gediminas, Duke of Trakai, co-ruler of Lithuania with his brother Algirdas.
[4] Algirdas (c. 1276–1377), brother of Kęstutis, Grand Duke of Lithuania 1345.
[5] 'Iron Wolf'.

MALAWI

The various struggles for independence in Africa have left a legacy of extensive minefields. From 1981 Malawi Railways diesel locomotives[1] were loaned to Mozambique to operate on the line to the port of Nacala, which allowed trains to avoid crossing Rhodesia following that country's unilateral declaration of independence from Britain. Since 1979 the other rail line leading to Beira had been put out of action by RENAMO.[2] Because of the political instability and the constant threat of attacks during the decade 1980–90, four Malawi Railways locomotives – Numbers 401, 402, 407 and 408 – were fitted with armour plates around the cab and certain fittings. Shire Class locomotives were also armoured in a similar fashion, and improvised armoured wagons provided protection for the trains.

SOURCES:
Bagshawe, Peter, private archives
Warner, Terry, 'Armoured Trains in Southern Africa', *Tank TV* (New Zealand) No 6 (June 1994, p 1.

One of the protection wagons on the Nacala line, fitted with the hull of a British Ferret armoured car.
(Photo: Peter Cooke)

[1.] The locomotives were 3ft 6in gauge units built by Metropolitan Cammell Carriage & Wagon Co Ltd of Birmingham/ Associated Electrical Industries (AEI), powered by a 1200hp Sulzer 6LDA28B motor.
[2.] Resistência Nacional Moçambicana.

On 22 November 1989, broken-down Zambesi Class Co-Co diesel-electric locomotive No 407 with its armour plating arrives at Blantyre towed by No 402. Diesel locomotives 401 and 408 were similarly armoured.
(Photo: Peter Bagshawe)

Shire Class Co-Co diesel-electric locomotive No 500 being armoured at the Limbe workshops in November 1989. The framework to support the armour plates has been fitted to the roof and hood, but it is not clear whether the intended all-round armour protection was ever mounted.
(Photo: Peter Bagshawe)

Another form of armour giving all-round protection to the cab of this Shire Class Co-Co diesel-electric locomotive No 501 seen at the Limbe workshops in 1989.
(Photo: Peter Bagshawe)

MALAYSIA

The British began to intervene actively in the affairs of the Malay peninsula from the end of the eighteenth century, and it was made a Protectorate in 1910. After the Japanese occupation during the Second World War, the Malayan Union became a colony in 1946, and two years later was replaced by the Malaysian Federation. A Communist uprising which began on 16 June 1948, and ended in 1960, plunged the country into a hard-fought counterinsurgency war (the 'Malayan Emergency'). It was during this period, on 31 August 1957, that the Federation gained its independence from Britain.

Following use by the British armed forces, a number of Wickham armed trolleys remained in the country, while others were sold on to countries[1] facing similar security threats and which, of necessity, used the same rail gauge. But the need for internal security continued even after the Communist guerrillas surrendered. Following the American withdrawal from Vietnam, the Malaysian authorities feared infiltration by guerrillas coming from Thailand. Therefore in 1978 they ordered a new design from Wickham, but in fact this was destined to remain on the drawing board. The machine was based on a development of the AT 105[2] armoured vehicle built by GKN Sankcy, to be mounted on a Wickham chassis. Powered by a Perkins V8/540 water-cooled motor, via a Clark 13-H-R 28314 gearbox with three speeds in both forward and reverse, maximum speed was 95km/h (60mph). The 16mm armour would offer protection against 5.56mm and

7.62mm projectiles fired from as close as a dozen metres (13 yards), with a floor 6mm thick. The turret was to have been armed with either one or two 7.62mm L 37 A1 machine guns

SOURCES:
Wickham Archives.
Malayan Railways.

Wickham trolley No 57 in Kuala Lumpur in December 1968. It has probably since been scrapped.
(Photo: Paul Middleton Collection)

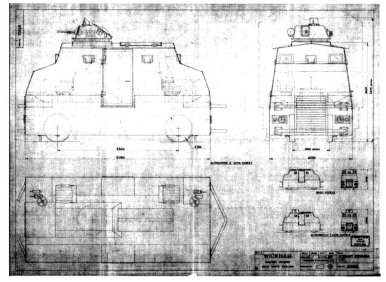

The original plan of the Wickham Project proposed to Malaysia in 1978.
(Plan: Wickham)

Three trolleys are still preserved in museums: AWT Nos 56, 60 and 63. Here is AWT No 63 in front of the Royal Malayan Police Museum in Lake Garden.
(Photo: http://zureuel.blogspot.fr/2008/05/wickham-trolley-legacy-of-malaysian.html)

An armoured brake van on display at Farlim. This type of armoured unit, of which several examples were probably constructed for use with goods trains, has never received as much attention as the offensive/patrol machines.
(Photo: Jaafar Amil)

---

[1] Vietnam, Thailand and Burma. Certain sources also mention Cambodia.
[2] Ultimately named the Saxon, this vehicle went into production in 1976, and several examples equip the Malaysian Army.

MAURITANIA

ARMOURED LOCOMOTIVES & ESCORT WAGONS (1978)

Iron ore represents some 50 per cent of Mauritania's exports, and the iron mines of Zouérate, run by the Company MIFERMA (Iron Mines of Mauritania Ltd) are connected by an extremely long railway line to the Atlantic port of Nouadhibou. In the 1970s the operator, Mauritanian Railways, was owned by MIFERMA.

Following Mauritania's occupation of the southern part of former Spanish Western Sahara in 1976, this crucial link came under regular attack by the POLISARIO Front, who were fighting to establish an independent Sahrawi Democratic Arab Republic (SDAR) in the occupied territories. Exchanging their camels for armed Land Rovers, the POLISARIO fighters launched lightning raids against the railway, causing significant damage to rolling stock and installations.

In 1978 the Mauritanians decided to armour the driving cabs of the locomotives and, at irregular intervals in the 2,500m (over one and a half miles) long iron ore trains they inserted improvised escort wagons. These were very summarily protected, by welding lengths of rail around the mineral wagon roofs to form a precarious shelter for the lookouts and gunners. The armament consisted of ex-Soviet 23mm cannon behind rudimentary shields.

In 1979 an armoured command wagon was constructed, and coupled near the end of the train. It was in direct radio commication with the locomotive. The ex-freight container which was used as the body was not fixed rigidly to the wagon chassis, in order to try to minimise the shocks felt when the extremely long convoy accelerated or slowed down. With 200 to 210 mineral wagons each weighing 83 tonnes, even a small gap of a centimetre between wagons, plus the spring effect of the couplings, would mean a to-or-fro movement at the rear of the train of 2–3m! This could produce a shock effect powerful enough to make an occupant of the command wagon lose his footing, if he were not prepared. The attacks ended when on 5 August 1979 Mauritania's new government signed a peace treaty with the POLISARIO Front, recognised the right to independence of the SDAR, and withdrew its own forces.

MIFERMA Class CC 01-21 diesel locomotive, based on the SNCF CC 65000 Class (Alsthom) with two diesel engines as per the French locos but of higher power output.
(Photo: Private Collection)

The damage caused by a POLISARIO raid on the locomotive depot.
(Photo: Private Collection)

The weight of the loaded iron ore trains required the use of three or four coupled locomotives. Note the powerful track-illuminating searchlight mounted lower down on the header loco, and therefore less vulnerable than on the standard production models. The superstructure fitted to the loco roof contained and protected the engine's vital air-filtration system.
(Photo: Private Collection)

Armour plating of the driving cab, with the offset spacing of 3mm just visible, and the company's livery continued over the armour.
(Photo: Private Collection)

Each train was made up of at least 200 wagons, among which armoured wagons were inserted at intervals. They would be withdrawn from service in 1979. The guards in their exposed positions were far more likely to flee or seek shelter than to fight back against raiders …
(Photo: Private Collection)

In 1979, an armoured command wagon was inserted in the convoys. The mineral wagon next to it is only lightly armoured, and is armed with a shielded 23mm cannon.
(Photo: Private Collection)

MEXICO

ARMOURED TRAINS AND TROLLEYS

The use of various armoured trains by the governments of the day and by certain revolutionary factions make the railways of Mexico one of the lasting symbols of South American revolutions. It is generally held that there were two principal revolutions: that of 1910–12 followed by civil war, and that of 1935–8, and in between the two the War of the Christeros.

Under the dictatorship of General Porfirio Diaz, the development of the railways was a mark of real progress: by 1910 Mexico had 20,000km (c. 12,000 miles) of railway lines, divided basically between two North American Companies, the 'Ferrocarril Central Mexicano' and the 'Nacional Mexicano'. But then the political situation deteriorated and the revolution broke out in November 1910, with the Maderists[1] rising up against the government, and the repression which followed. One of the future famous figures of the revolution, Francisco Villa,[2] joined the insurgents at the end of November in Chihuahua (North Mexico). In February 1911 Emilio Zapata began his agrarian uprising in Morelos, 80km (50 miles) to the south of the capital. In May, President Diaz resigned and left the country. Madero was elected and crushed the revolutionaries under Zapata who had risen up against him. In February 1913 Madero was assassinated, and was replaced by General Huerta. This saw the beginning of a long troubled period ('la decena tragica').

Pancho Villa waged a guerrilla war against the large landowners in Chihuahua. At the head of the División del Norte he captured the major rail junction of Torreón in late September, together with a huge collection of rolling stock. In December 1913 he became Governor of the State of Chihuahua. For his part Zapata continued his guerrilla struggle in the States of Pueblo and Guerrero. In April 1914 the Americans intervened for the first time at Vera Cruz, following the arrest of US sailors and to prevent the landing of a cargo of arms bound for the Federales. To force General Huerta to leave office, the Constitutionalists of Carranza, the troops under Villa (first allies then opponents of Huerta), and those under Zapata converged on Mexico City in a race to see whose forces would enter first. Between April and July 1915, in the struggle between the factions which began after the entry of the Zapatists and the Villaists (on 24 and 28 November 1914 respectively), the railways and the various types of armoured trains played a major role. With some difficulty, the central government progressively regained control of the country.[3] The railway system suffered heavily, with bridges demolished, lines torn up or dynamited, and rolling stock destroyed.

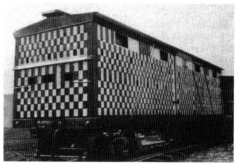

Two photos and a cutaway illustration of the armoured wagon specially camouflaged in a checkerboard pattern, so that at 30m (33 yards) range it was difficult to differentiate between real and dummy firing ports. The interior was sparsely equipped, but allowed the use of rifles at various firing positions. According to the magazine *Sciences et Voyages* (No 50 12 August 1920, p 337), this wagon could have been built by rebel forces. But another magazine *La Nature* (No 2053, 28 September 1912), described it as a government wagon, an identification confirmed on the cover of the *Illustrated London News* of 29 April 1911. This divergence is the proof that one must always verify journalists' comments, as they may be led astray by their local correspondents.

Shown here in 1912 is one of the numerous convoys which attempted to protect the railway. In fact the armoured trains of this period were never used in an offensive role but solely as one component of a means of transport. The protection formed by a wooden wall in the interior of the wagon is clearly visible. *(Photo: All Rights Reserved)*

[1.] From the name of Francisco Madero, the founder of the anti re-election party.
[2.] A well-known bandit, whose real name was José Doroteo Arango Arámbula. Better known by his popular nickname of 'Pancho Villa'.
[3.] Zapata was killed on 10 April 1919, Villa laid down his arms in June 1920 and was assassinated in 1923.

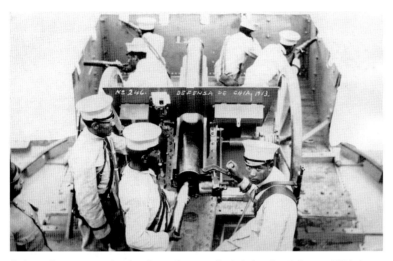

A view of an armoured wagon here photographed during the defence of Chia in 1913. In reality, the field gun would not fire directly over the heads of the infantrymen manning the front casemate, as the muzzle blast would be too dangerous.
(Photo: Philip Jowett Collection)

Built along similar lines to the one shown left, this armoured wagon lacks the firing ports in the front casemate. It appears the gun crew are removing the barrel rearwards, perhaps to change it.
(Photo: Paul Malmassari Collection)

The same wagon as above. The lowered side panels allowed for lateral fire, or they could be hinged upwards to protect the gun and crew.
(Photo: Philip Jowett Collection)

An undated view of a Federal wagon with unique armour protection, armed with a centrally-mounted field gun and machine guns at the four firing ports. The protection appears to be made of wood, and the canopy protects the crew from the sun. The person on the right appears to be an American.
(Photo: Philip Jowett Collection)

Federal armoured wagon with 80mm Mondragon field gun. That many of these scarce weapons are seen on armoured trains emphasizes their importance.
(Photo: Paul Malmassari Collection)

Mack-Saurer trucks, known as 'Rikers' from the name of their designer Andrew Riker, were converted to unarmoured rail trolleys to supply the American Expeditionary Force on the Mexican Border in 1916. On the Mexican side, at least one Riker was converted to an armoured trolley for use by the Constitutionalist Army,[4] and it appears the armour protection was installed by the North Western Railroad workshops in Juarez.

[4.] Ascribed by some sources to Pancho Villa.

The Riker on its road wheels. The Constitutionalist Army was created on 4 March 1913 by Venustiano Carranza who established a rebel government in the State of Sonora. This army was divided into divisions, brigades and smaller units, each one bearing the name of a geographical area. Villa was the commander of the Division del Norte.

(Photo: All Rights Reserved)

The same machine again, this time on its rail wheels. The inscriptions in the previous shot are just visible on the hull sides, along with part of the decoration of one wheel. This photo was perhaps taken just prior to it receiving its complete disruptive checkerboard camouflage. Magnification of the photo revealed the name 'Mack' on the wheel hubs.

(Photo: Paul Malmassari Collection)

The Mack-Saurer/Riker probably in its final configuration, with the lettering re-applied in a light colour over the (presumably black and white) checkerboard pattern. This is a form of disruptive camouflage – similar to the wagon shown earlier – intended to mask the actual firing points. On the other hand one must express astonishment at the wheel embellishments in the form of stars. Speed on the rails was estimated at 65–70km/h (40 to 45mph) and range as 350km (220 miles).

(Photo: Albert Mroz)

> « *Elle s'appelait Adélita*
> *C'était l'idole de l'armée de Villa*
> *Pancho Villa*
>
> *Des trains blindés portaient son nom*
> *Pour son caprice sautaient des ponts*
> *De toute la division du nord*
> *Oui c'était elle le vrai trésor . . .*»

> 'She was called Adélita
> The idol of the Army of Villa
> Pancho Villa
>
> Armoured trains bore her name
> At a whim she blew the bridges
> Of the whole Northern Division
> Oh yes, she was a real treasure . . .'.

During the Christiade[5] (1926–9) the Christeros rose in revolt in thirteen states of Central Mexico. Between March and May 1929, they conquered all of the west of the country (apart from the large towns), and attacked the communications networks. To assure free movement of its troops, the Government ordered the construction of armoured wagons. These units were clearly of much improved design compared with their earlier counterparts.

It only remains to cite the most recent mention of Mexican armoured trains. In the song *Adélita* by Julien Clerc (1971) we hear the words:

On the other hand the comic book *El Tren Blindado* only shows an *armed* train. But the title demonstrates how the image of the armoured train is indelibly stamped on the history of the Mexican Revolutions.

SOURCES:

Heigl, Fritz, *Taschenbuch der Tanks* (Munich: J. P. Lehmanns Verlag, 1935), Vol II.

Meyer, Jean, *La Révolution méxicaine* (Paris: Calmann-Lévy, 1973).

Mroz, Albert, *American Military Vehicles of World War I* (Jefferson [NC] & London, 2009, McFarland & Company, 2009).

Segura, Antonio, *El Tren Blindado* (Sueca: Aleta Ediciones, 2004).

---

5. A rebellion by the Christian Mexicans, against the presidency of General Callès. The rebels opposed the suppression of the Catholic Church, the closure of churches and the arrest of priests.

Near the end of the revolution, the security of travellers was assured by protection wagons inserted in the passenger trains. An American railroad company with connections into Mexico had these armoured wagons built.

(Photo: Le Miroir, No 326 [22 February 1920]).

Taken from Heigl's famous *Taschenbuch der Tanks*, this armoured wagon has been constructed on the base of the same type of bogie wagon as in the following shot, and is no doubt one of the wagons General Callès ordered to be inserted in all the trains in 1929.

This photo fits in completely with the notion of the 'rolling fortress' all too often applied to armoured trains. But the central structure with its firing ports is remarkable.

(Photo: Paul Malmassari Collection)

The influence of the Russian Revolution and the presence of Trotsky in Mexico inspired the title of this magazine created by Antonio Mella, of the Association of Proletarian Students. Here is Number 1 of September 1928.

MOROCCO

INSURRECTION 1952–1956

We have already examined the armoured train project conceived just before the Second World War (see the chapter on France). It appears that at last one armoured train from that period had been retained up until the events of 1952. The attacks in Morocco became more intense in July 1955, and measures were put in hand by the C.F.M. following the serious incidents at Oued-Zem, Khénifra and Kourigba. On certain routes trains no longer ran after dark, and security patrols commenced with two armoured trains which were reactivated in 1955.

These trains were made up of the following elements:

– a tank transporter wagon.
– an armoured diesel-electric locomotive.
– two bogie wagons with armour protection and internal equipment, transporting escort troops and a repair team.
– a second tank transporter wagon.

Trains of this type would be used during the Algerian War.

An armoured train of the type designed for Morocco, slightly modified after its transfer to Algeria, with an M3A3 light tank.
(Photo: Dejoux)

MOZAMBIQUE

ARMOURED TRAINS IN THE CIVIL WAR (1975–1992)

After Portugal granted independence to Mozambique on 25 June 1975, civil war broke out, which lasted up until 1992. The Limpopo railway line which ran between the port of Maputo and Zimbabwe, and also the line from Nacala in the north, were regularly subject to attacks, at least up until mid-1989. The locomotives were protected by steel plates, and the trains were preceded by ballasted flat wagons. The work of rebuilding the railway network began in 1990, with financial aid from several countries including France and India, under the protection of Zimbabwean troops.

Beginning in 1980, the company E C Lennings acquired several ex-Rhodesian armoured trolleys for use on the Beira corridor which linked Mutare to Beira. In 1992 the journalist Luca Poggiali published a study of the civil war in Mozambique, illustrated by a photo of an FPLM[1] 'armoured train' captured by RENAMO.[2] In addition, other means of protecting the rail traffic on this vital axis included reinforced bogie wagons armed with heavy machine guns.

[1] The FPLM (Mozambique Popular Liberation Forces) were the armed branch of FRELIMO (*Frente de Libertação de Moçambique*), Marxists.
[2] *Resistência Nacional Moçambicana*, the anti-Marxists.

SOURCES:

Lugan, Bernard, '1964-1992: Une Guerre de 30 Ans', *L'Afrique réelle* No 56 (August 2014), pp 13–15.

Poggiali, Luca, 'La RENAMO, victoire au bout du fusil', *Raids* (November 1992), pp 34–8.

Afrique Defense: various numbers.

Part of the armoured train captured by RENAMO. It is likely that these two Wickham armoured hulls were Nos 191 and 192, built in 1969 and transferred to Angola via the Beira corridor.

THE NETHERLANDS

ARMOURED TRAINS

The Second World War

In Holland itself, from September 1944 Dutch Railways were forced to fit shelters for the crews of civilian steam engines to protect them against the RAF who were systematically attacking all trains running in occupied Europe. These concrete shelters constructed on the tenders offered limited protection, and none at all if the boiler exploded, so instead the train crews preferred to jump from their engine. True Dutch armoured trains were designed and built only in the Dutch East Indies.

The armoured trains of the Dutch East Indies Railway Company (NIS[1])

In the Summer of 1941, two high-ranking officers of the Royal

[1] *Nederlandsch-Indische Spoorwegmaatschappij*, a private company.

Dutch East Indies Army (KNIL[2]) secretly made contact with the heads of the NIS in Semarang, in order to discuss the construction of two armoured trains to run on the Standard Gauge network (at that time the NIS operated two different gauges, metre gauge which was actually 1067mm or 3ft 6in, and standard gauge, 4ft 8½ins or 1435mm[3]), to meet the possibility of a Japanese attack on Java. The mission of the first train would be to prevent troops disembarking from seaplanes arriving on the lakes to the south of the line from Toentang to Willem I.[4] The other train was to operate on the Solo to Djokja[5] main line. In the event, a start was made on armouring only the first train, but the work would never be fully completed.

For this train, the NIS set aside 0-6-0 Tank Engine No 106, together with two platform wagons for the gun armament and a tank wagon to supplement the water supply of the engine. The 7mm armour protection for the engine was conceived by M. Ir. J C Jonker, chief engineer of the NIS, and made up in the Djokja workshops. The armour for the platform wagons was designed by the KNIL, and was to be constructed by the firm of De Vries Robbé in Semarang. The completed train was sent to Semarang, where it was planned to reinforce the suspension springs of the engine, to refit a lower, less conspicuous funnel, and to complete the wagons with a steel floor and arm them.

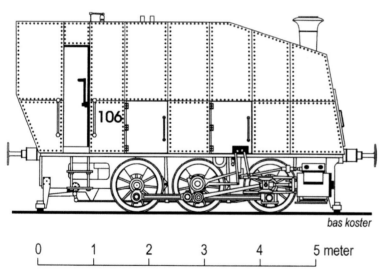

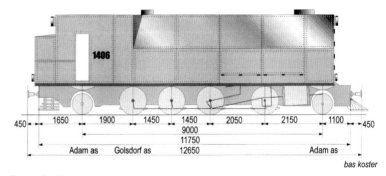

(Drawing: Bas Koster)

Following Pearl Harbor the project was re-examined, but what gave it a degree of urgency was the Japanese occupation of the Dutch part of Borneo. Within the available timescale, the only work which could be carried out was the armouring of Tank Engine No 106, and the train's proposed artillery armament was replaced by machine guns, protected only by sandbags. In the event, the armouring of the engine was still unfinished when the Japanese attack on Java began on 1 March 1942. It was therefore an old unarmoured Beyer Peacock 2-4-0 engine which was used to haul the sandbagged wagons to the lakes, where in fact the anticipated landings from seaplanes never

took place. On 5 March, the military crew abandoned the train and drew the fire in the firebox. They emplaced their machine guns in the mountains, and left the engine crew to return to their base on foot. As for No 106, after the surrender the Japanese removed its armour and returned the engine to normal use.

The armoured trains of the State Railway (SS[6])

The KNIL commanding officers also wanted to operate two armoured trains on the metre-gauge network. The first would operate in the western region of Java, and the second in the central and eastern regions. The trains were to be built in the State Railway workshops in Madioen in eastern Java, and in Mangarrai to the south of Batavia[7] in western Java. No information has come to light concerning the train constructed in Madioen, but the one built in Mangarrai is well-documented.

It was to be hauled by armoured 2-8-2 Tank Engine No 1406, one of a class of twenty-four engines built by Werkspoor in Amsterdam and by Hanomag in Hanover. Two reinforced flat wagons, armed with Madsen LMGs in revolving cupolas, two two-plank wagons protected by sandbags and armed with Breda machine guns for anti-aircraft defence, and an armoured command coach with most of the windows sealed off, formed the armoured train which became operational in November 1941. It was based at Tandjoeng Priok, the port of Batavia. On 22 February 1942 its crew of eighteen men (fourteen soldiers, two engineers and two train drivers) came under the orders of Infantry Sergeant W B Wisser, who was promoted to *Reserve Tweede luitenant* (temporary Second Lieutenant), on the day he took command. Despite the Japanese bombing, the train was brought to a state of readiness between 24 November 1941 and 2 February 1942.

[2.] *Koninklijk Nederlands-Indisch Leger.*
[3.] The first tracks were laid between 1864 and 1867 by a Dutch, German and British consortium, but the choice of standard gauge proved to be uneconomical. The narrower metre gauge was therefore used for the remainder of the network. Narrow gauge (70cm or 2ft 4in) was also used in the sugar-cane plantations on Java.
[4.] Present-day Ambarawa.
[5.] The present-day Soerakarta–Jogjakarta line.
[6.] *Staatsspoorwegen.*
[7.] Present-day Jakarta.

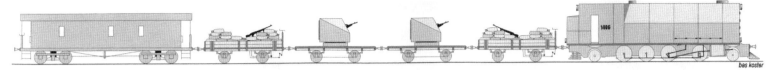

(Drawing: Bas Koster)

On 1 March, the Japanese began the invasion of Java, and on the 8th the Dutch garrison surrendered. During this week the Dutch carried out the destruction of elements of the rail infrastructure and the rolling stock was rendered unserviceable. At 02.00 on 1 March, the crew of the armoured train received orders to leave Batavia in order to reach Rangkasbetoeng, but it was halted at Paroengpandjang by the advance of Japanese forces. Returning the same day in the direction of Batavia, the train crew destroyed the bridges at Paroengpandjang and Serpong. Starting out on 5 March, the train offered protection to the transport by rail of the 11th Infantry Battalion between Tangerang and Soekaboemi, the armoured train following 5km behind the troop train. Near Tjitajam it was attacked by an enemy fighter, but the train rolling at 30 miles an hour (50km/h) took very few hits and in turn was unable to hit the aircraft. As the train accelerated to 40mph (65km/h) just before reaching Tjileboet, a bomb hit the track but without causing damage, and the armoured train was able to reach the station at Buitenzorg,[8] where it laagered for the night.

On 6 March the train received orders to escort a long military train (two locomotives and sixty wagons) between Buitenzorg and Bandoeng. Lieutenant Wisser learned that the track was blocked by a derailment near the Lampegan tunnel, and he saw that the work of clearing the track was taking longer than anticipated. While waiting, in order to avoid being spotted by the Japanese, who were actively hunting for the train, he distributed his armoured wagons around the depot at Soekaboemi. This was fortuitous, as four fighters bombed the depot and strafed it with cannon fire at around 09.00. At 16.00 a message informed the train that the Japanese had reached Tjisaät, only thirty minutes' march from Soekaboemi. At that moment the decision was taken to sabotage the train with explosive charges, which was completed by around 17.00. Although the Japanese managed to repair engine No 1406 late in 1942, to this day no trace of the rest of the armoured train has come to light.

The five armoured engines of the DSM

The private company DSM (Deli Spoorweg Maatschappi, based in the north of Sumatra, with its headquarters in Medan), operated a metre gauge network. In 1941 the decision was taken[9] to armour the cabs of five 2-6-4 tank engines, to protect the crews against

2-6-4 Tank Engine No 59 of the DSM (metre gauge) with partial armour protection, seen on Sumatra. These engines carried their armour plate from 1941 to 1953.
(Photo: Jan de Bruin Collection)

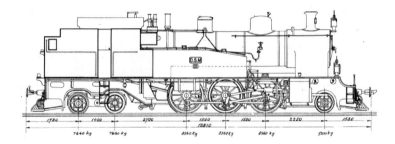

(Drawing: Bas Koster)

small-arms fire. The armour protection was left in place on these engines up to the end of 1953, as after the Japanese left, between 1947 and 1949 the region around Deli remained a hotbed of insurrection.

Fighting during the decolonisation period

On 17 August 1945 Indonesian nationalists declared independence from Dutch colonial rule, and began many acts of sabotage and outright attacks, which the Dutch countered with 'peacekeeping' operations. Colonial institutions such as the rail network were especially singled out for attack. The conflict[10] ended on 27 December 1949 when the Dutch recognised the independence of the Republic of Indonesia.

By July 1947 the majority of the 553km (344 miles) of the DSM Railway Company's routes on Sumatra were firmly in the hands of the Dutch authorities, but the free passage of trains was

8. Present-day Bogor.
9. It is not known whether the decision to fit armour plating originated with the KNIL or with the DSM.
10. Described as 'Révolusí' by the nationalists and as 'Politionele Acties' (Police Actions) by the Dutch.

disrupted by frequent attacks. A number of flat wagons armed with machine guns, and with the gunners protected by sandbags and overhead netting, were placed at the front of trains as pilot/safety wagons.

Protected DSM train on Sumatra, 1946.
(Photo: All Rights Reserved)

Pilot wagon at the head of a DSM train (metre gauge) on Sumatra in 1947.
(Photo: Jan de Bruin Collection)

DSM Armoured Jeep No P1 (*Pantservoertuig* nr 1)

On the most dangerous sections, a completely armoured Jeep preceded the trains. This unique machine complete with firing slits in a central armoured casemate was in fact based around a converted Jeep,[11] and was designed and built in 1947 by the DSM workshops at Poelau Brayan, near Medan. It was fitted with a special gearbox and a more powerful motor than usual. Propulsion was by the four central rail wheels mounted on the Jeep's axles, while the forward and rear axles of the platform wagon helped spread the weight of the complete vehicle. No trace of this vehicle can be found after 1949.

(Photos: Jan de Bruin Collection)

The situation on the Island of Java, August 1945–December 1949

After the Japanese surrender on 15 August 1945, the situation on Java became extremely complex: Sukarno declared independence on 17 August, and his supporters[12] took over control of the transport infrastructure, notably the tramways and the railways. In September the British attempted to seize control, and they were soon joined by Dutch PoWs freed from Japanese prison camps. The private and state railways were combined under a single body: the Unified Railway Authority,[13] abbreviated as 'VS', which worked in close co-operation with the Army. The reoccupation of Java took from

11. The result of co-operation between the Army which supplied the Jeep and paid for the modifications, and the DSM Company which built the vehicle.
12. The '*pemudas*' or 'youths'.
13. *Verenigd Spoorwegbedrijf* (VS).

December 1945 to December 1948, but railway traffic continued to be the target of continuing attacks, basically carried out using explosives seized from the Japanese. The principal method used by the nationalists was the traction bomb, activated by a wire stretched across the railway line. As on Sumatra, armed and protected flat wagons were propelled in front of the trains, and in the more dangerous zones, safety trucks were added in front of the flat wagons to protect the latter from mines.

Trolley-Jeep seen in the process of being armoured in the Manggarai workshops in 1947. Note that in this version only the two front seats are protected.
(Photo: Jan de Bruin Collection)

Armoured train on Java, in the early days of the rebellion, January–August 1946.
(Photo: All Rights Reserved)

The armoured trolleys on Java 1946–1949

Several Jeeps were armoured and converted to run on rails by the Dutch Army in workshops such as the one in Bandoeng, and armoured trolleys with two, or in the case of the heaviest, three axles were also built. Surprisingly, we do not know the total number converted, and the only proof of their existence which has come down to us are the photographs.

Two Trolley-Jeeps attached back-to-back, in the classic configuration allowing for rapid withdrawal under fire. Note the style of armour protection on the first of these two Trolley-Jeeps. The rear vehicle has an unarmoured rear platform.
(Photo: Jan de Bruin Collection)

Jeep converted to run on rails (metre gauge) seen at Manggarai.
Photo: Jan de Bruin Collection)

Trolley-Jeeps on patrol on Java, 1946–9.
(Photo: Jan de Bruin Collection)

A fully-armoured Jeep conversion with a third axle to carry the extra weight.

(Photo: All Rights Reserved)

To provide armour protection for flat wagons, one solution was to reuse the armoured hulls of Overvalwagen[14] vehicles bolted onto the wagon deck.

(Photo: Jan de Bruin Collection)

An Overvalwagen hull protecting a train on the Tjibatoe-Garoet line, Java, 1949.

(Photo: Jan de Bruin Collection)

Two 1980s views of BRAAT armoured hulls bolted to flat wagons, built in the Manggari workshops. Ultimately, the armoured hulls of some of these vehicles were cut in half and the halves joined end-to-end to create armoured trolleys. See the chapter on Indonesia.

(Photos: Tony Ford)

SOURCES:

Book:

De Bruin, Jan, *Het Indische spoor in oorlogstijd* (Rosmalen: Uitgeverij Uquiliar B.V., 2003).

Website:

http://www.overvalwagen.com

Preserved vehicles:

Jakarta Museum (BRAAT on a flat wagon)
Bandung Museum (Panser rel V16)

[14.] Literal translation 'attack wagon' . These armoured vehicles were also known by the designation 'BRAAT', from the N.V. Machinenfabriek BRAAT, a company with workshops in Soerabaja (eastern Java). They resulted from a design by Engineer Captain Luyke Roskott and were based on a Chevrolet COE chassis. The KNIL used several different versions of the Overvalwagen.

NEW ZEALAND

Already semi-autonomous since the end of the nineteenth century, New Zealand became an independent Dominion under the British Crown in 1907, and took part in both World Wars as part of the Commonwealth. During the Second World War, more than a quarter of the country's railway workers were in uniform, serving in the 16th and 17th Railway Operating Companies sent to the Middle East[1] as part of the MEF (Middle East Forces). In 1941–2 the theatre received forty-two Stanier 8F steam engines. In October 1942 during the British offensive following the second battle of El Alamein, the first train to roll westwards was hauled by one of these engines, with armour protection against aerial attack. In addition, two anti-aircraft detachments were included in all trains, in wagons attached at the front and rear of the rake. They were armed either with rifle-calibre Browning machine guns, or 40mm Bofors or 20mm Breda cannon.

[1.] These units were disbanded in 1943.

The armoured cab and front end of the tender. The following two tank wagons are being filled with additional water for the engine.
(Photo: All Rights Reserved)

Stanier 8F No 329 at El Alamein in November 1942, protected by concrete panels. The NZ Rly Op Coy (New Zealand Railway Company) were responsible for running this train and the railway system.
(Photo: All Rights Reserved)

Note the absence of armour protection over the top of the boiler unit, to avoid overheating problems.

(Photos: All Rights Reserved)

The 2-8-0 wheel arrangement is clearly seen in this side view.

(Photo: All Rights Reserved)

Above: A wagon converted into an anti-aircraft battery in Egypt, showing one of its two quadruple .30 calibre Browning mountings. The machine guns probably came from US-built tanks. The Brownings have not yet been fitted to the mounting at the rear. There are no known photos showing wagons armed with either Bofors or Breda cannons.

(Photo: All Rights Reserved)

Left: Ford trucks coupled back-to-back for patrol duties, with the central pillar mountings for machine guns.

(Photo: All Rights Reserved)

SOURCES:

Judd, Brendon, *The Desert Railway: The New Zealand Railway Group in North Africa and the Middle East during the Second World War* (Auckland: Penguin Group New Zealand Limited, 2004).

NICARAGUA

ARMOURED TRAIN 1912

Under the terms of a treaty signed on 6 June 1911, the Nicaraguan railway network was run by an American company. In July 1912 a political rival of President Diaz stirred up a rebellion, and the latter asked for American help to suppress it. Some 3000 American troops, mostly Marines, were sent to Nicaragua to restore order. One of their missions involved reopening the Managua-Granada rail link passing next to Lake Nicaragua. A special train was therefore assembled in September 1912: eight flat wagons followed by the first engine, then eight vans, the second engine and four other wagons bringing up the rear. The crew included 400 Marines (basically there to help push the train on the gradients!). The vans were unarmoured, but the wagons were protected by sandbags. The train's armament comprised no less than sixteen machine guns, some mounted on the van roofs. The town of Granada was finally captured by the government forces, after a five-day journey to cover some 20km (13 miles) of railway line.

SOURCES:

Thomas, Lowell, *Old Gimlet Eye, The Adventures of Smedley D. Butler* (New York: Farrar & Rinehart Inc, 1933).

Two poor-quality but nevertheless unique photos of the train in Nicaragua. This appears to show one end of the train, a bogie (?) wagon protected by a wall of sandbags. The machine gun is an American Vickers in .30/06 calibre, and centre-left is a US Marine (pointing towards the camera) wearing the traditional campaign hat. Given the preponderance of Nicaraguans it is probable this is the tail wagon. Interestingly the above photo is marked 'Rebel' armoured train.

(Photos: above, David Spencer; below, Paul Malmassari Collection)

NORTH KOREA (DEMOCRATIC PEOPLE'S REPUBLIC OF KOREA)

From 1905 up to the end of the Second World War, Korea was under Japanese rule. After the Japanese surrender, the country was declared independent on 15 August 1945. However, the Korean peninsula to the North of the 38th Parallel was occupied by Soviet troops, and the remainder to the South by US troops. In the South, the Republic of Korea was declared on 17 July 1948, while the North self-proclaimed the establishment of the Democratic People's Republic on 9 September of the same year, under the direction of Kim Il-sung who had led the anti-Japanese resistance.

Because of the railway connections between Korea and Manchukuo, the Type 94 Japanese armoured train had been captured intact in the Soviet Zone, and in fact in December 1945 it was photographed by an Official US Army Photographer.[1] During the Korean War, in the South, Japanese armoured wagons were put back into service to protect train convoys – see the relevant chapter on South Korea (1950–1953). The role of interdicting North Korean supply trains running along the east coast of the peninsula[2] was carried out principally by the UN naval forces[3] (among which the Canadian destroyer HMCS *Crusader* marked up the highest train-busting score), with the support of aircraft from TF 77. On at least one occasion, a North Korean armoured train was reportedly engaged and destroyed.

In the original 1989 edition of this encyclopaedia, various sources were quoted as having indicated the existence of eight North Korean armoured trains, information which to date has remained unverified. Numerous reports by foreign tourists visiting North Korea mention seeing goods wagons on which soldiers manned anti-aircraft machine guns against possible air attack, unsurprising in view of the fact that the North and the South are still officially at war, since at the time of writing no peace treaty has ever been signed between the two states. Finally, the armoured train of the 'Dear Leader' Kim Jong-il was widely described in the media on the occasion of his visit to Moscow in August 2011.[4]

SOURCES:

Directory of History and Heritage, Ministry of National Defence, *Le Canada et la guerre de Corée* (Montreal: Art Global, 2002).

The Japanese Type 94 train photographed in the Soviet Zone in North Korea.
(Photo: Don O'Brien)

[1.] Retired US Army Photographer Mr Don O'Brien at website https://www.flickr.com/photos/dok1/3894782980
[2.] As a priority those coming down from the North, as they were carrying front-line supplies furnished by the Soviet Union.
[3.] The UN Navies set up the 'Trainbusters Club', which by the end of the War had claimed twenty-eight trains destroyed.
[4.] Among other sources: https://www.lebuzzcontinue.wordpress.com/2011/12/19/kim-jong-il-a-quoi-ressemble-un-train-blinde-en-coree-du-nord/

NORWAY

ARMED TRAINS

This 75mm L/30 Schneider fortress gun was captured by the Wehrmacht and put back into service against Norwegian troops on 16 April 1940. Note the side plate which is perhaps not armour protection but probably a firing platform for the gun crew. We can also see the remains of an armoured shield.
(Photo: Paul Malmassari Collection)

A British 12pdr 12 cwt (3in) QF gun of the type fitted on British warships, and probably salvaged from one of the eleven A/S trawlers sunk or driven ashore by Luftwaffe aircraft,[1] has been mounted on a short bogie wagon. It is coupled to an NSB Type E1 4 electric locomotive.[2] It appears that both the gun and its locomotive have been sabotaged by their crews: the foreshortened barrel indicates it was first blocked and then a live round fired, and an explosive charge seems to have destroyed the centre section of the locomotive, followed by a fire.
(Photo: Paul Malmassari Collection)

It appears that the Norwegians never built classic armoured trains. On the other hand, from the time of the Great War, artillery pieces mounted on railway wagons and with minimal armour protection provided mobile defence on the Kiruna-Narvik (Ofotbanen) Line. In 1940, two such guns are recorded: a 75mm fortress gun and a British 3in.

SOURCES:
Website
http://forum.axishistory.com/viewtopic.php?t=114126&start=165 (also dealing with heavy railway guns)

[1.] The Norwegians had also mounted a German 3.7cm S.K. C/30 AA gun salvaged from one of the sunken destroyers in Narvik fjord on a rail wagon.
[2.] Built between 1925 and 1928, max. speed 60km/h (38mph), Type 1C+C1, overall length: 19.58m (64ft 3in).

OTTOMAN EMPIRE[1]

When Turkey allied with Germany during the First World War, the greatest threat to railway transport came from the Great Arab Revolt of 1916–18. The writings of Lawrence of Arabia detail attacks on Ottoman trains, but do not specifically mention armoured trains. However, it is certain that armoured trains were used by the Turks,[2] despite the fact that apart from the possible exception of the armoured wagon preserved in Syria, no photos have come to light.

In late 1917, French forces identified three armoured trains[3] at Medina, Boueir and Heddja. In addition, in almost all the stations, an armoured wagon (protected by iron plates or sandbags) was coupled to an engine with steam up, ready to intervene at any trouble spot.

In the same period armoured trolleys intended for the Middle East were built in Germany, although some were never delivered. At least two of these machines were captured by the Allies, one of which was in use hauling a train. The armoured bodies of two machines were converted by the French into armoured caissons mounted on flat wagons (see the chapter on France).

SOURCES:
Archives:
SHD: 4 H 27, Fonds Clémenceau, 6 N 191.

Books:
Strasheim, Rainer, *Panzer-Kraftwagen, Armoured Cars of the German Army and Freikorps*, Tankograd-World War One No 1007 (Erlangen: Verlag Jochen Vollert, 2013), p 73.
Das Ehrenbuch des Deutschen Pioniers (Berlin: Verlag Tradition Wilhelm Kolf, 1931).

[1.] The Ottoman Empire was abolished on 1 November 1922.
[2.] For example a coded message dated 10 November 1917 indicated a Turkish armoured train in combat on 12 and 13 October 1917 on the line from Antar to Boueit (Hedjaz). (SHD: 6 N 191)
[3.] SHD: 4 H 27.
[4.] Zone of activity of the *Freikorps* of General Märkers, which later became the 16th Brigade of the *Reichswehr*.

Ottoman armoured trolley, left-hand side, with its crew. Some photos show a German crew from the *Asien-Korps* commanded by Colonel von Oppen.
(Photo: Paul Malmassari Collection)

Armoured wagon on display in the Al Qadam Museum in Damascus. The origins of the wagon and the reason why it was constructed are unknown.
(Photo: All Rights Reserved)

Three views of armoured trolleys, the lower one showing one of these machines coupled as a train locomotive. This was perhaps the type of rake known as an 'armoured train' in contemporary reports.

(Photos: Australian War Memorial)

Right-hand front quarter of the armoured trolley, seen here between Rayack and Damascus.

(Photo: Das Ehrenbuch des Deutschen Pioniers)

This example has been converted to a road vehicle (probably the only one of its type!) and used by the police in Weissefels near Leipzig, as well as in Zella-Mehlis near Suhl in 1919.[4] It is likely that the rear of the armoured body has been reversed and has become the front end of this road version.

(Photo: Jochen Vollert)

PARAGUAY

THE ARMOURED TRAIN OF 1869, WAR OF THE TRIPLE ALLIANCE

This short-lived armoured train is believed to be the very first of its kind built in South America. Following territorial disputes, on 1 May 1865 war broke out between Paraguay, ruled by the dictator Francisco Solano Lopez, and the three countries of the Triple Alliance, Argentina, Brazil and Uruguay. The war began with a series of naval operations which resulted in the almost total destruction of the Paraguayan fleet on 22 March 1868, allowing the allies to take the Paraguayan forces in the rear and advance on the capital, which fell on 1 January 1869.

In the months which followed, the Paraguayans put together an improvised armoured train which went into action on 30 April 1869. It comprised two armoured wagons, each mounting a 3in gun, and in between the wagons an engine with an armoured cab, which had already seen distinguished military service: the *Piccadilly Pride*, a large single-driver constructed in 1854 in Crewe, had seen service (unarmoured) as Engine No 11 on the Grand Crimean Central Railway, built during the Crimean War to haul supplies from Balaclava. The armoured train counted among its crew another veteran of the Crimea, Major Hadley Baines Tuttle, who was to command the sortie.

The armoured train left the station of Cerro Léon and advanced into the Valley of the Pirayu in the direction of the Brazilian advanced post at Aregua. After the sentries had been overcome, it crossed the bridge of the same name and opened fire on the camp, killing and wounding around a hundred men. But after 20 minutes' combat, the Brazilians rallied, and three men in the wagon at the head of the train were killed. Running in reverse, the armoured train retreated, and the crew blew the bridge to prevent the Brazilians from following. Unknown to them, however, more than 250 cavalrymen of the Rio Grande do Sul Regiment had crossed the river and set up an ambush for the train alongside the track. Galloping on either side they hotly engaged the thirty unwounded survivors of the train's crew with carbine and revolver fire, but as the engine gained speed and their mounts tired they were gradually left behind. Unfortunately for the daring Paraguayans, a small group of cavalrymen had ridden on ahead, and had blocked the rails with a pile of logs. Unable to stop in time, the speeding train ran into the obstacle and derailed. *Piccadilly Pride* fell on her side, and her boiler, starved of water, exploded, killing two Brazilian ambushers as well as Major Tuttle.

SOURCES:

Capdevila, Luc, *Une guerre totale, Paraguay, 1864-1870. Essai d'histoire du temps présent* (Rennes University Press, 2007), p 514.
Meister, Jürg, *Francisco Solano Lopez* (Osnabrück : Biblio Verlag, 1987). 458 pages.
Uys, Errol Lincoln, *BRAZIL Book Five, Sons of the Empire* (Silver Spring, MD: Silver Spring Books, 2000).

PERU

ARMOURED TRAIN

From 1879 to 1883 Chile fought the War of the Pacific against Peru and Bolivia. The *casus belli* was the imposition by Bolivia of taxes on the transport of saltpetre extracted by two Chilean companies. Peru relied heavily on its railway network, and when the Chileans advanced on Lima, the militia and civilians defending the capital built an armoured train equipped with machine guns as well as the rifles of the troops on board. On 15 January 1881 the heavily-armed armoured train, carrying fresh troops, left Lima and set off for Miraflores, which was in Chilean hands. The Chileans attacked the train and forced it to retreat. When they entered Lima on 17 January, they discovered an additional five armoured wagons which had apparently never been put into service.

SOURCES:

Arana, Diego Barros, *History of the War of the Pacific* (Paris, J Dumaine: Vol I, 1881; Vol II, 1882).

POLAND

ARMOURED TRAINS[1] AND TROLLEYS[2] 1918-1950

Poland was reborn as an independent nation on 11 November 1918. Positioned in Central Europe, the country found itself hemmed in between Germany (including East Prussia) and Russia, and depending on the period, by its other neighbours Czechoslovakia, Hungary, Romania, the Ukraine, Belarus and Lithuania.

The Polish railway network reflected the various occupations of the country: the rail gauge in the region of Poznań (formerly Prussian Posen) and Galicia (formerly Austrian) was the standard 1435mm (4ft 8½in) whereas in Congress Poland (formerly Russian) it was the 1520mm (4ft 11¾in) broad gauge. Rail connections across Polish territory included five major junctions with the ex-German network but only two with the ex-Austrian lines. In 1915, the occupation of virtually all of what would become the new Poland by German troops led to the standardisation of the whole network on the European gauge, apart from the Ukrainian network which, after the Treaty of Brest-Litovsk, remained on the Russian broad gauge. The rolling stock accordingly originated from all the occupying or occupied countries: primarily German wagons in the region of Poznań and Prussia, plus Austrian, Hungarian, Russian and even Belgian rolling stock (the latter brought in from the Militär-Eisenbahn Direktion Brüssel). Even if the new Polish rail network offered few strategic advantages (compared to the German network which had been planned with mobilisation in mind), it remained the only sure means of transport in the absence of a good road system.

The employment of armoured trains, a weapon which was easily movable from one front to the other, was a reflection of the complicated and sometimes tragic story of this new country. They were therefore present from the very conception of the Polish Army of the Second Republic. In fact, the young Polish Army had to fight four wars almost simultaneously: the Polish-Ukrainian War of 1918–19, the Russo-Polish War from February 1919 to March 1921, the Silesian Uprisings from 15 August 1919 to 21 July 1921, and the Polish-Lithuanian War of August to 7 October 1920.

Then the Polish armoured trains settled down into the relative calm of the inter-war period, up until the German attack which started the Second World War. They were involved in the brief Polish campaign from 1 to 27 September 1939, then Poles in exile manned armoured trains in Britain between 12 October 1940 and November 1943. Finally they operated during the post-1945 internal security operations which were conducted by the Army and the Railway Guards up until the 1950s.

Armoured trains of ex-Russian Army Polish units

Even before the declaration of independence, Polish troops (who were not yet officially designated as the Polish Army) were engaged in frontier conflicts with their neighbours. On those fronts where good roads were the exception, the railway was the only means of moving armies, and the only mobile weapons of any power during that period were the armoured trains. The very first armoured train, *Związek Broni-Szeroki*[3] ('United Arms') operated as part of Polish I Corps. Its protection was provided by sandbags and trench shields on a flat wagon, and its weapons comprised a 76.2mm Model 1902 field gun, plus several 7.62mm Maxim machine guns including two in the twin turrets of a broken-down Austin (1st Series) armoured car.

During the Russian Civil War, five Polish divisions designated 'Siberian' fought alongside the Czech Legion on the Trans-Siberian Railway where they operated three armoured trains, named *Warszawa* ('Warsaw'), *Kraków* (Craków) and *Poznań*. When the last of these was lost, they captured an armoured train from Kolchak's forces and renamed it *Poznań II*.

The Polish Army of the Second Republic (November 1918 – September 1939)

In Poland proper, the new government set up an organisation tasked with creating and operating the growing fleet of armoured trains. In 1918, two Austro-Hungarian armoured trains, No III and

Armoured Train *Związtek Broni-Szeroki*, which had a brief existence between 10 February and 10 May 1918, when it was captured by German troops.
(Photo: All Rights Reserved)

---

[1] In Polish *Pociag Pancerny*, abbreviated as PP, followed by the number of the individual train.
[2] In Polish *Drezyna pancerna*.
[3] *Szeroki* = broad gauge. Added to the names of all trains operating on the Russian railway network.

No VIII (for their artillery wagons, see the chapter on Austria-Hungary), were in Polish hands. These formed the most modern units in service at the time, along with several former Russian wagons captured from the White forces. German armoured wagons (e.g. PZ 22) had also been abandoned in the Poznań region and in Prussia. A number of Russian, Ukrainian and Lithuanian wagons were also reused, plus civilian goods wagons and flat wagons seized by the Germans in Hungary, France and Belgium.

The first national armoured trains were built in Lwów,[4] then in Tarnow, Nowy Sacz, Warsaw, Poznań, Wilno and Slask. As the Poles lacked sufficient armour plate for entire trains, and which when it was available was used for the engines, the protection for the wagons initially consisted of concrete and sandbags, enclosing machine guns and field guns.

Between 1918 and 1920, the command of the armoured trains was in the hands of General Gawronski, Inspector of Army Railways, based in Warsaw. The Inspection Department then allocated them to the different military railway units: regiments, battalions, bridge guard detachments etc. Several trains were also made available to the Army High Command. In the course of the four wars which Poland fought, the armoured trains would pass from one Front to the other, would be broken up and distributed between other trains, or might be destroyed and ultimately pass on their name to a new train.

Before we begin to describe many of these trains, we need to detail the various conflicts which were all interlinked as part of the overall Russo-Polish struggle.

The Polish-Ukrainian and Russo-Polish Wars

The Polish-Ukrainian War (November 1918 – July 1919) was fought between Poland and the Popular Republic of Western Ukraine who each claimed Galicia. Captured Ukrainian armoured trains were incorporated in the Polish Army.

The Russo[5]-Polish War (February 1919 – March 1921) saw the young Polish Republic facing a Russia in the middle of civil war. Lenin in particular aimed at unleashing a worldwide revolution, and envisaged enrolling Germany by passing through Poland, which he regarded as 'White'. The first Russian offensive was halted and the victorious Poles advanced eastwards until May 1920. The Russians counter-attacked, and by July 1920 were close to capturing Warsaw. But the battle of Warsaw (13–25 August) was won by the Poles, thanks in part to supplies and aid provided by the Allied military missions. The Bolshevik retreat ended with the armistice of 12 October 1920. It is estimated that seventy armoured trains were employed by the Poles, plus some thirty

---

others captured from the Bolsheviks. In the course of the war, the Polish Army had lost at least eight armoured trains. The decision was therefore taken to build fifteen new armoured trains at the Cegielski factory in Poznań, where on 1 August 1920 the KBPP,[6] the military organisation responsible for armoured trains, was established, directed by Captain Stanisław Czerepiński. Many captured Russian armoured trains were recovered and parts of them or even entire trains were put into Polish service.

The first version of PP 1 *Piłsudczyk* formed from elements of the Austro-Hungarian armoured trains of the 3rd Detachment captured in Craków on 1 November 1918. The artillery wagon remained in service with this train up until 1939.
(Photo: Centralne Archiwum Wojskowe – CAW)

PP 2 *miały* was created after PP 1 was divided up into two separate parts on 26 October 1918. Note the Polish flag of the period and the wagon with turret at the rear of the train, probably inspired by a Russian vehicle.
(Photo: CAW)

Close-up of the artillery wagon of *miały* (note the number '2' on the wagon side), lacking its gun which was probably being repaired. This train was demobilised in 1923 or 1924.
(Photo: CAW)

[4.] Today modern Lviv in the Ukraine.

[5.] The term 'Soviet' cannot be applied to this conflict as the Soviet Union was not officially established until 30 December 1922.

[6.] KBPP = *woiskowe Kierownictwo Budowy Pociagów Pancernych* (Organisation for the Construction of Armoured Trains).

Following rebuilding, the new PP 1 *Piłsudczyk* was powered by a Class 73
engine, and was armed with a Soviet 122mm howitzer. The artillery wagon was
built in Lwów on the base of a German wagon in the Summer of 1920.
(Photo: CAW)

A fine profile view of the howitzer wagon of PP 1 *Piłsudczyk* (built on the base of
a German Type Ommku coal wagon at Lwów in September 1920).
(Photo: CAW)

Under the armour is an ex-Austrian engine: the kkStB Class 73 carried 15mm
armour, fitted in the workshops of Nowy Sacz. They hauled PP 1 *Piłsudczyk* (No
73.348) from August 1920 to 1921, in 1921 PP 18 *Huragan* (No 73.419, completely armoured), PP 25 *Stefan Czarniecki* in 1920, PP 7 *Smok* ('Dragon'), PP 6
Generał Iwaszkiewicz and PP 27 *Ochotnik* ('Volunteer', hauled by No 73.235
armoured at Lwów).
(Photo: CAW)

The third armoured train originally numbered PP 3, then from late April 1919 named PP 3 *Lis-Kula*, was built at Craków. The train was named in honour of
Commandant (Major) Leopold Lis-Kula, a war hero who died of his wounds on 7 March 1919 at the age of twenty-two.
(Photo: Artur Przeczek Collection)

One of the artillery wagons of PP 3 at Lwów in May 1919. Note that the 76.2mm field gun is carried complete with its wheeled carriage.
(Photo: CAW)

After the wars had ended, the crews of several armoured trains arranged for commemorative badges to be struck. Here is the one for PP 3 which needs some explanation: 'Pe Pe Trójka' means 'Armoured Train No 3'.
(Photo: Paul Malmassari Collection)

The leading artillery wagon of PP 3, armed with an Austrian 8cm M 05/08 gun. The cylindrical turrets were inspired by Soviet models.
(Photo: CAW)

PP 3 camouflaged, seen during the 1920s.
(Photo: Krysztof Margasiński)

This Austro-Hungarian engine No 180.533 was the sole example of this class armoured by the Poles at Nowy Sacz in April 1919. It was then attached to PP 3 *Lis-Kula*.
(Photo: CAW)

Right: The artillery wagon of PP 5 *Odsiecz I*. The layout of the main armament firing to the side indicates a defensive role, compared with the gun mounted in the chase wagon capable of firing along the track with the train advancing or withdrawing.
(Photo: CAW)

PP 8 *Rozwadowczyk* (later renamed PP 8 *Wilk*) at Nowy Sacz in February 1919, which served during the Polish-Ukrainian and Russo-Polish wars. It was powered by a Class 229 engine, and its wagons were armoured internally with cement.
(Photo: CAW)

PP 9 *Danuta*, built in Craków in January 1919. It took part in the defence of Warsaw against the Russians. It is headed by a Class 229 engine, followed by an ex-German armoured wagon (probably from PZ 22) and an armoured van.
(Photo: CAW)

Overall view of PP 10 *Pionier* ('Engineer'), which was built in Lwów in February 1919. It served during the Polish-Ukrainian War and the Russo-Polish War. Note the virtual symmetry on either side of the engine, apart from one additional wagon.
(Photo: CAW)

The engine of PP 11 *Poznańczyk*, originally a German Class G-5^2 with one of the first types of armour protection.
(Photo: CAW)

PP 10 *Pionier*, seen here in May 1919, had two artillery wagons (8cm Austrian guns) built on the base of German mineral wagons.
(Photo: CAW)

Built in Warsaw in late 1919, PP 11 *Poznańczyk* had a front turret armed with an Austro-Hungarian 8cm *Feldkanone* M05. Note the armour covering the axle boxes.
(Photo: CAW)

One of the wagons of PP 13 *Zawiska Czarny* armoured at Lwów in August 1920. The main weakness of these covered vans was the presence of ventilation slats, here seen covered by armour plates. The echeloned arrangement of the two sets of firing ports for riflemen was typical of Polish wagons.
(Photo: CAW)

Ex-Austro-Hungarian engine MÁV 377.402 originally with PP 1 *Piłsudczyk*, later attached to PP 5 *Odsiecz I*, seen here following Polish modifications such as the increased coal capacity. A second train was built under the name of *Odsiecz II*.
(Photo: CAW)

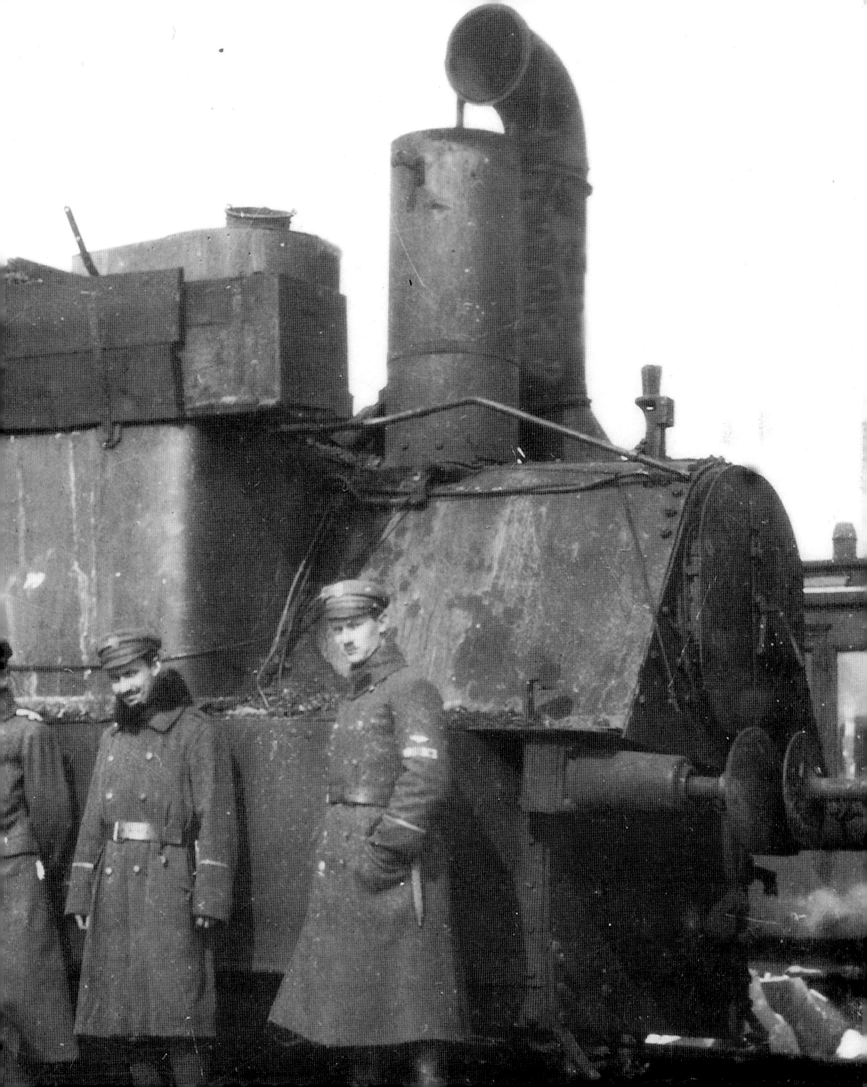

Class G3 engine of PP 14 *Zagończyk* which was damaged in the Autumn of 1920. Simple armour protection of this type allowed the production of a large number of armoured trains.

(Photo: CAW)

PP 15 *Paderewski*, built at Lwów in September 1919. It went into action on the Lithuanian frontier then took part in the battle of Warsaw against the Reds. It joined in the offensive against Wilno (Vilnius) in 1920 under the false name *General Żeligowski*.

(Photo: CAW)

One of the two Class 178 engines (this one is perhaps No 178.111) allocated to PP 15 *Paderewski*.

(Photo: CAW)

General view of PP 18 *Odsiecz II*, with the artillery wagon leading.

(Photo: CAW)

One of the six Class 178 engines armoured at Lwów. Here is No 178.95 allocated to PP 15 *Paderewski*, built in September 1919.

(Photo: CAW)

Artillery wagon of PP 15 *Paderewski*, probably armed with an Austrian 8cm gun, protected by steel plates and with a horizontal field of fire of some 270 degrees.

(Photo: CAW)

This 0-6-0 tank engine of PP 17 *Saper* was a kkStB Class 97. The train was built at Craków in March 1919. Here it is seen after having suffered collision damage in April 1919. It was repaired and put back into service. Note the smoke deflector (deactivated here, with the upper trap open) worked from inside the cab.

(Photo: CAW)

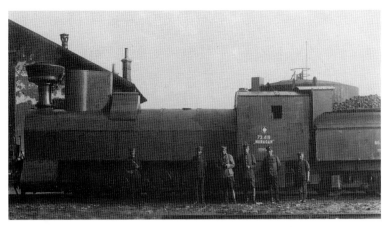

Engine 73.419 of PP 18 *Huragan* which was built in August 1920 at Nowy Sacz.
(Photo: CAW)

Armoured van of PP 18 *Huragan*, with its imposing roof casemate carrying an Austrian searchlight.
(Photo: CAW)

PP 19 *miały-Szeroki* was built in April–May 1919 using Russian units captured at Lida (in modern Lithuania). Although its shape is disguised, the engine was a Class O^v. This train went into action on 28 September 1919 at Dyneburg, then it was broken up and distributed among other trains at the end of April 1920.
(Photo: CAW)

7. 'Hunhuz' is the transcription of the Chinese word signifying 'red beard', used to describe the bandits infesting the Russian Far East in the nineteenth and twentieth centuries.

PP 20 *General Dowbor-Mu nicki-Szeroki* was powered by a captured Russian Class O^v steam engine, of the type as used on the *Hunhuz*[7] type of armoured trains. *Dowbor* was the former Ukrainian train *Sichovyi*, captured on 24 May 1919.
(Photo: CAW)

The artillery wagon of PP 20 *General Dowbor* was used unaltered from its Ukrainian configuration. The train was damaged in a fierce action against the Bolsheviks and was then captured on 23 June 1920.
(Photo: CAW)

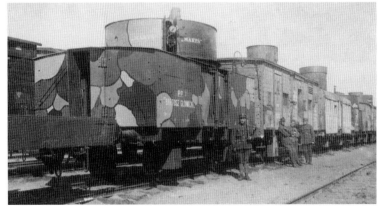

Of quite modern appearance, PP 20 *Bartosz Głowacki* was built in August 1920 at Craków. It had two artillery wagons armed with Russian 76.2mm guns, while the other wagons were covered vans of German origin, armoured internally with cement and sand. The two artillery wagons would later form the instruction school armoured train.

(Photo: Wawrzyniec Markowski Collection)

One of the artillery wagons of *Groźny-Szeroki* in 1920 from the captured Bolshevik armoured train BP 56 *Kommunar* and still armed with its Russian 76.2mm guns. After 1926 they were replaced with French 75mm.
(Photo: All Rights Reserved)

PP 23 *Sikorski-Szeroki* was composed of high-sided bogie wagons from a Russian armoured train captured in March 1920. It was equipped with a 76.2mm field gun in the chase position, and a second 76.2mm in a fully-revolving turret. It was destroyed on 25 June 1920.
(Photo: Artur Przeczek Collection)

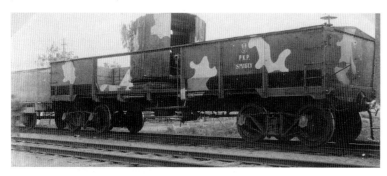

An impressive artillery wagon of PP 24 *Śmigły-Szeroki*, the ex-Russian BP N 45, captured in August 1919. Note the trench shields reinforcing the turret armour. This train was dismantled in June 1921.
(Photo: CAW)

Photographed at Nowy Sacz in September 1920, the central wagon of PP 25 *Stefan Czarniecki*, similar to that of PP 18 *Huragan*, with an identical casemate but without lookout shutters (probably used on *Huragan* to sight the searchlight when closed down).
(Photo: CAW)

The general layout of PP 25 *Stefan Czarniecki* (seen here at Nowy Sacz) was quite modern, armoured vans alternating with turreted wagons, heavily influenced by captured and partially reused Russian vehicles.
(Photo: CAW)

On this artillery wagon of PP 25 *Stefan Czarniecki*, note the casemates for machine guns. On these three photos, what might be mistaken for scratches on the negative at the bottom panels of the wagons are in fact foliage added for a ceremony.
(Photo: CAW)

Left: Not included in the classification of armoured trains, but fulfilling a similar role, the Craków Railway Batteries (*Krakowska Bateria Kolejowa*) were armed with Austrian 8cm casemate guns.
(Photo: All Rights Reserved)

The Polish-Lithuanian War (1920)

The short Polish-Lithuanian War (August – 7 October 1920) was fought to decide who would have possession of Vilnius. The dispute had been building up ever since April of that year: the Poles had captured Vilnius in April 1919, but the Lithuanians wanted to recover the city, which they considered their historical capital. When the Red Army invaded Poland the Lithuanians changed sides and supported the Russians. Between 2 and 27 September 1920 the Lithuanian Army launched its own offensive, but was defeated. A ceasefire was agreed on 7 October. Despite the wishes of the League of Nations, Vilnius remained a Polish city.

During this conflict the Poles captured the Lithuanian armoured train No 1 *Gediminas*, which was immediately renamed *Major Mond* before taking on its official designation of PP 27 *Jan Kili ski*.
(Photo: Krysztof Margasi ski Collection)

Third Silesian Uprising (May 1921)

The three Silesian Uprisings (15 August 1919 – 21 July 1921) were instigated by the Polish minority community to obtain the attachment of the rich mineral area of Upper Silesia to Poland. The Treaty of Versailles made provision for the holding of a plebiscite to determine the division of Upper Silesia between Germany and Poland. On the German side, the *Freikorps* (Free Corps) exerted pressure on the non-German population, while Poland promised to give full rights to the indigenous Polish inhabitants. The First Uprising began with a general strike by the Polish miners on 16 August. The 60,000 men of the *Reichswehr* crushed the revolt, which came to an end ten days later.

The Second Uprising broke out a year later. The plebiscite held under Allied (British, French and Italian) supervision on 21 March 1920 gave a large majority to the pro-German party. In August 1920, false rumours of the fall of Warsaw inflamed feelings on both sides. The Poles took control of administrative buildings in several towns without the Allied forces intervening. Following tense negotiations and a readjustment of the balance between Poles and German in the administration, the revolt began to calm down after

25 August, but the underground organisation created by the Poles remained.

This organisation was instrumental in starting the Third Uprising which began with the rumour that Upper Silesia was to remain German. In fact the French favoured the Poles while the British and Italians were co-operating with the Germans. What was at stake was possession of the rich industrial region in the Bytom-Gliwice-Katowice triangle. Against this background, the Uprising began on 3 May with the destruction of rail connections to block German intervention, notably by the *Grenzschutz* (Border Guard East). The revolt ended on 21 July with a ceasefire, following which the greater part of the disputed territory was given to Poland. In all these wars, the Poles made extensive use of armoured trains, and a selection of these is illustrated in the following section.

PP 14 *Zygmunt Powstaniec* during the Third Insurrection, on operations with the French, who are recognisable by their large berets and stripes on their sleeves, on the right. The armour of the engine was probably reinforced with trench shields. The wagons are of German origin, and the second one is armed with a gun in an open-topped turret.
(Photo: Paul Malmassari Collection)

PP *Kabicz*, built at Gliwice, was the only narrow gauge (7.85cm/2ft 7in) Polish armoured train. Here in May 1921 in Silesia, the train and crew are being blessed by a priest.
(Photo: Mariusz Zimny Collection)

Side view of *Kabicz*, with its ex-Prussian Class T37 engine.
(Photo: Mariusz Zimny Collection)

The Armoured Trains of the Polish Army in the Inter-War Period

Following the victory over Russia, the Polish trains were demobilised, except for sixteen units which remained in service. During the Winter of 1923/24 these units were grouped together into two regiments, each with four battalions of two trains. In addition in October 1927 two trains were dedicated to the training role with the 1st Training Division (*1 Dywizjon Pociagów Pancernych*) stationed at Jabłonna. In 1928 the six oldest trains were scrapped, and two armoured train divisions were formed (north of Warsaw and in Craków), which were integrated into the Armoured Force in 1930. Each armoured train formed the base unit, complemented by an instructional train, a support train and a reconnaissance company equipped with armoured trolleys. A modernisation programme was launched in 1931, intended to improve the trains' manoeuvring capabilities by reducing the numbers of wagons, while retaining two artillery wagons. A system of retractable lateral nacelles was introduced, permitting the machine guns to fire to front or rear along the sides of the train, the older artillery pieces were replaced with modern ones, and lastly the wagons themselves were replaced with more modern rolling stock.

Three classes of train were established:

Type I (Light).
Type II (Heavy).
Type III (Train composed of automotive units).

The Light Armoured Trains were composed of an infantry wagon and two artillery wagons, which kept the Austro-Hungarian and Russian artillery pieces, plus machine guns (from eight to sixteen on semicylindrical casemate mountings), and two anti-aircraft machine guns.

Their artillery wagons were of three types, inspired by the Soviet trains, classed Types I, II and III. Type I corresponded to the design of the *Sosnkowski* with two cylindrical turrets. Type II corresponded to the wagons of PP *Danuta* and *Poznańczyk*. Lastly the Type III corresponded to *Śmiały* and *Piłsudczyk*.

The Heavy Armoured Trains were more powerfully armed, with 100mm guns, and their machine guns were mounted in turrets. They had more powerful steam engines such as the Class Ti3 (ex-Prussian G53). After the First World War, Germany had delivered sixteen Prussian G53 engines as war reparations, of which six were diverted to the Polish Army. Beginning in 1920, two engines were armoured using Soviet engines as a reference, in the workshops of Warsaw-Praga, and these served as examples for the remainder, work on which began in 1926. The allocation of these engines was ordered on 20 November of that year, and the work was completed by 1932. In addition, two trains, *Zagończyk*[8] and *Stefan Czarniecki*,[9] were used for training before being broken up in 1928.

Their armament was standardised as:

– 100mm Skoda wz.1914/19, placed in the lowest turrets.

– 76mm Putilov wz.1902, replaced in 1926 by 75mm Model 1902/1926.

– 7.92mm water-cooled Maxim Mle 08.

For each armoured train plus its support train, the crew was fixed at eight officers, fifty-nine NCOs and 124 men.

The trains were numbered and named as follows:

PP 11 *Danuta*[10]
PP 12 *Poznańczyk*[11]
PP 13 *General Sosnkowski*[12]
PP 14 *Paderewski*[13]
PP 15 *Śmierć*[14]
PP 51 *Pierwszy Marszałek*[15]
PP 52 *Piłsudczyk*
PP 53 *Śmiały*[16]
PP 54 *Groźny*[17]
PP 55 *Bartosz Głowacki*[18]

PP 53 *Śmiały* dressed overall for Polish Army Day, on 15 August 1921. Its camouflage scheme would still be in use in the 1930s. Note the presence of a cowcatcher under the coupling hook. These wagons were armed with two types of Russian guns: a 122mm Model 1909 howitzer and a 76.2mm Model 1902 gun. In 1939 these pieces would be replaced by Polish 100mm and 75mm guns.
(Photo: Adam Jo ca Collection)

8. 'Adventurer'.
9. Polish nobleman (1599–1665), one of their most famous generals, who notably defended Warsaw against the Swedes in 1655.
10. A girl's name.
11. 'Connected to the town of Poznań', or 'The Poznanian'.
12. Kazimierz Sosnkowski (1885–1969), Polish nobleman, patriot, politician and general.
13. Ignacy Paderewski (1860–1941), the celebrated pianist, one of the political founders of Poland.
14. 'Death'.
15. 'First Marshal', after the first Polish Marshal, Józef Piłsudski (1867–1935), one of the founding fathers of the Polish State, then Head of State in 1918–22 and again in 1926–35. Also found written as 'I Marszałek'.
16. 'Audacious'.
17. 'Formidable'.
18. Bartosz Głowacki (originally Wojciech Bartosz, circa 1758–94) was a peasant ennobled for an act of bravery against the Russian cannons during the Kosciuszko Uprising in 1794.

Śmiały in 1934: note the modernisation of the artillery wagons with the installation of observation cupolas on the roofs. The wagon for the assault infantry has not yet received its lower armour protection.
(Photo: Mariusz Zimny Collection)

This and the other photos in a series of five show the methods of mounting the Maxim machine guns in the ex-Austro-Hungarian armoured wagons, including the retracting lateral nacelles, which stressed the importance of bringing fire to bear from all available weapons towards the front of the train, reminding us that an armoured train can be used as a means of surprise attack. The same types of mounting were standardised in all the trains.
(Photos: Mariusz Zimny Collection)

Below: PP 13 *General Sosnkowski*, seen here with an engine borrowed from another train. The Type I artillery wagons built in Pozna in 1920 on the bases of Russian wagons are armed with two 75mm wz.26/02 field guns (rebarrelled Russian 76.2mm Model 02). The safety flat wagons of the three trains in these photos are Type Pdkz VIIIC four-wheel flat wagons 13m (42ft 7¾in) long.
(Photo: CAW)

PP 15 *Śmierć.*

PP 14 *Paderewski* in a superb three-tone camouflage scheme: light green/olive green/red brown (the darker patches).

Light Armoured Train Project (Petrol-electric Armoured Railcar wz.28[19])

In 1928, armoured train studies turned towards automotive units (the Type III armoured train), comprising two vehicles and two safety flat wagons. The first vehicle was to be armed with a turret-mounted 75mm, and the second with a 37mm gun. Pddkz Type VIIc chassis, with two axles powered by tramway motors, were used for the prototype. The complete train was to be finished in August 1929. During the trials, its performance was far from impressive, one of the vehicles derailed, and the project was abandoned. The unit was not in fact dismantled, and was still on the roster of the armoured trains division in 1937, but it did not see service in September 1939.

Note the driver's vision slit front right. On this and the following three-quarters rear view, one can clearly see the two small lateral turrets intended for 7.92mm machine guns, and provided with virtually a 180-degree field of fire.
(Photo: Grzegorz Pomorski Collection)

Note that there are two hatches on the right hand side compared to just one on the left, and that the lower armour plating protects the whole vehicle.
(Photo: CAW)

[19.] Unofficial designation.

To the left of the entry door the auxiliary braking system can be seen.
(Photo: Artur Przeckek)

Petrol-electric Armoured Railcar wz.28	
Technical specifications:	
Overall length:	10.924m (35ft 10in)
Width:	3.150m (10ft 4in)
Wheelbase:	6.50m (21ft 4in)
Overall height:	3.850m (12ft 7½in)
Height from rail to vehicle roof:	2.93m (9ft 7¼in)
Armour thickness:	6–12mm
Weight:	Approx 25.9 tonnes
Crew:	1 officer and 12 men
Armament:	1 x APX 75mm Mle 97; 3 x 7.92mm wz.25 MG
Maximum speed:	32km/h (20mph)
Endurance:	Fuel for approx 10 hours

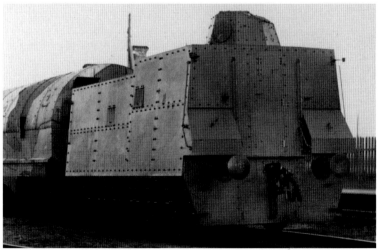

The second element of the Light Armoured Train project, armed with a 37mm gun in a turret. This vehicle seems to be much shorter. Note that it is coupled to an armoured wagon, perhaps from PP 53 *Śmiały*. It also appear to be much lower than the 75mm vehicle, probably to allow the heavier weapon to have a 360-degree field of fire.
(Photo: Adam Jo ca Collection)

Diesel-powered Armoured Train Project (1934)

In 1934, an article appeared in the military press mentioning a Polish project for a train without a locomotive, on which each wagon bogie would be powered by a diesel engine.[20] This train was to have weighed 1000 tonnes and be 150m (495ft) long; it would have reached a top speed of 130km/h (80mph). In order to save weight, only the crew compartments of the wagons would be armoured, the upper hull parts along with the roof being of duralumin, with the aim of allowing HE shells to pass completely through without setting off their fuzes. At each end there would be safety/protection flat wagons with machine-gun positions, and three or four armoured wagons: an infantry wagon (twelve men) with turrets and firing slits, an artillery wagon with two turrets, and a command wagon with an observation turret. If the commander of the group of armoured trains was present, a second command wagon could be inserted for him and his staff. It is not known whether this proposal formed part of project wz.28.

Armoured Trolleys and Rail Reconnaissance Units

In the early 1920s, the French company Crochat delivered ten light trolleys to the inspection department of the Polish Military Railways, in order to urgently make up for the lack of armoured trolleys. But the weight of the experimental armour fitted to one of the trolleys proved too much for the underpowered motor, so the machines were used as transport by the Engineers. We have no idea of what these machines looked like.

Tatra T-18 Armoured Trolleys

In November 1926 Poland acquired six Tatra armoured trolleys from Czechoslavakia, and they were allocated to the armoured trains School Battalion at Jablonna. Despite trials which revealed that these machines were underpowered,[21] nine additional trolley chassis were ordered, their armoured hulls being built and mounted by the firm CWS.[22] It was planned to replace the original turrets with those from the wz.28 armoured car, armed with a 37mm Puteaux SA-18 gun and two 7.92mm wz.25 machine guns, one to be used in an anti-aircraft role. The conversion, however, was never carried out.

One of the Polish Tatra T-18 trolleys, unmistakable due to the heraldic eagle attached to the turret. Note the four enormous 'headlamps' which in fact are white and red lanterns to signal the presence of the vehicle, protected by armoured glass 65mm thick.
(Photo: Adam Jońca Collection)

[20] Published in the *Red Star*, Moscow, May 1934.
[21] In April–May 1927 Poland purchased two unarmoured Austro-Daimler trolleys. They were tested by the armoured trains training formation, but no further orders resulted.
[22] *Centralne Warsztaty Samochodowe* = Central Car Workshops.

The 7.92mm Hotchkiss wz.25 machine gun in its two possible positions in the turret: above, arranged for anti-aircraft fire; below, for direct fire.
(2 Photos: Adam Jo ca Collection)

In a rare photo, a Tatra trolley wearing a typical Polish camouflage scheme is seen coupled to a Type 'R' trolley, on which the FT tank turret has rounded-off corners. This may mean it is a Polish-built CWS 'iron tank' or perhaps even a rebuilt Renault TSF wireless tank. This could be a view of one of the platoons of PP 13.
(Photo: Paul Malmassari Collection)

Several Polish T-18s carried names, as here, Żuk ('Scarab Beetle'). The jack handle visible on the left operated the lifting system for moving the trolley from one track to another.
(Photo: Janusz Magnuski Collection Via Mariusz Zimny)

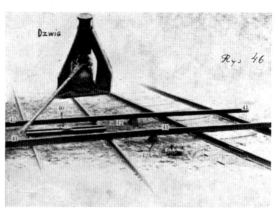

The equipment which allowed the Tatra trolley to move between parallel tracks. The turntable (item 40) and the rails (41) were carried on the sides of the hull, while the crank handle extension worked the jack.
(Photo: Adam Jo ca Collection)

A platoon of two Tatra trolleys was allocated to each of the armoured trains in the 1930s, but by 1939 these were only used with trains PP 13 and PP 15.

Tatra T-18 Armoured Trolley
Technical specifications (from Polish records):

Overall length:	3.55m (11ft 7¾in)
Width:	1.75m (5ft 9in)
Overall height:	2.14m (7ft 0¼in)
Armour thickness:	8mm sides; 5mm roof and floor
Weight empty:	3.45 tonnes
Crew:	3
Armament:	2 x 7.92mm MGs, either Maxim wz.08 (water-cooled) or Hotchkiss wz.25 (air-cooled)
Motor:	Tatra T-12, air-cooled
Maximum speed:	45km/h (28mph)
Range:	700km (435 miles)

In view of the poor performance of the Tatra trolleys, a road-rail machine based on the Vickers 6-ton tank was studied. It would have been armoured to 12mm on a weight of 7.5 tonnes, and its turret-mounted armament, comprising a 37mm Puteaux SA-18, would have provided reasonable firepower. Estimated speed on the road was 36km/h (22mph) and on rails 65km/h (40mph).

This illustration of the Vickers-based road-rail tank shows the turret armed with a 7.92mm wz.25 anti-aircraft machine gun. The changeover from rail to road was effected by lowering the tracked suspension, not by raising the rail wheels.
(Illustration: Tatra, via Marius Zimny)

Types 'R', 'TK' and 'TKS' Trolleys

At the same time, the innovative concept of tanks or tankettes with mixed road-rail propulsion was gaining in popularity. For example, as early as 1926 there were reports of various projects in Germany and France.[23] This type of machine was the subject of patents taken out in 1933 by Colonel Tadeus Kossakowski, inventor of the system shown in the following patent drawing. The prototypes of two rail chassis for the Renault tank and for the TK/TKS tankettes were ordered at the same time.

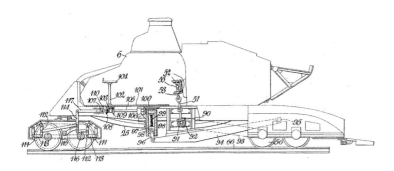

Drawing showing the operating principles of the armoured platform Type 'R', which led to the prototype. The production model arrangements would differ considerably.
(US Patent 2,014,769)

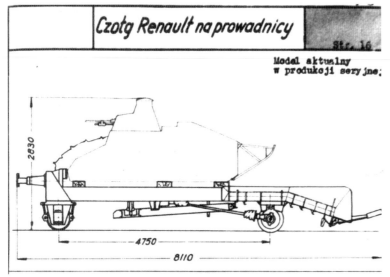

Outline drawing of the production model.
(Janusz Magnuski Collection via Mariusz Zimny)

23. An anonymous article 'Chassis sans moteur, pour le transport des chars d'assaut sur route et sur rails' which appeared on p 25 of *Le Génie civil* of 2 January 1927 referred back to the *Zeitschrift des Vereines deutscher Ingenieure* of 18 July 1926.
24. The CWS tanks were the Polish version of the Renault FT, of which twenty-seven examples were built in the CWS factory (*Centralne Warsztaty Samochodowe* = Central Car Workshops) in Warsaw. The small-link tracks designed in 1925 by Captain S. Kardaszewicz gave the tank a higher speed. But the steel used in the tanks' fabrication was not of armour quality, and these non-battleworthy machines were only allocated to training units.

The first prototype, *drezyna pancerna torowo – terenowa*, was built in 1932. It was not entirely satisfactory (even if it did move the lumbering Renault FT at 38km/h [23½mph]), principally because the platform was propelled by the revolving tracks of the tank turning rollers, transmitting the drive to the rail wheels through a system of chains and sprockets. This was a complex system, and had the disadvantage of wearing out the tank's tracks just as happened on the road. On the second prototype of 1933, the drive was transmitted from a connection on the gearbox via a hatch in the tank's floor (as shown on the original patent drawing), and speed rose to 45km/h (28mph) in either direction. After trials, the machine was accepted in 1938. More than thirty chassis were built in the Zieleniewski factory in Sanok and by Lilpop-Rau-Loewenstein in Warsaw. Two of these machines were allocated to each armoured train. Apart from the speed advantage compared

The prototype of the Type 'R' trolley. Here the tank is a Renault FT CWS[24] with small-link tracks. The chain final drive is clearly visible.
(Photo: Artur Przeczek Collection)

This arrangement of outside supports was seen only on the prototype. Note that the machine has a driving axle at the front and two carrying axles at the rear.
(Photo: Artur Przeczek Collection)

A Type 'R' trolley close to the definitive series production, with a Renault FT CWS tank. Note the reduced diameter of the wheels on the front axle.

(Photo: Janusz Magnuski Collection via Mariusz Zimny)

Rear view of the same machine, a much simpler arrangement than the prototype and at the same time more robust.

(Photo: Janusz Magnuski Collection via Mariusz Zimny)

with the previous Tatra trolleys (the platforms of the last batch reached 55km/h [34mph]), the idea was to be able to employ a railway reconnaisssance vehicle also capable of leaving the track to support assault troops disembarked from the trains. The unloading operation, as for that of loading, took less than three minutes.

Type 'R' Trolley
Technical specifications:

Length:	8.11m (26ft 7¼in)
Width:	2.04m (6ft 8¼in)
Height with tank:	2.83m (9ft 3½in)
Weight empty:	3.4 tonnes
Weight with tank:	10.5 tonnes
Crew:	2
Armament:	37mm L/21 Puteaux SA-18
Armour (FT tank only):	16mm (hull vertical plates), 8mm (top deck), 22mm (cast turret), 16mm (rivetted turret)
Maximum speed:	55km/h (34mph) in either direction

Platoon of Type 'R' and 'TKS' trolleys allocated to PP 54 in Biadoliny Station. The conversions of the Renault tanks were carried out in the Lilpop-Rau-Lowenstein factory. This and the following view show to good effect the front of the platform, painted in the three-tone camouflage.

(Photo: Paul Malmassari Collection)

Close-up of the front suspension of the platform. It is just possible to make out the registration plate on the right, and there is an immobilising shoe on the track, suggesting that the platoon and PP 12 would be remaining stationary for some time.
(Photo: Paul Malmassari Collection)

The Wehrmacht captured virtually all the trolleys used in action by the Polish Army in 1939. However, they showed no interest in these machines and none were put back into service. Note on this FT from PP 12 the unusual form of the exhaust pipe where it leaves the silencer.
(Photo: Paul Malmassari Collection)

It is difficult now after so many years to know whether this pileup was the result of an accident or sabotage to prevent the two trolleys (Type 'R' with Type 'TK' upside down behind it) from falling into German hands intact. The latter explanation seems the more likely, as the gun on the FT is in the full recoil position, and the tank itself is positioned at the rear of its platform, whereas the shock of a collision would have been expected to push it further forward. The trolleys are perhaps from PP 54.
(Photo: Paul Malmassari Collection)

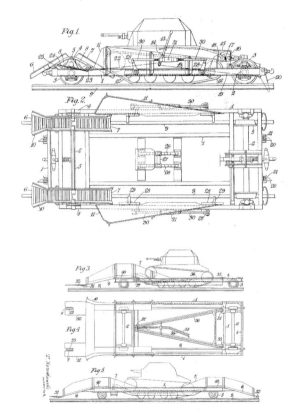

The three forms proposed for the guide platform for the TK tankette. The third solution was symmetrical to allow the tankette to dismount either forward or backward.
(US Patent 1,933,811)

The two prototypes for the TK and TKS[25] were completed in the Summer of 1932. The design was quite different to that for the Renault tank: instead of driving the rail wheels with the motor, the tracks remained in contact with the rails. The chassis built in this manner received the designation *prowadnica szynowa*, which translates roughly as 'guide on rails for tracked vehicle'. A hydraulic system allowed the tankette to descend from its guide platform in just one minute. In parallel, a model was studied having the tankettes back-to-back. The testing was carried out over four years, with eleven pre-production models (Version III) built between 1934 and 1935. The definitive model (Version IV) was adopted in 1936 and thirty-eight chassis were ordered, as well as four models in tandem. One tankette in two was equipped with a short-range radio set,[26] and all models were to have been modified to operate as trolleys, both independently and as part of an armoured train, with appropriate electrical and braking connections.

[25.] The TK tankette (known as the TK-3 when fitted with a Ford motor) went into production in 1931, followed by the TKS which was fitted with a Fiat 122 motor, an improved machine-gun mounting and new episcopes.
[26.] An RKB/c set, its presence evidenced by the box installed on the front left wing.

Type 'TK' & 'TKS' Trolleys
Technical specifications:

Length:	6.30m (20ft 8in)
Width:	2.15m (7ft 0½in)
Wheelbase (rail wheels):	3.855m (12ft 7¾in)
Height with tankette:	1.33m (4ft 4¼in)
Weight with tankette:	4.15 tonnes (the tankettes weighed 2.6 tonnes)
Crew:	2
Armament:	1 x 7.92mm wz.25 machine gun in front casemate and 1 spare 7.92mm wz.28 Browning machine gun
Armour (TK/TKS only):	8–10mm (hull vertical plates), 6mm (top deck)
Maximum speed:	46km/h (28.5mph). To travel in both directions, two TK or TKS trolleys would be coupled back-to-back.

A regulation platoon[27] of armoured trolleys was made up of two half-platoons: each one with one 'R' Type trolley and one 'TK' or 'TKS' trolley.[28] A fifth vehicle, a TK/TKS tankette, was held in reserve on the support train. In reality the Poles often made up combinations of 'TK-TK' without the Renault tank. Apart from the advantage of being able to travel in both directions, the tankettes would be carried with their tracks raised above rail level and could thus be disembarked very rapidly.

A 'TK' Type trolley.
(Photo: Adam Jońca Collection)

A 'TKS' Type trolley. There were three different versions of the TK-3 and TKS.
(Photo: Adam Jońca Collection)

[27.] A crew of one officer, six NCOs and ten men, plus the crew of the reserve vehicle.
[28.] Apart from PP 15 with two Tatra trolleys, and PP 13 with two Tatra trolleys and two TK/TKS.
[29.] *Dwuwieżowy* = double turret. An unofficial designation common today.
[30.] Only 137 7TP tanks were available in total.

In this photo of a captured trolley, note the extension which runs the length of the suspension beam, a sure way of identifying a TK belonging to an armoured train.
(Photo: All Rights Reserved)

The above and following photos show the prototype platform designed for the 7TP. Here, the trials are being conducted using a 6-tonne 7TP dw[29] (a Polish development of the British Vickers Mark E). This model was armed with a 7.92mm Model 30 (Ckm wz.30) machine gun in each turret.
(Photos: CAW)

Note beneath the chassis the connection between the motor of the tank and the final drive to the rear axle.

Trolley with 7TP Tank

This arrangement, similar to the platform for the C7P gun tractor was meant to supplant the Tatra T-18 and the TK-R-TK units. With its Bofors 37mm wz.37 gun this machine would have greatly increased the reconnaissance and raiding capabilities of the armoured trains. However, in light of the lack of 7TP tanks in the front line,[30] the project was dropped.

As a final note, since 1935 the Model 34 half-track trucks used by engineer and supply units could be fitted with a set of rail rollers. They do not, however, belong in the story of the armoured train.

A fine rear view of the trial tank mounting on its platform. The lateral guides help correct small errors in the approach lineup, inevitable since the the manoeuvre could be carried out without any member of the crew having to leave the tank.
(Photo: CAW)

Shown here for comparison, the transporter platform for the C7P artillery tractor, which had the same tracked chassis as the 7TP tank. Note that this platform appears slightly longer than the one carrying the tank.
(Photo: CAW)

Electric Armoured Trolley Project[31]

This eight-wheeled trolley was to have been armed with a 37mm cannon in a turret. The diagram top right gives the only known information on this project.

Diesel-Electric Trolley Project	
Technical specifications:	
Length:	7.92m (25ft 11¾in)
Width:	n/a
Height above rails:	4.40m (14ft 5¼in)
Weight:	32.5 tonnes
Main motors:	2 x 110hp diesel (?) driving 2 x 300V 240 amp generators
Axle motors:	4 x 550V 80 Amp
Crew:	5
Armament:	37mm Bofors wz.37 gun and 1 x 7.92mm wz.30 machine gun
Armour:	10–20mm
Maximum speed:	40km/h (25mph). The trolley was to have the capacity to haul armoured wagons of up to 110 tonnes.

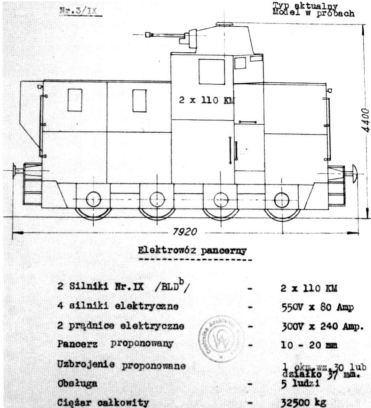

Draft outline of the electric trolley.
(Document: Adam Jo ca)

Unidentified Armoured Trolley

This machine, photographed in the early 1930s, was attached to the second armoured train unit. The turret is possibly one from a Samochód pancerny wz.28 half-track armoured car.
(Photo: Adam Jo ca Collection)

31. Probably diesel-electric, given the contemporary use of 110hp diesel engines in the 7TP tank

Armoured Trains During the Polish Campaign[32]

The ten armoured trains were mobilised between late August and the beginning of September 1939. Their numbering allocated during this period was a function of the division they were allocated to:

I *Dywizjon Pociągów Pancernych* – Nos 11, 12, 13, 14, 15.
II *Dywizjon Pociągów Pancernych* – Nos 51, 52, 53, 54, 55 (improvised armoured train used for training).
MDAL No 1, No 2 (Light Naval Artillery Armoured Rail Battery).

The improvised Armoured Rail Batteries for coastal defence were built in August and saw action in the Kartuzty region before being captured. The improvised training unit was assembled in September 1939 using rolling stock held in reserve. In action with German tanks at Jaroslaw, it was destroyed on 10 September. Another improvised train, *Smok Kaszubski* ('Dragon of Kashub'), was built in the Gdynia port workshops in September, using steel plates intended for the destroyers *Orkan* and *Uragan*, which were still on the slips. It was allocated to coastal defence and took part in fighting for a week before being destroyed. Lastly in September two other improvised armoured trains were built to defend Warsaw, but surviving information is sparse. One of these trains was armed with four 75mm guns on two wagons.

The two armoured wagons which composed the instructional Light Armoured Train were nonetheless fully armed. They were captured together by the Germans, repaired and incorporated separately in two German armoured trains: the wagon in the foreground of the above photo, with armoured axleboxes, was used in PZ 21, while the fully-protected wagon in the photo below went to PZ 22.
(2 Photos: Paul Malmassari Collection)

These two wagons were the former artillery wagons of PP *Bartosz Głowacki* dating from the Russo-Polish War, out of service until 1939. They had been built on the base of two Prussian Type Ommku mineral wagons.

Smok Kaszubski parked in Kartuzy Station. It is possible there is a second armoured wagon armed also with a 75mm on the opposite side of the platform.
(Photo: Mariusz Zimny Collection)

The use of the names of the armoured trains was abandoned shortly before the start of the Second World War in favour of numbers. However, to assist the reader we will continue to quote the former name along with the train number.

[32]. Known in Poland as the *Kampania wrze niowa or Wojna obronna 1939 roku*, the Defensive War of 1939.

Division	Number	Name	Allocation 1 September 1939	Type
I	11	*Danuta*	Poznań Army	Heavy
I	12	*Poznańczyk*	Poznań Army	Heavy
I	13	*Generał Sosnkowski*	Modlin Army	Medium
I	14	*Paderewski*	Modlin Army (reserve)	Heavy
I	15	*Śmierć*	Modlin Army (reserve)	Light
II	51	*Marszałek*	Craków Army	Medium
II	52	*Piłsudczyk*	Craków Army	Heavy
II	53	*Śmiały*	Łódź Army	Heavy
I	54	*Groźny*	Craków Army	Medium
II	55	*Bartosz Głowacki*	Prusy Army	Light

Out of some ninety actions in which the armoured trains participated, each time they came up against tanks, the latter suffered heavy losses. Seven trains had to be sabotaged by their crews, only one was destroyed by Luftwaffe attack and two others in ground combat.

PP 11 began the campaign in support of the 26th Infantry Division in the region of Chodziez-Szamocun and fought hard in support of the counter-offensive of 14–15 September towards the River Bzura. In the course of a bitter combat on 16 September near Jackowice, it was destroyed by the anti-tank guns of the 31st Infantry Regiment of the 24th Infantry Division.

PP 11 *Danuta* during its last fight on 16 September. The engine has been hit by anti-tank rounds, and its crew killed, making further movement impossible.
(Photo: Paul Malmassari Collection)

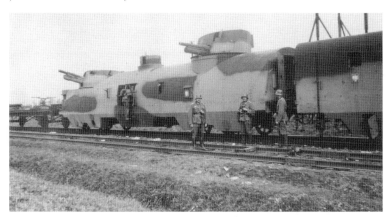

Above: The front section of PP 11 *Danuta*. Only this artillery wagon and the assault troop wagon seen on the right were salvageable, and they were incorporated in PZ 21. Note the hand-operated trolley carried on the safety/protection flat wagon. The gun in the lower turret is a 100mm wz.14/19P howitzer.
(Photo: Paul Malmassari Collection)

Rear view of the artillery wagon of PP 11 *Danuta* (identical to those of PP 12 *Poznańczyk*) prior to its inclusion in PZ 21. The upper turret is armed with a 75mm wz.02/26 gun (the Polish version of the 76.2mm Russian piece).
(Photo: Paul Malmassari Collection)

PP 12 supported the Wielkopolska Cavalry Brigade[33] in the region of Krotoszyn, Jarocina and Nowe-Miasto. It was employed during the offensive on the Szura then around 7 September in the Lowicz region. Damaged by artillery on the 9th, it was temporarily repaired at Błonie. On the 10th, the crew attempted to regain Warsaw, but Ołtarzew on their route had already been occupied by German forces. Its crew decided to sabotage the train and continued to fight the Germans on foot.

PP 12 *Poznańczyk* which had been sabotaged by its crew, damaged beyond hope of repair, apart from its engine which appears to have been towed to a depot.
(Photo: Paul Malmassari Collection)

Steam engines of Class Ti3 had been the standard propulsion unit for the Polish armoured trains since 1927. They were former Prussian Class G5 (built between 1903 and 1906). They moved the armoured trains at up to 45km/h (28mph). Here is the engine from PP 12 *Poznańczyk*.
(Photo: Paul Malmassari Collection)

The assault troop transport wagon of *Poznańczyk* moved to clear the track.
(Photo: Paul Malmassari Collection)

33. *Wielkopolska Brygada Kawalerii*, with its HQ in Poznań.

On 3 September **PP 13** took part in the defence of Giechanów then patrolled along the Narew and the Bug. On the 10th, it joined the 33rd Infantry Division retreating as far as Łochów Station. At around 14.00 the explosion of a bomb from a Stuka damaged the track and derailed the train, while other bombs set fire to the command/assault troop wagon. It was subsequently abandoned by its crew, who continued the fight on foot. It is certainly the most famous of all the armoured trains, as Hitler came to visit it on the 22nd, which generated hundreds of photos both official and private, reproduced in numerous publications.

PP 13 *Generał Sosnkowski* derailed. On the left is the command/assault troop wagon with its characteristic wire antenna.
(Photo: Paul Malmassari Collection)

The rear artillery wagon of PP 13 *Generał Sosnkowski*. Its turrets each had a 270-degree horizontal field of fire.
(Photo: Paul Malmassari Collection)

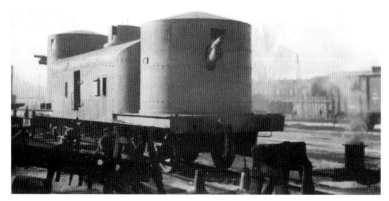

The same wagon following repairs (note the buffers have been removed). Based on an engraving published in a German newspaper, it is rumoured that PP 13 took part in the invasion of Denmark, but no photographic proof exists.
(Photo: Paul Malmassari Collection)

PP 14 was in action on 15 and 16 September at Łowicz. It began to withdraw, but near Jackowice its crew found themselves cut off from the rest of the retreating Polish elements. They abandoned the train between Jackowice and Rząśno.

Two photos of PP 14 destroyed between Jackowice and Rząśno.
(2 Photos: Mariusz Zimny Collection)

The last Polish armoured train remaining in action was PP 15 *Śmierć*. It was photographed in Modlin with an artillery wagon built in Lviv in 1920, then modernised, which had survived up until 1939. Its existence had long been ignored, for lack of previous photographic evidence. Its Class Ti3 engine has been set on fire.
(Photo: Paul Malmassari Collection)

The same artillery wagon seen from the opposite end. It is armed with a 100mm Skoda wz.14/19A howitzer. Note the state of the station roof with tiles blown off by artillery fire.
(Photo: Paul Malmassari Collection)

Initially held in reserve, **PP 15** went into action from 13 September in the defence of Modlin, where it was captured on the fall of the town.

Damaged by artillery fire near Wysoka on 2 September, **PP 51** *Pierwszy Marszałek* managed to reach Oświęcim. From 12 to 14 September it defended a bridge on the River San and supported the resistance of Army Group Sandomierz. On the 27th, near Przeworsk Station, it was either destroyed by a bombardment or abandoned by its crew – accounts differ. Recovered by the Soviets, it served with the 77th Regiment of the 10th NKVD Division and operated in western Ukraine (former Polish territory). On 5 July 1941 it was captured by the Wehrmacht during Operation 'Barbarossa', who put it into service as PZ 10.

Close-up of one of the artillery wagons of PP 51.
(Photo: Paul Malmassari Collection)

The rear artillery wagon of PP 15 *Śmierć*, originally an Austro-Hungarian wagon used on Polish trains since 1918, rearmed with a 75mm wz.02/26 gun.
(Photo: Paul Malmassari Collection)

PP 51 *Pierwszy Marszałek* captured by the Soviets (who renamed it BEPO 77), then by the Germans who took this photograph.
(Photo: Paul Malmassari Collection)

A view of what is obviously a rake of Polish armoured wagons on the way to a depot to be reconditioned. Behind the two wagons from PP 51 are visible those from PP 53, which together would eventually make up PZ 10.
(Photo: Paul Malmassari Collection)

PP 52 went into action on 1 September in the region of Mokre, in support of the 52nd and 53rd Infantry Regiments facing the 4th Panzer Division, where it was attacked by aircraft but escaped damage. It then took part in the fighting to prevent the Germans crossing the Warta, but it was forced to withdraw to the Laski-Łódź-Warsaw line. It was bombarded in the station at Laski, then when the tracks had been repaired it escorted the special train which evacuated the gold reserves from the Bank of Poznań. It next received orders to move to Siedlce because of the withdrawal of Polish forces, but the town had already fallen. Under the command of Colonel Więckowski, it formed the main element of an all-arms detachment which protected the pocket into which the Poles were withdrawing. Despite some successes (the destruction of reconnaissance vehicles and the capture of prisoners), its firepower was gradually worn down, until by 20 September only one turret with six shells and three machine guns remained operational. Too damaged to take part in a sortie, its crew sabotaged it with explosives.

Overall view of PP 52.
(Photo: Mariusz Zimny Collection)

PP 53 supported the Wolhynie Cavalry Brigade[34] on the morning of 1 September then took part in the battle of Mokra against the 4th Panzer Division. On the next day, it fought tanks of the 1st Panzer Division at Radomsko, then withdrew towards Lwów with PP 55. Arriving in the town on the 18th, the two trains were captured when Lwów fell to the Red Army.

In this view of the artillery wagon of PP 53, one can see the retractable nacelle system identical to that on the ex-Austro-Hungarian wagons.
(Photo: Paul Malmassari Collection)

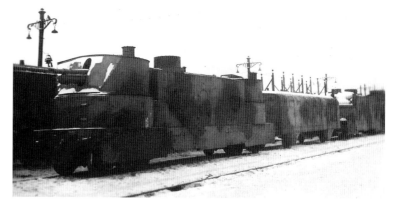

PP 54 Groz y seen at Cracóv in the Winter of 1939/40. The turret in the foreground is armed with a 100mm howitzer, and the other turret with a 75mm gun.
(Photo: Paul Malmassari Collection)

PP 54 went into action in Silesia from 1 September in support of the 75th Infantry Company at Kobiór, where it was damaged and its commander was killed. It withdrew towards Tunel and engaged several armoured units. On 17 September it was abandoned at Biadolina, being unable to cross the River Dunajec as the railway bridge had been cut.

Bombarded in Koluszki Station on the first day of the war, **PP 55** remained in reserve and patrolled in the region of Brześć. At Żabinka, it destroyed several armoured vehicles then withdrew to Kowel and Lwów with PP 53, where it was captured by the Soviets after being hit by artillery.

---

[34] Wołyńska Brygada Kawalerii, with its HQ at Lódż.

The Polish Armoured Train Battalions in Britain (12 October 1940 – November 1943

In 1940 the British built twelve trains to counter a threatened German invasion, by patrolling the coast from Cornwall in the West to the Moray Firth in Scotland. They were armoured at the Derby Carriage and Wagon Works of the LMS and at the Stratford Works of the LNER.[35] Of the 17,000 Polish officers and men who were stationed in Britain,[36] four battalions of the Polish Army of the West were assigned to the armoured trains from 1940 to 1942. They were organised as follows:

I *dywizjon*: Armoured Trains C, G and E.
II *dywizjon*: Armoured Trains A, D and F.
III *dywizjon*: Armoured Trains B, M and H.
IV *dywizjon*: Armoured Trains K, L and J.

In the early stages, to get round language problems, the Poles served their apprenticeship in armoured trains in Scotland, where there was the largest concentration of Polish units, liaising with the British crews of Armoured Trains Nos 10, 11 and 12. The Poles had completely replaced the British crews by April 1941, except for drivers and firemen transferred from the Royal Engineers, and for a few months longer, several radio operators.

From their long experience of armoured trains, the Poles rapidly suggested improvements to the rolling stock in their charge. Certainly the most active of the Polish officers was Colonel L Lodzia-Michalski, commander of the 1st Armoured Train Group. At countless meetings, he pressed for the augmentation of the trains' machine-gun and anti-aircraft armament; the amount of ammunition carried, including grenades and explosives for close combat, was greatly increased; and if it proved impossible to agree to his request for additional armour protection for the wagons, it was thanks to him that two basic improvements were put into effect: the enlarging of the gunshields on the 6pdr guns to improve crew protection, and the cutting of access hatches in the floors of the wagons to allow evacuation under fire.

Beginning in 1942, tracked and wheeled armoured vehicles were attached to the trains, to enable the trains to extend their zone of action, but also with a view to training the crews in armoured combat. This latter role gradually came to take precedence over the railway patrol function, and in 1942, the Polish train crews had absorbed sufficient training to be able to rejoin combat units. At that stage the armoured trains were transferred to British crews from the Home Guard.

[35.] LMS = London, Midland and Scottish Railway; LNER = London and North Eastern Railway.
[36.] Following their evacuation at the time of the Fall of France, along with many Polish airmen and seamen. The Government in Exile under General Sikorski had also left Paris for London.
[37.] The designation 'Bren' is an amalgam of the names of the towns of Brno where the ZB26 was made for the Czechoslovak Army, and Enfield, where the British version was manufactured.

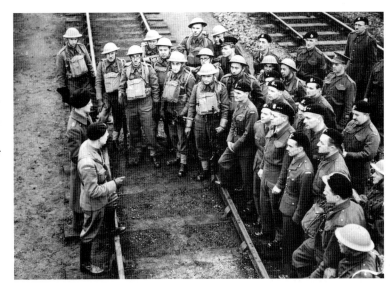

A briefing for the crew of an armoured train, allowing us a view of their British kit with certain additions and badges from Polish uniforms. *(Photo: IWM)*

In this view, the lack of a safety/protection flat wagon is not due to a request by the photographer, but a conscious decision on the part of the British General Staff. They considered the menace of mines so insignificant as not to warrant tying up much-needed transport wagons. The soldier climbing the ladder is carrying a .303in (7.7mm) calibre Bren[37] LMG. *(Photo: IWM)*

Bren gunners in firing position. Note the 'POLAND' shoulder flashes. *(Photo: IWM)*

The gun shield has been fitted with the extensions demanded by the Polish crews, who were very experienced and therefore critical of many of the original details of the British armoured trains. The photo was taken after the trains had been handed over to the Home Guard.
(Photo: IWM)

A Universal Carrier from Armoured Train G, belonging to a reconnaissance unit and used by the Poles in an effort to extend their zone of operations further away from the railway. Covenanter and Valentine tanks were also allocated to various trains.
(Photo: RAC Tank Museum)

Soviet Armoured Trains under Polish Command (1944–1945)

The part of the Polish Army which fell under Soviet control[38] took on the designation of the Popular Polish Army (*Ludowe Wojsko Polskie*, LWP). Despite the fact that armoured trains were not officially part of its establishment, during the 1st Byelorussian Front's offensive on the Vistula in September and October 1944, the 31st Special (Gorki) Armoured Trains Division and the 59th Armoured Trains Division were temporarily put under the command of the First Polish Army.

The 31st Division comprised the BP *Cosma Minin* and *Ilya Mouromietz*, plus various support units and reconnaissance trolleys. The armoured trains of the 59th Division were of Type OB-3, Nos 668 and 675, and they operated in the Warsaw region from September 1944 to January 1945.

The SOK[39] Armoured Trains (1945–1947)

After the official cessation of hostilities in Europe, parts of the new frontiers of Poland, in particular those to the south-east, were threatened by units of the Ukrainian Revolutionary Army (UPA[40]), who attacked the transport infrastructure, and principally the railway network. In the Autumn of 1945, the commander-in-chief of the SOK decided to set up his own armoured train units. A search for suitable rolling stock turned up several armoured wagons (primarily German but also Polish and Czech) scattered about the country (the German units still in good condition had been taken back to the USSR as war booty, and for study there). The remaining stock was identified, collected and repaired in the Ostrów workshops near Warsaw. The trains and their crews were brought together and formed in Warsaw and Craków, before being sent to the south-eastern regions.

The first SOK train (for the Russian broad gauge) was formed at Jaroslaw with a crew coming mostly from Szczecin, which gave the train its name *Szczecin*. It carried out patrols in the Medya-Lubaczow-Rawa Ruska region. In March 1946 its crew was replaced by personnel from Warsaw, then it returned to Ostrów for modification.

SOK Armoured Train No 2, later named *Grom* ('Thunderbolt') was put together in Warsaw in October 1945. Sent to Sanok where it came under the orders of the 8th Infantry Division, it patrolled between Sanok and Łupków and between Sanok and Ustinov. It went into action on several occasions notably at Olszanica, Stefkowa, Komańcza and Oslanica.

The future *Huragan* (Hurricane) which began as SOK Armoured Train No 3 was created in October 1946. In 1948 it was attached to the SOK training establishment at Toruń.

SOK Armoured Train No 4, the future *Błyskawica* ('Lightning') was created at the DOKP[41] near Kraków, using vehicles renovated in the Ostrów workshops. The former commander of Armoured Train No 1 took over control of SOK No 4, the train being allocated first to Zagora until June 1947, then to Zawada.

The existence of four armoured trains made it possible to create a SOK Division in early 1947, commanded by Captain M Jarosz, with its headquarters in the station at Zagórz, near Sanok. It was during this period that two newly-restored machines were allocated to it, one being a Steyr le.Sp trolley and the other, according to certain sources, being a Skoda trolley named *Baśka*

---

38. *Polskie Siły Zbrojne na Wschodzie.* In the West, a Polish Army Corps commanded by General Anders, called the *Polskie Siły Zbrojne na Zachodzie*, or Polish Army of the West, fought in Italy while other Polish units served at Tobruk.
39. *Służba Ochrony Kolei*, Railway Protection Service, reporting to the Interior Minister.
40. Українська Побманська Армія, established in October 1942 in Volhynie to fight against all the occupying forces (successively, Germans, Poles and Russians) and obtain independence for the Ukraine.
41. *Dyrekcja Okręgowa Kolei Pa stwowych*, State Railways Regional Management.

('Barbara'). In April 1947 this new division came under the command of Major-General Stefan Mossor, commander-in-chief of Operation 'Wisla' (*Ackja Wisła*) intended to eradicate the UPA.

Two of the trains (probably Nos 1 and 2) were placed under the orders of the Fifth Army Group (Craków). We have no information concerning the fate of these trains after 1947.

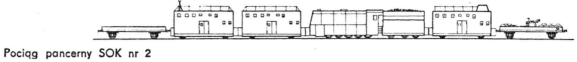

Pociąg pancerny SOK nr 2

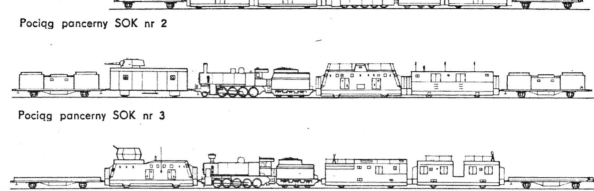

Profile views of three trains reconstructed by Janus Magnuski, in which it is easy to recognise ex-German vehicles, both armoured trains and anti-aircraft trains.

(Illustration: Wozy Bojowe, p 282)

Pociąg pancerny SOK nr 3

Pociąg pancerny SOK nr 4

The K-Wagen of SOK Armoured Train No 3.

(Photo: Janusz Magnuski Collection)

Train No 4 *Błyskawica* with its crew posing in front of a K-Wagen.

(Photo: Janusz Magnuski Collection)

This A-Wagen is one of the rare examples using a *Wirbelwind* turret. Note that it is oriented in the opposite sense to the original use of these wagons, which placed the 10.5cm turret in front. The crew members are wearing the *rogatywka*, the traditional Polish headgear.

(Photo: Janusz Magnuski Collection)

Note that the Steyr trolley used by the SOK units is one of the early versions with three rectangular plaques protecting the air intakes, as against the circular caps seen on the later series.

(Photo: Janusz Magnuski Collection)

Lokomotor Armoured Railcar WP870027 (ex-PT 16) & Armoured Wagon WP 870028 in Closeup

This railcar is described in the chapter on Germany. After the Second World War, this machine was used by a unit of the Polish Army based at Przemyśl-Bakończyce. It took part in Operation 'Wisla' then remained in service up until the 1960s. In 1982 it joined the collection of the State Railway Museum in Warsaw. It has not been possible to identify the train from which the armoured wagon derived. It appears that it too had served for many years before finding its way into the collection of the Railway Museum.

The turrets on both units are identical, seen here armed with Russian 76.2mm Putilov guns. The oval-shaped opening in the casemate side was cut after PT16 entered service, in order to make up for the absence of firing ports for close-in defence.

(Photo: Private Collection)

The three small square blocks just below the turret ring, which exist only on this side, are without doubt smoke extractor vents, connected to internal pipework, used when firing. The gun seen here is not the original.

(Photo: Private Collection)

SOURCES:
Archives:
SHD: 6 N 249, 7 N 2999, 7 N 3009/2, 7 N 3017, 7 N 3018.

Books:
Jo ca, Adam, *Renault FT 17/NC 1/NC 2/TSF, Renault R 35/40, Hotchkiss H 35/39* (Sandomierz: Stratus s.c., 2009).

_____, *Poci gi Pancerne Z Legionowa*, Wrzesień 1939 Vol 24 (Warsaw: Edipresse Polska SA, 2013).

Jurczyk, Jozef, and Margasinski, Krzysztof, *Dziennik pociagu pancernego Hallercsyk* (Cz stochowa: Towarzystwo Przyjacioł Czechowic-Dziedzic, 2010).

Konstankiewicz, Andrzej, *Bro strzelecka i sprz t artyleryjski formacji polskich i Wojska Polskiego w latach 1914-1939* (Lublin: Uniwersytetu Marii Curie-Skłodowskiej editions, 2003).

Krawczak T, and Odziemkowski, Jerzy, *Polskie pociagi pancerne w wojnie 1939* (Warsaw: Biblioteka Pami ci Pokole , 1987).

Kraśnickca, Urszula, and Filipow, Krzysztof, *Poci gi Pancerne 1918-1943* (Białystok: Ośrodek Bada Historii Wojskowej, 1999).

Kuntz, Captain Ch, *L'Offensive de l'Etoile Rouge contre la Pologne* (Paris: Lavauzelle, 1922).

Ledwoch, Janusz, *Polskie poci gi pancerne 1939* (Warsaw: Wydawnictwo « MILITARIA », 2015).

Magnuski, Janusz, *Poci g pancerny « ZYGMUNT POWSTANIEC »* (Warsaw: Wydawnictwo Ministerstwa Obrony Narodowej, 1981).

_____, *Poci g pancerny « DANUTA »* (Warsaw: Wydawnictwo Ministerstwa Obrony Narodowej, 1972).

_____, *Poci g pancerny « MIAŁY »* (Warsaw: PELTA, 1996).

_____, *Karaluchy Przeciw Panzerom* (Warsaw: PELTA, 1995).

_____, *Wozy Bojowe LWP 1943-1983* (Warsaw: Wydawnictwo Ministerstwa Obrony Narodowej, 1985).

Ostrówka, Adam Jacek, *Poci gi pancerne Wojska Polskiego 1918-1939* (Toru : Adam Marszałek, 2013).

Porte, Rémy, *Haute-Silésie 1920-1922* (Paris: Riveneuve Éditions, 2009).

Sikorski, Major General L., *La Campagne polono-russe de 1920* (Paris: Payot, 1928).

Journal articles:
Anon., 'Châssis sans moteur, pour le transport des chars d'assaut sur route et sur rails', *Le Génie civil* (2 January 1927), p. 25.

Anon., 'Trains blindés', *Revue d'artillerie* Vol 114 (July-December 1934), pp 93–4.

Anon., 'Panzerzüge in der polnischen Armee', *Militär-Wochenblatt* No 45 (1932), pp 1582–4.

Bulletin Vol 5 No 3 (1995), pp 5.31–5.32.

Jońca, Adam, 'The Polish Armoured Trolleys', *V.M.I.* (1989), No 3, pp 18–23; No 32, pp 18–19.

Magnuski, Janusz, 'Drezyna Pancerna SOK', *Militaria*, Vol 1, No 1 (1991), pp 37–9.

Surlemont, Raymond, and Pied, Robert, 'The German Armoured Train in the Railway Museum in Warsaw', *V.M.I.* (15 February 1988), pp 29–31.

Szychowski, 'Armoured Trains', *Pryeglad Artyleryiski* Volume IX, Fascicule 2 (1923), pp 162–80 (in Russian).

'The Polish Armoured Trains in the Campaign of 1939', *Lokotrans* (9/2009), pp 27–33 (in Russian).

Zaloga, Steven, 'Polish Armored trains in 1939', *AFV News* 12/3 (n.d.), pp 6–10.

_____, and Magnuski, Steven, 'Polish Armoured Vehicles of WW2', *Military Modelling* (October 1983), pp 730–3.

_____, 'Polish Armoured Vehicles of WW2', *Military Modelling* (November 1983), pp 843–5.

Website:
http://derela.republika.pl/

PORTUGAL

ARMOURED TRAINS AND TROLLEYS

Although they did not deploy armoured trains in Portugal proper, the Portuguese did use them in their colonies which were affected by anti-colonialist uprisings, which in chronological order were Goa, Angola and Mozambique.[1]

Goa, Portuguese Period

Goa was one of the three territories in the western part of India settled and exploited by the Portuguese since the sixteenth century.[2] After Britain granted independence to India in August 1947, nationalist movements attempted to disrupt communications between the three territories and Portugal by attacking economic targets and the transport system.[3] Goa itself was finally invaded and annexed by India between 17 and 19 December 1961.

Wickham armoured trolley supplied for use in Goa, with a different turret to the models built for Malaysia.
(Photo: Wickham)

[1] The fighting in Goa began in 1947, in Angola on 4 February 1961, and in Mozambique in September 1964. The last two wars ended with the Carnation Revolution of 1974.
[2] The Portuguese refused the annexation of its Indian territories on the grounds that when they had been established, India did not exist as a separate state, and therefore under international law India could not claim their return.
[3] Notably in July and August 1954, which led to the annexation of the two land-locked territories.
[4] Trolleys Nos 172 to 175, then Nos 181 to 190, with a question mark regarding trolleys Nos 171 and 186. Trolleys Nos 193 to 197 were ordered as bare rolling chassis to be armoured locally. (Information provided by Peter Bagshawe).

Angola, Portuguese Period

The first traffic on the Benguela Railway ran in 1905. The line was built following the discovery of copper in northern Rhodesia and Katanga in 1881. In the 1950s, the trains ran from Lobito to Elizabethville in the Belgian Congo. When the terrorist attacks began, armour plating was fitted to the cabs of the locomotives, and the inspection trolleys received complete armour protection. Additional trolley rolling chassis were ordered which were fitted with armour protection locally.[4]

Behind armoured Wickham trolley No 193, Garratt Class 10 B No 323, followed by Garratt Class 10 D No 386 (4-8-2+2-8-4), both with armoured cabs, depart Luso en route to Munhango.
(Photo: Peter Bagshawe)

Close-up of the armoured cab on Garratt Class 10 E No 389.
(Photo: Peter Bagshawe)

The classic arrangement in zones liable to attack: an open bogie wagon in front of a Garratt on the Munhango–Luso line photographed on 27 August 1972.

(Photo: Peter Bagshawe)

In Texeira de Souza Station, Class 9 A 4-8-0 engine No 209 with armoured cab.

(Photo: Peter Bagshawe)

A line of armoured Wickhams parked in Luso Depot on the evening of 24 August 1972, when the train services stopped for the night for security reasons.

(Photo: Peter Bagshawe)

A Wickham trolley leads 4-8-0 engine No 231 at the head of a Texeira–Lobito mail train, seen at Cangumbe Station.

(Photo: Wickham)

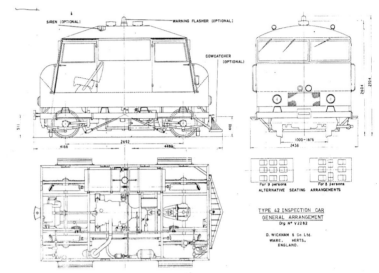

Wickham Type 42 Inspection Trolley (identical to the Wickham Type 40 Mk II), before the addition of armour protection.

(Document: Wickham)

Trolley No 83, delivered in November 1967. In around 1968 '100' was added to each serial number, which allows us to date this photo.

(Photos: Wickham)

Left: Armoured trolley No 172 in August 1972 at Munhango Depot, where a large number of these units were based.

(Photo: Peter Bagshawe)

Mozambique, Portuguese Period

Two Wickham running chassis (Nos 191 and 192 built in 1969) were ordered and sent to Mozambique to be locally armoured.

In 1972 Portugal entered into secret negotiations with the French firm of SOCOFER with a view to supplying the Mozambique colony with armoured trolleys, in the belief that France had retained a stock of trolleys left over from the War in Algeria. SOCOFER, based in the former Billard Works in Tours, carried out a design study, but the units were never built, as no official order was forthcoming. One unusual feature for an armoured vehicle at this late date was an open-topped hull covered with an awning, for ventilation in the hot climate.

Zorra was the name given to this armoured hull from an old Auto-Metralhadora-Daimler 4x4 Mod.F/64 (the Portuguese version of the British Dingo) mounted on a flat wagon. It offered scant protection against heavy weapons, but served as an excellent observation post for the five or six soldiers of its crew. Note the extra armour box added on top of the original hull.
(Photo: All Rights Reserved)

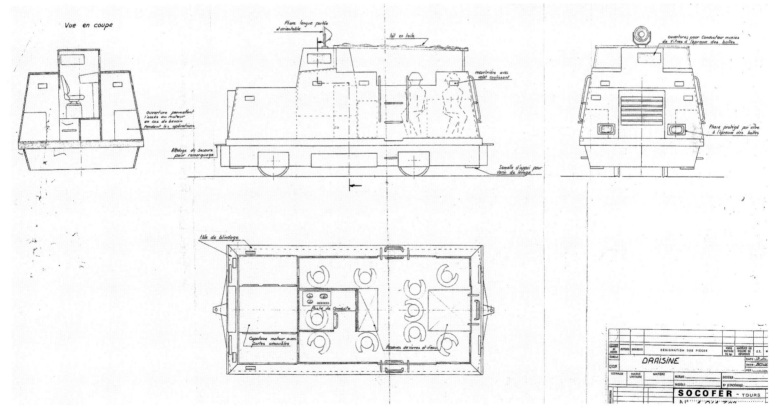

SOCOFER trolley design for Mozambique, which remained on the drawing board.
(Drawing: SOCOFER Archives, in the collection of Paul Malmassari)

SOURCES:

Harrison, Maurice A., 'Line across Angola', *The Railway Magazine* (September 1973), pp 446–9.
Wickham archives
The files of Peter Bagshawe.
'*Zorra*-The Railway Vixen', *Tank TV* No 2 (1992).

RHODESIA & ZIMBABWE[1]

ARMOURED TRAINS AND ARMOURED TROLLEYS 1972–1979

In our opinion, the defence of the railway network during the 1972–9 bush war in Rhodesia[2] by the security forces against the guerrillas of ZIPRA and ZANLA, who were armed respectively by the Russians and the Chinese,[3] is the rail conflict which produced the most innovations in armoured rolling stock.

The armoured trolleys[4]

The first attacks on commercial trains began in January 1975 on the line between Thomson Junction and Victoria Falls. At first security patrols were carried out using unarmoured Wickham inspection trolleys (Types 3, 4, 5 and 6), nicknamed 'Green Beans'. Very quickly it was realised that armoured rail vehicles would be required. The concept initially chosen would remain the standard for all subsequent vehicles, namely an armoured 'capsule' with a V-shaped cross-section, mounted on an existing chassis. The first type of armoured capsule, called the 'Rhino', was adapted to fit on the Land Rover LWB[5] chassis. The Rhino immediately attracted the interest of the railway operators, and late in 1976 three armoured capsules were delivered to the central railway maintenance workshops in Bulawayo for evaluation. During the war the MAP[6] vehicles were continuously developed, increased protection and an improved drive train being added to the Rhino and later designs, culminating in the ultimate armoured trolley, the Cougar.

The original Rhino model, with the turntable carried at the side together with one of the rails which allowed the trolley to drive onto the turntable, and the rail wheels fixed directly onto the axles without any intermediate drive system, which would cause many problems because of the vibration. Bringing up the rear is a Wickham Type 18 Mk VI inspection trolley.

(Photo: National Railways Museum, Bulawayo)

The first Rhino model was mounted on a standard Land Rover chassis, modified for use on the rails. The initial problem to be surmounted was the fitting of special rail wheels, because the Land Rover's wheelbase was wider than the local rail gauge of 1067mm (3ft 6in).

A wheel had to be designed with its rolling surface inboard of the outer end of the vehicle's axle. In addition, the four-wheel drive function, the steering and the rear hydraulic brakes were all discarded. The Rhino trolley entered service in early 1977. Initial reports mentioned cracks developing in the chassis, due to the constant jarring caused by the rail joints, and the first remedy was to weld on reinforcing plates. The second recurring fault was the breakage of the half-shafts, which had never been designed with rail use in mind. A new chassis layout was therefore designed for the Rhino, and this would prove entirely satisfactory in service.

Before the introduction of the revised chassis, a new crew capsule was designed, with multi-angle armour protection. This resulted in an interim model known as the 'Kudu', which offered better protection, but still on the original type chassis with its limitations.

The following model, nicknamed the 'O-Jay', used the multi-angled armour body of the Kudu, but profited from a modified transmission system: a V-belt transmitted the power from the axle flange to a pulley driving the rail wheel, thus avoiding the transmission of shocks back to the drive axle. The front axle was changed to the Wickham type. The layout was well-adapted to rail use, and was repeated on all the subsequent designs. The first O-Jay entered service on 26 April 1977.

In service, growing numbers of Rhinos and O-Jays began to fall victim to mine explosions, sometimes with dramatic results.

The Kudu, with the armoured body of the O-Jay on the chassis of the Rhino, with the good protection offered by the newer crew compartment, but retaining the Rhino's shortcomings, especially in regard to its turning capabilities.

(Photo: Boet Du Plessis)

Remedies were sought for each part of the trolley affected. Armour plate 10mm thick in the form of a 'V' was fastened beneath the vehicle, effectively protecting it from the radiator to the rear axle. However, if a powerful explosive charge was used, one of the wheels could be torn off, resulting in a violent shock when the front of the vehicle fell onto the rail sleepers or the whole vehicle became derailed. To prevent this happening, an anti-derailment device was designed, consisting of a square-tube frame fastened at a height of a few inches above the rail surface. Each tube was as wide as the trolley, with plates welded to the ends of the tubes in such a way that they extended out beyond the rails at each side. Thus, in the event a wheel became detached, the trolley would slide along on top of the rails and would avoid becoming derailed thanks to the plates at each side of the tubular frame, which would keep it more or less in a straight line. Next, a cow-catcher was attached to avoid the trolleys striking obstacles (such as animals) and derailing.

The explosion of the petrol tanks had resulted in some severe burns. The decision was taken to replace their rigid fixtures by sprung metal bands, held in place by 6mm 'veranda' rivets in such a way that, in the event of a violent shock, the tank would break free and be propelled some distance from the vehicle.

The question of how to turn the vehicle (since the Land Rover gearbox retained its four forward gears but only one reverse gear) was solved in the classic manner by the provision of a turntable. This was mechanically operated on the initial models and later hydraulically on certain subsequent models.[7] On the Rhino, the turntable was carried on the side of the vehicle, which had to be driven up onto it and fastened in place before being turned. On the other models, the device was integral to the chassis, which saved a great deal of time and reduced the risk of accidents from the trolley being badly placed or even falling off.

The next model was the 'Tusker', which used the same chassis as the O-Jay, but with a revised crew capsule offering improved protection.[8] Some Tuskers were used as transport by signals officers.

The last type of armoured trolley to be built was the 'Cougar', which incorporated all the previous improvements. In particular, it had a double braking system: hydraulic on the rear wheels and vacuum brakes on the front wheels. A radio-controlled trolley was also planned, remotely guided from a second trolley following some 500m behind, but it was not built.

Finally, the 'Jackal' was built in great secrecy. It was powered by a Leyland 680 diesel motor. Running 10 minutes in front of the postal train in the direction of Bulawayo, and then intended for use in the Beira Corridor, it did not prove to be a success, mainly because of its excessive weight. It could accommodate thirty-five fully-equipped troops, and was more akin to an armoured personnel carrier than a reconnaissance vehicle.

At midnight on 31 March 1980, all the armoured trolleys were withdrawn from service, with the exception of two Cougars made available to the engineers at Rutenga, and a third Cougar intended for the National Railways Museum, Bulawayo.

[1.] Rhodesian railways changed names twice following political changes. From Rhodesian Railways (RR) they became Zimbabwe Rhodesian Railways (ZRR) between 1 June 1979 and 30 April 1980, and then National Railways of Zimbabwe (NRZ).
[2.] The country itself underwent several changes of name: from Southern Rhodesia (1923–64) to Rhodesia (from 1964), then Rhodesia-Zimbabwe (1979) and finally Zimbabwe (from 18 April 1980).
[3.] The Zimbabwe African National Liberation Army (ZANLA) was the military arm of the Zimbabwe African National Union (ZANU), and the Zimbabwe People's Revolutionary Army (ZIPRA) was the military arm of the Zimbabwe African People's Union (ZAPU).
[4.] The Rhodesians used the term 'security trolley'.
[5.] Long Wheel Base.
[6.] Mine and Ambush Protected.
[7.] At one time it had been planned to install turntables at several pre-determined points on the railway network, but the project was abandoned because of the excessive costs involved.
[8.] For example, provision of a motorcycle helmet for the driver, the fitting of safety belts, and the inclusion of first-aid kits, etc.

A Kudu parked up, seen from inside a trolley.

(Photo: Horst Schobesberger)

A photo of the O-Jay armoured trolley, showing the disk brakes fitted after it had entered service, and the deliberately flimsy fastening of the petrol tank. For scanning the track the central searchlight was preferred to the fixed front headlights. The 'V' form of the lower armour is clearly visible.

(Photo: National Railways Museum, Bulawayo)

Armoured locomotives and wagons

While the trolleys are well known, it should be remembered that the locomotives were also armoured, basically around the cabs and other vulnerable areas. To accompany goods trains, a certain number of platform wagons were fitted with heavy weapons and provided with an armoured shelter at each end and between the gun mountings.[9] The wagon crews were drawn from the six specialist Railway Defence Companies of the Guard Force – the fourth element of the Rhodesian defence forces. They operated from Gwelo (Somabula) towards Rutenga and Beitbridge on the South-African border.

The twelve daily goods trains ran loaded in one direction during the night, and returned empty back south during the day. They followed each other at very short intervals to prevent the rebels from profiting from the five or six minutes necessary for planting explosives.[10] This was the same procedure as used by the French 'Rafales' in Indochina. In addition, the armoured trolleys would run at an interval of about four minutes in front of each train. However, the system was not foolproof, as there were usually more trains than serviceable trolleys. The solution was to run patrols at random, to confine the goods trains to daytime runs, and use the trolleys to patrol during the nights.

Ever since Mozambique had obtained its independence in June 1975, the zone most at risk was the south-eastern section of the railway network carrying the trains vital for Rhodesia's survival. Therefore the majority of the armoured vehicles were concentrated on the Somabula-Beitbridge line, while the rest were divided between the Bulawayo-Plumtree line to the south and the Bulawayo-Victoria Falls line heading north, except for a few units on the east-bound line to Gwelo and Gatooma. All the armoured units were now linked by radio to the CTC (Centralised Traffic Control). In addition, by passing an electric current through the rails the CTC knew immediately if a section of rail had been cut, or if a trolley had been derailed, and they could despatch reinforcements to the point of attack. For this system to work, the trolleys were fitted with metal brushes on bars just behind the front wheels and just in front of the rear wheels, adjustable so that they would touch the rails and thus close the electric circuit. After independence was declared on 18 April 1980, the attacks by dissident elements led to the re-commissioning of certain units and their despatch in the direction of the Beira railway network.

In conclusion, it is clear that such a technical and tactical evolution of armoured rail units has rarely been achieved elsewhere, and in such a short time span. In the multiple attacks, not one single trolley crewmember was killed. Again, all of the damaged units[11] were

able to be repaired and returned to service thanks to their robust construction. One must also remember that these developments took place at a time when Rhodesia was suffering under international sanctions aimed at disrupting the supply of spare parts and technology transfer.

The armoured hull of the Tusker, carried on the standard-type chassis incorporating all the improvements found wanting in the original Rhino, was reputed to offer better protection to the crew, especially with the introduction of the netting to protect against the hollow-charge warhead of the RPG-7 with which the terrorists were well supplied. Of note is the rear door which was the sole means of access on all the armoured trolleys.
(Photo: National Railways Museum, Bulawayo)

A Tusker with a different design of motor compartment protection. These vehicles were painted in the contemporary British Army bronze green finish.
(Photo: Horst Schobesberger)

In this view of the Jackal (here with the rear wheels removed) of note are the access stairs which double as cowcatchers. The anti-derailment bars are here clearly visible, with the small plates welded on at each side, intended to keep the unit in a straight line in the case of one wheel being blown off.
(Photo: National Railways Museum, Bulawayo)

[9.] Known as 'K Wagons', ('K' for 'Kill').
[10.] A line breakage would need on average 24 hours' work to repair.
[11.] It is estimated that half of all the trolleys fell victim to an attack, except for the Cougars which entered service only a short time before the end of hostilities.

This photo of the opposite side of the Jackal on display in Bulawayo shows the different lower section.

(Photo: Glöckner)

The final type of trolley, the Cougar, incorporating all the modifications resulting from the experiences of the bush war.

(Photo: National Railways Museum, Bulawayo)

Another photo of a Cougar, parked in front of a fully-armoured Wickham trolley.

The Cougar preserved in the Bulawayo Museum. Unfortunately, the interior of the vehicle is in poor condition.

(Photo: Olivier Grognet)

A closeup of the drive train, with a V-pulley which helped reduce the hammer blows caused by the rail joints and also to save the transmission from damage in the event of a derailment. Unfortunately the very first models had a tendancy to shed their belt.

(Photo: Olivier Grognet)

A photo taken in April 1980 showing one of the Garratts hired by the ZRR from South African Railways between August 1979 and September 1981. On these locomotives only the cab was armoured.

(Photo: Peter Bagshawe)

Two DE9A[12] armoured locomotives, Nos 1959 and 1957, at Heany Junction in April 1980. The armour plating serving no further use was removed a few months after this photo was taken.

(Photo: Peter Bagshawe)

Two K Wagons, each armed with a 20mm cannon and a 7.62mm MAG. One of these wagons is preserved in the Bulawayo Museum.

(Photo: Horst Schobesberger)

Two shots of the crew of a K Wagon.

(Photos: Horst Schobesberger)

Two diesel locomotives with armour protection (on the left an English Electric Class D.E.2 and on the right a Brush Class D.E.4) used on the Beira Corridor in July 1987.

(Photo: John M. Batwell)

SOURCES:

Books:

Bryer, Tom, *Terror on the Tracks: a Rhodesian Story* (Rothershorpe, Paragon Publishing, 2011).

Hamer, E D, *Locomotives of Zimbabwe & Botswana* (Malmö: Frank Stenvalls Forlag, 2001).

Website :

http://www.rhodesiansoldier.com/hist-bush-war-railway-security.html

---

12. Built in Spain by Babcock & Wilcox.

ROMANIA

During the Russian Civil War, a Romanian Legion of some 3000 men was formed in Siberia from the elements of different units of the former Austro-Hungarian Army. It came under the orders of the Czech Legion. They protected the Trans-Siberian Railway between Taychet and Nizhneudinsk, and possessed at least one armoured train. The men were repatriated to Romania in May 1920.

At the end of the First World War, many of the former Austro-Hungarian armoured trains were in Romania, and they were retained in service. Little information is available as to their fate, other than the existence of a 'Group' composed of three armoured trains reported by the French Military Attaché in 1924.

In early 1919, a British officer, Captain Kyle, was tasked with studying whether the Jassy and Bender workshops were competent to produce armoured locomotives and rolling stock. He concluded that it would be possible to form two trains each composed of a locomotive and three or four wagons, and proposed that the execution of the work be carried out by a French officer.[1] The armour plates to be used would be those originally intended for the protection of lorries in the Nicolina workshops. Despite the fact that the Minister of Public Works ordered the Romanian railways to carry out the work, we do not know if these new trains were actually constructed. The Romanian archives describe only one train, composed of an engine and two armoured wagons, based at Târgoviste in 1921, and attached to a tank regiment. This train was in a poor state of repair, missing parts of its armour protection, and lacking vital equipment such as lighting, automatic brakes, running lights and so on.

In 1926 records show that the Armoured Train Battalion contained four trains, two narrow gauge and two standard gauge. Each train was composed of ten armoured wagons (with two 76.2mm guns, six machine guns and two LMGs), and two engines. Their armament could be supplemented by attaching wagons with two 120mm naval guns, a 75mm gun and eight machine guns.

In a later (undated) development, the number of armoured trains increased to seven, each one being composed of two distinct parts: the combat unit with one locomotive and two wagons, and the support unit with accommodation and supplies.[2] If no photographs have come to light, the Romanian archives hold details of their composition, summarised in the following table drawn up in 1934. The armoured wagons once more fell into disrepair, and in 1935 studies were begun with a view to overhauling them.

[1.] At the time two countries, France and Great Britain, were active in helping Romania.
[2.] The support wagons provided sleeping accommodation, ammunition magazines, a galley, office, storeroom, eating area, baths and washbasins, and a flat transporter wagon.

One of the Austro-Hungarian armoured wagons left behind in Romania, a standard component of the Romanian armoured trains during the inter-war period.
(Photo: Paul Malmassari Collection)

Train	Locomotives and Wagons	Armour Protection	Armament			Wagon dimensions		
			76.2mm/ 909 gun*	8mm MG Saint-Etienne	8mm LMG Gladiator⁰	Length	Width	Height
No 1	Tank engine No 375.809	Iron plates, but lower parts not protected						
	Wagon 169.043		2	6	4	7.70m (25ft 3in)	2.35m (7ft 8½in)	2.20m (7ft 2½in)
	Wagon 271.004		2	6	4	7.70m (25ft 3in)	2.35m (7ft 8½in)	2.20m (7ft 2½in)
No 2	Tender engine No 325.240	Minimal protection						
	Wagon 434.525	Internal armour	3	4	4	8.80m (28ft 10½in)	2.10m (6ft 10¾in)	2.00m (6ft 6¾in)
	Wagon 162.151		1	4	4	6.25m (20ft 6in)	2.25m (7ft 4½in)	2.35m (7ft 8½in)
No 3	Tender engine No 326.109	Minimal protection						
	Wagon 594.660	Iron plates	1	4	4	6.25m (20ft 6in)	2.25m (7ft 4½in)	2.35m (7ft 8½in)
	Wagon 65.814	Unarmoured	3	3	4	7.50m (24ft 7¼in)	2.55m (8ft 4½in)	2.30m (7ft 6½in)
No 4	Tender engine No 326.003	Minimal protection						
	Wagon 58.514	Iron plates, crushed concrete, timber	1	4+2	4	6.51m (21ft 4¼in)	2.20m (7ft 2½in)	2.17m (7ft 1½in)
	Wagon 135.304		2	5	2	7.35m (24ft 1½in)	2.50m (8ft 2½in)	2.25m (7ft 4½in)
No 5	Tank engine No 377.417	Complete overall protection						
	Wagon 556.160	Mixed, timber and iron plates	1	5	4	6.15m (20ft 2in)	2.10m (6ft 10¾in)	2.35m (7ft 8½in)
	Wagon 426.558		3	4	4	8.85m (29ft 0½in)	2.17m (7ft 1½in)	1.96m (6ft 5in)
No 6	Tender engine No 326.470	Minimal protection						
	Wagon 555.968	Iron plates	1	5	4	6.00m (19ft 8¼in)	2.25m (7ft 4½in)	2.30m (7ft 6½in)
	Wagon 65.548	Unarmoured	3	4	4	7.50m (24ft 7¼in)	2.55m (8ft 4½in)	2.30m (7ft 6½in)
No 7	Engine No 376.508	Complete overall protection						
	Wagon 15.752	Well-arranged but not complete	2	4	2	7.37m (24ft 2in)	2.40m (7ft 10½in)	2.25m (7ft 4½in)
	Wagon 116.620		2	5	2	7.35m (24ft 1½in)	2.45m (8ft 0½in)	2.25m (7ft 4½in)

*Model 1909   Ø Known in Romania for the Gladiator cycle factory where most Chauchats were made

Studies were also conducted into eventually replacing the trains by armoured trolleys, or even by motorised platform wagons with removable armour protection, capable of carrying tanks armed with 57mm or 75mm guns. It is clear these plans showed Polish influence, as the Type TK, TKS and R trolleys were thought superior to the classic type.

SOURCES:

Romanian Military Archives (File references 3831/3330/15-17 and 3059/361/7-8; 100-105; 150-151).
SHD: 7 N 3063.

RUSSIA, THE USSR AND THE RUSSIAN FEDERATION

ARMOURED TRAINS,[1] RAILCARS AND TROLLEYS[2] 1900–2016

For ease of historical reference, this chapter has been divided into three separate periods: the Tsarist period which lasted up until 25 October 1917, the Russian Civil War and the Second World War (1917–45) and from the Cold War until the present day. But these divisions are simply labels, behind which the development of armoured trains proceeded in leaps and bounds: for example the First World War saw the introduction of armoured trolleys and railcars, while the Civil War and the Great Patriotic War marked turning points in the strategic and tactical use of armoured trains, as well as in their technological development. Furthermore, the wide expanse of Russia gave rise to a great diversity in the design of the trains, and certain types can be identified as belonging to specific regions. Faced by the large number of armoured trains and motorised rail vehicles built in a variety of factories, or locally improvised using materials to hand, or captured from enemy forces, plus the huge variety of armoured wagons, we have been obliged to feature certain units while leaving others in the shade. The following chapter, while not comprehensive, will nevertheless form a visual guide complete enough to aid future researchers building on the work and publications of specialists such as Maxim Kolomiets.

The Russian Railway System

The USSR was the country which made the most use of armoured trains, bringing improvements not only to their technical aspects but also their tactical deployment. They were used not only as short- and medium-range mobile artillery, but were also manoeuvred like the ships of a land-based fleet. Given the vast expanse of its territory, Russia was the country most likely to make maximum use of its railway system. From a late start compared with Western Europe, the Tsars created and expanded the network, but even so, when the Revolution began, the system was still underdeveloped in relation to the huge distances to be covered. Nonetheless, all the battles and campaigns of the Civil War would see the use of armoured trains, as much by the Reds as by the Whites. The larger towns and industrial areas were in fact linked by railway lines rather than by roads, which even where they existed were impassable in wet weather.

The Armoured Trains of Tsarist Russia

The history of Russian[3] armoured trains began well before the First World War, as a consequence of the Boxer Uprising of 1900 in China. The Russian contingent in Beijing, which was the largest of the Legation forces, was charged with the defence of the railway

station which was on the other side of the river from the Legations. In order to secure communications with the coast, an armoured train was therefore improvised, which could transport 200 troops. Then during the Russo-Japanese War, to protect trains from the depredations of the Khunkhuz bandits, armoured wagons were inserted in the rakes, working in conjunction with the *radziesd*, blockhouses armed with artillery and machine guns built along the line of the Trans-Siberian Railway. Then in 1907, the military press reported on the order by General Rennenkampf for armoured wagons to be armed with artillery and machine guns.[4]

Armoured wagon of the type attached to rakes on the Trans-Siberian Railway, at least one of which was in service with the armoured train *Mstitiel* during the Civil War. The armament is given as a revolver cannon which could fire from the front hatch (closed in the photo) or from the sides. Note the method of applying the brakes.
(Photo: Enrique Rostagno, from Les Armées russes en Mandchourie, *p 34)*

[1.] Armoured train = *Broniepoezd*.
[2.] Armoured railcar = *Motorbronievagon* (Self-propelled armoured wagon). Armoured trolley = *Broniedrezina*.
[3.] Here we will use the description 'Russian' when referring to the Imperial Army then to the Army post-1991, 'Red', 'Bolshevik' or 'White' when referring to the Civil War period, and 'Soviet' for the period 1922 to 1991.
[4.] *Neue Militärische Blätter*, 26th Year, Vol 70 (17 February 1907), p 70.

The Russian Army built several improvised armoured trains on the outbreak of the First World War. After studying their performance, from June 1915 it built fifteen more. Seven of these were of a similar design to the Austro-Hungarian trains. Their makeup was straightforward: an artillery wagon/steam engine/artilley wagon. The first was christened *Khunkhuz* after the bandits who had harassed the Trans-Siberian, and this train gave its name to the class.

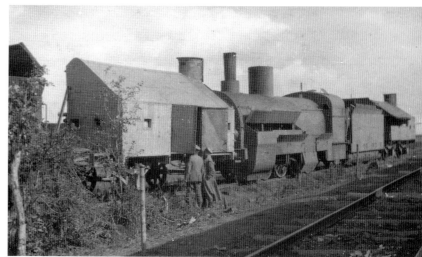

This improvised armoured train, first built by the Austro-Hungarians, was equipped with a Russian engine from a Khunkhuz-type train after being captured by the Bolsheviks, who named it Train No 56 (*Red Peasant*). It was captured in turn by the Poles on 28 May 1920 and later served with the Ukrainian Army.
(Photo: Paul Malmassari Collection)

The first improvised armoured train of the war: designed by the 9th Railway Battalion, it had two artillery wagons armed with captured 8cm Austrian field guns, as seen here, an infantry wagon, and at first an Austrian engine which was later changed to a Russian one.
(Photo: Maxim Kolomiets Collection)

General Dowbor in Polish service.
(Photo: Maxim Kolomiets Collection)

The first train of the standard series, produced in 1915. Its artillery wagons had several firing embrasures along the sides of the casemate section. The revolving turret, which could train through some 270 degrees, did not extend to the roof level, on which was a small observation cupola.
(Photo: Maxim Kolomiets Collection)

These trains would be destroyed or captured during the first months of the Civil War. Train No 2 became the Red '2nd Siberian Armoured Train' after modifications at Tsaritsyn, which principally involved rearming its turrets with 76.2mm Model 02 guns and adding two flat wagons carrying 3in guns. Captured by the Whites, it was renamed *Officier*. Another example became the famous Czechoslovak train *Orlik*, and a third, the Polish *General Dowbor*.

One of the two wagons built by the 4th Railway Battalion in November 1914, in the region of Łód . The Arbel-Fox bogie coal wagon is armoured with 7mm and 12mm plates, and carries a naval 37mm Hotchkiss gun and four machine guns. The next wagon in line is armed with an Austrian 8cm Feldkanone M.5.
(Photo: Paul Malmassari Collection)

Left: View of the rear wagon of the armoured train of the 4th Siberian Railway Regiment, seen in the Summer of 1916. Designed by Engineer Balla, the train was armed with two 76.2mm Model 1902 guns. Built during the Summer of 1915 at Kiev, it later served with the Ukrainian Army. The armoured engine is a Class Ow, and the second wagon in line is a six-wheeler armed with nine machine guns, one of which is on an anti-aircraft mounting. Note the false embrasures painted black.
(Photo: Maxim Kolomiets Collection)

Below: Armoured Train *General Annekov* of the 8th Railway Battalion of the Russian Army. It was in action on the South-West Front where it was captured by the Bolsheviks. It was then sent to fight in Finland.
(Photo: Maxim Kolomiets Collection)

The first armoured trolleys

The Russian Army rapidly recognised the need to deploy motorised combat vehicles on the railways, which did not emit the telltale smoke of steam engines. Several trolleys were built in the workshops in Vologda, Odessa and Kiev, but they were restricted to secondary duties on account of their weak armament. The Army's desire to deploy more powerful units led to the design of the *Zaamuriets* railcar. At the same time, fifteen unarmoured trolley chassis were ordered from the British firm Drewery Car Co. Ltd., to be built by Baguley Cars Ltd (Burton-on-Trent), in 1917–18, and to be armoured on their arrival in Russia. With the outbreak of the Revolution, only chassis Nos 906 to 913 had been shipped from Liverpool, and the others remained in England. It is not known whether the armoured hulls were mounted on any of the chassis. Lastly, armoured trolleys were built according to local requirements and resources.

One of the two trolleys built in Odessa during the Revolution. Weighing 7 tonnes and armed with two machine guns in turrets, they had a maximum speed of 40km/h (25mph). This one is named *Strela* ('Arrow').
(Photo: Maxim Kolomiets Collection)

Armoured trolley of the Russian Army built in Kiev, bearing the insignia of the railway troops. It appears to be heavily armed, with four Colt Browning machine guns in turrets, and has a cupola in the centre between the turrets.
(Photo: Maxim Kolomiets Collection)

Two of the four trolleys designed by Captain Mescherinov[5] from February 1915. They appear to be armed with Vickers machine guns. Trials took place using three Russo-Balt Type C armoured cars and one Renault. In June 1916 a platoon was formed which continued to carry out experiments but with some difficulty due to the extremely slow delivery of materials. In April 1917, the unit was to have been sent to the Romanian front, but with the stirrings of the Revolution it remained in action with the 2nd Railway Brigade during the following Summer. The ultimate fate of these trolleys is not known.
(Photo: Paul Malmassari Collection)

[5.] We are unsure whether he was the same Mescherinov who proposed a design in France in October 1924 (see the chapter on France).

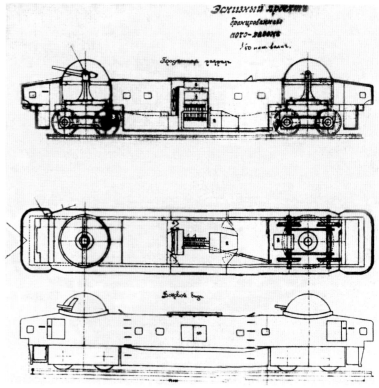

Above: The draft plan for the *Zaamuriets* railcar. The semi-spherical turrets have not yet been raised. The overall form of this 'motorised wagon' – to use the contemporary description – is quite modern.
(Drawing via Maxim Kolomiets)

Zaamuriets prior to its conversion by the Czechoslovaks. The 57mm guns are still in place. The Czechs would replace them with 76.2mm Putilovs (see the chapter on Czechoslovakia), but the heightening of the turrets was carried out in Odessa.
(Photo: Paul Malmassari Collection)

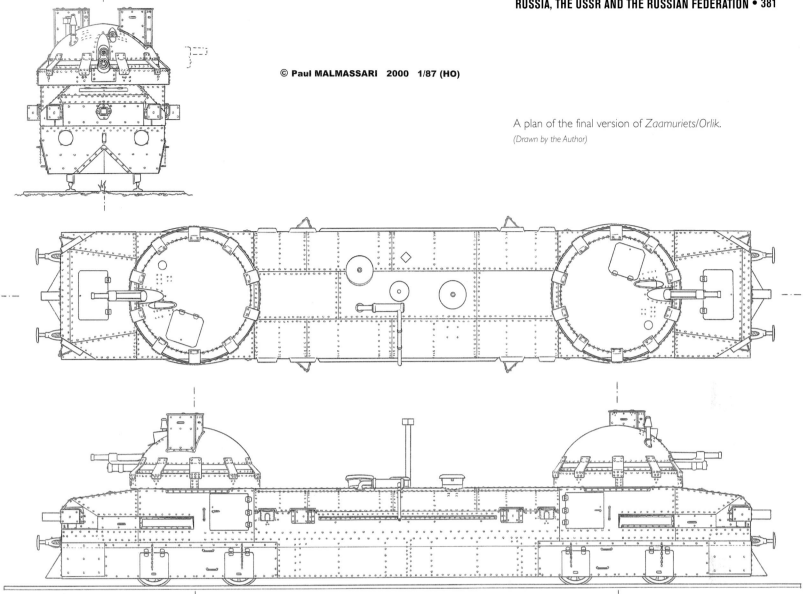

© Paul MALMASSARI 2000 1/87 (HO)

A plan of the final version of *Zaamuriets/Orlik*.
(Drawn by the Author)

From the Civil War to the Great Patriotic War (1917–1945)

The Red armoured trains of the Civil War

At the beginning of 1917, Russia possessed 500,000 wagons and 20,000 steam engines. By 1919, there remained just 30,000 wagons and 2,000 engines in service, thanks to the failings of the new organisations which had been created, despite the fact that ironically the railway workers had been the group most heavily indoctrinated by the Bolsheviks in the years leading up to the Revolution. Despite the scarcity of rolling stock for the transport of essential goods, the first armoured trains of the Revolution had to be converted from existing wagons, on the orders of the Soviets. These trains were created in Petrograd in November 1917, under the direction of the VBK, the Provisional Armour Bureau. On 20 December 1917, the Executive Committee elected during the Second Pan-Russian Congress on Armoured Vehicles received the task of organising the armoured units. But systematic construction did not begin until the formation of the military technical organisa-

tion 'Centrobron', on 31 January 1918. By that date, twenty-three trains were already in service, with a large number under construction. The best-equipped factories were the naval construction yards and the railway workshops, such as those in Kharkov, Leningrad, Putilovak, Isorak, Balhjska and Skorochod.

An improvised Bolshevik armoured train (note the numerous red flags), converted from modified covered vans, probably at the start of the Revolution: they have thick internal armour as can be seen in the embrasure, and the roof has an opening for deploying a light artillery piece.
(Photo: Paul Malmassari Collection)

A basic division into two classes was introduced to try and standardise the anarchic proloferation of armoured wagons:

1st Class
Train No 1: safety wagon/ artillery wagon (75mm)/armoured engine/safety wagon, the armament also including twelve machine guns and two mortars.
Train No 2: safety wagon/partially-armoured artillery wagon (100mm or 150mm gun)/armoured engine/safety wagon.

2nd Class
Train No 3 in support with ammunition and supplies.

On 6 October 1919, a partial reform laid down the composition of the 'Desantniy Otryad' or Assault Detachment. With a strength of 160 infantrymen, plus forty-seven mounted men and a two-gun machine-gun section, this substantial reinforcement allowed a major increase in the radius of action of the train, extending its reconnaissance range and assuring close-in protection. To carry the men and horses, between twenty and thirty wagons were added to each train. For long-range observation, certain trains carried captive balloons of German (Parseval) or French (Kako) manufacture, linked to their train by telephone.

On 5 August 1920, the Revolutionary Council established three categories of train:

1) Heavy Assault Armoured Trains Type A1 (in wartime, crewed by 162 men) or Type A2 (with a reduced crew of eighty-six men), to comprise:
– safety wagon(s).
– artillery wagon (two 76.2mm Model 02 guns in turrets and five to eight machine guns).
– armoured engine.
– second artillery wagon armed similarly to the first.
– safety wagon(s).
The assault detachment of Type A1 Trains comprised 265 infantry and thirty-five cavalry; that of Type A2 Trains would comprise only infantry, totalling 234 men.

2) Light Armoured Trains Type B (subdivided into categories B1 to B6 according to the gun calibre, crewed by forty-three men), to comprise:
– safety wagon(s).
– artillery wagon (two turret-mounted guns with a calibre less than 152mm).
– armoured engine.
– safety wagon(s).

3) Light Armoured Trains Type V (subdivided into categories V1 to V6 according to the gun calibre), to comprise:

– safety wagon(s).
– artillery wagon (one turret-mounted gun with a calibre less than 152mm and one machine gun).
– armoured engine.

In these defined configurations, the trains would carry out only combat functions, logistics being catered for by accompanying trains which would be unarmoured, carrying the men's kit, the galley, the cells, sleeping accommodation and repair equipment. Accordingly, the Type A1 Trains would be accompanied by a support train of twenty-three wagons, and the Type A2 by a train of twelve wagons. Type B and Type V Trains would be supported by rakes of nine wagons.

Within the Red Army, each separate army formation (made up of five army corps) had an armoured train brigade under its command. In action, the basic formation was the section, in which Types B and V trains provided support to Type A trains. When necessary, they provided artillery support to disembarked assault groups. The reconnaissance function devolved to a squadron of aircraft which could act as necessary as fighters or bombers for attacks on enemy trains or stations and key lines.

When advancing, the section spread out as follows, using one or two tracks:

– armoured reconnaissance trolleys 1–2km in advance.
– light armoured train.
– heavy armoured train.
– support train.
– rearguard light armoured train.

Trains armed with artillery were divided into two broad categories:

– the 'Bepo' Trains (abbreviated to 'BP') which were armed and armoured trains, utilised for attacks and raids.
– the 'BB' Trains which were composed of railway guns. This second classification included Type M Trains defined under the 1920 rules as intended for coastal defence.

Red armoured train captured by the Czechoslovaks. The armoured wagon is a wooden variant of the metal-panelled mineral wagons.
(Photo: Paul Malmassari Collection)

A far superior design, issuing from an efficient technical/industrial base, the revolving casemate of this train is carried on a ten-wheel wagon. Note the two complete rounds of ammunition presented for the photographer.
(Photo: Maxim Kolomiets Collection)

The 'Sormovo' type wagons, named for the factory which built them, were typical of the high quality of the armoured trains of the young Red Army. A central observation tower would be added in 1931 when these wagons were modernised in Military Depot No 60. Note the profile of the armour on the engine. The guns are 76.2mm Model 1902s.
(Photo: Maxim Kolomiets Collection)

The White armoured trains

The Red Army, which despite the best efforts of Trotsky was in a chaotic state of disorganisation, faced the Army of Volunteers, better known as the Whites. Formed mostly of officers who had escaped the Communists, the White Army attempted to overthrow the new regime by carrying out a pincer movement against Moscow from the south and the east. Their first armoured trains were war prizes, which were immediately turned against their former Red owners, then as they went from success to success, the recapture of stations and railway workshops allowed the Whites to improvise new trains of their own.

On the Siberian Front, the situation was different in that, by tentative agreement between the Allies, the role of guarding the railway network and in particular the Trans-Siberian Railway, was undertaken by the Czechoslovaks and the Japanese. It seems that the White army of Admiral Kolchak possessed no proper armoured

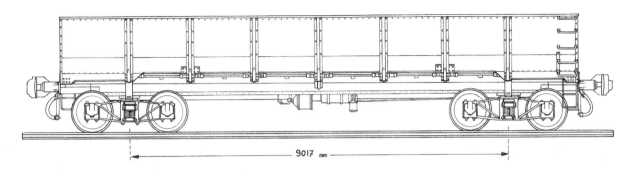

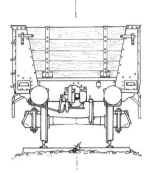

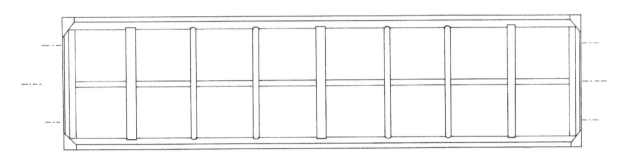

General arrangement drawing of the standard bogie wagon which would serve as the base for armoured trains built by the Russians, the Czechoslovaks, the Japanese etc, from the Russian Civil War to the Second World War.

(Drawing by the Author)

trains, while another White leader, Ataman Semenov, had seven. There was no love lost between the trains of Semenov and the Allies, especially the French and the Americans. Their career ended badly: sent to crush the revolution in Irkutsk on 26 December 1919, they were blocked by the derailment of a goods engine sent to crash into them. Withdrawing to the East, they began fighting with American troops at Verkhne-Oudinsk and, according to one American source, were 'taken out with grenades'.

Denekin's army, operating on the Southern Front, had very few armoured trains, apart from those captured from the Reds. Under Wrangel, the Army of the South had eight armoured trains, including three commanded by Captain Wagner, a German officer fighting in the White ranks. The fiercest fighting they endured took place between 25 and 27 October 1920 on the Sivasch Dike, the last link between the Crimea and Northern Tauride.

Above: A wagon from one of the Red trains captured by the Whites, probably No 96 *Red Hurricane*. The upside-down chevron insignia of the Whites became the emblem of the Armed Forces of Southern Russia (formed in April 1919), until it was replaced in April 1920 by the white, blue and red roundel. Recaptured by the Reds, this train was renamed *Béla Kun* (after the Hungarian Communist leader in power from March to 1 August 1919, who later became a political commissar in the Red Army).

(Photo: Pierre Touzin Collection)

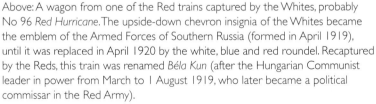

Left: One of the armoured trains controlled by Ataman Semenov. Note the effective protection for the bogies on the van, which has internal armour. On the other hand, the artillery piece on the leading flat wagon, at least at the time this photo was taken, has no protection at all, lacking even a gun shield.

(Photo: Paul Malmassari Collection)

203mm naval gun of the 2nd Heavy Battery in 1917. It fought the Germans in February 1918 at Pskov then served during the Civil War.
(Photo: Paul Malmassari Collection)

This railway gun platform of the Russian Navy, cut down from a high-sided bogie wagon, is curiously armed with a British 60-pounder BL gun (127mm calibre). Note the white flags with the blue cross of Saint Andrew, used by the Russian Navy since 1712.
(Photo: Paul Malmassari Collection)

The final Red offensive, launched with 85,000 men on 15 October 1920 in temperatures of -15°, pushed the White forces back and threatened to cut off their retreat to the Crimea. The famous cavalry under Budenny, 25,000 strong, was repulsed on the 17th, but renewed their attack on the 20th. Out of eight White trains, five had to be abandoned together with many guns and their ammunition. While Wrangel sought sufficient ships to evacuate his troops and civilians, the last armoured trains *Ivan Kalia*, *Dimitri Donskoï* and *Officier* fought a delaying action on the dike. On the Red side, the troops were supported by eight armoured trains. At dawn on the 26th, the White trains enjoyed the support of the artillery batteries harassing the Reds. The latter, however, succeeded in landing 4km to the east of the railway line, which rendered the White positions untenable. At 10 o'clock on the 27th, the *Dimitri Donskoï* was destroyed by artillery fire. The surviving two trains slowed down the Red advance up until 3 November 1920 which saw the end of the White presence in the Crimea.

The campaigns of the Red Army

The civil war against the Whites ended in 1920, but the Bolshevik leaders, driven by their crusading zeal, decided to export their revolution, so the young republic attacked Poland, the Baltic States, the Ukraine and Finland, in the hope of creating a wave of Communist uprisings throughout Europe.

The Polish campaign began with a Polish raid which got as far as Kiev in April 1920. In response, two Red armies threatened Warsaw from the end of July up until 13 August. Commanded by Piłsudski, and aided by the French, the Polish Army regained the upper hand, turning the Russian withdrawal into a rout. During

the two months of warfare, the railways played a key role. The Polish railway network was the result of construction by three companies which were formally Prussian, Austrian and Russian respectively. Of the three regions, the first was the densest and the best maintained, while the third was handicapped by the interaction of the standard gauge with the broad gauge, installed according to the whims of the occupying powers. This gauge difference in what was the principal combat zone would be a constant problem when deploying armoured trains. On the Russian side, a state of siege was declared in a zone reaching 50km on either side of the rail tracks, in order to discourage sabotage. As a result of the Polish victory, the captured Bolshevik armoured trains would be taken into Polish service and renamed.

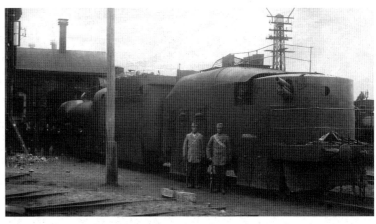

The Red armoured train (initially named *General Annenkov*) following its capture by the Finns. It was subsequently used by the Germans of the *Freikorps*, before being incorporated into the Finnish Army which used it, regularly modernising its wagons, up until the Second World War. Note that in its initial form the roof had only one walkway with a single handrail. The gun is a Russian 76.2mm.
(Photo: Paul Malmassari Collection)

On the Finnish front, the war there also ended with the defeat of the Red forces. The armoured trains in this theatre were essentially the arm of the Reds. Russian intervention was restricted basically to technical support, the railway workshops which were now Finnish having been Russian up until the Revolution. On the other hand, the direct railway link between Petrograd and Viipuri allowed the Bolshevik trains to come to the aid of the Finnish Reds. It seems that the latter received three or four trains during the war. One of them was captured at Säiniö in 1918. Comprising an armoured engine and two modern armoured wagons each with two turrets armed with 76.2mm Model 02 guns, it was named *Kerenski*. It was employed in the attack on Lahti and had to cross the bridge over the Koria River in three sections due to its weight. It was finally captured intact on the afternoon of 23 March, after its crew had fled.

An example of the significance of the armoured train in Soviet revolutionary mythology: the play by Svevolod Ivanov,[6] *Armoured Train 14-69*, seen in the above photo being performed on 11 December 1934, and below is the commemorative stamp issue which was dedicated to the playwright in 1965. Despite the fact that the armoured wagon on the stamp appears to be of a later type, the play was set during the Revolution.

(Photo and postage stamp: Paul Malmassari Collection)

In 1975, the myth was revived by the publication of the novel *Our Armoured Train* Nicolaï Grigoriev. Note the resemblance between the leading wagon and the casemate wagon of the armoured train of the 4th Siberian Railway Regiment.

(Illustrations: Paul Malmassari Collection)

[6.] Vsevolod Viatcheslavovitch Ivanov (1895–1963).

The end of the Civil War and the Reforms of 1929

Despite the Bolshevik victory, even while the final Cossack and separatist revolts were coming to an end, fighting continued between the Red Army and various 'Green' peasant factions, and local bands of thieves and bandits. The improvised armoured wagons were returned to civilian use, while the better-designed trains were carefully preserved. It is thought that by the end of the conflict with the Whites, 103 armoured trains had been built and used. During the period 1921 to 1941, the best trains were retained, new wagons joined the fleet, and an ongoing attempt at standardisation was made in order to rationalise production. Thus, the construction of the engines was divided between three principal centres: Podolsk for the Class PB, Kolona for the Class KB and Kharkhov for the Class KhB. In 1923, the armoured trains came under the control of the Artillery Department.

The results obtained thus far encouraged the authorities to improve this arm. An operational study resulted in the Provisional Rules of June 1926, which were immediately put to the test in the Summer Manoeuvres. The definitive version was published in August 1929, in the same volume as that for Tanks and Armoured Cars. The new organisation was laid down as follows:

– light armoured train Type A.
– heavy campaign armoured train Type B,
– special armoured train Type ON.

Their composition was to be:

1) Light armoured train Type A (160 men) supported by a supply train of twenty-nine wagons (or eleven wagons depending on the size of the crew):
– safety wagon.
– safety wagon.
– artillery wagon (two 76.2mm Model 1902 guns and eight Maxim machine guns).
– armoured engine of Class PB, KB or KhB.
– artillery wagon identical to the first.
– safety wagon.

Between 1926 and 1939 new gun wagons were built in order to increase the anti-aircraft capabilities of the trains: armament was the heavy 12.7mm machine gun together with the 76.2mm ZP Obr. 1914g., or even two 37mm Zenitnaya Pushka Obr. 1939g. cannon.

2) Armoured train Type B (supported by a rake of twelve wagons):
– safety wagons.
– artillery wagon (106.7mm Pushka Obr. 1910/30g. gun or 121.9mm howitzer).
– armoured engine of Class CH or KB-2.

– artillery wagon (106.7mm and 76.2mm ZP Obr. 1914g. guns).
or
– artillery wagon (122mm Gaubitza Obr. 1910/30 gun/howitzer, then an Obr. 1909/37g.)
– safety wagons (152mm howitzers could be mounted on these wagons).

3) Armoured train Type ON (the descendant of the Type 'M' trains, supported by a rake of twelve wagons):
– armoured or partially-armoured engine.
– two armoured wagons (106.7mm or 121.9mm gun).
– armoured wagon (76.2mm gun).
– three armoured ammunition wagons.
– two searchlight wagons.
Additional armament included a Maxim anti-aircraft machine gun.

A new tactical organisation was also introduced. The basic tactical unit would now be the battalion, composed of two light trains and one heavy train. In Europe, it was envisaged to use the armoured trains in support of the ground troops, while in Asia they would form the central part of forces committed to an attack. In combat, the five trolleys of the section, grouped together for administrative purposes, would be divided between the trains, primarily for reconnaissance, then to act as liaison and maintenance units.

At the time of the Reform, it was estimated that there were thirty Type A, twelve Type B and nine Type ON trains in service. Several series of manoeuvres enabled the new organisation to be tried out, notably those of September 1929, during which the stated objective was to test 'the co-operation with the infantry and the cavalry'. The principal problem noted was the lack of liaison between the infantry and the armoured trains group, whose commanders were not part of the decision-making process. The result was that during withdrawals, the trains tended to be left behind without covering units. Lastly, the capacity to transport cavalry during an advance was felt to be essential.

In 1931, the Red Army began research into special ultra-light wagons for armoured trains, and some were even built in Leningrad. Military Depot No 60 in Briansk was primarily responsible for studying the new equipment. Their research momentarily halted the reorganisation which was underway, and had an influence on the type of armament carried. In particular, the heavy armoured trains saw their artillery reduced to two heavy guns, four heavy machine guns and thirty-two anti-aircraft machine guns. It was estimated that in 1931 the Red Army could count on the use of forty trains, of which twenty-five were light, twelve heavy and from three to six Type ON, all under the Army Motorisation and Mechanisation Command. By 1932/33, there were sixty trains in service, and by 1934, ninety-two.

Although this Reform changed little in the ongoing rebuilding of the force, it did however define the assignments of the command structures of the battalions and regiments, at a time when interest in this arm of service was turning more towards the kind of usage envisaged by the Western Powers, namely anti-partisan action and keeping the railway network open. Finally, it introduced the Type W train, designed for combat roles requiring armament and armour protection similar to that of railway guns. Their composition was to be the following (plus a ten-wagon supply train):

– armoured engine.
– two armoured wagons carrying 152mm or 203.2mm artillery pieces.
– one armoured ammunition wagon.
– one armoured trolley.

Captured near Tallinn after it had been immobilised following the destruction of a bridge (or perhaps even following sabotage by the crew), this train corresponds to Type W.
(Photo: Paul Malmassari Collection)

Below: Several wagons for the Type W trains were stored at Revall (Tallinn), which principally came from the Estonian arsenal. The armament appears to be 130mm Vickers naval guns.
(Photo: Paul Malmassari Collection)

Right: Shortly after its capture, the engine seen here was put back into service by the Wehrmacht. But note that the lower armour panels have not been refitted, probably due to damage suffered during the derailment. One can read the class designation 'Oz'[7] on the buffer beam.
(Photo: Paul Malmassari Collection)

7. O = *osnovoĭ* or 'principal engine', of 0-8-0 configuration. The letters 'b', 'v' or 'z' indicate a variant of the basic class.

Building of the Type BP-35 armoured trains began in 1933 in the 'Krasnoye Profintern' factories in Briansk. In all, forty-seven units were delivered to the Red Army. Production ended with the evacuation of the workshops in August 1941. Their successors are described below.

BP-35 type armoured train, with wagons from Military Depot No 60, recognisable by their cylindrical turrets, here seen armed with 76.2mm M. 1902/30 guns. From four to six machine guns were divided between the hull and the turrets. The engine in the middle is a Class PR-35 which carried either 10 tonnes of coal or 6 tonnes of fuel oil.
(Photo: Paul Malmassari Collection)

In its heavy version, the train comprised two wagons similar to these shown here, armed with a 107mm Model 1910/30 gun. An armoured train of this type weighed 400 tonnes and could cover a distance of 120km (75 miles) at a maximum speed of 45km/h (28 mph) between refuellings.
(Photo: Paul Malmassari Collection)

The Finnish War and the Great Patriotic War

For the war with Finland, the Soviet Union deployed the 8th Special Armoured Trains Division in the Karelia Isthmus from January to March 1940, with the MBV-2 prototype and the sixteen (light) and twenty-one (heavy) armoured trains used for artillery support.

At the time the Soviets mobilised to face the German invasion in June 1941, there were nine armoured train battalions in existence (the 4th and 5th in the West, the 1st at Kiev, the 7th in the Caucasus, the 10th in Western Asia and the 9th in the Far East), with a training regiment at Briansk, one battalion of armoured trolleys, thirteen independent light armoured trains and

A Soviet engine captured by the Finns at Karhumäki on 9 November 1941. The panels giving access to the wheels and rods appear to generate a great deal of interest.
(Photo: Paul Malmassari Collection)

Although we are in 1941 here, these wagons were directly derived from their counterparts in the Civil War. The small number of loopholes piercing the sides is surprising, especially as it is obvious that plates have been fixed over former openings. It appears that an access hatch has been fitted under the floorboards.
(Photo: Paul Malmassari Collection)

An NKVD armoured train complete with safety wagons, the unarmoured engine in the middle and two heavy trolleys. The second of these has suffered severe damage to the point where a part of the hull has collapsed.
(Photo: Paul Malmassari Collection)

two independent heavy trains. The Red Army and the NKVD each had their own armoured trains, but the NKVD was orientated towards internal security rather than front-line combat. The Army had nineteen heavy trains, thirty-four light trains,[8] nine trolleys and a certain number of armoured railcars. For its part the NKVD had thirty-six railcars, twenty-five armoured engines and thirty-five wagons, as well as infantry and cavalry units.

Evidently after the launch of Operation 'Barbarossa' local authorities decided to create a number of new armoured trains in the factories capable of constructing them. A wide range of different designs resulted, in which one can recognise features from previous trains from the Civil War up to the BP-35s. The creation of a certain number of new trains was evidently decided upon following the German invasion, on the initiative of the local authorities and in those factories capable of building armoured trains. A great variety of different designs resulted, in which one can recognise several distinct features of previous trains from the time of the Civil War up to the BP-35. They all demonstrated a remarkable ability for adaptation, to the detriment of the quality of finish which took second place given the urgency of the situation. During the Great Patriotic War the armoured trains were employed in groups, and supplied fire-support for attacking troops, and if necessary they covered troops forced to break off contact, the trains pulling back after the main body had withdrawn. But apart from desperate situations, standard Soviet tactics forbade the trains from taking up static defensive positions or engaging in delaying actions, which would have risked their loss. One constant feature was that most wagons were equipped with two turrets, and in exceptional cases with three.

The gunlayer who aimed a HE shell at the cab window must have been a crack shot. But the solidity of the Russian armoured trains, and their resistance to the guns employed by the German Army in the early stages of the campaign, must have been a surprise similar to that of the first appearance of the T-34 tanks.
(Photo: Paul Malmassari Collection)

Unidentified armoured train captured at Nikolaïev in the Ukraine. The turrets which equip two of the four wagons are similar to those on the trains built in the Crimea. To our knowledge, no photo shows which engine would be attached.
(Photo: Paul Malmassari Collection)

All the units which were available and capable of combat were thrown into the fray. The Germans encountered wagons which sometimes dated from the Civil War, such as these two shown here. This confirmed in the minds of the Germans that this type of arm was definitely obsolete, and led to them delaying the creation of their own modern armoured trains.
(Photo: Paul Malmassari Collection)

8. In total 106 wagons and fifty-three engines.

This armoured train captured at Kiev in August–September 1941 is armed with a turret from a T-26 tank on the leading wagon, and three turrets from captured Polish 7TP tanks. The engine is apparently armoured only around the cab, which is probably the result of its urgent conversion.
(Photo: Paul Malmassari Collection)

The T-26 Model 1933 turret in the chase position with its 45mm gun (here destroyed by its crew) gives anti-tank capability, and the first compartment of the following wagon carries an unidentified gun, possibly a 57mm naval piece arranged for plunging fire.
(Photo: Paul Malmassari Collection)

This photo of the second wagon shows two interesting features. Firstly the curved armour protection, which is quite rare (see the chapter on China), and secondly the mounting of two turrets from Polish 7TP (twin-turretted) tanks. The right-hand turret on this wagon, and the turret on the wagon in front of the engine, both come from the 2nd prototype 7TP. This tank had served at No 1 training centre in 1939 before being captured by the Russians. Note the slot in the turret appliqué armour which allowed the fitting of a 13.2mm Hotchkiss heavy machine gun in Polish service.

(Photo: Paul Malmassari Collection)

Another type of train, this time built on the lines of the BP-35, with two turrets (here from two different T-26 tanks: on the right a T-26 Model 36, on the left a BT-5 or T-26 Model 35) and four machine guns in the hull.
(Photo: Paul Malmassari Collection)

An armoured train for the narrow gauge captured at Tallinn (Reval up to December 1918) in Estonia.

(Photo: Paul Malmassari Collection)

One of the turretted wagons of the narrow-gauge train. A trolley was also captured on the same day.

(Photo: Paul Malmassari Collection)

The only photo we know of this wagon of unusual dimensions, and also an end door with identical doors at the sides. It appears that the turret from a tank or an armoured car has been mounted in the centre of the roof.

(Photo: Paul Malmassari Collection)

Armoured Train No 1 of the 66th Battalion, famous for its turret from a KV-II tank. In the centre, the turret from a T-34/76 model 40, without its usual mantlet, and fitted instead with a 45mm gun for anti-tank use. In the front turret is a 76.2mm gun.

(Photo: Paul Malmassari Collection)

At the rear of this train is a wagon built on the lines of the BP-35, armed with a 76.2mm M1902/30 Divisional Gun, the modernised version of the First World War weapon. The polygonal turret is mounted on the engine tender, and just visible is a T-34 turret identical to that on the front wagon.

(Photo: Paul Malmassari Collection)

An armoured train captured incomplete in the ruins of a factory in Kerch. Note the imposing size of the command tower built on top of the tender, and the 76.2mm gun. The central turret is from a T-26 S.

(Photo: Paul Malmassari Collection)

An identical wagon which saw action in May 1942. Evidently the Germans felt they were of interest as shortly afterwards both wagons were to be found at Rembertow. Note that the gun is a 76.2mm M1902/30, production of which ended in 1937.

(Photo: Paul Malmassari Collection)

A mixed armament wagon with a 37mm anti-aircraft gun, of Armoured Train *Tambow Kholkhose*. The panels were folded downwards when the gun was used in a ground role. It appears that vertical armour plates protect the rear of the firing position.

(Photo: Paul Malmassari Collection)

Armoured Train *For Stalin* was captured with its two anti-aircraft wagons. Its engine may have inspired the design of the Class BR57 engines of the future Panzerzug BP 42 and BP 44.

(Photo: Paul Malmassari Collection)

Armoured Train *Ordshonykydshoviek* seen here in November 1941, built in the naval yards in the Crimea. Its naval origins are betrayed by the armament in gun shields and the cylindrical observation cupola. These dual-purpose guns were capable of firing against ground and air targets.

(Photo: Paul Malmassari Collection)

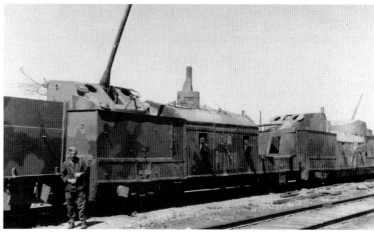

Armoured Train *Za Rodinu* ('For the Motherland') carrying the same armament as in the previous photo, captured at Bataisk (south of Rostov-on-Don).

(Photo: Paul Malmassari Collection)

The armoured trains built in the Crimea had a particular design which gave them the appearance of belonging to a family of such units, despite differences in detail. The guns are naval 76.2mm 34-K anti-aircraft weapons, with a ceiling of 9500m (almost 31,200ft).

(Photo: Paul Malmassari Collection)

Another type of wagon, armed with two 76.2mm/30 Lender (8-K). In 1943, at least six of these wagons would be converted by the Wehrmacht and included in PZ 21, 23 and 26.
(Photo: Paul Malmassari Collection)

An armoured train knocked out of action in the Crimea in 1941. The intact wagon would be put back into service with the engine seen in the following photo, to form a train used for security patrols (designation unknown).
(Photo: Paul Malmassari Collection)

The gun shield is open at the rear, another naval feature of these trains. The top surface of the breech is seen here with the 76.2mm gun at its maximum elevation of 85 degrees.
(Photo: Paul Malmassari Collection)

This wagon from Armoured Train *Voykoviec* is built to the same design but the casemate on the right is armed with either a 76mm M/14 Putilov anti-aircraft gun or a field gun on a wheeled carriage, hidden in this photograph.
(Photo: Paul Malmassari Collection)

The engine of one of the Crimean trains. Its design does not follow that of the 'continental' trains and its armour is much smoother. In particular note the lack of inspection hatches for the wheels and rods.
(Photo: Paul Malmassari Collection)

Armoured Train *Worker of Kolomna* has a design which is totally different to that of its contemporaries (January 1942), even if the wagons still have two turrets, armed with 152mm Model 1916 howitzers. Built in Kolomna, it belonged to the 55th Independent Armoured Train Battalion.

(Photo: Maxim Kolomiets Collection)

In the direct line of descent from the armoured trains of the Civil War, certain trains were built in workshops with less sophisticated equipment, using materials at hand: a turret from a KV-1 tank, and 76.2mm/30 Model 1914/1915 Lender (87-K) anti-aircraft guns.

(Photo: Maxim Kolomiets Collection)

NKPS-42 Type armoured train in its standard configuration. Note the similarity with the older BP-35, of which they were a simplified, but better protected, version.

(Photo: Paul Malmassari Collection)

During the first months of the German invasion, the armoured trains of various types which we have examined in the previous pages played an important role in resisting the invaders, even if a large number were destroyed. The locomotive repair facility at Poltava designed a new armour layout based on that of the BP-35. Designated NKPS-42, it offered better protection, but the lack of good-quality armour plate meant that the appearance of the trains tended to vary.

On a PT-33 wagon, this 76.2mm Model 1939 Divisional Gun in an NKPS-42 turret is an unusual combination, due to the differing availability of artillery pieces in the particular region.

(Photo: Paul Malmassari Collection)

This view of a turret from Armoured Train *Marshall Budenny* allows us to note the protection afforded to the gun in an NKPS-42 turret.

(Photo: Paul Malmassari Collection)

Coupled to an NKPS-42 type train, this engine seems to be equipped with a condensing tender. The USSR began to show interest in this technique in 1935, which had the dual advantage of reducing the plume of smoke, while tripling the range before stopping to take on water, due to the recycling system. Apart from this feature, the remainder of the engine is classic, with a command cupola on the cab roof and an anti-aircraft position on the tender.

(Photo: Paul Malmassari Collection)

A wagon typical of the Type OB-3 trains. The armament, served by twelve men, could vary to a surprising degree according to the local supply situation: 76.2mm Model 1902 guns, 76mm Model 1927, 76mm anti-aircraft Model 1914 and 76mm L/10 tank guns. As in this photo, even French or Polish 75mm Model 1897s from the Civil War were carried.

(Photo: Paul Malmassari Collection)

Engine of a Type OB-3 armoured train painted with one of the many personal, geographic or patriotic slogans. Here we see the popular 'For Stalin', used on several trains.

(Photo: Paul Malmassari Collection)

The engine normally used was a Class Ov or Ok, armoured to between 30mm and 80mm. Some twenty Type OB-3 trains would be destroyed or captured, mainly in 1942, like this train photographed in April 1942.

(Photo: Paul Malmassari Collection)

The Type OB-3 trains were designed to overcome the problems experienced with the NBP-35 and NKPS-42 wagons due to their dimensions and their weight, and also the fact that bogie wagons were much more difficult to re-rail than four-wheelers. To meet the production target of sixty-two armoured trains (thirty-two battalions) to be ready by 1 January 1942, the State Defence Committee decided to standardise on the Type OB-3 train. The artillery wagons were shorter, armoured from 30–80mm, and armed with a single gun. The production of the Type OB-3 was undertaken in nine factories and forty-three rail depots, but by the planned date only two complete trains had been produced, with another twelve, seventeen and then twenty-six arriving in the next three months respectively.

The Type BP-43 trains would be the final type built during the war on the Soviet side (twenty-one for the Red Army and a few for the NKVD). They represented a development of the OB-3: each wagon carried only one turret and three machine guns, and two coupled together provided the equivalent firepower of an old BP-35 wagon, but offering a smaller target. One of the more ingenious wagon designs, and one which offered the heaviest firepower, was incontestably the mixed armament wagons mounting sixteen M8 rocket-launcher racks, together with two 37mm Zenitnaya Pushka Pbr 1939g. anti-aircraft cannon. These wagons were produced for Trains No 659 *Kuzma Minin* and No 702 *Ilya Mouromets*.

The PL-43 wagons which made up these trains were examples of the simplified solution which had been sought: the T-34 turret had an anti-tank capability, and it was mounted on a wagon offering a much reduced silhouette. The round opening in the side of the hull was a mount for a machine gun.

(Photo: Maxim Kolomiets Collection)

Seen here in the factory and below during a parade probably preceding departure on a mission, this type of wagon is derived from the hull of a T-34 tank, with the lines elongated to form an armoured wagon. In the photo below, on the right is a line of armoured wagons based on old T-28 tanks. Perhaps this is a changeover ceremony from the old wagons to the newer type.

(Photos: Paul Malmassari Collection)

A PL-42 wagon from *For Stalin* built at Kolomensa. The 76mm guns in T-34 turrets gave these trains powerful anti-tank firepower. Similar wagons were included in Armoured Trains *Kuzma Minin* (in the next photo) and *Ilya Mouromets*. The central observation tower varied from wagon to wagon, as well as the lower armour skirt.

(Photos: Paul MALMASSARI Collection)

A sketch showing the basic method of mounting the 'Stalin Organ' in a wagon, allowing 360-degree training. The same Soviet publication featured other mountings, for example on a river gunboat.

(Illustration: All Rights Reserved)

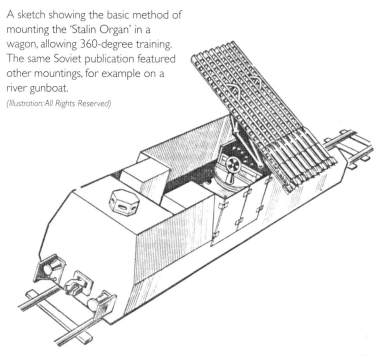

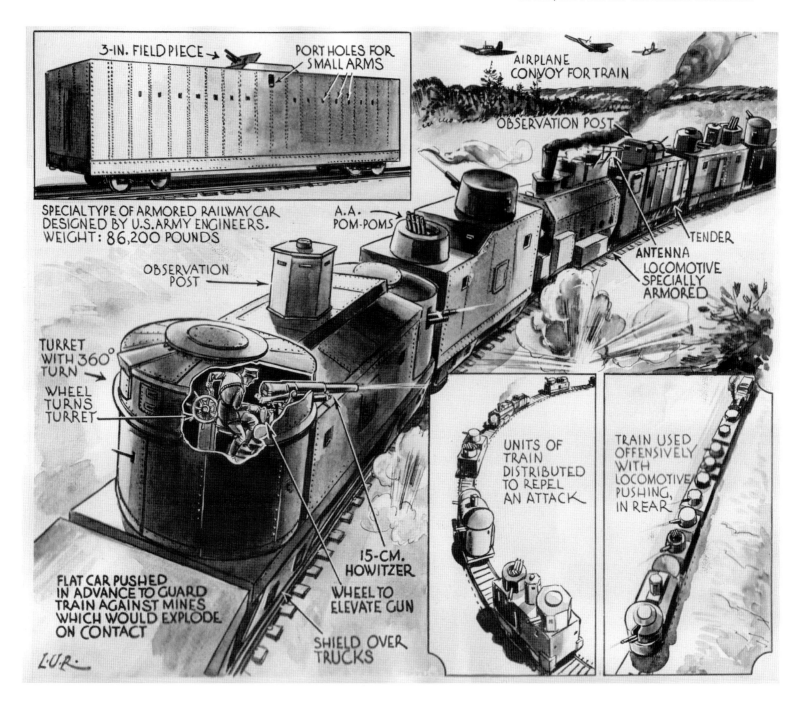

Within the illustration:

- 3-IN. FIELD PIECE →
- PORT HOLES FOR SMALL ARMS
- SPECIAL TYPE OF ARMORED RAILWAY CAR DESIGNED BY U.S. ARMY ENGINEERS. WEIGHT: 86,200 POUNDS
- AIRPLANE CONVOY FOR TRAIN
- OBSERVATION POST
- A.A. POM-POMS
- TENDER
- ANTENNA
- LOCOMOTIVE SPECIALLY ARMORED
- OBSERVATION POST →
- TURRET WITH 360° TURN →
- WHEEL TURNS TURRET
- UNITS OF TRAIN DISTRIBUTED TO REPEL AN ATTACK
- TRAIN USED OFFENSIVELY WITH LOCOMOTIVE PUSHING, IN REAR
- FLAT CAR PUSHED IN ADVANCE TO GUARD TRAIN AGAINST MINES WHICH WOULD EXPLODE ON CONTACT
- 15-CM. HOWITZER
- WHEEL TO ELEVATE GUN
- SHIELD OVER TRUCKS
- L.U.R.

ARMOURED TRAIN ANTI-AIRCRAFT DEFENCE

Despite continuous growth in on-board anti-aircraft armament, the majority of Soviet armoured trains lost fell victim to air attack. In the battle for Smolensk alone, six were lost, all to Luftwaffe attacks. Although each armoured train carried its own anti-aircraft armament, special armoured wagons were built, which became more and more elaborate with greater and greater protection.

In addition, specialised anti-aircraft trains were introduced as a separate branch of the Soviet armoured train organisation, and some 200 such trains in all would be formed. The standard composition of each train was an engine and five wagons. Although the wagon chassis were unarmoured, the guns were provided with side armour protection generally 15mm thick, sheltering the gunners from bomb and shell fragments and small-arms fire. Their

In late September 1941 the American illustrator Logan Reavis represented this tactical employment of Russian armoured trains. (For comparison he added a view of the last type of American Army armoured wagon, as used on the Mexican border.) With a certain degree of artisitic licence, the separate missions are reasonably well displayed, apart from the group of wagons spread out to repel an attack: such deployment was a favourite theme in illustrations intended for the public at large, but would have found little favour with armoured train commanders.

(Illustration: Paul Malmassari Collection)

armament varied, and initially comprised 76.2mm guns, 37mm cannon and 12.7mm DShK heavy machine guns.

As a general rule, as each new armoured train battalion was formed it was allocated a PVO-4 AA defence wagon, for example initially armed with two 37mm cannon or two 12.7mm heavy machine guns. Each Type BP-43 train had two anti-aircraft wagons.

These two guns on anti-aircraft mountings are installed in a wagon at the rear of an unidentified armoured train (perhaps the train armed with a KV-II turret). Note the crude appearance of the gun tubs with their unfinished edges.
(Photo: Paul Malmassari Collection)

A derailed PVO-4 wagon, allowing us a view of the internal arrangements, and the side panels in the lowered position. The 37mm cannon is mounted on a circular platform.
(Photo: Paul Malmassari Collection)

The anti-aircraft wagon coupled to *For Stalin* with its 37mm Model 1939 cannon, followed by a second quite different wagon which was unique to this particular train.
(Photo: Paul Malmassari Collection)

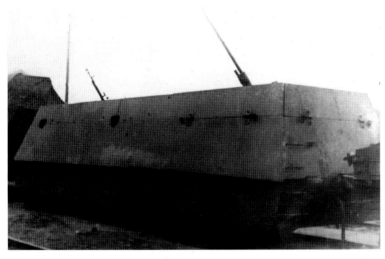

This wagon attached to Armoured Train No 339 photographed in 1942 carries a mixed anti-aircraft armament: a 37mm 61-K and a 12.7mm DShK Model 1938. It is probable that for the sake of standardisation, the base chassis was the same for both the OB-3 train wagons and the PVO-4 AA platforms.
(Photo: Maxim Kolomiets Collection)

Narrow-gauge armoured train or anti-aircraft train at Tallinn in Estonia. The open-backed shield is of naval origin, with a 76.2mm (34-K) AA gun. An ex-tank or armoured car turret is mounted for local defence.
(Photo: Paul Malmassari Collection)

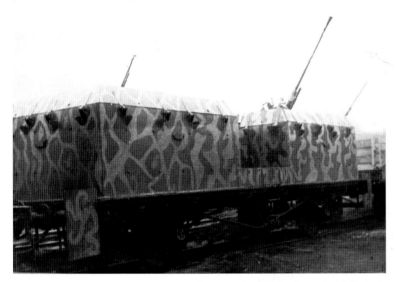

The same armament is mounted on a different style of PVO-4 seen in 1942. An example of this design is on display in the Armed Forces Museum in Moscow.
(Photo: Maxim Kolomiets Collection)

This anti-aircraft defence train is armed with 85mm M1939 guns. The unarmed wagons alternating with the gun wagons are equipped with rangefinders and other viewing devices, plus maintenance materials. Note that the base used for the conversions is the standard Russian Railways bogie flat wagon.
(Photo: Paul Malmassari Collection)

The same type of wagon today in Moscow with two 37mm cannon. The other wagon on the left is a BP-43 type, modified with armoured compartments replacing the open end platforms.
(Photo: All Rights Reserved)

Right: This wagon armed with two 37mm cannons has also three machine guns for close-in defence (one on each side and one in a turret). It is coupled in OB-3 type train No 664, and was built in the Kolomna factories. Note the similarity of its form with *Worker of Kolomna* illustrated above.
(Photo: Private Collection)

The armoured railcars and trolleys of the Red Army and the NKVD

As with other armies, the Red Army had noted that the vulnerabllity of armoured trains derived in part from their heavy weight and relative lack of flexibility. On the other hand, railcars (irrespective of their weight classification) had the speed needed for carrying out reconnaissance of the tracks. Contrary to the desire for standardisation, as far as possible armoured trolleys had used parts and equipment available in the areas where they were designed and built: motorised chassis, turrets and weapons, armour plates. In parallel, trolleys were developed from road-based armoured vehicles.

In 1938, the S.M. Kirov factory in Leningrad built several 'motorised armoured wagons' (MBV) which reached 80km/h (50 mph) and carried a dual-purpose armament for ground and anti-aircraft use. The base vehicle used components and three turrets from T-28 tanks (which had been built in the same factory). The tank turrets were armed first with the 76.2mm PS-3 gun then the longer L-11 and F-34. The secondary armament comprised 7.62mm DT machine guns divided between the turrets, rear and sides, and anti-aircraft defence was provided by a quadruple Maxim mounting situated between No 2 turret and the command cupola. With a crew of just forty men, the railcar was practically the equal in firepower to an armoured train, being self-sufficient in ammuni-

tion with 365 shells, 10,962 rounds for the DTs and 22,000 for the Maxim machine guns carried on board, but was a great deal more versatile. The armour protection ranged from 16–20mm on the sides, the central command cupola and the turrets. The roof was armoured to 10mm. The whole machine weighed 80 tonnes and could reach 120km/h (75mph) on the 400h of its M17-T petrol engine. The prototype was tested during the Finnish War on the Viipuri-Viborg-Leningrad line in March 1940.

Several models of armoured trolley were developed, using proven components, notably the turrets from T-26 or KV-1 tanks. One of the latter was mounted for example on the *Red Star* railcar featured below. Other turrets were intended solely for use on special machines such as the D-2 railcars.

An unique example built in the Winter of 1942 and named *Krasnaya Zvezda* ('Red Star'), with the designation KZ-1 painted on all four faces), this machine was equipped with a turret from a KV-1 tank, armed with a 76.2mm ZiS-5 gun. 11.72m (38ft 5½in) long by 2.48m (8ft 1½in) wide and 2.70m (8ft 10¼in) high, it weighed 60 tonnes in working order. Powered by two V-2K diesel motors it could reach a maximum speed of 43km/h (27 mph). One of its four 7.62mm calibre machine guns is visible here. It is not known whether it saw any action.

(Photo: Maxim Kolomiets Collection)

Above: Viewed from the front, the MBV-2 was a battleship on rails. This version is the one equipped with T-28 turrets, and immediately noticeable are the false rails painted on the camouflage whitewash. Each electrically-operated turret had a limited training arc, from front to rear respectively, of 280, 318 and 276 degrees. The twin-axle bogie was motorised whereas the three-axle bogie was simply a load carrier.

(Photo: Maxim Kolomiets Collection)

This machine was famous enough to feature on a Russian stamp issued in 2014 (part of the series on Glorious Towns, this one commemorated Tikhvin), along with a 203mm M1931 (B-4) howitzer and the Petlyakov Pe-8 bomber.

(Stamp: Paul Malmassari Collection)

The D-2 railcars were produced in the factories in Lugansk and Orsk, which between them received orders for 200 units. They were armed with two 76.2mm guns and four machine guns. One successful innovation was the installation of a generator producing green smoke, which proved very successful in trials. There was no separate chassis, the running gear being bolted direct to the armoured hull as with the British Daimler Dingo. Used principally by the NKVD, many of these these railcars would be captured in 1941, and several were re-used by the Wehrmacht (as PT 17 to 23).

(Photo: Paul Malmassari Collection)

A BD-41 armoured trolley immobilised near the NKPS-42 armoured train to which it was assigned. This machine belonged to the 7th Independent Armoured Train Battalion. The turret comes from a T-26 Model 1931 tank, with a 37mm cannon and a 7.62mm DT machine gun. Around twenty BD-41 trolleys were built in Moscow in early 1942, and the last were still in service in 1944.
(Photo: Paul Malmassari Collection)

This version is fitted with armour protection for the recoil cylinder, an arrangement rarely seen on armoured trains.
(Photo: Paul Malmassari Collection)

DTR armoured trolley. An example was included in PZ 10 (see the chapter on Germany).
(Photo: Paul Malmassari Collection)

The BDT trolley was designed in 1935. It used the turret of a T-26 tank.
(Photo: Maxim Kolomiets Collection)

Alongside the 'compact' trolleys built in workshops and intended solely for rail use, certain machines were converted from road armoured cars, such as the FAI-ZhD.[9] There were two rail versions of the BA-64 ZhD, both based on the wide wheelbase variant. The first was designed by the Vyksinky factory in July 1942 and consisted of fastening rail wheels to the outside of the road wheels, a lengthy procedure similar to that used for the BA-20 ZhD. Although the forward speed was 85km/h (43mph), speed in reverse was only 13km/h (8mph), a derisory performance when high speed in both directions was required for a rail reconnaissance vehicle. In addition, the gearbox broke down after prolonged driving in reverse, the engine cooling was insufficient when moving backwards, and the machine continually fell off the rails due to the wheel rims being too small.

9. ZhD = *Zheleznaya Doroga*, road wheel/rail wheel.

The shape of the FAI-ZhD was somewhat archaic, and even the wire wheels for use on rails appear fragile.

(Illustration: All Rights Reserved)

On this BA 20M (recognisable by its frame antenna) we can clearly see the three attachment points for the wheels not in use: one on each side of the bonnet and a long axle rod with a hook at the rear, above the petrol tank.

(Photo: Paul Malmassari Collection)

The first model BA 20M was rarely photographed by the Germans, being already very old by the time of 'Barbarossa'. It was easily identifiable by its cylindrical turret.

(Photo: Paul Malmassari Collection)

This second BA-64B rail prototype from the GAZ factories was designed in June but only emerged from the Gorki works in November 1942.

(Photo: All Rights Reserved)

A production-model BA20 trolley with conical turret, in its road configuration, and the rail wheels attached to their standard fittings. Note the base of the movable antenna on the left-hand side.

(Photo: Paul Malmassari Collection)

The second version had better on-rail stability but the problem of rearward driving remained, and no production models were built. However, in the Summer of 1944, the Moscow wagon repair depot did fit several BA-64 and BA-64B models with rail wheels for use with armoured trains.

A small production series of BA-6-ZhD models was produced in 1936, convertible by fastening rail wheels to the outside of four of the road wheels. This method was continued for the BA-10 armoured cars.

The BAD-2 ZhD was as interesting as it was bizzarre. It was developed from the original BAD (*Brone Avto Drezine*) armoured car designed in 1932 at the 'Bolshevik' factory in Leningrad. Its boat-shaped hull was designed to give it amphibious capability, which was the subject of many research projects during the 1930s. The rail conversion was studied by the 'Izhorski' factory and was added to a well-armed vehicle, which could be considered as

The BAD-2 measured 5.28m (17ft 3¾in) long by 2m (6ft 6¾in) wide and 2.36m (7ft 9in) high. It weighed 4.6 tonnes, and was armed with a 37mm (Hotchkiss) cannon in the turret plus two 7.62mm machine guns. It was capable of maximum speeds of 65km/h (40mph) on rails and 50km/h (30mph) on roads.
(Photo: All Rights Reserved)

A BA-10 ZhD on road wheels, with its four rail wheels fastened to the hull rear. Note the lengths of caterpillar tracks also carried above these wheels. The machine has just been hit, and a crew member was cut down as he tried to exit the vehicle.
(Photo: Paul Malmassari Collection)

This view of a BA-10 ZhD being turned shows to advantage the large diameter of the rail wheels which would be fastened to the outside of the road wheels, thus avoiding a lengthy wheel change. The trolley version ran on only four rail wheels, two at the front and two at the rear.
(Photo: Maxim Kolomiets Collection)

The rear turret armed with a 7.62mm machine gun could train over a wide field of fire. The propeller for amphibious operations is just visible beneath the hull.
(Photo: All Rights Reserved)

suitable for its proposed role. In fact, the machine was never adopted, despite operational trials in 1932–4.

Among the wide range of different machines built to face the advancing Wehrmacht, we also find unidentified models of trolleys.

It is interesting to note several projects which were studied during the war. The MBV-2 railcar gave rise to a variant mounted on the same two- and three-axle bogies, but more lightly armed, as shown by the scale model at centre right on page 406.

One Soviet engineer even proposed building a railcar of exceptional size, with a very heavy armament. Three turrets armed with 76.2mm guns were to be mounted on the cylindrical hull. Each of these main turrets was to have carried a smaller turret on top, the sub-turrets at the ends to be armed with four anti-aircraft machine guns and the central one with a pair of 45mm anti-tank guns. Twelve machine guns were to be mounted in the hull sides, plus two flamethrowers in unspecified locations. The armour protection was to have been 25mm, 30mm on the turrets. The electric drive would produce 950hp, propelling the machine at up to 55km/h (34mph). This is illustrated by the scale model on page 406 (bottom).

Among other design projects was one based on the NKVD D-2 railcars, but with four turrets, and an armament ranging from 76.2mm up to 127mm, on a total length of some 20m (65ft 7½in).

Two different views of a Soviet trolley captured and marked with large crosses in chalk. Note that the attached wagon differs in the two photos, which would indicate that the trolley has seen some use after being captured.

(Photos: Paul Malmassari Collection)

Note the completely unarmoured radiator projecting from the hull side.

(Model by Paul Malmassari to 1:200th scale)

This machine was probably a front-line improvisation. The turret appears to belong to the BT-2 series of light tanks.

(Photo: Paul Malmassari Collection)

Below: This proposed design would have measured 24m (78ft 8¾in) in length, weighing 145 tonnes, with a crew of thirty-four men. The cylindrical hull would have carried three T-28-type turrets, themselves carrying separately trainable sub-turrets. The ladders on the model give some idea of the gigantic propostions of the project, which however displays a streamlined modern shape.

(Model by Paul Malmassari to 1:200th scale)

Armoured Trains from the Cold War to the Present Day[10]

The end of the Great Patriotic War did not see armoured trains disappear from the Soviet inventory. An armoured train was active during the suppression of the Hungarian Uprising in 1956 and also, up until the 1960s, another was permanently parked in a tunnel in a suburb of Berlin, according to former East German railway workers. Three important periods mark the modern history of these trains: the Sino-Soviet conflict, the wars in Chechnya (1994–6 then 1999–2000), and since 2010, the maintenance of order in the face of the growing insecurity in the republics to the south of Russia (Chechnya, Daghestan and Ingushetia). In addition, the continuing latent rebellion in the Caucasus region requires that appropriate railway security measures remain in force.

Between the late 1950s and the early 1960s, tension between the Soviet Union and China mounted over the question of the delini-ation of the frontier between the two countries, and in particular the status of the island of Damansky (Zhenbao to the Chinese) situated on the River Ussuri which separates the two countries.[11] In March 1968, two weeks of fighting ended in a Soviet victory, but both sides continued to build up their forces for a future confrontation. On the Soviet side, the under-developed state of the region[12] made the garrisons almost entirely dependent on the Transbaikal and Trans-Siberian railway lines, as much for resupply as for troop movement. The latter line is situated only some 100km (63 miles) from the frontier and is therefore vulnerable to a mass attack. With the whole railway network plus 1,200 sensitive points to protect, only armoured trains had the necessary firepower, flexibility and mobility.

Locomotive Design Bureau No 65 at the Kharkov factory, which had specialised in the production of T-64 tanks and locomo-tives since it was opened, was charged with the design work. Railway and armoured vehicle components were taken 'off the shelf', copying the ideas followed during the Great Patriotic War. Initially, the turrets were to come from T-55 tanks and ZSU 23-4 *Shilka* anti-aircraft armoured vehicles, armed with four 23mm AZP-23[13] cannon. The use of a diesel locomotive circumvented the problems of electricity or alternatively water supply. The locomo-tive was built in Lioudinovo, and the armoured wagons in Kalinine and Marioupol. The train was ready in 1970 and was tested, but never entered service as the frontier tensions had decreased.

When tension once more increased, the employment of armoured trains was again considered during the establishment of the Far East central command structure in February 1979.

The new concept was modular: each armoured train was to comprise a central train and several autonomous units, with tanks embarked. Each of these armoured attack groups was to be formed with a TGM-14 armoured diesel shunter, positioned in between two flat wagons carrying T-55 or T-62 tanks. At the rear of each platform wagon, a demountable armoured casemate was intended for an infantry detachment, who could observe using periscopes, communicate by radio and fire through loopholes. Each train could include up to five groups of two tanks plus twenty-five men. Thus organised, a train could cover 500km (300 miles) of the rail network, each group covering 100km (60 miles).

One of the prototype tank transporter flat wagons. Note the two unloading ramps, made practicable by the central coupling gear and the lack of buffers.
(Photo: Maxim Kolomiets Collection)

The tank transporter wagon carrying a T-55 is being towed by a BTR40-ZhD. Here the armoured case is not intended for transporting troops.
(Photo: Maxim Kolomiets Collection)

[10.] Here we will not be examining the twelve Molodets 15P961 ballistic missile trains which existed from 1987 to 1994, nor the new ballistic missile system being set up at the time of writing.
[11.] In 1991 Russia under Boris Yeltsin recognised Chinese sovereignty over the island, which was retrospectively ceded to China.
[12.] At that time no motorways existed between European Russia and the Far East.
[13.] This was probably what inspired the artwork illustration in the article 'Panzerzug – Neuauflage' (in the East German journal *Armee Rundschau* 8/1976) showing a modern train equipped with turrets from T-62 tanks and ZSU 23-4 armoured vehicles. We know of no photo of such an armoured train.

One of the production tank transporter wagons with the lateral armoured panels hinged upwards, seen here with a T-62 fitted with side bars as protection against RPGs. Note the armoured casemate immediately behind the tank. The unloading ramps are clearly visible in front of the tank. In operational use, a guard rail would be fitted at the rear of the tank to prevent the turret from firing into the rest of the train.

(Photo: Maxim Kolomiets Collection)

Armoured TGM-14 diesel shunter which propels the attack group.

(Photo: Athol Yates Collection)

A still from the propaganda film *Heirs of Victory*, in which three combat groups are seen on exercises, with the two tank transporters coupled in front of and behind the TGM-14 diesel locomotive.

(Film still: All Rights Reserved)

The central train was formed from an armoured TG-16 diesel locomotive, a command wagon protected against NBC (Nuclear Bacteriological and Chemical) effects, since it was thought these trains could enter contaminated zones in the event of a nuclear attack. The wagon was armed with two 23mm ZU[14] 23-4. Additional anti-aircraft defence was provided by an armoured wagon equipped with either two ZU-23-4 or ZU-23-2 mounts. The reconnaissance element was provided by two flat wagons transporting PT-76 amphibious tanks which were protected by lateral armour plates 2m (6ft 6in) high, and able to disembark. The rail reconnaissance company was formed from eight BTR-40 ZhD vehicles, which could be carried over longer distances on flat wagons fitted with rails. In 1969, several BTR-40s were converted into trolleys by using the same method developed by GAZ for the wartime BA64-ZhD. Disembarking them took less than five minutes.

The flat wagon transporting the PT-76 opens at the front or rear to allow the tank to disembark. On the left is the anti-aircraft wagon.

(Photo: Maxim Kolomiets Collection)

The BTR-40 ZhD is the road-rail version of the 4x4 troop transport. The conversion, which is permanently fixed, consists of adapting two rail guide axles in front of and behind the driven wheels, which remain in contact with the track and provide the motive power. The two cutaway steel plates attached to the rear of the hull are devices which, when fastened to the track, form a small oblique ramp to facilitate mounting onto and descending from the rails.

(Photo: Maxim Kolomiets Collection)

[14.] ZU = *Zenitnaya Ustanovka*, or anti-aircraft system. ZSU = *Zenitnaya Samokhodnaya Ustanovka*, or self-propelled anti-aircraft system.

The version A of the BTR-40 ZhD was armed with a twin-barrelled 14.5mm KPVT anti-aircraft mounting. It is not known how many of these conversions made in 1969 were attached to the armoured trains. This example is on display in the armour collection at Kubinka. The two rail versions of the BTR-40 remained in service up until 1991.

(Photo: Paul Malmassari Collection)

BTR-40 ZhD Technical specifications:

Length:	5m (16ft 4¾in)
Width:	1.9m (6ft 2¾in)
Height:	1.75m (5ft 9in) without armament
Ground clearance:	27.6cm (10.9in)
Wheelbase:	2.7m (8ft 10¼in)
Weight:	5.8 tonnes
Crew:	10
Max speed (rails);	65km/h (40mph)
Max speed (road):	75km/h (47mph)
Range (road):	430km (270 miles); probably x 3 on rails
Armour:	4mm to 15mm
Armament:	1 x 7.62mm SGMB machine gun
	(BTR-40-A): 2 x 14.5mm KPVT heavy machine guns

of the trains helped with clearing the track of derailed rolling stock in 1986. In January 1990 they were reactivated to go into action during the uprisings in Baku and Sumqayit, to keep open the two key routes linking the South Caucasus with Russia. They arrived on station after the recapture of Baku, but remained active to protect the railway convoys. At the end of their tour of duty, they were gradually dismantled, with the exception of the locomotives.

When the Chechen war began, the railway engineers put a certain number of specialised trains into service, incorrectly described as 'armoured trains', which were intended to maintain and repair the rail network and remove mines. It was only at the end of 2002 that four genuine armoured trains were employed, named *Amur*, *Baikal*, *Don* and *Terek*. Only the last of these included armoured wagons from trains previously taken out of service.

Their composition was generally as follows, with variations in the number and order of the wagons:

– flat wagon with ZU-23-2.
– flat wagon with BMP-2.
– flat wagon with T-62.
– armoured wagon, with fixed turret, for infantry weapons and grenade launchers.
– equipment wagon.
– one or two coaches for the crew.
– two or three safety wagons (carrying sand or ballast).
– one or two flat wagons carrying a signals vehicle.
– locomotive.

The four trains which were built never went into action, and were stored at Chita, being regularly used for exercises. One

These TGM-14 diesel shunters and TG-16 locomotives were photographed in storage in a military depot in the Zabaikalsk district, after the four armoured trains were taken out of service. Note that the diesel shunter in the foreground does not have an armoured cupola.

(Photo: Athol Yates)

Above: Armoured Train *Baïkal* in Chechnya. Note the makeshift nature of the armour with two turrets and lateral sponsons. The body has been hastily constructed and attached to a commercial bogie flat wagon.

(Photo: Maxim Kolomiets Collection)

Below: The *Terek* communications wagon is based on an armoured tank platform on top of which a ZIL radio truck is secured and protected with planks and makeshift armour, including concrete blocks. The tarpaulin is probably used to break up the silhouette and certainly provides the crew with protection from the elements.

(Photo: Maxim Kolomiets Collection)

As originally built, this command wagon was armed with two twin 23mm ZU-23-2 or quadruple 23mm ZU-23-4 mountings. In the absence of an air threat in the Caucasus, here the crew of *Terek* has replaced the AA mountings with observation positions and embrasures for firing at ground targets. Note the ventilators on the roof.

(Photo: Maxim Kolomiets Collection)

Directly inspired by the anti-aircraft wagons of the Great Patriotic War, originally this armoured wagon also mounted 23mm cannon. These various wagons are all based on the same design of bogie flat wagon.

(Photo: Maxim Kolomiets Collection)

A view of the interior of an anti-aircraft wagon. Here the original multiple-barreled heavy weapon has been replaced by either an NSV[19] 12.7mm heavy machine gun, or a Kord.

(Photo: Maxim Kolomiets Collection)

19. The acronym comes from the names of designers G I Nikitin, Y S Sokolov and V I Volkov.

In October 2002 a fifth train, the *Cosima Minine*,[15] joined the base at Hankala,[16] which served as the supply depot for the trains. It had been built by an OMON[17] unit on the base of commercial rolling stock, armoured with all the materials that could be found on site. In particular it transported a BMP-2 with additional protection provided by sleepers and other materials, which were also used on the other wagons of the train.

The armoured trains in the Caucasus are credited with an impressive performance, such as the clearing of mines from 1000km (over 600 miles) of track, the escorting of 100 troop trains, and reconnaissance missions covering the 32,000km (20,000 miles) of track between Russia and Chechnya.

Since 2004, the Russian Army has had a specialised railway unit, the ZhDk (*Zheleznodoroznhiki*), split into four railway corps, twenty-eight brigades and an unspecified number of units, in charge of military transportation, and responsible for their correct functioning and their protection. The two armoured trains in the North Caucasus (Ingushetia) were activated by the 76th ZhDk based at Volvograd.

With the return of insecurity in 2010, the *Cosima Minine*, the sole armoured train deployed by the Interior Ministry, was reconstructed and fitted with modern equipment. For mine clearance work, it is equipped with an M4K Kamysh which interferes with the radio detonation of mines up to 20km (12.5 miles) away. Its anti-aircraft defence is provided by two ZPU-4 armoured vehicles, ten AGS-17 automatic chaff launchers and a number of machine guns. Firepower is provided by a 30mm 2A42 cannon, and the 9P135 M anti-tank missiles of a BMP-2 armoured vehicle carried on a flat wagon and protected by a side wall of sandbags. As necessary, one or two T-62 tanks (115mm gun) can be added to the train. On its return to service[18] in around December 2013, it was stationed either at Hankala to the west of Grozny or at Mozdok in North Ossetia, along with other armoured trains.

The other trains were supposed to have been dismantled after the end of the operations in the Caucasus. At the time of writing that order has been rescinded, the Russian Defence Minister having announced their reactivation as part of the modernisation of the armed forces. Certain sources consider that, apart from their value in assymetric warfare, they could form excellent platforms for the transport and firing of self-propelled artillery pieces such as the brand-new 152mm 2S19 Msta-S howitzer.

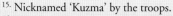

[15.] Nicknamed 'Kuzma' by the troops.
[16.] Sometimes written as 'Alkhan-Kala'.
[17.] Otryad Mobilniy Osobogo Naznacheniya, or special missions mobile unit, reporting to the Interior Ministry.
[18.] For an estimated cost of $635,000.
[19.] A new town named in 1964 after Palmiro Toggliati, one of the founders of the Italian Communist Party, who passed away in the town in that year, while holidaying in the USSR. The former town, Stavropol-on-the-Volga, had been covered by the waters of a dam.

Above: For railway maintenance and repair missions in high-risk areas, in response to an order placed by the Gorki Railway company, the firm of Arzamas produced this GAZ-5603J based on the BTR80 troop transporter. In fact the system of auxiliary rollers is identical to those used on the road-rail vehicles which can be seen in every modern railway worksite.
(Photo: Alain Dupouy Collection)

Left above: On display outside the Auto Vaz technical museum in Togliatti,[19] this type of armoured train is clearly intended to protect a military zone or base, as the height of the wagons and the anti-aircraft turret would preclude them from operating within the normal railway loading gauge.
(Photo: All Rights Reserved)

Left below: The great length of the wagon allows for the loading of an armoured intervention vehicle with the use of inclined ramps. The turret appears to be an automatic 2M-3, armed with two 25mm 110 PM cannon.
(Photo: All Rights Reserved)

This armoured wagon on display today in the Ukraine, in the Armed Forces Museum in Kiev, raises several queries. The height of the T-10 turrets and the lack of lower armour skirts leads one to think this is a training vehicle. Note the external ladders and the handgrips on the sides at the level of the open-topped infantry compartment.
(Photo: Paul Malmassari Collection)

A photo of the railway version No 2 with its inspection platform deployed. The same chassis has been offered as a fire engine by the same factory, under the designation GAZ-59402.
(Photo: Alain Dupouy Collection)

A modern reproduction of an armoured train of the Great Patriotic War. We can pick out the features of several wagons: the one behind the safety wagon is a mix of Baltic-type wagons with the small lateral turret, and Armoured Train *Khunkhuz*. The other wagons demonstrate the different combinations used at the time.
(Photo: Private Collection)

On 30 April 2015, to mark the 70th anniversary of the victory of 1945, Russia issued a set of postage stamps commemorating military equipment, of which four featured armoured trains. From top to bottom are: *Moskovski Metropoliten* ('Moscow Metro', Type BP-43), *Moskvitch* ('Muscovite', Type OB-3), *Istrebitel Nemetskikh Zakhvatchikov* ('Destroyer of the German Invaders', Type OB-3) and the *Kuzma Minin* ('Cosima Minine').

(Stamp issue: Paul Malmassari Collection)

SOURCES:
Works partly covering armoured trains

Books:

Body, Marcel, *Un Piano en bouleau de Carélie, Mes années de Russie 1917-1927* (Paris: Hachette, 1981).

Bullock, D, *Armored Units of the Russian Civil War, Red Army* (Oxford: Osprey Publishing Ltd, 2006).

_____, and Deryabin, A, *Armored Units of the Russian Civil War, White and Allied* (Oxford: Osprey Publishing Ltd, 2003).

Dupouy, Alain, *Les Engins blindés à roues Tome I: historique* (Grenoble: self-published, 1999).

_____, *Les Engins blindés à roues Tome II: automitrailleuses et autocanons* (Grenoble: self-published, 1999).

_____, *Les Engins blindés à roues Tome III: le BTR-40 et le BTR-152* (Grenoble: self-published, 1997).

_____, *Les Engins blindés à roues Tome VI: le BTR 70 et le BTR 80* (Grenoble: self-published, 1997).

Kinnear, James, *Russian Armored cars 1930-2000* (Darlington, MD: Darlington Productions, Inc., 2000).

Pasternak, Boris, *Doctor Zhivago* (Paris: Gallimard, 1959).

Rostagno, Enrique, *Les Armées russes en Mandchourie* (Ixelles-Bruxelles: A Beuer, 1909).

Vollert, Jochen, *KV-2 Soviet Heavy Breakthrough Tank of WWII* (Erlangen: Tankograd Publishing, 2004).

Zaloga, Steven J, and Grandsen, James, *Soviet Tanks and Combat Vehicles of World War Two* (London: Arms and Armour Press, 1984).

Journal Articles:

L'Appel des Soviets No 13 (15 October 1929), cover page.

Vaucher, Robert, 'La Route de Petrograd', *L'Illustration* No 3929 (22 June 1918), pp 607–9.

Works exclusively or principally covering armoured trains

Books:

Kolomiets, Maxim, *Sowieckie samochody pancerne vol. 1* (Warsaw: Wydawnictwo Militaria, 2005).

_____, *Sowieckie poci gi pancerne vol. 1 1930-1941* (Warsaw: Wydawnictwo Militaria, 2006).

_____, *Les Trains blindés de l'Armée rouge 1930-1941* (in Russian) (Moscow: Frontline Illustration, 2006).

_____, *Les Trains blindés de l'Armée rouge 1941-1945* (in Russian) (Moscow: Frontline Illustration, 2007).

Kopenhagen, Wilfried, *Sowjetische Panzerzüge und Eisenbahngeschütze 1917-1945* (Wölfersheim-Berstadt: Podzun-Pallas-Verlag, 1995).

Journal Articles:

Brauer, 'Do we need armoured trains?' (in Russian), *Техника и снабжение красной армии* ('Techniques and Supply of the Red Army') (August 1923), pp 27–9.

Koenig, Alan R, 'Glass-Jawed Goliaths: Red Army Artillery Armored trains in World War II', *The Journal of Slavic Military Studies* Vol 14, No 4 (December 2001), pp 144–61.

'Le train blindé *Cosima Minine*', *Modelist Konstruktor* (1980-5), pp 4–9.

McGregor. Andrew, 'Russian Interior Ministry Revives Its Armored Train in the North Caucasus', *Eurasia Daily Monitor* Vol 10, Issue 91 (14 May 2013).

Malmassari, Paul, 'Les Trains blindés soviétiques', *39-45 Magazine* No 45 (1989), pp 30–5.

Maurin, 'Installation of large calibre artillery pieces on armoured trains' (in Russian), *Техника и снабжение красной армии* ('Techniques and Supply of the Red Army') (September 1922), p 14.

Trojca, Halina and Waldemar, 'Der Panzertriebwagen Kirowski', *Modell-Fan* 4/94, pp 53–5.

Zaloga, Steven, 'Soviet Armored Trains', *AFV News* 17/2, pp 5–11.

Zhilin, Gennady, 'Baikal, Terek and Co.', *Tankomaster* No 7 (2003), pp 2–14.

Play:

Vsevolod, Ivanov, *Le Train blindé n° 14-69* (Paris: Librairie Gallimard, 1922).

Film:

Heirs of Victory (1975), 60 minutes.

Websites:

https://reibert.info/threads/bronepoezda-belyx-armij.116097/
http://en.zabmodels.mybb.ru/viewtopic.php?id=262

SLOVAK REPUBLIC[1]

ARMOURED TRAIN *OROL*

Created following the dismantling of Czechoslovakia, the Slovak Republic under Monsignor Tiso briefly joined in the attack on Poland in September and October 1939. During the campaign the Slovaks put back into service *Bernolak*,[2] a former Austro-Hungarian armoured train.[3] It appears that a second train was improvised at Zvolen for the same campaign. The latter unit was composed of locomotive No 310.422 and wagons numbered U-7,76290 and 7,17369. To date no photo of either armoured train has come to light.

On 23 June 1941, the Slovak Republic declared war on the Soviet Union, and in the occupied zone which comprised the northern part of the Ukraine and the southern part of Byelorussia, Slovak troops quickly came into conflict with communist partisans. The German armoured train PZ 25 was the main means of securing the zone of operations. Major Martin Strapak, commander of the 1st Battalion of the 102nd Slovak Infantry Regiment, was so impressed by the performance of the German train that he set about improvising a Slovak armoured train[4] for the 'Orol' (Eagle) Security Division in the Spring of 1942. To protect his train, he used armour plate and turrets recovered from destroyed and abandoned Soviet tanks, plus a complete BT-5 cruiser tank.

The train immediately went into service on the line between Pinsk and Gomel, and its first major action took place in August 1942 in conjunction with PZ 25. *Orol* was regularly targeted by partisan attacks, and they succeeded in derailing it several times, in particular following the withdrawal of PZ 25 which was sent to France. The Winter of 1942/43 was a period of relative calm, but on 22 March *Orol* was seriously damaged in a derailment. Finally, on 27 May 1943, 3km (2 miles) to the north of Slavečna, it was irreparably damaged by the partisans.

[1.] In post-war literature also known as the Slovak State (*Slovenský štát*).
[2.] After the name of the Army Group.
[3.] Crew: forty-six officers and men; armament: seven 7.92mm Schwarzlose Model 7/24 heavy machine guns, two 7.92mm ZB vz.26 LMGs, and one 37mm KPÚV vz.37 anti-tank gun.
[4.] In Slovak: *Improvizovaný Pancierový Vlak* (IPV).

This view showing the rear of the tank demonstrates the weak protection of *Orol* in its initial form. The BT-5 was armoured to a maximum of 13mm at the front, but the sides and rear were much thinner. The partisans succeeded in blowing up the train at least three times.

(Photo: Pavel Mičianik)

Orol in September 1942, in its initial configuration, with a Class BR 57 locomotive, and a lead wagon with a complete BT-5 Soviet tank protected by vertical armour plates at the leading end of the wagon only. This type of platform was also armed with 81mm mortars and a 37mm anti-tank gun.

(Photo: Pavel Mičianik)

Orol in its second configuration: the wagons had internal timber walls with the space between the inside and outside faces filled with stone ballast. The turret is from a T-28 or T-35 Soviet tank. Occasionally, individual wagons were detached from the complete train and coupled in supply trains.

(Photo: Pavel Mičianik)

Above: In the Autumn of 1942, the train was rebuilt with improved armour protection, seen here in the workshops.
(Photo: Martin Lacko)

The photos right and below show the armoured wagon completed and bearing the emblem of the Slovak Republic.

(Photo: Martin Lacko)

SOURCES:

Mičianik, Pavel, 'Improvizovaný pancierový vlak zaist'ovacej divízie "Orol"', *Vojenská história* 4, 12 (2008), pp 10–19.

(Photo: Paul Malmassari Collection)

SOUTH AFRICA

ARMOURED TRAINS[1] AND TROLLEYS

Southern Africa was the scene of bitter fighting between the Boer Republics of the ZAR and the Orange Free State against the British from 1899 to 1902 during the Second Boer War. The armoured trains engaged in this conflict are described in the chapter on Great Britain. Having gained its independence under the South Africa Act of 31 May 1910, the Union of South Africa took part in the First World War. In 1939 the country once more went to war with Germany as part of the Commonwealth. On 31 May 1961, South Africa became an independent republic and left the British Commonwealth. The uprisings of the ANC and the nationalist movements against the apartheid policies of the white government which began in 1960 led to several declarations of a state of emergency. In 1966 fighting broke out on the frontiers of South Africa, and the state had to exert considerable effort to protect its infrastructure from attacks and sabotage by terrorists, at least up until 1989.

The First World War and the Boer Rebellion

In 1914 South Africa joined in the First World War, attacking and capturing the German colony of South West Africa (SWA, present-day Namibia), and fighting alongside other Commonwealth forces in the Somme. In Africa several armoured trains, of which certain elements dated from the Second Boer War, were put into service on the country's narrow-gauge network (1067mm/3ft 6in). They were used to fight the German colonial troops, but first they had to protect rail transport during the Maritz Rebellion of a group of Afrikaners which took place between September 1914 and February 1915.

Armoured Train No 5 *Schrikmaker*, built in Pretoria, which was used in German South West Africa. It was armed with an artillery piece, seen here surrounded by a group of officials and officers.
(Photo: S.A.R.)

[1] In Afrikaans *Pantsertrein*.

This involved officers and men who had fought the British during the last Boer War, notably Brigadier-General Christiaan Frederick Beyers, the commander-in-chief of South African forces, who resigned his commission to lead the rebellion, and also many officers such as Generals de Wet, Kemp and Maritz, the latter lending his name to the movement. Repeated defeats led to the collapse of the uprising, the last *kommando* surrendering on 8 February 1915.

Five armoured trains were built in 1914: *Trafalgar* (His Majesty's Armoured Train No 1, completed on 22 October), *Scot* (No 2, 6 November), *Erin* (No 3, 9 November), *Karoo* (No 4, 6 November) and *Schrikmaker* (No 5, 18 November). However, at the time there was no rail link between South Africa and SWA. Huge efforts were expended between 15 August 1914 and 25 June 1915 on the construction of a rail link, including deviations and secondary lines, in order to deploy armoured trains. *Erin* remained in reserve in South Africa, while the other four were used for patrol missions and for support of the ground troops. For this latter function seven armoured railway batteries were employed, often coupled to the armoured trains. But it appears that fire support by these batteries usually required their emplacement on the ground, as firing from the wagons proved impractical.

A modified version of the wagon shown below placed at the head of H. M. A. T. No 5 *Schrikmaker*, with additional facilities to ensure the comfort of the crew, in the form of two timber shelters and a framework to hold a canvas covering to protect from the sun and rain. Nineteen such wagons were converted and divided between the Transvaal and the Orange Free State.
(Photo: S.A.R.)

A similar wagon, the sandbags providing both protection (descending behind the wagon sides) and also a rampart to support the weapons. The troops carry the SMLE (Short Magazine Lee Enfield) Mk III adopted in 1907 and are supported by a Lewis Gun at each end.
(Photo: S.A.R.)

Above: The 12pdr artillery wagon of H. M. A. T. No 1 *Trafalgar*. Note the armoured side plates which hinge down to form the firing platform.
(Photo: IWM)

Below: The three leading wagons of Armoured Train No 3 *Erin*. The composition of the armoured trains was relatively standard: for example AT No 5 comprised an armoured engine, an artillery wagon, a support wagon, three bogie wagons (one of which transported draught animals), a water tank wagon, and a short wheelbase wagon. Searchlights had to be purchased from the local mining companies to increase the effectiveness of night patrols.
(Photo: S.A.R.)

Left: Armoured wagon built in Bloemfontein for *Erin* at the end of 1914. Two similar wagons were also built, each coupled to an unarmoured engine to form an armoured reconnaissance train.
(Photo: S.A.R.)

Below: A 6in naval gun mounted on a five-axle wagon: the two axles furthest from the camera are a locomotive leading truck and the other three are a tender chassis, seen in 1915.
(Photo: Revue du Génie Civil)

Active at Johannesburg. The bogie wagons, although armed with captured German Maxim 08 MGs such as the one mounted on the right, and .303 calibre Lewis Guns (the barrel of one of which can be seen behind the head of the fourth officer from the right), do not present a formidable appearance, as their armour protection is hidden from view behind the side plating.
(Photo: S.A.R.)

The Inter-War Period

Drawing on the experience of the First World War, it was decided to establish the Railways and Harbour Brigade (R & HB) to take charge of all forms of transport, including its two armoured trains, No 1 (*Active*) based at the Cape, and No 2 at Johannesburg. In 1928, the R & HB was dissolved and the two armoured trains were transferred to the Active Citizen Force.[2]

The Second World War

South Africa declared war on Germany on 6 September 1939. On 1 April 1940, the R & HB was reactivated: with its HQ at Johannesburg the Brigade comprised two infantry battalions, four armoured trains and an Engineers detachment (which would give rise to railway regiments and a regiment in charge of the ports). AT No 1 was based at the junction at Milner Park (Johannesburg) and No 2 at Durban, with volunteer crews manning them on a part-time basis. In August 1940, AT No 1 was moved 35km (28 miles) from its home base to Mapleton, which was also the training centre of the R & HB. In 1942, modernisation of the Brigade involved the dismantling of AT No 2. AT No 1 remained active up until 1 January 1946, when it was withdrawn from service.

Although the country was part of the Commonwealth, as in 1914 a large part of the white population did not support the dec-laration of war, and the government, fearing acts of rebellion and sabotage, decided to take steps to protect the rolling stock. Steam engine No 1554 was therefore partially armoured in August 1940, in order to haul an armoured train. Stationed at Mapleton with a view to patrols on the main line in Natal, this train, about which little information has come to light, was protected in a similar manner to the engine, by plates 25mm thick intended to resist small-arms fire. Its principal armament would have been a 18pdr QF field gun on a naval mounting, plus Vickers and Lewis machine guns. Later on in the war, this train was used to support the war effort by making runs from the Union of South Africa into Rhodesia, but it never saw action. Finally, the armour protection was removed from the engine and it returned to civilian use.

[2] The Defence Act of 1912 had created the South African Army or UDF (Union Defence Force) composed of the Permanent Force, a standing army of professional soldiers, and the Active Citizen Force, composed of recruits and volunteers.

Above: Class 4 engine No 1554, partially armoured.
(Photo: Terry Hutson)

Right: Active's 18pdr Ordnance QF Mk II field gun on one of the two bogie wagons numbered 41101Z and 41102Z.
(Photo: All Rights Reserved)

Below: An interesting document: cigarette card N° 17 from Hortors Ltd with a fair representation of the artillery wagon of this train. Despite the crew being out of proportion, the original shows the train in camouflage colours, in contrast to the engine and tender which are still painted in charcoal grey.
(Card: Paul Malmassari Collection)

In 1942, a Marmon-Herrington Mk I armoured car (No U1341) was converted to run on rails. No details of this machine are known, apart from a silhouette showing the unmistakable twin turret hatches, seen in the background of a photo of engine No 1554, and the fact that it was disposed of by auction at Lyttleton in 1952.

At the end of the Second World War, South African author and poet Roy Campbell[3] penned the following lines, which show how much the armoured trains featured in the imagination of the country: 'Against a regiment I oppose a brain / And a dark horse against an armoured train'. These verses also inspired the 1954 painting by Alex Colville *Horse and train*.[4]

The Frontier War (South African Border War)

This conflict lasted more than 20 years (August 1966 – September 1980) and involved South West Africa (the future Namibia[5]) and Angola, both supported by revolutionary independence movements (SWAPO in Namibia from 1962, and UNITA in Angola from

1966). These terrorist groups infiltrated South Africa to attack the economic and cultural infrastructure, and in particular the transport network, with increasing severity during the mid-1970s.

This background prompted several quite original armoured responses, comprising road/rail armoured vehicles and trains specially conceived for maintaining public order.

The BOSPADDA[6] convertible armoured vehicles

The two machines known as *Kobus* (No SAS R 810494) and *Chris* (No SAS R 810493) were used by the South African Rail Police (SAS:[7] *Suid Afrika Spoorwegpolisie*) to protect the lines during crisis periods. Their conception and construction took place under the direction of Mr Chris van der Merwe in the Langlaagte workshops,[8] based on the combined experience of the railway police, the Army Engineers, the South African Armed Forces and the CSIR.[9] One of these vehicles was therefore baptised as *Chris*, in honour of its designer, and the other as *Kobus*, in honour of Dr Kobus Loubser, former president of the South African Railways.

As designed, these machines were dual road-rail convertible configuration: during road travel the rail wheels were retracted underneath the hull; for rail travel they were hydraulically lowered onto the rails to act as guide wheels, traction on the rails being provided by the road wheels. At an unknown date, this system was removed due to supposed hydraulic problems (but possibly also the problem of using the road wheels as source of traction beside the track). Thereafter *Chris* and *Kobus* became simply armoured railcars mounted on traction bogies.

Today *Chris* is preserved on display in front of the TransNamib Museum in Windhoek. *Kobus* is still in working order, assigned to the Braamfontein Memorial Marshalling Yard.

Here *Kobus* is being presented to the authorities in 1978.
(Photo: S.A.R.)

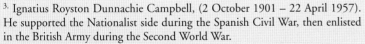

Above: Chris and *Kobus* were equipped with six-cylinder diesel engines, giving them a maximum speed of 60km/h (37mph) and a range of 1000km (620 miles) on rails and 750km (466 miles) on roads. Here one of the rail guide wheels is clearly visible in its lowered position.
(Photo: S.A.R.)

One of the remarkable features of these machines is that all of the 6800 or so component parts which make up each one were designed and built in the workshops without any external help, during a period of severe international sanctions against South Africa.
(Photo: S.A.R.)

[3.] Ignatius Royston Dunnachie Campbell, (2 October 1901 – 22 April 1957). He supported the Nationalist side during the Spanish Civil War, then enlisted in the British Army during the Second World War.
[4.] Art Gallery of Hamilton.
[5.] German South West Africa was conquered in 1915 and was made a South African protectorate in 1920. After the Second World War, South Africa demanded the annexation of the territory. But the United Nations took SWA under its guardianship in 1966 and renamed it Namibia in 1968. From 1967 SWAPO began its guerrilla operations. In 1971 the International Court of Justice declared the South African presence in the territory to be illegal. Namibia finally achieved independence on 21 March 1990.
[6.] 'Bush Frog' in Afrikaans.
[7.] The railway police were absorbed into the national police in 1986.
[8.] South of Johannesburg, in the Road Mechanical Vehicle Workshops of the SAR&H.
[9.] Council for Scientific and Industrial Research.

In this photo of *Chris* preserved in Windhoek, note the road mudguards are still in place, but the drive train has been converted from road wheels to rail bogies. The steps welded on the buffer beam at each end do not appear on *Kobus*.

(Photo: All Rights Reserved)

In comparison, *Kobus* has been retained in full working order, and its protruding road mudguards have been removed. The road wheel arches have been covered by protective grills, again no doubt for health and safety reasons.

(Photo: Petrus Botha)

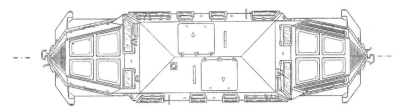

© Paul MALMASSARI 2004 1/87 (HO)

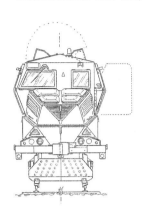

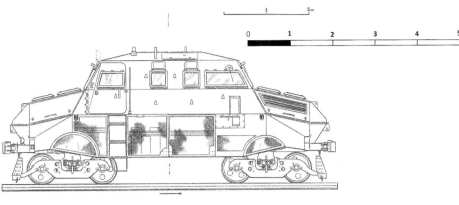

This frontal view of the machine taken in 1995 emphasises its aggressive appearance, which fits in well with its intended mission. It was designed to protect the crew from the explosion of a 7kg charge of TNT. The central knuckle allows for coupling wagons or for towing the machine in the case of breakdown.

(Photo: Petrus Botha)

A close-up of the driving bogie on *Kobus*.

(Photo: Petrus Botha)

Interior view of *Kobus* at Braamfontein. Note the padding which covers much of the inside of the machine.

(Photo: Johannes Botha)

Above: Right side view of *Kobus*: the two sides of the machine are different as regards the lower central section, the doors are offset to the left on each side, and the front can be recognised by the motor cooling slots. The central observation windows, however, are symmetrical.
(Photo: Petrus Botha)

Below: Left side view taken on 9 August 1996: Note that the square lamps have been moved from the roof to the front and rear hoods.
(Photo: Petrus Botha)

The Inspection Trolleys

Several small inspection trolleys were built, some fitted with platforms. The latter were intended for inspection of the 3000-volt overhead catenary cables which powered the main lines and the depots, and to repair damaged sections when thieves had risked stealing the copper cables.

Turntable on the left-hand side of *Funkey*. Apparently this device was not automatically fitted to all of these machines.
(Photo: Petrus Botha)

10. State-owned company responsible for rail freight, which became Transnet in July 2007.

One of them called *Funkey* seems to have lent its name to all of these machines. Here we can make out painted on its sides the emblem of the South African Railways (Spoornet)[10] during the 1990s.
(Photo: Petrus Botha)

The inspection platforms were designed by the Electrification Department of Spoornet.
(Photo: Petrus Botha)

The Riot Trains: ('Ghost Trains'[11])

During the 1960s, it was planned to build armoured trains, but the idea was dropped. On the other hand, four trains designed to control rioters were built, and partially armoured, in the 1970s. Generally, they were composed of the following units:

– a Type DZ-7 bogie wagon ballasted with gravel and equipped with cowcatchers.
– coaches for the riot police.
– a water tank and fire-fighting equipment.
– a diesel locomotive or steam engine.
– at the rear a second ballasted Type DZ-7 bogie wagon.

These trains could also be used for the transport of munitions, and to ensure their security the orders to move would be given only an hour prior to departure. When transporting munitions, the trains could be organised in the following formation, to provide maximum security to the personnel:

– diesel locomotive.
– ballasted Type DZ-7 wagon.
– the explosives transport wagon, followed by the second ballasted Type DZ-7.

[11.] Not to be confused with the 'Phantom Trains' covered in the Belgian chapter, which were used as rams or indendiary trains.

One of the four 'Ghost Trains' powered by a Class 25 NC steam engine, preceded by its ballasted bogie wagon.
(Photo: Petrus Botha)

Two standard Class 38 dual power diesel-electrics double-heading this riot train and followed by two personnel coaches. Note the cowcatcher at the front of the Type DZ-7 bogie wagon.
(Photo: Petrus Botha)

The driving cab of this standard Class 38 diesel-electric prime mover is armoured against small-arms fire. The leading loco is 38-002 followed by 38-003.
(Photo: Petrus Botha)

Class 34 diesel-electric locomotive, which alternated with a Class 15 F steam engine on 'Ghost Trains' Nos 3 and 4.
(Photo: Petrus Botha)

The Class 25 NC steam engines were modified to spray water to help fight fires and also to serve as a water cannon to repel rioters who approached too close to the engine, which is here N° 3475 *Braamfontein*. Class 15 steam engines were also employed on Trains 1, 2 and 4.
(Photo: Petrus Botha)

Close-up view of the hot water nozzle on the left side of the engine, and the long jet of steam it produced (below).
(Photos: Petrus Botha)

This Type X-17 water tank wagon has been modified with a water jet for use in fighting fires, with a nozzle similar to that on the steam engine fitted to the top of the central ladder. The wagon is in the orange and white livery of Spoornet.
(Photo: Petrus Botha)

Close-up of the front end of one of the Type DZE-7 bogie wagons. The cowcatcher reaches down quite far below the wagon and is fitted with reinforced rubber extensions.
(Photo: Petrus Botha)

No 9246, one of the self-propelled Class 2M1 electric units, converted into a riot coach. Note the circular ports for weapons in each of the armoured windows. When these coaches were used as motor units for suburban trains (note the folded pantograph), the driver's cab in this photo dating from 1996 would be on the right.

(Photo: Petrus Botha)

Internal view of one of the armoured coaches, the seated troops facing outwards towards attackers. Note the grills covering the windows. The armour protection consisted of 3mm steel plates on the outside of the wooden coach sides plus 5mm steel plates on the inside surface.

(Photo: Petrus Botha)

SOURCES:

Book:

Camp, Steve and Heitman, Helmoed-Römer, *Surviving the Ride* (Johannesburg: 30° South Publishers (Pty) Ltd, 2014).

Journal Articles:

Bouch, Lieutenant R J, 'The Railway and the War Effort 1914-1915', *Militaria* No 4/4 (1974), pp 1–14.

_____, 'The Railway and the War Effort 1939-1945', *Militaria* No 5/2 (1975), pages 66–75.

'E J', 'Capetown: A correspondant writes', *S.A. Railways & Harbour Magazine* (May 1928), pp 848–50.

___, 'With the Armoured Train at Potchefstroom', *S.A. Railways and Harbour Magazine* (May 1930), pp 697–9.

Harrigan, Anthony, 'The Armoured Train', *Commando* (March 1963), pp 19–21.

Revue du Génie Civil (23 October 1915).

Rhind, D M, 'The Mystery of 4AR No 1554', *World War Two Railway Study Group Bulletin* Vol 8 No 1 (1998), pp 8.19–8.21.

'Veelsydige Pantserwa om Treindienste te Beskerm', *SASSAR* (July 1978), pp 681–3.

SOUTH KOREA

ARMOURED TRAINS (1950–1953)

The North Korean Army began the invasion of the South on 25 June 1950. The US Army's 772nd Military Police Battalion (Railway Security) made up of four companies with a total complement of thirty-eight officers and 412 men, left its base in Maryland in September and landed at Wonsan. Their initial role was to help stop the advance of the North Korean divisions, and ensure the security of road communications. They also took charge of refugees and prisoners of war. In December, they handled security during the retreat of the United Nations Forces, faced with twelve Chinese divisions, up until the fall of Hamhung. At that point, the United Nations' lines of communication were being threatened by the presence of North Korean units[1] as much as 150km (93 miles) behind the front lines. The 772nd Battalion, which had been evacuated to Pusan, was charged with the role of protecting the MSR, the principal supply route for the United Nations forces. Company D became responsible for protecting the railway line between Ulsan and Chechon, then from January 1951 as far as Seoul. In August 1951, the role of the battalion was changed, and all four Companies were dedicated to protecting the railway network, from their HQ in Taegu, under the overall command of the 3rd Transportation Military Rail System.

Company A was posted to Taejon, Company B to Pusan, Company C to Tongdong-Po, and Company D remained at Yongchon. In all, they were responsible for the security of almost 1,700km (1,050 miles) of track.

Their rolling stock comprised bogie wagons reinforced internally with sandbags and nicknamed 'rolling foxholes'. Company B at least put back into service a Japanese armoured wagon, which ran in front of the locomotive and was itself preceded by a safety bogie wagon. The unit remained in Korea after the armistice of 27 July 1953, and was demobilised on 11 June 1955.

SOURCES:
Book:
Mesko, Jim, *Armor in Korea, a Pictorial History* (Carollton, Texas: Squadron Signal Publications Inc. 1984).

Websites:
http://www.military.com/HomePage/UnitPageHistory/1,13506,10 4826|797829,00.html
http://www.transportation.army.mil/museum/transportation%20m useum/korearail.htm

American and Korean members of Company B, 772nd MP Battalion (Railway Security) in front of their ex-Japanese armoured wagon.
(Photo: Paul Malmassari Collection)

The ex-Japanese armoured wagon and the rear of the safety wagon.
(Photo: Paul Malmassari Collection)

[1.] With a strength equal to three divisions.

SOUTH SUDAN

ARMOURED TRAIN, 2001

South Sudan became independent of the North on 9 July 2011. At the time of writing the only railway line possessed by the South is the 248km (154 miles) stretch of the Babanousa line from the frontier to Wau, built between 1959 and 1962 to a gauge of 1067mm (3ft 6in).

A decade prior to the division of the country, the only mention of armoured trains is an Internet article by M. Brice Lalonde[1] dated 3 September 2001, in which he mentions that each

year an armoured train, escorted by militia cavalry, was despatched by the Khartoum Government to resupply the garrisons in Southern Sudan. Probably for security reasons, no photograph of this operation has come to light.

[1] French politician, former Secretary of State then Minister for the Environment from 1988 to 1992. He founded the Europe Ecology Party, of which he was the President at the time he wrote the article.

SPAIN

ARMOURED TRAINS[1]

As with many of the other major European powers, Spain first employed armoured trains in its colonial empire (Cuba and Spanish Morocco), then afterwards at home during the Civil War of 1936–9. Although during the Carlist Wars of the nineteenth century certain railway stations had been protected by small fortifications, there is no evidence that armoured trains were used at that time.

The Defence of Cuba

The transport network in Cuba comprised almost 1500km (930 miles) of railway lines, shared between sixteen small operators. During the Ten Years War (1868–78), which started with an uprising then the declaration of independence by the province of Oriente on 10 October 1868, armoured wagons were built and mustered in train rakes, to defend against sabotage. After several years of peace, on 24 February 1895, a new uprising led by a political exile named José Marti[2] started with a landing by a small group of his followers at La Playitas de Cajobabo in the east of the island. Faced by a worsening of the situation, the authorities established a co-ordinating body, the *Sección de Intervención de la Intendencia Militar*. Patrol trains made up of troop coaches and

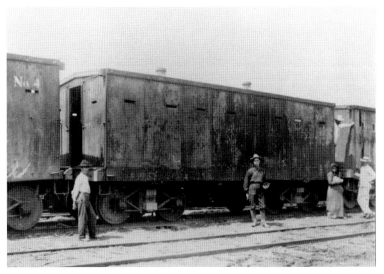

Numbered armoured wagons photographed at Saguä la Grande in Cuba on 5 March 1898. They appear to be of classic construction, well protected against small-arms fire.

[1] In Spanish: '*Trenes Blindados*'.
[2] He was killed in action on 19 May 1895.

Armoured train in Cuba in 1898. Note the firing loopholes in the wooden sides of the wagon.

(Photo: Archivo General Militar de Madrid, F.05933)

several armoured wagons were assembled, and used on the defence line established by General Campos, backed by a network of small forts built along the tracks. These measures did not succeed in stopping the rebel advance, and in April 1898, following the controversial destruction of the battleship USS *Maine*, the Americans decided to intervene. At the end of the ensuing Spanish-American War, under the Treaty of Paris signed on 10 December 1898, the Spanish gave up their colonial empire.

Operations in Spanish Morocco

The Rif War began on the morning of 17 July 1921 when a column of 200 troops was attacked by the fighters of Abd El Krim. There would be considerable fighting involving French and Spanish forces before the war ended with his surrender on 27 May 1926.

The Spanish railways in Morocco were operated by several companies: the 24km (15-mile) line of the Compañia de Minas del Rif (60cm/1ft 11½in gauge) ran between Melilla and Avanzamiento; the 30km (18.6-mile) line of the Compañia de Minas del Rif (metre/3ft 3¼in gauge) between Melilla and Afra; and finally the Linea des Estado (metre gauge) between Melilla and Tistutin, which ran for 36km (22.5 miles).

After the military disaster of Anoual on 21 July, the Spaniards tried to react. On 15 August 1921, the *1st Regimento de Ferrocarriles* was charged with extending the line from Melilla, and with constructing a platform for unloading equipment. As each night the Rif fighters dismantled the track, each following morning a repair team was put to work under the protection of an armoured train. The town of Nador was attacked on 17 September. Two armoured trains (one on the 60cm gauge and the other on the metre gauge) were in action in support of the troops. However, the 60cm gauge armoured train was stopped by demolitions. The second train

managed to arrive in Nador, and another train for the metre gauge was built by cannibalising parts of the immobilised 60cm-gauge train. These two armoured trains were then used up until the end of December to reconquer territory as far as Avanzamiento and Titustin. We have no information on the technical details of these improvised trains, which apparently carried no artillery.

The Spanish continued to lose ground to the rebels. In October 1924, an armoured train (60cm gauge) was assembled at Tetouan to relieve the besieged garrison at Zinatz. Two partially-

The '*Tortillard*' ('Local Train') on the Taza run. An armoured train was known to operate on the Taza run in July 1926, but it is not known whether it was the same as one recorded in 1921.

(Photo: Via JMAM – Jacinto M Arévalo Molina)

Card No 17 from an Orús (Barcelona) chocolate bar, showing one of the armoured trains in Spanish Morocco.

(Card: Paul Malmassari Collection)

The engine of the armoured train (60cm gauge) built to relieve the garrison at Zinatz.

(Photo: via JMAM)

armoured (front and sides) steam engines formed the head and tail of the train. In between were nine wagons protected on the sides with sandbags, carrying four machine guns, medical teams and signallers. During the retreat from Xauen in December 1924, it seems that an improvised armoured train was used.

Revolt in the Asturias

In October 1934, a general strike declared in some regions of Spain turned into armed confrontations between the workers and the forces of order. The strike was quickly broken, except in Catalonia and in the Asturias. After several incidents of street fighting, the revolt ended in Catalonia, but the situation in the Asturias worsened to the point where the Army had to intervene. At least three armoured trains were used alongside armed trains. The first encounter took place on 7 October 1934, when a lightly-armoured train left the machinery depot of la Argañosa for the Norte Company station where the crew fought with the strikers. The most well-known of these trains was the one hauled by the steam engine *Grado* on the metric gauge Vasco-Asturiano railway, which left the Vega factory on 9 October and was in action the following day against strikers in the suburb of Pelayo. Several days later, a broad-gauge[3] train was in action at Vega del Rey Station but was hit in the boiler by a shell and was forced to withdraw. During the night of 14/15 October, the opponents of the Army put together an armoured train at Trubia to help the strikers in Grado.

[3.] The Spanish gauge was wider than that in France: 1668mm (5ft 3¾in) as against 1435mm (4ft 8½in).

The armoured train built at Oviedo on the Ferrocarril Vasco-Asturiano, with its steam engine *Grado*, used in October 1934.
(Photo: Paul Malmassari Collection)

In the foreground is steam engine No 2544 *Cervera* of the Northern Company. In front and behind the engine is a low-sided flat wagon, each one carrying a Landesa armoured tractor, with a ball mount for a 7mm Hotchkiss machine gun. If necessary, this train could act as an armoured train.
(Photo: All Rights Reserved)

The Spanish Civil War

The Nationalist revolt began on 17 July 1936 in Spanish Morocco, led by Colonel Francisco Franco Bahamonde, commander of the troops in Morocco. Faced with the refusal of the Republican Government to issue arms to the general population, the people took advantage of those areas where the Army garrisons were weak to seize arms for themselves. Among the many emergency measures put in place by the Government from the very early days of the Army revolt was the construction of armoured trains, alongside many other types of improvised armoured vehicles. They were used almost exclusively by the Republican side.[4] They operated either independently, or under the command of the local majority trade union or workers' committee. In late 1936, specialised units were created within the Madrid Army Corps, including a Railway Brigade which grouped together the Railway Militias, the Railway Shock Battalion, the armoured trains and the railway workshops. The Railway Brigade deployed its personnel as and when necessary to the construction of armoured trains, and when the *Ejercito Popular* (Army of the People) was formed, the experienced and disciplined railway units were successfully integrated.

In fact, on 10 January 1937, a former trade unionist, Narciso Julián Sanz, was charged with regrouping all the armoured trains in a new unit. In Madrid, experienced soldiers were to train the various specialist crewmen: troops, railway workers, engine drivers, gunners, assault infantry, signallers, sappers to defuse mines and to repair the tracks, cooks, nurses etc. In February 1937, the Railway

Brigade formed an independent unit in the Army of the Centre, then in May it became the Railway Battalion with a strength of 1798 men. This battalion, which for the whole period of the Civil War would be commanded by Sanz, was one of the formations under the overall command of Colonel Tomás Ardid, head of the Engineer Services of the Army of the Centre. If at the end of the Civil War, ten armoured trains remained operational, we know that a total of thirty had been built during the war, of which up to the present time twenty have been identified. However, the defeat of the Republican side, when the trains were all demobilised and the rolling stock was returned to commercial use, means that with rare exceptions they were never photographed.

Despite the very real existence of these well designed and assembled trains, and in some numbers, relevant documentation is sadly lacking, preventing a full description of their story, or indeed correct attribution of their identifying numbers and letters. The following outline description is based on the remarkable work undertaken by Sr. Jacinto M Arévalo Molina, as well as on the articles and reconstitutions of Sr. Francisco Cruzado Albert.

The armoured trains of the Sierra de Guadarrama[5]

Starting in Madrid, a railway line crossed the Sierra de Guadarrama and divided into two branches at the level of Villalba, one of which passed through a tunnel under the Alto del León and continued towards Segovia. The other branch passed by way of El Escorial, Robledo de Chavela and Las Navas del Marques and arrived in Avila. The first actions involving armoured trains took place on these two branches. On 23 July 1936 the first train, which was hastily protected with mattresses, tabletops, beams and steel plates, was put into service, and on the 26th it took part in the defence of Alto de Léon, but was a failure. On 5 August the first properly-

The badge of the *Brigada Ferroviaria de Trenes Blindados y Especialidades* printed as a title of a review published in June 1937. It is noticeable here, as on the game boards reproduced in Appendix 1, that a railway gun means more to the uninformed observer than an armoured train with its less prominent characteristics. *(Reconstruction by JMAM)*

A fine view of the engine of Armoured Train 'A' in August 1936, in Los Molinos Station, which shows off well the camouflage scheme and the armoured casemate at the front.

(Photo: All Rights Reserved)

[4.] Certain reports mention the existence of four Nationalist armoured trains, only one of which went into action, the other three lasting only a short time.
[5.] The region to the north-west of Madrid.

constituted armoured train came out of the workshops of the Compañia del Norte. It had been designed by Engineer Lieutenant-Colonel D Ramón Valcárel, and comprised four wagons and a steam engine, all armoured, and armed with two 70mm guns, nine machine guns and eighty-nine rifles, considerable firepower for the period. It was designated *Tren blindado* 'A', which was later changed to Armoured Train No 1 and finally by the end of the war,

to Armoured Train No 5. This train, along with one or two motorised wagons used for reconnaissance, remained on this line for the whole of the war and patrolled from Torrelodones towards Cercedilla and El Escorial. A short time later, a similar train (Armoured Train 'B') was built, and after remaining on this front for a short time, moved to the Talavera line in October 1936.

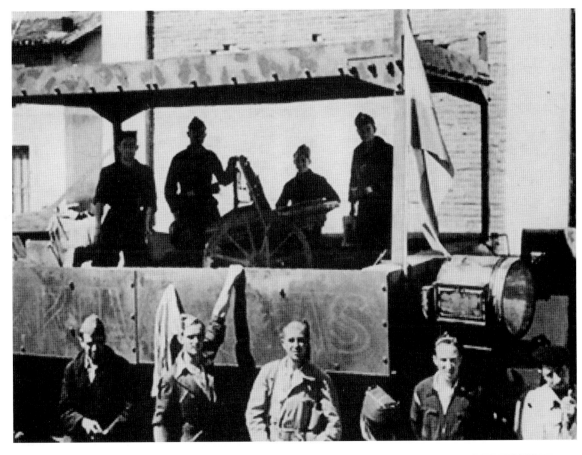

Close-up of an end compartment of the artillery wagon of Armoured Train 'A', based on a Type MMG bogie well wagon of the Norte, before the inscriptions were painted on. (Note the outlines of the letters chalked on the metal as guidelines). It is armed with two 70mm guns. The red-yellow-red Spanish national flag hangs from one of the corner pillars. The photo was taken on 5 September 1936.
(Photo: Archivo General de la Administración, AGA)

The stamp used by Armoured Train 'A' showing the composition of the crew and their political affiliation.
(Illustration: JMAM Collection)

A photo apparently taken by a member of the Condor Legion in the Sierra de Guadarrama. The artillery wagon converted from a Type Rrf well wagon with six-axle bogies has obviously been damaged by fire, as there are smoke marks above the firing slits and the embrasure.
(Photo: Paul Malmassari Collection)

The armoured trains of San Sebastián

There are a few brief details of the existence of two armoured trains during the short-lived fighting in the Basque Country. In August 1936, the Nationalist troops from Pamplona under General Beorlegui headed in the direction of Vera to capture Irún. A narrow-gauge train was quickly fitted with several steel plates, planks of wood and sandbags, and armed with machine guns. We know that it was in action on the 12, 15, 19, 20 and 26 August, before withdrawing into the town before it fell. In addition, there is some information concerning one or two armoured trains operating on the broad-gauge line to Oyarzun and Tolosa, used to transport ammunition and support troops with their machine guns.

[6.] UHP = *Unión de Hermanos Proletarios*, the Union of Proletariat Brothers; UGT = *Unión General de Trabajadores*, the General Workers Union; CNT = *Confederación Nacional del Trabajo*, National Working Confederation; AIT = *Asociación Internacional de los Trabajadores*, the International Workers Association.

2-6-0 Tank Engine *Zarauz*, armoured in a simple manner but with protection certainly proof against light weapons. Note the armoured blockhouse carried inside the high-sided wagon marked 'Bidasoa'. The markings painted on by the trade unions[6] are typical of armoured trains at the start of the Civil War. *(Photo: Paul Malmassari Collection)*

The armoured trains of Aragón

In his book *Diario de la guerra española* (Paris: Ruedo Ibérico, 1963, and Editorial Akal, 1978), the Russian journalist Mikhail Koltsov relates how on his arrival in Tardienta on 13 August 1936, he saw his first armoured train. At the end of that month, it went into action against the Nationalist forces which were attacking the village, but without tangible results. On 28 August 1936 an armoured train built by the workers of the firm Construcciones Devis, S.A. of Valencia appeared. It was made up of an engine and two armoured wagons. It left for Teruel and then disappears from the records. Then in December, several newspapers mentioned the existence of a 'Phantom Train' in the area of Aragon. But then a long period passed without any information on these trains, apart from a photograph taken by a member of the Lincoln Brigade (15th International Brigade in the Quinto Zone) showing a well-built armoured train. Finally in March 1938 the town fell, and the Nationalists discovered two abandoned wagons and a broken-down tank.

This train (perhaps the 'Phantom Train') was possibly employed near Barcelona. Note it still bears the initials of the trade unionist political organisations, which would soon be in conflict inside the Republican faction. Despite the poor quality of the photo we can clearly make out two wagons fitted with a turret in front of the coach.

(Photo: Puig Ferrán printed in La Vanguardia, Barcelona, No 22692 [5 December 1936], p 4 and also in La Gaceta del norte, Bilbao, No 12099 [30 December 1936], p 10 in the Hermeroteca Municipal de Madrid (HMM), via JMAM)

Right and above: Two photos taken on 13 August 1936 showing the armoured train built in Tardienta, in response to the advance of the Nationalist forces. The rustic construction of the armour protection is typical of the very first armoured trains, but the following trains would show astounding progress.

(2 Photos: Fundación Tierra y Libertad, via JMAM)

The armoured train built in the workshops of the Devis Company in Valencia, seen on the day it was presented to the press.

(Photo: Ahora (Madrid) No 1771 [ND] via JMAM)

The armoured trains of Talavera and the region to the south of Madrid

To the south of Madrid, three railway lines branched out towards Estremadura passing by way of Torrijos and Talavera de la Reina; towards Ciudad Real, and towards Cuenca by way of Aranjuez. One armoured train operated on each line. On 26 August 1936, in the face of the unstoppable advance of the rebel forces to the south-west, Armoured Train 'B' was transferred from the Sierra de Guadarrama line to Talavera de la Reina, a move given wide press coverage, and immediately entered Oropesa where it went into action for the first time. Meanwhile in Madrid, a series of armoured trains was being built, designated by a letter: we know of Armoured Trains 'H', 'I', 'J' and 'K', but there were several others which have not so far been identified.

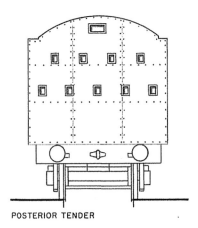

POSTERIOR TENDER

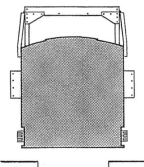

LATERAL

(TRACCION DEL TB "H")

SECCION

A view of Armoured Train 'H' in October 1936 near Toledo on the approach to Talavera Station. The artillery wagon is the six-axle bogie type.
(Photo: AGA)

Armoured Train 'H' with a different armoured engine, this time propelling an artillery wagon converted from a four-axle bogie well wagon.
(Photo: AGA)

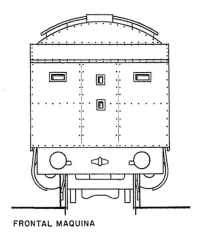

FRONTAL MAQUINA

A clear view of the front of the engine of Train 'H', with an armoured cab. The usual slogans and initials of the political parties and trade unions on the Republican side are clearly visible.

(Photo: AGA)

Technical drawing by Sr. Francisco Cruzado Albert.

LOCOMOTORA BLINDADA 240 Cia. OESTE (1936)   1/87

5 m.

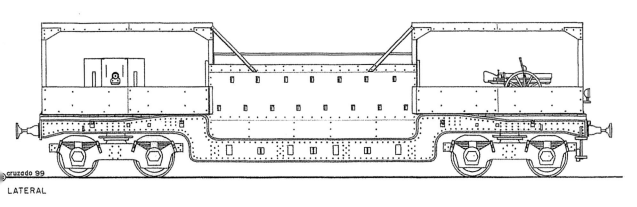

cruzado 99

LATERAL

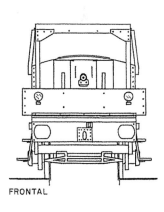

FRONTAL

Technical drawing by Sr. Francisco Cruzado Albert.

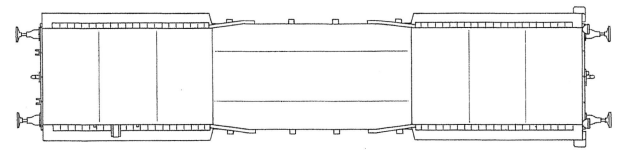

PLANTA

EN CABEZA TB "H")

VAGON BLINDADO DE ARTILLERIA (1936)   1/87

5 m.

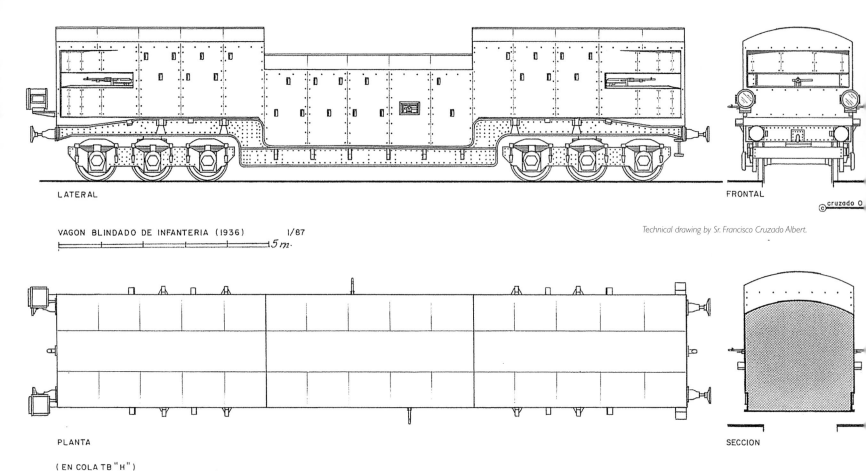

LATERAL

FRONTAL

©cruzado O

VAGON BLINDADO DE INFANTERIA (1936) 1/87

Technical drawing by Sr. Francisco Cruzado Albert.

5 m.

PLANTA

(EN COLA TB "H")

SECCION

The Republican forces lost control of Talavera de la Reina and pulled back towards Torrijos with the support of armoured trains which helped with the transport, made themselves useful, supported operations, but all in vain. When Toledo was captured in early November 1936, the line to Aranjuez was cut between Toledo and Algodor, then in November at Getafe when the Nationalists attacked Madrid, and finally to the south of Ciempozuelos during the Battle of the Jarama in February 1937, severely curtailing the actions of the train. On the other hand, the Algodor-La Flamenca-Aranjuez-Seseña line remained in the hands of the Republicans, and in that zone they had the use of two new armoured trains. The older armoured train, which was large and heavy, was replaced by two smaller, lighter trains which were more effective. Armoured Train No 10 (2nd Battalion, incorporated in III Army Corps) was stationed at the Farm of La Flamenca. Armoured Train No 11 (1st Battalion, incorporated in II Army Corps) was stationed at Aranjuez Racecourse. The high standards maintained in the Aranjuez workshops permitted these two trains to remain in good working order right up to the end of the war.

Armoured wagon captured at Griñón (to the south-west of Madrid) on 28 October 1936.

(Photo: Diniz Salgado, via JMAM)

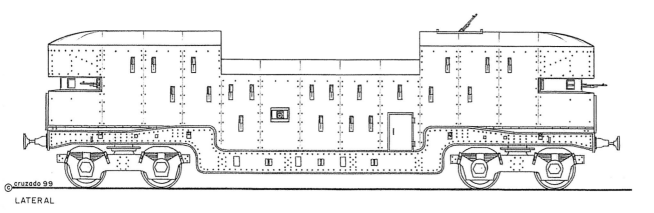

LATERAL

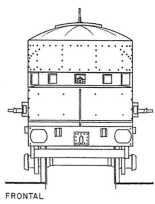

FRONTAL

© cruzado 99

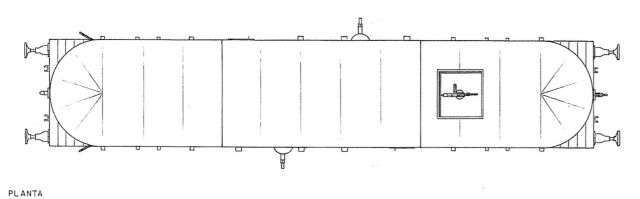

PLANTA

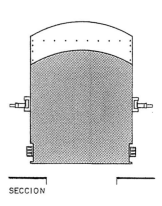

SECCION

Technical drawing by Sr. Francisco Cruzado Albert.

(EN CABEZA TB "K")

VAGON BLINDADO DE INFANTERIA (1936)   1/87

5 m.

A shot of one of the very first armoured trains of the Civil War, seen here at Aranjuez in October 1936. Note the impression of power and at the same time protection offered by the elaborate form of the armour, which however leaves the coupling rods of the engine exposed.
(Photo: AGA)

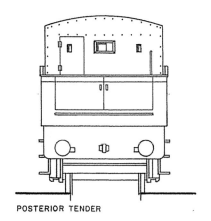

POSTERIOR TENDER

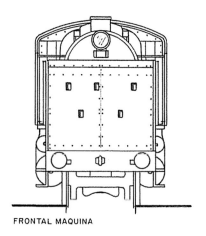

FRONTAL MAQUINA

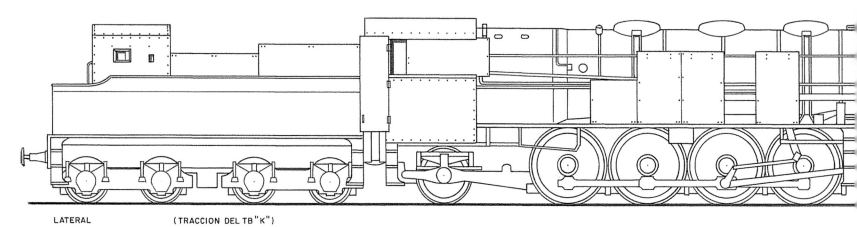

LATERAL   (TRACCION DEL TB "K")

Technical drawing by Sr. Francisco Cruzado Albert.

LOCOMOTORA PROTEGIDA

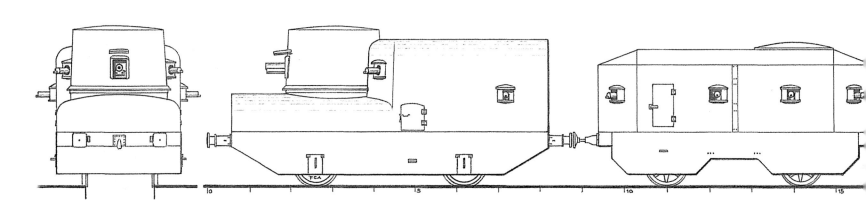

Tentative technical drawing by Sr. Francisco Cruzado Albert.

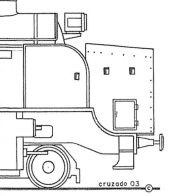

Cia. NORTE (1936)   1/87
5m.

Armoured Train No 10, or the Train of Aranjuez. Little information is available on this train, which had a quite modern appearance.
(Photo: Paul Malmassari Collection)

Armoured train employed in the Asturias.
(Photo: Ahora (Madrid) [14 April 1937], p 12 in the Hemeroteca Municipal de Madrid (HMM), via JMAM)

The trains of Oviedo[7]

When the Civil War began, almost the whole of the Asturias remained loyal to the Government, except for the capital and a corridor joining it to Galicia, which meant that Oviedo found itself in a state of siege for several months. In September 1936 a rudimentary armoured train was built by the workers in the La Algodonera workshop depot near Oviedo, to bolster resistance against Nationalist attacks, especially from 21 February 1937 onward. A second train was also built, to operate on the Vasco-Asturiano metre-gauge network. The two trains were in action around Oviedo on several occasions. In early 1937 a new metre-gauge train was built (or indeed it may have been a conversion of the broad-gauge train). In May, the two trains went into the workshops for repairs, and no further trace of them is recorded.

7. Capital of the Asturias.

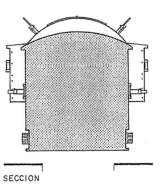

SECCION

The trains of Guadalajara

In July 1936, the railway militia were transported by train to occupy the town of Sigüenza (Guadalajara) and took up position there. Clashes with the rebels coming from Saragossa along the line of the railway began several days later. The siege (known as the battle of Sigüenza) lasted from 7 September to 15 October and ended with the surrender of the defenders. The armoured train from the Talavera line, which at the time was under repair in Madrid, was hurriedly put back in service due to the urgency of the situation, and tried to support the besieged forces. It succeeded in helping a number of militiamen to escape.

After the fall of Sigüenza, the front line moved towards Jadraque where Armoured Train 'B', a more modern and more powerful unit, with artillery platforms on six-axle bogie wagons, was stationed. After the Battle of Guadalajara, the Republican front line recoiled even further near Humanes. This front was subsequently patrolled by Armoured Trains 'E' and 'K'. In June 1937 these two trains were re-designated Armoured Trains No 9 and No 10 respectively. Finally, beginning in mid-1938 and up until the end of the war, only Armoured Train No 7 remained on this line, along with railcars, one of which was lightly armoured to undertake reconnaissance missions, as well as artillery platform wagons used for firing trials.

The trains at the siege of Madrid

In November 1936, the Nationalist forces arrived on the outskirts of Madrid, but despite the fact that they succeeded in creating a bridgehead in the University campus, they were unable to extend it,

Armoured Train 'B' in January 1937 at Jadraque. The three safety flat wagons at the front of the train can be clearly seen, and the high visibility of a moving armoured train is amply demonstrated. *(Photo: Narciso Julián via JMAM)*

and the front lines remained virtually unchanged up until the end of the war in April 1939. Armoured trains operated on the following lines departing from Madrid:

– on the line of the Norte towards Villalba, which was cut quite close to the capital at the Pont des Français on the River Manzaranes, an armoured train operated throughout the entire war (firstly Armoured Train No 4 then later No 6). The train distinguished itself in the fighting on 8 November, then in April 1937 during the fighting at Cerro Garabitas.
– on the Almorox metre-gauge line, an armoured train (No 12) operated between Goya Station and the suburb of Aluche. In 1937, the train was hit by friendly fire from Republican artillery and was put out of action.
– the lines from Andalusia and Estremadure were cut a short distance from the capital, but at least three armoured trains operated on them near the suburbs of Delicias and Villaverde.
– on the line from Valencia, also cut a short distance from the capital, one train was in action for the entire duration of the war.

All of these trains were kept in operational condition during the last two years of the war, but they were gradually taken out of service,

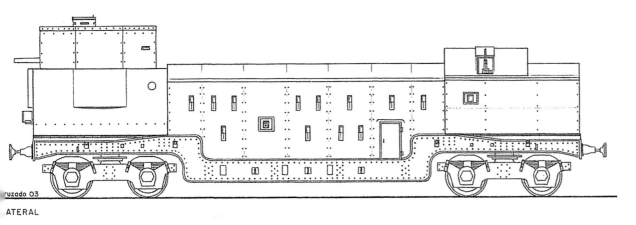
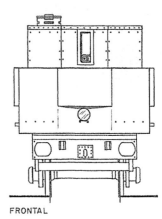

ATERAL

FRONTAL

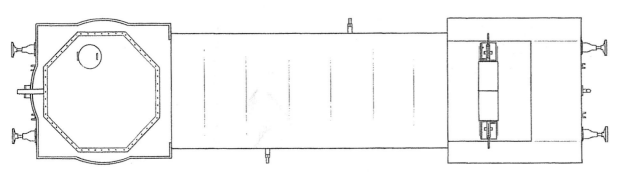

ANTA

Technical drawing by Sr. Francisco Cruzado Albert.

due principally to a lack of coal. Thus by February 1939 only a single unit of the Armoured Train Brigade remained in service, in the Northern Station.

The armoured trains of Andalusia and Estremadura

From Madrid, a railway line ran towards Cabeza de Buey and Almorchón, then two branches continued towards Badajoz and Cordoba. Because the lines in the south of Estremadura and those of the north-west of Andalusia were quite close together, armoured trains constantly moved from one front to the other. The study of these trains is therefore treated as if they ran in one single zone.

In 1936 and early 1937, we know that an armoured train was in action in Andalusia, but we have no details of its composition, just as for a train which arrived from Madrid in September 1936 and was in action on the Oropesa and Talavera de la Reina front.

In early 1937, two trains were armoured at Águilas (Murcia), using two diesel shunting locomotives and wagons built as lightly as possible (because of the limited power of the shunters[8]). Armoured Train No 7 was sent to Estremadura for the operation on the Tage in May 1937, and No 8 went to Andalusia. Shortly afterwards, they were employed paired with steam-hauled armoured trains.

Diesel shunter T.M. 2201.
(Photo: MTZ-Motortechnische Zeitschrift, Heft 12 [1942], p 489)

[8.] With a power output of only some 200hp.

An interesting shot of one of the two armoured diesel shunting locomotives (10011 and 10012, built in 1935) used on Armoured Trains Nos 7 and 8. Note the rails fixed to the roof to simulate a length of track when seen from the air. Carrying 27 tonnes of armour plate, this machine weighed a total of 57 tonnes, for an overall length of 7.30m (23ft 11½in).

Near Villanueva de la Serena, we also know of the actions of several special trains, on one of which members of the crew were trained for special operations such as the capture of prisoners – ideally officers to obtain intelligence from them. Nicknamed the 'Band of Crows' after their train, this unit was disbanded following unauthorised behaviour.

Another train was crewed by Catalan volunteers, controlled by the powerful 'National Railway Union' from the 9th (Barcelona) Zone. They conducted their own private war as they did not acknowledge the authority of the Armoured Trains Brigade. This situation was tolerated up until the end of 1937, when the Brigade Commander demanded that the command detachment of the train be relieved of duty and be replaced by an experienced team. The train thereafter became Armoured Train No 13Bis, and carried out its missions effectively.

The actions of the trains on the metre-gauge Peñarroya-Puertollano line deserve special attention and will be described later.

From the moment when Armoured Trains Nos 7 and 8 were sent to the Spanish Levant in mid-1938, up until the end of the war only Armoured Train No 3 stationed at Km Post 308.9 on the Madrid-Badajoz line, and Train No 4 stationed at Los Pedroches remained in the Andalusia /Estremadura Zone.

Armoured Trains No 7 and No 8 (Diesel)

By the end of 1936, the workshops had acquired a certain amount of experience with armouring steam engines, and their limitations had been recognised, such as the lack of range due to the amount of fuel and water which could be carried on board, and their high visibility due to the smoke and steam from their chimneys. Tests carried out with 40- or 60-horsepower shunters revealed that they would be incapable of supporting the weight of the armour. Studies were then made into the possible use of 200-horsepower shunters, of which two examples were available. In early January 1937 the 210hp diesel locomotive No 2201 was sent to Águilas (Murcia), for conversion in the central railway workshops of Lorca in Baza. There it received its armour, which was also fitted on two mineral wagons chosen to be the lightest and smallest capable of carrying the required loads. The result was a train of reduced dimensions but

Close-up of the safety chariot at the front of Armoured Train No 8 (Diesel), an arrangement which was unique in the history of armoured trains.

(Photo: Mi Revista, Barcelona [15 June 1937], HMM via JMAM)

Above: A rare profile shot of the complete Train No 8 (Diesel). Its well-designed layout in our opinion classes it among the most modern of its period. Note the armoured walkway between the two wagons.

(Photo: Mi Revista, Barcelona [15 June 1937], HMM via JMAM)

Below: The complete Armoured Train No 7 which sought refuge at La Tour de Carol in 1939. It would be interesting to know its ultimate fate: was it given back to Spain, as the different rail gauge prevented its use in France, or was it cut up for scrap?

(Photo: L'Illustration, [4 March 1939])

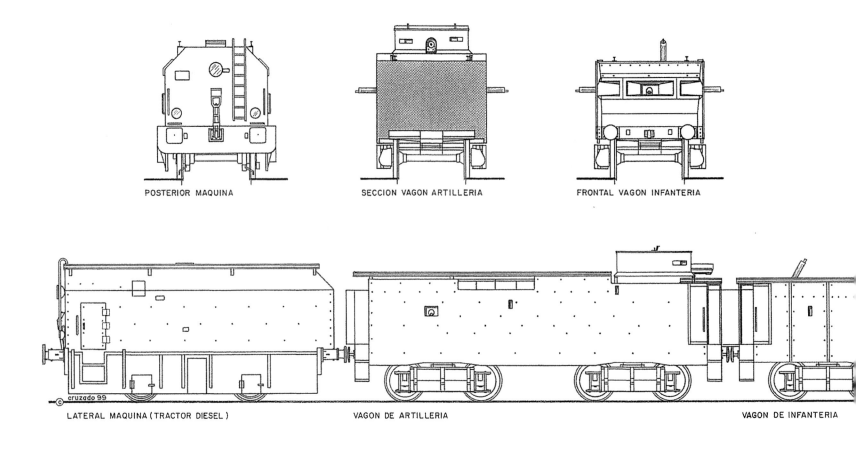

POSTERIOR MAQUINA   SECCION VAGON ARTILLERIA   FRONTAL VAGON INFANTERIA

LATERAL MAQUINA (TRACTOR DIESEL)   VAGON DE ARTILLERIA   VAGON DE INFANTERIA

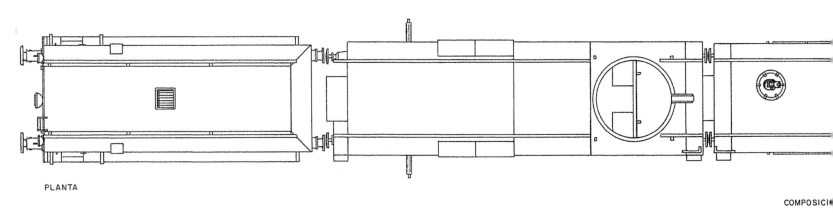

PLANTA

COMPOSICIÓ

Technical drawing by Sr. Francisco Cruzado Albert.

heavily armed, capable of immediate intervention in a threatened area as it could be started up in several minutes, compared to the several hours needed to start a steam train. Its crew consisted of a captain, two lieutenants, two drivers, twenty-four militiamen, six gunners, two radio operators, three optical signallers, a doctor, two cooks, an ordnance specialist and an armourer. It was given the number 8, and was placed under the orders of the Tank Brigade. As its conversion was being completed, a second diesel shunter was taken in hand for armouring, becoming the future Armoured Train No 7.

The projected armoured train on the Peñarroya-Puertollano line

The metre-gauge line known as 'Peñarroya to Puertollano' ran to the north of the province of Córdoba. The war had cut it in two, with 90km (55 miles) on the Nationalist side and 140km (88 miles) on the Republican side. In mid-1937, the town of Pozoblanco became the base of the Eighth Army. A year later, a scantily-protected train was built using 2-8-0 tank engine No 22 at the town station, to which was coupled a wagon protected with wood, the latter armed with machine guns protected with sandbags. Even though this train saw little use, apart from patrol duties, it gave birth to a more ambitious project.

Above: In this view, compared with the original design sketch used by the author, the armour of the engine is higher than that on the armoured wagon. As the turret was to have 360-degree traverse, it was therefore necessary to increase the height of the turret.
(1/72nd scale model by Paul Malmassari)

Below: Another view of the 1/72nd scale model built by the author, which was intended to copy as closely as possible the characteristic features of the design sketch. Building in three dimensions meant correcting the approximations of the flat drawing. This was at the limit of this type of reconstruction, but shows it to advantage.
(1/72nd scale model by Paul Malmassari)

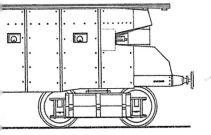

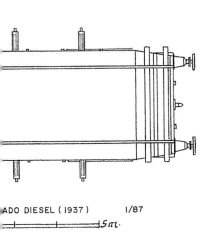

ADO DIESEL (1937)   1/87

5 m.

Captain A Cueto, a technician in the Armoured Trains Brigade, proposed the construction of a short train, of reduced dimensions but powerfully armed. Therefore engine No 22 would be completely covered by armour, formed of nickel-chrome plates 14mm thick on the exterior and 7mm on the interior, the 80mm space between the plates being filled with reinforced concrete. This armour would be inclined to increase the degree of protection. The engine would be coupled semi-rigidly to a short wagon, similarly armoured, designed to carry the main armament. The armour protection would weigh 7.4 tonnes for the engine and 11.15 tonnes for the artillery wagon. The armament was to be either a 70mm mountain gun or a 57mm naval gun. Two light machine guns were planned to be fitted at the front and the rear, and two 7.62mm heavy machine guns would be in ball mounts on the sides of the wagon. According to several eyewitnesses, this train was actually built and used up until the end of the war, but no surviving document produced by the Armoured Trains Brigade makes mention of it.

The armoured trains of the Spanish Levant

At the start of the Civil War several trains transferred militiamen from the Levantine areas to the Aragon front, and the action of the

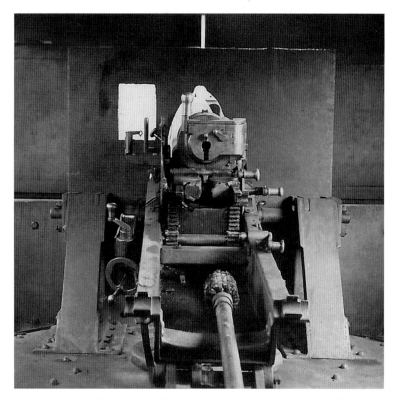

A photo taken inside Armoured Train No 8 when it was part of an exhibition of captured equipment in Valencia Station, on 5 May 1939.

(Photo: Eduardo Rubiales Rascón Collection, via Artemio Mortera)

armoured train built in Valencia has been already mentioned above in the paragraph dedicated to Aragon. Up until mid-1938, the region saw no military operations, apart from several air raids, but with the arrival of Nationalist troops at Vinaroz, the Republican zone had been cut in two, with Catalonia to the north and Valencia to the south.

During the conquest of Valencia, which began with a powerful Nationalist offensive on several fronts and notably in the Province of Castellón, at least three armoured trains were in action: Armoured Train No 1 from the Army of the Centre (Madrid), Armoured Train No 8 (diesel) from the Estremadura-Andalusia front, and Armoured Train No 12, which was the most powerful and the most modern, having been built in the Sagonte steelworks. Fighting took place on the Sagonte-Teruel line and on the Valencia-Sagonte-Tortosa line, the trains changing from one sector to the other depending on the operational situation. One of the hardest fights took place at Alcalá de Chivert where Train No 8 was derailed and remained under enemy fire for two days before it could be recovered. This front was the subject of propaganda articles in the press, which reported the destruction of several trains. However, the supporting photos always showed the charred remains of wooden wagons, and in one case an engine, and none showed an actual armoured train.

Armoured Train No 8 had first been allocated to the Almorchón-Córdoba line, but it also fought near Toledo in early May. Armoured Train No 7 then rejoined the zone which extended

as far as Peñarroya, La Granjuela and other peripheral zones where some hard fighting took place. In April 1938, Armoured Train No 8 rejoined the Valencia-Tarragona line and it was here, near Alcalá de Chivert that it was derailed as mentioned above. Armoured Train No 7 also intervened in that zone, including the battle of the Ebro where it was used to transport ammunition to the troops. The three armoured trains finished the war in this zone, Train No 7 withdrawing to the French frontier in early March 1939 (see the earlier photo taken at La Tour de Carol). Train No 8 remained in the province of Valencia after the bridge over the Ebro had been cut. Along with Train No 12 it was photographed in Valencia Station several days after the capitulation, in a display of captured enemy equipment.

Armoured Train No 12

By mid-1937 the Popular Army of the Republic had gained valuable experience in the employment of armoured trains, and had developed new designs such as the diesel trains. A new project was undertaken in the factory at Sagonte (Fábrica de Guerra Número 15) which was extremely advanced as regards its protection as well as in its overall concept. The armour was to be sloped to obtain the greatest possible protection without too great an increase in weight, and the steel chosen was of the best quality, with thicknesses varying from 20mm to 23mm on the turrets, to 7mm to 14mm on the side panels.

A precise description was written by Political Commissar Manuel Rodriguez Bastante. According to him this train carried four Skoda 76mm guns in single turrets, two Vickers 40mm pom-poms for anti-tank and anti-aircraft protection, behind armour 23mm thick, sixteen Maxim machine guns (made in Czechoslovakia) and a mortar at each end of the train. A command cupola was fitted between the engine and tender, with a modified submarine periscope. The crew was divided according to specialisations: a section of four groups of artillerymen, one section of mortar crews, two sections of machine-gunners and anti-aircraft gun crews, one section of infantry and one for repair work. These last two, armed with infantry weapons, would also form a ground assault unit.

The train came out of the factory on either 14 or 15 April 1938 and was to join the eastern front (Andalusia and Estremadura), but on the very same day the Nationalist forces cut communications between the Catalonia-Aragon region and the centre-south of Spain. The train therefore remained based at Sagonte, which was the junction of the two operational lines of the Centre-South Group of the Republican Army of the Levant: the Valencia-Barcelona line and the Valencia-Teruel line. As the line was cut at Vinaroz, the train went into action notably at Alcalá de Chivert, where its guns inflicted heavy losses on the Nationalist 4th 'Navarre' Brigade.

The construction of the train had been lengthy and difficult:

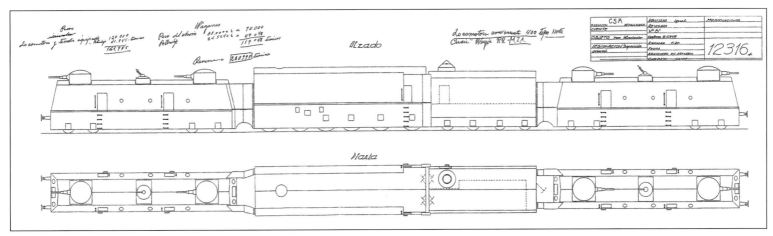

the initial plans are dated July 1937[9] and the train not was completed until April 1938. For example, the original Type 400 engine of the Norte had to be replaced by a *Garraf*; also, the long recoil of the Skoda guns prevented their installation in the turrets as designed, and they had to be reworked. Again, differences between engineers as regards the technical aspects and tactical requirements had delayed the design work. However, in the end the completed armoured train, 50m (164ft) long and weighing 300 tonnes, was a success, and its fighting capacity far exceeded that of previous trains.

The original design from 1937 for Armoured Train No 12, showing the small planned turrets. The complete train weighed around 300 tonnes, and the 4-8-0 engine No 2.074 of the Central Aragon Railway was capable of hauling it at up to 115km/h (72mph).
(Drawing via JMAM)

Right: One of the artillery wagons as built, with Skoda 80mm guns. Note how, compared with the original plan of 1937 shown above, the casemates carrying the turrets have been increased in width, because of the need to install larger turrets to cope with the guns' long recoil. Note also the inclined armour side walls.
(Photo: Eduardo Rubiales Rascón Collection, via Artemio Mortera)

The armoured engine of Train No 12 photographed in Valencia on 5 May 1939, during the display of captured Republican equipment. In the background is an artillery wagon, then elements of one of the diesel armoured trains, probably No 7.
(Photo: Eduardo Rubiales Rascón Collection, via Artemio Mortera)

9. It is interesting to note that the French Military Attaché in Spain reported on the construction of this train in July 1937, and considered 'its form to be well-designed', but the armour protection failed badly: during trials the plates had resisted 20mm to 37mm shells fired at them, but shells from field guns 'shattered them like glass'. Lastly, he mentioned a French engineer as having participated in the design of the train, without naming him, but the Spanish archives give his name as a certain M. Lempereur (Letter by Colonel Morel No 502/A of 7 July 1937, 7 N 2755, SHD). In general, the Attaché considered the war as he observed it to be incomprehensible, for example because of the negligence of the belligerents in not destroying the tracks.

The armoured trains of Catalonia

Several armoured trains built in the workshops of *La Maquinista Terrestre y Maritima* at San Andrés had operated in support of the anarchist columns which left Barcelona for Aragon and Estremadura during the initial months of the Civil War. At some date between late 1937 and early 1938 the construction of at least three more armoured trains had begun in the same workshops, intended to equip the Catalan Army (Catalonia, having declared its independence, had formed its own government and army). The known photographs of these trains, taken in or outside the workshops, shown semi-artistic flowing forms, with novel technical features such as periscopes or weapons in ball mounts. However, these trains never became part of the Armoured Trains Brigade, and in fact it is not certain whether any were used in combat, since no photo showing a complete train or one at the front has come to light.

We do know that Armoured Train No 7 (Diesel) arrived to support the troops on the Ebro (between July and November 1938) before withdrawing to seek refuge at La Tour de Carol in France at the time Catalonia fell to the Nationalists.

An armoured train photographed during the battle of the Ebro. Note what appears to be an armoured cupola on a four-wheel flat wagon in front of the steam engine, then a wagon with a turret resembling that of the 'Phantom Train' shown earlier. The engine is a 4-8-0 of the 1400 Series, from the MZA Company.
(Photo: All Rights Reserved)

Seen here in January 1938, this type of armoured wagon built in Barcelona seems to be the only design to have two cylindrical gun tubs. Note it carries a different style of camouflage to the two in the preceding photo, more akin to the 'speckled' scheme seen on engine No 4.069 in the following shots, and its machine-gun ball mounts are also the same type. Note how the vertical sides curve inwards at the ends to increase the machine guns' field of fire.
(Photo: Mi Revista, Barcelona, No 30, p 78 via JMAM)

Note the extremely elaborate camouflage scheme which effectively breaks up the outlines of the artillery wagons. In this photo we can see lower and upper rows of firing loopholes plus the machine-gun ball mount.
(Photo: All Rights Reserved)

Two views of engine 4.029 of the Norte Company, photographed in the workshops of La Maquinista Terrestre y Maritima in Barcelona.
(Photo: Luis del Valle Mendiburo, via Francisco Cruzado Albert)

The camouflage scheme is highly elaborate. Note the well-finished rounded corners of the forward casemate which are evidence of a sophisticated industrial capability, together with the machine-gun ball mounts, each one paired with a sighting/observation aperture to its right

(Photo: Luis del Valle Mendiburo, via Francisco Cruzado Albert)

The tender fitted with a machine-gun turret as well as the installation of a machine-gun casemate at the front of certain engines are characteristic features of the trains of the Spanish Civil War.

(Photo: Luis del Valle Mendiburo, via Francisco Cruzado Albert)

The Republican armoured trains as objects of propaganda

In the propaganda field, the following song was one of the success stories of the Spanish Civil War:

Translation:

El Treno Blindado	**The Armoured Train**
Yo me subí a un pino verde	I climbed a green pine tree
Por ver si Franco llegaba	To see if Franco was coming
Y sólo vi un tren blindado	And I only saw an armoured train
Lo bien que tiroteaba.	Its machine guns firing
Anda jaleo, jaleo, jaleo,	Anda fuss, fuss, fuss
Silba la locomotora	Whistled the engine
Y Franco se va a paseo	And Franco went away
Y Franco se va a paseo.	And Franco went away
Por tierras altas de Burgos	On the high ground of Burgos
Anda Mola sublevado,	Away went Mola angry
Ya veremos cómo corre	We clearly saw how he ran
Cuando llegue el tren blindado.	When came the armoured train
Anda jaleo, jaleo, jaleo,	Anda fuss, fuss, fuss
Silba la locomotora	Whistled the engine
Y Mola se va a paseo	And Mola went away
Y Mola se va a paseo.	And Mola went away
Yo me fui en el tren blindado	I went in the armoured train
Camino de Andalucía	On the way to Andalusia
Y vi que Queipo de Llano	And I saw how Queipo de Llano
Al verlo retrocedía	At the sight of it ran away.
Anda jaleo, jaleo, jaleo,	Anda fuss, fuss, fuss
Silba la locomotora	Whistled the engine
Y Queipo se va a paseo	And Queipo went away
Y Queipo se va a paseo.	And Queipo went away

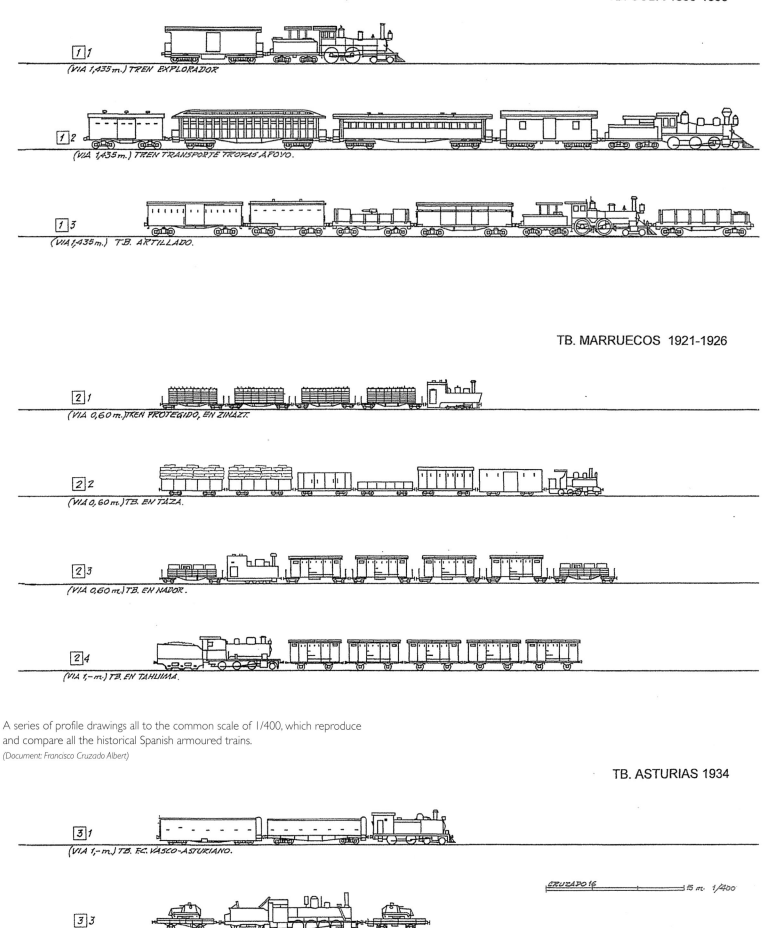

TB. CUBA 1895-1898

1 1 (VIA 1,435 m.) TREN EXPLORADOR

1 2 (VIA 1,435 m.) TREN TRANSPORTE TROPAS APOYO.

1 3 (VIA 1,435 m.) T.B. ARTILLADO.

TB. MARRUECOS 1921-1926

2 1 (VIA 0,60 m.) TREN PROTEGIDO, EN ZINAZT.

2 2 (VIA 0,60 m.) T.B. EN TAZA.

2 3 (VIA 0,60 m.) T.B. EN NADOR.

2 4 (VIA 1,- m.) T.B. EN TAHUIMA.

A series of profile drawings all to the common scale of 1/400, which reproduce
and compare all the historical Spanish armoured trains.
(Document: Francisco Cruzado Albert)

TB. ASTURIAS 1934

3 1 (VIA 1,- m.) T.B. F.C. VASCO-ASTURIANO.

CRUZADO 16 _____ 5 m. 1/400

3 3 (VIA 1,672 m.) TREN ARMADO F.C.NORTE.

TB. GUERRA CIVIL 1936-1939

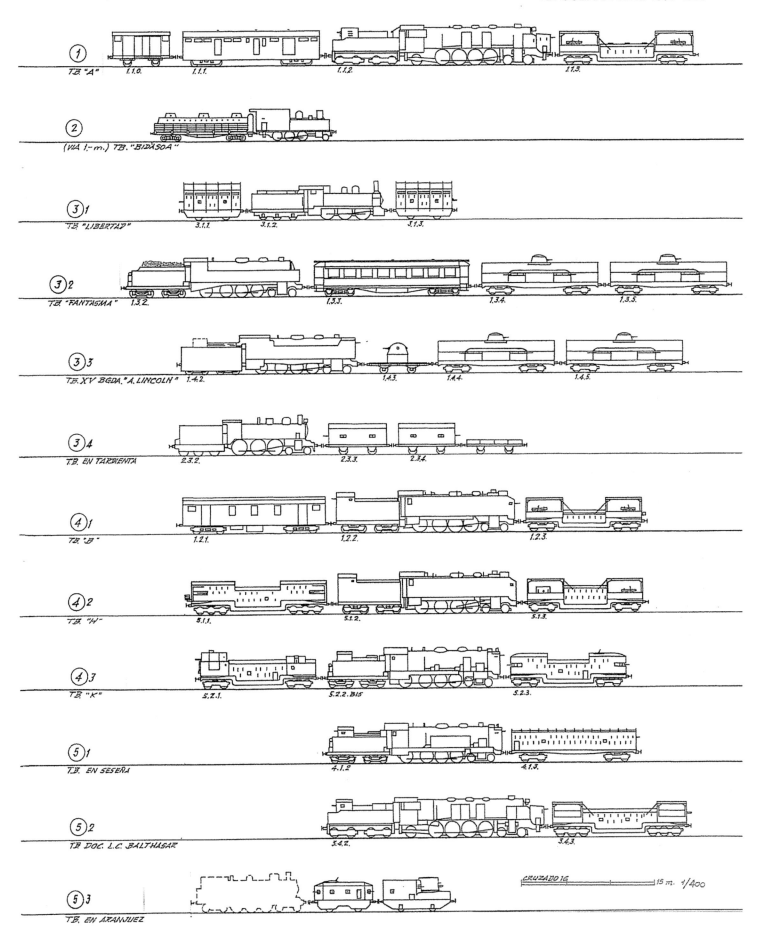

1   TB. "A"   1.1.0.   1.1.1.   1.1.2.   1.1.3.

2   (VIA 1-m.) TB. "BIDASOA"

3 1   TB. "LIBERTAD"   3.1.1.   3.1.2.   3.1.3.

3 2   TB. "FANTASMA"   1.3.2.   1.3.3.   1.3.4.   1.3.5.

3 3   TB. XV BGDA. "A. LINCOLN"   1.4.2.   1.4.3.   1.4.4.   1.4.5.

3 4   TB. EN TARDIENTA   2.3.2.   2.3.3.   2.3.4.

4 1   TB. "B"   1.2.1.   1.2.2.   1.2.3.

4 2   TB. "H"   5.1.1.   5.1.2.   5.1.3.

4 3   TB. "K"   5.2.1.   5.2.2.BIS   5.2.3.

5 1   TB. EN SESEÑA   4.1.2   4.1.3.

5 2   TB. DOC. L.C. BALTHASAR   3.4.2.   3.4.3.

5 3   TB. EN ARANJUEZ   CRUZADO 1G   15 m. 1/400

TB. GUERRA CIVIL 1936-1939

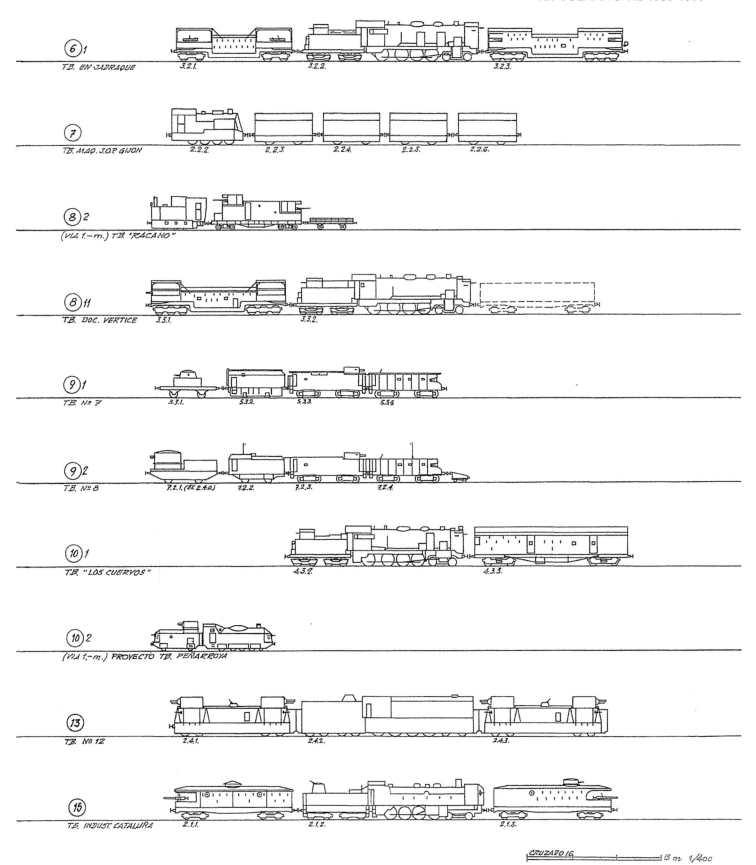

6 1
TB. EN JADRAQUE   3.2.1.   3.2.2.   3.2.3.

7
TB. MAQ. J.O.P GIJON   2.2.2.   2.2.3.   2.2.4.   2.2.5.   2.2.6.

8 2
(VIA 1.-m.) TB. "RACANO"

8 11
TB. DOC. VERTICE   3.3.1.   3.3.2.

9 1
TB. Nº 7   5.3.1.   5.3.2.   5.3.3.   5.3.4.

9 2
TB. Nº 8   7.2.1.(EX 2.4.0.)   7.2.2.   7.2.3.   7.2.4.

10 1
TB. "LOS CUERVOS"   4.3.2.   4.3.3.

10 2
(VIA 1.-m.) PROYECTO TB. PEÑARROYA

13
TB. Nº 12   2.4.1.   2.4.2.   2.4.3.

15
TB. INDUST. CATALUÑA   2.1.1.   2.1.2.   2.1.3.

CRUZADO 16   15 m. 1/400

SOURCES:

Archives:

Archivio General Militar de Madrid (AGMM), Madrid, Spain.
Archivio General de la Administración (AGA), Alcalá de Henares, Madrid, Spain.
Hemeroteca Municipal de Madrid (HMM), Madrid, Spain.
SHD, 7 N 2755-EMA/2ème bureau.

Books:

Arévalo Molina, Jacinto M, *Los Trenes Blindados Españoles* (Gijón: Ediciones Trea, S.L., 2003).
Cruzado Albert, Francisco, *Carros de combate y vehículos blindados de la guerra 1936-1939* (Barcelona: Borrás ediciones, 1980).
Fernandez Sanz, Fernando, and Reder, Gustavo, *Historia de la tracción vapor en España. Tomo VI, 1936-1941* (Madrid: Proyectos Editoriales S.L, 2014).
Kondratenko, R V, *Ispanso-Amerikanskaya Voína 1898 Goda* (St Petersburg: Tsitadel 2000).
Mortera Pérez, Artemio, *Los Carros de combate 'TRUBIA' (1925-1939)* (Valladolid: Quirón Ediciones, 1994).
Taylor, Thomás L, *Los Ferrocarriles en la Guerra* (Barcelona: Administración de la revista científico-militar, 1885).

Journal articles:

Afán Alcáraz, Juan, 'Trenes Blindados en la Guerra Civil', *Carril* No 14 (December 1985), pp 23–7.

Arévalo Molina, Jacinto M, 'El tren que nunca existió', *Revista Española de Historia Militar* (September 2001), pp 109–11.
_____, 'La Brigada de Trenes blindados 1936-1939', *Memorial del Arma de Ingenieros* (December 2000), pp 99–110.
_____, 'Los Ferrocarriles militares en la guerra de Cuba', *Memorial del Arma de Ingenieros* (June 1999), pp 139–45.
_____, 'Los Trenes blindados en la Guerra Civil Española', *Revista de Historia Militar* No 88 (2000), pp 181–206.
Cruzado Albert, Francisco, 'España: Guerra Civil 1936/1939', *Hobby Tren* No especial 150 (April 2006), pp 58–67.
_____, 'Tren Blindado, España: Guerra Civil 1936/1939 (I)', *Hobby Tren* No 169, (November 2007), pp 66–75.
_____, 'Tren Blindado, España: Guerra Civil 1936/1939 (II)', *Hobby Tren* No 170 (December 2007), pp 44–53.
_____, 'Trenes Blindados', *Trenmania* No 7 (2001), pp 57–66.
Surlemont, Raymond, 'Republican Armoured Trains in the Spanish Civil War 1936-1939', *Tank TV* No 6, (June 1994), pp 5–7.

Sound recordings (partial list):

CNT. FAI. 1936. The Spanish Revolution, by The Ex, AK Press, San Francisco, 1997 (2 CDs).
Chants de la Guerre d'Espagne, Le Chant du Monde, ref. LDX-S 4279, 1963 (vinyl).
España en el Corazón, Bear Family Records GmbH, 2014 (CD + DVD).

SWEDEN

ARMOURED TRAINS AND TROLLEYS 1905–1960

The Crisis of the Union (1905)

As a consequence of the crisis of the Union[1] in 1905, which obliged Sweden to take steps to defend its new frontier to the south-west with Norway, the railway network took on a new strategic importance. The task of guarding the line was given to the Wärmland frontier detachment under the command of Major Arvid Wester, who had served as an observer during the Boer War and who was therefore well aware of the capabilities of armoured trains. In addition to the fortifications he had built in the region of Eda and also Charlottenberg, he decided to construct an armoured wagon to provide a means of mobile defence. An old wagon from Göteborg was sent to Charlottenberg where it was fitted with 8mm-thick plates and armed with a Hotchkiss Model 1897 machine gun (known in Sweden as the ksp:/1900). It appears that neither this wagon nor any subsequent units actually entered service.

This view could depict the armour being either fitted or removed (but in our opinion probably the latter), showing the wooden planking at one end. The large number of fixation holes for the plates would indicate that they were hurriedly adapted from boiler plate or constructional panels.

(Photo: Sveriges Järnvägs Museum)

The 1905 armoured wagon as built.

(Photo: All Rights Reserved)

'Landsverk 320' Armoured Trolley[2]

In 1931 the firm of Landsverk carried out a design study of an armoured rail trolley intended for reconnaissance and for guarding railway infrastructure such as bridges. Its main armament was to comprise a 20mm cannon and coaxial machine gun in each of two turrets. The description specified that the armament disposition allowed for end-on fire by three machine guns and a cannon, and lateral fire by both cannon plus five machine guns and small arms per side. The trolley design was symmetrical, and it was to be driven from the central armoured cupola where the vehicle commander/driver sat on a pivoting seat. In addition, it was proposed to attach anti-aircraft armament on top of the turrets. This design was offered to Ireland, but seems not to have been proceeded with.

[1.] The Union between Norway and Sweden was concluded on 4 November 1814. Sweden had forced Norway into a personal union with a common monarch and foreign policy, but the Norwegians resented the breakup of their previous union with Denmark which had lasted for 434 years. Disagreements between the two countries, notably over Norway's demand for separate consular services to oversee its large merchant marine, increased to the point where a plebiscite in August 1905 formally recognised that the Union had ceased to exist.

[2.] In Swedish, *Pansar-Dressin*.

Technical specifications:	
Gauge	1435mm (4ft 8½in)
Wheel diameter	0.7m (2ft 3⅓in)
Overall length	6.20m (20ft 4in)
Hull width	2.025m (6ft 7¾in)
Overall width	2.30m (7ft 6½in)

Wheelbase	2.80m (9ft 2⅛in)
Armament height	Swivelling MGs 2m (6ft 6¾in)
	20mm cannon & coaxial MGs 2.5m (8ft 2½in)
Overall height	3.05m (10ft)
Weight in working order	13.2 tonnes
Motor	6-cylinder 60/70hp at 1200/1400 rpm
	Electric starter
Range	800km (500 miles)
Gearbox	1st = 10.5km/h (6.5mph)
	2nd = 20.5km/h (12.7mph)
	3rd = 30.5km/h (19mph)
	4th = 50km/h (31mph)
Minimum track radius	65m (213ft 3in)
Armour protection	Sides and ends, turrets: 14mm
	Command cupola, access doors, cowcatchers: 10mm
	Roof: 6mm

Armoured Trains *Boden* and *Kiruna*

In 1940, General Douglas, commanding officer of the Great North Army Group, decided to build four armoured trains: *Kiruna*, *Boden*, *Malmö* and *Österlund*, all bearing the name of their home base, but the last two would not see the light of day. *Kiruna* was built in the workshops of the LKAB Mining Company, using two Type Or flat wagons. The armour protection was 15mm thick (5mm for the roofs). The wagons of *Boden*, built in the SJ workshops in Notviken, were of a quite different design. This train had three open-topped armoured wagons, with the anti-aircraft wagon being placed immediately in front of the engine. For both trains, the engines chosen were 2-6-4 types of Class J, partially armoured. *Kiruna* was completed on 20 May 1940 and *Boden* the following month.

Kiruna patrolled the Kiruna-Narvik mineral line and *Boden* the Boden-Haparanda line. There is very little surviving information on the actions of these trains, apart from 20 May 1940 when *Kiruna*, in Vassijaure Station 7km (4.3 miles) from Narvik, and an anti-aircraft battery exchanged fire with a German aircraft.[3] In the course of this action a Swedish soldier by the name of Sven Sjöberg was killed. In 1945 the two trains were demobilised, but they were maintained in reserve up until 1949, before being scrapped in around 1960.

[3.] Certain sources mention a Dornier Do 26, a four-engined flying boat armed with a 20mm cannon in a nose turret and several machine guns. Both the V1 and the V2 were operating in the Narvik area up to their destruction on 28 May 1940 by RAF Hurricanes.

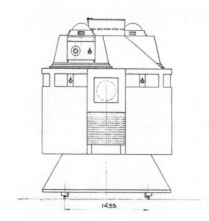

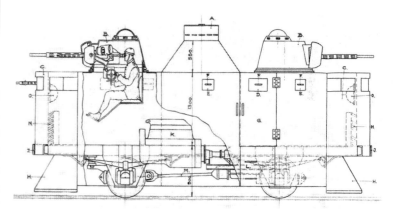

The domes on the turrets had vision slits and the lateral loopholes allowed the use of personal weapons as well as one machine gun per side. The siting of the entry doors beside the offset turrets would appear to make for difficult access given the position of the gunner's seat, but this arrangement would permit the swivelling of the lateral machine gun on the opposite side.
(Landsverk drawing: Paul Malmassari Collection)

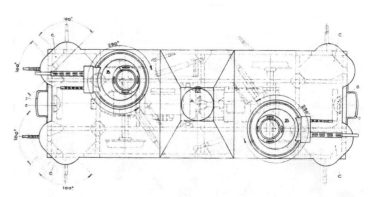

The central cupola was equipped with an emergency escape hatch. Note the horizontal fields of fire: 290 degrees for the turrets; 180 degrees for the corner casemates (by dismounting and repositioning the MGs); 90 degrees for the side-mounted MGs.

Crew member armed with an m/37-39 sub-machine gun, made by Husqvarna and modified to fire the 9x19mm Parabellum round.
(Photo: Sveriges Järnvägs Museum)

The importance given to these armoured trains can be gauged by the fact that in 1939 there were only twenty 57mm guns in service in the whole of Sweden.
(Photo: Sveriges Järnvägs Museum)

The 57mm gun on *Boden* had a restricted firing embrasure allowing limited traverse and even less elevation. It had a range of 4000m (4375 yards).
(Photo: Sveriges Järnvägs Museum)

The engine of *Boden* was Class J No 1390, with armour protecting only the coupling rods and the cab. The three wagons were built by placing armoured hulls on Type Mas 6-wheel flat wagons.
(Photo: Sveriges Järnvägs Museum)

Right: The twin-handed 8mm Kulspruta m/36 Lv Dbl anti-aircraft machine guns on *Boden*. Note the fixed radio antenna behind the gun position.
(Photos: Sveriges Järnvägs Museum)

A fine profile shot of *Kiruna*, showing the anti-aircraft mounting on the roof of the rear wagon. The engine is partially-armoured Class J No 1343.
(Photo: F.M.W.)

The 37mm gun which armed the leading wagon had a practical range of 4000m (4375 yards).

(Photo: Sveriges Järnvägs Museum)

In this shot the 37mm Bofors has not been mounted. Because the gun was offset to the left to allow space for the machine gun mounted in the front right corner embrasure to swivel, there was no room available for a corner embrasure on the front left. The armoured wagons were constructed using Type Or flat wagons.

(Photo: Sveriges Järnvägs Museum)

Kiruna at Riksgränsen[4] in 1941. Note the lack of lamps and also of cowcatchers beneath the buffer beam of the front wagon. The gun is the 37mm *pansarvärn-skanon* m/38 (or m/37), and its barrel is closely enveloped by the two sliding shutters when these are closed.

(Photo: Sveriges Järnvägs Museum)

SOURCES:

Berggren, Jan-Gunnar, 'Pansartåg, järnvägsartilleri och järn-vägsluftvärn', *Militärhistorisk Tidskrift* (2004), pp 111–59 (translated by Captain Valérie Cagnard).

Furugård, Bo, 'Pansartåget Kiruna', in Hultstrand, Birger, *Kungl. Norrbottens regementes historia 1841-1966* (Boden: Kungl. Norrbottens regementes kamratfören, 1972), pp 359–65.

'Pansansartagen Kiruna och Boden', *Pansar* (1983/4), pp 16–19.

4. A town on the frontier with Norway, and 40km (25 miles) to the east of Narvik.

SWITZERLAND

To the best of our knowledge, Switzerland has never employed armoured trains. On the other hand, a work dealing with the employment in Switzerland of railways for troop transportation and other military operations, inspired by the American Civil War and published in Basle in 1868, outlined proposals for the use of locomotives running light for reconnaissance missions by officers, and for wagons fitted with armour protection. The carriage of an assault team was also envisaged, for ground combat in the case of the train meeting a serious obstacle.

Analogous to the use of guns mounted in armoured trains to provide mobile firepower, we need to record the two platform wagons used at Fort Dailly between 1884 and the end of the Second World War. Running on rails in a cutting, the guns were on disappearing mountings, being reloaded beneath the armoured roof, rising in order to fire and retracting under recoil. When not in action they were housed in a tunnel with armoured doors.

SOURCES:

De Montet, Lt Col Jean, *Les Bouches à Feu de l'Artillerie Suisse 1919-1939* (Lausanne: Editions du Centre d'Histoire, 1980). Hoffmann-Merian, Theodor, *Die Eisenbahnen zum Truppen-Transport und für den Krieg im Hinblick auf die Schweiz* (Basle: Schweighauser, 1868).

The two disappearing mountings on a track at Fort Dailly, Emplacement E3. The guns were 12cm/L25 Krupp Model 1882s on Saint-Chamond coast-defence disappearing mountings. One gun and its mounting, without the wagon, is on display at the entrance to the fort.
(Photo: Heer Kommando Festungswachtkorps, FWK Region 2)

THAILAND

Sulzer 450hp A1A-A1A locomotives, used in Siam from 1931 to the 1990s, were fitted with armour-plated cabs, possibly as early as the Second World War. From 1960 Thailand suffered continuous threats to its security, fomented by Communists, some being militants fleeing Malaysia and others being opponents of the Vietnam War, as between 1965 and 1975

Thailand was a base for the US Air Force. Several Wickham trolleys were obtained from Malaysia. The state of insecurity continued until just before the date of writing, notably in the South, with few details being released. Three armoured trolleys survive, No 50 at Thung Song, and two others in Bangkok at Bang Sue and Hua Lamphong.

A view of an armoured wagon preceded by a flat wagon loaded with a Vickers 6-Ton Mark E Type B tank, armed with a 47mm gun and a coaxial machine gun to the right of the main gun. Siam (renamed Thailand from 1939) possessed eighteen of these tanks prior to the Japanese invasion.
(Photo: All Rights Reserved)

Before restoration, Wickham No 50 at the loco depot of Yhung Song, seen from the right-hand side.
(Photo: All Rights Reserved)

On this trolley seen from the front (with the driving position on the right), the .50 Cal machine gun is still in place, and there is a warning horn on the right-hand side of the turret.
(Photo: All Rights Reserved)

Several restorations later, and fitted with a fake gun, it has finally benefitted from a livery in Thai national colours,[1] which detracts somewhat from its martial appearance.
(Photo: All Rights Reserved)

A trolley in a sorry state in Bang Sue Station (Bangkok).
(Photo: All Rights Reserved)

[1.] The red symbolises the earth and the people, the white the religions and the blue the monarchy.

TUNISIA

With the rise of nationalism, a 'Battle of the Rails'[1] began in 1952, but it turned out to be less serious than the attacks on the railway network in Algeria. The first incident took place on 21 January when a section of rail was unbolted, resulting in traffic being held up for five days. From April 1952, the role of guarding the tracks was confined to 'security groups', but from May onward the running of trains at night was stopped. This measure continued up until July 1953 for freight trains and until January 1954 for passenger trains. In addition, armour protection was added to the motor units.

Following the war of independence, certain elements in Tunisia who supported the FLN in Algeria remained hostile to the continued French presence. On at least one occasion this anti-French sentiment led to the use of armed rail wagons.

In 1961 Air Base No 156 at Sidi-Ahmed was due to receive Mystère IV fighters to replace its force of Mistral fighter-bombers. From 13 June, threats to the security of the base increased to the point where, on the evening of 19 June, the 2nd RPIMa (Marine Infantry Parachute Regiment) dropped onto the base, which by then was surrounded and under fire from Tunisian artillery. The Tunis-Bizerte railway line which ran alongside the base allowed the Tunisians to install mortars in rail wagons. In the course of this operation, enemy fire caused a number of casualties, with two men killed and twenty-three wounded, and hit or destroyed five Noratlas transports.

SOURCES:

Bucher, Antoine, 'Mémoire des évènements de Bizerte vécus au sein de la compagnie de défense CD30 de la base de Sidi-Ahmed', *La Charte* No 7 (November 1998), pp 21–2.

Patrick-Charles, Renaud, *La bataille de Bizerte (Tunisie)* (Paris: Harmattan, 2011), p 20.

Railwaymen extend the bodyline red band around the frontal armour added to one of the seventeen Alsthom/Sulzer BB diesel-electric locomotives of the 'Overseas' type belonging to the Gafsa[2] Phosphate & Railway Company in May 1953. The locomotives were numbered 201 to 217.
United Press Photo: Paul Malmassari Collection)

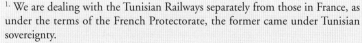

[1.] We are dealing with the Tunisian Railways separately from those in France, as under the terms of the French Protectorate, the former came under Tunisian sovereignty.

[2.] More commonly known as the Sfax-Gafsa line, abbreviated to S.G.

UKRAINE

ARMOURED TRAINS

The history of the Ukraine is complex, and requires a brief introduction in order to be able to understand the tortuous story of its armoured trains.

The territory of the Ukraine was fought over first by Germany and Austria-Hungary, then by the nations and various factions which were born or profited from the dismantling of the Russian and Austro-Hungarian Empires: Poland, Romania, Bolshevik Russia, Red Ukrainians, Nationalist Ukrainians, the White Russians, the Anarchist Black Army of Makhno, independent Cossacks and assorted atamans (warlords).

The Ukraine (less Galicia and the Crimea) declared its independence on 1 November 1917, while the Bolsheviks created their own republic in the east of the country, as did other local power groups. On 22 January 1918 the Rada (Ukrainian Parliament), under pressure from the Reds and the Black Anarchists under Makhno, was forced to leave Kiev. In addition, territorial claims based on the presence of large ethnic minorities led Romania to seize first Bessarabia then Bucovina in January 1918.

Following the capture of Kiev by the Germans on 1 March 1918, three different states coexisted: a Bolshevik government under Christian Rakowski, centred on Kharkov; a Popular Ukrainian Republic (Ukraine of the Dnieper) controlled by the warlord Symon Petlioura; and then from 1 November 1918 a Popular Republic of Western Ukraine with its capital at Lvov headed by Jevhen Petrouchevitch.

Conscription was introduced on 13 November 1918 to establish the Western Ukraine Army,[1] in order to counter the Polish separatists in Lvov. In December 1918 an Allied force under French command landed on the shores of the Black Sea to counter Bolshevik progress. But in 1919, part of the Carpathians was given to Czechoslovakia, and on 14 February 1919 Galicia was made a part of Poland. By late 1919, the Ukraine, with the exception of the Crimea, was in the hands of the Bolsheviks. In February 1920, part of the Western Ukrainian Army was incorporated by force into the Red Army[2] and became the Ukrainian Red Army of Galicia. In April 1920 two of its brigades surrendered to the Poles when Poland and the Ukraine signed a treaty to drive out the Bolsheviks. However, the Ukrainian forces were beaten in November 1921 and Poland signed a separate treaty with the Bolshevik Party of the Ukraine. Reduced to guerrilla operations only, the remaining Ukrainian forces were crushed by Bolshevik cavalry on 17 November 1921.

Armoured trains continue to play a major role in Ukrainian folklore. In September 2013, a tramcar was converted into a replica armoured train in honour of the train *Za Batkivshchnynu* ('For the Mother Country') which saw combat in July 1942.

Armoured Trains of the Ukrainian Army of Halych (UHA) or the Ukrainian Army of Galicia

During the First World War, Galicia was the scene of bitter fighting between Russia and the Central Powers. After having beaten the Austro-Hungarians in 1914, the Russians took over most of the region, but they were chased out by an Austro-German offensive between the Spring and Summer of 1915.

Fighting between Poles and Ukrainians started up again on the night of 31 October/1 November 1918 with attacks on Lvov by the Sich Riflemen and other units. In 1918 the western part of Galicia was incorporated in the new state of Poland which also absorbed the short-lived Ruthenian National Republic of the Lemkos.[3] The Treaty of Riga signed on 18 March 1921 assigned Galicia to Poland.

The Galician railways used rolling stock left behind by the former German and Austro-Hungarian occupying forces to form their armoured trains. Many improvised trains were built in the industrial centres such as the Drohobycz Refinery or the railway workshops at Sambor. All the armoured trains of the UHA were captured by the Poles. The River Zbrucz[4] marked the limit of the standard gauge, after which the Russian broad gauge applied, which prevented the Ukrainian armoured trains from retreating across the river with the rest of the army.

[1.] Also known as the Ukrainian Army of Galicia – *Ukrayins'ka Halyts'ka Armiya* (UHA). It was the regular army of the Western Ukrainian National Republic – *Zakhidnoukrayins'ka Narodna Respublyka* (ZUNR). This army existed during and after the Polish-Ukrainian War.
[2.] It should also be noted that a Red armoured train named *Ukrainski Revolutsija* ('Ukrainian Revolution') was captured by the Finns near Antrea in late March 1918. This was obviously an honorific designation, as neither the train nor its crew had any connection with the Ukrainian Front.
[3.] 5 December 1918 – 23 January 1919.
[4.] Tributary of the Dniestr, in the western part of modern Ukraine, which marked the frontier between the former Austro-Hungarian and Russian Empires.

Armoured Train No 1 of III Corps of the UHA, near Lvov in December 1918.

(Woodcut: Alexander Diedyk Collection via Krzysztof Margasinski)

Austro-Hungarian wagon of an improvised armoured train of the UHA. This photo is of poor quality but interesting as it shows the exact moment of firing: the barrel of the 76.2mm field gun is seen at maximum recoil.

(Photo: Alexander Diedyk Collection via Krzysztof Margasinski)

A woodcut showing a similar gun on a UHA train, fighting an oncoming Polish armoured train.

(Woodcut: Alexander Diedyk Collection via Krzysztof Margasinski)

Armoured Train No 212 of I Corps of the UHA, halted and then captured by the Poles on 15 May 1919. Note the improvised protection consisting of trench shields fastened to the sides of the vans and wagons.

(Photo: Mariusz Zimny Collection)

A view of a Ukrainian armoured train, converted from German Type Om high-sided wagons, captured by the Poles on 9 July 1919 near D uryn (Buczacz region) during the Polish-Ukrainian War. Note the thickness of the protection and the plates extending above the wagon sides, probably trench shields.

(Photo: CAW)

The Armoured Trains of the UHA in Transnistria[5] (July 1919 – January 1920)

Despite its retreat behind the line of the Zbrucz, the UHA was not defeated. It regrouped in the Kamenets-Podolski region and formed three army corps. Along with about a hundred field guns and 390 machine guns, in late 1919 I Corps possessed an armoured train (Russian gauge), named *Halatschina*, which the UHA had captured during its offensive towards Kiev in August of that year.

The Armoured Trains (Russian Gauge) of the Army of Petlioura

On 23 June 1917, the National Ukrainian Republic[6] was proclaimed. After the Russian Revolution, for a time it formed part of Russia. Several armoured trains were operated, and they ranged in quality from improvised wagons or units built in naval workshops such as in Odessa, to refined and well-armoured units captured from the Bolsheviks and Denikin's White forces.

The train in the photo below began life as Russian Armoured Train No 1 *Chunchuz*, immobilised in No Man's Land by hits from Austro-Hungarian artillery on 24 September 1915. After repairs, it was used by the Bolsheviks, then became Ukrainian Armoured Train *Sichevik*[7] of the Petlioura Army. Captured by the Poles on 24 May 1920, it was used against the Russians under the name of *Krechowiak* – as in the photo below – then later as *General Dowbór*. Then on 6 June 1920, it changed hands for the last time, being captured by the Red Cossacks of Budenny's First Cavalry Army. It appears to have suffered no serious damage, as its latest owners managed to repair it. It apparently remained in Russian service right up to the beginning of the Second World War.

Armoured train captured from the Whites by the Sich Riflemen at Kiev and then renamed *Sichovy Strilets*. The inscription '*strilets*' (riflemen) can be made out on the wagon's side. Note the fake firing slots painted in black to deceive enemy snipers.
(Photo: All Rights Reserved)

Armoured train *Krechowiak* seen in May 1920.
(Photo: CAW)

5. Today situated in the north-west of modern Moldavia.
6. Українська Народня Республіка (УНР), *Ukrayins'ka Narodnia Respublika* (UNR).
7. The name given to the members of the Sich Riflemen (derived from the term for a Cossack encampment).

Captured following the action by Colonel Wolf at Schepietovka in August 1919, this is the train christened *Wilna Ukraina* ('Free Ukraine'). The design of the train is the same as several examples built in the railway workshops in Kiev, powered by Class O steam engines, such as Communist Korosthenskovo Rayona ('The Communists of the Korosten Region') and *Karl Liebknecht*.

(Postcard: Paul Malmassari Collection)

Bolshevik broad-gauge armoured train captured from the Petliura Army in 1919. Here its high-sided bogie wagon has been fitted with crude armour and a Canet naval gun.

(Photo: Krzysztof Margasiński Collection)

Ukrainian Armoured Trains Co-operating with the Polish Army, 1920.

In the combat zone where the Polish forces and the Ukrainians of Petlioura operated side-by-side from April 1920, notably in Podolia,[8] the railway network was dual gauge, both Russian broad gauge and European standard gauge.

Russian broad-gauge Armoured Train *Ukraine* (note the inscription in Cyrillic and roman letters) seen in late 1920. The high-sided bogie wagon is fitted with a turret armed with a 76.2mm Model 1902 field gun.
(Photo: Krzysztof Margasiński Collection)

A meeting of two famous personalities, Józef Piłsudski of Poland and Symon Petliura of the Ukraine, at Stanisławow on 5 September 1920, on the occasion of the commissioning of the Ukrainian Armoured Train Кармелюк (Karmeluk), built in the local railway workshops.
(Photo: Krzysztof Margasiński Collection)

[8.] A region which became Polish in 1919 after having formed part of the Western Ukrainian Republic. The Soviets briefly occupied it during the Russo-Polish War.

The Modern Period

The Ukraine's desire for closer ties with the European Union, as opposed to its traditional ties with Russia, saw the sporadic reappearance of attempts to build armoured trains, such as this high-sided bogie wagon with roughly-cut firing embrasures, emplaced as a roadblock in the Lugansk region. Note the damage from a shell or RPG.

SOURCES:
Archives:
Polish Historical Service (CAW).

Books:
Krotofil, Maciej, *Ukraińska Armia Halicka 1918-1920* (Toruń: Wydawnictwo 'Adam Marszałek', 2002).
Tynchenko, Yaroslav, *Armored Trains and Armored cars in the War of Liberation 1917-1920* (Kiev: Tempora, 2012).

Journal Articles:
Diedyk, Alexander G, 'Armored Trains of the UHA. The war on railway tracks', *The Red Kalyna Chronicle* No 6–7 (1992).
Wolos, Mariusz, 'Sortir de la guerre à Lvov', *Revue historique des armées* [online] 251 (2008), put online 9 June 2008, URL : http://rha.revues.org/323

Video:
http://ukstream.tv/en/videos/ukrayins_ki_viis_kovi_znishchili_bro niepoyizd_iekstriemistiv_u_slov_ians_ku_05_05_2014#.VOcXtyy bfc

Website:
http://www.encyclopediaofukraine.com/default.asp

UNITED STATES OF AMERICA

ARMOURED TRAINS, RAILCARS AND TROLLEYS

Initial projects

In 1845, the *Journal des sciences militaires*[1] described a project by a contributor to the *United Service Magazine* which fell halfway between railway artillery and armoured trains. He proposed defending the coastlines of the United States by means of a 'railway wide enough to allow the passage of wagons of large dimensions, similar as far as possible to the deck of a warship, open on the landward side and armed with cannons pointing out to sea'. The wagons were to be protected by an armoured side pierced by loopholes. A wall or dike of stones would be built to protect the railroad. Fortified stations set every 20 miles would enable the artillery wagons to intervene at any point on the coast within a maximum delay of fifteen minutes.

The American Civil War (12 April 1861 – 9 May 1865)

(For the armoured rail vehicles used by the South during the Civil War, see the chapter on the Confederate States of America)

From the very beginning of the war, the employment of railway batteries in the form of guns placed at the head of trains came into use at several different locations on the front line, either on the initiative of the high command or of especially inventive local commanders. For example, in May 1861, in order to protect the network of the Baltimore & Ohio Railroad, Union General McClellan ordered the mounting of artillery at the head of troop trains. The *Dictator* was another example, made famous during the siege of Petersburg between June 1864 and March 1865. This 13in coast-defence mortar lacked armour protection, and fired from a simple platform wagon. However, in this chapter we will confine ourselves to an examination of those armoured artillery batteries which demonstrated the modern aspects of the American Civil War, and which provided the inspiration for similar construction in many future conflicts, beginning with the Franco-Prussian War, until surpassed in ingenuity during the Boer War.

During the very first days of the war the Federal Government ordered the construction of an armoured wagon to protect the track workers on the Philadelphia, Wilmington & Baltimore Railroad. It was placed under the orders of General Herman Haupt, a renowned railroad engineer, but he refused to use it, considering the wagon to be a 'white elephant'. Nevertheless, the idea of armouring railway vehicles had taken root.

The Union Army built several armoured wagons. In the Summer of 1862, General Burnside[2] ordered the construction of

armoured wagons to counter the incursions of guerrillas and Southern raiders, but they were not meant to resist artillery. These wagons were mainly built in the workshops of the Baltimore & Ohio Railroad.

In 1862 a captain in the 23rd Massachusetts Volunteer Infantry Regiment designed an armoured artillery wagon which was built by the Atlantic & North Carolina Railroad and used for patrolling the line to the west of Newberne, where the Confederates were posted in some force. Propelled ahead of an engine with an armoured cab, this wagon bore the name *Monitor*. The wagon front, sides and rear were all inclined vertically inwards by some 15 degrees, and were painted black, with red firing loopholes. Its front end, pierced by an embrasure for a small naval gun, was armoured with vertical rails, and the sides and rear by boiler plate. The sides were bulletproof, and the front armour resisted projectiles from field guns. The roof was left open for ventilation and light, and

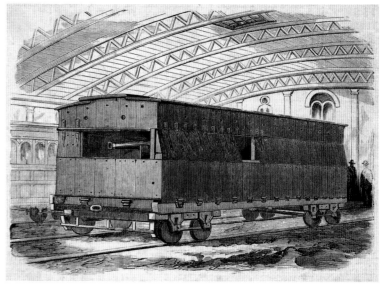

One of many illustrations featuring the armoured wagon for the Philadelphia, Wilmington & Baltimore Railroad. This one shows the wagon parked in a station, while others show it from the same angle but in the countryside, demonstrating how much this new mechanised warfare held a fascination for the journalists and the readers of the period. The chase gun, with its muzzle swell, is likely a 10pdr Parrott rifle, capable of firing out of ports to each side as well as to the front. Note how the artist has exaggerated the width of the flat car used as the base.
(Illustration: Paul Malmassari Collection)

1. 'Emploi de l'artillerie sur un chemin de fer pour la défense des côtes [des USA]', *Journal des sciences militaires* No 66, Third Series, Vol XXII (1845), p 304.
2. Who, from his famous side whiskers, popularised the fashion of 'sideburns'.

Another engraving, this time by William C Russell, showing a similar armoured artillery wagon, based on an eighteen-stave flatcar, with the Parrott rifle capable of forward and lateral fire. The sides of this wagon were trapezoidal, allowing for space alongside the gun for the gunners (shown under-scale!). The raised roof section allows light to enter and smoke to escape. The artist has represented a line of loopholes in the upper part of the sides, but the holes are too small to allow for sighting rifles. The weakest point on these trains was the engine's boiler and prominent smokestack.

(Engraving: Paul Malmassari Collection)

covered by a tarpaulin. One Confederate artillery lieutenant expressed puzzlement and alarm at the first appearance of what the Southerners called the 'Yankee gunboat on wheels'.

Faced by the cottonclad wagon of General Finegan (see the chapter on the Confederate States of America) during the Confederate attempt to recapture Jacksonville, in Union hands ever since 10 March 1863, the Northerners built their own armoured railway battery, armed apparently with a 10pdr Parrott rifle. The fighting between the two was the first example of combat between armoured railway wagons. The siege of Jacksonville would be lifted by the Union forces on 29 March.

In the same year, the *Scientific American* described trials by the Northerners of an armoured engine named *Talisman*, on which the cab and connecting rods were protected by an iron plate four-tenths of an inch (10mm) thick, on the advice of General Haupt. However, the trials showed that only small-arms projectiles would be stopped.

A Union armoured train was built by the Baltimore & Ohio Railroad with the aid of the 2nd Maryland Regiment, and was given the task of protecting the region around Cumberland. The train was arranged symmetrically on either side of the engine,

This armoured wagon precedes and protects its train with a gun mounted so as to allow virtual all-round fire. This arrangement on the other hand has the inconvenience of exposing the gun crew to hostile fire when loading or when using their small arms. The armour protection would probably be constructed using inclined rails fastened to a wooden structure.

(Engraving: Harper's Weekly, 1862)

A close-up detail from an Andrew J Russell photo, showing the first train over the repaired Bull Run Bridge in the Spring of 1863, allows us a glimpse of an armoured artillery wagon, constructed on a twelve-stave railroad flatcar. Note the typical inset halfway up the armoured sides, and the gun emerging from hinged ports. It appears this was a two-gun wagon, so a similar piece would be mounted to fire from the front set of ports faintly visible in the photo (here probably trained to cover the opposite side of the track).
(Photo: Library of Congress)

which had an armoured cab. At front and rear there was an armoured battery protected by rails on three sides, the roof and rear of the wagon being left open, and then an armoured van with firing loopholes. In spite of its armour, a projectile in the boiler of the engine followed by a second striking an armoured wagon led to its destruction by the Confederates in July 1864.

The siege of Petersburg (June 1864–April 1865) saw the employment of railway artillery by the Union forces who wished to

A 32pdr gun arms this battery used by the Union forces during the siege of Petersburg in 1864–5, mounted on seven axles. The use of wood for protection was widespread, and iron protection was much rarer.
(Photo: Library of Congress)

seize this strategic railroad centre where five major lines converged. The United States Military Railroad (USMR) which was by this time fully operational, deployed these weapons to such good effect that the Confederate Army was gradually cut off from outside aid. The town fell on 3 April 1865.

Alongside these units actually built, there existed a range of proposals put forward by enthusiastic citizens. For example, the project for a 'travelling battery' proposed by Charles Perley of New York, would have had the advantage of being able to move on rails (of different gauges) and on roads, the wheels being wide enough for these multiple roles. The inventor proposed to use such a wagon in front and to the rear of the engine. In the event of the wagon being uncoupled, the removable floor section would allow the crew to descend to rail or ground level and to push the vehicle, or even repair the tracks under cover. The armour protection was to consist of iron or steel plates fastened to a wooden frame. In addition to the light guns, firing loopholes were to pierce the sides, and four lengths of spare rail (marked No 4 on the plan) would be carried for track repair or replacement.

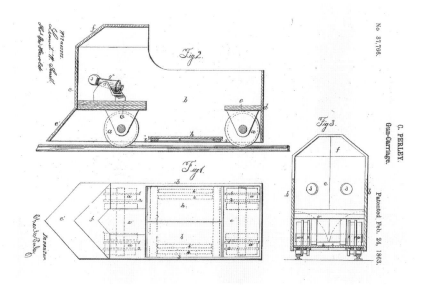

Plan attached to Patent 37.766, registered by Charles Perley, granted on 24 February 1863.

Between the Civil War and the First World War

Armoured trains in Panama, 1885 and 1903

Prior to the opening of the Panama Canal, the railway line linking Colón (Aspinwall to the Americans) in the north of the isthmus with Panama City in the south was of great strategic importance. To counter the attacks on the railway infrastructure of the Panama Railroad Company by revolutionaries struggling against the Colombian Government, the United States decided to intervene by sending by sea a contingent of 740 men (two battalions of Marines and sailors used to handling Gatling guns). The troops landed at Panama on 7 April 1885 then at Colón on 15 April. Between these

American armoured wagon in Panama.
(Engraving: Harper's Weekly, *30 May 1885)*

two dates, on the night of the 10th/11th, two armed and armoured wagons were built under the supervision of Lieutenant Kimball, US Navy. From the 11th onward, order was gradually restored, and normal railway traffic could recommence, now under the protection of the armoured wagons.

These wagons were armoured with steel plates 3ft 7¼in (1.10m) high and four-tenths of an inch (10mm) thick; each wagon was armed with a 37mm Hotchkiss QF gun, a short Gatling on its mounting, and a 12pdr smoothbore howitzer. The latter could be deployed in a ground role. The crew comprised forty-two US Marines and fifty-eight sailors.

In September 1902, the region was shaken by revolutionary movements, and in November 1903 a contingent of Marines and sailors landed once more, took up position in Colón and put into service armoured trains about which virtually no information is available.

(No Model.)

J. BECK.
MILITARY RAILROAD CAR.

No. 540,134.   Patented May 28, 1895.

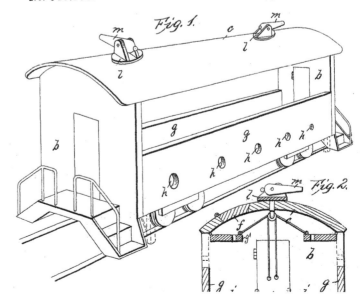

Engraving attached to Patent 540,134 of 28 May 1895.

Project by John Beck

In 1895, a native of Pennsylvania, a certain John Beck, obtained a patent for an armoured wagon armed with guns on the roof, aimed and fired by remote control. The upper halves of the armoured sides had panels which hinged upwards to allow salvo firing by the crew, while gunports in the lower halves allowed for firing small-calibre guns. Recoil was to be catered for by stabiliser legs at each corner of the vehicle. Surprising for such a late date, the small-calibre guns in the patent drawing would not have been out of place in the Civil War thirty years earlier. Probably the drawing was purely indicative, but they detract from the overall impression.

Armoured cruiser on rails of the electoral campaign of William McKinley, Governor of Ohio, 1896

This tramcar converted into an armoured cruiser is purely anecdotal, and would have no place in the overall story of the armoured train had it not raised interest in the possible employment of such vehicles during civil disturbances.

To publicise the presidential election campaign of Republican candidate William McKinley in 1896, a tramcar had been converted into an armoured cruiser, using pasteboard according to some sources, or metal according to others. Designed by naval architect Henry P Lapointe, it was built and ran in the town of Fitchburg,[3] Massachusetts. The idea originated with a supporters' club who set up a company to participate in the election campaign, and elected as its 'captain', a certain Major Charles K Darling.[4] The 'warship' was 37ft (11.28m) long, 9ft (2.74m) wide and 12ft (3.65m) high. It was powered by two 30hp electric motors. The basic idea was to show that it would be possible to construct an armoured vehicle on tramway rails to intervene in urban riots. It could also be used to rapidly and securely transport a body of troops up to company size, plus artillery, between towns. This idea would be revived again in 1938, when 'a fleet of such trolleys, a new step in the progress towards mechanised warfare' was suggested. After McKinley's presidential election victory in 1896, certain sources indicate that the 'armoured cruiser' was put afloat on Lake Whalom, in a park belonging to the tramway company, while others claim it was left to fall to pieces.[5]

In 1899, shortly after the Spanish-American War, the Americans decide to take control of the former Spanish colonies. In

The tramcar, loosely inspired by the armoured cruiser USS *Brooklyn*, described as having a white hull, green superstructure (which in fact would have been buff yellow) and black armament and portholes.

(Engraving: La Nature No 1247 [24 April 1897], p 336)

3. By the Fitchburg & Leominster Street Railway Company.
4. *The Fitchburg Daily Sentinel*, 13 and 21 August 1896, p 6.
5. All the sources consulted remain quite vague, but it is not the job of journalists to record history.

the Philippines, the Nationalists, with their capital at Manolos, refused to accept what they considered a new colonial yoke, and took up arms against the American forces concentrated in Manila. The latter advanced along the railway, using an improvised armoured train initially armed with a naval 6pdr gun and two Gatling guns firing to the sides. This armament was later augmented by a Hotchkiss revolver cannon. Their advance on Manolos was delayed by several lines of resistance but the town was taken. The rebels changed their tactics and began attacking the railway behind the American lines. On 25 April 1899 the armoured train was in action at Calumpit, pushed by Chinese workmen, in support of 400 troopers of the 4th Cavalry fighting dismounted. During that battle, it seems the firepower of the train was a major factor in inducing the Filipinos to withdraw. The war dragged out in the mountains, and the armoured train having no further useful employment, the individual wagons were probably returned to civilian use at the end of 1899.

We have no information on this American armoured train design, which is probably intended for coast defence given the similarity of its components to those of warships. Stated to be a project dating from 1898, it could in fact be a revival of the original project of 1845.

(Engraving: All Rights Reserved)

An engraving showing the armoured train, made up of four wagons, the leading wagon armed with a 37mm Hotchkiss revolver and a Gatling gun. In the absence of a steam engine, it was pushed by hand by Chinese labourers during the fighting on the Bagbag River during the Battle of Calumpit.

(Engraving: Paul Malmassari Collection)

The 'Bull Moose Special'[6] Armoured Train of 1913

In West Virginia, coal miners went on a long drawn-out strike, lasting from 18 April 1912 to the end of July 1913. On one side were some 8000 strikers, demanding equality of pay with miners from the surrounding areas, an end to the practice of compulsory purchase in the company shops, and regulated coal-weighing procedures. They faced 300 private guards from the notorious Baldwin-Felts Detective Agency, brought in by the mining companies, supported by 1200 Federal troops. In order to protect strike-breakers, the Agency guards organised the construction of an armoured train in the workshops of the C&O[7] Railroad Company at Huntington. The train consisted of a steam engine, a passenger coach and a van protected by steel plates. On the night of 7 February 1913, in retaliation for an attack on an ambulance and the depot near Mucklow, this train was used in a raid by private detectives, policemen and mine operators led by Kanawha County Sheriff Bonner Hill. They fired a hundred rounds from a Colt machine gun into the timber-framed house of a striker, Cesco Estep, killing him and wounding several others.

Miners' armoured train, September 1913

Another dramatic incident took place during this period, when violent clashes broke out in Southern Colorado, in particular in a lengthy strike involving the coal mines owned by the Colorado Fuel & Iron Corporation, where the miners were stung by the murder of one of their number. On one occasion during a raid on the strikers' tent encampment by guards recruited by the company, the miners improvised an armoured train, and used it to attack strike-breakers. The strike continued into the Spring of 1914 and ended in the 'Ludlow Massacre' in which twenty-six miners along with several women and children perished.[8]

Although not strictly speaking armoured, the train which had transported the Colorado Militia to attack the tent camp at Ludlow was deliberately halted by its driver in front of the Militia machine gun emplacements, thus covering the escape of many strikers and their families.

In 1914 the US Division of the German firm Orenstein Arthur Koppel in Pittsburg built an armoured wagon with firing loopholes arranged in a quincunx layout, as used in the trains of the Boer War a dozen years earlier. As at that moment the US Army had no operational requirement for such a vehicle, it was probably sold to a foreign country, perhaps in South America.

The Mexican Border Patrols

After troops under Pancho Villa had massacred Americans on a civilian train, then carried out the raid against the town of Columbus, New Mexico, on 9 March 1916, the USA decided to send a force under the command of General Pershing to eliminate the guerrilla menace. For this operation, in 1916 the American Army acquired some thirty Mack-Saurer trucks, known as 'Rikers' (from the name of their designer Andrew Riker). Several would be converted for use on rails, but were employed only in supply missions on the railway networks in New Mexico and Texas, since the Constitutionalist Government had forbidden American forces to use the Mexican railways.

An artist's impression showing the interior of the Standard Steel Co. patrol wagon. The machine guns shown here were the Machine Rifle Model of 1909 (Benet-Mercié Hotchkiss Portative), the unjustly maligned 'Daylight Gun' of the Pancho Villa raid on Columbus, New Mexico.
(Illustration: Popular Science Monthly Vol 89 [1916])

Side elevation and end view of the patrol wagon.
(Drawing: All Rights Reserved)

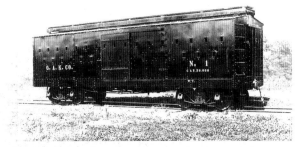

Orenstein Arthur Koppel Armoured Car No 1.
(Photo: All Rights Reserved)

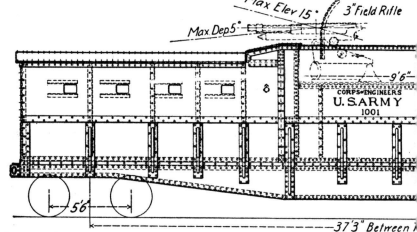

6. So named from the mine owners' links with the Progressive Party of West Virginia, known as the 'Bull Moose Party' after the popular nickname of presidential candidate Theodore Roosevelt.
7. The Chesapeake & Ohio Railroad, founded in 1869.
8. Some sources quote a total of sixty-six deaths.

The hulls of these two armoured railcars have a similar roof layout and lower armour protection to the 1916 Standard Steel armoured wagon. The lack of vertical T-section straps on the sides and driving positions in each corner follow the arrangement of the Hall-Scott Type 11.001 railcar. The gun in the nearer of the two wagons is not the US 3in, but the Model of 1917 (the British 18pdr converted to fire French 75mm ammunition), which entered service in February 1918, and .30 Cal Browning MGs are mounted in the gun well. This armament would suggest a date in the 1920s, and the railcars could conceivably be retained for Mexican Border patrols. Note the smoke from the roof exhaust pipe. A coloured version of this photo was issued as cigarette card No 99 by Lloyd Zigaretten.
(Photo: El Paso Public Library)

The Board of Engineers of the American Army had noted the armoured wagons built by the Villa forces, including an armoured version of the Riker truck (see the chapter on Mexico). So to secure the Mexican border during the crisis, the Engineers designed an armoured wagon, and gave the contract to the Standard Steel Company, which turned out the vehicle in just twenty-seven days. Its mission was to defend the railway lines and the nearby installations, rather than carry out offensive raids. The armour provided protection against small-arms fire only, and it was pierced by twenty firing loopholes at standing height for light machine guns and rifles. The central part held a stock of ammunition in its lower level, and the upper part formed a firing position for a 3in (76mm) field gun, served by three gunners. On patrol, the crew totalled a dozen men, who were provided with benches, a toilet and a tank of drinking water. The whole wagon weighed 44 tons. Although the cutaway illustration from *Popular Science Monthly* shows the wagon being propelled by an armoured steam engine, in fact the latter was never built. An identical wagon mounting a searchlight was however built, and this was propelled by a rail trolley.

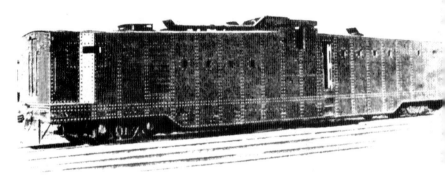

Similar in layout to the Standard Steel armoured wagon, but self-propelled and therefore more versatile, this is the Hall-Scott Type 11.001 Armoured Railcar. Note the driving positions at each corner, the centre of each end being taken up by a communicating armoured door when multiple units were coupled together.
(Photo: All Rights Reserved)

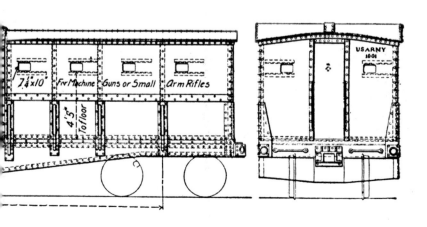

A second prototype armoured railcar was also commissioned by the US Army Corps of Engineers, and this time built by the General Electric Company. It is a more compact, traditional design, also mounted on bogies, but lacking a field gun.
(Photo: All Rights Reserved)

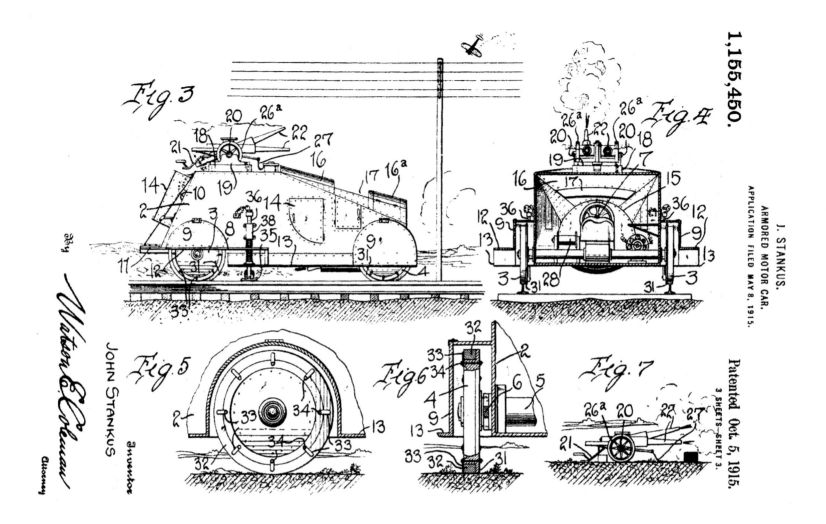

1,155,450.

J. STANKUS.
ARMORED MOTOR CAR.
APPLICATION FILED MAY 8, 1915.

Patented Oct. 5, 1915.
3 SHEETS—SHEET 3.

The Armoured Trains of the First and Second World Wars

Drawing forming part of the patent granted to John Stankus on 5 October 1915.

The First World War 1917–1918: Proposals imaginative and practical

Although the Americans only entered the First World War on 6 April 1917, several patents for armoured rail vehicles had been applied for since 1914, for example one by a certain Mr Bellamore of New York for a system of standardised armoured panels. In 1915, John Stankus of Pennsylvania proposed an armed and armoured road-rail vehicle. The conversion was effected by attaching rubber tyres on the rail wheels (US Patent 1,155,450).

On 17 July 1918 Frederick W Wagner applied for a patent for an ambitious machine: armed with quick-firing guns, it travelled on the road, and was also equipped with tracks to cross wet ground. In addition, its wheels allowed it to travel on rails. The patent was granted on 21 January 1919, too late for the war, under Number US 1,292,170. It is illustrated below.

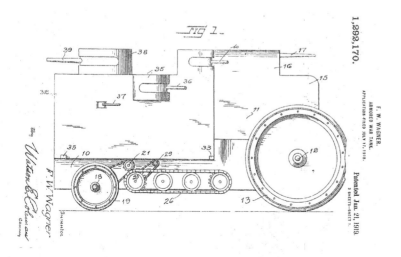

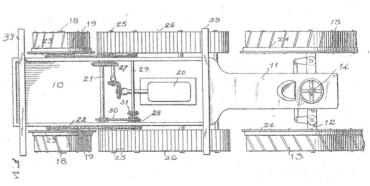

1,292,170.

F. W. WAGNER.
ARMORED WAR TANK.
APPLICATION FILED JULY 17, 1918.

Patented Jan. 21, 1919.
3 SHEETS—SHEET 1.

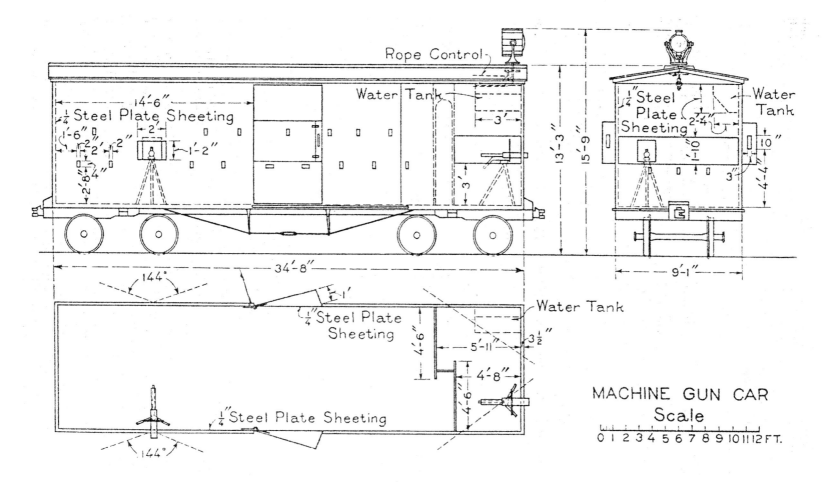

Rope Control

Water Tank

14'-6"

¼" Steel Plate Sheeting

1'-6"

2"

13'-3"

15'-9"

3'

¼" Steel Plate Sheeting

Water Tank

2'-4"

2"

1'-10"

10"

3'

34'-8"

9'-1"

144°

1'

¼" Steel Plate Sheeting

Water Tank

4'-6"

5'-11"

3½"

4'-8"

4'-6"

¼" Steel Plate Sheeting

144°

MACHINE GUN CAR
Scale

0 1 2 3 4 5 6 7 8 9 10 11 12 FT.

In 1917, directives were issued laying down rules for the rapid conversion of armoured wagons in an emergency. The plan annexed to these proposals harked back to the wagons built during the Boer War, down to the roof-mounted searchlight and the arrangement of the firing loopholes in the armoured sides (drawing above).

Tractors for the 60cm gauge were built for service at the front, on the model of the British Simplex, and were used notably in the Meuse-Argonne offensive. They had a maximum speed of 8mph (12.9km/h) and a total weight of 6.35 tons.

A more practical proposition, as planned in 1917. Note the curious representation of the machine guns.
(Drawing: All Rights Reserved)

Baldwin built 126 narrow gauge Type MM8 tractors, with an output of 50hp, for use by the American army in France, but apparently only one example was armoured.

In 1919, the Americans intervened alongside the other Allies against Bolshevik Russia. The American Expeditionary Force (AEF)

The prototype of the Baldwin MM8 armoured tractor.
(Photo: DeGolyer University)

An improvised armoured train used by the American contingent in Russia in 1920.
(Photo: IWM)

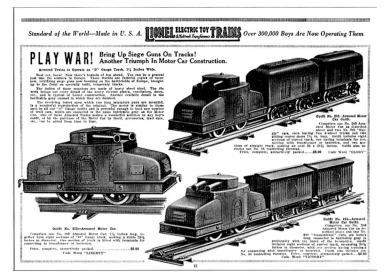

The page from the Lionel Catalogue of 1917. The turret guns were fitted with red lights which flashed as the turret was turned.

(Catalogue Page: via Bill Schmeelk of The Lionel Collectors' Club of America)

The card model from February 1941.

(Sheet: Paul Malmassari Collection)

was in action in the Murmansk region where, to protect the rail network, it put into service at least one armoured train.

Armoured trains featured prominently in the popular press during the early years of the First World War, so it was inevitable that an electric train set would be produced by the Lionel Company. The set complete with armoured locomotive (which presaged the form of the Crochat armoured tractors which would appear a year later) was first offered in the Lionel Catalogue of 1917, and remained on sale through 1919. It has recently been reissued by a modern American manufacturer.

During the Second World War, the Americans did not use armoured trains in an offensive role. On the other hand, they did employ passive protection, particularly on locomotives. Certain Whitcomb 65-DE-14 diesel locomotives were armoured, being the units deployed to the North African theatre (nineteen in 1942 and seventeen in early 1943). In all, in order to provide protection against air attack, fifty complete sets of armour were ordered from Whitcomb, to protect the driving cab and the ends of the machine.

Although the Americans did not use armoured trains (the special armoured coach built by the LNER for General Eisenhower is described in the chapter on Great Britain), armoured trains

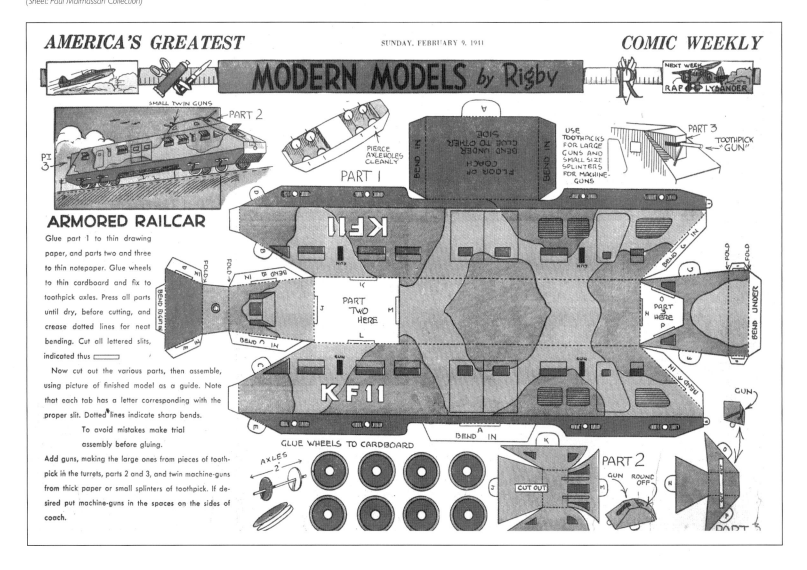

remained part of popular imagination, and continued to appear in toy form. Metal being in demand for war construction, card cutouts became very popular, as shown by this sheet issued in February 1941. Even if it is not based on any specific prototype, the camouflage scheme of green and earth upper surfaces is very British!

The Armoured Trains of the Cold War Period

Characteristic of the Cold War Period is the 'White Train' designed for the transport of nuclear material. The Safe Secure Railcar (SSR) wagons were built by the Thrall Car Company of Chicago, Illinois, by reinforcing and armouring modified bogie wagons. Design studies began in the 1950s and took two years to complete. Built initially for the transport of nuclear weapons, the older wagons were later used to carry military nuclear waste from the Rocky Flats site in Colorado to an underground repository in Idaho.

Eighty-three of the ATMX 500 Series were built, followed by fourteen ATMX 600 Series. They possessed several security measures to prevent terrorists from gaining access to the cargo. The inclined shape of the wagon ends is intended to minimise the results of a collision, by allowing the end of one wagon to slide up over the rear of the preceding one. Overall structural strength was also enhanced by the fact that loading took place through openings in the roof which were closed by riveted plates.

Running in complete designated rakes and not coupled in commercial trains, the nuclear wagons formed an armoured train rolling at up to 35mph (55km/h), stopping only to refuel the locomotives, and protected by armed guards aboard wagons at each end. The normal configuration was: locomotive/escort wagon/shock-absorbing wagon/nuclear munitions transport wagon/shock-absorbing wagon/escort wagon. Empty wagons would be coupled in with the loaded ones. The crew had at their disposal HF, VHF and CB Band radio equipment, and remained in constant communication with a network of intervention teams. The employment of each train was the responsibility of the Operations Bureau of the DOE (Department of Energy) in Albuquerque, which also controlled road movements. The eleven surviving wagons were preserved at the National Atomic Museum on Kirtland Air Base near Albuquerque, before being transferred to the Amarillo Railroad Museum.

Technical details (ATMX-600 Series)	
Length:	59ft 10in (18.24m)
Width:	10ft 0in (3.05m)
Height:	13ft 10in (4.22m)
Carrying capacity:	45.95 tons
Loaded weight:	99.79 tons

Nuclear Weapons Transport Car TSSX 557.
(Photo: Amarillo Railroad Museum)

Armoured Escort Wagon TSSX G-33, showing its openings, firing loopholes and radio antenna.
(Photo: Amarillo Railroad Museum)

Special Vehicles

For the sake of completeness, we need to mention certain special armoured rail vehicles, such as the presidential carriage *Ferdinand Magellan*, converted and armoured for President Franklin D Roosevelt, or armoured postal or cash transfer wagons, an American speciality which was the subject of many Patents between the late nineteenth and early twentieth centuries. Below is just one example, taken from 1888, which bears more than a passing resemblance to certain military contemporaries.

In 1919, a newspaper article described one of these protection wagons in great detail, probably to dissuade potential hijackers. At right we see a guard firing a pump-action shotgun, as used by prison guards, through an armoured embrasure. The same article was even copied in 1924 in a popular French review!

Finally, we note that an armoured railcar was put into service on the Metroliner network, but we have no details concerning it.

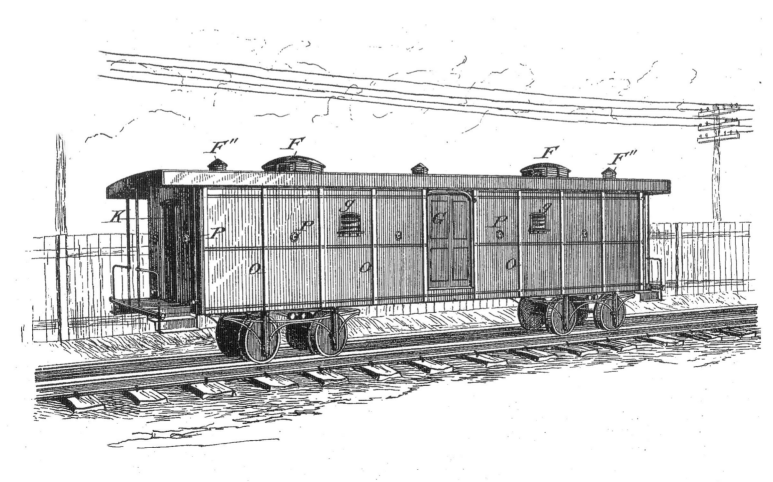

Right: Armoured Whitcomb railcar belonging to the United Fruit Company, built in 1928.

(Photo: All Rights Reserved)

SOURCES

Archives:
DeGoyler Library
Library of Congress
US National Archives
US Patents Office

Books:
Alexander, Edwin P, *Civil War Railroads & Models* (New York: Clarkson N. Potter, Inc./Publishers 1977).

Drumm, Nelde K, and Harley, Margaret P, *Lunenburg – The Heritage of Turkey Hills 1718-1978* (Lunenburg, MA: Lunenburg Historical Society, 1977).

Heimburger, Donald J, and Kelly, John, *Trains to Victory: America's Railroads in WWII* (Forest Park, IL: Heimburger House Publishing Co, 2009). 380 pages.

Hodges, Robert R Jr., *American Civil War Railroad Tactics* (Oxford: Osprey Publishing, 2009).

Koenig Alan R, *Ironclads on Rails: Railroad Weapons of the American Civil War, 1861-65*, Doctoral History Thesis, University of Nebraska-Lincoln (E-U.), under the supervision of Dr Edward Homze, 1995.

Journal articles:
Hall, James D., 'Armored Trolley', *Railroad Magazine* (1938), pp 93–4.

Stanitz, Jim, and Moon, Paul F, 'Safe Secure Rail Cars', *NMRA Bulletin* (September 1980), pp 33–4.

Waite, Thornton, 'ATMX Covered Hoppers, a Special Car for Nuclear Shipments', *Mainline Modeler* (August 2001), pp 69–72.

Walsh, Paul V, 'A US Armoured Train in the Philippines, 1899-1900', *AFV News* 28/2 (May-August 1993), pp 10–11.

'A Trolley Man-of-War', *Literary Digest* Vol XIV, No 10 (9 January 1897), pp 304–5.

'Emploi de l'artillerie sur un chemin de fer pour la défense des côtes [des USA]', *Journal des sciences militaires* No 66, Third Series, Vol XXII (1845), p 304.

'Our First Armored Car', *Popular Science Monthly* Vol 89 (1916), pp 388–9.

'Parades américaines, un navire de guerre à trolley', *La Nature* No 1247 (24 April 1897), p 336.

'Trains blindés d'Amérique', Lecture pour tous (November 1924), pp 180–2.

'Trains, Boats and Guns–Armour in Panama, 1885', *Tank TV* No 23 (September 2000), pp 1–4.

Papers on Naval Operations, Chapter II, Navy Department, 1885.
Fitchburg Daily Sentinel, 11 September 1896
Harper's Weekly, 1862.
Harper's Weekly, Vol XXIX, No 1484 (30 May 1885), p 349.
Metal Trades (February 1919), pp 94–5.
Modern Mechanics (February 1919).

Websites:
www.amarillorailmuseum.com
www.youtube.com/watch?feature=player_detailpage&v=kz54FcA4wqA

VIETNAM, REPUBLIC OF

ARMOURED TRAINS

Vietnam gradually regained its sovereignty during the War in Indochina, and the ARVN (Army of the Republic of Viet Nam) was created on 1 January 1949.[1] Between June 1954 and October 1955, Vietnam was ruled by Emperor Bao Dai, who was deposed in a coup which created the Republic of Vietnam. Proclaimed on 26 October 1955, the Republic, also called South Vietnam, disappeared with the fall of Saigon on 30 April 1975.[2]

Even before complete independence had been achieved, in 1953 the (French) armoured trains began to be transferred to the ARVN's 1st Armoured Cavalry Regiment, which was the successor to the 4th Dragoon Regiment. On 16 August 1954, the armoured train detachments of the 5th Cavalry Regiment (Armoured Train No 5, on the line to Loc Nonh) and of the 2nd Foreign Legion Infantry Regiment (Armoured Trains Nos 2 and 3, on the line to Nha Trang), were transferred to the 1st Escort Squadron Group (1er G.E.E.) of the ARVN. In about October 1954 this unit became the 1st Vietnamese Dragoon Regiment, and assumed the role of ensuring the security of the railway network.

[1] Article 60 of the Constitution of the Fourth Republic stipulated that the French Union was formed, on the one hand by the French Republic, and on the other hand by the territories and states associated with France, among which were the three states of the Indochinese Union created in 1887.

[2] Unification of North and South Vietnam was proclaimed on 2 July 1976.

[3] Created in 1890. The gold symbolised the ruling dynasties and the three red bands, Tonkin, Annam and Cochinchina.

Saluting the flag in Phan Thiet in October 1954, in front of Armoured Train No 3. The Vietnamese flag, yellow with three red bands[3] is being hoisted.
(Photo: Private Collection)

Armoured wagon armed with the turret of a Coventry armoured car, seen during an exercise at Govap.
(Photo: Private Collection)

The crew of Armoured Train No 3 with its French officers in charge of handing over the equipment and training the Vietnamese. The insignia is that of the 1er G.E.E., also known as the 'Black Dragon Squadron'.
(Photo: Private Collection)

The wagons still carry their French names given to them by the 4th Dragoon Regiment.
(Photo: Private Collection)

Note the insignia of the 1er G.E.E. attached to the casemate of what is certainly the the wagon of the train commander. *(Photos: Private Collection)*

During the Vietnam War, passenger and goods trains were protected by the insertion of armoured wagons in the rakes, manned by men drawn from eight companies of civilian guards. In addition, reconnaissance runs were carried out by Wickham armoured trolleys purchased from Malaysia in 1962.

As the war progressed, the railway network shrank to the point where, at the fall of Saigon, the only line still in use was the one linking the capital to Bien Hoa, a distance of just 30km (18.5 miles). Despite their chequered career, the French armoured wagons had remained in service for thirty years.

This is probably the all-metal Type GGy, which does not appear to have been modified – apart from the radio equipment – since its days in French service.
(Photo: Critical Past)

It is just possible that this wagon is the one named 'Paimpol', photographed twenty years earlier. One wonders what happened to these wagons. They were probably cut up for scrap or reconverted to goods traffic use. The armoured body of one has even been observed grounded for use as a guard post.
(Photo: Critical Past)

SOURCES:
Archives:
SHD (10 H 1276, 10 H 1729, 10 H 4477, 10 H4559).
Private archives.

Videos:
Military History Video: *'Railroad Support Vietnam'* (506th Field Depot, 1967, 45 minutes)

The overall condition of these trolleys owes much to the disastrous effect humidity has on modern equipment. The significance of the lettering 'DBD' is unknown. The third trolley in line shows that the drivers' positions were offset front and rear.
(Photo: All Rights Reserved)

Armoured wagon constructed on the chassis of a Type HHy bogie wagon. At the side we can see an extension to the casemate which allowed for observation and firing along the axis of the train.
(Photo: Critical Past)

Phu Bai, 1969. This shows the classic layout of two safety wagons preceding the train. The first of the two wagons has an observation cab. It appears that the locomotive is a General Electric Type U8B.[4]
(Photo: AWM)

---

4. Built in 1963, forty-eight units were delivered to the Vietnamese Railways. In 1975, they were re-designated as Type D9E.

YUGOSLAVIA

ARMOURED TRAINS[1] 1918–1992

Yugoslavia was created by the Treaty of Versailles[2] and broke up in 1992. In order to correctly allocate the armoured trains, this chapter will cover the Yugoslav trains up to the officially recognised disappearance of this state. Because of the various territorial partitions and accidents of history which affected the state of Yugoslavia, the Croatian armoured trains of the Independent State of Croatia (1941–5) and of the Croatian War of Independence (1991–5), plus the Serb armoured trains of the Republica Srpska[3] (situated in Bosnia-Herzegovina) and the Serbian Republic of Krajina[4] (situated in Croatia) are described separately.

From the End of the Great War to the End of the Second World War

At the end of the First World War, it appears that only the Austro-Hungarian PZ V remained on the territory of the future Yugoslavia. It was taken over by the new Yugoslav Army, although no details of its use have come to light, apparently together with the artillery wagon from PZ I – but the only proof that this wagon was in Yugoslav hands is the photographic record. In March 1921 the French Military Attaché reported that '3 or 4 armoured trains could be formed'. On 27 October 1936, the new establishment of the Yugoslav Army included them in its 'special combat equipment'. However, there is no proof that these armoured trains had actually been put into service. At the time of the German invasion, several wagons were captured in Belgrade and from November 1941 were added to PZ 25. In addition, the pilot wagon of the ex-Austro-Hungarian PZ I was put back into service by the Wehrmacht, only to be lost on some unknown date.

Yugoslav armoured train captured in Belgrade in 1941. Note the modification to the wagon originally part of PZ V which now appears to have been fitted with a turret, possibly for anti-aircraft defence.

(Photo: Wolfgang Sawodny Collection)

Above and below: Two views of the armoured artillery wagon from the old ex-Austro-Hungarian PZ I, left behind in Yugoslavia after 1918, fitted with buffering gear and brake hoses, and put back into service after the German invasion of Yugoslavia. Note that its 7cm gun has been removed: the wagon is now armed with an MG34.

(Photos: Paul Malmassari Collection)

[1.] In Serbian: *Oklopni Voz, OKV.*

[2.] The Principality of Serbia was created in 1815 and became independent from the Ottoman Empire in 1878. The Kingdom of Serbia was proclaimed in 1882, and then in 1918 the gathering of the Southern Slavs gave birth to the Kingdom of the Serbs, Croats and Slovenes, which became the Kingdom of Yugoslavia in 1929. During the Second World War its territory was divided up by the Axis powers, then in 1945 its territorial integrity was re-established as the *Federativna Narodna Republika Jugoslavija* or FNRJ (Federal People's Republic of Yugoslavia). Following the war of 1991 to 1995, then the subsequent independence of Montenegro in 2006, Serbia inherited what was left of the old Yugoslavia.

[3.] Unilaterally declared in May 1992 and officially recognised within Bosnia-Herzegovina on 14 December 1995 by the Dayton Accords.

[4.] The 'Autonomous Serb Region of Krajina' seceded on 1 April 1991, transformed itself into the 'Serbian Republic of Krajina' on 19 December 1991, and was completely overrun by the Croats in early August 1995.

During the Second World War, there were reports of a 'partisan armoured train', today preserved in the Narrow Gauge Railway Museum in Požega, situated in the Belgrade-Bar adminis-trative district. It was used in the region of Uzice before that area was retaken by the Wehrmacht.

These two photos show the locomotive, on which only the cab is armoured, and a bogie low-sided wagon filled with sand, protecting a central open space. The collection also includes an armoured covered wagon with the same type of firing loopholes.

(Photos: Philippe Tomatis)

After the Second World War

At the end of the Second World War a number of Croatian, German and Italian armoured trains and trolleys were captured, and some at least were put back into service.[5] The majority of the units had been seized in Slovenia, and for the first year of the post-war period, they remained either in the zone where they had been captured, or otherwise were stored at the VTZ[6] '21 October'[7] in Kragujevac. On 24 May 1946, General Koca Popovic, Chief of the General Staff, gave orders to the commanders of the armoured and motorised units (KTJM[8]), to place all the various scattered armoured rail units under the responsibility of the RVK,[9] to report back on the numbers of units extant, and to evaluate their current state in order to establish a repair and maintenance programme. At that stage, in the zones of the First, Second, Fourth and Fifth Armies it was reported there were in existence a total of 242 armoured wagons and three armoured locomotives. However, of these some 60 per cent were unusable.

At the VTZ in Kragujevac alone there were around a hundred armoured wagons of which forty had concrete armour. After months of work at the VTZ, thirteen Steyr (in Serbian, *Štajer*) light trolleys (le.Sp) were considered ready for use along with seven Fiat trolleys. The VTZ also had several examples of heavy trolleys (s.Sp) and Italian LibLi (Ansaldo Fossati ALn56) railcars.

In August 1946 these units were sent to the central armoured workshops (CTR[10]) to be fitted with the equipment they lacked, notably machine guns and radios. It was planned to form one squadron of light Steyr trolleys,[11] then a second one with Fiat AB 41 trolleys. The towed armoured units were to be used by the Army battalions as command wagons, as troop transports or as workshops. At Sarajevo, where eighty-nine armoured wagons were concentrated, sixteen were selected to form a batallion for use on the narrow (76cm) gauge, with six wagons in combat configuration and the remainder in a support role. On the other hand, three armoured locomotives were transferred back to civilian use, as it was planned to use the Steyr trolleys as tractor units for the Narrow Gauge trains. In order to put the units in hand in a fit state to use, the KTMJ decided to cannibalise obsolete units and to produce or purchase the equipment which was missing. The batallions of armoured trains were to be attached to the Third, Fourth and Sixth Armies. The first formation was to be established at Sremska Kamenica.[12]

The General High Command issued a notice which indicated that the armoured trains had as their 'principal mission to ensure transport, communications security and combat on the internal front'. It also laid down, however, that no new trains were to be built, and that repairs to existing trains should be carried out only where the end result justified the effort. Lastly it ordered the KTJM to constitute three narrow-gauge (76cm/30in) divisions at Belgrade (or Karlowitz), Zagreb and Sarajevo. The fate of the units in excess of these requirements (seventy-three wagons at Sarajevo, thirty-

seven at Kragujevac and an undisclosed number at the VTZ '21st October') was to be decided by the Transport Ministry. No record exists, however, to prove that these armoured trains were ever formed, or that the proposed organisation had been set in motion. On the other hand, in July 1949 armoured trains featured in the inventory of the People's Corps for the Defence of Yugoslavia (KNOJ[13]) and were deployed in four divisions for the purposes of internal security:

7th Division: two armoured trains made up of Fiat trolleys at Bosanski Samac and Bihac; two Steyr trolleys at Banja Luka.

11th Division: one platoon at Nis; two armoured trains made up of Steyr trolleys at Skopje.

27th Division: one platoon of three Steyr armoured trains at Batajnica.

16th Division: one Steyr platoon at Vinkovci; three Fiat armoured trains at Ljubljana, Ogulin and Zagreb.

PanzerZug (s.Sp) 201 destroyed in Cacini Station on 14 April 1945. Several of these heavy trolleys were recovered in working order by the new Yugoslav Army. *(Photo: MRN via Bojan Dimitrijević)*

5. For example: PZ (le.SP) 301 at Kraljevo on 11 November 1944, PZ (le.SP) 302 at Kosovo Polje on 12 November 1944, PZ (s.Sp) 201 at Čačincima on 15 April 1945, and PZ 6 destroyed in Serbia on 1 October 1944. At the capitulation the largest number of prizes seized was at Celje and Dravograd (on the Austro-Slovene frontier) when twelve armoured trains and various railcars surrendered, in particular PZ 73 which had been put back into service in the region of Gôrz. An extremely accurate list is given in Bojan Dimitrijević's book *German Panzers and Allied Armour in Yugoslavia in World War Two*.
6. VTZ = *Vojno Tehnički Zavod*, Military Technical Institute.
7. October 21st could be a reference to the massacre of 21 October 1941, when the German Army killed more than 6000 civilians in reprisal for Chetnik and Partisan actions against them in the area (the number varies according to the sources). It could also be a reference to 21 October 1944, day of the liberation of the city.
8. KTMJ = *Komanda Tenkovskih I Mehanizovanih Jedinica*.
9. RVK = *Rezerva Vrhovne Komande*, Reserves High Command.
10. CTR = *Centralna Tenkovska Radionica*.
11. In reality, the Steyr trolleys were not defined as 'heavy' or 'light' in the archives, but instead were classified according to their armament. In certain cases it is impossible to be certain which type is mentioned.
12. Today a suburb of Novi Sad.
13. Created on 15 August 1944 to operate in liberated areas.

In 1950, an article in the *Chicago Daily Tribune* described 'several armoured trains . . . One of which was on a storage siding outside Belgrade . . . '.[14] In 1953, the KNOJ was dissolved and the armoured train units were integrated into the Yugoslav armoured forces, where the Department of Armoured and Motorised Units was charged with drawing up the doctrine for their emplyment. As the result of this reorganisation, the armoured trains were integrated into the various divisions as follows:

17th OKD:[15] two armoured trains, one made up of five Steyr trolleys (three artillery and two MG units), and the other of three Steyr trolleys (two artillery and one MG units) based at Batajnica.

20th OKD: three Steyr trolleys (MG units) at Zagreb; two Fiat trolleys at Ljubljana.

26th OKD: three Fiat trolleys (including one without armament) at Nis (transferred to Batajnica in November 1953 in exchange for three Steyr trolleys); two Steyr trolleys (MG units) at Pristina; two Steyr trolleys (MG units) at Skopje.

In the 7th Military Region (Bosnia-Herzogovina and Montenegro, where no armoured divisions were stationed): six Steyr trolleys (MG units) equally divided between Sarajevo, Banja-Luka and Vinkovci. These latter units would eventually rejoin the 20th OKD in the 5th Military Region.

In mid-October 1954, the armoured trains were gathered together in Zagreb East Station, and on 22 November 1955 the order was given to withdraw all the armoured trains from active service. Their armament and motors were taken out and stored, the armaments at Zagreb (at VR[16] No 69) and the motors at the TRZ[17] at Bregana. Two years later, on 22 October 1957, it was decided to restore an s.Sp heavy trolley (the 75mm gun version) to working order, using the services of the armoured forces and the Army technical department. However, the lack of spare parts, and the recent manufacture of more modern arms and equipment, led to the abandonment of the project. All the armoured rail units were therefore scrapped.

One of the seven LiBli armoured railcars (known as *Panzertriebwagen*) Nos 30 to 35 and 38, captured in Slovenia in May 1945.
(Photo: MRN via Bojan Dimitrijević)

Above: The first of three photos of captured German vehicles integrated into the Yugoslav armoured train units. Above is an alignment of ten s.Sp trolleys, of which at least four have a turret, photographed from a train passing in front of the CTR at Mladenovac, 56km (35 miles) to the south of Belgrade in 1946. Note the line of tanks in the background, among which are former French armoured vehicles.
(Photo: Bojan Dimitrijević Collection)

Below left: Two PanzerJägerWagen preceded by a Croat wagon.
(Photo: Bojan Dimitrijević Collection)

Below right: A German armoured artillery wagon with its distinctive turret. The Yugoslav Army was not interested in the complete armoured trains. In comparison the autorails and trolleys were felt to be more useful.
(Photo: Bojan Dimitrijević Collection)

SOURCES:

Archives:
SHD DAT 7 N 3200, 7 N 3202.

Books:
Dimitrijević, Bojan, *Modernizacija i intervencija, Jogoslovenske oklopne jedinice 1945-2006* (Belgrade: Institut za savremenu istoriju, 2010).

_____ (with Savić, Dragan), *German Panzers and Allied Armour in Yugoslavia in World War Two* (Erlangen: Tankograd Publishing, 2013).

Journal article:
Grognet, Olivier, 'Les musées ferroviaires yougoslaves', *La Feuille*, AJECTA newsletter No 87 (December 1997), pp 5–6.

14. Cass, Donn, 'Transport Poor in Russia and Balkan Lands', *Chicago Daily Tribune*, 3 January 1950, p 4.
15. OKD = *Oklopna Divizija*, Armoured Division.
16. VR = *Vojna Radionica*, Military Workshop.
17. TRZ = *Tehnicki Remontni Zavod*, Technical Repair Workshops.

APPENDIX 1

ARMOURED TRAINS IN ART AND PROPAGANDA

Postcards were an excellent means of spreading a propaganda image, a role taken over today by postage stamps. Much rarer were commemorative objects such as this East German stylised model train of the Leuna Arbeiter uprising of 1919.
(Photo: Paul Malmassari Collection)

AUSTRIA-HUNGARY

This section presents a series of classic postcards of the Great War period. The Austro-Hungarian armoured trains were more impressive than their German counterparts, and were the subject of a great many reproductions aimed at the general public.
(Postcard: Paul Malmassari Collection)

Type A armoured train in combat with Russians.
(Postcard: Paul Malmassari Collection)

A patriotic German postcard, using the image of an Austro-Hungarian Type B armoured train, which was evidently felt to be more impressive, and more symbolic of armoured trains in general, than their own. In actual fact French soldiers wearing blue and scarlet uniforms, typical of the early months of the war, never came into contact with Austro-Hungarian armoured trains. In addition, the artist has represented the observation cupola as a chimney.
(Postcard: Paul Malmassari Collection)

Above: A fine composition showing a Type B PZ brushing aside Russian obstacles during the fight for Wilna. However, when the town did fall, on 19 September 1915, it was captured by German troops.
(Postcard: Paul Malmassari Collection)

Right: Here PZ I / IX is the subject of a postcard which is strikingly faithful to the actual appearance of the train.
(Postcard: Paul Malmassari Collection)

A patriotic postcard, with three national flags behind the cartouche of the armoured train: German on the right, Ottoman in the centre and Austro-Hungarian on the left. The black and gold which were the colours of the House of Habsburg between 1804 and 1866 continued to be used when representing the Emperor.

(Postcard: Paul Malmassari Collection)

An illustration of a Austro-Hungarian armoured train used by the French popular press to portray the intervention of a German train. In truth the images of the German trains lacked the visual impact necessary for efficient propaganda. The resulting scenario is certainly aesthetic, but it contains numerous inaccuracies, notably the long-barrelled gun in the position where one would find the engine, and the common misconception that the observation cupola was a chimney.

(L'Illustration National No 42: Paul Malmassari Collection)

A fine heroic engraving of fighting between Italian soldiers and troops disembarked from an Austro-Hungarian armoured train. The action took place on the night of 12/13 September 1915, when the Austrians advancing from Gorizia attempted a surprise attack on Zagora. Note that the engine is not the actual type which would be used with these wagons.

(Engraving: La Domenica del Corriere, No 39, XVIIth Year [26th September–30 October 1915]: Paul Malmassari Collection)

An original watercolour signed Linebauer, which is perhaps unfinished, but which clearly shows one of the early Austro-Hungarian armoured trains. Note the rear armoured wagon depicted as having three lateral machine-gun positions but lacking a cupola.

(Watercolour: Paul Malmassari Collection)

This small collectors' card (original size 5.8cm × 4.8cm/2¼in x just under 2in) faithfully depicts PZ II, but during its Czech period as Train No 1, with minor differences.

(Card: Bilderdienst Schienen Wunder, Berlin, No 288: Paul Malmassari Collection)

BELGIUM

Left and right: The impressive appearance of the Belgian armoured trains (as with their Austro-Hungarian contemporaries) inspired many artists, and in almost all types of media. The illustration on the right taken from a popular publication details the colour of the Belgian uniforms, with Royal Navy gunners manning the guns. The view on the left is an engraving which appeared in *La Domenica del Corriere* dated 17 January 1915.

(Both illustrations: Paul Malmassari Collection)

A Heavy Armoured Train on a collectors' card painted by Nathan. It draws inspiration from an original photo which was widely printed in the contemporary press; this can be seen in the Belgian chapter, page 61.

(Illustration: Paul Malmassari Collection)

This postcard takes up the same view as the Belgian Army train depicted on page 61, but this time attributing the train to the German Army.

(Postcard: Paul Malmassari Collection)

CAMBODIA

Armoured Train in Action, by the Italian Futurist Gino Severini, 1915, oil on canvas, 115.8cm by 88.5cm.

(Museum of Modern Art, New York)

The insecurity of a period that required armouring locomotives featured on a Cambodian stamp issue of 1984. The date of '1966' refers to when these locomotives were first introduced rather than to the date they received their armoured cabs.

(Paul Malmassari Collection)

ESTONIA

Patriotic postcard of the Estonian War of Independence, showing the action at Petserimaal in March 1919, near the end of the Bolshevik offensive.

(Postcard: Paul Malmassari Collection)

FRANCE

A dramatic engraving showing the dangers which still threatened civilian trains in the 1920s in Algeria.

(Cover of the Petit Journal of 19 December 1920)

A detail from *Asnières vue des bords de la Seine pendant l'insurrection le 22 mai 1871*, by H Charles (Asnières seen from the banks of the Seine during the insurrection on 22 May 1871). The artist has deliberately omitted the roof of the railway battery on the right to show the interior details.

(Painting: Collection du Ministre, 7 M B 335, SHD)

GERMANY

German South West Africa during the Herero revolt: railway workers repairing the track (note the detached rails lying on the left) covered by the armoured train and men of the *Schutztruppe* on 13 January 1904.

(Illustration: Paul Malmassari-DGEG Collection)

Front cover of issue No 111 of the series *Heinz Brandt der Fremdenlegionär* (up to No 80, Heinz Brandt, the hero of the story, was a French Foreign Legionnaire, but when the First World War broke out, he deserted and joined the German Army. Between 1914 and 1921 the series ran to 332 issues). This illustration demonstrates how the armoured train was recognised as part of the 'normal' armament of the countries of the period.

(Cover: Paul Malmassari Collection)

GREAT BRITAIN

An example of British use of armed trains at the end of the nineteenth century is evoked by this postage stamp issued to commemorate the Alderney Railway's 1890 wagon armed with a QF gun for coastal defence, supplementing the fortifications built between 1847 and 1857. It appears there is a second such wagon partly obscured by the Queen's head.

An engraving from across the Atlantic which is a fine depiction of the Anglo-Belgian armoured trains.

(Image: Scientific American, Vol CXII, N° 18 of 1 May 1915)

HUNGARY

A postcard commemorating the Hungarian 'Red' Armoured Trains.

(Postcard: Paul Malmassari Collection)

JAPAN

These two patriotic postcards illustrate the same theme in a contrasting serious and comical manner. Apart from their historical interest, they give an impression of the colours used in the camouflage schemes.

(Two postcards: Paul Malmassari Collection)

An example of the use of official photos to create postcards for the soldiers of the Emperor (the original photo can be found on page 293).
(Postcard: Paul Malmassari Collection)

Another postcard view inspired by the same train, this time including a rangefinder in the nearer artillery wagon.
(Postcard: Paul Malmassari Collection)

Here is an infantry wagon at the head of a train, with an understandably nervous officer bottom left, as they have no safety wagon preceding them.
(Postcard: Paul Malmassari Collection)

Two of the many propaganda postcards published during the war.

(Two postcards: Paul Malmassari Collection)

This illustration of a railway guard in winter kit and the engine of an armoured train is from the cover of a packet containing a set of patriotic postcards.

(Illustration: Paul Malmassari Collection)

MEXICO

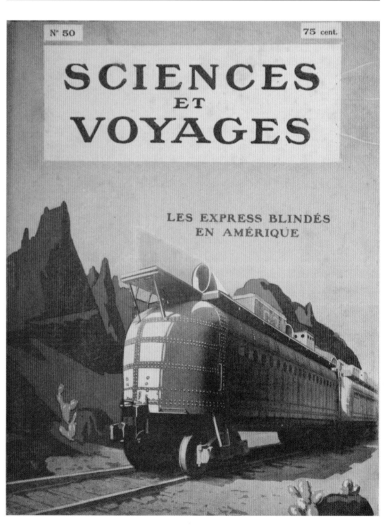

The striking appearance of the American-built armoured protection wagons inserted into passenger trains during the Mexican revolution made a big impression. Here they feature in a popular magazine of the 1920s. See page 321 for further details.

(Illustration: Paul Malmassari Collection)

RUSSIA

Intended as publicity for their airships, this German postcard also features the Russian defences, and curiously uses identical turrets on both the fort and the train, probably inspired by a similar use of the German Gruson turrets.

(Postcard: Paul Malmassari Collection)

A heroic rendering of the capture of a White armoured train by Budenny's cavalry, in this contemporary engraving. The wagon is a mixture of 'White' and 'Red' train designs, not unusual during a period when the capture and return to service of the trains was commonplace.

(Engraving: Paul Malmassari Collection)

Wartime propaganda revived the myth of the armoured trains : here an OB-3 is saluted by the civilian population.

(Postcard dated 1943: Paul Malmassari Collection)

Even Stalin got in on the act: on this postcard dated 1942, he is seen (with his arm raised), supposedly commanding on the Tsaritsyn Front in 1918. The armoured train takes second place just behind him.

(Postcard: Paul Malmassari Collection)

An extremely odd train (perhaps intended to be a railcar) features on this postcard from 1942, with a chimney smoking in front of the armament, and the main cannon flanked by two others. But note the red star and red banner proudly displayed.

(Postcard: Paul Malmassari Collection)

This BTR which features on the cover of *Soviet Military Review* N° 3 (1975) is rail-mounted. The date could correspond to a period of experimentation, but it could also be used as a means of training troops to mount and dismount from a moving vehicle.

(Illustration: Paul Malmassari Collection)

SPAIN

Left: An illustration included in American chewing gum packets, showing an episode from the Civil War.

(From the Series 'Horrors of War', N° 215, Gum Inc., Philadelphia, Pennsylvania, 1938, Paul Malmassari Collection)

Below left and right: These two illustrations show armoured trains in board games, the one on the right being a form of snakes and ladders, with symbols rarely found in such games: a head wearing a Phrygian bonnet (symbolising the Republic), or a crown (the Monarchy), and the initials and devices of political parties and trade unions. The one on the left celebrates the courage of the city of Madrid, 'Muy heroica cuidad'.

(JMAM Collection)

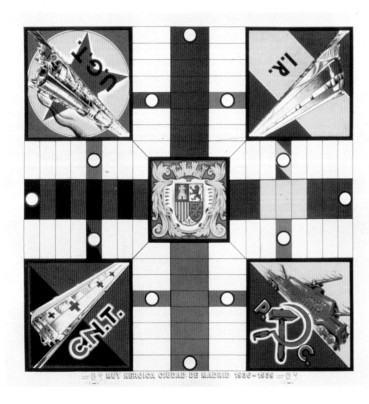

Armoured Trains in Comic Books

There are as many genres of comic books as in 'classic' literature. From the past to the future, thus from history to science fiction, passing by way of politics, it is no surprise to find armoured trains represented, either to illustrate an actual historical event, or an adventure frozen in time, or to support a proposition. With rare exceptions, the armoured train is not an object of humour! In every case, it does not appear by accident in a cartoon strip: its impact is always linked to its impressive, even menacing aspect. And artists never hesitate to (deliberately?) exaggerate its dimensions or juggle with the chronology. The illustrations we have chosen, displayed chronologically in their order of appearance, are far from being exhaustive (*Entremondes*, or *Grêlé 7-13* spring to mind among others), but are intended to give food for thought.

Even though many armoured trains appear in *Corto Maltese en Sibérie*, we might grumble about their simplified representation – but the atmosphere of the 'end of the world' is well rendered (1971, p 51).

The accuracy of Hergé's drawings is evident in this image, despite the fact that this train of the time of the Manchurian Incident is actually Chinese (Fengtian Army) and not Japanese. However, the two did occasionally work together! (*Le Lotus bleu*, 1946).

In *Pâtée explosive* (1971) the armoured train is a classic design and well represents the type used up until the end of the Second World War.

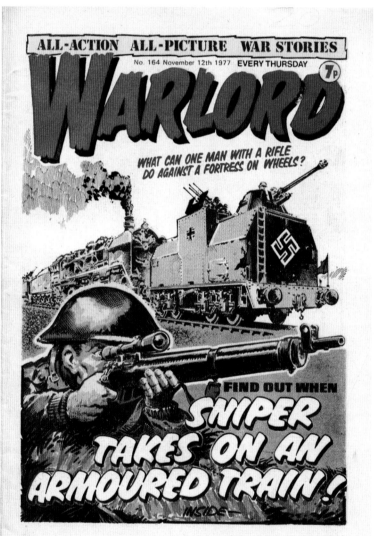

In 1977, this German armoured train inspired by the BP 42 type is doomed to meet its fate at the hands of a single sniper, in the spirit of the super-hero but fitting in well with the overall genre. *Warlord* was published from 1974 to 1986.

CE GROUPE RECEVRAIT L'APPUI DES TRAINS BLINDÉS "H" "Y" "K".

Left: Here is a faithful represen-tation of the virtually unknown Spanish armoured trains, rendered by Antonio Hernandez Palacios in *Eloy* (1981, p 40)

Right: In *Rails* (*2. La Garde Blanche* [1993], p 25) we see the gigantic aspects of science-fiction armoured trains, coming close to that of *La compagnie des glaces*.

Below: In *L'Encyclo-B.D. des armes*, Jacques Devos uses the comic strip for educational purposes: here are the first armoured trains rendered in humourous style (1985, p 59)

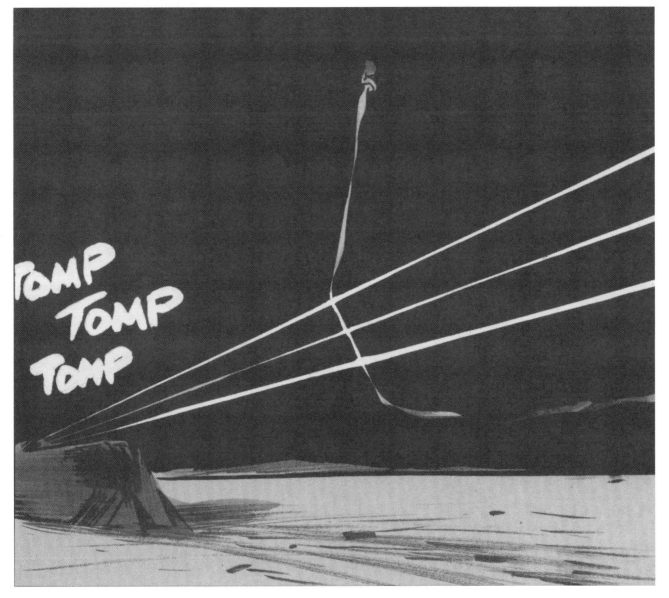

Above: Because the story takes place in Russia, the armoured trains in *Harry Dickson, la conspiration fantastique* (1999, p 19) are obviously Russian, though the tank-transporter wagon with the armoured cars unloading is clearly German. But then of course the Soviet trains of the 1970s had carried BTR 40 ZhDs and unloaded them in a similar manner! (See the chapters on Germany and Russia.)

Left: In *Transperceneige*, the train is armoured as much against some of its passengers as against an invincible enemy. The armament is the only element which disturbs the purity of its smooth outline. (2000, p 58).

Above: In *YIU, premières missions, l'armée des néo-déchets*, the train, menacingly armed and armoured since it is on the side of the 'baddies', is far removed from historical armoured train designs (2003, p 12).

Left: An astounding mix of historical 'faction' and fascination for the nineteenth century of steam, wild inventions and unlikely machines, Volume 4 of *Hauteville House* plunges us into an American Civil War even more modern than the 'real' version, and reminds us of the 1999 film *Wild Wild West* by Barry Sonnenfeld (2007, cover illustration).

Below: An armoured train the Confederates and Union forces could not have imagined in their wildest dreams ... (*Hauteville House* Vol 4 [2007], p 12).

Les Armées blanches 1917-1921 (2008) faithfully depicts the impressive appearance of the armoured trains of the Russian Revolution and Civil War, the only contemporary land machines capable of moving over such enormous distances to rain fire and devastation. The idea of the 'moving fortress' is well rendered here.

In *Svoboda!*, the armoured trains are the stars, but aesthetics wins out over chronology and geography: the Austro-Hungarian armoured trains, as impressive as they were, could not operate in Russia, given the distances to cover and the different rail gauge ... (Vol 1 [2011], p 26).

As for the 6 August 1914 in Prague Station, the supposed date of the scene depicted, the Austro-Hungarian trains did not yet exist, and the train shown is one from the Russian Civil War ... (*Svoboda!* Vol 1 [2011], p 29).

With *La Rafale*, the cartoon strip depicts history, despite taking several liberties with the depiction of the train, and even with the title itself (see the chapter on France for the true meaning of the word 'Rafale' in Indochina), but captures well the essence of these trains. (2014, p 18).

SUGGESTIONS FOR FURTHER STUDY:

Arnaud, G J, *La Compagnie des glaces*, 15 volumes in 3 series (adapted from the eponymous novels) (Dargaud 2003–2009).

Chaboud, Jack, and Dupuis, Dominique, *Quai des Bulles – Le train dans la bande dessinée* (Paris: La Vie du rail, 1985).

Chauvel, Simon, and Findakly, *Rails 1 à 4* (Tournai: Guy Delcourt Productions, 1993).

Cothias, Patrick, Ordas, Patrice, and Winoc, *La Rafale* (Charnay-Lès-Mâcon: Grand Angle/Bamboo Editions, 2012, 2013, 2014).

Devos, Jacques, *L'Encyclo-B.D. des armes* (Paris: Editions Jean Dupuis, 1985).

Di Marco, 'L'Odyssée du convoi Apfelkern', *La Vie du rail*, numéro hors-série (23 August 1964).

Duval, Gioux, Quet, Beau, *Hauteville House* Vol 4 (Atlanta, Tournai: Guy Delcourt Productions, 2007).

Hergé, *Le Lotus bleu* (Tournai: Casterman, 1946).

Hombourger, François, *Maknovtchina Ukraine 1919* (Saint-Georges d'Oléron-Paris: Drapeau Noir, 1985).

Jacobs, Edgar P, *Le Secret de l'Espadon* Volume 3 (Brussels: Le Lombard, 1950).

Joly, Octave, *Reporter et train blindé*, Les belles histoires de l'Oncle Paul, *Spirou* No 946 (Paris: Dupuis, 31 May 1956).

Lob, Jacques, and Rochette, Jean-Marc, *Le Transperceneige* Vols 1–3 (Paris: Casterman, 1984, 1999 and 2000).

Palacios, Antonio Hernandez, *Eloy* (Paris: Les Humanoïdes associés, 1981).

Pendanx, Jean-Denis and Kris, *Svoboda!* Vols 1 and 2 (Paris: Futuropolis, 2011, 2012).

Pratt, Hugo, *Corto Maltese en Sibérie* (Paris: Casterman, 1979).

Ray, Jean, Vanderhaeghe, Christian, and Zanon Pascal J, *Harry Dickson, la conspiration fantastique*, Vol 6 (Paris: Dargaud, 1999).

Rochette and Legrand, *Transperceneige 2-L'Arpenteur* (Tournai: Casterman, 1999).

'Sniper takes on an Armoured Train', *Warlord* No 164 (12 November 1977).

Tehy, Vax, and Vee, *YIU, Premières missions, l'armée des néo-déchets* (Toulon: Soleil Productions, 2003).

Temglit, Hadi, and Lehideux, Guy, *Les Armées blanches 1917 – 1921* (Paris, Editions du Triomphe [collection Histoire], 2008).

Tillieux, *Gil Jourdan N°12 Pâtée explosive* (Paris: Dupuis, 1971).

_____, *Au pays du matin calme* (Paris: Dupuis, 1986).

Armoured trains in films

Several historical or fictional films, documentaries and cartoons, bring to the screen armoured trains, real or reconstructed or imagined for the needs of the script. The very fact that these films exist and the way the trains are depicted tells us much about the way the average filmgoer imagines armoured trains. As with comic books, the priority is the impression of power which they represent, and by so doing enhance the courage of their adversaries who have to face them.

In *Goldeneye* (1995) we are on the fringes of science-fiction. But the brutal-looking train which bears comparison with its Russian counterparts as described in the appropriate chapter, deserves a second glance from armoured train enthusiasts. *(Photo: Nene Valley Railway via Angie Nurse)*

In 1964, the images of the real armoured trains and in particular the train in *La Bataille du rail* (1945) were still fresh in filmgoers' minds. This mock-up made for *The Train* was directly inspired by the real thing as the German armoured wagon depicted here existed as part of PZ 32.

Two T-34 tank turrets are a classic icon of the Soviet armoured train, but even though there are few tunnels on the Steppes, the need to respect loading gauge limits to pass under over-bridges and other structures would have forbidden such a lofty construction! We can guess at the mineral wagon base beneath the 'armour'. (*Stalingrad*, 2001).

In 1965, *Doctor Zhivago* marked generations of cinema fans. The scene when the hero comes face-to-face with Strelnikov's armoured train is a cult moment. The armoured wagon looked the part of a Bolshevik train, even though the coaches and engine would have severely restricted its fields of fire! A wonderful memory which feeds our imagination.

Viewed from this angle, the turrets and the armoured wagons of *The Last Armoured Train* (2006) are really believable, and in fact the whole train is very convincing. After a period of 'artistic licence', it seems the film industry is once again becoming preoccupied with historical realism.

SUGGESTIONS FOR FURTHER VIEWING:

Bosna, Bernard-Henri Levy, Arte-Video, 1994. 117 mins.
Castle in the Sky, dir. Hayao Miyasaki, Studio Ghibli, 1986. 124 mins.
Cuba, dir. Richard Lester, United Artists, 1979. 122 mins.
Doctor Zhivago, dir. David Lean, Metro-Goldwyn-Mayer, 1965. 192 mins.
Goldeneye, dir. Martin Campbell, EON Productions, 1995. 130 mins.
La Bataille du rail, dir. René Clement, Coopérative Générale Française du cinéma, 1945. 90 mins.
La Cour secrète des arcanes, dir. Pascal Morelli, Gebeka Films, 2002. 95 mins.
Notre Train blindé (in Russian: Наш бронепоезд), Mikhail Ptachouk, 1988 (presented alongside the competition entries at the Russian Film Festival in Vyborg, 9 to 16 August 2003).
Reds, dir. Warren Beatty, Paramount, 1981. 187 mins.
Stalingrad, dir. Jean-Jacques Annaud, Pathé Distribution, 2001. 131 mins.
The Last Armoured Train, dir. Zinovii Roizman, Belpartner TV, 2006. Four episodes of 52 mins.
The Train, dir. John Frankenheimer, Associated Artists Productions, 1964. 133 mins.
Young Winston, dir. Richard Attenborough, Columbia Pictures, 1972. 157 mins.

Young Winston (1972) includes the incident when the future Prime Minister is on an armoured train in South Africa which the Boers attack and cause to derail. The same episode appears in Octave Joly's comic strip in *Spirou* (listed above). Here, the steam engine is hauled into position for filming by a diesel, which the British would dearly have liked to possess in 1900!

(Photo: Didcot Railway Centre via Frank Dumbleton)

APPENDIX 2

SELECTED ORIGINAL FACTORY DRAWINGS OF ARMOURED TRAINS AND TROLLEYS

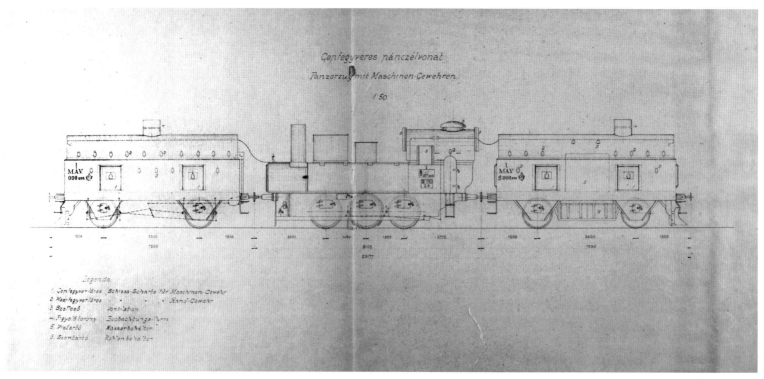

Above: Profile view of the first series of Austro-Hungarian armoured trains, Type A, later re-classified as 'Light Armoured Trains'. Note the command cupola on the roof of the engine cab, and the different positions of the observation cupolas on the two machine-gun/infantry wagons.

(Rajzalbum RA-581 01 19150804)

Below: Profile view of the later Type B Austro-Hungarian Heavy Armoured Trains built by MAVÁG, showing the telephone intercom wires connecting the units. Note the machine-gun embrasures moved further to the ends of the central wagon.

(Rajzalbum RA-581 01 191509xx)

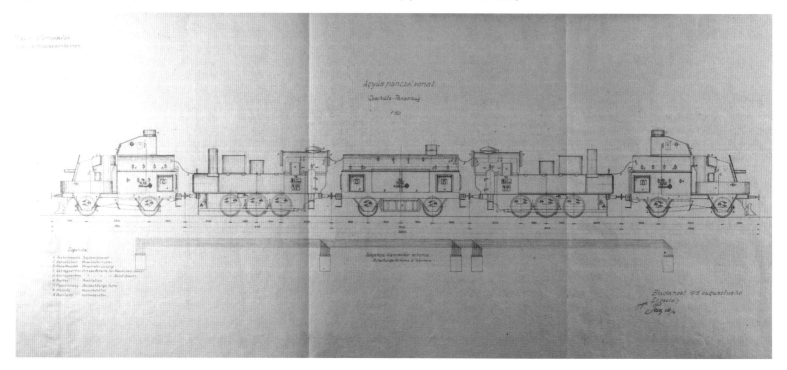

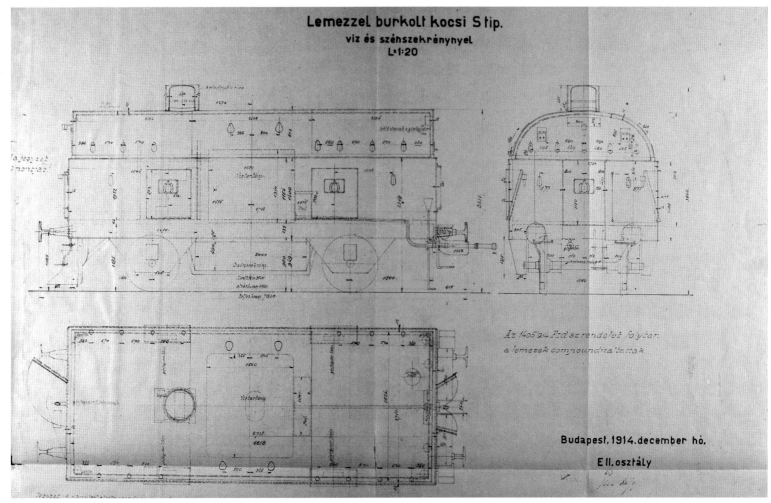

Above: Three-view drawing of an early S-Type machine-gun/infantry wagon, with the firing embrasures sloping inwards at the top. Note the central water tank (with coal locker underneath) and the offset observation cupola.

(Rajzalbum RA-581 11 19141209)

Below: Below: Three-view drawing of an S-Type wagon showing the braking system. Note the access ladder to the central observation cupola.

(Rajzalbum RA-581 12 19141209)

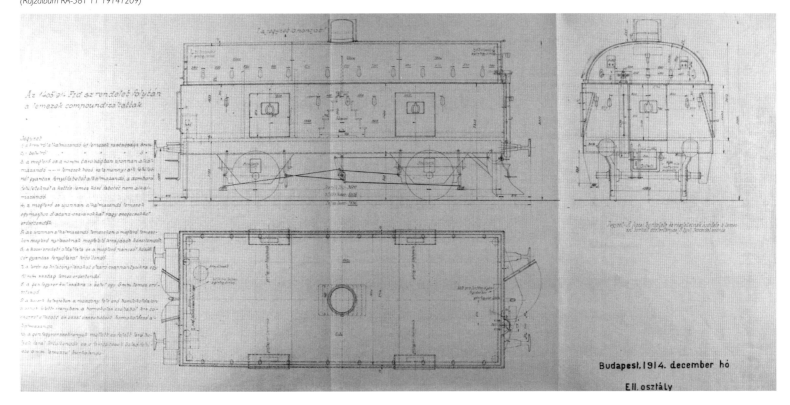

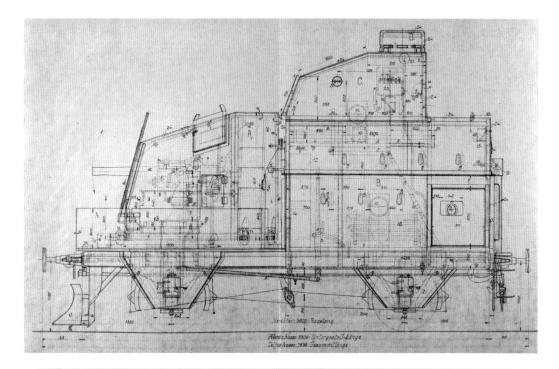

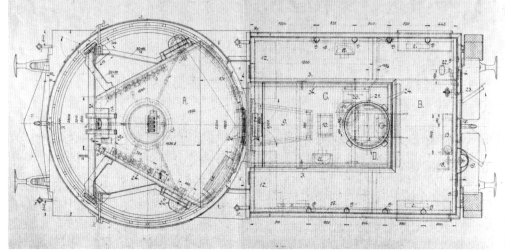

Complete set of original drawings for the artillery wagon of the Type B Heavy Armoured Trains. Note the braking system, with its armoured housing at the rear, and the system of travelling clamps to lock the rotating turret when not in action.

(Rajzalbum RA-581 12 19150620)

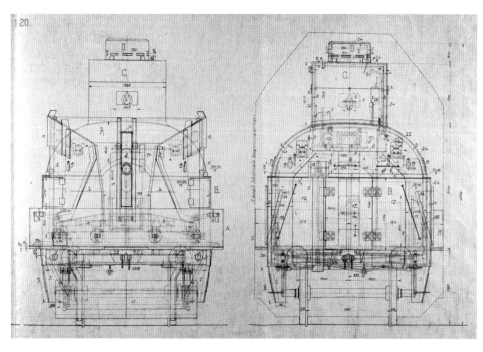

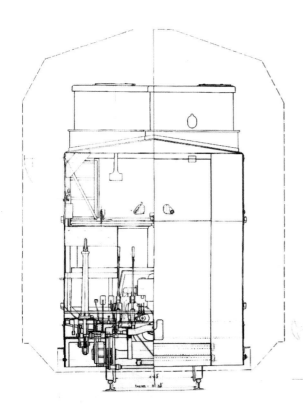

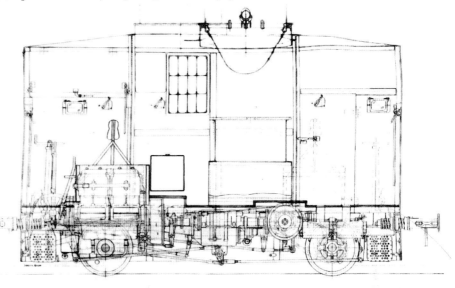

General arrangement sectioned drawings of the Drewry trolley ordered for the British Army in Mesopotamia. The plans which were almost 100 years old are slightly distorted, but give a good impression of this small machine, with a 9ft (2.736m) wheelbase. The gunners in the twin turrets had a Lewis Gun each, but would be obliged to perch on the leather strap hung from one side of the turret base to the other, just as on the Renault FT light tank of 1917.

(Drawings: The Industrial Railway Society via Staffordshire Record Office)

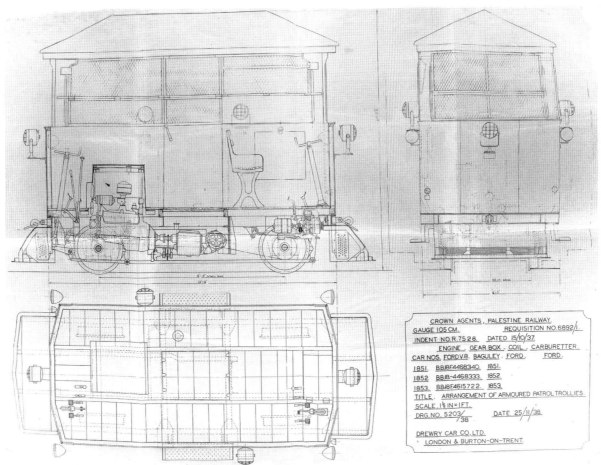

Factory drawing of the 1938 Drewry Light Trolley for Palestine, with 8ft 0in (2.438m) wheelbase

(Plan: Industrial Railway Society via Staffordshire Record Office)

Sources

Archives of the Hungarian Museum of Science, Technology and Transport, Budapest.
Staffordshire Record Office, Stafford, UK.

INDEX

ACKNOWLEDGEMENTS

This encyclopaedia represents more than thirty years of research. The assembling of such a vast collection of documents, photographs, drawings, technical details and personal reminiscences, from all the various original sources, would not have been possible without the support and help given by a large number of correspondents in many countries worldwide.

We would like to specially mention Mr Roger Branfill-Cook who has done much more than simply translate these texts, he is an armaments specialist always on the lookout for details hidden in photographs, an utter perfectionist and an uncoverer of secrets! Thanks must also go to our Editor, Mr Robert Gardiner, who with Roger Branfill-Cook insisted that this book, which initially we planned as just a simple updating of our 1989 edition, should be completely revised and expanded. My research efforts have been supported by historians and specialists in the realms of armoured trains and railway artillery, and by railway experts who have written about the rolling stock of their own country, or have created a specialised series of documents. In particular I must mention Messrs Illès András, Jacinto M Arévalo Molina, Peter Bagshawe, Carlos Stephani Bastos, Brian Baxter, Johan Botha, Petrus Botha, Jan de Bruin, Guy Chabot, Francisco Cruzado Albert, Bojan Dimitrijović, General Guy François, Daniele Guglielmi, Tomáš Jakl, Tony Hill, Adam Jońca, Alan Koenig, Maxim Kolomiets, the late Janusz Magnuski, Krzysztof Margasiński, Pavel Mičianik, Tiit Noormets, the late Nicola Pignato, Artur Przeczek, Wolfgang Sawodny, Tamara Štefanac, Marcel Verhaaf, Steven Zaloga and Mariusz Zimny. My thanks go to them all for their unfailing support.

We have also been able to count on the constant support and patience of Mme Laure Dubus, and on her expertise in international relations.

Our gratitude goes to the curators and archivists of the museums, archives and private companies, who have replied to our requests for information or have pointed us in the direction of contacts we would not otherwise have known about. Every effort has been made to correctly ascribe credit for the photographs and documents. Nonetheless, certain documents, the origin of which we have been unable to identify, have been used here because of their rarity or their historical interest. We trust their originators and owners will readily excuse us, and see in our use of them our recognition of the quality of these items.

We must also mention all the penfriends and correspondents who have helped us over the years and please accept our apologies in advance if anyone has been accidentally omitted: Alain Alvarez, Reginaldo Bacchi, John Batwell, the late Yves Bernard, Luc Binet, Captain Valérie Caniart, Colonel Fillipo Capellano, Frédéric Carbon, Jean-Christophe Carbonel, Emmanuelle Chanteranne, Peter Cooke, Paul Coterell, Pascal Danjou, Stephen Dartnell, the late Yves Debay, Henry Dropsy, Rob Dickinson, Marcel Duflot, the late Alain Dupouy, Patricia Durrieu, Matthew Ecker, Barba Ekmane, Konstantin Fedorov, Tony Ford, the late Andrew Gillitt, Florian Grupp, Frederic Guelton, Olaf Güttler, Georges Handrinos, Michael Hansson, David Hills, Stuart Jefferson, the late Jean-Gabriel Jeudy, John Jolly, Jacques Jost, Philip Jowett, Hans Kohit, Bas Koster, Günther Kraus, Martin Lacko, Eric Laugier, Colonel (Hon) Dominique Loiseau, Denis MacCarthy, Walter McGrath, Wawrzyniec Markowski, the late Georges Mazy, Jürgen Meister, Chen Melling, Candice Menat, André Meyer, Paul Middleton, Albert Mroz, John Murphy, Paul Napier, Général Pierre Nicolas-Vullierme, Kevin Patience, Walter Piringer, Lieutenant-Colonel Rémy Porte, Gérard Pouilé, Michel Protat, Uzi Raviv, Werner Regenberg, Charles Rickwood, Stuart Robinson, John L Rue, Max Schiavon, Bill Schmeelk, Horst Schobesberger, Aleksandar Smiljanić, Prakash Tendulkar, Philippe Tomatis, Gerry Van Tonder, Véronique De Touchet, Pierre Touzin, François Vauvillier, Jochen Vollert, Paul V Walsh, Hal Walters, Athol Yates and Chen Yichuan.

We dedicate this book to all the crews of armoured trains, who carried on the railway war which was as difficult and as dangerous as those of their comrades in arms in other branches, without however receiving the accolades that armoured trains so richly deserved. Our hope is therefore that this book will open up new and multiple avenues of research, and we remain open to all constructive criticism.